THE VERB 'BE' AND ITS SYNONYMS

(6)

THE VERB 'BE' IN ANCIENT GREEK

FOUNDATIONS OF LANGUAGE

SUPPLEMENTARY SERIES

VOLUME 16

To Henry and Danuta Hiż
in friendship and affection

EDITORIAL PREFACE

The present volume is the sixth of a series of studies analysing the verb 'to be' and/or synonyms in a number of languages; in contrast to preceding volumes, it is devoted to one language only: Ancient Greek. It is expected that these studies will provide some of the necessary foundational research in logic, the theory of knowledge, and ontology; and possibly in other philosophical disciplines. The concluding volume will attempt to assess the linguistic and philosophical impact of all the contributions; one more volume will precede the concluding volume, i.e. a study on 'to be' in biblical Hebrew and biblical Greek, by James Barr.

JOHN W. M. VERHAAR

PREFACE

This book began unintentionally in 1964, when I tried to put together a brief description of the pre-philosophical uses of the Greek verb *be* in order to lay the groundwork for an interpretation of the more technical use of the verb by the philosophers beginning with Parmenides. But the task was harder and longer than I thought, and it gradually became clear that no adequate description of the Greek data could be given without confronting a number of major issues in linguistic theory and in the philosophy of language. As often happens in so-called empirical research, the terms in which the problem is posed and the recognition of what might count as a solution turn out to depend upon certain theoretical assumptions about the nature of the subject matter and the appropriate form for description, analysis, and explanation. In this case there was the preliminary question of an appropriate method for describing and classifying the different uses of the verb, and the closely connected question of the relationship between a syntactic or formal analysis of these uses and a semantic account in terms of difference of meaning. Similar questions would arise in the study of any verb. But the verb *be* poses specific philosophic problems of its own: how are we to define or clarify the concepts of subject, predicate, copula, and verb of existence? And there is the problem of the verb *be* itself: in what sense is this system of distinct uses a unity? Is the possession of a single verb *be* with such a diversity of uses only a historical accident of Indo-European? And does it follow that the concept of Being is only a philosophic illusion?

Although I have been obliged to deal with these wider issues, and as a result have seen (with some dismay) my early sketch give way to a study of quite different scope and dimensions, the focus has remained on the original goal: to give an account of the ordinary, non-technical uses of the Greek verb. Of course it was the philosophic career of *be* which motivated the study in the first place, and I have tried throughout to point the analysis in a direction that will be useful for work in Greek philosophy.[1] But the book remains a study of the verb *be* in Greek, not in philosophic Greek. Furthermore, by dealing extensively with the earliest evidence (from Homer)

---

[1] My preliminary results for the philosophical interpretation were given in "The Greek Verb 'to be' and the Concept of Being", *Foundations of Language* **2** (1966), 245–65. The application to Parmenides was published as "The Thesis of Parmenides", in *Review of Metaphysics* **22** (1969), pp. 700–24, and "More on Parmenides", *ibid.* **23** (1969), pp. 333–40.

and by referring to parallel evidence in cognate languages, I have tried as far as I could to make this a study of the Indo-European verb *be*. Although the Greek verb has a strong personality of its own, most of the characteristic uses have striking parallels in other languages of the same family, and particularly in those for which archaic texts are available. I hasten to add, however, that I am not a comparative linguist, and all conclusions offered here that go beyond the Greek evidence can be regarded only as hypotheses for specialists to confirm or refute.

The core of the book is the descriptive account of the various uses of εἰμί, presented in Chapters IV, VI, and VII. In order to organize this data in a coherent way and to provide some reasonably clear analysis of the copula, existential, and veridical uses of the verb, it was necessary to employ a theory of syntax more carefully articulated than what we find in Kühner-Gerth or Schwyzer-Debrunner. What I have used is a modified version of the transformational grammar of Zellig Harris, as formulated in his article "Transformational Theory" (in *Language*, 1965) and in his book *Mathematical Structures of Language* (1968).

My use of this theory may be a stumbling-block to some readers, particularly to Hellenists trained in traditional grammar, who may wonder why I have encumbered the description with such bizarre items as kernel sentence forms and transforms, zero pronouns and sentence operators. Let me say only that I do not believe any simpler theory can classify the copula uses in a rational way or can give any analysis at all of the existential uses and their relation to the copula. The notion of a kernel or elementary sentence is really the traditional notion of a simple sentence given a precise formulation. I hope that some of the preliminary difficulties can be overcome by a careful reading of Chapter I §§6–7, where I describe Harris' theory in outline and explain the notion of transformation which will be used here. One difficulty calls for special mention, however, since it may perplex many philologically trained readers. This is my systematic use of the term "derivation" in the absence of any historical evidence that what I call a derived form appears later than its alleged transformational "source". To forestall misunderstanding, let me insist that the relevant sense of "derivation" is neither chronological nor psychological: it is a technical concept defined by the syntactic theory. Perhaps the closest analogy would be to the sense in which the theorems of geometry are "derived" from the axioms of the system. In Harris' system of grammar, the elementary sentence forms serve as the axioms, so to speak, from which more complex sentence forms are derived. And the rules of derivation are precisely the transformations defined in the system. To say that the passive sentence form *Caesar was stabbed by Brutus* is transformationally derived from the active form *Brutus stabbed*

Caesar is not to say that the latter form is historically older (though this might be true). Nor is it to say that a speaker first thinks of the active sentence pattern and then constructs the corresponding passive (though a child presumably learns to use the active form first). To say that the passive is a transform of the active is to say (i) that the active is simpler (in an intuitive sense, which the theory can articulate), and (ii) that there is a grammatical rule, i.e. a regular transformation, to get from one form to the other. This and no more is what is meant by "derivation" here, when I am using the term in a technical sense.

Another class of readers may ask not why I use transformational grammar but why I use it in this particular form, rather than in one of the more familiar generative systems developed by Noam Chomsky and his school. Why transformational grammar without tree diagrams and without rewrite rules? My answer is that I learned this theory from my friends and colleagues in Philadelphia, that I found it easy to use because it has so much in common with traditional grammar and easy to apply to the Greek texts because it sticks relatively close to the surface structure of actual sentences. I do not mean to take up any position on the relative merits of different theories of modern syntax. But I will be happy if one of the side-effects of my work is to remind some readers of the fact that transformational grammar, of which Harris is the pioneer, is not simply co-extensive with the theories of Chomsky and his followers. For those readers who are familiar with generative grammar I should point out that my use of the term "deep structure" (or "underlying structure") is somewhat narrower than that to which they may be accustomed. The deep structure of a given sentence is simply the elementary sentence form (or forms) which constitutes its source, plus the transformations by which it is derived from this source. In no case does the term "deep structure" refer to a semantic level that might be "deeper" than the kernel sentences of the language with their elementary vocabulary. One of the advantages of this theory, to my mind, is that it implies no concept of meaning which goes beyond the sentences of the language, except in terms of paraphrase relations between sentences. (I do make use of a more extended notion of meaning in what I call strong semantics, to which I will refer in a moment. There we are no longer in the domain of syntax or linguistics proper but are concerned rather with the logical and philosophical analysis of the concepts under discussion.)

For readers whose interest is primarily philosophical rather than linguistic, I have tried to separate the discussion of theoretical issues from the detailed description of Greek sentence types. Thus the concepts of subject and predicate are treated in Chapter II, the general theory of the copula in Chapter V, and the unity of the system of *be* in Chapter VIII. Unfortunately it was not possible to make such a clear separation between theory and description in discussing the uses of *be* as an expression for existence and truth. Thus the theory of the existential verb is given within the largely descriptive Chapter VI (especially §§19–21); and my remarks on the concept of truth are contained within the account of the veridical uses in Chapter VII (see §§2–3 and 7).

In dealing with the different "senses" of the verb *be* I have not developed or assumed any general theory of meaning. But the problem of meaning does arise, for example in dealing with the existential verb, which is clearly a semantic rather than a formal or syntactic notion. My procedure in Chapter VI has been to attack the problem by successive levels of analysis, each of which attempts to specify the meaning of the verb by a different method. The first analysis is carried out in terms of paraphrase value or dictionary meaning. This is the kind of semantics (I call it weak semantics) that is standard practice in philology and traditional linguistics. Thus I distinguish four nuances or paraphrase values for the existential uses of εἰμί (Chapter VI §§3–4). The second stage of analysis is syntactic as well as semantic: I define different existential "uses" of the verb on the basis of distinct sentence types, each with its own syntactic description (Chapter VI §§5–18). The assumption here is that while not every intuitive difference of meaning for the verb can be accounted for by a syntactic difference, the more relevant distinctions we can make in syntactic terms the firmer will be our grasp on differences of meaning. Here and elsewhere, transformational syntax provides us with a powerful tool for making our intuitive distinctions more precise and more general. (I believe this is also true for the analysis of periphrastic uses of the copula in Chapter IV §§14–17, and for the discussion of impersonal constructions in Chapter IV §§27–30.) Finally, I ask what is the logical function of the existential verb, in the context of "strong semantics" where we are no longer satisfied with a paraphrase or translation equivalent as an account of what the word means. As understood here (following Henry Hiż), strong semantics makes use of logical notions such as truth, reference, and entailment. I claim no originality for the logical account of existence sentences offered in Chapter VI §20. I do hope to have clarified the relationship between (1) this logical or semantic concept of existence, (2) the syntactic analysis of existential sentences, and (3) their intuitive meaning as rendered in paraphrase or translation.

Two points on technical matters. I have used the Oxford text of Greek authors wherever possible. And I have been rather unsystematic in the use of quotation marks. It is standard practice in linguistics to present sample sentences in italics, and I have followed this practice as far as I could. I have made no use of single quotes. Double quotes serve for translations of Greek samples, for genuine quotations, for words or phrases mentioned rather than used, and for a variety of purposes often referred to under the title of "shock quotes".

It remains only to express my gratitude for aid received from various quarters. The first material was collected when I was an A.C.L.S. research fellow in 1963–64; the bulk of the manuscript was drafted when I was on scholarly leave from the University of Pennsylvania in 1968–69. It was John Verhaar who, as editor of the monograph series on the verb *be*, first urged me to present my study in this series and sustained me with steady encouragement as the work dragged on. I am most grateful to K. J. Dover, who wisely rejected for publication my earliest attempt to treat this topic in 1964 and has since been willing to do unjust penance by reading the whole manuscript and improving it by his criticism and suggestions. Other friends and colleagues who have read substantial portions and helped to remove some of the imperfections include Diskin Clay, S.-Y. Kuroda, Jon Moline, Martin Ostwald, and Ernst Tugendhat. George Cardona has generously helped with information on Sanskrit and other points in comparative grammar. I have profited from individual comments by more people than I can name. Much of the initial stimulus for my work came from the writings of Émile Benveniste, and he showed great kindness in discussing these matters with me on several occasions. Among my students Joan Kung, Richard Patterson, and Blair Edlow have helped with the preparation of the manuscript. Finally, I dedicate the study to Henry and Danuta Hiż who instructed me in the rudiments of transformational grammar, without which this book could not have been written.

Philadelphia, September 3, 1971   CHARLES H. KAHN

TABLE OF CONTENTS

Editorial Preface   VII

Preface   IX

Analytic Table of Contents   XVII

CHAPTER I.   The Problem of the Verb 'Be'   1

CHAPTER II.   Subject, Predicate, Copula   38

CHAPTER III.   Application of the Transformational Analysis to Greek   60

CHAPTER IV.   Description of the Copula Uses   85

CHAPTER V.   The Theory of the Copula   184

CHAPTER VI.   The Verb of Existence   228

CHAPTER VII.   The Veridical Use   331

CHAPTER VIII.   The Unity of the System of 'Be' in Greek   371

APPENDIX A.   On the Accent of ἐστί and Its Position in the Sentence   420

APPENDIX B.   On the Theory of the Nominal Sentence   435

APPENDIX C.   The Nominalized Forms of the Verb: τὸ ὄν and οὐσία   453

Bibliography   463

Indices   468

ANALYTIC TABLE OF CONTENTS

I / THE PROBLEM OF THE VERB 'BE'

§1. The verb *be* and the question of linguistic relativism. Is Greek ontology a projection onto the world of the peculiar categories of Indo-European languages? 1

§2. The concept of Being and the challenge of philosophic analysis. How can there be a single concept corresponding to such diverse notions as existence, predication, identity, and class inclusion? 3

§3. Leśniewski's Ontology as an illustration of the possibility of systematic interconnections between the different uses of *be*, taking the copula use as central. 4

§4. Gilson's philosophical defense of the linguistic view of *be* (I.-E. **es-*) as primarily a verb of existence. 7

§5. Preliminary requirements for a description of εἰμί in Greek: the choice of the Homeric poems as primary corpus and the use of transformational grammar for a framework of description. 9

§6. Outline of the transformational system to be used here: an adaptation of the theory expounded by Zellig Harris in "Transformational Theory" (1965) and *Mathematical Structures of Language* (1968). 10

§7. Kernel sentence forms for English and a transformational analysis of the English verb *be*. A formal definition of the copula for elementary sentence forms and a definition by analogy for derived forms of copula *be*. We notice eight distinct uses of *be*:

    (1) the elementary copula in kernel sentences

    (2) the copula in a broad sense, including a number of distinct derivative uses of *be* whose surface structure is analogous to that of the elementary copula

    (3) the dummy verb, where *be* may be paraphrased by *take place* or *occur*, and where it is followed by a temporal phrase (*The fire was yesterday*)

    (4) the existential operator, *there is*

    (5) the vital use: *She is no more.*

    (6) the sentence operator: *That is so, Thus it was that...*

(7) as an example of idioms or minor uses: *He is to go tomor-row*.

(8) the *it*-extractor: *It is here they did it*.   17

§8. Survey and classification of the copula uses of *be* according to transformational principles. Elementary and second-order copulas. Adjectival copula, noun copula, and locative (or quasi-locative) copula.   24

§9. Non-copulative uses of *be*: the dummy-verb with temporal "predicates" (*The meeting is tomorrow*) and the existential phrase *there is*. Sentences with *there is* are analyzed as transforms of sentences with *be* as copula.   30

§10. Two special cases of the copula: the impersonal construction *It is hot (today)* and the nuncupative use *I am Charles*.   35

II / SUBJECT, PREDICATE, COPULA

§1. Formal definitions of "subject", "predicate" and "copula". On the basis of the transformational analysis we make use of the general formula for sentencehood $NV\Omega$ to define the subject as N and the predicate as the verb phrase ($V\Omega$). For the special case of the copula sentence N *is* Φ, the definitions of subject and copula are obvious. For the term "predicate" there are two senses, one narrower (excluding the copula *be*) and one broader (for the whole verb phrase). For sentences of the form N *is* N, the normal word order in English specifies initial N as subject, but some ambiguity may arise in Greek because of freer word order.   38

§2. The distinction between syntactical, semantical, ontological and judgmental (or "conceptual") predication. The four corresponding notions of subject and predicate are all distinct from the concepts of *topic* and *comment* as used in some recent linguistic literature.   40

§3. The terminology for subject and predicate in Aristotle. Syntactic subject and predicate are designated by ὄνομα ("noun") and ῥῆμα ("verb") respectively. The terms ὑποκείμενον and κατηγορούμενον, from which we derive "subject" and "predicate", properly refer to an extra-linguistic subject and to a semantical (linguistic) predicate or to an ontological attribute or characteristic (species, genus, action, etc.).   46

§4. Towards a general definition of subject and predicate. The occurrence of a formal or distributional contrast between the word classes of nouns and verbs in all, or nearly all, languages

is correlated with the semantical (referring) function of nouns and
the syntactical (predicating, sentence-forming) function of verbs.
Although nouns and verbs can be defined in some I.-E. languages
(including Greek) on the basis of declensional suffixes alone, any
more general definition must rely on distributional differences
which reflect the subject-predicate structure of sentences: the
finite verb is the form which can be predicate only, never subject.
This syntactical asymmetry indirectly reflects a semantic asymmetry: the noun and not the verb can designate or refer to individual objects in the world.   48

§5. Some restrictions on the universality of the noun-verb or subject-
predicate sentence structure. There are languages such as Nootka
where the noun-verb distinction may not be a necessary or even a
useful part of a syntactical theory for describing sentence structure. But this strictly linguistic question is independent of the
properly philosophical issue whether or not there is a fundamental distinction to be drawn between the linguistic functions
of referring and predicating. For if there is, then the noun-verb
or S.-P. structure of I.-E. syntax is of philosophic importance
just because it gives a clear and natural formal expression to this
basic distinction.   54

III / APPLICATION OF THE

TRANSFORMATIONAL ANALYSIS TO GREEK

§1. Survey of this chapter.   60
§2. The basic principle of analysis: the underlying sentence forms are
the same for Greek as for English, although the surface expression differs markedly in the two cases. In kernel structure there are
no verbless sentences and no one-term sentences except for a few
impersonal verbs.   61
§3. The notion of a minimal sentence with no eliminable elements presupposes the theoretic concept of a normal or zero context.   66
§4. Narrower and broader senses of the term "ellipse". The notion of
semantical completeness and the Stoic view of the sentence as
"the expression of a complete thought".   67
§5. Understood subject and grammatical antecedent. The two notions
are clarified by the principle of referential constancy, illustrated in
the analysis of a referential chain in the opening episode of the
Iliad. The theory of grammatical reference requires a sharp dis-

tinction between the *context* and the extra-linguistic *situation of utterance*. 70

§6. Summary of conclusions on verb forms with understood subject. 74

§7. First-order nominals, abstract nouns and sentential subjects. Sentences with εἰμί will be classified according to the nature of the subject term, whether expressed or understood. 76

§8. The problem of organizing the data for εἰμί. The copula/existential-verb dichotomy is inapplicable in its usual form. I make use of a purely syntactical distinction between copulative and non-copulative constructions of the verb. An outline of the major uses, and the distribution of material here between Chapters IV, VI, and VII. 80

§9. Comparison with the classification of uses of εἰμί in Liddell-Scott-Jones, Ebeling's *Lexicon Homericum*, and two more recent Lexicons. 82

IV / DESCRIPTION OF THE COPULA USES

§1. The traditional distinction between verbal and nominal sentences is restated as a contrast between kernel sentence forms with and without an elementary verb, between $NV\Omega$ (where V does not include the copula *be*) and N *is* Φ. From Homer on, εἰμί is primarily used in the copula construction: 80–85% of all occurrences in *Iliad* 1–12. 85

§2. Plan of the present chapter. Outline of the major subdivisions of the nominal copula: N *is* Φ, with Φ ranging over N, A, pronoun or participle (in the same case as subject N). 87

§3. First subclass of nominal copula: the adjectival copula (*cop A*) for personal subjects, i.e. N *is* A with N as personal noun. The distinction between *elementary* and *transformationally derived* *uses* of the copula. Sample sentences **1–2**. 89

§4. The class of personal nouns and the extra-linguistic category of *persons*, both defined by reference to the use of first- and second-person forms (verbs and pronouns) as expression of the speaker-hearer framework of discourse. Doubts as to the general applicability of the concept of "animate noun". Personal nouns are the paradigm subclass of first-order nominals. Nominals in the widest sense (N^*) include first-order nominals, abstract nouns, and sentential subjects. 90

§5. Illustration of N *is* A for first-order N, abstract nouns, and for some borderline cases. Sentences **3–11**. 94

§6. *Cop A* for sentential subjects. We may have exactly the same underlying structure for sentences with and without expressed pronoun τό, with an infinitive preceding or following the copula, or with sentential subject in a separate clause. Sentences **12–21**.   97

§7. Conclusion of *cop A*. This construction is the most common of all uses of εἰμί. Since the subject is most often a personal noun, Aristotle's example ἄνθρωπος λευκός ἐστι, "(a) man is pale," represents what is in fact the most typical use of the verb *be* in Greek.   101

§8. The general distinction between nouns and adjectives: adjectives are normally restricted to predicate (or attributive) position, while nouns can stand alone as subject or object of a verb.   102

§9. Second major subclass of the nominal copula: the substantival copula (*cop N*) whose form is *N is N*. This is most common with personal and sentential subjects. The form is illustrated for personal subjects with various types of predicate noun, elementary and derived. There is a problem in the analysis of nuncupative sentences: *This is Ajax*. Metaphorical use of abstract predicates with personal subjects. Sentences **22–35**.   104

§10. Abstract *N* as predicate with abstract and sentential subjects. The most interesting case of *N is N* is the construction of certain modal terms (θέμις, μοῖρα, ἀνάγκη, χρεώ, etc.) with an infinitival clause, with ἐστί expressed or omitted. The problem: whether the abstract noun is subject or predicate of ἐστί. The solution: this surface ambiguity is trivial, since deep structure and meaning are the same in either case; the noun serves as modal sentence operator on the infinitival clause. Decay of this sentence type in post-Homeric Greek. Sentences **36–50**.   109

§11. Third subclass of nominal copula: pronouns as predicate. Where a pronoun occurs in predicate position, we can usually derive the sentence from one with the pronoun as subject. When the predicate is a demonstrative pronoun, the distinction between subject and predicate in effect lapses, since ἐστί here can be construed as the *is* of identity. Instead of distinguishing between "S". and "P". we may often analyze these sentences in terms of the rhetorical-psychological distinction of "topic" and "comment". In a use of special interest for the future development, τίς occurs as predicate in the question *Who (what) is it?* Two groups to be distinguished. Sentences **51–54**.   118

§12. τίς ἐστι; (group 1): questions of personal identity. Stereotyped forms in Homer for questioning strangers. The answer need not

specify the personal name, but generally names the father, the
family and the local group. Greater importance of the personal
name in the fifth century. Sentences **55–59**.   121

§13. τίς ἐστι; (group 2): interrogations of surprise and concern. The
pre-philosophic background of the Socratic question τί ἐστι;
Sentences **60–63**.   124

§14. Fourth subclass of the nominal copula: the periphrastic construction with εἰμί as "auxiliary verb" and with a participle as
predicate. Importance of this construction from a philosophical
point of view. The philological discussion of this use has been
inconclusive and often incoherent, because of a confusion between semantic, stylistic, and syntactic criteria in the definition
of periphrasis. I propose a purely syntactic definition, and thus
admit the possibility of a periphrastic construction with a strong
lexical value for εἰμί. Examples of non-periphrastic conjunction
of verb and participle (not involving εἰμί). Sentences **64–67**.   126

§15. Application of the definition to εἰμί. (1) Non-periphrastic
constructions of εἰμί with participle. (2) Unitary periphrasis
where *copula + participle* may be regarded as the equivalent of a
single finite verb form. Sentences **68–75**.   130

§16. Copulative periphrasis, with the participle assimilated to an
adjective. This assimilation is never complete, and so-called
"adjectival periphrasis" must be included among the other,
properly periphrastic uses. Adjectival and unitary periphrasis may
coincide in a single example. Sentences **76–79**.   133

§17. Affinity of the periphrastic construction for perfect participles.
The "static" effect of periphrasis. Some special cases: periphrasis
with an existential or veridical value for the verb; with εἰμί in
initial position. Present periphrasis in Homer. Except with perfect participles, periphrasis remains rare. Sentences **80–85**.   137

§18. The articular participle in predicate position is not a case of
periphrasis but a statement of identity, one term of which is provided by the subject of the source sentence underlying the articular
participle. Sentences **86–89**.   142

§19. Generalization of the analysis of periphrasis: an auxiliary verb
is simply a special case of a verb operator or sentence operator.
We have transformationally comparable uses of εἰμί with agent
nouns and adjectives, with adjectives in -τός and verbals in -τέος.
Sentences **90–92**.   144

§20. The nominal copula concluded. Summary of verb and sentence-
operator uses of εἰμί alone. Comparable uses of εἰμί together

with adjective as compound verb operator: δῆλός (φανερός) εἰμί +*participle*. *Cop A* and *cop N* construction with sentential subjects (§§6 and 10) belong here as compound sentence operators (εἰμί +*adjective/noun +infinitival clause*). Sentences **93–94**. 147

§21. Copula constructions with adverbial "predicate" (*cop adv*). The use of personal subjects with adverbs meaning "silent", "in silence" seems to reflect a concrete sense of the verb: *to stand, remain, persist* in a certain state or condition. Sentence **95–97**. 150

§22. The copula with adverbs of manner in -ως; personal and sentential subjects, and some impersonal uses (κακῶς ἦν "things went badly"). Related uses with nouns of action. οὕτως ἐστί and the veridical construction. Sentences **98–111**. 152

§23. The locative copula. Traditional theories of the copula overlook either the general parallel or the systematic distinction between the nominal and locative copulas. The further distinction between locative adverb and prepositional phrase is superficial and will be ignored here: *N is PN* will serve as a general formula for the locative construction. "Pure" locative uses of the copula are relatively rare, but they include uses of the compound verbs ἄπ-ειμι πάρ-ειμι. Sentences **112–118**. 156

§24. Paralocative uses of *N is PN*. (1) Pregnant uses of the locative, where the literal sense of place is appropriate but does not give the primary or the full meaning of the construction. (2) Metaphorical uses, where the literal sense is inappropriate. Extensive development of the latter in post-Homeric Greek. Sentences **119–128**. 159

§25. Locative-existential uses. Overlap with the possessive construction. Occurrences of the nominal copula with an existential sense. Sentences **129–139**. 164

§26. The predicate genitive. This is a semi-copulative use of εἰμί, with various special senses: (1) partitive genitive, (2) genitive of source, ancestry, material, (3) genitive of measure and price, (4) genitive of belonging to (as property or distinctive mark). A contrast with the dative of possession. 167

§27. The impersonal construction. Importance of the general problem, as a challenge to the traditional view that a proposition necessarily consists of subject and predicate. The problem is clarified by the transformational distinction between elementary and derived sentences, since many impersonal constructions are secondary transforms of S.-P. sentences. We recognize three types of impersonal construction and one type misleadingly described as impersonal (with a true subject vaguely determined). We shall note the rarity of the first two impersonal forms in Homeric Greek.   169

§28. Impersonal constructions of elementary form (Type 1): expressions for weather and time. Meteorological verbs are never impersonal in Homer (Ζεὺς ὕει "Zeus rains"). Impersonal sentences of time (ἀμφὶ ἡλίου δυσμὰς ἦν "it was about sunset") are well established in classic prose, but at best incipient in Homer. Sentences **140–141**.   173

§29. Impersonal variants on *NVΩ* sentences occur as an optional or stylistic transformation (Type 2). This secondary use of the impersonal form is common in Attic, but there are only two examples in Homer. Initial ἔστι in singular with plural "subject" may be considered a weak form of this transformation. Sentences **142–143**.   176

§30. Impersonal sentences operators (Type 3). *Cop A* and *cop N* with sentential subjects (or "bound infinitives") might be classified here; also the potential construction (ἔστι + *infinitive*) to be described in Chapter VI. We may imagine an historical development of the impersonal potential use of ἔστι out of elementary constructions of the verb together with an epexegetical infinitive. We note the use of ἐστί with impersonal verbal in -τέον or -τέα. Antecedents for this may be found in the epic use of adjectives in -τόν and -τά. Our general formal definition of the impersonal construction is: the use of a finite verb where no subject expression is provided by the context. Nearly all examples of this for εἰμί fall under the three types recognized in §§28–30, but there are some difficult cases (e.g. κακῶς ἦν) which do not seem to be of elementary form (Type 1), but which are not easily analyzed either as transforms (Type 2) or as sentence operator uses of εἰμί (Type 3). Compare the "redundant" use of εἶναι as articular infinitive construed adverbially (τὸ νῦν εἶναι). Sentences **144–155**.   178

V / THE THEORY OF THE COPULA

§1. The traditional concept of the copula is reformulated to apply explicitly to locative as well as to nominal predicates. The notion of predication in turn is generalized to apply to all sentences. It is the finite verb, and not the copula as such, which then becomes *the sign of predication*. We distinguish (1) the syntactic role of the copula, providing the verb form required for sentencehood, and (2) the semantic role, providing the indicative mood form which is the mark of *declarative* sentence or truth claim. Truth claim of sentences is distinguished from assertion by speakers.   184

§2. Why is a finite verb generally required for declarative sentence-hood? The answer lies in the efficiency of the I.-E. system of verb endings as markers of person, tense, mood, and number. The indicative mood is the general mark of the declarative register, including question, supposition, etc. However, these other uses of the indicative may be regarded as secondary modifications of *statement*, or positing as true, which is the fundamental mode of descriptive and quasi-descriptive speech.   187

§2a. Digression on the general theory of moods. The link between the copula function and veridical use of εἰμί will be better understood if we recognize that the fundamental function of the verb in I.-E. is the expression of sentential truth claim. This follows from the fact that the unconditional declarative sentence is the primitive sentence form, upon which all modal forms (including question, wish and command) are to be defined. The formal description of moods within a particular language requires for its semantic interpretation a general theory of logical, epistemic and intentional modalities. The morphology of the Turkish verb offers a suggestive illustration. The analysis of performative verbs recently proposed by G. Lakoff is compatible with my claim of a fundamental role for the declarative form in any general theory of the sentence.   191

§3. Why is it precisely the verb *es- in I.-E. which occurs with non-verbal predicates? It has been suggested (by Meillet) that *es- was preferred because of its relatively slight meaning as verb of existence. The aspectual value of the verb is emphasized in Lyons' account of the general contrast between static and kinetic aspects: *is* stands to *becomes* as *has* to *gets* and as *is located in* to *goes (comes) to*. In Greek, these three aspectual oppositions for location, possession and nominal predication can all be expressed by the contrasting pair εἰμί-γίγνομαι.   194

§4. Hence, without having a definite "meaning of its own" *be* as copula nevertheless contributes something to the meaning of the sentence, in virtue of (1) its verbal marks of person, tense, etc. including the indicative mark of truth claim, and (2) its aspectual value *static*, as verb of state or station. The traditional hypothesis of the development of the copula role of *es- from some earlier use as verb of existence alone is to be rejected for Greek at any rate, in view of the overwhelming predominance of the copula construction in Homer (some 80% of all occurrences of the verb). 198

§5. The developmental view of the copula must be rejected also on transformational grounds: of the two alleged sources of the copula construction with *be*, (1) apposition presupposes the sentence type with *be*, and (2) the nominal sentence represents merely the zero form of the copula. The relation between apposition and copula is brought out by Jespersen's analysis of "predicatives of being" in English. 201

§6. *Be*-replacers (like *stands, remains, becomes*) are distinguished from *be*-modifiers (like *seems, appears, is known/thought/said to be*, etc.). The latter behave like other verb operators such as *begins, wants, tries* (to do such-and-such). Like the appositive construction, the *be*-modifiers also presuppose a copula construction in their transformational source. We are left with the question of a small group of static copulas as *be*-replacers (*stand, lie, sit*) and a comparable group of kinetic copulas or *become*-replacers (*turns, grows, goes*). Are these two groups to be derived from *be* and *become*? And is *become* in turn to be derived from *be*? 203

§7. Being is conceptually prior to becoming: *X becomes Y* implies or presupposes *X was not Y* and *X will be* (*begins to be*) *Y*, but not conversely. So in I.-E. there is a single, universal root for *is* (namely, **es-*), but a shifting set of *become*-verbs whose lexical value is determined in each case by their syntactical parallel and aspectual contrast with **es-*. *Becomes* could be analyzed as a verb operator on *be*, comparable in structure to *begins (to be)* or *comes (to be)*. 205

§8. The theoretical concept of the verb *be* as required in transformational grammar. The most purely empirical concept of the verb, e.g. as the total actual occurrences of the various forms of εἰμί in the text of Homer, contains a theoretical element in its selection of relevant forms, and even more so in its identification of *the text* of Homer (as distinct from particular copies or tokens). But transformational analysis requires a further theoretical extension in the reconstruction of *zero forms* in addition to actual occurrences. It is these zero forms which are presupposed in ellipse, in apposition, and in the nominal sentence. 207

§9. The proposal to eliminate copula *be* from deep structure leads in fact to a further generalization of the notion of *be*, completely

divorced from the concrete forms of *es- in I.-E.: "the *is* of predication", as represented by the generalized sentential scheme *Fa*.
This is the form of predication as such, as in the Port Royal
theory of the copula which is generalized for predicates of any
type. We must distinguish this from the actual use of *es-* as
copula in I.-E., which is restricted to non-verbal predicates.
There seem to be natural languages which approximate to a
general, uniform predicative scheme, as in the case of copulative
suffixes in Turkish. The Greek philosophers regarded the verb
εἰμί in just this way, as the generalized form of predication.   211

§10. Comparison with more restricted copula verbs in other languages.
Ewe has one copula verb for predicate nouns, another verb for
predicate adjectives and locatives (and this verb expresses existence and possession as well). Classical Chinese has no copula
with adjectives; however it has (or develops) a substantival copula,
and has a distinct locative verb. The I.-E. solution of a single
copula for nouns, adjectives and locatives, though not a sufficient
condition, was probably a necessary one for the generalized conception of Being in Greek philosophy.   215

§11. A survey of *be-* and *become*-replacers in Homer. The chief replacers of *es-* as static copula (in Homer and in I.-E. generally) are
the three verbs of posture: *sit*, *lie*, and *stand*. For the mutative
become-verbs the principal representative outside of Greek is
bhū- (the root of φύω, φύομαι "generate," "grow"). In Greek
the principle *become*-verb from Homer on is γίγνομαι/ἐγενόμην
"be born". Other verbs like τρέφομαι, πέλομαι, τελέθω, τέτυγμαι
serve as expressive or poetical equivalents for *be* or *become*. Of
these, only γίγνομαι has an important copula use in Attic prose.   217

§12. The vital-static-locative value *be alive, live, stay (in a place)*
is tentatively reconstructed for εἰμί as the center of the copulative
system in Greek. This hypothetical value is partially confirmed
by the Homeric use of εἰμί for "I am alive", and by various suppletive verbs for *be* in I.-E.: *wes-* in Germanic (originally "stay"
or "dwell"); *stato, été, estar* in Romance languages (from *stare*
"stand"). This gives us statements of place for personal subjects
as the paradigm form of predication with εἰμί. In summary,
we have three concepts of *be* as sign of predication: (1) predication in the widest sense as declarative sentencehood, i.e. truth
claim for a sentential structure of arbitrary form and content
(cf. veridical εἶναι in Chapter VII); (2) predication in the traditional sense, as a two-term syntactic form (*Fa* or *X is Y*) with

the corresponding semantic interpretation (F is true of a, Y is true of X). This corresponds to εἶναι in the sense of Aristotle's Categories, i.e. to the copula construction understood as the underlying form of *all* sentences; (3) the actual use of *es- as copula in I.-E., defined by contrast to sentences with "full" verbs. It is here, in the specific I.-E. data, that we have the copulative system of *be-become* verbs centered on εἰμί, which is in turn a verb with certain non-copulative uses.   222

VI / THE VERB OF EXISTENCE

§1. In addition to existential uses the non-copulative uses of εἰμί include the possessive, potential, and veridical constructions. The present chapter deals with all non-copulative uses except the veridical. Existential uses are more difficult to analyze than the copula constructions of Chapter IV, since the concept of existence is lexical or semantic rather than syntactic. The procedure to be followed here is (1) to give an informal account of the lexical nuances expressed by εἰμί in the so-called existential uses, (2) to isolate five or six characteristic sentence types in which the verb has an existential value, and (3) to specify in logical or semantic terms the force of the verb in each type.   228

§2. The difficulty in finding any general description or paraphrase value for the existential uses. The term "existential" is itself misleading as a description of the Greek usage of εἰμί.   230

§3. Informal description of the four nuances which can be distinguished in the lexical value of εἰμί as existential verb: vital, locative, durative, and existential in the strict sense (as represented by the existential quantifier in logic).   232

§4. Illustration of the four nuances: Sentences **1–13**.   235

§5. Preliminary sketch of six existential sentence types with εἰμί.   239

§6. Type I (the vital use), including the marginal case where εἰμί can be rendered "dwell, live (in a place)". Sentences **14–26**.   240

§7. Type II. Mixed assertions of existence for singular subjects, including subtype IIA with a topographical item as subject, and subtype IIB where subject is a person. Sentences **27–42**.   245

§8. Syntactical analysis of Type IIB: a locative sentence with an expressive ("existential") transformation marked by initial position for the verb, or a mixed example of copula-existential overlap.   251

§9. Analysis of Type IIA along the same lines.   255

§10. Post-Homeric parallels to Type II. Sentences **43–50**. 258

§11. Sentence Type III: the plural form of Type II and its affinity with the larger class of locative-existential uses; the problem of quantifier adjectives (*some, many, two*). Sentences **51–58**. 261

§12. The possessive construction (εἰμί with dative *x*, rendered as "*x* has"), including four distinct types: (i) ownership of property, (ii) kinship relations, (iii) part-whole relations, and (iv) surface possession, with abstract noun as subject of εἰμί and no possessive construction in the source sentence. Sentences **59–72**. 265

§13. Negative forms corresponding to Types II–III: denials of presence and relative denials of existence (denials of presence for a *sort* of thing in a given place). The relevant distinction between definite and indefinite syntax for the subject of εἰμί is not always clearly marked in Greek. Various forms of overlap between the existential value ("there is") and the copulative construction with either locative or nominal predicates. Sentences **73–83**. 271

§14. Type IV: the existential sentence operator (οὐκ) ἔστι ὅς (τις)+ *clause*, the analogue in natural language to the existential quantifier in logic: (∃x) *Fx*. Sentences **84–96**. 277

§15. Type V: εἰμί as surface predicate or verb of occurrence with abstract noun as subject. The verb is to be analyzed as sentence operator ("it occurs that") with the verb of the operand sentence transformed into subject noun of Type V. Thus κλαγγὴ νεκύων ἦν "There was a clamor of the dead" is a transform of νέκυες ἔκλαγξαν "The dead clamored". Sentences **97–107**. 282

§16. The concrete use of abstract nouns, and other problem cases connected with Type V. Sentences **108–111**. 288

§17. The potential construction: ἔστι +*infinitive*. Its similarity to and divergence from Type V. Sentences **112–120**. 292

§18. The post-Homeric Type VI: οὐδ' ἔστι Ζεύς "There is *no* Zeus"; εἰσὶ θεοί "The gods exist". The early examples of this type are generally associated with some scepticism concerning the existence of the traditional gods. Sentences **121–127**. 296

§19. The distinction between existence₁ (for individuals), as in Types II–IV, and existence₂ (for events, properties, states of affairs) as in Type V. We may speak of two senses or uses of "exists" corresponding to the lexical and syntactical divergences between these two. But the logical or semantical role of the verb is the same in both cases. 307

§20. The semantic role of the existential verb. We distinguish between the descriptive content (expressed by the operand sentence or sentences) and the semantic component (expressed by ἔστι or οὐκ ἔστι). The descriptive content may be of unlimited diversity, but the semantic component takes only two values: positive and negative. The differences between existence₁, existence₂, and the notion of truth correspond to syntactical differences in the form of the operand sentence in Types IV, V, and the veridical construction. But the semantic role of ἔστι/οὐκ ἔστι is the same: to posit or deny the realization of the descriptive content in the world.   310

§21. The problem of a semantic analysis for Type VI existentials. Four alternative construals of the underlying operand, one of which takes account of the intuitive connections between existence and location. The fourth construal emphasizes the generality of Type VI: the operand may be of *any* form. On all four views the verb ἔστι in Type VI is an existential sentence operator, and Type VI has the same general structure as Type IV.   315

§22. On the historical origins of Type VI. Approximations to the later existential sentence type in Homer. Sentences **128–129**.   320

§23. Appendix on mixed existential uses and on some apparent approximations to Type VI in Herodotus. A sample confirmation of the adequacy of the Types recognized here for the analysis of existential uses of the verb in post-Homeric Greek. Sentences **130–143**.   323

VII / THE VERIDICAL USE

§1. Veridical nuance and veridical construction. The use of εἰμί with the lexical value "is so," "is true" is wider than the veridical construction as a definite sentence type. The former has long been known; the latter is to be defined here for the first time and clearly distinguished from the copula and existential uses.   331

§2. Illustration and formal definition of the veridical construction. ἔστι ταῦτα and ἔστι οὕτω can both be derived from the fuller form ἔστι ταῦτα οὕτω ὡς σὺ λέγεις "These things are just as you say (that they are)." This veridical sentence type is defined by the following three conditions: (1) the construction of εἰμί is absolute; (2) the subject of the verb is a sentential structure, and (3) a demonstrative-comparative adverb such as οὕτως joins the clause with εἰμί to another clause with verb of saying (or thinking). The essive clause (with εἰμί) may have nearly the same structure as a Type V existential. Sentences **1–9**.   334

§3. Restricting the definition of the veridical construction to the "veri-

dical proper", where it coincides with the veridical nuance, may
not be possible in formal terms alone: the crucial feature is that
the intentional clause (of saying or thinking) must refer to a statement or to its cognitive analogue, a belief. Consideration of standard
formal variants on the veridical construction explains the close
affinity, but not identity, between the essive clause of the veridical
and a Type V existential use. Sentences **10–17**.   342

§4. The veridical construction in participial form, meaning "the
truth" or "the facts". This occurs once in Homer, frequently in
Attic and Ionic. The participial use is illustrated in detail from Herodotus. Further connections with Type V existential uses of εἰμί and
γίγνομαι as verb of occurrence. Sentences **18–27**.   349

§5. The veridical use and the copula construction. An underlying
sentence with nominal copula may have a veridical construction
superimposed upon it when this sentence is correlated with a clause
of saying or thinking. In this case the use of εἰμί in the essive clause
has the internal structure of the ordinary copula. Perhaps we may
speak of an *implicit* veridical construction in every instance where
εἰμί bears a distinct veridical nuance. In other cases where there is
no correlation with a clause of saying or thinking, a strong initial
position for the copula may carry a nuance of emphatic assertion
which underlines the truth claim of the sentence as a whole.
Sentences **28–36**.   355

§6. Parallels to the copula-veridical overlap in Homer. Sentences **37–41**.   360

§7. Some polemical reflections on the Greek notion of truth. The naive
analogue to a correspondence theory of truth ("Things are just as
you say") can be traced from Homer to Aristotle, and it is probably
prehistoric. Heidegger's view of ἀλήθεια as the "unhiddenness"
or self-disclosure of things does not give a correct account of the
Homeric use of this term; and in any case ἀλήθεια is only one
word among several for "truth" in Homer.   363

§8. Some uses of veridical εἶναι in Greek philosophy. The negative
form (οὐκ ἔστι ταῦτα, τὸ μὴ ὄν) is extremely rare in non-technical
literature, but systematically introduced by the philosophers next
to the affirmative formula. Some examples in Aristotle of εἶναι and
μὴ εἶναι for the general form of a proposition or a fact. A similar
use in the *Theaetetus*. This use is not strictly veridical: it represents the underlying function of the verb as sign of propositional truth claim. The properly veridical uses thematize this claim
and bring in the notion of truth by a comparison between what is
and what is claimed or thought to be.   366

VIII / THE UNITY OF THE SYSTEM OF 'BE' IN GREEK

§1. The plan of this chapter. Different points of view on the unity of
the system of εἰμί will be developed in turn, beginning with an
etymological inquiry as to the original meaning of *es-, and
concluding with a discussion of the conceptual unity of the system
in philosophical terms.   371

§2. The search for the original meaning of be (*es-) in Indo-European.
Attempts to discover an etymology have generally assumed that
the oldest meaning must be vivid or concrete. Hence the most
plausible candidates are the vital use (εἰμί = "I am alive") and the
locative-existential (εἰμί = "I am present," "I am at hand"). It is
fairly easy to construct an hypothesis according to which all uses
of εἰμί developed gradually from an original local-existential sense.   373

§3. Some general reasons against taking the suggested etymology of
be at its face value, as a chronological development of "abstract"
meanings from an original "concrete" sense. This view is based upon
a myth of primitive univocity. The examination of a few I.-E. roots
with known etymologies shows that some more general or abstract
meaning is present in the oldest and most concrete applications.
Thus *krei-, the root of criterion, implies a clear principle of
discrimination even in its etymological value "to sift, separate",
as applied to the operation of separating grain from chaff.   380

§4. The reinterpretation of the developmental hypothesis in synchronic
terms: spatial imagery is somehow fundamental in our thinking
generally, and in our concept of existence in particular. Philosophers have constantly made use of local metaphors in expressing
the idea of exists.   385

§5. The unity of εἰμί as a linguistic system: the aspectual contrast
stative-mutative defines the relationship between be and become, not
only in the predicative, locative, and possessive branches of the
system but also in the vital use (lives-is born), the existential (there
is-there occurs), and the veridical (τὰ ὄντα "the facts" as against
τὰ γεγονότα or τὰ γενόμενα "what occurred"). In addition, the
system of τίθημι (I.-E. *dhē-), put/make, parallels that of εἰμί
over almost its entire range. Put/make serves as causal-factitive
operator on be. We have a tripartite system for the expression of
state (εἰμί), change of state (γίγνομαι) and cause of state (τίθημι).
A further dimension of the system is indicated by the cognitive
operator seems/believes (δοκέω). These parallels help to determine
the position of εἰμί as the basic (stative-intransitive) verb in the

central system of verbs in Greek. Within the system, the philosophic antitheses of *Being-Becoming* and *Reality-Appearance* are
largely prepared.   388

§6. Transition to the final stage of the discussion. Abandoning the
traditional view that the existential uses are primary, we recognize the copula construction as central for the uses of εἰμί.
Three senses of *sign of predication* are distinguished, of successively
wider generality. A review of the syntactic division into first-order
(elementary) and second-order (derived) uses of εἰμί shows that
all properly existential uses are second-order, as is the veridical
use. We speak of veridical and existential constructions together
as the semantic uses of the verb.   394

§7. The copula and the semantic uses of *be*. A case is presented for
recognizing the triple use of *be* for predication, existence and truth
as a philosophical asset in Greek, a fortunate "accident" which
brings together concepts that are logically interdependent. This
interdependence is illustrated by an analogy with Quine's notion
of ontological commitment. Taking the elementary copula
construction of εἰμί as our point of departure, we see that the
function of the veridical and existential uses is to make explicit and
general what is implicit and particularized in the copula. These
semantic uses of εἰμί thus serve to express the fundamental conditions for the success of descriptive language as such.   400

§8. Concluding remarks on the static character of *be*, and on the absence
of a concept of ego or Self in Greek ontology. The principle of
stability seems to be fundamental in the scientific attempt to
understand the world, and in the concept of truth itself. The sharp
contrast between what "Being" means for the Greeks and what it
means for Heidegger reflects a fundamental disparity between ancient and modern metaphysics. There is no concept of a personal
self or ego in Greek theories of Being: no analogue to "cogito ergo
sum." The Greek philosophers failed to develop an ontology of
persons; but the verb *be* is not responsible.   415

ACKNOWLEDGEMENT

The University of Chicago Press has kindly granted permission to quote
extensively from Richmond Lattimore's translation of the *Iliad*.

CHAPTER I

INTRODUCTION

THE PROBLEM OF THE VERB 'BE'

La structure linguistique du grec prédisposait la notion d' "être" à une vocation philosophique.

ÉMILE BENVENISTE

§ 1. THE VERB *be* AND THE QUESTION OF LINQUISTIC RELATIVISM

Any linguistic study of the Greek verb *be* is essentially conditioned, and perhaps ultimately motivated, by the philosophic career of this word. We know what an extraordinary career it has been. It seems fair to say, with Benveniste, that the systematic development of a concept of Being in Greek philosophy from Parmenides to Aristotle, and then in a more mechanical way from the Stoics to Plotinus, relies upon the pre-existing disposition of the language to make a very general and diversified use of the verb εἰμί. Furthermore, insofar as the notions expressed by ὄν, εἶναι, and οὐσία in Greek underlie the doctrines of Being, substance, essence, and existence in Latin, in Arabic, and in modern philosophy from Descartes to Heidegger and perhaps to Quine, we may say that the usage of the Greek verb *be* studied here forms the historical basis for the ontological tradition of the West, as the very term "ontology" suggests.

At the same time it is generally recognized that this wide range of uses for the single verb εἰμί in Greek reflects a state of affairs which is "peculiar to Indo-European languages, and by no means a universal situation or a necessary condition."[1] The present monograph series on "the verb 'be' and its synonyms" shows just how far the languages of the earth may differ from one another in their expression for existence, for predication with nouns or with adjectives, for locative predication, and so forth. The topic of *be* can itself scarcely be defined except by reference to Indo-European verbs representing the root *es-*. The question naturally arises whether an historical peculiarity of this kind can be of any fundamental importance for general linguistics and, even more pressing, whether a concept reflecting the Indo-European use of *es-* can be of any general significance in philosophy. A philosophic linguist surveying the situation in Chinese can conclude:

---

[1] É. Benveniste, "Catégories de pensée et catégories de langue", in *Problèmes de linguistique générale* (Paris, 1966), p. 73.

"There is no concept of Being which languages are well or ill equipped to present; the functions of 'to be' [sc. as verb of predication in I.-E.] depend upon a grammatical rule for the formation of the sentence, and it would be merely a coincidence if one found anything resembling it in a language without this rule."[2] Philosophers and linguists alike have observed that Aristotle could scarcely have formulated the same doctrine of categories or the same substance-attribute metaphysics if his native language had been Ewe, Arabic, or Chinese. Given these facts of linguistic relativism it is a natural step, and one that has often been taken, to infer that the concepts and doctrines of traditional ontology simply represent the projection onto the universe of the linguistic structures of Greek or of Indo-European.

Taken literally, this strong thesis of linguistic determinism is clearly false, for it implies that all speakers of the same language must share the same metaphysics. But the ontologies of Plato and Aristotle, of Epicurus, Chrysippus, and Plotinus differ from one another in radical ways which can no more be accounted for by differences in the common language which these philosophers utilize, than the structure of English can account for philosophical disagreements between Whitehead, Quine, and Strawson. In a weaker form, however, the thesis is more convincing. Surely the structure of a language, the pattern of its syntax and vocabulary, tends to exert some deep influence upon philosophical reflection by the distinctions which it systematically makes or fails to make. And this influence is likely to be all the greater when, as in the case of Greece, the philosophers are familiar with no language but their own and make no use of a technical terminology derived from another tongue. So much, and no more, will we concede to the "linguistic relativity" of B. L. Whorf.

We may pass over more subtle forms of linguistic relativism, since they do not concern us directly. Thus one might claim that each language has a built-in conceptual structure which can be described as a *tacit* metaphysics and which is unconsciously presupposed by all thinkers who articulate their doctrines in that tongue. In the case of Greek, for example, the explicit disagreements among philosophers might be regarded as comparatively superficial: the deeper conceptual commitments would be the ones which they all take for granted. This thesis could be rendered more complicated, and more plausible, by introducing a relativised version of Strawson's distinction between descriptive and revisionary metaphysics. A descriptive ontology for Greek would be a theory like Aristotle's, which remains more faithful to the tacit metaphysics of the language, whereas a revisionary ontology like Plato's seems to go against the linguistic grain.

[2] A. C. Graham, "'Being' in Classical Chinese," *The Verb 'be' and its Synonyms*, Part I (1967), p. 15.

My own view is that no such claims are tenable, since they presuppose a degree of coherence and consistency in the tacit conceptual scheme which is simply not to be found in the case of a natural language. The truth is that the structure of any given language exhibits various conceptual tendencies, many of them in conflict with one another, and that different philosophers develop these tendencies in different ways. In this sense, a large number of alternative ontologies are "latent" in the language; but the task of philosophers is not only to bring these tendencies out of hiding but to give them rational form by articulating them in systematic theories. It is more by accident than by necessity that some arguments and evidence for or against such theories may in fact depend upon peculiarities of a given language.

§ 2. THE CONCEPT OF BEING AND THE CHALLENGE OF PHILOSOPHIC ANALYSIS

We agree, nevertheless, that the resources and tendencies of a philosopher's language are among the conditions for his philosophical activity. We may say, then, that the development of a general concept (or concepts) of Being in Greek philosophy is made possible by the system of uses of the Greek verb *be*, even if these linguistic facts do not determine the specific ontological doctrines of Parmenides, Plato, or Aristotle. They could not have a theory of τὸ ὄν or οὐσία at all if they did not have a verb εἰμί to provide them with a present participle and with a nominal derivative in -ία. There is no doubt that the unity of the concept expressed by these nominalized forms depends in some measure (and in ways which vary from thinker to thinker) upon the unity of the linguistic system associated with the verb, or more generally with the morpheme family ἐστί/εἶναι/ἐών, a system which is in its broad outlines Indo-European though some of its features are peculiarly Greek. The question we must ask, then, is whether this system of uses is unified *only* by the fact that a single sign (or family of signs) happens to serve these various linguistic functions, or whether they constitute a conceptual unity of some intrinsic philosophical importance. It would seem that only if there is some deep logical connection between these various uses could the traditional concept of Being remain a viable topic for philosophic discussion. If this system represents only an accidental bundling of essentially diverse and unrelated notions and functions, if the linguistic system unified around εἰμί in Greek (and more generally, around *es- in I.-E.) is merely a superficial and provincial fact about a certain family of languages, then the task of philosophy is rather to isolate the disparate members of this conglomerate and to clarify them separately.

Such has been the predominant view in British philosophy since John

Stuart Mill first emphasized the contrast between the existential and copulative functions of *be* and denounced "the frivolous speculations concerning
the nature of Being... which have arisen from overlooking this double meaning
of the word *to be*; from supposing that when it signifies *to exist*, and when
it signifies to *be* some specified thing... it must still, at bottom, answer to
the same idea, and that a meaning must be found for it which shall suit all
these cases."[3] So Russell, even when he continued to use the language of
"being," was careful to point out the range of ambiguity.

> The word *is* is terribly ambiguous, and great care is necessary in order not to confound
> its various meanings. We have (1) the sense in which it asserts Being, as in "A is"; (2) the
> sense of identity; (3) the sense of predication, in "A is human"; (4) the sense of "A is a-man"...
> which is very like identity. In addition to these there are less common uses, as "to be good
> is to be happy", where a relation of assertions is meant, that relation, in fact, which, where
> it exists, gives rise to formal implication. Doubtless there are further meanings which have
> not occurred to me.[4]

Since Russell, most philosophers of logic have agreed that we must distinguish at least three and perhaps four senses of "to be": (1) existence as
expressed by the quantifiers, (2) predication, as in Fx, (3) identity, as in
$x=y$, (4) class inclusion, symbolized as $x \subset y$. Russell once described it as
"a disgrace to the human race" that it has chosen to employ the same word
"is" for two such entirely different ideas as predication and identity.[5] The
general tendency of analytic philosophy in the twentieth century has been
to emphasize that, although there may or must be a philosophic account
of existence, of predication, of identity, and of class inclusion, there can be
no single concept of being which groups them all together.[6] Such nullifying
conclusions drawn from the logical analysis of notions ordinarily expressed
by *be* thus tend to reinforce the conclusions of linguistic relativism that show
how the functions grouped together by a single I.-E. verb are distributed
otherwise, among diverse and unrelated features of vocabulary and syntax,
in other languages such as Turkish or Chinese.

§ 3. Leśniewski's ontology as an illustration of the possi-bility of systematic interconnections between the differ-ent uses of *be*, taking the copula use as central

However, not all logicians have agreed to anatomize the venerable body of
Being in this drastic way and to exchange the erstwhile unity for the new

[3] *A System of Logic*, Book I, ch. iv, sect. 1. "Nature and Office of the Copula."
[4] *The Principles of Mathematics*, (London, 1903), p. 64n.
[5] *Introduction to Mathematical Philosophy*, (London, 1919), p. 172.
[6] See, e.g. the references to Carnap and Stegmüller given by E. Tugendhat, "Die Sprachanalytische Kritik der Ontologie", in *Das Problem der Sprache*, Achter Deutscher Kongress
für Philosophie, Heidelberg 1966, pp. 484 and 488.

disiecta membra. We must take note of an important enterprise carried out by the Polish logician Leśniewski from 1920 to 1939, which might be described as a counter-attack in defense of ontology. Leśniewski actually used this term "ontology" as a title for his own system of set theory. The term reflects his desire to reconcile the basic insights into being and predication contained in the Aristotelian tradition with the new logic of Frege and Russell. Thus he made use of a primitive relation of singular predication, represented by an epsilon, which functions like the traditional copula after singular subject terms, with a nominal predicate that may be either singular or general. In Leśniewski's usage, "$x \varepsilon y$" may take as true substitution instances "Socrates is wise," "Socrates is Socrates," "Socrates is the husband of Xanthippe," or "The husband of Xanthippe is wise." Identity (for individuals) is defined as a special case of the epsilon relation, namely, the case where "$x \varepsilon y$" and "$y \varepsilon x$" are both true; and what Russell regarded as "a disgrace to the human race," the use of a single sign for predication and identity, is thus in part justified.[7]

On the basis of this primitive copula for singular subjects or individuals, higher levels of predication can be defined for subjects and predicates of other semantic categories, for example, a second-order *is* joining functors or predicate-expressions.[8]

It is also possible to define "x exists" in terms of the ε-relation, with or without the use of quantifiers.[9]

In the semantic interpretation, the existence of an individual x is among the truth conditions for "$x \varepsilon y$". Thus, although only the ε-relation is formally primitive, the semantic interpretation introduces the notions of truth for sentences and existence for singular individuals, as subjects or elements of the domain of the elementary ε-relation.

Leśniewski's Ontology shows how all or most of the uses of *be* in Indo-European languages can be derived from three basic notions: truth, predication for singular subjects, and existence for singular subjects. This reduction is clearly Aristotelian in spirit. And it may prove suggestive for our own

---

[7] There is a conscious approximation to Leśniewski's view in Quine's use of the same symbol ("ε") for class-membership and identity, in *Mathematical Logic* (2nd ed. Cambridge, Mass. 1951), p. 122. For Leśniewski's theory, see E. C. Luschei, *The Logical Systems of Leśniewski* (1962), pp. 144ff. and C. Lejewski, "On Leśniewski's Ontology", *Ratio* 1 (1958), 150–76.

[8] See Lejewski, "Proper Names", *PAS* 1958, pp. 247–49, where "Man is a species" is interpreted by the use of a second-level "is" between two functors: "Form-the-class-of-men is form-a-species." This corresponds (though in a different grammatical category) to the *is* of "To be good is to be happy," whose distinct character was recognized by Russell in the citation on p. 4 above.

[9] Where x (and y) is a first-order noun, "x exists" is defined by the formula for *ob x*:
x exists $\equiv x \varepsilon x \equiv (\exists y) \, x \varepsilon y$.

theoretical articulation of the Greek use of εἰμί. In passing, we may observe
a kind of echo of Leśniewski's scheme in Quine's own notion of ontological
commitment as expressed in the slogan "to be is to be the value of a variable."
Given the apparatus of predication and quantification together with the
notion of truth, what a theorist is committed to, according to Quine, is the
existence of those entities which figure irreducibly as the values of bound
variables in the formulas that he soberly accepts as true. Here the Aristotelian
inspiration has vanished but we are left again with the three fundamental
notions of existence, predication, and truth.[10]

This brief glance at Leśniewski's Ontology is designed to provide some
counter-weight to the dominant tendency in the Mill-Russell-Carnap tradition which insists upon the *diversity* of meanings and functions for *be*. The
spokesmen for this tradition often assume, for example, that because the
"is" of the copula and the "is" (or "there is") of existence are distinct
in meaning and in grammar, there can be no wider conceptual system that
relates them to one another. Thus they overlook the possibility that, even
if the system of *be* cannot be reduced to a single unambiguous meaning,
it may nevertheless exhibit *some* conceptual unity. The ontology of Leśniewski, and perhaps also that of Quine, suggests how the various uses and senses
of *be* need not be taken as sheerly equivocal (as the dominant tradition tends
to suppose), but that they may be recognized as distinct and nonetheless
related to one another in a systematic way. In that case the concept of Being
might be salvageable after all as a higher-order notion, not simply reducible
to existence or predication or truth or assertion, but representing a complex
system within which the various kinds of *is* might be interdefined or mutually
explicated.

Something like this was explicitly claimed by Aristotle in the doctrine
which G. E. L. Owen has baptized "focal meaning," a theory of the semantic
status of certain terms that represent neither synonyms nor homonyms but
πρὸς ἓν λεγόμενα, a plurality of uses and senses unified by reference to a
single base.[11] For Aristotle, all senses of "to be," or rather all modes and

---

[10] Not only does Quine take *to be* in the now rather uncommon sense of *to exist*; he also
uses the term "ontology" in a way which was frowned on by Carnap but which, as Quine
rightly remarks, preserves a traditional sense that "has been nuclear to its usage all along".
See "On Carnap's Views on Ontology", reprinted in *The Ways of Paradox, and other
Essays* (New York, 1966), p. 127.

[11] See *Met.* Gamma 2, 1003a33–b10. Strictly speaking, for Aristotle it is not the word "being"
which has a systematic diversity of meanings but rather *things* of different kinds and orders
which are said *to be* (are called "beings") in different ways, by reference to one fundamental
kind of being, that of substances. As different individuals and kinds of things are called
"homonyms" if they share a name only, "synonyms" if they share both a name and a
definition (or an explanatory paraphrase of the name), so they are πρὸς ἓν λεγόμενα if (1)
they share a name or designation, let us say "φ", and (2) do not share a definition or a

kinds of being, were related in this way to a fundamental base or focus, which he identified as the being of individual substances, a fused notion of being which includes both the *existence* of these objects as distinct individuals and also their *being-such-and-such* or *being-of-a-certain-kind*, e.g. their being men or being horses. The parallel between Aristotle and Leśniewski may be brought out if we think of the former as having one fundamental concept, the being of particular substances, where Leśniewski has two: singular existence and predication for singular subjects in the ε-relation.

I do not propose to take Aristotle's analysis of εἰμί for granted, any more than I take for granted Russell's analysis of *be* or Leśniewski's account of predication. But I do intend to explore the possibility that there is *some* systematic unity of a logical or philosophically relevant sort underlying the Greek uses of this verb, that the uses to be studied here are not related to one another in a merely accidental and historical way. Such an assumption may be provisionally defended as a heuristic device, since it encourages us to look for some systematic unity and perhaps to find it.

§ 4. Gilson's philosophical defence of the linguistic view of *be* (indo-european *es-) as primarily a verb of existence

Here at the outset we wish to leave open the question as to which use of εἰμί is to be regarded as most basic or whether several cases are to be recognized as equally fundamental. Hence it is well to make explicit, and thus open to critical discussion, two contrasting views as to the fundamental use of the verb *be*. If we regard Leśniewski's Ontology as an account of the systematic unity of *be*, we can say that the adoption of a primitive epsilon (in a basic formula such as "AεB") represents the claim that the primary case of *is*, the central focus or base of the system is to be located in the copulative construction of *is* with nominal predicates. A rather similar emphasis on the copula is suggested by the familiar logical expression for predication or being-such-and-such in the form "*Fx*". Whereas other verbs would be

---

single explanatory paraphrase corresponding to this name, but have diverse accounts (λόγοι) of what it means for them to be φ, and yet (3) these different accounts are related to one another by the fact that they all refer to one primary case of being φ (e.g. to substances, where "φ" is "being"). Thus the doctrine of πρὸς ἕν λεγόμενα is properly a concept in what Henry Hiż has called *strong* semantics, where an extra-linguistic notion such as truth or reference is involved; it is not a concept in *weak* semantics, explicable in terms of linguistic paraphrase values alone, since neither the ἕν nor the λεγόμενα represent linguistic expressions, nor even "meanings," but things and kinds of things. Hence the term "focal meaning" may be misleading insofar as it suggests or admits an interpretation in weak semantics only, involving only linguistic expressions and their paraphrase values.

analyzed as distinct predicates (like nouns or adjectives) and symbolized as "*F*", the verb *be* vanishes into the bare form of predication itself.[12]

This analysis, which treats verbal and nominal predicates as logically comparable or formally equivalent but sharply distinguishes both of them from the verb *be*, may be regarded as a natural outcome of the medieval theory of the copula, as reformulated in grammatical terms by the Port Royal *Logic*. According to this view there is, strictly speaking, only one true verb, *is*, which serves for predication (or rather for "affirmation" in the Port Royal doctrine): every other verb can be analyzed as a combination of *is* with a nominal concept. Thus *John runs* represents *John is running* or *John is a runner*: "C'est la même chose de dire *Pierre vit*, que de dire *Pierre est vivant*."[13]

In view of this constant tendency in the Western logical tradition to treat *be* as different in kind from other verbs and to assimilate the latter to nominal predicates, it is worth bearing in mind the spirited defense of the properly verbal function of *be* (in its strong sense of "to exist, to be something real,") formulated by Gilson in one of the concluding chapters of *L'être et l'essence*. He contrasts the logician's desire to reduce *be* to a copula, and all other verbs to nouns, with a more faithful linguistic account that sees *to be* or *to exist* as the primary intransitive verb, the expression of the most fundamental "subjective action" (that is, an intransitive action which terminates in the subject and does not involve an object). "Que l'on dise *il est*, *il existe*, ou *il y a*, le sens reste le même. Toutes ces formules signifient l'action première que puisse exercer un sujet. Première, elle l'est en effet, puisque, sans elle, il n'y' aurait pas de sujet."[14] The verb *be*, in its existential use, is thus the verb *par excellence*, not because it affirms or predicates some attribute of the subject but because it poses the subject itself, as agent in the "primary act" of existence and hence as a possible subject for the secondary acts or operations signified by other verbs.

[12] Thus Quine's dictum, "to be is to be the value of a variable," represents a quite different interpretation of *be*, one which takes as its focus the existential "there is an *x* (which is F)" rather than the copulative "*x* is *F*." Of course the two interpretations are compatible, if we do not insist that some one use of *be* is more fundamental than all the others.

[13] *La logique ou l'art de penser*, IIe Partie, ch. 2: "Du verbe." The Aristotelian background of this doctrine is familiar: (see below, p. 215, n. 45). Note however that what Aristotle claims is that every verbal predication can be paraphrased by a sentence with *be* + nominal predicate; and so much remains true. What the Port Royal grammarians seem to hold, however, is that the *be* + *nominal* form is in every case more basic or fundamental than its verbal equivalent. And here they are in conflict with the analysis given by modern grammar, which excludes *be* from elementary or kernel sentences wherever the nominal predicate itself is derivative from an elementary verb. Thus the *is* in *John is running* and *John is a runner* is not the elementary copula but the result of a transformational derivation: the elementary or kernel form of both sentences is *John runs*. See below, Section 8.

[14] *L'être et l'essence* (1948), p. 275. Gilson is appealing to the analysis of French verbs by Ferdinand Brunot.

Gilson's interpretation of the verb *be* is metaphysically motivated, but it may usefully serve to remind us that εἰμί and its cognates are, after all, unquestionably verbal in form and morphologically parallel to other old verbs signifying "go" (εἶμι, ἰέναι), "make to go," "send" (ἵημι, ἱέναι), "say" (φημί, φάναι), "set upright," "stand" (ἵστημι, ἱστάναι, aor. στῆναι), "place" (τίθημι, τιθέναι, θεῖναι) and "give" (δίδωμι, διδόναι, δοῦναι). Hence students of comparative grammar have always assumed that the independent and "existential" uses of the verb *es-* in Indo-European are more ancient and fundamental than the copulative use, and that the latter is a late and secondary development. This is a thesis which we will have occasion to challenge in Chapters V and VIII. For the moment I simply note that, although the independent, non-copulative uses of *be* are more important in ancient Greek than in a modern language such as English, the copulative uses are still vastly more frequent in every attested state of Greek, beginning with the *Iliad*.

§ 5. PRELIMINARY REQUIREMENTS FOR A DESCRIPTION OF εἰμί IN GREEK

The question of a systematic unity for the uses of εἰμί cannot be discussed further until we have described these uses in their factual diversity. And here a method of linguistic description is required. First of all, in the absence of living speakers of ancient Greek we need a fixed and manageable corpus as the basis for our description. We also need a linguistic theory to provide us with the terms and concepts for the description.

As my primary corpus I choose the two Homeric epics, the *Iliad* and the *Odyssey*, as the earliest monuments of the language in usable form. (The older documents from the Linear B tablets do not provide us with sentences illustrating the verb εἰμί in any interesting way.) We want to study the uses of the verb *before* it became a topic for philosophical discussion, and the Homeric poems provide the only substantial body of pre-philosophical literature. We are concerned here with the ontological predispositions of the Greek language, and not with the philosophic doctrines that exploit these linguistic possibilities. On the other hand, the philosophical discussion exercised only a marginal influence even on literary usage, and I will not hesitate to consider examples from post-Homeric Greek. In fact I systematically include specimens of classical prose and poetry, to illustrate both the underlying continuity between the Homeric and classical uses of εἰμί and also the development of new complexities (or occasionally, simplifications) in the later stage of the language.

Another reason for concentrating on a relatively complete description of the Homeric usage is to obtain results that will, as far as possible, reflect the wider Indo-European situation. Many of the facts concerning εἰμί are also facts concerning I.-E. *es-. As a general rule, it is in these archaic texts that such facts emerge most clearly.

My method of description will be inspired by some of the recent work in transformational grammar, insofar as this can be used to sharpen and clarify the familiar insights of historical philology. I have no intention of throwing overboard the fruits of classical scholarship, historical knowledge, *Sprachgefühl*, and literary sensitivity. I do intend to add the rudiments of a grammatical theory along the lines of current work in English syntax, because I think that this will often help to make precise what classical scholars have always known in their bones. As Chomsky has observed, traditional grammar was implicitly transformational.[15] The advantage of transformational theory is to develop certain familiar principles in an explicit and systematic way. I shall borrow and where necessary construct such a theory, but only insofar as this seems helpful for the immediate purpose at hand, namely, to describe and classify the attested uses of εἰμί. I shall certainly not construct or even sketch a general transformational syntax for Ancient Greek. I do not know whether this can be done at all for a language with no living speakers, but insofar as it is feasible, the job will be done by professional linguists, and not by an amateur like myself.[16] The grammatical principles used here will consist only of a few elementary concepts borrowed from current work in English syntax and applied in an obvious way to the Greek material. For readers unfamiliar with the work of Zellig S. Harris, I briefly describe the theory from which I shall be borrowing.

§ 6. OUTLINE OF THE TRANSFORMATIONAL SYSTEM TO BE USED HERE

The beginnings of contemporary syntax can be dated to 1946, when, in Harris' paper "From Morpheme to Utterance," the formal techniques of descriptive linguistics, originally developed for the study of phonemes and morphemes, were for the first time applied in a systematic way to the analysis of syntax and sentence structure.[17] These new methods, which center on the concept of grammatical transformation, have been elaborated over the last twenty years in two distinct directions by Harris and by his former student Noam Chomsky. Since both schools of transformational grammar are in a

---

[15] "A Transformational Approach to Syntax," in Fodor and Katz, *The Structure of Language* (Englewood Cliffs, N. J., 1964), p. 211 n. 2.

[16] For a professional attempt to cover some of the field for Latin from a rather different transformational viewpoint, see Robin T. Lakoff, *Abstract Syntax and Latin Complementation* (Cambridge, Mass. 1968).

[17] *Language* 22 (1946), 161–183, reprinted in Z. S. Harris, *Papers in Structural and Transformational Linguistics* (Dordrecht, 1970), pp. 32–67.

rapid state of development, only partially reflected in available publications, it is perhaps too soon to say how far the differences between them are due simply to two contrasting temperaments and styles of exposition, or how far they reflect two fundamentally distinct views of the scope and nature of linguistic theory. In my own analysis I shall draw largely on Harris' version of the theory, in part because I am better acquainted with it as a result of conversation with my colleagues in Linguistics at the University of Pennsylvania, but also because it is simpler, less abstract, and hence more immediately applicable to the descriptive task before us.[18]

Chomsky describes his enterprise as "generative grammar": the construction of an abstract system of symbols and rules which, when applied in a specified order, will generate every grammatical sentence of a language (e.g. of English) together with a structural description of each sentence, and which will generate no non-sentence. Here the actual sentences of a given language appear only among the end-products of the theory and as an empirical test of its adequacy. In Harris' analysis, on the other hand, one begins with given sentences of any degree of complexity, and proceeds to decompose them, via transformations, into one or more simpler sentences of certain fixed types, the so-called kernel sentences of the language. The theory of kernel sentences is essentially a more precise reformulation of the familiar notion of *simple sentence*; the concept of transformation is a theoretical elaboration of the idea that all compound and complex sentences can be derived from or constructed out of simple sentences in a regular way. The entire grammar thus consists of only two parts: the set of kernel sentences, subdivided into types or elementary sentence forms, and the set of transformations that operate either on kernel sentences or on previously transformed kernels, to produce all the sentences in the language. Hence Harris' theory can also be interpreted as "generative," if one begins with the kernel sentences and derives the rest by transformation. It can be equally well seen, however, as proceeding in the opposite direction, from a given sentence of arbitrary structure to its decomposition into underlying elementary sentences – what Harris calls the factoring of a given sentence into its prime sentences – in other words, into kernels which, together with some of the transformations,

---

[18] For Chomsky's own statement of the historical connections between his work and that of Harris, see his remarks in "Current Issues in Linguistic Theory," reprinted in Fodor and Katz, *The Structure of Language*, p. 83, n. 29; also, in the same anthology, p. 128 n. 23 and p. 223, n. 23. Several of the earlier papers of Harris and Chomsky are reprinted in this work. For fuller statements of Chomsky's theories see *Syntactic Structures* (1957) and *Aspects of the Theory of Syntax* (1965). The views of Harris used here are those expressed in "Transformational Theory," *Language* 41 (1965), 363–401, and *Mathematical Structures of Language* (New York, 1968). Since this was written, "Transformational Theory" has been reprinted in the collected *Papers* mentioned in the preceding note; but my page references are to the original publication in *Language*.

bear all the information of the original sentence. The theory is thus capable, in principle, of providing a program for the computerized analysis of ordinary English texts by their decomposition into kernel form.[19] And insofar as the kernel sentences and transformations of one language can be correlated with the kernel sentences and transformations of another much more effectively than the individual words or arbitrary sentences can be correlated from one language to another, the technique of transformational decomposition into kernels perhaps offers a promising basis for a procedure of mechanical translation between languages – in that remote day when the preliminary mechanical *analysis* of each language has been achieved.

I shall begin with a rather technical discussion of transformations in order to do justice to the rigor of the theory and also in an attempt to clarify the difference between transformations as envisaged by Harris and by Chomsky.[20] In the next Section (§7) I shall apply the theory in a description of *be* in English.

Harris defines a transformation as a relation of equal acceptability between two sentence forms A and B with respect to a single set of words to be inserted at the corresponding places in the two forms. Thus if A and B are two sentence forms that constitute a transformation, and if A_1 and A_2 are the two sentences which result when a given set of words is inserted in each form, then if A_1 is a normal sentence, B_1 is normal also; if A_1 is marginally acceptable, B_1 is marginally acceptable; if A_1 is limited to a special kind of discourse, B_1 is also so limited. To take a familiar example, the active-passive transformation is represented by the relation between the normal sentences *John loves Mary* and *Mary is loved by John*, between the marginal sentences *The bone bites the dog* and *The dog is bitten by the bone*, and between the technical sentence *This set satisfies the specified condition* and *The specified condition is satisfied by this set*.[21] More generally, the active-passive transformation can be defined as the relation between the two English sentence forms N_1VN_2 and N_2 *be Ven by* N_1 (where N designates the word-class of nouns, V the class of verbs, *Ven* the participial forms such as *loved* and *bitten*, and the subscripts indicate successive occurrences of members of the same class). The relation preserves sentencehood, since for any set of

---

[19] See Danuta Hiż and A. K. Joshi, "Transformational Decomposition: A simple description of an algorithm for transformational analysis of English sentences, *Proceedings of the 2nd Intern. Conference on Computational Linguistics*, Grenoble, France (Aug. 1967).

I apologize to my purist friends for the use of the term "kernels" as a convenient shorthand for "kernel forms" or "elementary sentences."

[20] Chomsky's own statement of the difference in 1962 (Fodor and Katz, p. 83 n.) is inapplicable to the recent formulations of Harris' theory.

[21] See Harris, *Mathematical Structures* 4.1.2 to 4.1.4; "Transformational Theory," 367–371. In summarizing the theory here I omit a number of complications explicitly treated in Harris' discussion.

words representing the classes *N, V, N* (e.g. *John, love, Mary*, or *bone, bite, dog*) the resulting pair of utterances has like acceptability as sentences of English. Transformations are thus defined as a relation of equal acceptability between (1) two sentence forms, (2) two sets of sentences realizing these forms, by the insertion of actual words for the class-symbols *N, V,* etc., and (3) any pair of sentences produced by inserting the same words for the same symbol in each form. Normally we will consider transformations in the most concrete and specific form (3), as a relation between a pair of particular sentences.[22] Thus we speak of the transformation relation between two sentences *John loves Mary* ↔ *Mary is loved by John*, and may describe either sentence as a transform of the other.

So much for the concept of transformation in a very general sense, as a kind of (grammatical) equivalence relation between sentences. The concept becomes much more interesting, however, when we regard the relation as dynamic rather than static, when we treat one of the two sentences as primitive, the other as derived, and thus define the transformation as an *operation* that acts, in our example, on the active sentence (the operand) to produce the passive version (the derived sentence, or transform). When transformations are conceived in this way we draw the arrow in one direction only: *John loves Mary → Mary is loved by John*.[23] In this form there is an obvious similarity between transformations in Harris' system and in Chomsky's, although for the latter transformations are defined not on sentences but on "phrase-markers" (i.e. on structural descriptions of strings of symbols which become actual sentences only when the terminal string of symbols is converted into a *phonetic* description by the final application of morphophonemic rules). For Chomsky the active-passive transformation, even if written in the same way, viz. as $N_1 V N_2 \rightarrow N_2$ *be Ven by* N_1, represents not a relation between two English sentences but a rule for changing a structural description in the course of generating the second sentence, not from another given sentence but from the symbol "S" (for *sentence* in general). Thus where a transformational derivation for Harris begins with kernel sentences (such as *John loves Mary*), Chomsky's generative derivations begin with abstract rules such as $S \rightarrow NP + VP$, ("*Sentence* becomes *Noun phrase + Verb phrase*"). For Harris, transformations are defined either as relations or as operations between sentences, sets of sentences, or sentence-forms. For Chomsky both transformations proper and the more basic "rewrite rules" of the type just

---

[22] For simplicity, I ignore for the moment the case of binary transformations, where one sentence is derived from two kernels. See the example of sentence (3) on p. 14.

[23] For transformations as operations whose direction is defined by the nature of the "trace" or formal difference between the two sentences, see *Mathematical Structures*, 4.1.5.2.

quoted are defined only as operations upon strings of symbols with associated structural descriptions.[24] In general I shall follow Harris' terminology and speak of transformations only between two sentences or sentence-forms. But there are some cases where this strict limitation on the use of the term proves inconvenient, for example for nominalizations. Thus the relation between (1) *John loves Mary* and (2A) *John's loving Mary* or (2B) *that John loves Mary* or (2C) *for John to love Mary* is not a transformation for Harris, since (2A-C) are not sentences. Harris calls these "deformations" of (1). In the interests of a simplified terminology I shall here use "transformation" more loosely, so that we may describe (2A-C) as nominalized transforms of (1). Since in a nominalizing operation like *John loves Mary → John's loving Mary* the operand at any rate is always a grammatical sentence, this departure from Harris' terminology seems relatively trivial, and is in any case not without precedent.[25] A similarly extended use of the term "transformation" is also convenient when we are describing the derivation of a phrase or subordinate clause from a sentence. For example, the sentence (3) *A tall man entered the room* may be decomposed into the two kernels (3A) *A man entered the room* and (3B) *A man is tall* (with the meta-linguistic restriction that *a man* in the two kernels refers to the same individual). The derivation of (3) from (3A) and (3B) is a (binary) transformation in the strict sense, where one sentence form AN_1VN_2 is derived from two kernel forms, N_1 *is* A and N_1VN_2 (A representing adjectives). But I will also want to say that the phrase *a tall man* is derived "by transformation" from *a man is tall*, although the "transform" in this case is not a sentence. Analogously, I will describe the formation of a relative clause as a transformation, e.g. *A man entered the room → The man who entered the room*.

Once transformations are conceived as operations that derive some sentences from others, it is possible to define a set of kernel sentences, the elementary sentences or sentence-forms of the language, from which all other sentences may be derived (or into which they may be decomposed) by grammatical transformation. Note that the set of kernel sentences is determined only *relative to the transformations*: each time a new transformation is defined, the number and variety of elementary sentences is reduced. Recent work on the definite article in English suggests that *the* can usually be transformationally derived; hence kernel sentences will in general not

---

[24] For a more adequate account of transformations in Chomsky's theory see his "A Transformational Approach to Syntax," in Fodor and Katz, *The Structure of Language*, pp. 211–245; and, for a less technical account, see John Lyons, *Introduction to Theoretical Linguistics*, pp. 249–269.
[25] See, for example, Zeno Vendler, *Adjectives and Nominalizations*, (The Hague, 1968) p. 31 and passim.

contain the definite article.[26] Harris proposes that pronouns, numbers, and most plurals be introduced by recognized transformations and need not be admitted into the kernel. "The kernel sentences are not only short and of simple form, but are also composed of a restricted and simple vocabulary: mostly concrete nouns and verbs and adjectives, and mostly unimorphemic words. Most morphologically derived words are not in the kernel.... The kernel words are mostly concrete, because action nouns, nouns of result, and many abstract nouns are in general nominalizations of sentences under [certain] operators," and many expressions of mode, aspect, or "propositional attitude" (like *S is a fact, John believes that S*) can be transformationally derived.[27]

The concept of elementary or kernel sentence (and I shall here use "elementary" and "kernel" as interchangeable) is of great linguistic interest, and also of considerable importance for philosophy, insofar as philosophers are concerned with the syntax of sentences in a natural language. It is true that much of the work on "the logical syntax of language" in the Frege-Russell-Carnap tradition is primarily concerned with the simplified or purified syntax of *formalized* languages, designed as a canonical notation for science; and here there will only be a general analogy, say, between the atomic formulae of the notation and the kernel sentences of English. But much that has been thought of as philosophical grammar in the ordinary-language tradition is in fact an amateurish or at least pre-scientific exploration of the domain of empirical syntax for natural languages. And now that the main outlines of a scientific syntax for English (at least) are becoming apparent, it should be possible for philosophers to profit from this theory in order to increase the rigor of their own syntactic analyses, and in order to reformulate those problems which turn out to be not questions of grammar after all. The philosophical analysis of language will not disappear simply because syntax has become rigorous, any more than the philosophy of nature was eliminated by the rise of physics and biology as autonomous sciences. But at least there is no longer any excuse for speaking metaphorically of the logical or philosophical "grammar" of a natural language, once its actual grammar can be adequately described – in depth – by theoretical linguistics.

---

[26] See Beverly Robbins, *The Definite Article in English Transformations* (The Hague, 1968).
[27] "Transformational Theory", p. 385. Kernel sentences have also appeared, though not in so conspicuous a place, in Chomsky's early version of the theory. See, for example, his reference to "simple, declarative active sentences with no complex noun or verb phrases," in Fodor and Katz, p. 129; for Chomsky kernel and derived sentences are distinguished by the fact that the former are generated by obligatory transformations only, the latter by optional transformations as well, *ibid.* 223. But this distinction has perhaps disappeared from Chomsky's theory in *Aspects of Syntax*.

The new concept which is of greatest philosophical significance, in my opinion, is Harris' theory of kernel sentences, even if the set of such sentences is not exactly delimited. This is not a defect of the theory, for in fact the set of grammatical sentences is also not exactly delimited. Given the grammatical sentences of English (i.e. the sentences acceptable to a native speaker), the kernel sentences are determined just to the extent that we have an adequate account of all the transformations. For, when any particular sentence is given, we can decompose it into one or more simple, declarative sentences with a concrete vocabulary, together with the relevant transformational history (i.e. together with a partially ordered list of the transformations by which the given sentence is derived from the reconstructed kernels). The fact that kernel sentences can be determined even in a relative or tentative way should prove useful for the discussion of many philosophical questions. It may very well turn out that no problems in logic or epistemology can be solved (or even dissolved) by the discovery that sentences such as *I know that it rained yesterday, That it rained yesterday surprised me,* and *That it rained yesterday is a fact* are derived from the elementary sentence *It rained yesterday* by transformations of the same grammatical type. And yet this grammatical discovery should at least help to clarify the philosophic discussion. Thus the transformational data suggest that *This sentence is true* or *This sentence is false* is grammatical only to the extent that *I know this sentence* and *This sentence surprised me* are also grammatical.[28] Similarly the fact that all questions and commands can be derived from declarative sentences by what Harris calls "performative operators" should shed some light both on the logic of questions and imperatives and also on Austin's theory of performatives.[29] Again, many philosophers have sought to reduce statements that refer to attributes or abstract properties, such as beauty or illness, to other statements where these properties appear only in predicate form. Thus, instead of saying "Supreme beauty was manifest in Helen," or "Helen's beauty exceeded that of all other women," they would insist upon formulations of the type: "Helen was supremely beautiful" or "Helen was more beautiful than all other women." Russell once wrote that "All propositions in which an attribute or a relation *seems* to be the subject are only significant if they can be brought into a form in which the attribute is attributed or the relation relates."[30] Not all philosophers will agree on this need for reparsing attribute-nouns as predicate expressions, but it is surely of interest to note that such a reduction is automatically carried out when a sentence containing an action noun or quality noun is decomposed into its kernels. For predicate

[28] See *Mathematical Structures*, 5.8.3, and "Transformational Theory", pp. 375–77.
[29] See "Transformational Theory", pp. 391 f. and below, Chapter V §2a.
[30] *Logic and Knowledge* (ed. R. C. Marsh), pp. 337f.

phrases like *is beautiful, is sick,* but not property-words like *beauty* and *sickness,* will belong to the kernel vocabulary. These "abstract" nouns will be analyzed as nominalized transforms of the adjectival predicates, just as *blushing* or *explosion* will be derived by nominalization from *blushes* or *explodes.*[31] Examples such as *beauty* and *sickness* show very clearly that morphological derivation may, but need not, coincide with syntactical derivation, and that the syntactical (transformational) derivation is always of greater philosophic interest when the two diverge. In the nominalized forms *sickness, illness, ugliness,* syntax and morphology are at one, since these forms contain the predicate-morpheme *sick, ill,* etc. plus the property-forming morpheme *-ness.* In the case of *beautiful,* however, the situation is apparently reversed: it is the property-word *beauty* which serves as the morphological base for the adjectival-predicate form. But this situation is the result of a secondary development: in the older French form *beauté* the derivation of the property-word from the corresponding (predicate) adjective *beau* is transparent. (The adjective-forming morpheme *-ful,* as in *grateful, merciful, fanciful,* is simply a device for providing concrete predicate forms for property-words which have lost their adjectival base or which have developed from some other, more complex source.) And in contemporary use *beauty* is related to *beautiful* just as *sickness* is related to *sick.* The transformational analysis, in terms of the nominalization of predicate forms, preserves the primacy of syntactical derivation regardless of such morphological vagaries. For these reasons, and for others like them, I suggest that the definition of kernel sentences in transformational theory represents the most important contribution to the philosophical search for a ground-level "object language" *within* natural languages since Aristotle's account of the basic forms of predication in his *Categories.*

§ 7. KERNEL SENTENCE FORMS FOR ENGLISH AND A TRANSFORMATIONAL ANALYSIS OF THE ENGLISH VERB *be*

Let me breathe a little life into this skeletal outline of transformational theory by illustrating the kernel sentence forms currently recognized, and suggesting what light this sheds on the analysis of *be* in English, where the material is immediately familiar to us. Before listing the kernel forms, however, I should emphasize once more that the set of kernel sentences is determined only in relation to a given state of transformational theory; and as long as

[31] This, at least, is my view of the matter. The parallel between nominalizations from nominal predicates (i.e. from elementary nouns and adjectives) and from verbs has not been treated systematically, as far as I know. It is mentioned by Vendler, *Adjectives and Nominalizations,* p. 50. It will be more fully dealt with below. See Chapter III §7.

the analysis of transformations is subject to revision or reformulation, the same will be true of any account of kernel sentences. Furthermore, even apart from a definite *advance* in the theory as represented by the discovery and definition of a new transformation, the theory at a given stage will admit of alternative formulations corresponding to different considerations of convenience, simplicity, or clarity. In this case I follow Harris' formulation in *Mathematical Structures*, because it clearly distinguishes the role of *be* from that of other verbs in the kernel.

In the following list, symbols stand for word-classes as follows (where each class is in principle to be defined extensionally by a complete list of its members): N stands for elementary nouns, V for elementary verbs other than *be*, P for prepositions, A for adjectives, N_{rel} for a subclass of elementary relational nouns, and D_{loc} for locative adverbs. The seven or eight kernel sentence and infra-sentence forms are then:

1. *NV: A man arrives.*
2. *NVN, NVPN: John loves Mary.*
    John looks at Mary. $\Big\}$ verbal sentences

3. *NA: A man (is) tall.*
4. *NN: A man (is) a mammal, John (is) a man.* $\Big\}$ nominal sentences
5. *NN_{rel}PN: John (is) the son of Jones.*

6. *ND_{loc}: A man (is) here.*
7. *NPN: John (is) at home.*
    A tree (is) near the brook.[32] $\Big\}$ locative sentences

[32] For the list, see *Mathematical Structures*, 6.5. I ignore various complications, including the status of the articles, tense of the verb, etc., and also the subclassification of "classifier noun" which Harris specifies for the second N in form 4. I have reordered Harris' list for the sake of the discussion which follows.

This was written after *Mathematical Structures* appeared (in 1968) but before the publication of "The Elementary Transformations" in Z. S. Harris, *Papers in Structural and Transformational Linguistics* (1970), pp. 482–532. The more elaborate account of elementary sentence forms given in this latter paper lists eleven kernel structures, as follows:

	Σ	V	Ω_1	Ω_2	
1.	N	V_o			A man came.
2.	N	V_n	N		The man found gold.
3.	N	V_p	PN		The man relied on gold.
4.	N	V_{np}	N	PN	The man attributed the letter to Shaw.
5.	N	V_{nn}	N	N	The man gave Shaw a letter.
6.	N	be	N		A whale is a mammal.
7.	N	be	PN		The book is on the desk.
8.	N	be	A		The box is small.
9.	N	be	D_e		The box is here.
10.	It	V_{it}			It rained. It's May 8.
11.	There	V_{th}	N		There's hope.

The list calls for certain comments. In the first place, its full significance can be established only by two procedures which are not in order here: (1) to show in some detail what words figure as members of the elementary classes *N*, *V*, *A*, etc., and (2) to show how all other words and sentence-forms in English can be derived by precisely defined transformations.[33] In the second place, this list differs from earlier accounts of the kernel forms by containing no *V* in forms 3–7, and thus abstracting from the rule that every English sentence must contain a verb.[34] Hence, strictly speaking, these forms are more general than the kernel forms for English. Forms 3–7 are directly applicable to sentences in languages with the so-called nominal sentence; in English, they represent infra-sentence forms, requiring the insertion of "a single stop-gap verb" *be* in order to satisfy the condition for sentencehood.[35] This analysis of kernel types also succeeds in distinguishing the grammatical form of *NVN*, *John sees a man*, from that of *N (be) N*, *John (is) a man*, whereas earlier lists of kernel forms made no

---

(I omit the tense morpheme "*t*" before *V*.) Here Σ stands for subject, Ω for object, and the *V*-subscripts for subcategories of *V*. (E.g. V_{nn} is "a small subcategory of dative verbs": see Harris, *Papers*, p. 484.) For our purposes, the only interesting innovation, besides the recognition of an impersonal sentence form 10, is the admission of *There is N* as a distinct kernel form 11. I will suggest below, in §9, that most examples of this form can be transformationally derived.

[33] There is an interesting exception to the statement that all English sentences can be derived by transformation from the kernel forms. The exception is provided by the so called "primitive adjuncts", certain optional (deletable) additions, mostly adverbial modifiers, which distinguish "near-kernel" sentences from their kernels; e.g. for a sentence of the form *NV*, *A man arrives*, we have the near-kernel variants *NVD* and *NVPN*, where *D* and *PN* represent adverbial words and phrases of time, place, and manner: *A man arrives quickly*, *A man arrives at 2:00 P.M.*, *A man arrives quickly at the station at 2:00 P.M.* We are free to treat this last sentence either as a compound of several near-kernel forms or simply as an optional variant on *NV*, where the latter is thought of as containing a specified number of places for adverbial modifiers. Adopting the second alternative, we might redefine *NV* as the zero form for a kernel structure $NVD_{loc}D_{temp}D_{manner}$ (where *D* stands for adverbial phrases as well as single words); and similarly for the other kernel forms. The statement that all sentences are derived by transformation from kernels might then stand without qualification. This is my own suggestion: as far as I know, no theoretical solution has yet been accepted for this problem. Harris' suggestions go along different lines; see, e.g. *Papers*, pp. 486, 644, and 652.

[34] Contrast the statement in D. Hiż and A. K. Joshi, "Transformational Decomposition" (1967), p. 1: "The kernel sentence forms (for English) are defined as the string of class marks *NtV* followed by one of the kernel object strings: *Q, N, NN, NPN, ND, PN, D, A*" (where *t* stands for *tense/auxiliary* and *Q* for *zero*).

[35] Compare the remarks of A. C. Graham, *The Verb 'be' and its Synonyms* I, p. 15, who in effect illustrates the kernel forms *NV*, *NN*, *NPN*, and *NA*, and defines the copula by reference to the insertion of a "stop-gap" verb in the last three forms. Graham's conception of the copula is essentially the one proposed in the text, except that he does not explicitly distinguish between kernel and non-elementary forms.

such distinction.[36] Thus we draw a sharp line between elementary *be*, as inserted in the kernel forms 3–7, and all other elementary verbs (V) which occur in forms 1–2. This has an obvious importance for the study of *be*. Another advantage of this analysis is to indicate that every verb other than *be* which may be inserted in forms 3–7 (for example, *gets* or *becomes* in *NA* and *NN: Tom gets tired, John becomes a father*) is derivable by regular transformation from a form N *(be)* A or N *(be)* N: *Tom (be) tired, John (be) a father*, with *gets* and *becomes* as transformational operators on the kernel. We thus eliminate from the kernel all "predicative" verbs except *be*; the class of quasi-copulas like *seems, becomes, looks, feels, smells, turns, grows, etc.*, (as in *looks green, turns green, grows green*) can now be systematically treated as "container-verbs," i.e. as verb operators on *be* in the kernel.[37]

This account of kernel forms thus provides us with a sharp formal definition of the copula in English, namely, the verb *be* introduced into sentence forms 3–7. In a transformational perspective this elementary copula is clearly distinct not only from the (non-elementary) verb-operators *seems, becomes,* etc., but also from other kernel verbs like *arrives, sees, gives,* which appear as V in forms 1–2. Furthermore, this formal distinction corresponds to the intuitive semantic fact (in a loose sense of "semantic") that, unlike *be* in forms 3–7, these elementary verbs carry independent lexical information. Similarly, the non-elementary verb-operators *become, seem,* etc. also provide independent lexical content. In more traditional terminology, the verb-operators *become, seem, turn,* like the elementary verbs *run, love, give,* (but unlike *be*) have a "meaning of their own" over and above their function of providing a verb for the sentence. Thus our transformational definition of the copula as the verb *be* inserted in the infra-sentential kernel forms 3–7 corresponds quite well with the usual notion of the copula as a purely formal or "empty" syntactical device, inserted to satisfy a rule of sentencehood in English or in other languages where the verbless sentence is not grammatically acceptable. (By analogy, we may define a non-verbal copula for languages

---

[36] The distinction between *NVN* and *N be N* might seem to be artificially imposed on English if we consider the kernel forms only. While in more inflected languages the grammatical case of the second N will distinguish the predicate of *be* from the object of V (as in Latin, *est homo* from *videt hominem*), in English there is no such overt contrast between *James is the professor* and *James sees the professor*, or even between *The professor is me* and *The professor sees me*. It is one of the merits of transformational analysis to show that nevertheless the grammatical distinction between these two sentence forms is every bit as real in English as in Latin. Thus *NVN* but not *N (be) N* takes the passive transformation; *N (be) N* but not *NVN* takes the mutative copula *becomes*; after causative sentence-operators, *be* but not V will be zeroed (i.e. *The University made him a professor*, but *The chairman made him see a professor*), etc.

[37] See Harris, *Mathematical Structures*, Ch. 6, n. 11. In Chapter V §6 I distinguish these quasi-copulas into *be*-modifiers and *be*-replacers.

where it is a pronoun or a participle that is required or permitted in kernel forms *NA*, *NN*, *NPN*, etc. See the literature on the nominal sentence cited in Appendix B.)

What we have defined, however, is only the *elementary* copula, the verb *be* inserted into kernel sentences. Our analysis will distinguish this from other uses of *be* which are superficially like the copula (in that *be* is followed by a nominal form such as a participle, or by a prepositional phrase) but which are transformationally derived from a kernel *NV* that does not contain *be*. Thus we have *be* in the passive transform *Mary is loved by John* ← *John loves Mary*, in the progressive *John is arriving* ← *John arrives*, and other versions to be mentioned shortly. We may describe these as near-elementary (but transformationally derived) uses of *be*. We must also distinguish a second-order copula where the subject noun is itself derived by transformation from a more elementary verb or sentence: *Mary's singing is beautiful* ← *Mary sings (beautifully)*. Here again the underlying kernel sentence contains no *be*. Other cases of the second-order copula will be more complex, for example in *Virtue is happiness*. I sketch a possible analysis in order to illustrate the status of *be*:

> *Virtue is happiness*
> ← *To be virtuous is to be happy*
> ← *If a man is virtuous, he is happy*
> ← *A man is virtuous* + *A man is happy* under an *if-then* binary transformation involving cross-reference.[38]

In this case we can see that the underlying kernel forms do contain an elementary copula, but that this is *not* the source of the higher-order copula in *Virtue is happiness*. That is evident from *To be virtuous is to be happy*, where we find both the elementary copula (preserved in infinitival form) and the second-order copula side by side. The *is* introduced here is a new transformational operator, although its "surface syntax" is modelled on that of the elementary copula in *N be N*, the infinitive being treated like a kind of noun.[39]

With these cases in mind we may define the copula in the widest sense as any use of *be* which has the surface syntax of the kernel copula, i.e. which takes a nominal form (noun, adjective, participle, infinitive, gerund), a

[38] I.e. here we need some metalinguistic equivalent to quantification. Compare Harris' theory of "carrier-sentences" in *Mathematical Structures*, esp. 5.8.2, "Reference to individual."

[39] This new transformational operator corresponds to the *is* between infinitives whose distinct character was recognized by Russell in the passage quoted above in Section 2, p. 4. Henry Hiż informs me that every variety of *is* which can be distinguished in transformational terms can also be given a formal definition in Leśniewski's system.

locative adverb, or a prepositional phrase as its "predicate," without regard
to transformational derivation. Thus sentences like *It is hard to know what
to say, It is twelve o'clock, Democracy is chaos, The meeting is in the next
room, The explosion was at 8:00 A.M., Her singing is too loud*, all represent
be as a copula in this widest sense. As we shall see, this sense is really too
wide to be retained. (We cannot accurately describe *at 8:00 A.M.* as a
"predicate" in *The meeting is at 8:00 A.M.* And to what kernel form is this
use of *be* analogous?) Yet this wide sense does correspond to a traditional,
vague use of the term "copula" – a use which we are here trying to make more
precise.

I shall now sketch an analysis of *be* in English along transformational lines.
I first briefly survey the different uses to be recognized and then, in the next
sections, give a more detailed account of the copulative and existential
constructions, that is, of the copula in the broad sense and of the locution
"there is."

We begin, then, with the copula broadly understood, including (1) the
elementary copula in kernel sentences and (2) a number of distinct, transformationally derivative uses of *be* which are sufficiently analogous to the
elementary copula for us to assign to the verb the same (superficial) syntactic
role, i.e. we can describe the surface structure of these sentences as comparable to that of kernels with *be*. From these I distinguish (3) what has
sometimes been called a temporal copula and what I shall call a dummy-verb,
namely, the use of *be* in the case just mentioned: *The meeting is at 8:00 A.M.,
The celebration was last Tuesday*. Here the analogy with (1) breaks down.
There is no elementary sentence of the form *John is at 8:00 A.M.*[40] The
notion of a temporal copula is based upon a false analogy between adverbials of time and place. Only local adverbs may occur as predicate with
be when the subject is an elementary or first-order nominal. The distinct
structure of the so-called temporal copula is revealed by the fact that in
this case the verb *be* may be paraphrased by other dummy-verbs such as
occur, take place. Next we have (4) the existential operator, "there is." These
four uses will all be discussed further in the next two sections. First I complete
my survey.

(5) We have a rare and literary use in which *be* is construed absolutely,
i.e. with no predicate or complement other than a few fixed temporal adverbs
such as *no longer: To be or not to be*; *Lucy is no more*. Since here *be* may
generally be replaced by *live*, I call this the "vital" use and we shall find it

---

[40] Such sentences do occur, of course, but only in special contexts where they can be
transformationally derived. For example: *The dentist has two appointments early in the
morning*; *John is at 8:00 A.M., Peter at 8:30*. Thus the source of *John is at 8:00 A.M.* is
John's appointment is at 8:00 A.M., or something of that sort.

much more abundantly documented for Greek. (The use is so fossilized in English that I am willing to suppose it is a literary survival from classical antiquity.) Note that in (5), unlike (3), the verb cannot take specific date phrases (like *today*, *tomorrow*). Furthermore, since – again unlike (3) – the verb in (5) takes an elementary ("human") noun as subject, it is in effect a rather frozen form of *elementary verb*, and perhaps represents the only kernel use of *be* in English other than the copula (1).[41]

(6) Another isolated but somewhat more frequent use of the verb occurs in expressions like *So be it* or *That is so*, with which we may probably connect phrases like *Thus it was that*. I shall deal with some Greek parallels to this under the title of the "veridical" use in Chapter VII. For the moment I simply observe that the *it* (or *that*) in such cases serves as pro-word or dummy-subject for a *that*-clause or a nominalized sentence, and hence we may refer to this as a sentence-operator use of *be*. By this designation we bring the apparently isolated use of the verb in *It is so* into connection with the larger group of sentence-operators recognized by Harris, many of which happen to include *be: It is necessary that, It is possible that, It is surprising that*. Similarly, these sentence-operators also appear in predicate position after a *that*-clause or nominalized sentence: *is a fact, is true, is possible, is surprising*, etc., to which we now add: *is so*.[42]

(7) As a specimen of a minor or idiomatic use that might deserve closer study, I mention: *He is to go tomorrow, She was to have done that yesterday*. *Be* functions in this case as a modal auxiliary (compare *should*). We may be tempted to regard *is* as elliptical here for *is supposed (to), is obliged (to)*; but the parallel of *He has to go* points in a different direction.

(8) Finally, I mention the very generalized use of *be* in what has been called the "*it*-extractor:" an initial phrase *it is* that serves to bring forward or emphasize any word in the sentence. (This is the phenomenon known as a cleft sentence in Chomsky's terminology.) Examples: *It is here that the British stopped, It is the British who stopped here, It was a century ago that they came, It was a fort they built, not a town, It was by land they came, not*

---

[41] Thus I interpret otherwise the facts that lead J. Lyons to suggest "that *live* and *exist* (the former restricted to animate subjects) are the temporal copulas occurring with first-order [= elementary and near-elementary] nominal subjects. Like *be* in locative sentences, they are purely grammatical 'dummies'." (*Introduction to Theoretical Linguistics*, 1968, p. 349.) *Exist* is a different matter; but surely *live* is as much a member of the class of elementary *V* as *die*! Lyons has ignored its lexical content by transferring this value implicitly to the "animate" character of the subject noun. (For a criticism of this notion of animate noun, see below, Chapter IV §4. For Lyons' view of the verb *live* see Chapter VI, n. 21.) And I believe his parallel between temporal and locative copulas is misleading, precisely because temporal complements do not appear as predicate (with *be*) in kernel forms.

[42] For the class of sentence-operators, see "Transformational Theory," pp. 375–377. For a more detailed analysis of *is so*, see my account of ἔστιν οὕτω in Chapter VII.

by sea. Since *be* can here be followed by almost any portion of the operand sentence and hence by an expression of almost any form, there is no general analogy with the copula construction.

§ 8. SURVEY AND CLASSIFICATION
OF THE COPULA USES OF *be*
ACCORDING TO TRANSFORMATIONAL PRINCIPLES

So much for a partial survey of the uses of *be* in current English. There would be no point in aiming at completeness. Our English verb is heir to three I.-E. roots, **es-*, **bhū-* and **ves-*, and a glance at the data recorded in the Oxford English Dictionary will show that the mass of idiomatic, dialectal, or literary uses representing one or more of these roots is too various for any systematic and comprehensive analysis. If out of this great medley I have picked the vital use and the veridical sentence-operator for special mention, it is with an eye to the Greek analysis that lies ahead. For these uses, which are relatively isolated or fossilized in English, are part of the living language in Homer, Herodotus, and Plato. Here the fresher and clearer Greek evidence helps us to see our way through some decayed and dust-covered stretches of English. By contrast, the existential *there is* is more clearly defined in English as a standard transformation, and the copula is at least as important today as it was in antiquity. Hence we may pause to look more closely at these uses in English, and to consider them as a possible point of comparison and a source of clues for organizing and interpreting data in an ancient language whose living usage is so remote from us.

By far the most productive and diversified use of *be* in English is the copulative construction, where "copula" is understood in the broad sense I have indicated, including the elementary copula as a special case. A very small statistical sample tends to confirm my impression that over 90% of the occurrences of *be* in current English are instances of the copula in this sense. (What portion of these uses represent an elementary or near-elementary copula will depend upon the style and subject of the discourse. Kernel uses are relatively frequent in children's books and in straightforward narrative, relatively rare elsewhere.)

In order to survey this mass of copulative uses at a glance, I suggest the following simplified picture. First of all, we distinguish two strata, depending on whether the subject of *be*, that is, the noun which precedes it in normal declarative order, is a member of the elementary class *N* (including concrete nouns, both count nouns and mass words, together with proper names and personal pronouns of the first and second person), or whether this subject of *be* is a nominalized derivative of a verb, adjective or elementary noun (e.g.

explosion, teaching, bravery, manhood). In the first case, where the subject belongs to *N*, I shall speak of a first-order copula; in the second case, where the subject is an action nominalization, a quality-noun, or an infinitive, I speak of a second-order copula. (This corresponds roughly to John Lyons' distinction between first-order and second-order nominals.)[43] Drawn in this way, the division is not exhaustive. I am ignoring an intermediate but philosophically (and perhaps grammatically) uninteresting case where the subject of *be* is an agent nominalization like *teacher* (← *he teaches*), *writer*, *bookkeeper*, e.g. *The bookkeeper is in the office*. Since these nouns are still concrete, in the sense that they refer to the same individuals referred to by instances of elementary *N* – e.g. by *man, brother, John*, etc. – I count such use of *be* as essentially indistinguishable from the use with elementary nouns. (In Lyons' terminology, these agent nouns are still first-order nominals.) But action nouns and quality nouns are a different matter. The distinction between first-order and second-order copulas is, from an intuitive point of view, the difference between sentences with concrete and those with abstract subjects (counting action and event nouns as abstract, for our purposes).[44] The transformational analysis permits us to draw this intuitive distinction more precisely. In fact, I think we rely upon this abstract-concrete intuition in setting up our class of elementary *N* in the first place. But to a large extent, even this basic intuition can be clarified by criteria of co-occurrence and of transformational behavior.

Within these two levels of the copulative use – first-order copula with concrete subject, second-order with nominalized subject – various substrata may be recognized depending upon the kind and number of transformations that have operated on a given sentence. For the purposes of this sketch I indicate only two substrata within each level. Thus within the range of the first-order copula we distinguish (i) elementary uses of *be*, where the subject is an elementary *N* and where the predicate (that is, the expression following *be*) is one of the kernel forms *A*, *N*, D_{loc}, or *PN*, and (ii) near-elementary uses, where the subject is an elementary *N* (or, more generally, a first-order nominal like *teacher* and *bookkeeper*), but where *is* + predicate is not a kernel form but a transformational derivative of some elementary *V*. Among these verb-operators which introduce *be*, are, as we have seen, the progressive, the passive, and a third type that produces a stylistic or morphological variant of *V* in the form *be PN*.

---

[43] See his *Introduction to Theoretical Linguistics*, p. 347. For a more elaborate development of this distinction for Greek, see below, Chapter III §7 and Chapter IV §4.

[44] Later, in Chapter VI §18 and Chapter VII §6, I employ the terms "first-order" and "second-order" uses of εἰμί in a slightly different sense. The difference is that I there count as first-order only those uses where εἰμί is not introduced by a transformation. This excludes some sentences with concrete subjects, for example in the periphrastic construction.

> *Progressive: John is sitting ← John sits.*
> *Passive: Mary is loved by John ← John loves Mary.*
> *Morphological variant: John is in love (with Mary) ← John loves (Mary).*[45]

These transformations all operate on *NV* or *NVN* (where of course *V* excludes copula *be*), and hence our verb does not normally occur in the kernel. The progressive is a partial exception, since here we may find an operator *is* next to the transform of a kernel *be*:

> *Joan is being sweet today ← Joan is sweet (today).*

Shifting our attention to the second-order copula, the variety of subdivisions becomes bewildering as a result of the complex phenomena of nominalization.[46] By definition, every second-order copula has a nominalized subject. I shall limit myself to one subdivision, determined by whether or not the predicate is also second-order. By a second-order predicate I mean one which does not normally or typically co-occur with a first-order nominal as subject. Thus in *The singing is beautiful, The excitement is next door*, we have second-order subjects but first-order predicates: compare *Mary is beautiful, John is next door*. But in *To see her is bliss, His success is unlikely*, the predicates are no longer first-order: *Mary is bliss, John is unlikely* are marginal or abbreviated sentences in a way in which the preceding examples are not. Thus within the second-level copula I recognize two substrata: (i) the *mixed* second-order copula, where the subject but not the predicate is second-order, and (ii) the *pure* second-order copula, where both nominal terms are second-order, i.e. where the subject is an "abstract" nominalization and the predicate also is an expression that does not generally apply to concrete subjects.

These four divisions can be represented schematically as horizontal strata of increasingly "abstract" uses of the copula. (In the following list, the more concrete uses come first, the more abstract ones last.)

I. First-order copula

(i)   Elementary copula: *John is tall, Mary is a girl, Mary is the sister of John, A girl is here, A boy is in the hall.*

---

[45] The near-kernel forms of *be PN* will be described below as quasi-locatives. Many examples can be derived from *V* (e.g. *John is on the march ← John marches*), but perhaps not all. I am willing to accept the following derivations: *John is in pain ← Something* (or *It*) *pains John, John is in trouble ← Something troubles (gives trouble to) John.* But the problem deserves more attention than I can give it.

[46] For a systematic survey of verb- and sentence-nominalizations (i.e. "event" and "fact" words), see Z. Vendler, *Adjectives and Nominalizations*, 1968. Vendler also mentions, but does not analyze in detail, the quality, state, and property words (such as *sweetness, presidency, manhood*) that derive from adjectives and from predicate nouns.

(ii) Near-elementary copula: *John is coming, Mary is observed by a boy, A man is in love with Mary.*

II. Second-order copula

(i) Mixed cases: *The meeting is gay, The celebration is across the street, The delegation is on its way here, The demonstration is being watched by small boys.*

(ii) Pure second-order copula: *Shrewdness is a virtue, To see her is to love her, The discussion is an exercise in futility, The meeting is pointless.*

This scheme makes no claim to completeness; it serves only to give a somewhat more structured idea of our loose notion of copula.[47] For this view of the copula to be even approximately accurate, however, we must combine our initial division into horizontal layers with a further vertical classification determined by the word-class of the predicate. I draw this vertical division in detail only for the lowest stratum, the elementary copula, and shall simply allude to the projection at the upper stories. Since we have five kernel sentence forms into which *be* is inserted (NA, NN, $NN_{rel}PN$, ND_{loc}, NPN), we might recognize five corresponding forms of the kernel copula. In fact, however, I propose that we reduce these to three. For present purposes there seems to be no significant difference between a predicate N and a predicate $N_{rel}PN$. Similarly I shall combine *(be)* D_{loc} and *(be)* PN into a single copula type. After *be* in the kernel, D_{loc} would be represented by only a very few forms (such as *here, there, nearby*); whereas the prepositional phrase in kernel N *(be)* PN will, I think, always be locative in meaning. (This is largely an intuitive hunch, but I assume that we can exclude from the kernel such sentences as *John is in trouble* and *James is out of the question* on respectable transformational grounds.) Thus I distinguish three kinds of elementary copula, corresponding to the five kernel types 3–7:

(A) the adjective copula, or *be* inserted in form NA

(B) the noun copula, *be* in forms NN and $NN_{rel}PN$

[47] I mention two complications among many. 1) *Mary is perplexed by his question* ← *His question perplexed Mary* ← *He asked Mary a question*, etc. The form *be* is introduced here by a passive transformation on a sentence with a second-order nominal for subject. Since the derivative subject is concrete, the result resembles a near-elementary use of the copula (I. ii), but the nominalized subject of the source or operand sentence suggests a mixed second-order case, like II. i. above. 2) I have entirely ignored further transformations of the copula at all levels, under the operation of "container-verbs" and the like: *She noticed that John was tall, Mary has the reputation of being kind, She wants to be an actress, The police allowed the demonstration to be interrupted.* Since these transformations apply quite generally to other verbs as well as *be* (e.g. *She wants to leave Philadelphia, The police allowed the demonstration to continue*), they do not belong specifically to an analysis of our verb, although they help to account for most of its actual occurrences in English.

(C)   the locative copula, *be* in ND_{loc} and *NPN*.

Examples are:

(A)   *James is tall, Socrates is wise.*
(B)   *James is a man, Socrates is the husband of Xanthippe.*
(C)   *James is here, Socrates is in Athens.*[48]

Since (A) and (B) often behave alike, in contrast to the locative (C), I shall
for convenience group them together under the title of the nominal copula
(where "nominal" refers to adjectives as well as nouns, as in the phrase
"nominal sentence"). In many languages outside of I.-E., these two nominal
kernel forms *NA* and *NN* are treated quite differently. Even within I.-E.,
Spanish, for example, draws a radical line between the two. Thus for predicate
adjectives in Spanish there is a choice between *ser* and *estar* as copula verbs,
depending upon an aspectual contrast; for predicate nouns, however, only
ser is acceptable as the copula.[49] In English too there are some clear transformational differences between the forms *NA* and *NN*. Thus, while the verb-
operator *becomes* may apply equally to both *(John becomes wise, John
becomes a man)*, the application of *seems*, by contrast, is normal in one case,
but may be marginal in the other: *Tom seems (to be) tired, Tom seems (to be)
a man*. And for other "predicative" verbs, the operation is strictly limited
to *N (be) A: The tomato smells fresh*, but not **The tomato smells a fruit*; and
whereas in *The bush grows green*, the verb *grow* has the syntax of *seems,
becomes*, etc., in *The bush grows leaves* the syntax is *NVN* with elementary *V*.
Similar, but less radical differences might be noted between the transformational properties of ND_{loc} and *NPN*. Hence where I speak simply of nominal
and locative copulas I intend to leave open the possibility that a more
refined classification might be desirable for specific purposes, as it clearly is
for the theory of verb-operators or container verbs. For some generalizations,
however, we may ignore even the basic distinction between nominal and
locative copulas. Thus in *all* kernel uses, whether nominal or locative, *be* as
copula serves on the one hand to make a grammatical sentence out of infra-
sentence forms that carry all the lexical information (and hence the verb
can be omitted in telegraphic style, as in newspaper headlines); while as a

---

[48] Compare T. Langendoen's distinction between the copula construction with predicate
nominals, with adjectives, and with locatives, in "The Copula in Mundari," *The Verb 'be'
and its Synonyms*, Part I (1967), pp. 83ff. If this triple division of the copula is not universal,
at least it extends well beyond Indo-European.
[49] The exception to this rule is of course only apparent in the case of noun forms used
adjectivally, e.g. *Está muy presidente hoy*, "He is very presidential (= acting like a president)
today." (I am indebted here to Gregory Rabassa of Columbia University.) Note that participles in Spanish, as in I.-E. generally, behave like adjectives rather than like nouns: they
admit *estar* freely.

declined form it carries the indications of tense, number, and mood that are normally associated with *V*. And this statement applies not only to the kernel use of *be* but to the copula in the widest sense. If it were true of no other form in the language, this might serve as a general definition of the copula. But unfortunately, this description is much *too* general. And hence I see no possibility of defining the copula in the broad sense, except by analogy with the elementary copula strictly defined for the kernel forms.[50]

It is obvious that the distinction between noun copula, adjective copula, and locative copula just sketched at the elementary level can be projected up through the higher stories of our stratification, since it depends simply upon the word-class of the predicate. As we move upwards, the intersection of this division with the near-elementary forms of the first-order copula is relatively simple. 1) *Be* in the passive and progressive is strictly analogous to the adjectival copula; i.e., *be + participle* is analogous to *be A*. 2) *Be* in the morphological variant on *V* (or on other kernel predicates) is generally analogous to a locative form: *John is in love, Peter is out of his mind, Mary is on the way*. 3) At first sight, there seems to be no analogy to *be N* at this level. But the analogy is quickly found if we agree to regard agent nominalizations as transformationally derived from their underlying verb phrase. We then have *John is a teacher ← John teaches, The man is a gardener ← The man works in the garden*.

At the level of the second-order copula things are more difficult because of the general difficulties concerning second-order nominals; and the details could not be profitably worked out except in the context of a full-scale study of English nominalizations. I simply mention that the tripartite division re-appears even at the level of the pure second-order copula: *Spitting is a habit* (noun copula); *Spitting is unlawful* (adjective copula); *Spitting is against the law* (quasi-locative). The rising level of the strata corresponds to increasing transformational remoteness from kernel form and, in intuitive terms, to an increasingly "abstract" function of the copula. In the case of the locative copula, the more abstract or derivative sentence form often corresponds to a metaphorical value in the use of prepositions: contrast *Spitting is against the law* with *The shovel is against the wall*. Something very similar occurs when elementary verbs are used with second-order nominals: *Spitting wins the prize, Power slipped into the streets, Sincerity frightens him*. There is of course no simple, linear correlation between the intuitive contrasts of

---

[50] To see that the generalized definition suggested above does not apply exclusively to copula *be*, consider a newspaper headline BIG FIRE IN CENTER CITY. I am more likely to reconstruct this as a sentence by prefixing *There is a* (or by inserting *rages* or *breaks out* after *fire*) than by inserting a copula *is*. But surely we cannot be satisfied with a definition of the copula that applies equally well to *there is*.

concrete-abstract or literal-metaphorical and the formal syntactic contrast of elementary-derived, but the correlation does seem massive enough to deserve investigation. The phenomenon in question is a general feature of the language and not a special fact concerning the verb *be*. But precisely this general consideration must be borne in mind if we are to raise the question of a concrete or "literal" use of the verb *be*. For any form which occurs in a variety of transformational functions or levels, the question of concrete or literal meaning can be coherently posed, in the first instance, only for the elementary uses.

§ 9. NON-COPULATIVE USES OF *be*: THE DUMMY-VERB WITH
TEMPORAL "PREDICATES" AND THE EXISTENTIAL PHRASE *there is*

Just as actions, events, and states may be dated, so elementary verbs may take temporal modifiers and, at a higher level, an action or event noun may receive a temporal "predicate": *John arrives tomorrow → John's arrival is tomorrow*. But the terminology of copula and predicate is here abused, since we can no longer find any precise analogy to a kernel use of *be*. There is no elementary sentence of the form *John is tomorrow*.[51] In this use, *be* is a paraphrastic equivalent for *occur, take place*, as I mentioned in Section 6. I call this use the "dummy verb" to indicate that *be* is here construed without a predicate – i.e. without a form that is structurally analogous to a kernel predicate – but with a temporal modifier; and thus it behaves superficially like a normal *verb* rather than a copula. But it is a mere dummy in that the kernel contains no *be* (or no *occur* or *take place*), and the *be*-transformation adds no new meaning or lexical content to the kernel; it may on the contrary add ambiguity or reduce precision:

> *John begins tomorrow → John's beginning is tomorrow*
> *They attacked three days ago → Their attack occurred three days ago.*

Note that the tense of *be* (or its replacer) will reflect the tense of the kernel verb.

Because of the lack of analogy to any kernel use of *be*, this transformational use as dummy verb should be clearly distinguished from copula *be* with the same nominalized subjects: *John's beginning is a calamity, Their attack was brief*. Nevertheless, to insist that the second-order copula and

---

[51] Such sentences do occur, of course, marginally. They may in most cases be analyzed as abbreviating transformations of the use with nominalized subjects: e.g. *Mr. Jones is tomorrow ← Mr. Jones' speech (arrival) is tomorrow ← Mr. Jones speaks (arrives) tomorrow*.

the dummy verb are distinct is not to deny that in some cases the distinction is not a sharp one. Consider the case where the subject of *be* is a nominalization of the kind just illustrated and where the "predicate" is a locative expression: *The meeting is in the next room, The singing is in the hall.* Are we to regard *is* here as a dummy verb, replaceable by *takes place* or *occurs*? Or are we to regard it as a locative copula, analogous to *The delegates are in the room, The singers are in the hall*? Since a kernel locative expression may also occur as adverbial modifier with an elementary verb, there is no general answer to this question. In other words, we do not know whether the derivation is *The delegates meet in the room → The meeting is in the room*, in which case we recognize a dummy use of *be*, or whether it is *The delegates meet + The delegates are in the room → The meeting is in the room*, in which case, since we have a locative copula in the source, we may legitimately recognize a copula in the result.[52]

Philosophically, the most interesting case of *be* is in the initial phrase *there is*. Note that this "existential" use of *there* is not identical with (though it must be historically derived from) the local adverb *there*: the former is unstressed, the latter stressed.[53] From the point of view of contemporary English, we might describe *there is* as a device for permutational transformation bringing the verb ahead of its subject, as with initial adverbs in German or certain constructions in French. (Compare *Nun lacht Anna* or *Ainsi font les marionnettes*.) The historical origins of the usage seem to confirm this view of its function. In Middle English the order *NV* (including *N be*) is the more common, but inversion of verb and subject noun occurs

---

[52] Thus John Lyons' parallel between temporal and locative copulas *(The parade was in Central Park, The demonstration was on Sunday)* is, from my point of view, ambiguous. *(Introduction to Theoretical Linguistics,* pp. 345f.) If on the one hand the locative after *be* represents a kernel locative with an elementary verb *(They paraded in Central Park),* then the parallel to *on Sunday* is exact and in both cases we have a dummy use of *be.* But if the locative represents a kernel locative with copula *be,* the parallel breaks down. For a plausible derivation of this type, consider

The demonstration is in the courtyard (now, after having gathered on the
street) ← They demonstrate + They are in the courtyard (now).

In this case, the verb *is* serves indeed to locate the demonstration by locating the persons who are demonstrating, precisely as if we spoke of the demonstration as *approaching* or *scattering*. In the dummy-verb case, by contrast, it is not the persons as such but the act or event of demonstrating which is located.

This distinction may be of little importance in English, but it is essential in Greek. For εἰμί can be used as dummy-verb (= "occurs") even *without* temporal or locative complements. And such uses would normally be regarded as existential, not copulative at all. See Type V in Chapter VI §15, where I describe this use of εἰμί as surface predicate or verb of occurrence.

[53] This was pointed out to me by Henry Hiż. Yuki Kuroda adds that the distinction is clearest when both occur in the same sentence: *There is a book there.* For the function of the first *there*, compare Jespersen, *Philosophy of Grammar*, pp. 154–156; Lyons, *Introduction*, p. 393.

in many circumstances, including those in which the sentence begins with an adverbial expression. Declarative sentences beginning with the verb are still found in Middle English. "But quite early the verb tended to be preceded by the characteristically Modern English pseudo-subject *there*": *ther were twey* (two) *men of holy wyl that levyd togedyr* (lived together); *ther fel a gret hungre* (famine) *in that lond* (land).[54]

Thus as the inverted order *verb-subject* began to be felt as odd, it was supported by an initial dummy-subject *there*. In origin, then, the transformation *There is a man at the door* ← *A man is at the door* must be regarded as strictly comparable to *There came a knight ariding on his horse* ← *A knight came ariding on his horse*. In current English, however, initial *there is* (together with its modifications, such as *there seems to be*) is so common while the parallel permutation with other verbs is so rare that it is probably more accurate to treat *there is* separately, and to regard *There came a knight ariding* and *There dwelt a man in this town* as vestigial or literary. The transformational properties of *there is* are rather complex and have apparently not been studied in detail.[55] Hence I offer these remarks only as a preliminary survey.

In order to point out some of the characteristic features of this transformation, it will be useful to have in view the whole range of sentences to which it might be applied. Hence I shall first summarize the preceding analysis of *be* together with the kernel forms for other elementary verbs. Since *there is* does not normally act on sentences with proper names or "definite descriptions" as subject, I illustrate *N* in each case as a common noun with the indefinite article.[56]

I. Kernel forms

   A.   Verbs other than *be*.

            NV   A man arrives.
            NVN   A man loves the woman.
            NVPN A man looks at the woman.

---

[54] Fernand Mossé, *A Handbook of Middle English* tr. by J. A. Walker (Baltimore, 1952), p. 128 (§174). Mossé remarks that "alongside *ther*, the neuter pronoun *(h)it* was also used with the same force up to the 13th century ...: *of hise mouth it stod a stem* 'from his mouth there came a ray'."

[55] Compare the very brief and tangential comments on "existential extraction" by Zeno Vendler in *Linguistics in Philosophy* (1967), pp. 64–69. Vendler also describes *There is an N wh*... as a "transform" of the original sentence with *N*.

[56] It is of course possible to find special contexts in which *there is* may occur with proper names. For example "Who's coming to dinner tonight?" "Well, there is John (who is) coming, there is Peter, etc." Similarly for the definite article: "Who can we find to take the message?" "There is the old man across the street (who can do it)."

B.   Nominal copula

NA   *A man is tall.*[57]
NN   *A trout is a fish.*
$NN_{rel}PN$ *A man is father of the boy.*

C.   Locative copula

ND_{loc} *A man is here.*
NPN   *A man is near the tree.*

II. *Near-kernel uses of "be"*

A.   Progressive   *A man is arriving.*
                            A man is looking at the woman.

B.   Passive   *The woman is loved by a man.*

C.   Morphological variant of *V* *A man is in love with the woman.*

III. *Second-order copula, with nominalized V as subject*

A.   Nominal copula ($\approx$I.B)
       A meeting is successful, is a disappointment, is the beginning of a plot.

B.   Locative copula ($\approx$I.C)
       A meeting is here, is in the next room.

C.   Progressive ($\approx$II.A)
       A meeting is coming to an end.

D.   Passive ($\approx$II.B)
       A meeting is interrupted by a telephone call.

E.   Morphological variant of *V* ($\approx$II.C)
       A meeting is under consideration.

IV. *Second-order nominal as subject with verbs other than "be"*

       A meeting begins at 2:00 P.M., A meeting decides policy.

V. *Second-order nominal with "be" as dummy verb*

       A meeting is at 2:00 P.M., A meeting is tomorrow.

Now at first sight it seems that *there is* can be prefixed to any one of these

---

[57] Or *A certain man is tall*, to make the example seem more natural. The occurrence of the article in kernel forms raises difficult problems which cannot be dealt with here. Since *the* is known to be transformationally introduced in most cases, I usually give the indefinite article in examples of kernel form, even if in some cases the result is not a wholly natural sentence.

sentence forms, with the operand verb phrase transformed into a *wh*-clause, as in the case of the *it is* "extractor" (see above, Section 7): *There is a man who loves the woman, There is a man who is father of the boy, There is a man who is looking at the woman, There is a meeting which is successful,* etc. In some cases, however, the result is a marginal sentence: *?There is a trout that is a fish.* In other cases the result seems incomplete or pointless without a special context: *There is a man who arrives, There is a (certain) man who is tall, There is a meeting which is here.* This seems to run counter to the definition of a transformation as a relation preserving sentence-acceptability. I am unable to account for all the discrepancies, but some can be smoothed out by two considerations.

(1) In several cases we get a more acceptable sentence if we assume that the *wh*-pronoun and operand *be* are zeroed after *There is: There is a man here* ← *There is a man who is here; There is a meeting under consideration* ← *There is a meeting which is under consideration.* This is equivalent to regarding *there* simply as a permutational operator on *be* in the original sentence, without bringing in a *wh*-clause in the first place: *There is a man at the door* ← *A man is at the door.* It is the locative sentences which are most naturally treated in this way: *There is a man here, There is a lecture in the next room;* and the quasi-locatives such as *There is a meeting under consideration.* Note that the nominal copula resists this simple permutation of *is* and zeroing of *wh- is:* *There is a meeting (which is) successful, *There is a man (who is) tall, *There is a trout (that is) a fish.* These sentences remain dubious even if the position of the predicate is shifted: *?There is an unsuccessful meeting, ?There is a tall man.*

(2) In many cases the *there is* transformation is natural only, or primarily, as an introduction to further discourse with the same noun as subject: *There is an unsuccessful meeting in the next room, There is a tall man who* .... In such cases, the *there is* permutation on a nominal copula is fully acceptable when it occurs as a transform of the first operand in a binary transformation, with a second kernel to be supplied: *A meeting is unsuccessful + A meeting is in the next room* → *There is an unsuccessful meeting in the next room.* This works smoothly for the adjectival copula, but for a *there is* transform of noun predicates we need to allow for apposition: *There is a man, a father of a boy, who* ....[58] It seems that *there is* must single out one and only one noun from the kernel sentence on which it operates, and that it introduces this noun as a subject for further discourse going beyond the kernel. Hence the typical

---

[58] Hence this is one case where the two forms of nominal copula diverge in their transformational behavior, just as both differ here from the locative. And our sample of *NN*, *A trout is a fish,* apparently remains unsalvageable for the *there is* transformation, even with apposition, unless we exchange subject and predicate: *There is a fish, the trout, which (is abundant in these streams).*

role of *there is* at the beginning of a narrative: *Once upon a time there was a beautiful princess who* ... . Note that this introductory function is also possible, but by no means necessary, in the case of the locative copula. A *there is* transform of a locative kernel may introduce a further clause; but it may equally well stand alone: *There is a man here (who ...), There is a meeting in the next room (which ...).*

Perhaps we may conclude, then, that the *there is* prefix represents (1) a normal transformation on *be*-locative sentences, yielding an acceptable permutation of *be* and its subject, and (2) an extension of this to other types of sentences, including the use of *be* as nominal copula, where the result is fully acceptable only as first member of a binary transformation or of some more extended discourse. These conclusions will apparently be confirmed by our analysis of comparable uses of εἰμί in Chapter VI.

§ 10. TWO SPECIAL CASES OF THE COPULA: THE IMPERSONAL CONSTRUCTION AND THE NUNCUPATIVE USE

Before leaving the topic of *be* in English, I want to mention two special versions of the copula that raise questions of some theoretical interest. The first case is the very common use of a kernel copula in impersonal form: *It is hot (in the room), It is dark (here), It is humid (today).* I take these to be true impersonals (in a sense to be further defined in Chapter IV §§ 27–30), since the subject *it* does not occur here as a pro-word for anything else. Whereas in a sentence like *It is an awful book* we may perhaps recognize a transform of *A book is awful,* i.e. of a regular *N (be) A* kernel, in the case of *It is dark* we are obliged to admit a kernel form *it (be) A* where the subject expression cannot plausibly be replaced by any ordinary noun. This is the impersonal kernel copula, corresponding to an impersonal use of *V* for a limited class of "meteorological verbs:" *It rains, It thunders.* Note that the unmistakable examples of the impersonal copula just cited are also in a sense "meteorological," describing the weather or the conditions of temperature, visibility, etc. Other cases are more dubious. Thus one may hesitate to regard *It is two o'clock, It is Sunday* as examples of the impersonal kernel copula, insofar as they represent natural answers to the questions *What is the time?* and *What is today?* In view of this fact, the *it* of the answer can be interpreted as a pro-word transform of *time* and *today.* There is perhaps no clear borderline here between normal and impersonal forms of the copula, as we may see from the perplexing *it* in *What time is it?*

Finally, I mention the case of *N (be) N* where a proper name or personal pronoun appears in predicate position: *The man who walked away is Paul, The culprit is you.* In many cases it is possible to derive such sentences from

more elementary forms in which the pronoun or name occurs as subject:
Paul walked away, You are the culprit. Where transformational grammar
takes this course, it finds itself in the company of Aristotle, who described
sentences of the first type as "accidental predication" and would recast them
as predication proper (κατηγορεῖν ἁπλῶς) in the second form, where proper
names and pronouns appear only as subject of *be,* just as adjectives and verb
forms (such as participles) appear only as predicates.[59] To this extent
Aristotle's conception of proper or scientific predication anticipates the
transformational concept of kernel sentence form. It seems, however, that
neither Aristotle nor transformational theory can decompose *I am Charles*
into a sentence where the proper name does not occur as predicate, unless it
is into the metasentence *"Charles" is my name.* Whatever theoretical solution
is adopted, sentences where *be* is followed by a proper name or personal
pronoun represent an interesting special case of the copula, perhaps the
only definite grammatical equivalent in natural language to the logical
notion of an *is* of identity. We shall have occasion to return to this "nuncupative" use of *to be,* as I shall call it following Abelard. (See Chapter IV § 9.)
As for the other case of so-called singular terms in predicate position, what
Russell called definite descriptions (as in "Scott is the author of *Waverley*"),
the linguistic problems raised here belong rather to the theory of the article
than to the verb *be.* The *is* in question is a non-kernel copula introduced
together with an agent-nominalization of some elementary *V* (or, in other
cases, from an operation on an elementary copula, as in *John is the tallest
man in the room,* from underlying kernels which include *John is a man, John
is tall* and *John is in the room*). Thus the introduction of *is* in *Scott is the
author of Waverley,* from a kernel form *Scott wrote Waverley,* is not different
in principle from *Scott is an author (of books) ← Scott writes books.* The
logically relevant difference concerns *the* and *a,* not *be.*

In concluding this survey of *be* in English let me add a word of caution.
In the last chapter of this work I shall explore the possibility that the Greek
uses of εἰμί are interrelated in a systematic way which is of some philosophic
interest. At a certain level of generality, what is true for Greek εἰμί should
be true for English *be,* since we are dealing in both cases with an inherited
system of uses for I.-E. **es-* which is surprisingly conservative. In detail,
however, the two verbs look very different. For one thing, our English verb
is heir to three distinct I.-E. roots, **es-, *bhū-,* and **ves-,* whereas only the
first is represented in the forms of εἰμί. Insofar as forms like *is* and *be*

---

[59] Compare *Prior An.* I 27, 43ᵃ32–36 with *Post. An.* I 22, 83ᵃ1–21: "That white (thing) is
Socrates" and "What approaches is Callias" are instances of accidental predication, just
as "The white (thing) is a stick" or "What walks (there) is a man" are accidental variants
on "The stick is white" and "A man walks (there)."

are regarded as lexically equivalent, the aspectual contrast between *es- and *bhū- which is so strictly preserved in Greek is largely lost in English (though it may still reappear in the contrast of be and become). Probably no philosopher innocent of our ontological tradition would rediscover the concept of Being on the basis of the modern linguistic data from English, or from any comparable language. The ancient system, as preserved in Greek, has been dislocated by the gap between a copula verb and the fixed formulaic use of there is which seems almost to be a distinct morpheme (like hay in Spanish or il y a in French). The system has been altered by the appearance of an independent verb to exist which takes over some of the original function of *es-, and by other developments the most notable of which is the decay of the participle. Whereas the participle of εἰμί is a supple instrument of grammatical transformation and the source of a nominalized form τὸ ὄν that retains regular connections with nearly all uses of the verb, the form being in English is a relatively inert fusion of participle and gerund, whose use as a substantive is extremely restricted, whether in the abstract action nominalization (as in the concept of Being) or in the concrete "agent" form (a human being, a being from another planet).

The fate of the English participle (which is partially paralleled, for example, by that of étant in French) is a symptom of the decay of the ancient system. Considered as an instrument of philosophic conceptualization, the modern verb be is a shadow of its ancient self – at any rate a shadow of the system as represented in Greek εἰμί.

CHAPTER II

SUBJECT, PREDICATE, COPULA

§ 1. FORMAL OR SYNTACTIC DEFINITIONS OF "SUBJECT," "PREDICATE," AND "COPULA"

In Chapter One I made free use of the terms "subject," "predicate," and "copula" in describing the transformational behavior of *be* in English, and the same terms will be required for our account of the Greek verb in the chapters which follow. In view of the debate and confusion which have often surrounded these terms, it is best to clarify our use of them before proceeding further. First of all I indicate how the terms may be defined for the purposes of syntactical analysis.

Because of the fixed word order for nouns and verbs in a normal declarative sentence in English, it is easy to give a formal definition of "subject," "predicate," and "copula," at least for sentences of more or less elementary form, on the basis of the transformational syntax sketched in the previous chapter. (See Chapter I § 7.) Thus in the general formula for sentencehood $NV\Omega$, we identify the initial N as subject in every case. The copula is defined for the special case where V is *be* and where Ω – or as I shall say in this case, Φ – ranges over adjectives, nouns, local adverbs, and prepositional phrases. Thus the copula is the verb *be* in the sentence form N *is* Φ. This is the elementary or near-elementary copula. By analogy with this elementary case we can define the copula in a wider sense, where the position of N can be taken by any noun-like form, including whole clauses, and where Φ may range over participles, infinitives, clauses, and other nominalized forms. For example in the sentence *The reason why he arrived late for the meeting was that his train had been delayed*, the verb *was* is a non-elementary or second-order copula, with the *that*-clause as predicate and the complex phrase beginning with *The reason why* as subject.

So much for the definition of subject and copula. The predicate may be defined in either of two ways. Taking it narrowly, we identify the predicate as Φ in the form N *is* Φ, excluding the copula. Or taking the predicate broadly to include the copula, we define it as *is* Φ in the same formula. This broader definition preserves the analogy with the general sentence form $NV\Omega$, where we want to say that $V\Omega$ is the predicate. The broader definition is essentially the same as that offered by Chomsky in terms of noun phrase and verb phrase; and it corresponds to traditional usage in grammar. As just indicated, it has the merit of maintaining the analogy between *John/reads*, *John/is reading*, and *John/is tall*, where in each case (on the broader definition) the sentence divides cleanly into subject and predicate, without remainder. (I assume that an object noun, where it occurs, will also be included in the predicate, e.g. *John/reads the book*. Other definitions are obviously possible here, but since our discussion of εἰμί does not require an analysis of sentences with direct objects I shall not pursue the question.)

On the other hand, there is something to be said for the narrower sense of "predicate" that excludes the copula, as in the *S is P* analysis of traditional logic. Not only in logic but in grammar as well we want to keep the familiar terminology of "predicate noun", "predicate adjective", "predicate phrase", and to be able to speak more generally of "the predicate" without specifying its form. In doing so, we presuppose the alternative analysis of *N is Φ* not into subject-predicate but into *subject + copula + predicate*. To avoid this ambiguity, Jespersen introduced the term "predicative" to apply to predicates in this narrow sense that excludes the copula. But once recognized, this ambiguity is harmless and I propose to tolerate it here. Thus I shall speak of predicate in both the broader and the narrower sense, according as the copula is or is not counted as part of the predicate.

In English the subject *N* is unambiguously indicated by initial position in normal declarative word order and thus formally distinguished from predicate *N* in a sentence of the form *N is N: Nixon is president*. In Greek where the word order is much freer, ambiguity may arise for this copula type (and for this type only). Ambiguity as to which noun is subject will normally be avoided by some indication from the context, or by the use of the definite article with one of the two nouns. Thus in a sentence like ὁ ἀνήρ ἐστι στρατηγός, "The man is a general," the article identifies ἀνήρ as the subject regardless of permutations of word order.[1] But we must be prepared to admit that in some cases of *N is N* sentences in Greek the distinction between subject and predicate noun may be undefined. These are in general the cases where *is* may be read as *is identical with*.[2] Even in such cases the English word order provides us with a purely formal distinction between subject and

---

[1] Because of the syntactic neutrality of Greek word order in this respect, I generally follow the English order *N is Φ* in citing an arbitrary Greek example. The most common Greek order is *N Φ is*, ὁ ἀνὴρ στρατηγός ἐστι. See Appendix A.

[2] The cases of *N is N* which I have in mind include those where the subject "noun" is a nominalized adjective, participle or infinitive, as marked for example by the article, which in Greek tends to specify the subject term. Consider this complex specimen of *N (is) N* with omitted copula from Euripides' *Bacchae* 395f. τὸ σοφὸν δ᾽ οὐ σοφία/τό τε μὴ θνητὰ φρονεῖν, where I take σοφία as the predicate whose subject is given by the two articular forms: "Cleverness is not wisdom, nor is thinking high thoughts (the same as being wise)." For the nominalized or substantival use of the adjective, see below, Chapter IV §8.

On the other hand, there are certainly *some* cases where the article goes with the predi-

predicate noun. It is another question whether any importance is to be attached to the distinction in this case.[3]

These formal definitions of subject, predicate, and copula are easily extended to other I.-E. languages, and indeed to any language in which the word-classes *noun, adjective, verb*, etc. are recognized. For example, the copula can then be defined as any device – whether verb, pronoun, pause or inflection – that serves to make grammatically acceptable sentences out of the infra-sentential forms *noun-adjective, noun-noun, noun-prepositional phrase*, etc.[4] And in a language where there is no special device required for sentences of the form *noun-noun* or *noun-adjective* which distinguishes them from the form *noun-verb*, we may speak if we like of a zero copula. It is in this sense, I suppose, that the term "copula" is used in reference to languages outside of I.-E., insofar as it is used in any precise sense at all.

§ 2. THE DISTINCTION BETWEEN SYNTACTIC, SEMANTIC ONTOLOGICAL, AND JUDGMENTAL (OR CONCEPTUAL) NOTIONS OF SUBJECT AND PREDICATE, AND A CONTRAST WITH THE LINGUISTIC TERMS "TOPIC" AND "COMMENT"

This treatment of subject and predicate in purely formal or syntactical terms leaves certain deep issues untouched. In some cases we want to identify the subject of a sentence not as a word or expression but as a definite person or object in the world. I shall argue later that this is often the case when we

---

cate, not the subject. See Newman's note to Arist. *Politics* 1276ᵇ29 κοινωνία δ᾽ ἐστὶν ἡ πολιτεία, where the construction is disputed: "The association is a constitution"? or conversely? Newman cites 1278ᵇ11 πολίτευμα δ᾽ ἐστὶν ἡ πολιτεία "The supreme authority virtually is the constitution," and 1283ᵇ42 where the definition of "citizen" begins πολίτης δὲ κοινῇ μὲν ὁ μετέχων τοῦ ἄρχειν καὶ ἄρχεσθαί ἐστι "In general, the citizen is one who shares in ruling and in being ruled."

In such cases, the apparent distinction of subject and predicate is perhaps really one of topic and comment.

[3] Compare Jespersen's account of grammatical subject in *Philosophy of Grammar* (2nd ed. 1934, pp. 150–4), where the criterion is explicitly semantic: the subject term is the one with narrower extension. This generally gives the same results as the formal definition which I have proposed in the text, but it tends to diverge precisely in the case of *N is N* sentences. For identity statements where Jespersen's criterion might seem to lapse, he gives interesting reasons for regarding a proper name as subject whenever it appears with *be*. Hence in the case of an English sentence like *The conqueror of Gaul was Julius Caesar*, Jespersen's criterion and mine result in a different choice of subject noun. But Jespersen does not consider the difficulty of applying his second criterion to what I call the nuncupative sentence: *I am Charles*.

[4] If we regard these infrasentential forms as unordered pairs (or triplets, etc.) of word-classes, we may also include *word order* among the devices that serve as copula in the sense defined.

speak of an "understood subject" that does not appear in the sentence. To take an example which will concern us in Chapter VI, we want to say – and a lexicon may in fact say – that the verb εἰμί means (i.e. may be translated as) "is alive" only when the subject is a person, and that it means "occurs, takes place" only when the subject is an action, situation, or event. But persons and events are not linguistic expressions which occur in sentences. It is, I think, only an apparent solution to this problem if instead of speaking of persons and events as subject of the verb we talk only of "human nouns," "animate nouns," or "action nouns." In many cases what we really mean by such expressions is not a formal distinction between different types of nouns but a semantic or extra-linguistic distinction between words that refer to *persons*, that refer to *living things*, that refer to *actions* or *events*.[5] There is a genuine ambiguity here in the concept of subject which parallels an ambiguity that has often been noted in the case of predicate.[6] This ambiguity must be frankly recognized, and I propose to distinguish four or five senses of the terms "subject" and "predicate", only one of which is covered by the formal definitions given in the last section. (Here I limit myself to subject and predicate; there is to some extent a corresponding ambiguity of the term "copula", as we shall see in Chapter V §§ 1–2; but I neglect this problem for the time being. In what follows, I shall frequently abbreviate "subject" and "predicate" as "S." and "P.")

The chief point is to avoid confusion between the grammatical subject of a sentence and what I shall call the extra-linguistic subject, i.e. the person, thing, or event which the sentence is "about" and to which the linguistic or grammatical S. refers. When the distinction is baldly stated, it seems impossible to miss. Who can confuse the sense of "subject" in which the *word* "Napoleon" is subject of the sentence "Napoleon died on St. Helena," with that other sense in which Napoleon *himself*, the man who died in 1821, is subject of the same sentence? In principle, to distinguish Napoleon from his name is no more difficult than to distinguish that tiny island in the Atlantic from the syllables which refer to it. Yet it is precisely this confusion which infects the grammatical discussion of *understood subject*, and which often arises also when linguists speak of a *psychological subject*: is it a word or a thing which the speaker "has in mind"? Even philosophers, when they talk of logical subjects, do not always seem to be perfectly clear on this point.

I shall treat S. and P. as correlative terms and describe the relation or tie between them as *predication*. In speaking of a relation of predication between

---

[5] For more on human or animate nouns, see below, Chapter IV §4.
[6] Thus Geach observes (*Reference and Generality*, Ithaca, New York, 1962, p. 23) that even in the work of "logicians as distinguished as Aristotle and Russell" we are sometimes unable to tell whether, when they speak of predicates, they are referring to linguistic components of sentences or to some extra-linguistic concepts or entities.

A and B, or in saying that B *is predicated of* A, I mean nothing more than when I say that A is the subject of B, or that B is the predicate of A. What we need now is to distinguish four kinds of predication (or four senses of the word "predication"): a syntactic, a semantic, an ontological, and a conceptual or judgmental relation. The syntactic and semantic forms of the S.-P. relation are required in any theory of language; the ontological and judgmental versions of predication must be mentioned here if only because of their historical importance and the consequent need of distinguishing them from the other two. In each case, S. and P. may be defined relatively to the sentence (proposition, judgment) in which they occur, as "subject of the sentence" and "predicate of the sentence."[7] It is simpler, however, and more in accord both with traditional usage and with the etymology of the terms, to define them relatively to one another, so that for example in a simple noun-verb sentence like *John runs* we speak of the noun as "subject of the verb *runs*". Of course we may speak derivatively of the noun in such a case as subject of the sentence. We are also obliged to take account of a fifth notion, the topic-comment relation, which tends to replace the subject-predicate terminology in contemporary linguistic theory. I shall describe this as a rhetorical relation since it is properly a question of emphasis, focus of attention, or *mise en relief* within a given context.

(1) Syntactic predication is a relation or tie between linguistic parts of sentences, i.e. between expressions. Thus in the sentence *Napoleon died on St. Helena*, the noun *Napoleon* is the syntactic (or grammatical) S. and the verb phrase *died on St. Helena* is the syntactic (or grammatical) P. There is an obvious analogy to this grammatical conception in the use of the term "predicate" in predicate logic. It is this syntactic or grammatical notion of S. and P. for which we have given formal definitions in the preceding section.

(2) Semantical predication, on the other hand, is a relation or tie between a linguistic and a non-linguistic item. The S. here is an extra-linguistic object (e.g. a person or thing), whereas the P. is a word, phrase, or sentence that describes this entity or that says something about it. Thus in our sample the extra-linguistic S. is the man Napoleon, of whom "died on St. Helena" (or "He died on St. Helena") is predicated. For any singular sentence of S.-P. form, we may say that the extra-linguistic S. is the person or entity (if there is one) to which the grammatical S. refers or, in an older terminology, the object which it denotes. Note that in both (1) and (2) the term "predicate" designates a linguistic expression, and that will be my use of the term throughout this study. In the case of "subject" where confusion is possible I speak of "grammatical S." when I mean the syntactic relatum (e.g. the word "Napoleon")

[7] So Chomsky, *Aspects* pp. 68 ff.; cf. p. 106.

and "extra-linguistic S." when I mean the person or thing that a grammatical subject-expression refers to. (The terms "syntactic S." and "semantic S." might serve as well to make the same distinction.)

(3) To do justice to the traditional usage we must also recognize the concept of predication as an ontological relation where neither term is a linguistic expression, namely the relation that holds between a person or object or other entity and *what is said of it*, where the thing said is not an expression but a property, action, or state. In this sense, which has a respectable tradition behind it going back to Aristotle's use of τι κατά τινος κατηγορεῖσϑαι in the *Categories*, and which is still alive in the philosophical literature, we may say that the act or state of *dying* (and not the verb "died") is predicated of the emperor Napoleon (and not of his name). I shall make little or no use of this third sense in my own discussion, but its existence and distinctness from the other two should be clearly recognized.[8] Its importance lies not only in the influence it has exerted but also in the resistance which it calls forth and which has often been transferred to the S.-P. distinction as formulated in linguistic terms. It should be pointed out that neither the grammatical sense of subject and predicate in (1) nor even the semantic concept of an extra-linguistic subject in (2) depends upon the substance-attribute or thing-property ontology which figures in (3), although both (1) and (2) might be used to support or recommend the latter. As we shall see, *some* ontological conceptions are probably required for any general definition of the subject-predicate relations (1) and (2). But I think that a rather common-sense ontology of particular objects or individuals will suffice, without any appeal to the existence of properties or universals. I propose to make use of the notion of extra-linguistic S. by relying upon the general concept of *reference* or *reference to particulars* as used (in rather different ways) by Quine and Strawson. It is this notion we employ when we say that, for any simple sentence of S.-P. form, the extra-linguistic subject is the particular (or particulars) referred to by the grammatical subject. But I shall leave the notion of grammatical predicate without any ontological explication. I would hope that we do not need to tackle the problem of universals or to answer

[8] This third, properly Aristotelian interpretation of "P. is predicated of S." is itself more complicated than might at first appear. We must distinguish (i) the ontological relation as such, i.e. the complex subject-attribute fact or state of affairs corresponding to a true sentence of the form "S. is P."; and (ii) the assertion or claim that such a relation holds, as made by a speaker (or by a statement-form "S. is P."), without prejudice as to whether this claim is true or false. It is in the second sense that a proposition of the form "S. is P." functions as premiss in a syllogism, e.g. in the *Prior Analytics*, where the truth value of the proposition is left indeterminate. But Aristotle often uses κατηγορεῖται to mean "is truly predicated of", e.g. in the *Categories*, where it is (i), the ontological relation as such, which he has in view.

the question "What do predicate expressions stand for?" in order to analyze the use of εἰμί in Greek.

(4) I shall avoid the terms "logical S." and "logical P.", since there seems to be no general agreement as to whether logical subjects are to be understood as linguistic expressions, as persons and things in the world, or perhaps as something in between, like the "terms" of an abstract proposition or judgment. Instead I shall speak of "conceptual S." and "conceptual P.", where these are understood as constituents of a judgment or "thought" (in Frege's sense of *Gedanke*), taken as the *meaning* of a declarative sentence. A few historical remarks may shed light on some of the things recently said by linguists and philosophers in terms of logical S. and P.

By "conceptual S." and "conceptual P." I mean the notions of S. and P. which figure in the classical theory of judgment, as we find it expressed for example in the *Logic* and *Grammar* of Port Royal. In this theory, which perhaps owes more to the Stoics than to Aristotle's own very brief remarks on psychological "signs" at the beginning of the *De Interpretatione*, the *terms* of a proposition in syllogistic analysis are interpreted as "ideas" or concepts combined in the act of judging. In order to avoid the notorious difficulty of situating attributes or predicate concepts either in human thought or in the world of nature, the Stoics had sought to define a new realm of logical or semantic objects – their λεκτά, i.e. "sayables" or "meanings" – among which not only predicates but also judgments or propositions (Stoic ἀξιώματα) and arguments as well could be located. The Stoic λεκτά reappear (and are reinterpreted) in medieval Aristotelianism as the *intentiones* or concepts in the intellect which are regarded as the primary and universal natural signs, signified in turn or (as we would say) "expressed" by the secondary signs which are words in a particular language. It is this post-Aristotelian theory of meaning conceived in psychological or epistemological terms that is reformulated in the Port Royal doctrine of the union of subject concept (or subject term) and predicate concept (or term) in the act of judgment.[9]

Now in this theory of judgment the S.-P. relation properly belongs neither to the structure of things and events (as with Aristotle) nor to the purely grammatical pattern of utterances, but to some mental or intellectual structure underlying the expression of thought in words. Insofar as the deep structure of language as Chomsky conceives it is constituted by linguistic universals, a tacit knowledge of which is presupposed in the child as part of his innate language-acquisition system, Chomsky's theory of deep structure must likewise be regarded "as a specific hypothesis, of an essentially ratio-

---

[9] For further discussion of the post-Aristotelian theory, see below Chapter IV §27. Aristotle's own doctrine is briefly described in the next section of this Chapter.

nalist cast, as to the nature of mental structures and processes".[10] And as he formulates it, the notion of "logical S." and "logical P." as constituents of deep structure must also be interpreted in conceptual or mental terms.

For strictly linguistic purposes, however, Chomsky's notion of logical S. and P. can be construed in a purely syntactic way as the grammatical S. and P. in a canonical rewriting of the sentence. In the transformational system used here, this means that the logical S. or P. of a given sentence will be the grammatical S. or P. of its elementary source. For example, the logical (or "conceptual") S. of a passive sentence will be recognized in the grammatical S. of the underlying active form. This corresponds exactly to Chomsky's observation that in the sentence *John was persuaded by Bill to leave* it is *John* which functions as grammatical S. (in the surface structure of the sentence) but *Bill* which functions as logical S. – in other words, as grammatical S. in the deep structure.[11] For us the deep structure is given by the elementary source, plus transformations. This possibility of reconstruing the logical or conceptual S. and P. in purely syntactic terms means that we need make no use here of the former notion.

(5) The terminology of topic-comment as it has developed in recent years represents an attempt to salvage the older notions of "psychological" (sometimes "logical") S. and P., or of similar notions such as *theme* and *rheme*, in order to make them useful in formal linguistics. The aim was first of all to get rid of the traditional logical and ontological associations of the S.-P. terminology, and at the same time to define a more general notion of which the I.-E. "subject" and "predicate" (as noun and verb, respectively, in a noun-verb sentence) would be a special case. These two aims are in part incompatible, and they have resulted in two distinct notions circulating in contemporary linguistics under the term "topic". One is a rhetorical (or in some cases psychological) notion which is concerned with the focussing of attention, the expectations of the hearer, what can be taken for granted from the context, and so on. In this sense, the *topic* is described as what is given in the preceding context as the background of the utterance; the *comment* is what is new, unpredictable, or in the foreground of attention. This rhetorical contrast has no intrinsic connection with the syntactic S.-P. relation and it may in fact interfere with it, for example by altering the word order of a standard sentence in English. Thus in Hockett's example, *That new book by Thomas Guernsey I haven't read yet*, the position of the object before subject and verb might be explained as the result of emphasis or focus on this part of the sentence.[12] A rhetorical analysis of this kind is essentially concerned

---

[10] *Aspects.* p. 53; cf. pp. 25ff.
[11] *Aspects*, p. 70.
[12] See the discussion by Lyons, *Introduction*, pp. 334–7, who underestimates the difference

not with the internal structure of given sentences out of context but with the interrelations between several sentences in a connected discourse. It may thus throw light on such phenomena as word order, deletability (or zeroing), pro-wording, and sentence intonation or stress.

Entirely different in principle is the properly syntactic concept of *topic* which some linguists have used to describe any expression in a sentence that receives a specified formal treatment, such as the nominative case in many I.-E. languages, initial position for a noun in languages like English, certain suffixes in Korean.[13] This syntactical conception, which can be regarded as a generalization of the traditional notion of grammatical *subject*, may of course coincide in the case of some sentences with the rhetorical notion of topic as an item in low relief, or which is given by the preceding context. But whereas the syntactic topic can be defined so as to coincide with the grammatical subject in *all* cases where the latter is defined, the rhetorical topic is essentially a factor of stylistic focus that varies independently of the S.-P. structure of the sentence.

§ 3. THE TERMINOLOGY FOR SUBJECT AND PREDICATE IN ARISTOTLE

In view of our special interest in the Greek material and by way or preparation for a general consideration of S. and P., it may be well to call to mind the original Greek discussion of the S.-P. relations. The distinctions made in the previous section should help to clarify some obscurities in the modern interpretation of this ancient doctrine. For one thing, it has not been generally noticed that, although both Plato and Aristotle may be said to have recognized the syntactical relation of predication, neither of them describes this relation in terms of "subject" (ὑποκείμενον) or "predicate"

---

in principle between the rhetorical topic-comment notion and the traditional syntactic analysis into S. and P. But Lyons rightly remarks that without a special context a sentence like *John ran away* is "structurally 'unmarked' for the distinction of topic and comment" (*ibid.* p. 336).

Note that the sentence given above is an example of Harris' permutation transformation. We may compare its rhetorical effect to that of the transformation known as the *it*-extractor: *I read that book → It is that book (which) I read.* In both cases we can give a formal definition of the phenomena which are rhetorically described in the terminology of topic and comment. But the formal definition presupposes normal word order in the source of the transformation, where the grammatical subject will be represented by the first *N* in the sentence.

[13] See Harris, *Mathematical Structures*, p. 112, n. 2, and compare the discussion of "primary topicalization" in Fillmore, *Universals in Linguistic Theory*, p. 55. Fillmore's "secondary topicalization" (p. 57) is closer to the rhetorical concept of topic which I have just distinguished above. Chomsky's remarks on topic and comment in *Aspects* (pp. 220ff. n. 32) seem to hesitate between the syntactical and the rhetorical conception.

(κατηγόρημα, κατηγορούμενον). The terms are Aristotle's invention, apparently, and Plato does not use them at all. Both philosophers, however, when they clearly are concerned with the analysis of a sentence (λόγος) into grammatical S. and P., designate these as ὄνομα and ῥῆμα respectively.[14] The terms ὄνομα and ῥῆμα are normally translated as "noun" (or "name") and "verb," and Plato's very brief discussion is compatible with this rendering. In Aristotle's usage, however, there is no question that ῥῆμα may extend to what we call adjectives as well, when these occur in a predicative role.[15] It is essential to both discussions that nouns and verbs are considered not simply as word-classes but as syntactic constituents of sentences. We may say that Plato and Aristotle set out to distinguish syntactical subject and predicate, and could do so only by distinguishing noun and verb (or noun and adjective) in kernel sentences of the noun-verb (or noun-adjective) type: *Theaetetus flies, (A) man walks, A man (is) tall.*

On the other hand, when Aristotle introduces the terms from which our "subject" and "predicate" are derived by loan-translation, it is not to designate the syntactic but the ontological relation of predication, what we have distinguished as sense (3) in the previous section. Hence his term ὑποκείμενον properly designates the extra-linguistic S. only, and never the grammatical S. The ὑποκείμενον of the *Categories*, which is a "primary substance" (πρώτη οὐσία), is of course the *man* Socrates and not his name or description. It is because his ὑποκείμενον is properly an extra-linguistic S., and in the primary instances a particular individual in the world, that Aristotle in *Categories* 2 can contrast "being said of a subject," in a specially restricted case of the ontological sense (3) of predication, with "being present in a subject," without shifting the meaning of ὑποκείμενον.[16] The rudimentary

---

[14] See *Sophist* 261D–263D and *De Interpretatione* 2–5.

[15] See L. S. J. s.v. ῥῆμα, and John Ackrill, *Aristotle's Categories and De Interpretatione* pp. 118–20. The first example of a ῥῆμα offered by Aristotle in the *De Int.* is apparently λευκός at 16ᵃ15, and his first examples of complete declarative sentences again take as their "verb" λευκός: see the quantified versions of ἄνθρωπος λευκός (ἐστι), "man is white," in ch. 7. On the other hand, in *Poetics* 1457ᵃ14–17 (as generally in the post–Aristotelian usage) λευκός is unambiguously classified as a noun, for the obvious reason that it does not satisfy the definition of ῥῆμα given in *De Int.* 3: it does not indicate time or tense. The different senses of ῥῆμα in Aristotle are carefully distinguished by Ammonius (*in De Int.* 52, 32–53, 7): 1) any word indicating tense, including past and future forms and negated verbs, 2) the narrower sense specified in *De Int.* 3, limited to unnegated verb forms in present tense, and 3) any word in predicate position: πᾶσα φωνὴ κατηγορούμενον ἐν προτάσει ποιοῦσα. Note that Ammonius, unlike Aristotle, uses κατηγορούμενον for a *syntactic* predicate. This development was no doubt facilitated by certain tendencies in Aristotle's own usage. As a systematic terminology, however, the use of κατηγόρημα and κατηγορούμενον for a syntactic or judgmental predicate is post-Aristotelian.

[16] For an example of confusion on this point see the remarks of Chung-Hwan Chen, in *Phronesis* 2 (1957), p. 149, who claims that "the term ὑποκείμενον is very equivocal." In

ontological theory of the *Categories*, in which attributes are predicated of extra-linguistic subjects, underlies the logico-grammatical analysis of the *De Interpretatione*, in which nouns are combined with verbs to compose sentences. Hence a verb is said to be "always the sign of attributes (τῶν ὑπαρχόντων), namely of those predicated of a subject (τῶν καϑ᾿ ὑποκειμένου)" in the ontological sense (*De Int.* 16ᵇ10). Originally, then, the term "subject" applied only to the extralinguistic subject, so that the correlative "predicate" (κατηγορούμενον) designated either the expression applied to (or true of) an object, in the semantic sense of "predication", or else the ontological attribute or characteristic (genus, species, quality, action, etc.) signified by this expression. In the *Categories*, at any rate, the subject-predicate terminology is used only for predication in the semantic sense (2) or the ontological sense (3) distinguished in § 2.[17] In their more elaborate theory of language the Stoics make use of Aristotle's subject-predicate terminology in a new way: for them ὑποκείμενα are bodies and κατηγορήματα are λεκτά or propositional "meanings". But *neither* term designates words or expressions as syntactic parts of sentences, and to this extent the Stoics are faithful to the original Aristotelian usage.

§ 4. Towards a General Definition of Subject and Predicate

It is a matter of historical fact, then, that Aristotle followed Plato in designating the syntactic constituents of sentences as noun (ὄνομα) and verb (ῥῆμα), whereas the term "subject" (ὑποκείμενον), and to some extent the whole subject-predicate terminology, was introduced to denote the extra-linguistic analogues of nouns, verbs, and adjectives. It is perhaps an historical accident that the situation has now been reversed, so that we think of the S.-P. distinction as primarily grammatical. But it is no accident that an abiding connection seems to be felt between the syntactic analysis of simple sentences into noun-verb (or noun-adjective) and the extra-linguistic distinction between things or objects and their actions, states, or properties. It

---

fact the equivocation is not between two senses of ὑποκείμενον but between predication in the modern, syntactic sense (1) and in Aristotle's own ontological sense (3). Aristotle may himself confuse the two from time to time, but not as frequently as his interpreters do. For exceptional cases where Aristotle seems to use ὑποκείμενον for grammatical subject (or for some comparable syntactic notion) see *De Int.* 10, 19ᵇ37; 12, 21ᵇ29, 22ᵃ9.

[17] Thus I agree in part with Lejewski, who understands Aristotle's notion of *being predicated of* as "a semantical relation, i.e. a relation that holds between an expression of a language and a non-linguistic entity .... We *predicate* expressions of things" ("Proper Names", *Proceedings Aristotelian Society* 1958, p. 230). But in Aristotle's own intention this concern with the semantical relation is probably subordinate to the study of ontological relations, in which *things* (species, genus, quality, action, etc.) are predicated of things.

has often been supposed that a substance-attribute metaphysics or, more generally, an entity-property distinction is a projection onto the world of the noun-verb or subject-predicate structure of sentences in Greek and cognate languages. What I want to propose is the contrary hypothesis: namely, that the appearance in many or most languages of a noun-verb distinction, and hence of a subject-predicate sentence structure as well, is the reflection within grammar of certain fundamental conditions underlying all human use of language.

The conditions I have in mind include such facts as these: a language is employed by individual human beings to speak to one another; speaker and hearer must be able to talk not only about themselves and other persons, but also about the animals, plants, artifacts, and other relatively durable objects which make up their world. Hence they must have some device for mentioning or referring to these objects, for singling them out and calling them to mind as a basis for further discussion. The class of nouns (in the general sense, which includes not only common nouns and proper names but also personal pronouns) is the fundamental linguistic device for this purpose: nouns, or more exactly, elementary nouns (primitive N) constitute the nucleus class of referring expressions, which may of course be supplemented by demonstratives, articles, numbers, verb-clauses, etc. for greater precision. The reason, I suggest, why nearly every language distinguishes a word-class of nouns or nominal forms is just that every language requires a class of referring expressions to denote persons (e.g. the speaker and hearer), horses, sheep, houses, boats, weapons, and other particulars, both singly and in groups.

These facts are sufficiently obvious, and they suggest the general definition of *noun* as a word-class of referring expressions, with a characteristic subclass (the elementary nouns or first-order nominals) whose members denote individual persons, places or things.[18] This may not seem a satisfactory definition, since it presupposes the concepts of (1) denoting or referring, and (2) individual persons and things. The second notion seems to me sufficiently primitive to require no further discussion here;[19] but the concept of referring might itself be explicated or illustrated by a consideration of the subject-predicate structure of sentences; and this in turn can be explained in terms

18 This is what Lyons calls a "notional" definition of noun, where for "notional" I would say "semantic."

19 By taking the common-sense notion of individual thing or physical object as primitive I do not mean to suggest that this notion is sharply defined. There are many clear cases; in addition to people, we surely include cows, trees, vases, and spears. But what about rivers, cities, and clouds? I tend to be generous in my use of the concept, and for present purposes would count these as individual things. But I exclude numbers, thoughts and events.

of the elementary sentence forms *noun-verb* or *noun-adjective*, as we have seen in the Greek discussion in the previous section. It might be argued that the concept of noun as a word-class in general linguistics (in contrast to verb or other non-nominal form), the concept of referring or denoting as a semantic (extra-linguistic) relation between word and thing, and the syntactic concept of S.-P. sentence structure are all *equally* primitive, in this respect, that one cannot give an adequate account of any one of these three concepts without making use of the other two.

It is often the case that within a given language the noun-verb distinction can be made in purely formal terms, on the basis of such criteria as grammatical suffixes or the forms used for negation.[20] And it might appear that we can generalize this distinction, without relying on any extra-linguistic considerations, by the following observation: given the noun-verb distinction for a particular language, as a division of word-classes on formal grounds alone, we call one of these classes "noun" and the other "verb" simply because most of their members will be translated by nouns and verbs respectively, in English or a cognate language. I do not believe this formal account goes to the heart of the matter. Why do we translate the putative proper names (of individuals or tribes) by proper names in our own language, a word for an animal species by a common noun, a morpheme or word indicating the speaker by the pronoun "I"? These questions may be ignored; but they cannot be answered, they cannot even be formulated, without introducing the notion of reference and considering the nature of the extra-linguistic items referred to.

The interconnection between the lexical, syntactical, and semantical analyses is roughly this. Given the basic word classes and a simple two-term sentence of the form *NV*, e.g. *Socrates sits, (A) man stands*, we define the grammatical S. as the noun and the grammatical P. as the verb in the given sentence. (In Greek, the noun-verb distinction is easily drawn on the basis of suffixes; in English we would need distributional criteria.) We may then extend these concepts to more complex sentences, retaining the (in English) initial noun phrase as S., and the expanded verb phrase as P.[21] By introducing the concept of reference we can define the extra-linguistic S. of the sentence, the ὑποκείμενον or entity we are talking about. And if we choose, we can similarly introduce the ontological version of P. as the action, state, or property signified by the linguistic predicate. And this procedure, from

---

[20] For an example of the latter, see A. C. Graham's account of the noun-verb distinction in Chinese: *The Verb 'be' and its Synonyms*, Part I, pp. 2f.

[21] At this point my account follows Lyons, *Introduction*, pp. 338f. at least in part. See also his "Towards a 'notional' theory of the 'parts of speech,'" *Journal of Linguistics*, 2 (1966), 209–36. As will appear in a moment, we are both following Sapir.

morphologically or distributionally defined word-classes to syntactic components of sentences, and from syntactic S. and P. to particular entities and their properties, is roughly the course followed by the development from Plato's discussion in the *Sophist* to Aristotle's doctrine in the *Categories*. From the point of view of general linguistics, however, this has the disadvantage of not affording us any general characterizations of noun and verb, so that as soon as we abstract from morphological peculiarities of familiar languages, the whole analysis is left hanging in the air. On the other hand, if we take for granted the syntactic analysis of sentences into S. and P., we can define nouns as the word-class that can occupy both S. position and P. position, whereas verbs can occupy P. position *only*.[22] Finally, if we choose to take as primitive the notion of expressions referring to or denoting persons, places, and objects, we can define the class of (elementary) nouns as the word-class of referring expressions and can define a verb as a form which, when added to a noun, produces an acceptable sentence. Any one of these approaches may reasonably be preferred for a particular purpose, although I believe the third is philosophically the most illuminating. My present aim is simply to show that the concepts of noun-verb, S.-P., and reference to objects (in conjunction with the concept of sentencehood), represent three points of departure for covering essentially the same ground.

The interdependence of these lexical, syntactic, and semantic (or extra-linguistic) concepts is vividly reflected in a well-known passage of Sapir which I shall quote at length as a kind of concluding "authority" for my discussion of S. and P. Sapir has just remarked that "no logical scheme of the parts of speech... is of the slightest interest to the linguist. Each language has its own scheme."

Yet we must not be too destructive. It is well to remember that speech consists of a series of propositions. There must be something to talk about and something must be said about this subject of discourse once it is selected. The distinction is of such fundamental importance that the vast majority of languages have emphasized it by creating some sort of formal barrier between the two terms of the proposition. The subject of discourse is a noun. As the most common subject of discourse is either a person or a thing, the noun clusters about concrete concepts of that order. As the thing predicated of a subject is generally an activity in the widest sense of the word, a passage from one moment of existence to another, the form which has been set aside for the business of predicating, in other words, the verb, clusters about concepts of activity. No language wholly fails to distinguish noun and verb, though in particular cases the nature of the distinction may be an elusive one.[23]

---

[22] It is in this respect, and in the perspective of transformational grammar, that adjectives belong with verbs (as essentially predicate expressions) rather than with nouns. See Lyons' proposal to classify adjectives under the broad category of "verb" in *Introduction*, pp. 323–5, and in the article quoted in the preceding note. The same point can be made in terms of Harris' kernel analysis by observing that *NN*, *NV* and *NA*, but not *VN* or *AN*, represent elementary sentential forms.

[23] Edward Sapir, *Language*, Harcourt Brace paperback, p. 119.

In several respects this passage is very carelessly written. Sapir would have taken greater pains with it if he had foreseen how often he would be quoted! We must forgive the more-than-Aristotelian *insouciance* with which "the subject of discourse" is identified as a noun in one sentence and a person or thing in the next.[24] But if we introduce the necessary distinctions, we see that Sapir is accounting for the universality of the noun-verb opposition by pointing to its function in the syntactic relation of predication, taking as his specimen a two-term sentence with intransitive verb; and that he is explicating this in turn by appealing to the semantic relation involving reference (where the "subject of discourse" is a person or thing, not an expression), and even to the ontological relation, where the "thing predicated" is "an activity in the widest sense, a passage from one moment of existence to another."

Despite its deficiencies of formulation, this statement of Sapir is a precious one, coming as it does from a master of exotic languages who was of all men the one least inclined to see the universal laws of thought embodied in the idioms of Indo-European. All the more remarkable, then, that he should in effect have endorsed the Platonic-Aristotelian analysis of the sentence into noun and verb on the basis of extra-linguistic considerations quite similar to those from which the classical analysis arose. We can summarize Sapir's position, which is essentially the view defended in this section, by the following four points.

(1) Certain universal features or tendencies in word classes and sentence structure are conditioned by the existence of individual objects such as persons and things, which any language must be able to talk about, i.e. must be able to take as extra-linguistic subjects for declarative sentences, questions and the like.

(2) This distinction between things and what we say about them is reflected in the grammatical S.-P. structure of some sentences in every language, i.e., there will be some sentences in which one term serves to refer to an individual person or object and another term can be construed as predicated of – as true or false of – the object referred to by the first term.

(3) In the context of general linguistics, independently of the morphological and syntactic peculiarities of any given type of language, a noun may be defined (in the first instance) as a word class some of whose members function typically as referring expressions to designate or identify persons and things as extra-linguistic S. (By introducing transformational considerations which Sapir did not envisage, we may sharpen this as follows. A class of elementary or first-order nouns may be defined as the words that refer to persons or

[24] For a more conscientious distinction on Sapir's part between "objects, actions, qualities to talk about" and "their corresponding symbols" in words, see the same work, p. 93.

individual things in the way indicated. An extended class of nouns may be defined to include all words morphologically and syntactically analogous to the elementary nouns, e.g. words that can occur in some of the same environments, or in environments of the same general form.) The class of verbs (or, in Lyons' sense, "predicators") is distinguished as the class of words that combine with a noun to give a simple two-word sentence.

(4) This difference in function of the expressions in a simple two-term sentence type is such a fundamental feature of discourse that it receives a formal expression in most languages by some distinction between nominal and verbal forms, i.e. between typical S. expressions and typical P. expressions.[25]

It must be observed that I have not, after all, formulated any general definition of S. and P. What I have tried to do, informally, is to indicate two ways in which such a definition might proceed, on the one hand by considering the word class distinction in the two-term sentence of noun-verb form, and on the other hand by the distinction between a referring expression (or noun) and what must be added to it (namely, a predicate) to make a sentence. I have suggested that the second procedure, which combines semantic with syntactic considerations, in fact underlies the first. This second line of definition is also more general, since it recognizes an S.-P. relation even in the case of the so-called nominal sentence, where the predicate constituent is, or might be, a referring expression as well. Thus a noun may serve as a predicate in the narrow, and perhaps also in the wider sense distinguished above in Section 2; but a (finite) verb can never be the subject of a sentence. There is only an apparent exception in the case of quoted words, e.g. "*Runs*" *is a verb*. When a verb form functions as a S. expression, we for that very reason describe it as "nominalized." It is this syntactic asymmetry which determines the universal character of the noun-verb opposition, if anything does. And this syntactic asymmetry is indirectly correlated with the semantic asymmetry that is constituted by the referring function of nouns. Verbs cannot occur as subject of a sentence because they do not refer to or denote objects. And in the more elementary cases, the function of the subject expression is precisely to denote the object that the sentence is "about".

[25] A stronger version of this thesis is offered by Lyons: "*Every* language may be assumed to have, as its *most* typical sentence-type of minimal syntactic structure, a class of sentences whose nuclei are composed of a nominal and a verb (the term 'nominal' is intended to include nouns, pronouns, and noun-phrases; and the term 'verb' is understood in the wider sense which also embraces adjectives)" (*Introduction*, p. 339, with emphasis added here). The italicized words probably make the statement too strong, as we shall see in the next section.

§ 5. Some restrictions on the universality of the noun-verb or subject-predicate sentence structure

Before turning to the Greek material, it will be useful to consider a pointed objection to the general claims about the S.-P. structure of sentences that were presented in the preceding section. In a recent article in *Mind*, Ian Hacking has challenged the thesis that all languages make some use of the S.-P. (or nominal-verbal) sentence type. Ironically enough, Hacking's challenge is based upon evidence from the language on which Sapir was the unrivalled authority: the speech of the Nootka Indians on Vancouver Island.[26] A brief look at Hacking's argument will help to clarify the import of Sapir's claim, and also lead us to qualify it in a significant way.

Hacking does not doubt that the Nootka Indians live in a world full of individual things, which they succeed in talking about. Thus he does not deny claim (1) in our statement of Sapir's position (above, p. 52). But he does deny (2), that the language contains terms which are properly described as referring expressions used to identify persons or objects as the extra-linguistic S. of a given sentence, expressions which, in Strawson's phrase, "serve to introduce particulars."[27] Above all, he wants to deny (4) by showing that the language makes no S.-P. distinction within the sentence since, in fact, it makes no distinction between nominal and verbal forms. Thus Hacking agrees with Sapir and with the view maintained here that, in the context of general linguistics, the paired concepts of noun-verb and S.-P. stand or fall together.

Now Nootka is certainly one of the languages Sapir had in mind when he recognized that in some cases the nature of the noun-verb distinction may be elusive. Hacking quotes Boas' statement for the related language of Kwakiutl: "All stems seem to be neutral, neither noun nor verb, and their nominal or verbal character seems to depend solely on the suffix with which they are used, although some of the suffixes are also neutral." Hacking adds: "And this 'character' is not internal to the language, but arises from how we translate it."[28] He concludes that the Nookta sentence is best understood in terms of what Strawson calls feature-placing, where we have the report of a state or process to be found in some place and time, without a S.-P.

[26] See "A Language without Particulars," *Mind* 77 (1968), 168–85, cited below as "Hacking."
[27] In this connection it is curious that Hacking fails to consider Nootka stems classified as proper names, personal suffixes such as the 1st pers. sing. *-ah*, and an important "indirect reference stem" such as *'o-* "he, she, it, they," with corresponding interrogative forms "who?" or "what?" See M. Swadesh, "Nootka Internal Syntax," in *International Journal of Amer. Linguistics* 9 (1938), p. 98. These forms would, I think, present some difficulties for Hacking's thesis. And compare Swadesh's (perhaps unconvincing) attempt to distinguish a semantic class of "entity stems," *ibid*. p. 99.
[28] Hacking, p. 178.

structure, as in the English sentences "It is snowing" and "There is water here." (I waive the question whether, from a syntactical point of view, the latter sentence is really devoid of S.-P. structure. On the analysis presented in Chapter I § 9, *There is water here* is derived from (*Some*) *water is here* in precisely the same way as *There is a man at the door* is derived from (*A*) *man is at the door*. In the deep structure of *There is water here*, the noun *water* is subject, just as (*a*) *man* is the underlying subject of *There is a man at the door*. The fact that the underlying subject is in the latter case a count noun and in the former a "mass word" seems irrelevant to the question of S.-P. structure.)

We cannot decide whether or not Hacking is right about the logical syntax or deep structure of Nootka and Kwakiutl. This is, after all, not a matter of linguistic fact so much as a question of the appropriate grammatical *theory* in which to describe the phenomena of sentence formation in languages very different from our own. All we can attempt to do is to see why Sapir, who knew the facts, nevertheless thought Nootka no exception to his generalization about the universality of the noun-verb or S.-P. distinction. For Sapir describes in detail how a particular stem, repeatedly suffixed, may yet remain neutral as far as this distinction is concerned. The radical element *inikw-* "fire," when augmented by the suffix *-ihl* "in the house," pluralized by -*'minih*, given diminutive form by -*'is*, and even modified by the preterit tense suffix *-it*, is still open to both nominal and verbal determination. (This, presumably, tells against any universal connection between verb and tense.) For Sapir the word becomes nominal when the articular ending *'i* is added: "*inikwihl'minih'isit-'i* means 'the former small fires in the house, the little fires that were once burning in the house.'" But it becomes an "unambiguous verb" when by the addition of a modal suffix "it is given a form that excludes every other possibility, as in the indicative *inikwihl-minih'isit-a* 'several small fires were burning in the house'" (*Language*, p. 134). It is surely misleading to suggest, as Hacking does, that "nominal suffix" in Nootka means simply "a suffix which appended to a stem gives something we translate as a noun" (Hacking, p. 180). That we call it a noun is of course correlated with the fact that we translate it by a form which in our own language we recognize as nominal. But underlying the use of "nominal" in both cases is the recognition that a term which may be used with an article has a semantic function comparable to that of a name or *nomen*: it may serve as a referring expression to "introduce particulars", i.e. to identify them as extra-linguistic subjects for further discourse. Similarly, if a form determined by a given suffix always translates into English as an indicative verb, that translation reflects the fact that such a form suffices (either alone or with a nominal) to make a declarative sentence, i.e. a statement with a truth claim. (This seems to be the most general characterization of a verb: it is an adaptation of Benveniste's definition, below, p. 57.) Hacking's attack on the noun-verb distinction in Nootka and Kwakiutl falls short of its goal because he fails to see that underlying the morphological and lexical contrast of nominal and verbal forms is the functional opposition between a referring expression (signalled in Sapir's example by the article-suffix, which we may regard as an element of weak deictic reference) and the sentence-forming role of a predicate expression (signalled here by the indicative or assertive ending). Thus Swadesh can illustrate Nootka sentence structure by showing how two stems, for "man" and "large" or "man" and "working," can be used alternately as S. and P. depending upon which stem receives the articular or modal suffix.[29]

But perhaps Hacking is right on a key point, and the Nootka word-sentence that translates as "several small fires were burning in the house" cannot reasonably be regarded as S.-P. in form. There is no distinction within such a sentence between an element which identifies the fires and an element which says that they burn, a morpheme which singles out an object and another which describes some state or activity of that object: the stem *inikw-* does both jobs at once. The feature-placing character of the sentence is perhaps revealed by a translation that attempts to render the morphemes one by one: "Fire-burning, in the house, several, small, past, it-is-so." The best English parallel seems to be of the form "It snowed lightly in the woods for a long time." (The fit is not perfect, since we cannot pluralize meteorological verbs in English.)[30]

What Hacking has shown is that a language capable of distinguishing nominal and verbal forms need not always, or even normally, use them in such a way as to construct its sentences in the S.-P. pattern. And this version of his conclusion is perfectly compatible with the passage quoted from Sapir in Section 4. (It may even be compatible with Strawson's view, which is the direct target of Hacking's attack.) My own cursory acquaintance with Nootka texts (as published by Sapir and Swadesh) leads me to believe that many sentences can naturally be construed on the nominal-verbal or S.-P. pattern, but that this is not the predominant shape, even for sentences like "The fire is burning in the house" which one might reasonably regard as (slightly expanded) kernel sentences of the language. Hacking's suggestion that the fundamental sentence pattern is a one-term feature-placing con-

[29] See "Nootka Internal Syntax," p. 78.
[30] Is it an accident that Sapir illustrates noun-verb neutrality in Nootka by a term for fire, the Heraclitean symbol for a process ontology? Perhaps the "feature-placing" tendencies of Nootka make this a *typical* reality pattern in that language, as the S.-P. structure of Indo-European presents the thing-property or agent-action pattern as typical.

struction may serve as a useful hypothesis for anyone who undertakes a new theoretical description of Nootka syntax.

For our own purposes, we may draw one definite conclusion from this discussion of the Nootka material. Even if Sapir and others are correct in supposing that the S.-P. pattern in its basic form, as a two-term nominal-verbal sentence type, is universal in the sense that it has left its trace in every language, it does not follow that this is the typical or predominant sentence form in all of them. And even in those languages like Greek in which the S.-P. form is clearly predominant, it may not be the *only* fundamental type, even in deep structure. We should expect at least one other basic form, the one-term or purely verbal sentence, with no grammatical or extra-linguistic S. In some I.-E. languages we actually find such sentences, as in Greek νείφει or Spanish *nieva*, "it is snowing." In English syntax (as in German or French) the S.-P. pattern is so imperious that we are constrained to introduce the dummy S. expression *it*: *It is raining, It thunders*. We have already encounter-ed this dummy subject in our discussion of the impersonal copula in *It is dark here* or *It is chilly today* (see Chapter I § 10). We recognize this pronoun as a dummy for we know that there is not, even in principle, any sort of extra-linguistic S. which the *it* might naturally be taken to refer to. We cannot answer, nor even seriously ask, the questions: *What is dark? What is chilly? What is raining?* The inappropriateness of the question shows that *it* here is not a pro-word for some referring expression but a mere form imposed by the S.-P. pattern. The failure of the question is a linguistic test that reveals the absence of an extra-linguistic relation of referring to or denoting individ-ual objects in the world. (For more on the topic of impersonal sentences, see Chapter IV §§ 27–30.)

In a language like Greek, the verb in such a case will stand alone as an "impersonal" form, i.e. as a predicate without a subject: ὕει, νείφει.[31] Or rather, since we have defined P. and S. as correlative, and cannot properly speak of one without the other, let us call this simply the one-word sentence. I suspect that in every language in which the noun-verb distinction can be applied in a general way, the word-sentence will be classified as a verb. This is what is implied by Benveniste's general definition of the verb as "the element which is indispensable for the constitution of a finite assertive utterance."[32] And it is in this sense that the concept of verb can be defined independently of a S.-P. sentence structure. In Strawson's terminology, an

---

[31] For the moment I ignore the fact that a Greek *can* say Ζεὺς ὕει, "Zeus is raining." Even in English we can say in certain cases. *The room is dark, The air is chilly*, perhaps even *The sky thunders* but certainly not *The sky rains*!

[32] See "La phrase nominale," in *Problèmes de linguistique générale* (1966), p. 154. However, the application of this definition to the predicate term in a nominal sentence gives para-doxical results.

impersonal verb is the natural expression for a "feature-placing" assertion, in contrast to a S.-P. statement that describes the properties or characteristics of an identifiable, discrete object. It is clear that in I.-E., and above all in early Greek, such impersonal, one-word sentences have been reduced to a minimum. But there may well be other languages such as Nootka in which the contrast between nominal forms for reference and verbal forms for predication plays no fundamental role in sentence structure – that is to say, where the introduction of the word-classes *noun* and *verb* may be of no theoretical utility in describing the sentences of the language. It may be that in such languages the one-term feature-placing sentence is the elementary unit of syntax, so that most of the actual sentences of language are formed by stringing together such units (with secondary modifications or supplementary "case-forms") in chains of various length and complexity, in which expressions that we will translate by a proper name and by a verb seem to be treated as formal elements of the same type. Such a language would call for a syntactic theory very different from that which is based upon the noun-verb or subject-predicate structure familiar to us from I.-E. An appropriate theory for such a language might take the form which Charles Fillmore has recently proposed in "A Case for Case." [33]

This question of the universality of subject-predicate sentence structure in the context of general linguistics is of course not directly relevant to the task

---

[33] *Universals in Linguistic Theory*, ed. Bach and Harms (New York, 1968), pp. 1–88. Fillmore wishes to regard "subject of" (verb or sentence) as "exclusively a surface-structure phenomenon" (p. 17), to be replaced in deep structure by a variety of case relations (agentive, instrumental, dative, locative, etc.) associated with a kernel verb. However, Fillmore's theory apparently preserves the fundamental asymmetry between verbal and non-verbal or nominal forms, since there will be one (and only one?) verb in every kernel structure, whereas the number of the nominal forms will vary with the case relations that characterize a particular verb type.

I note in passing that much of what I have said about the subject-predicate structure of noun-verb sentences can be reformulated in Fillmore's theory for the special case (which I would regard as the subject-predicate case *par excellence*) where the extra-linguistic subject is a person and the predicate is a non-stative, non-psychological verb like *walks*, *gives*, or *strikes*. Fillmore's agentive case can be defined as the relation of subject noun (i.e. I.-E. nominative case form) to verb in sentences of this type. For non-personal subjects and for verbs like *sees*, *believes*, *wants*, *knows* the corresponding case-relation in his theory is no longer the agentive, and hence the S.-P. structure of such sentences as *The river flows into the sea* or *I see the picture* could be described as secondary (or "surface") extensions of the nominative case-finite verb correlation which "properly" expresses agency in I.-E. – an extension which suggests or presupposes an analogy between *The river flows* and *I see* on the one hand, and *I walk*, *I strike* on the other.

Hence, although Fillmore's theory might at first suggest that the noun-verb distinction is after all more general than S.-P. structure, I would deny this even within the context of his theory, at least for that class of sentences which admit the agentive case. For those sentences the S.-P. relation in deep structure is just the agentive-verb relation (with all other cases treated as subordinate to the verb).

of describing the uses of the verb *be* in Greek. But it is indirectly relevant insofar as the notion of predication associated with the verb in grammatical and philosophic theory implies a sentence structure of S.-P. form. As we shall see in Chapter V, this is only partially the case. And some uses of the verb, such as the veridical uses described in Chapter VII, are so general in form that they abstract from any internal structure of the sentences whose truth or falsity is expressed by ἔστι. However, insofar as the primary and predominant use of εἰμί is that of the copula verb as defined above in §1, the theory of this verb inevitably involves a subject-predicate analysis of the sentence. Hence the question of the universality of this structure is, after all, part of the question of the universality of the functions of the Greek (or I.-E.) verb *be*. That issue cannot be settled here. What I have tried to do is to distinguish this strictly linguistic question, whether a noun-phrase verb-phrase theory of sentence structure is adequate and appropriate for the *description* of all languages, from the properly philosophical question, whether the S.-P. structure which is so natural in I.-E. syntactic theory does not reflect an asymmetry in the basic linguistic *functions* of referring (i.e. identifying objects for discourse) and predicating (or saying something about them which may be true or false). It seems likely that, even if the answer to the linguistic question is "no" or "maybe not", the philosophical question must still be answered in the affirmative. And if, as I suppose, the distinction between referring (naming, denoting) and predicating (sentence-formation, statement-making) is so fundamental that it must be recognized in any theory of language, then the noun-verb or S.-P. structure of sentences in I.-E. is a happy peculiarity, for it permits us to recognize and express this distinction in a perfectly natural way. And of course one of the most natural expressions for it is a sentence of *N is Φ* form.

CHAPTER III

APPLICATION OF THE TRANSFORMATIONAL
ANALYSIS TO GREEK

§ 1. Survey of this Chapter

In Chapter II I argued that the noun-verb or subject-predicate sentence form, although it may not in fact be linguistically universal as the dominant sentence pattern in all languages, is nevertheless of fundamental importance for philosophy because it reflects the perfectly general distinction between two linguistic functions – the function of reference (and in the primary case, reference to individuals) and the function of predication or sentence-formation – which must be performed in any language. The capacity of referring to individual men or sheep or baskets and the capacity to make sentences, and in particular declarative sentences which can be true or false, represent two minimum conditions that every human language must satisfy. It is another question whether they are in fact always satisfied by a pair of contrasting forms or word classes comparable to the distinction of nouns and verbs in I.-E.

The burden of my argument can be summarized as follows (considering only the simplest case of the two-term declarative sentence with intransitive verb): whether or not the S.-P. or noun-verb sentence pattern can be regarded as in fact universal, it has the same general importance for a theory of language as do the predicate forms Fa and Fx in logic. Nouns and verbs, and more generally subjects and predicates, are the functional equivalents in natural language for the predicates and variables or individual constants in logic: verbs and verb phrases correspond to "F", nouns in subject position correspond functionally to "a" or "x".

Although I do not intend to abandon this general point of view, we must now turn more specifically to the situation in Greek. My primary concern in this chapter will be to clarify the conceptual foundation for the description of Greek usage to be given in the chapters which follow. I shall assume that the general form for elementary sentences and for most non-elementary sentences as well, in Greek as in English, is the subject-predicate or noun phrase-verb phrase pattern, which I symbolize by Harris' formula $NV\Omega$ (noun-verb-object). Here "object" (Ω) is taken in the broadest sense, to include predicate nouns, adjectives, and adverbs in the case where V is the verb *be*. To indicate this special case of the copula sentence, instead of $NV\Omega$ I shall write N *is* Φ (where "Φ" stands for "predicate," in the narrower sense specified in Chapter II §1). In other cases the value of Ω is either (1) empty, in the two-term sentence with intransitive verb, *John runs*; (2) *N* (noun) in *John loves Mary*; (3) *PN* (prepositional phrase), *John goes to town*; or (4) *NPN, John takes Mary to town*. (Compare Chapter I §7.)

With an appropriate modification we can also apply this general formula to the impersonal construction, where the initial *N* position will be empty: ( ) *V*, ὕει, "(it) is raining". Such impersonal constructions, already mentioned in Chapter II §5, will be further discussed in Chapter IV §§27–30. It is important to distinguish this impersonal construction, where the subject position in the *underlying* structure of the sentence is genuinely empty (even if in some modern languages we have a surface subject like *it*) from the case of ellipse or zeroing of the subject expression in a sentence of the form *NVΩ*. By "zeroing" of the subject I mean the absence of any nominal term corresponding to *N* in the text of a sentence whose underlying form is *NVΩ*.[1] This is, roughly speaking, the phenomenon of the "understood subject." In Sections 4–6 I discuss this and related topics, including the concepts of ellipse, the Stoic notion of a "complete" and "incomplete" sentence (or proposition), and the general principle of referential constancy over a given stretch of discourse. I shall give my reasons for preferring the transformational method, which takes the *NVΩ* form as fundamental and explains most deviations from it as instances of zeroing, to the alternative approach to Greek sentence structure that takes the one-word verbal form (e.g. ἔρχομαι) and the nominal or verbless sentence pattern (σοφὸς ὁ Σωκράτης) as the two minimal sentence forms with no eliminable elements.

In Section 7 I prepare the syntactic analysis by distinguishing three types of sentences on the basis of the subclass of *N* which figures in subject position: first-order nominals, abstract nouns, and sentential subjects.

Finally, in Sections 8–9, I discuss the problem of classifying the uses of εἰμί in Greek and outline the organization of the following chapters.

§ 2. THE BASIC PRINCIPLE OF ANALYSIS: THE UNDERLYING SENTENCE FORMS ARE THE SAME FOR GREEK AS FOR ENGLISH

Throughout this study I shall take for granted that the elementary sentence types in Greek are identical with those defined by Harris for English,

---

[1] Strictly speaking, the term "zeroing" refers only to the omission of a word or phrase that can be reconstructed (or "understood") from the context. "Deletion" is a more general term for any transformational omitting of material, whether or not the deleted form can be reconstructed by the hearer or reader.

except for one or two kernel forms which we must add to Harris' list.[2] As just indicated, this means I assume that the underlying structure of any given sentence, or of its constituent kernels, is of the form $NV\Omega$, and that only in the case of an impersonal construction can N be regarded as empty.

At first sight this assumption may seem in plain conflict with the linguistic facts. In the Homeric poems which constitute our primary corpus, most sentences have no subject N expressed, and many sentences with predicate nouns and adjectives have no copula ἐστί. Yet it is an essential part of the linguistic theory which I use in *describing* the syntactic data to assume that the underlying structure is always $NV\Omega$ or N *is* Φ. I suggest that no coherent description of these sentence structures can be given without this assumption, or, to put the point more mildly, that no alternative account can have the generality and simplicity of the transformational description which relies on such an assumption.[3]

The proof of the pudding is in the eating, and I might here pass directly to the application of my theory in the next chapter. However, in order to show more clearly what is at issue, and also as an act of *captatio benevolentiae* in the direction of philological readers who may be inclined to cast up their hands in despair at this point, I shall contrast my assumption with what seems to be the more natural alternative, a traditional analysis in terms of two minimal sentence forms. As an historical account, this view has been influential in comparative linguistics for over a century, and it was recently formulated as a synchronic theory of Latin syntax by Maurice P. Cunningham.[4]

---

[2] These differences are largely due to the richer system of case forms in Greek. Specifically, the possessive sentence form with the dative ἔστι μοι χρήματα "I have money" is not paralled by any form in English. Note that the related construction in French is of the form N *is PN (C'est à moi)* ; that is to say, the dative case is replaced by a preposition. Similarly for the predicative genitive ἀγαθοῦ πατρός εἰμι "I am (come) of a good father" (Chapter IV §26). Here the English equivalent is of the form $NVPN$.

[3] My remarks are not directed against a theory like Fillmore's, in "A Case for Case" (*Universals in Linguistic Theory*, ed. Bach and Harms, New York, 1968), where the $NV\Omega$ pattern appears as one particular form of the general sentence structure that consist of a verb and one or more case categories. Fillmore's theory represents a wider generalization; it would require an analysis like Harris' at a more "superficial" level in order to describe the situation in I.-E.

[4] "A Theory of the Latin Sentence," *Classical Philology* 60 (1965), 24–8; see p. 25: "The two most basic sentence forms in Latin are the simple verbal sentence and the simple predicate sentence." For the first case, compare Munro, *Homeric Grammar* p. vii: "The simplest possible sentence … consists of a verb … containing in itself … a subject and a predicate." A view of this kind also underlies Meillet's account of verbal and nominal sentence structure in I.-E. The oldest systematic formulation of this theory of two minimal or primitive forms seems to be that of L. Lange in *Verhandlungen der XIII. Versammlung deutschen Philologen … in Göttingen, 1852,* cited and summarized by J. Kinzel (see below). I paraphrase Kinzel's summary: the simplest, least developed form of sentence is the finite

This alternative view takes as basic the two following sentence types:

1. the finite verb alone, e.g. ἔρχομαι "I go", "I am going".
2. two non-verbal forms juxtaposed, with one as predicate of the other, e.g. σοφὸς ὁ Σωκράτης "Socrates is wise."

This view regards as secondary variants the two fuller forms:

1A. finite verb with nominal subject: ἐγὼ ἔρχομαι "I go".
2A. a copula verb added to 2 above: ὁ Σωκράτης ἐστὶ σοφός[5]

Now 1A has the form *NV* and 2A has the form *N is Φ*; thus both may be seen as cases of the general sentence form *NVΩ*. The difference between the transformational approach adopted here and the more traditional view under consideration is that I take forms 1A and 2A as elementary and basic, whereas the traditional view takes them as secondary and derived. Hence I regard the nominal sentence form 2 as the result of zeroing of the verb, just as I regard the one-word sentence type 1 as containing a nominal subject in zero form. In each case the underlying sentence structure can be indicated by writing the deleted form in parenthesis. Thus I would rewrite 1 and 2 above as follows:

1*. (ἐγὼ) ἔρχομαι
2*. σοφός (ἐστι) ὁ Σωκράτης

Concerning the nominal sentence (type 2) I shall have more to say later. (See Chapter V §5 and Appendix B.) Considering for the moment only sentences 1 and 1*, as representing the traditional and the transformational description of the minimal verbal sentence in Greek, we can describe the difference between them as a difference between surface structure and deep structure. On the surface, there is an unquestionable empirical contrast between verbal sentences in Greek and English, since a one-word sentence like ἔρχομαι is perfectly acceptable in Greek (or Latin or Spanish) whereas the corresponding sentence in English (or French or German) must contain two terms, including a pronominal subject: *I go, je vais*. The difference is unmistakable, since the addition of the pronoun to the Greek sentence results in an contrasting emphasis on the subject which does not characterize the English form: ἐγὼ ἔρχομαι means not simply "I go" or "I am

---

verb, which contains the subject-element in its personal ending, the predicate element in its root or stem; the second sentence form consists of two juxtaposed nouns (or nominals, *nomina*), one of which functions as S. the other as P. See Josef Kinzel, "Die Kopula bei Homer und Hesiod," *Jahresbericht des k.k.K. Franz Joseph Staatsgymnasium in Mährisch-Ostrau* (Schuljahr 1907–1908), pp. 1–2.

[5] See Chapter II, n. 1, for my convention of following the English word order *N is Φ* in giving sample copula sentences for Greek.

going" but rather "*I* am going" or "Whatever you or anyone else may do, I am going." In posing *NV* (that is to say, sentence 1* above) as the underlying form of ἔρχομαι I do not intend to deny this obvious difference. I mean rather to spell out, in syntactic terms, the implications of the usual view that in a form like ἔρχομαι the subject is somehow "contained" or "morphologically expressed" in the finite verb-ending. What is contained, of course, is the marker for first person singular. This is a linguistic category not a subject, but it *specifies* a definite (extra-linguistic) subject, to wit, the speaker, in any given situation of utterance. Thus the personal ending performs exactly the same function as the corresponding personal pronoun *I* in English: both forms identify the speaker as subject when they are used in an actual speech situation. It is because of this referential function of the marker for first and second person that it makes sense to speak of the subject as hidden or contained in the verb-ending. And it is because this function is adequately performed by the finite verb alone that the personal pronoun is added only when some special effect of emphasis or contrast is intended.

Yet it is convenient to assume a pronominal element "(ἐγώ)" in the underlying structure of ἔρχομαι and thus to preserve the sentence pattern *NV*. This is so, in the first place, because the verb ending is marked for the grammatical category of person, and this category is most naturally expressed by a pronominal element *N*, as in the pronouns *I*, *you*, *he*. This makes it at least plausible to analyze ἔρχομαι into two elements *N* and *V*. But in the second place, both elements are *necessary* if we want to regard ἔρχομαι "I go" as the transformational source of the derived sentences φησί με ἔρχεσθαι "He says (that) I go", ἀνάγκη μοι ἔρχεσθαι "It is necessary for me to go," as well as of the nominalized forms ἡ ὁδός μου, τὸ ἐμὲ ἔρχεσθαι, "my going;" for in all of these transforms a pronoun explicitly appears. Where did it come from if it was not present in zero form in the source? Similarly, if the basic form is transitive, as in ἔβαλες τὸν ἄνθρωπον "You struck the man," the pronominal subject will appear as agent in the passive transform ὁ ἄνθρωπος ὑπό σου ἐβλήθη, "The man was struck by you." In positing the invisible pronoun "(ἐγώ)" in the underlying structure of ἔρχομαι, our theory simply unifies the description of this transformational series within Greek; and by the same token it indicates the obvious syntactic parallel between I.-E. sentences like ἔρχομαι on the one hand and *I go, je vais* on the other.[6]

[6] My view of the zero pronoun is influenced by Lyons' discussion; see his *Introduction*, p. 281. I differ from Lyons only in regarding his "abstract 'pronominal' element" as a member of the class of *N*, i.e. as an ordinary pronoun even if invisible, rather than some pre-lexical theoretical entity, whose nature and status remain undefined.

Since this introduction of zero pronouns seems to provide a stumbling block for otherwise sympathetic readers, let me point out that it makes no practical difference if one prefers to regard the verb stem (ἐρχ-) as the predicate element and the personal ending (-ομαι)

In this transformational perspective, all of the differences between the normal form for verbal sentences in Greek and English will be retained, but they will be redescribed as features of the surface structure only: for example, as the result of a rule which specifies that the pronominal subject is reduced to zero form (or "deleted") in the elementary occurrences of $NV\Omega$ for first and second person, when no special circumstances of emphasis or contrast call for its expression. Thus between the transformational and the traditional view of a one-word sentence like ἔρχομαι there is no disagreement as to the facts but only as to the theory of sentence structure in terms of which these facts are best described.

Similar considerations apply in the case of type 2, the nominal sentence. Thus the invisible copula "(ἐστί)" posited by our theory will actually put in its appearance in the usual transforms, e.g. in a participial clause (Σωκράτης, σοφὸς ὤν, "Socrates, being wise") and usually in indirect discourse (φημὶ τὸν Σωκράτη σοφὸν εἶναι "I say Socrates is wise"). Indeed, the verb becomes visible in the indicative in most cases where the subject is in the first or second person, and in nearly all cases of past and future tense and non-indicative mood. The theoretical need for a unified description of this syntactic system would therefore induce us to posit a zero form of the verb in the third person present indicative even if the verb in these forms *never* appeared – even if, as in Russian, the standard copula verb had no forms in the present indicative.[7] In Greek, where the present indicative forms not only exist but are found more frequently than the verbless sentence type in all cases except the third person singular, the situation is simpler still: the verbless examples are naturally regarded as instances of a zero or deleted verb-form. Otherwise we would have to suppose that the underlying structure of the third person singular sentence is *different in principle* from the other persons of the present indicative. But the concept of a verbless sentence type existing only in the third person, and above all in the singular, with a *distinct* (but otherwise parallel) copula sentence type covering all three persons both singular and plural, is a concept that is hard to make sense of in transformational terms.

---

as the grammatical subject or referring element in a sentence like ἔρχομαι "I am going". From the point of view of syntactic theory, however, the two-term analysis with (invisible) pronominal subject has the advantage of clarity and generality, for reasons given both here and below, in the discussion of a referential chain in §5. These reasons are reinforced by our general considerations on the respective functions of nominal and verbal forms in Chapter II §§4–5. I suggest, then, that the development from sentences like ἔρχομαι or Latin *eō* to the more "analytic" forms *I go* and *Je vais* has the effect of bringing the deep structure to the surface.

[7] Compare the remarks of Horace G. Lunt, *Fundamentals of Russian* (New York, 1958), p. 33: since there are explicit forms for the copula *be* (i.e. *byl*) in both past and future, "it is convenient to say that the 'zero verb-form' of the present is a unit in the normal three-way past-present-future system."

We account for the facts most naturally by admitting an optional transformation that may delete the verb form in the unmarked case of third person singular, and in other cases when the indication of person and number is given independently.[8]

§ 3. THE NOTION OF A MINIMAL SENTENCE WITH
NO ELIMINABLE ELEMENTS

It should be clear that I am not rejecting the traditional account of one-word and nominal sentences as a description of surface phenomena in Greek syntax; but I do consider these unacceptable as a general theory of sentence structure. Since the traditional account relies upon the somewhat deceptive notion of a sentence "with no eliminable elements," a notion which gives the impression that this account reflects only the bare facts undistorted by any theoretical reconstruction, it is worth submitting this notion to closer analysis.

If we take an English sentence like *Odysseus, attacking from his chariot, hit the first man in the chest with his spear*, which we analyze on the basis of the kernel form *NVN*, *Odysseus hit (a) man*, it might seem that we reach the kernel structure by stripping away every eliminable element. And here the significant difference between the English and Greek data immediately emerges. For any further elimination gives grammatically unacceptable (subsentential) forms in English, e.g. *Odysseus hit* or *hit a man* or *hit* (the last two being acceptable only homonymously, as imperatives), whereas the corresponding abridgements of the Greek sentence are frequent and "normal." The divergence between surface syntax in Greek and English shows up precisely in the fact that ἔβαλε "(He) hit (him)" can occur alone as a nondeviant sentence.

On the other hand, ἔβαλε will in fact occur as a one-word sentence only in a context where subject and object are indicated by some other means. The notion of eliminability is not absolute, but relative to a certain context. And the notion of a *normal context* is one which has to be specified theoretically. For there is always some context in which a given element may be eliminated. Thus in response to the question *Who among the gods set them to quarrelling?* the utterance *Apollo* or *The son of Zeus and Leto* is entirely grammatical, whether in English or in Greek (compare *Iliad* 1.9). Thus the

---

[8] For further discussion of this problem, see Chapter V §5 and Appendix B on the theory of the nominal sentence. An author like Callimachus mechanically omits the third person present indicative of εἰμί in all forms, both singular and plural. But in Homer the situation is more complex. The verb in the plural is omitted about as often as not, whereas in the singular sentence omission is much more common than occurrence, in a ratio of 2:1 for main clauses. See the statistics from Lasso de la Vega, cited below, pp. 440 and 444.

verb itself is apparently eliminable from the verbal sentence. The abridged answer is of course understood as equivalent to *Apollo set them quarrelling*, and the transformational analysis will derive the answer from this fuller form by a rule for zeroing the verb phrase when the latter repeats material from an immediately preceding question. (And in this case we can describe the zeroing as "ellipse".) Furthermore, both noun and verb are eliminable in certain standard replies, for example *Yes* or *Right*! in English (and corresponding Greek forms like οὕτω, πάνυ μὲν οὖν), which are logically equivalent to the reassertion of a preceding sentence. In these circumstances it is possible to "preserve" a sentence of any given structure while eliminating *all* of its original elements.

In order to avoid this *reductio ad absurdum* of the notion of eliminable elements, we must insist that the eliminations in question shall not depend upon any special context. But as soon as we impose this restriction upon our data – as we must, for *any* grammatical description – we have moved away from the mere recording of factual occurrences towards a theoretical framework within which kernel forms can be defined. For it is characteristic of kernel sentences that they are "maximally independent of each another" and of any particular context: they are reconstructed "by the removal of dependences on other sentences in the course of transformational analysis."[9]

The method by which we define ἔβαλε as a minimal sentence in Greek (in contrast to other forms like τοῦτον which we do not count as sentences) and the method by which we define its underlying structure as *NVN* are the same in principle, although they imply different theoretical restrictions on the context.

§ 4. THE NARROWER AND BROADER SENSES OF "ELLIPSE"

The notion of ellipse which I make use of, and which was illustrated in the preceding section, is a notion restricted to the case where (1) a non-occurring word or phrase would be expected in virtue of the underlying structure of the sentence, and also (2) the same or a very similar form actually appears in the context, usually in a parallel construction, and is thus easily "understood" in the place where a form is omitted. Thus ellipse is a special case of zeroing, namely the case where the occurrence of the form would constitute a repetition within the context. The typical examples of the nominal sentence are non-elliptical, since they are not cases where ἐστί or εἰσί occurs nearby;

[9] Z. Harris, "Co-occurrence and Transformation in Linguistic Structure," in Fodor and Katz, *The Structure of Language*, p. 206 with n. 63.

and the absence of an overt subject for a sentence like ἔρχομαι is also non-elliptical in this sense.

In a looser sense, any omission of an expected form, and in particular any omission of the subject expression or copula, could be (and often has been) described as a case of ellipse.[10]

As a matter of terminology, this broader use is not to be recommended, since it would oblige us to find a new term for the *narrow* sense of ellipse just specified. And for the broader notion the terms "zeroing" and "deletion" are both in current use.[11] But as a matter of historical fact, it is the broad sence of ellipse which answers to the original Stoic notion of an "elliptical" or defective sentence, an ἐλλιπὲς λεκτόν which has not received complete expression.[12] The standard Stoic examples concern precisely the omission of the subject. For the Stoics, a sentence like γράφει "(He) writes" is defective; whereas γράφει Σωκράτης, "Socrates writes" is complete and independent (αὐτοτελές). This is the doctrine which underlies the traditional description of the sentence as "the expression of a complete thought." We might interpret this Stoic view in terms of the contemporary contrast between surface and deep structure: the form without a subject noun is defective not because it is ungrammatical in any ordinary sense but because it does not fully reflect the underlying subject-predicate (*NV*) structure. But the Stoics were philosophers, not linguists, and the decisive considerations here must be logical rather than grammatical.

Probably the motive of the Stoics (and of Plato and Aristotle before them) for regarding as incomplete a sentence like γράφει, "(He) writes," is that such a sentence *is not determined as to its truth conditions*, cannot be either true or false, until its subject is specified.[13]

---

[10] See, e.g. Kühner-Gerth I §352, "Ellipse des Subjekts"; §345, "Ellipse des Verbs εἶναι."
[11] For the distinction between zeroing and delection see above, n. 1.
[12] Diogenes Laërtius VII. 63 ἐλλιπῆ μὲν οὖν ἐστι τὰ (sc. λεκτὰ τὰ) ἀναπάρτιστον ἔχοντα τὴν ἐκφοράν, οἷον Γράφει· ἐπιζητοῦμεν γάρ, Τίς; αὐτοτελῆ δ'ἐστὶ τὰ ἀπηρτισμένην ἔχοντα τὴν ἐκφοράν, οἷον Γράφει Σωκράτης.
It is this sense of ἔλλειψις which is taken over by the Greek grammarians. See, e.g. Apollonius Dyscolus, *Syntaxis*, ed. Uhlig p. 7, where the nominal sentence πάρα δ'ἀνήρ (Od. 16.45) is described as a case of ἐλλείπειν ῥήματι.
[13] Strictly speaking, to determine the truth conditions of a sentence what we must specify is an extra-linguistic subject and not merely a subject expression. For, without further information, ἄνθρωπος γράφει "(A) man writes", or ἐκεῖνος γράφει, "*He* writes" are equally indeterminate. Hence the Stoics describe these as "indefinite" propositions; but they regard them as formally complete, perhaps because the occurrence of a grammatical subject in these sentences testifies, in principle at least, to the need for specifying the individual referred to. And the sentences in question become true or false for some definite specification of ἄνθρωπος or ἐκεῖνος. (I should add that Michael Frede has convinced me that the MSS. of Diogenes Laërtius VII. 70 are probably corrupt and that the Stoics very likely did *not* regard ἐκεῖνος κινεῖται as "indefinite".)

The one-word sentence with an unspecified subject is logically or semantically incomplete, because we do not know what it affirms or denies, i.e. we are unable to specify its truth conditions. Semantical completeness in this sense, and considering only the simplest case of an elementary *NV* sentence, requires (1) that an extra-linguistic subject of reference be specified, normally by means of *N*, and (2) that something be predicated or asserted of this subject, e.g. by the verb *V*. (Note that the sense of predication required here is what I have called *semantic* predication in Chapter II §2.) Like the notation *Fa* in logic, the sentence type *NV* in a natural language represents the simplest form of syntactic predication, i.e. declarative sentencehood for two-term sentences. When it is interpreted with regard to truth and falsity, this formula also represents the basic *semantic* relation designated as "satisfaction" in Tarski's terminology, the relation between term and object which Quine calls "is true of." [14] Adapting a formula from Quine we may say that *syntactic predication here joins a noun and a verb to form a sentence that is true or false according as the verb is true or false of the object (or extra-linguistic subject), if any, to which the nominal term refers.* [15] Thus the syntactic and the logical or semantic analysis of predication – in the notion of "completeness" for elementary sentences – fit together. But this fit can be properly appreciated only if the two concepts are first grasped in separation. Syntactic predication is the device for expressing *within* language, by joining noun and verb within the sentence, the semantic relation that holds (or is said to hold) between language and the world, i.e. between the linguistic predicate or verb and the object referred to by the subject noun. The permanent interest of the subject-predicate concepts for the philosophy of language, and the widespread (if not universal) importance of the corresponding distinction between noun and verb (or between *referring-expression* and *predicator*), are both founded on this fact, that syntactic predication reflects within the structure of the sentence the basic semantic relation involving truth and falsity, the relation upon which all descriptive use of language depends.

For this relation to be clearly articulated the sentence must consist of two distinct expressions (as in the logical form *Fa* for atomic sentences). Hence we can understand why a Stoic might consider a sentence like ἔρχομαι "(I) go" as *defective*, even though the "complete" form ἐγὼ ἔρχομαι is in no way less vague or ambiguous. In an actual utterance, of course, neither form is at all ambiguous. In both cases, the extra-linguistic subject is uniquely specified by the verb ending (and in the second case redundantly specified by the pronoun) only and always in its functional, deictic connection with the

---

[14] See *Methods of Logic*, p. 65.
[15] Compare *Word and Object*, p. 96.

situation of utterance.[16] Yet the philosopher interested in truth conditions will prefer to see this semantic relation articulated in a two-term sentence with pronominal subject, rather than in the fused form of the finite verb alone. Hence his analysis rejoins (but with an entirely different motivation) the conclusions of the linguist who, in order to account for the transformational results, assumes that the underlying structure of a sentence like ἔρχομαι contains a first person pronominal form.

§ 5. "UNDERSTOOD SUBJECT" AND GRAMMATICAL "ANTECEDENT"

The notion of ellipse in the broad sense covers all cases of an "understood" subject or verb. Since in many of the sentences studied here the subject must be understood (or "provided") from the context, it will be well to clarify this notion before preceding.

First of all, it is essential to establish a sharp terminological distinction between the *context* and the *speech situation* or framework of utterance. The context of a given sentence consists of other sentences, coming before and after. The *situation of utterance* consists not of sentences but of speakers, hearers, and the circumstances under which they address one another. This distinction is essential for any theory of the personal pronouns and verb endings, and for any understanding of the way in which these endings "contain" or specify the subject.

In the case of first and second person pronouns, it is the situation of utterance and not the context which determines their reference. These pronouns are not properly "pro-words" standing for names or nouns occurring elsewhere in the text. In their primary use, words like *I* and *you* are entirely independent of the context: their referential function depends *only* on the actual speech situation, within which they specify their extra-linguistic subjects as speaker and hearer respectively at the moment of utterance. (The context can affect their meaning only in an indirect way, by specifying a speech situation and identifying the interlocutors. Thus at *Iliad* 1.29 τὴν δ'ἐγὼ οὐ λύσω "I shall not let the girl go," the first person ending and pronoun refer directly to Agamemnon as speaker; they do not refer back to any word or phrase in the context. But it is the context which *tells* us that Agamemnon is speaking, and in this sense the reference of ἐγώ is specified by the earlier occurrence of the name *Agamemnon* in 1.24, followed by the mention of his speech.) Hence in syntactical terms the first and second person

---

[16] On the important grammatical category of *deixis*, of which demonstratives are the most conspicuous representatives, see Lyons, *Introduction*, pp. 275–81.

pronouns are members of the elementary class of nouns, like proper names. They are not transformationally derived (as are third person pronouns like *he*) as pro-words for other expressions, and the simplest sentences in which they occur are themselves elementary sentences.[17]

The situation is entirely different for the third person. The third person is an unmarked category, specified only by contrast with the first two as *neither speaker nor hearer*.[18] In semantic terms, the reference of a third person form can never be specified by the situation of utterance alone. Hence the subject of the verb is "contained" in the first and second person endings in a strong sense which does not hold for the third person. When a one-word sentence like ἔρχομαι "I am going" is actually uttered, the personal ending alone serves to specify the extra-linguistic subject of the verb. But nothing of the sort is true for the third person ending; at the very least, the speaker who pronounces the sentence ἔρχεται "(he) is going" must accompany his utterance by a glance or a demonstrative gesture, by some kind of pointing at the person or thing intended as subject. Hence it is only natural that in place of the third person pronoun for which there is no inherited I.-E. form we should find demonstratives like ὅδε (*hic*), οὗτος (*iste*), and ἐκεῖνος (*ille*). These forms correspond to the minimum deictic indications which, within a situation of utterance, permit speaker and hearer to identify the extra-linguistic subject of a verb in the third person.[19]

If the third person subject is not directly available for pointing, the speaker must generally refer to it by a name or description. Once such an identification has been made, of course, it can be taken up by anaphoric pronouns like *he*, or *they*. In Greek one may also use the finite verb alone and leave the subject to be "understood." In either case, the understanding of such sentences presupposes what I shall call a principle of *referential constancy*. This is an assumption involved in the very notion of an anaphoric pronoun and its antecedent, as for example in *I saw John as soon as he entered the room*. Intuitively expressed, the principle of referential constancy means that two linguistic expressions, in this case *John* and *he*, are understood as referring to the same individual; in other words, that the extra-linguistic

---

[17] My remarks apply strictly only to first and second person *singular*. The reference of the plural forms is partly determined by the identity of speaker and hearer, but it naturally depends on other factors also, which may be specified in the context.

[18] See É. Benveniste, *Problèmes de linguistique générale*, pp. 225–36 and 251–66.

[19] I do not mean to suggest that the Greek demonstratives ὅδε, οὗτος and ἐκεῖνος behave just like the three Latin pronouns. But ὅδε and *hic* generally refer to a person or object close at hand or otherwise connected with the speaker, and hence are sometimes called "first person demonstratives". οὗτος often applies like *iste* to a subject near or closely related to the hearer ("second person demonstratives"); whereas ἐκεῖνος and *ille* look away from both speaker and hearer.

subject of *He entered the room* is the same as the (extra-linguistic) object of *I saw John*.[20]

For various purposes it may be possible to give a formal account of referential constancy without bringing in the notion of denotation or reference *to the same individual*. But in the more elementary cases, for example where we are speaking of a particular person, the notion of reference as a many-one relation between expressions (i.e. between utterances or occurrences of expressions) on the one side and a single individual on the other seems to me intuitively clear, and in any case fundamental. However formulated, this principle is presupposed not only in the use of anaphoric pronouns but in all transformations involving noun-sharing, zeroing of nouns, relative clauses and the like: for example, in the derivation of *A man came and went* from *A man came* and *A man went*, or *The man whom I met was bald* from *I met a man* and *He* (or *the man*) *was bald*.

Generally stated, the principle in question implies that, under certain circumstances specified by the grammar, nouns or noun phrases occurring at different positions in a text or in a discourse will be *referentially equivalent* to one another. A special case is the referential equivalence of a pronoun and its antecedent, including our zero pronouns posited for a verb form like ἔρχεται "(he) is going." In describing the actual use of such sentences, we often say that their subject is to be understood from the context or that the pronoun refers back to an antecedent. If we examine the situation for pronoun use, for example in Homer, we find an ambiguity in this notion of antecedent which reflects the ambiguity between grammatical and extra-linguistic subject discussed in Chapter II.

Consider the opening scene of the *Iliad*, in which the priest Chryses comes to ransom his daughter, is rebuffed by Agamemnon, and prays to Apollo for vengeance on the Achaeans (*Il.* 1.43):

> ὣς ἔφατ᾽ εὐχόμενος, τοῦ δ᾽ ἔκλυε Φοῖβος Ἀπόλλων
> "So (he) spoke in prayer, and Phoebus Apollo hearkened to him."

What is the antecedent of the pronoun τοῦ "to him"? Our theory permits us to say that it is the zero pronoun *he* which we recognize as invisible subject

---

[20] Grammarians will naturally prefer to formulate this principle in less ontological terms. Thus Harris suggests an explication of reference to "same individual" by "counted in the same counting act" (*Mathematical Structures*, p. 143). Henry Hiż has undertaken to construct a theory of referential terms or cross-references without any reliance on the notion of (extra-linguistic) reference. See his paper "Referentials," *Semiotica* I (1969), pp. 136–66.

of ἔφατο "(He) spoke." But this in turn is an anaphoric pronoun, referring back to the speaker of the prayer, who has just been identified as ὁ γέρων and ὁ γεραιός "the old man," in verses 33 and 35. Within his prayer we have another reference to the priest but now of course in the *first* person (κλῦθί μευ, "Hearken *to me*" in verse 37, answered by "Apollo hearkened *to him*" in the verse quoted). In his earlier exchange with Agamemnon, the priest was addressed by the king in the second person: "Let me not find *you*, old man, among the ships" (μή σε, γέρον, v. 26). These and all other pronouns indicating the priest in this episode form a referential chain whose first link is the initial introduction of the priest by name in verse 11: οὕνεκα τὸν Χρύσην ἠτίμασεν ἀρητῆρα, "because Agamemnon dishonored *him*, the priest Chryses. For he came to the swift ships of the Achaeans" (ὁ γὰρ ἦλθε θοὰς ἐπὶ νῆας Ἀχαιῶν, v. 12).

If we ask now, what is the true antecedent of τοῦ in our original quotation from verse 43 at the end of this episode, we see that there are several different answers. The first and most obvious is the one we have already given: τοῦ refers back to the invisible subject *he* or "(ὁ)" which is "contained" in the immediately preceding finite verb ἔφατο, "(he) spoke." But this answer merely specifies the next link in the chain. This zero pronoun is in turn an anaphoric pronoun, referring us back across the speech of Chryses to the preceding designation of the speaker as "the old man." And it would be arbitrary to stop here. For this designation itself echoes Agamemnon's reference to Chryses as "you, old man," where the bearing of the second person pronoun is fixed by the dialogue situation created by Chryses' initial appeal to the Achaeans (v. 15 καὶ λίσσετο πάντας Ἀχαιούς). In one sense, the antecedent of τοῦ at the end of the episode is the whole chain of referential expressions (nouns, personal pronouns, zero pronouns) running back to the initial quasi-deictic mention of "him, Chryses the priest." What we have is an equivalence class of referential forms. It is convenient to choose the proper name *Chryses* as the paradigm specimen of this class, and it is no accident that the name (with the demonstrative-article τόν) is the first member of the class to occur in the narrative. But the privileged position of the proper name should not obscure the more general role of referential constancy here, which we can most naturally interpret as a many-one relation of different linguistic forms converging on a single extra-linguistic individual over a given stretch of discourse. For the function of proper names itself depends upon a similar principle of constancy: different tokens of the same name-type constitute an equivalence class of names (exemplify "the same name" in a special, narrow sense) just insofar as they stand in a many-one relation to the same nominatum. It is only because such referential constancy can be presupposed for names, pronouns, and the like that Homer's narrative, or any descriptive use of language, is intelligible at all.[21]

Since it is precisely the constancy of the extra-linguistic referend that holds the entire chain together, in a deeper sense the antecedent of the pronoun τοῦ in our example is not any expression in the context but the common referend of them all: the priest Chryses, and not his name.

§ 6. Conclusions on verb forms with understood subject

We can sum up our results in the last section as follows. First and second person verb forms "contain their subject" in two senses: (1) the personal ending is functionally equivalent to a pronominal element which we therefore posit as a zero (invisible) grammatical subject: (ἐγώ), (σύ); and (2) in an actual situation of utterance, these endings specify the extra-linguistic subject as speaker and hearer, respectively.

Verb forms of the third person contain their subject only in the first sense. To specify an extra-linguistic subject they require either an extra-linguistic gesture of pointing or, more commonly, some referring expression, i.e. some name or description in the context. In this case the zero pronoun or the third person ending functions anaphorically, and specifies its extra-linguistic

[21] This is a point which Plato made a great deal of in his criticism of a certain theory of Heraclitean flux; see especially *Cratylus* 439 D–E. But the point as I am urging it is not as ontologically oriented as might appear. I would admit that the general principle of referential constancy is indifferent to the question whether the object of reference (the right-hand term of the many-one relation) really exists or is merely presupposed within the semantic framework of a certain narrative or literary text. In the Homeric passage above, the priest Chryses functions as a constant object or target of reference somewhat as an actor on the stage represents for the audience an imaginary person who remains self-identical throughout the scene or scenes in which he appears. The logic of reference is the same in fiction and in history, in the theater and in everyday life. *Ajax* functions as the name for two distinct warriors in Homer's epic just as *Richard* functions as name for thousands of men and boys today. But it is clear that we construct and understand the fictional use of names and pronouns by analogy with their primary use in everyday situations. It is only because we take for granted referential constancy in everyday life that we can also take it for granted in literature.

The description of the referential function of a name by means of a many-one relation, with the named person as second term, is at best a convenient simplification. In fact this function consists in singling out or identifying one individual among others; and in this respect there seems to be no difference in principle between the function of names and that of ordinary descriptions. Suppose while I am waiting in an anteroom someone enters and calls out "Charles!" This will do if no one else in the room answers to the same name. If there are two of us, some further specification is required, e.g. the family name. Compare this with the situation in a waiting room where one summons "The applicant for the job!" If there are two applicants or two jobs involved, the description must be made more specific. Names and descriptions both operate not so much by aiming at their referend as by discriminating it from others. And their discriminatory power in any given case will naturally depend upon the situation, that is upon the number and variety of the other objects of reference in sight.

subject via the preceding name or description, in virtue of the principle of referential constancy.[22] In this case the subject of the verb is "understood" from the context, and in both senses of *subject*: the grammatical subject of the verb is identified as the antecedent name or description; and the extra-linguistic subject will be the individual denoted by this name or description. First and second person pronouns do not depend upon the context in this way. In cases of actually occurring speech they do not depend upon the context at all; in cases of reported speech, they depend upon it only for the identification of speaker and hearer. In a strict sense, it is from the speech situation (actual or reported) and not from the context as such that the reference of first and second person forms is understood.

For third person forms there is another kind of "understood subject" which I mention here in order to round off the topic, although this case does not directly concern the verb *be*. It does have a bearing on the confusion between grammatical and extra-linguistic subject.

In the cases we have so far considered, third person sentences without expressed subjects do in fact refer to specific individuals (such as the priest Chryses) who are named or described in the context. There is another use of the third person in which the specific identity of the subject is of no importance: it may be anyone within a certain range of appropriateness indicated by the verb itself. Hence in this case we can say that the subject is understood *from the verb alone*, without reliance on the context. The standard Homeric example is *Od.* 21.142.

> ἀρξάμενοι τοῦ χώρου ὅθεν τέ περ οἰνοχοεύει
> "Beginning from the place whence (one) pours wine."

There is no antecedent and no trace of any grammatical subject for οἰνοχο-εύει beyond the zero pronoun posited by our theory. The understood subject is not a linguistic expression at all but simply some person who pours wine. The verb specifies this subject in a general way, just as a subject noun like οἰνοχόος "wine-pourer" would do. Similarly in the textbook case from Xenophon: ἐσάλπιγξε "(one) blew the trumpet:" it is a trumpeter – a man and not a word – which is understood as the subject.[23]

In sentences such as this it would be ludicrous to speak of an *impersonal* construction: no grammatical subject is expressed, but the sentence really has an (extra-linguistic) subject, which is in most cases a *person*.

---

[22] For details of the referential mechanism of the third person pronouns in Homer, see Chantraine, *Grammaire homérique*, II, Chapter 10, esp. pp. 158ff.

[23] See this and other examples in Kühner-Gerth, I, 32, §352b; Schwyzer-Debrunner 621.2. In some cases the subject is understood not from the verb alone but from some other word or phrase in the sentence: *Il.* 22.199 ὡς δ᾽ ἐν ὀνείρῳ οὐ δύναται φεύγοντα διώκειν, "as in a dream (the dreamer) cannot catch the man who flees."

§ 7. FIRST-ORDER NOMINALS, ABSTRACT NOUNS AND SENTENTIAL SUBJECTS

In Sections 1–3 of this chapter I gave my theoretical reasons for applying the $NV\Omega$ sentence pattern to the analysis of Greek texts, even in the case of those sentences where a subject noun or copula verb is omitted. The discussion of ellipse, anaphora, and "understood" subjects in Sections 4–6 was designed to clarify some of the assumptions which are involved in this kind of analysis. The practical relevance of the entire discussion so far lies in the fact that I shall classify sentences with εἰμί according to certain distinctions in the nature of the subject, even where no subject is *expressed*. In such a case either we have a first or second person verb, and hence a person as "understood" subject, or else we have a third person verb whose subject is specified by the context. It is in the case of third person verbs alone that the relevant distinction arises. This is the distinction between *first-order nominals, abstract nouns*, and *sentential subjects*.

My concept of first-order nominals (which is inspired by that of Lyons) is broader than the notion of an elementary noun but it includes the latter.[24] Elementary nouns are defined relatively to a specified set of transformations: they are those which are not to be derived from verbs, adjectives, etc. by transformational operations. Thus (*a*) *man* is an elementary noun, but (*a*) *mortal* is not, since it may be derived from the adjective *mortal* by zeroing of the noun in *a mortal man*, or alternatively from some verb like *dies*. So *runner* or *worker* is non-elementary, since it is derived from *runs* or *works*; and *kinsman* is non-elementary if it is derived from *akin to*, and so forth. Yet *mortal, runner, worker*, and *kinsman* are all first-order nominals. Various formal definitions of this class can be given on the basis of distributional criteria: for example, a first-order noun is one which can occur in the same sentential neighborhoods as an elementary noun, i.e. one which can replace an elementary noun in a sentence of the same general form, as *worker* or *plumber* can replace *man* in *The man came home tired*.[25] More intuitively, we can describe a first-order noun as one which refers to individuals, i.e. to persons, animals, places and discrete objects or artifacts such as *rock, helmet, house*. In classifying occurrences of εἰμί according to the subject, the notion

---

[24] See Lyons, *Introduction*, pp. 347ff.

[25] Lyons' distributional criterion between first-order and second-order nominals depends upon whether or not the noun can be followed by an adverbial expression of time; thus *John was yesterday* is ungrammatical (and hence *John* is first-order) but *The demonstration was yesterday* is acceptable (and hence *demonstration* is second-order.) But this test would count *sum* (as in *the sum of two and two*), *beauty, virtue*, etc. as first-order nominals, which seems undesirable. In fact Lyons' test isolates only a sub-class of second-order nominals, namely action nouns correlated with verbs.

of a first-order nominal turns out to be more useful than that of elementary noun. This is in part due to the fact that the class of elementary nouns is really specified only in connection with a full transformational analysis of the language, which I do not undertake. And in any case, the notion of elementary noun is essentially dependent upon a given state of transformational theory. But the distinction between first-order and higher-order nominals lies somehow "in the nature of things," insofar as the distinction between individuals and non-individuals also depends upon the nature of the objects in question and not upon the theory in terms of which they are described.

Among elementary and first-order nouns, the privileged class is that of *personal nouns*, or nouns referring to persons. In I.-E., this seems to be the only subclass of first-order nouns (other than elementary *N*) which can be defined on formal grounds alone, in terms of co-distribution or replacement relations with the personal pronouns *I*, *you*, *he*, *she*, or with the personal relative *who* in contrast to *which* or *what*. (See Chapter IV §4.) By contrast, the notion of *animate* noun as currently used in general linguistics seems to have no formal or syntactic status in I.-E. (It does of course have a formal definition if used in the traditional sense, as the class of masculine and feminine substantives in contrast to neuter forms. But this does not correspond to its function in contemporary grammatical theory.) [26]

I define an abstract noun as one which is syntactically (and in many cases, also morphologically) derived by the nominalization of a verb, an adjective, or an elementary noun in predicate position: *murder* from *murders*, *anger* from *is angry*, *manhood* and *brotherhood* from *is a man* and *is a brother*. The subclass of abstract nouns with which we shall be particularly concerned as subjects of the verb εἰμί are action nouns or verbal nouns, the *nomina actionis* of traditional grammar. As abstract nouns these must be distinguished from the corresponding agent nominalizations which count as first-order nominals: *murder* is an abstract action noun, while *murderer* is a "concrete" (first-order) agent formation from the same verb. And so for (*the*) *running* in contrast with (*the*) *runner*, *rule* in contrast with *ruler*, etc. In my view, quality nouns like *courage*, *virtue*, *hardness* and the like are abstract in the same way, and are to be derived from the corresponding predicate adjectives,

---

[26] In some recent work, following Chomsky's *Aspects of Syntax*, an attempt has been made to correlate classes of nouns such as animate or human with restrictions on the selection of subjects for certain verbs. The violation of such restrictions would constitute the grammatical analogue to Ryle's notion of a category mistake. I find such attempts almost uniformly unconvincing. A sentence like *The tea-cup delivered a lecture on astrophysics* or *The bone ate the dog* is probably always false (though it might be presented as true in a children's book or some form of humorous fiction); but I cannot see that it violates any rule of grammar.

like *anger* from *is angry*. All abstract nouns can thus be seen as nominalizations of predicate expressions, whether the predicate is of the form $V\Omega$ or *is* Φ. In fact, however, I shall deal only with action nouns derived from V.

This general conception is essentially that of W. Porzig, whose analysis of abstract nouns was transformational *avant la lettre*.[27] Porzig pointed out that an action noun must in general be regarded as the syntactical derivative of the corresponding verb, even when the verb happens to be *morphologically* derived from the noun in question. This point is essential. Syntactical derivation and morphological derivation do not necessarily coincide. The morphology of a word is a function of its position in the lexical structure of the language as a whole, independently of any particular arrangement in sentences. But the syntactic derivation of an expression can only be given relative to a specified sentence or sentence type.[28] If a noun regularly functions syntactically as the nominalization of an underlying verb phrase, then it is an (abstract) action noun, regardless of its etymology. In many cases the derivative status of the action noun is also clear at the formal level, as when the noun κλαγγή "shriek, outcry" serves as nominalization of the verb κλάζουσι, "They shriek, cry out." In other cases, it is the action noun which serves as basis for the formation of a corresponding verb. Thus Porzig rightly saw that ὅμαδος, "uproar, tumult," must be regarded syntactically as the nominalization of the verbal idea expressed by ὁμαδέω, "to be in an uproar, in tumult," although the *verb* in this case is morphologically derivative. For the syntactical relationship between ὅμαδος and ὁμαδέω is precisely the same as between κλαγγή and κλάζω.[29]

Porzig extended his analysis to quality nouns like ἀρετή "courage, excellence, virtue," which he related to the corresponding predicate adjectives (in this case ἄριστος, "best, most noble"), just as action nouns are related to their verbs. If we add the more limited class of noun forms derived from predicate nouns, we have in principle a general account of abstract nouns as transformational derivatives (nominalizations) of underlying predicates.[30]

---

[27] See *Die Namen für Satzinhalte im Griechischen und im Indogermanischen* (1942), esp. pp. 11ff., 31f., 39–42; followed by Schwyzer-Debrunner, pp. 356f. Compare my own discussion of abstract nouns in English, above, Ch. I §6 (pp. 16f.); and see also below, Ch. IV §4.

[28] The distinction between the two forms of derivation is roughly de Saussure's contrast between "rapports syntagmatiques" and "rapports associatifs," the latter being morphological (at least in part); see *Cours de linguistique générale*, 2e Partie, Ch. V.

[29] "Es handelt sich um eine auch sonst ganz geläufige Erscheinung. Im Nhd. ist z.B. zweifellos *Zorn* das Nomen actionis zu *zürnen*, trotzdem das Verbum von Nomen abgeleitet ist." Porzig, *op. cit.* p. 24.

[30] The formation of an abstract noun like ἀνδρότης from a substantive (ἀνήρ) is isolated in Homer, though similar forms are more frequent later, especially in philosophical authors. See Chantraine, *La formation des noms en grec ancien* (Paris, 1933), p. 296.

Such a syntactical definition of the class of abstract nouns or second-order nominals leaves many philosophical problems untouched, for example the status of numbers as abstract objects. (It will be relevant, however, to recall that cardinal numbers appear in Greek and cognate languages as quantifier-adjectives rather than as nouns.) But the transformational analysis does suggest that philosophers are ill-advised to discuss such quality nouns as *roundness*, *beauty*, and *bravery* without recognizing that their syntactic relation to the predicate adjectives (*is*) *round*, *beautiful*, *brave* is exactly parallel to the relation between action nouns like *clamor*, *love*, or *fighting* and the corresponding verbs. For our purposes here it is only the action nouns which come into consideration: quality nouns like ἀρετή "excellence" rarely occur as subjects of the verb εἰμί outside of philosophical contexts (and almost never in Homer).

To describe action and event nouns as abstract may seem philosophically odd but it is linguistically sound. In I.-E. languages an action is represented as fully concrete and particular only when it is expressed by a finite verb – in other words, only when it appears as predicate. (In a way the opposite is true for concrete nouns like *man*, *soldier*, which normally refer to individuals in subject but not in predicate position.) The nominalization of a verbal predicate has the formal effect of generalizing the verbal idea, for it eliminates the specification of subject and time. These specifications may of course be reintroduced by supplements or completives attached to the action noun, as when we render *I went yesterday* by *my going yesterday*. But this is a secondary fact; by itself, the shift from *went* to *going* automatically eliminates tense, number and person. (This is a much more conspicuous feature of nominalization in an inflected language like Greek, with its richer stock of personal verb endings.) Hence action nouns, like infinitives, may properly be regarded as abstract, not only because they do not refer to individuals in the intuitive sense, but also because they abstract from the particularizing features of the conjugation: they represent the verbal idea without the specific determinations of person, number, mood and tense.

Finally I distinguish *sentential subjects* which are constituted by the nominalization not of a single word or predicate phrase but by that of a sentence as a whole. These are typically represented in Greek by infinitival clauses and in English by *that*-clauses. In many cases, however, the sentential subject of the verb εἰμί appears not as an infinitival clause within the same sentence but as a neuter demonstrative τό, τοῦτο, τάδε (expressed or "understood"), which refers back to the content of a previous sentence or, in some cases, refers forward to a following clause or sentence. The demonstrative adverb οὕτω "so, thus" can also function as a pro-word referring to a near-by sentence. The situation is comparable in English, where we have sentential subjects of the verb in *That happened yesterday* or *So be it*.[31]

This description of the concepts of first-order nominal, abstract noun, and sentential subject, is necessarily sketchy and preliminary. The notions will become clearer when I apply them to the analysis of specific sentences, beginning in Chapter IV §§4–6.

§ 8. THE PROBLEM OF ORGANIZING THE DATA FOR εἰμί

We turn now to the concrete data for analysis: the sentences with εἰμί in Homer and in selected samples of classical Greek. We ask first of all how this mass of material is to be organized for description.

Since Mill, the theory and description of the verb *be* in I.-E. has been dominated by a basic distinction between the copula and the existential verb. This dichotomy has certain radical disadvantages, both in principle and in descriptive practice. On the one hand, it is possible to specify the copula uses of *be* in syntactic terms alone, by reference to the sentence form *N is Φ* with certain definite values for *Φ*. But the existential uses of εἰμί cannot be specified in this way, for they depend upon the *meaning* of the verb: the notion of existence is essentially lexical or semantic, not syntactic. The copula-existential verb dichotomy cannot be applied in practice because it is vitiated in principle by a confusion between syntactic and semantic criteria. The traditional assumption has been that the copula uses are those in which the verb is devoid of meaning, whereas the existential uses are just those where the verb has " meaning of its own" and is not "a mere copula." As far as the Greek verb is concerned, however, both assumptions are false. In many copula constructions the verb has an existential or other "strong" sense; and in some non-copulative uses the verb is also non-existential (viz. in the possessive, potential, and veridical constructions). Hence any description based upon the copula-existential dichotomy is necessarily incoherent. In practice, this means that any attempt to apply this dichotomy in the classification of actual sentences must allow for a wide spectrum of "other" uses, which do not fit under either branch. (I illustrate this fact in the next section.)

In my own organization of the data, I take as fundamental the syntactic distinction between those uses which are and those which are not copulative in the formal sense. Under the copulative uses we must be prepared to

---

[31] The concept of a nominalized sentence and its pro-word can obviously be generalized to include sentential objects of the verbs as in *I know it* or *I told you so*. But I shall not need this wider concept, sine εἰμί does not take a construction with an object of this form.

recognize both pure and mixed cases: sentences in which εἰμί seems to function *only* as copula verb and sentences in which distinct verbal meanings (such as *exists, belongs to*) are also suggested. Under the non-copulative uses I recognize a variety of existential sentence types and three non-existential uses: the possessive construction (ἔστι μοι "I have"), the potential construction with the infinitive (οὐκ ἔστι Διῒ μάχεσθαι "One cannot fight against Zeus"), and the veridical construction which occurs typically in conjunction with a verb of statement or cognition (οὕτω τάδε γ᾽ ἐστί,, ὡς ἀγορεύεις "These things are as you say;" cf. *Il.* 24.373: below, Chapter VII, sentence **1**). The non-copulative uses can be distinguished from one another in a preliminary way by a difference in meaning; thus in the veridical use the verb means "is true, is so." But in each case a more precise definition will be offered in terms of a sentence type with a certain syntactic description.

Under the copula uses I distinguish not only pure and mixed cases, but also elementary uses and those which are transformationally derived, such as the periphrastic use of εἰμί with a participle and the sentence-operator use with an infinitival clause or other sentential subject (e.g. μόρσιμόν ἐστι + *infinitive*, "It is fated that..."). Among the elementary or basic uses of the copula I recognize the five sentence types defined by Harris for English, to which we must add two others, as has been seen:

1.	*N is A*	Socrates is wise
2.	*N is N_{classifier}*	Socrates is a man
3.	*N is N_{rel}PN*	Socrates is son of Sophroniscus
4.	*N is PN*	Socrates is in the agora
5.	*N is D_{loc}*	Socrates is here

And in addition:

6.	*N is D_{manner}*	ἀκὴν ἔσαν, "They were silent"
7.	*N is of-N*	(predicate genitive) Σωκράτης ἐστὶ πατρὸς ἀγαθοῦ "Socrates is of-a-good father"

For clarity we group these seven types as follows:

(A) Nominal copula (types 1–3)
(B) Locative copula (types 4–5)
(C) Adverbial copula (type 6)

The predicate genitive of type 7 can perhaps be grouped under (B) as "para-locative." (See Chapter IV § 26.)

The general scheme for classifying sentences with εἰμί can thus be given in the following outline:

I. Copulative uses (Chapter IV)

   A. Nominal copula (Ch. IV §§3–20)

      1. with predicate adjectives (§§3–7)

      2. with predicate nouns (§§9–10)

      3. with pronouns as predicate (§§11–13)

      4. periphrastic construction with participles (§§14–17)

      5. with articular participle (§18)

      6. copula as sentence-operator with various predicate nouns and adjectives (§§19–20)

   B. Adverbial copula (§§21–22)

   C. Locative and para-locative copula (§§23–24)

   D. Various mixed uses of copula, coinciding with existential or other "strong" sense (§25)

   E. Predicate genitive (§26)

   F. Impersonal construction of copula (§§27–30)

II. Non-copulative uses

   A. Existential sentence types (Ch. VI) (including vital use of ἔστι "is alive")

   B. Possessive construction (ἔστι μοι "I have") (Ch. VI §12)

   C. Potential construction (ἔστι +infinitive) (Ch. VI §17)

   D. Veridical construction (οὕτω τάδε γ᾽ἐστί... ὡς ἀγορεύεις) (Ch. VII)

Further refinements of this scheme will appear in the course of the description, including those which depend upon the distinction between first-order nominals, abstract nouns, and sentential subjects. As may be seen, the copula uses are described in Chapter IV; the various existential uses, together with the possessive and potential constructions, in Chapter VI; the veridical use is treated in Chapter VII.

§9. COMPARISON WITH THE CLASSIFICATION OF εἰμί IN LIDDELL-SCOTT-JONES AND OTHER LEXICONS

We may confirm our criticism of the copula-existential dichotomy by a brief glance at a few standard attempts to organize the material concerning εἰμί. Thus the relevant article in the Liddel-Scott-Jones Lexicon is divided under three main headings, as follows:

   A. as the substantive verb, *exist ... be the fact* or *the case* ....

   B. most frequently, *to be*, the Copula connecting the predicate with the Subject, both being in the same case.

   C. εἶναι is frequently modified in sense by the addition of Adverbs or the cases of Nouns with or without Prepositions.

In this classification, L.S.J. lists the potential construction under A, but the adverbial copula, the predicate genitive and the possessive construction under C, where we also find examples of what I would call paralocative uses of the copula with prepositions. (See Chapter IV §24.) This system is plainly inspired by the copula-existential opposition, represented by headings A and B, whereas section C represents a makeshift category that groups together whatever does not fit either under the existential verb (A) or under the *mere* copula (B). The artificial nature of this category is clearly brought out by a good recent lexicon like G. Italie's *Index Aeschyleus* (1955), which generally follows L.S.J. in grouping the uses of εἰμί but replaces rubric "C" with various other subdivisions, thus:

I. substantivum: esse exstare
II. copula
   2. in periphrasi
III. cum adverbio
   2. cum genitivo
IV. cum dativo
V. cum praepositionibus.

Italie, like L.S.J., takes account only of the nominal copula (subject and predicate "being in the same case"): the locative and paralocative copula is not recognized as such but dispersed among existential uses (ἔτ' ὢν ἐν σπαργάνοις, ἐν τάφοις), under adverbial uses (ἐγγύτατα εἶναι), and under prepositional constructions (πρὸς τῶν κρατούντων ἐσμέν, *a victoribus stamus*). It should be clear, I think, both on syntactic and on lexical-semantic grounds that these three uses belong together.

Consultation of other lexicons would only strengthen our impression that the traditional theory of the verb cannot provide the basis for a rational classification of the actual uses. This fact is implicitly recognized in Powell's Lexicon for Herodotus, which takes note of a few special constructions (such as the possessive, the periphrastic, the potential), but is resigned to list the bulk of examples – 507 out of 631 occurrences of enclitic ἐστι – under the neutral title "*is* both copulative and substantive"! Powell has, in effect, given up Mill's dichotomy altogether.[32]

More helpful because essentially closer to the facts of Greek usage was the older procedure represented in Ebeling's *Lexicon Homericum*, which lists the passages for εἰμί under 15 distinct headings:[33]

---

[32] For accented ἔστι Powell does admit an existential heading (III.1) "emphatic, *lives, exists.*" But he assigns to this category only 13 examples of ἐστι out of 811 occurrences of the third-singular form; and in fact these 13 cases are rather different from one another. See their analysis below, Chapter VI §23.

[33] I ignore items 16–18 in Ebeling's article, since these are of the nature of supplementary comments rather than distinct uses of the verb.

1. vivo et vigeo
2. il y a, es gibt
3. ἔστι τινί est ei, habet
4. ἔστι cum infinitivo, fieri potest
5. es findet statt, tritt ein
6. ἔκ του oritur a
7. του oriundus a quo
8. cum substantivo
9. cum adjecto
10. cum pronomine
11. (with dependent infinitive)
12. cum adverbiis loci
13. cum adverbiis temporis aliisque
14. cum praepositionibus
15. (periphrastic construction with participles)

Ebeling's 1, 2 and 5 belong under existential uses; 8–10 and 15 under nominal copula; 6, 12 14 under locative copula. Ebeling recognizes the possessive construction (3) and the potential (4), as well as the adverbial copula (13) and the predicate genitive (7). He has missed the veridical use as such, listing some examples of it under the existential (5), others under the adverbial construction (13). Except in this point – and apart from inevitable errors of detail – Ebeling's classification is an admirable preliminary stage for a rational organization of the material. In order to advance beyond Ebeling's classification, an adequate theory of syntax was required. None was available before Harris' account of kernel sentence forms and transformations.

CHAPTER IV

DESCRIPTION OF THE COPULA USES

§1. THE COPULA CONSTRUCTION

In the last two sections of Chapter III I argued that the only satisfactory general classification of the uses of εἰμί is the formal division into copulative and non-copulative constructions, and that the question of an existential sense or use of the verb must be left open as a problem to be clarified. Thus on the one hand we are obliged to recognize non-copulative uses which are not clearly existential in meaning (the potential, possessive, and veridical constructions), while on the other we find instances of the copula construction where the verb seems at the same time to carry some existential value or some other "concrete" meaning.

In this chapter I describe the uses of εἰμί that are copulative in form. In Chapter V I attempt to sketch a general theory of the copula verb (in Greek, or in I.-E.) which sets these uses within a wider perspective and suggests an answer to questions such as the following. In what sense is *be* a sign of predication? Is the copula verb a purely formal device, or does it have a meaning of its own? In Chapters VI and VII I describe the non-copulative uses; and in the concluding Chapter VIII I discuss the connection between these various uses, and ask why it is that a single linguistic sign (the I.-E. root *es-*) can serve as copula verb and also as an expression for existence and truth.

According to a traditional doctrine of comparative grammar, the syntax of Greek and of Indo-European generally is characterized by a contrast between two sentence types, the verbal and the nominal. In the verbal sentence the predicate is a finite (i.e. a personal) form of the verb; in the nominal sentence it is generally a noun, adjective, adverb, or prepositional phrase.[1] At the theoretical level the terminology of "nominal sentence" leads to confusion, and I propose to avoid it as far as possible.[2] But the contrast in

---

[1] See Meillet, "La phrase nominale", *Mémoires de la Société de Linguistique de Paris* 14 (1906), 1–26; with further literature in Schwyzer-Debrunner, 622f.

[2] In particular, the theory of the nominal sentence tends to confuse two quite distinct contrasts: (1) between a sentence with an ordinary verb and a copulative sentence with *be*, and (2) between a sentence with any finite verb (including *be*) and a sentence with none. Meillet's terminology "pure nominal sentence" and "nominal sentence with copula" suggests that the first opposition is the more fundamental but that it would normally

question is a real one, and it reappears in transformational theory as a distinction between two classes of kernel sentence forms. On the one hand we have the sentence forms containing an elementary verb V: NV, NVN, $NVPN$. On the other hand we have infrasentential forms which contain no V and which become sentence forms for English with the insertion of *be*: NA, NN, ND_{loc}, NPN.[3] We have defined the elementary copula as the verb *be* (εἰμί) introduced into these infrasentential kernel forms; and by analogy we define a near-elementary and a second-order copula as the verb *be* introduced into similar forms where N is non-elementary or where the elementary predicate is replaced by a transformationally derived form such as the participle. Thus *John (is) tall* is an elementary use of the copula; whereas *John (is) singing* is near-elementary and *John's singing (is) off key* is a second-order copula. (These distinctions in the transformational status of the copula were sketched in Chapter I §8, and will be developed further in what follows.) In each case, the insertion of the verb *be* makes a sentence out of what would otherwise be an infrasentence form (in English at least), since it would lack a finite verb.

From the grammatical point of view, then, the distinctive function and importance of the verb *es- lies in the fact that it bridges the gap between "nominal" and "verbal" sentences. Because of this fact *be* appears as the most universal of verbs, the verb *passe-partout*, the verb *par excellence*, or – in the doctrine we have cited from the *Logic* of Port Royal – as the only *true* verb, the one which is implicit in every sentence and every clause, since all other verbs, for example *sits*, can be analyzed into two concepts, a nominal form such as *sitting* and a verbal *is*. The question naturally arises, why should it be precisely the verb *es- that plays this universal role? Or to put the question in another form, what is the relationship between εἰμί and other, more typically elementary verbs in Greek? In what sense is *be* a verb like other verbs?

An answer to this question can emerge only at the conclusion of our study. In this chapter I attempt to give a sharper form and content to the

---

(in the "pure" case) be *expressed* in the form of the second opposition between a verbal and a verbless sentence. More recent discussions tend to restrict the concept of nominal sentence to the second opposition only: "En indo-européen, la proposition pouvait présenter une double structure: verbale, lorsqu'elle comporte une form personnelle du verbe; nominale, lorsqu'elle n'en comporte pas" (Chantraine, *Grammaire homérique* II, 1). In a transformational perspective, however, it is only the first contrast (between ordinary verb and copula sentence) which is important for deep structure, and it is just this contrast which I am referring to here. The presence or absence of a copula verb in a sentence of the form N *is* Φ is simply a matter of surface variation on a single underlying sentence type. See above, Chapter III §2; below, Chapter V §5 and Appendix B "On the Theory of the Nominal Sentence."

[3] See above, Chapter I §7; cf. Harris, *Mathematical Structures*, p. 171.

concept of a copula verb by a full description of the copula uses in Greek. These uses are overwhelmingly more numerous than the non-copulative uses in every phase of the language which I have studied. On the basis of my own statistics for *Iliad* 1–12, the proportion of copula constructions in Homer is at least 80% and perhaps over 85% of all instances of the verb. (The variation in percentage depends upon how certain mixed or dubious cases are to be counted.) The nominal copula alone – the copulative construction in the narrow sense, with a noun, adjective, pronoun, or participle as predicate – represents over 65% of all occurrences of εἰμί in Homer. These facts justify us in beginning our description with the copula construction, as the *principal* use of εἰμί from a purely quantitative point of view. It is also the easiest use to define in formal terms.[4]

§2. PLAN OF THE PRESENT CHAPTER

As the basis for our description we take Harris' five kernel sentence forms with *be* in English, plus the two forms which we are obliged to add for Greek: the predicate genitive and the adverbial copula. (See Chapter III §8.) Taking *N is Φ* as our general formula for the copula construction, we can group the major types as follows:

(i) Nominal copula
  a. Adjectival copula: *N is A*
  b. Noun copula: *N is N, N is $N_{rel}PN$*
(ii) Locative copula
  N is $D_{locative}$, N is PN

The use of εἰμί with predicate pronouns or participles represents an obvious variant on the nominal copula. But neither the predicate genitive nor the adverbial copula fits neatly into this scheme. Intuitively, and perhaps formally as well, the predicate genitive seems closest to certain paralocative constructions which fall under (ii); and it is in this connection that I describe it below in §26. The adverbial copula is naturally regarded as an intermediate case between (i) and (ii), more akin to the locative copula in form (since there too the predicate is "adverbial") but to the nominal copula in sense. And so I describe it (in §§21–22) after the nominal and before the locative construction. Adding the further considerations of mixed cases and im-

---

[4] The statistics given here and throughout this study are based upon the following samples: *Iliad* Books 1–12, including 562 occurrences of εἰμί; Lysias I and XIII.1–95, including 150 occurrences of the verb; and Xenophon, *Anabasis*, I.1–3.16, 8.13–10.19, and II.1.2–3.4, again with 150 occurrences.

personal construction, we have the following general outline for the contents of this chapter:

1. Nominal Copula (§§3–20)
2. Adverbial Copula (§§21–22)
3. Locative Copula (§§23–25)
   (a) pure locative (§23)
   (b) paralocative uses (§24)
   (c) predicate genitive (§26)
4. Mixed Cases (overlap of nominal and locative copula, of copula and existential force) (§25)
5. Impersonal constructions of the copula (§§27–30)

Within the description of the nominal copula (which accounts for the bulk of this chapter as it accounts for the majority of copula uses) further distinctions will be necessary. The major divisions of the exposition correspond to differences in the grammatical form of the predicate; i.e. these divisions are determined by the word class of Φ (in N is Φ). Thus we consider first those uses in which the predicate is an adjective (*cop A*, §§3–7), then those in which it is a noun (*cop N*, §§8–10), a pronoun (§§11–13), a participle (§§14–18), a verbal in -τός or -τέος (§19), and a complex construction consisting of adjective and participle (§20). In analyzing these cases we make use of another principle alluded to, namely, the transformational status of the construction. In this connection we distinguish between cases where the subject noun is or is not a first-order nominal. When the subject is first-order, we must make a further distinction between constructions in which εἰμί occurs as copula in an underlying kernel and those in which it is introduced by a transformational operator. If the subject is second-order, the copula will always be analyzed as the product of a transformation. The same distinctions apply equally to the analysis of the locative copula in §§23–25. And in discussing the impersonal construction at the end of this chapter (§§27–30), we introduce a corresponding distinction between elementary and transformationally derived forms of the impersonal sentence type.

For the sake of clarity, I here list the major subdivisions in the following description of the nominal copula:

A. Adjectival copula (abbreviated *cop A*): *N is A* (§§3–7)
B. Noun copula (abbreviated *cop N*): *N is N* (§§8–10)
C. Periphrastic copula, construed with a participle: (§§14–17)
   N is Ving, Peter is fighting
   N is Ved, Peter is wounded
D. Copula with verbals in -τός and τέος (§19)

E. Copula with adjective and participle: δῆλός ἐστι ποιῶν "He is obviously doing (such-and-such)" (§20)

The discussion of sentences with pronouns in predicate position (§§11–13) may be regarded as an appendix to the description of *N is N*, just as the account of the articular participle (§18) represents an appendix to the periphrastic construction.

§3. THE ADJECTIVAL COPULA *(cop A)* FOR PERSONAL SUBJECTS: ELEMENTARY AND DERIVED USES

The use of the copula in sentences of the form *N is A* can be analyzed from two points of view: according to the structure of the subject *N* or according to that of the predicate *A*. The second form of analysis would require a complete transformational theory of adjectives which I cannot develop here. Let me suggest only what would be involved in such an undertaking.

Consider two examples of *cop A* from the first speech of Agamemnon in the great quarrel scene of the *Iliad*:

1 *Il.* 1.114

ἐπεὶ οὔ ἑθέν ἐστι χερείων
"(I wish to keep the girl) since she is not inferior to her
(sc. to my wife Clytemnestra)"

2 *Il.* 1.118

ὄφρα μὴ οἶος
Ἀργείων ἀγέραστος ἔω
"(Prepare me another prize) lest I only among the Argives be prizeless"

The comparative adjective χερείων in **1** presupposes a kernel of the form *She is (not) poor (in some quality)*, with an adjectival predicate corresponding in meaning to κακός. The syntactic derivation of the comparative construction is rather complex.[5] Nevertheless, since the elementary source of **1** includes a sentence of the form *N is A*, the copula construction as such is not derived from subsequent transformations.

In the case of **2**, on the other hand, the *N is A* form is transformationally introduced, since the adjective ἀγέραστος is a negative compound based upon the noun γέρας "prize of honor." Hence the source sentence would be of the form *I receive no prize* or *I have a prize (no longer)*, where we might encounter a possessive construction of εἰμί (ἔστι μοι γέρας) but certainly not a copula sentence *N is A*.

---

[5] Compare Harris, *Mathematical Structures*, pp. 75f.

Neither **1** nor **2** is an elementary sentence: but **1**, unlike **2**, has in its transformational source an elementary sentence of the form *N is A*. Hence I shall describe **1** as an elementary use of the (adjectival) copula, even though the sentence as such is not elementary. In **2** on the other hand we have a transformationally derived copula. A complete transformational grammar would require such distinctions to be worked out in detail for all the adjectives in the language, or at least for all the principal types. I shall subsequently refer to one of these types whose structure is particularly transparent, namely the "agent adjectives" derived from corresponding verbs, as *studious* is derived from *(he) studies*. (See below, Section 19.) In general, however, I shall simply ignore the transformational status of the predicate phrase *is A* and restrict my attention to the subject *N*.

Now neither in **1** nor in **2** is this subject *N* directly expressed within the sentence. Nevertheless, we are entirely justified in providing such an *N* in the syntactic analysis, as I have argued in Chapter III. For **1** the underlying grammatical subject is the phrase κούρη Χρυσηῒς "the girl Chryseis" uttered earlier in the same speech (verse 111); the real or extra-linguistic subject is the girl herself. In **2** we may provide as grammatical subject the zero pronoun (ἐγώ).[6] The real subject is of course the speaker, Agamemnon.

I note in passing that I pay no attention to the subjunctive mood of ἔω in **2**, any more than to the participial form ἀγαθός περ ἐών ... Ἀχιλλεῦ "noble as you are, Achilles" in 1.131 or the future tense in 1.583 ἵλαος Ὀλύμπιος ἔσσεται ἡμῖν "The Olympian (sc. Zeus) will be gracious to us." These variations of mood and tense, like the transformation into participial form, follow the general rules of Greek grammar and are of no special relevance to our study of εἰμί. For our purposes these may count as ordinary examples of the *N is A* sentence form. Almost the same thing can be said for the infinitival construction in 1.91 ὅς ... ἄριστος Ἀχαίων εὔχεται εἶναι "(Agamemnon) who claims to be the best of the Achaeans". Here we have a kernel *N is A*, "I am best", under the sentence operator for indirect discourse. According to the general rule for cases where the underlying subject *N* of the kernel is identical with that of the verb of speaking, the subject of εἶναι here is "zeroed", i.e. left unexpressed. In general, I abstract from all such complexities which do not specifically concern the verb *to be*, and I cite a sentence like ἄριστος εὔχεται εἶναι simply as an example of *N is A*.

§4. PERSONAL NOUNS AND FIRST-ORDER NOMINALS

In the examples considered so far the subject of εἰμί is a person; that is to

---

[6] For zero pronouns, see Ch. III §2.

say, the grammatical subject is a member of the class of personal nouns. The concept of a *person* (i.e. a human being or a god) is an extra-linguistic category, but the corresponding class of personal nouns happens to admit of a purely linguistic or formal definition. This definition makes use of the fact that first and second person forms of verb and pronoun apply specifically to subjects which we recognize as *persons*, whereas the so-called "third person" forms are actually unmarked for this category of *person* as such.[7] (In this context I write *person* in italics for the extra-linguistic category including human beings, gods and the like, as distinguished from the morpho-syntactic system of first, second, and third person forms.) Hence a personal noun in Greek may be defined as one which can normally co-occur in the nominative or vocative with verb forms in first or second person. The same definition can be formulated more generally, without reference to the case forms and personal endings of ancient Greek, in terms of co-occurrence with the personal pronouns *I, we, you*: a personal noun is one which can normally occur in apposition with, or as predicate of, these first and second person pronouns.[8] The class of personal *N* is thus the class of nouns which can occur in the sentence forms *I am N, You are N*. In some modern languages, but not in ancient Greek, there is an even neater linguistic test which gives the same results: a personal *N* is one which can replace or be replaced by the interrogative-relative pronoun *who* in contrast to the interrogative *what* or the relative *which*. (So also French *qui?* in contrast to *que?* or *qu'est-ce qui?*) But in Greek this test, for example by reference to τίς/τί, specifies only the class of animate nouns in the purely grammatical sense: that is to say, masculine and feminine nouns as distinct from those of neuter gender.[9]

---

[7] See the remarks of Benveniste, "Structure des relations de personne dans le verbe", *Problèmes de linguistique générale*, p. 228.

[8] The qualification "normally" here is intended to exclude nouns which are "personified" in poetical or rhetorical contexts, for example in an apostrophe like Aeschylus *P.V.* 88–92 ὦ δῖος αἰθὴρ καὶ ... ποταμῶν τε πηγαί ... ἴδεσθε με "Divine sky and river streams ... behold me!" I would not in general count αἰθήρ, ποταμός etc. as personal nouns, though the text in fact addresses them here as *persons*. Insofar as this form of address constitutes not a poetical posture but a genuine prayer to sky and rivers, the second person form shows that these cosmic powers are indeed regarded by the speaker as *persons* ("hearers"); so that under these archaic or religious circumstances the nouns in question would have to be counted as personal *N*. It is an essential characteristic of mythopoetic thought and speech that all nouns are (at least potentially) personal, that is, that all objects and concepts are conceived as analogous to *persons*.

[9] The grammatical efficacy of the distinction between personal and non-personal nouns can be illustrated for certain nouns which are "reclassified" as personal in special uses (namely, when they refer to *persons*). Contrast *the swine who said that* with *the swine which followed Eumaeus*, and similarly *the star who made that movie* with *the star which shines in the zenith*. When the Greek interrogatives τίς and τί are used without an associated noun, the animate-inanimate distinction corresponds closely to the personal-nonpersonal contrast of *who?* and *what?* Compare τίς ἐποίησε; "Who did it?" with τί ἐποίησε; "What did

Once we realize that the third person forms are unmarked for *person*, we see that there is more than a word play involved in the homonymy of grammatical person and the ontological (or logical) category of *person*. The grammatical concept of first and second person contains an essential reference to the role of speaker and hearer. Hence the proposed definition of personal nouns suggests the following philosophical account for the concept of *person*: a *person* is an extra-linguistic subject that can speak or be spoken to. Etymologically, the concept of person is associated with the actor's mask or role (Latin *persona*, Greek πρόσωπον); historically, it is connected with a certain legal status and in Christian doctrine with a certain theological "role". For the purposes of a general definition, however, the grammatical notion of first and second person, as speaker and hearer, seems to suggest the most satisfactory analysis of the concept of *person* as it is used today. If anything in language is universal, this pair of notions (*I-you*, speaker-hearer), must be, since it specifies the dialogue framework for a situation of utterance, the minimum condition for the existence of speech as such.

For this and other related reasons, I regard the category of *persons* as paradigm subjects of discourse (that is, extra-linguistic subjects of sentences) and, correspondingly, the class of personal nouns as the privileged subclass of first-order nominals. Privileged these nouns are in any case, since they admit a more precise and more general formal definition than any other class of nouns; and furthermore they provide the grammatical subjects for the great mass of sentences in Homer, and perhaps in non-technical literature generally.[10] This predominant role of personal nouns can be attributed in part to their fundamental connection with the speech situation, and in part to a link between the grammatical function of subject and the underlying

---

he do?" But we always have the possibility of a purely formal agreement by attraction to the gender of a co-referential noun, e.g. τίς (ἐστι) ὁ τρόπος τοῦ τάγματος; "What kind of arrangement is this?" This failure of a formal test for personal nouns suggests that my distinction is of no grammatical significance in Greek, although it remains useful for our semantic analysis (in terms of *persons* as extra-linguistic subjects).

A certain borderline class of uses occurs in English, which has an analogue in semi-poetic or metaphorical Greek expressions like πᾶν ἐστι ἄνθρωπος συμφορή "man is sheer accident" (Hdt. I.32.4). So in unpoetic English we may say *You are an animal who (which?) walks on two legs, You are a heavy object which (who?) tends to fall to the earth.* Depending upon the context, such nouns may be more or less reclassified as personal, i.e. they may take *who* rather than *which*.

For the metaphorical use of abstract nouns as predicate with personal subjects, see below §9, sentences **33** and **34**.

[10] In *Iliad* 1, I count 20 sentences with personal subjects out of 30 instances of *N is A*; in Lysias I the ratio is 14 in 26; in Xenophon, *Anabasis* II (1.2–3.4) it is 14 in 18.

semantic concept of *agent*. For the latter is essentially a personal (or perhaps more broadly an animate) category.[11]

The class of personal nouns could be defined within the class of elementary nouns, but it can also be defined more widely within the class of first-order nominals, as will be done here. The elementary nouns are those which are formally primitive in the sense that they are not derived by nominalization (or by pro-wording) from verbs, adjectives or other nouns.[12] This concept must be fundamental in any complete system of transformational syntax, but not in the more informal analysis pursued here. Instead we take as our basic class of N the set of first-order nominals, corresponding to the intuitive notion of a concrete noun: proper names, personal pronouns (except for the third-person pronouns, which are to be regarded as pro-words for other nominal forms), count nouns and mass nouns like *water, dirt, snow*. The members of this basic class can be informally described as designations for persons, places, and things, i.e. for men, divine beings, animals, plants, artifacts, and natural objects such as rivers, hills, and islands. More generally, we can say that first-order nominals refer to "enduring and recurring physical objects" (in Quine's phrase), that is, to things that have a certain spatial position and physical substance which they conserve or change in a continuous way in the course of time.[13] Within this basic class we recognize a nuclear sub-class of personal nouns, defined by the possibility of co-occurrence with first and second person forms in the way we have specified. This class of personal N is included in a wider subclass of animate nouns, which can be described informally as nouns referring to animals, or perhaps to living things. However, I have found no formal criteria that would permit us to define the class of animate nouns in this sense in I.-E. (See above, p. 77 with n. 26.) The concept of animate noun seems to be relative to certain language families, and its unrestricted use in general linguistics appears to be dubious, if not illegitimate. The class of human nouns, which is often mentioned in contemporary work in linguistics, seems to me simply an inaccurate description of the class of personal nouns as defined above. There is no linguistic difference of a general sort between names like *Zeus*

---

[11] I think in this connection of Fillmore's theory of cases, where the notion of agentive case is the most important correlate in universal deep structure for the I.-E. concept of subject noun, as specified by the nominative case in Greek or initial position in English. See *Universals in Linguistic Theory*, ed. Bach and Harms, pp. 1–88, and above, Chapter II n. 33.

[12] For a more formal statement of this definition, see Beverly L. Robbins, *The Definite Article in English Transformations*, p. 59. Note that only the first and second person pronouns figure as members of elementary N, together with proper names and certain mass nouns and count nouns.

[13] Compare *Word and Object*, pp. 92 and 94. For first-order nominals see above, Chapter III §7.

and *Agamemnon*, or between nouns like θεός and ἄνθρωπος. The class of personal *N* is the only generally recognizable subclass of elementary and first-order *N*, and its definition is in practice more precise than that of either of the two wider classes.

In contrast to this basic class of first-order *N*, I recognize a wider class of nominals in general, symbolized here as *N**, which includes abstract nouns and sentential subjects. The abstract nouns which will chiefly concern us as subjects of εἰμί are action nominalizations of verbs, like γένεσις ("birth") and ὄλεθρος ("destruction", "death"), but the class also includes nominalizations of underlying adjectives and nouns, like ἀρετή ("courage", "excellence") and ἱπποσύνη ("horsemanship"). The class of sentential subjects, on the other hand, does not consist of individual *N* at all, but only of infinitives, clauses, and whole sentences taken as syntactic subjects for other verb phrases or predicates. Excluding infinitives and the like, which are not properly members of *N* (i.e. nouns with case declension in Greek) but only of the wider class of *N** (nominals generally), the class of nouns divides into first-order nominals and abstract nouns. (It is these two subclasses which will be symbolized here as *N*.) I take it that the distinction between first-order (or "concrete") and abstract nouns is clear enough in principle, even if in some cases it is not easy to decide to which class we are to assign a given form (say μῦθος "speech" or μένος "force", "fury"). Sentential subjects will be described in further detail below. For the concept of abstract noun I refer back to the discussion in Chapter III §7.

§5. *Cop A* FOR FIRST-ORDER AND ABSTRACT NOUNS

Before passing to the more complex phenomena of sentential subjects I here list a representative selection of *N is A* for first-order nominals, abstract nouns, and certain special or border-line cases.

3 *Il.* 1.176

> ἔχθιστος δέ μοί ἐσσι διοτρεφέων βασιλήων
> "To me you are the most hateful of all the kings whom the gods
> love".   (tr. Lattimore)[14]

4 *Il.* 12.12

> τόφρα δὲ καὶ μέγα τεῖχος Ἀχαιῶν ἔμπεδον ἦεν
> "For this time the great wall of the Achaians stood firm"
>   (Lattimore)

---

[14] In order to avoid imposing my own interpretation on a passage cited, I generally give a standard English translation, usually Richmond Lattimore's for the *Iliad* and G. H. Palmer's for the *Odyssey* (as edited by Howard N. Porter, Bantam Books, 1962). Where not otherwise indicated, the translations are my own.

5 Xenophon *Anabasis* I. 9.27

ὅπου δὲ χιλὸς σπάνιος πάνυ εἴη

"Where fodder was very scarce"

6 *Il.* 9.25

τοῦ γὰρ κράτος ἐστὶ μέγιστον

"Since his (sc. Zeus') power is greatest"

7 *Il.* 10.383

μηδέ τί τοι θάνατος καταθύμιος ἔστω

"Let death be not at all in your thoughts"

8 Lysias 1.29

ἐγὼ δὲ...τὸν δὲ τῆς πόλεως νόμον ἠξίουν εἶναι κυριώτερον

(sc. τοῦ ἐκείνου τιμήματος)

"I held the law of the city to be more authoritative

(than his offer to compensate me with money)"

In **3** we have a case of *N is A* for personal *N*: the underlying subject is *you, Achilles*. In **4** we have a first-order nominal referring to an inanimate object, the wall built by the Achaeans at Troy. Note that a stronger sense for ἦν here, brought out in Lattimore's translation "stood (firm)", does not affect the copulative syntax. I cite **5** as an example of a mass-word (χιλός "fodder") as first-order subject. In **6–8** we have abstract nouns as subject of the adjectival copula. I take it that just as θάνατος is the action nominalization (*nomen actionis*) of the verbal root *θαν-/θνη- so νόμος is the nominalization of the verbal idea expressed in νέμω, νομίζω and κράτος is the action or quality nominalization corresponding to the adjective κρείσσων, the verb κρατέω or the frozen participle κρείων. (The etymological dictionaries would separate this last form from the other two, for reasons which are not clear to me.) In these constructions the *N is A* sentence form can be derived from an underlying kernel where instead of the abstract *N* we have a corresponding verbal or adjectival predicate.

6A   *Zeus is stronger than all others.* (κρείσσων or κράτιστός ἐστι)

  or: *Zeus prevails over all others.*   (κρατεῖ, κρείων)

7A   *Don't think that you will die.* (θανεῖν)

  or: *Don't be afraid to die.*   (μὴ θάνῃς)

8A   *I acted according to the law (prescription) of the city ← I acted as the city prescribes*

  (ἔπραττον κατὰ τὸν τῆς πόλεως νόμον ← ἔπραττον ᾗπερ νομίζει ἡ πόλις)

Note that the corresponding kernel is not usually of the form *N is A*, even though it may be so in some cases (as in **6A**). In general, the *cop A* construction with abstract subjects will be transformationally derived. (This is doubly true in **7**, where the predicate *A* is itself transparently derivative.) In **6** and **7** the motivation for the transformation is essentially stylistic; that is to say, it is a matter of convenience rather than necessity for the language to nominalize and thus "thematize" the predicate concepts of dominating and dying. In the case of **8**, however, the need for nominalization goes deeper. It is not only that the concept of νόμος is an essential one in Greek political life, and that in **8** the noun has the special sense of "statute" which does not belong to the verb. In addition the very sentence form, with its second-order comparison between the legal punishment for adultery and an alternative course of action on the speaker's part, would become almost unbearably complex if the language did not possess nominalizations of the form νόμος and τίμημα. It is in this strictly intentional realm of judgments about principles and plans of action or conduct, and perhaps also in the institutional realm of concepts like legislation, that abstract nouns seem to be most indispensable. Whereas the substitution for **6** and **7** of the underlying forms **6A** and **7A** with personal subjects might result in a weaker sentence from the literary point of view, there would be no clear loss of meaning or content. In the case of **8**, on the other hand, the decomposition to sentences with first-order *N* as subject, such as is hinted at in **8A**, makes the thought of the original sentence almost unrecognizable. This suggests that what we have in **8** is not only a much more complex derivation but an essentially different function of abstract *N*, for talking about relations between abstract entities – what may be described as an intrinsically second-order use of *N is A*, in contrast to the stylistic or optional use of a second-order construction in **6** and **7**.

As problem or borderline cases of *N is A* I list the following:

9 *Il.* 1.107

> αἰεί τοι τὰ κάκ᾽ ἐστὶ φίλα φρεσὶ μαντεύεσθαι
>
> "Always the evil things are dear to your heart to prophesy"
>
> (Lattimore)

10 *Il.* 11.793

> ἀγαθὴ δὲ παραίφασίς ἐστιν ἑταίρου
>
> "The persuasion of a friend is a strong thing"
>
> (Lattimore)

11 Lysias XIII.23

> ὁρῶντες τὰ πράγματα οὐχ οἷα βέλτιστα ἐν τῇ πόλει ὄντα
>
> "Since they saw that matters in the city were not as good as they might be"

In **11** we have a construction of the form *matters are (not) good*, where the subject *N* may be analyzed as an action nominalization of the verb πράττω: the underlying personal sentence could be of the form **11A** πράττουσι οὐ καλῶς ἐν τῇ πόλει, *Men (in power) in the city are not acting rightly* (i.e., not acting in the public interest). Thus πράγματα as a nominalization of **11A** can count as an abstract noun. But it may also be regarded as a catch-all or dummy form which, like ἔργα in Homer or *the situation, the state of affairs*, in English, serves as a convenient covering term for particular actions or events that are (or might be) specified by other sentences in the context. We are thus on the borderline between an abstract *N* and a sentential subject. So also in **10** where παραίφασις ἑταίρου is only a slight formal variant on the infinitival clause παράφασθαι ἑταίρῳ (ἕταιρον) "to persuade one's friend" (or, taking ἑτέρου in **10** as subjective genitive, "for one friend to persuade another"). The *cop A* construction with abstract *N* in **10** is practically equivalent to the construction of φέρτερόν ἐστι with infinitival-sentential subjects as illustrated in the next section.

The construction in **9** is doubly complex. In the first place we have as subject not a noun but an adjective κακά used substantively with the article-pronoun τά, which suggests some general classifier like *things* as underlying subject *N*. In the second place, although the predicate *A* φίλα agrees with κακά as subject, this is a fact of surface concord only, and it leaves undetermined the precise syntax of μαντεύεσθαι as epexegetical infinitive. The underlying relationship between κακά and this infinitive is clearly represented only if we construe κακά as direct object: *Prophesying evil is dear to you*, i.e., *You like to foretell disastrous events*. But if κακά is thus understood as object of the infinitival clause, what we have as underlying subject of the copula phrase *is dear to you* is neither a noun nor an adjective but the whole infinitival clause, (τοι) κακὰ μαντεύεσθαι, "(you) prophesying evils", i.e., a sentential subject.[15]

§6. *Cop A* FOR SENTENTIAL SUBJECTS

The typical form for sentential subjects in Greek, corresponding to *that*-clauses in English, is the infinitival clause. (Under "infinitival clause" I include the occurrence of the infinitive alone, without a subject in the accusative

---

[15] The close connection between abstract nouns and sentential subjects – between nominalized predicates and nominalized sentences – is reflected in Porzig's title for what I call abstract *N*: "die Namen für Satzinhalte". (See the reference in p. 78 n. 27 above.) Porzig's study makes clear how abstract nouns can appear as (direct or indirect) object as well as in subject position, and in general in any position where a first-order nominal could stand. Sentential "subjects" can also appear in object position (e.g., in indirect discourse) even in Homer. With the post-Homeric development of the articular infinitive, the infinitival clause acquires the full syntactic flexibility of an abstract noun.

or dative case, since this can always be treated as the reduced form of an infinitival clause with zero expression of the subject *N*.) The sentential subject of εἰμί may be specified either in this form with the infinitive, or by a distinct clause with a finite verb, or by one or more separate sentences. (We must also take account of the case where the copula phrase itself is reduced to a verbless form, in this instance to an adjective alone. But for the moment I consider only examples where εἰμί is expressed.) Since infinitival clause, verbal clause, and separate sentence all serve the same general function, the following examples of *cop A* may be regarded as equivalent in regard to their underlying sentence structure.

(a) The copula verb has as its expressed subject a demonstrative-anaphoric pronoun τοῦτο, τό, ὅ, etc. referring to a separate sentence or string of sentences.

12 *Il.* 7.28

   ἀλλ᾽ εἴ μοί τι πίθοιο, τό κεν πολὺ κέρδιον εἴη ·
   νῦν μὲν παύσωμεν πόλεμον καὶ δηϊοτῆτα
   σήμερον

   "But if you might only do as I say, it would be far better.
   For this day let us put an end to the hatred and the fighting"
   (Lattimore)

(b) The verb has no expressed subject, but the reference to a clause, sentence, or sentences in the context is given by ὡς, οὕτω, or ὧδε.

13 *Il.* 8.473

   οὐ γὰρ πρὶν πολέμου ἀποπαύσεται ὄβριμος Ἕκτωρ,
   πρὶν ὄρθαι παρὰ ναῦφι ποδώκεα Πηλεΐωνα,
   ἤματι τῷ ὅτ᾽ ἄν...μάχωνται
   ...περὶ Πατρόκλοιο θανόντος,
   ὡς γὰρ θέσφατόν ἐστι

   "For Hector will not sooner be stayed from his fighting
   until there stirs by the ships the swift-footed son of Peleus
   on that day when they shall fight ... over fallen Patroklos.
   So is it fated."

   (Lattimore, adapted)

14 *Od.* 6.145 (≈ 5.474: cf. *Il.* 14.23)

   ὡς ἄρα οἱ φρονέοντι δοάσσατο κέρδιον εἶναι,
   λίσσεσθαι ἐπέεσσιν ἀποσταδὰ μειλιχίοισι

   "It seemed to him on reflection better thus: to stand apart and
   entreat (Nausicaä) with gentle words."

(c) The verb has no expressed subject, but the zero pronoun posed as subject of the verb must be understood as referring to a sentence or sentences in the context.

15 *Il.* 5.201

ἀλλ' ἐγὼ οὐ πιθόμην· ἦ τ' ἂν πολὺ κέρδιον ἦεν

"I did not let him persuade me, and that would have been far better" (sc. to bring my horses and chariot to Troy)

(Lattimore)

16 *Il.* 3.40

αἴθ' ὄφελες ἄγονός τ' ἔμεναι ἄγαμός τ' ἀπολέσθαι·
καί κε τὸ βουλοίμην, καί κεν πολὺ κέρδιον ἦεν

"Better had you never been born, or killed unwedded.
Truly I could have wished it so; it would be far better"

(Lattimore)

(Note that here the sentential subject of κέρδιον ἦεν is identical with the *object* of βουλοίμην, and that sense and syntax are the same whether or not τό is expressed as subject: compare **12** above.)

(d) The verb has no expressed subject, but the reference of the zero pronoun *it* is specified by a following infinitive. This is the typical case in Homer.

17 *Il.* 6.410

ἐμοὶ δέ κε κέρδιον εἴη / σεῦ ἀφαμαρτούσῃ χθόνα δύμεναι

"And for me it would be far better / to sink into the earth when I have lost you."

(Lattimore)

More unusual is the sequence in which the infinitive precedes the copula phrase:

18 *Od.* 8.549

φάσθαι δέ σε κάλλιόν ἐστιν.

"(Do not refuse to answer:) it is better for you to speak up."

(e) Another form, in which the unexpressed subject of the copula is spelled out by a subordinate noun clause with finite verb, is poorly represented in Homer, whose sentence structure tends to "parataxis" rather than to subordination. The classical form is illustrated from Xenophon:

19 *Anabasis* II.3.1

ὃ δὲ δὴ ἔγραψα ὅτι βασιλεὺς ἐξεπλάγη τῇ ἐφόδῳ, τῷδε δῆλον ἦν

"And as to what I wrote above that the King was dismayed by the attack, it was clear from the following"

There has been much discussion of the differences between these forms. Some authors would make a sharp distinction between sentences where a pronoun like τό is expressed and the "subjectless" construction where we have what I call a zero pronoun; and again between the cases where the infinitive precedes and those in which it follows the predicate adjective: in the former but not in the latter case it would be regarded as subject.[16] But the presence or absence of an explicit pronoun is of no deeper syntactic interest here than in the parallel case of pro-words for personal subjects. The uses of *cop A* in sentences **12–18** are obviously built according to a formal analogy with the *N is A* constructions for the first-order or abstract noun in **1–11**. The question whether or not the infinitive in a case like **17** or **18** is "felt as subject," or whether it is only "the apparent subject" cannot be answered, for it is falsely posed.[17] The notion of grammatical subject is a tool of theoretical analysis and not a category of the naive *Sprachgefühl*. Our theory posits a zero pronoun even where no subject is expressed. But this pronoun – like the explicit τό or the English *it* – is a mere pro-word, and the question whether or not we have a "real" subject or an impersonal construction is the question whether or not this pro-word refers forward or backward to some other expression which specifies its content. In sentences like **17** and **18** there is a clear connection between the verb (via its zero pronoun, or by the referential function of its third person ending) and the infinitive clause; and this is recognized by Hermann and other writers who speak in such cases of a "gebundener Infinitiv." The situation is no different when the pronoun is expressed:

> **20** *Od.* 1.370
>
> ἐπεὶ τό γε καλὸν ἀκουέμεν ἐστὶν ἀοιδοῦ
>
> "For this is a fine thing, to hear such a singer"

The form of **20** makes explicit what I take to be the common pattern of all sentences with *cop A* and infinitival clause, as in **17** and **18**. We may describe the surface structure here by saying that the infinitive stands in apposition to a pronoun subject, which is either expressed or implicit in the verb ending. But since this third person form τό or (τό) is itself a pro-word, standing for

---

[16] For this view see Ed. Hermann, "Die subjektlosen Sätze bei Homer," *Nachrichten Gesells. der Wissenschaften Göttingen*. Philol.-Hist. Klasse (1926), pp. 265–97. For the opinions cited, see pp. 272–3. Hermann's otherwise valuable discussion suffers from an inadequate analysis of the notion of *subject*.

[17] Compare the remarks of D. B. Munro on ἀργαλέον ἐστὶ θέσθαι, which he renders "it (the case, the state of things, etc.) is hard in view of making": "the impersonal form ... makes it easier for the Infinitive to become the Subject in sense, while it is still grammatically a word limiting the vague unexpressed Subject" (*A Grammar of the Homeric Dialect*, 2nd ed. Oxford 1891, p. 200, §234(2), cited hereafter as *Homeric Grammar*). If by "Subject in sense" one understands subject position in the underlying syntax, Munro's view is compatible with the analysis suggested here. But we must ignore his misguided speculation concerning "the original character of the Infinitive" as a dative form (p. 199; cf. p. 196). For the modern rejection of this view of the Greek infinitive, see below, p. 179, n. 108.

a fuller expression, it is the infinitival clause that represents the subject in deep structure. The underlying relationship here is precisely the same as when a preceding pronoun is spelled out by a first-order nominal:

21 *Il.* 4.20

αἱ δ᾽ ἐπέμυξαν ᾿Αθηναίη τε καὶ ῞Ηρη·

"They muttered, Athene and Hera."

The construction differs in **12, 15** and **16** only to this extent, that the underlying subject clause is not embedded in the *cop A* sentence in infinitival form but is expressed even more paratactically, as a sentence in its own right. The general development of the language is from such paratactical forms, with syntactic relations only loosely expressed in the surface structure by juxtaposition, to an increasingly precise indication of these relations by more explicit formal devices. Thus the underlying role of the infinitive as subject of *cop A* comes to the surface in the later use of the articular infinitive:

νέοις τὸ σιγᾶν κρεῖττόν ἐστι τοῦ λαλεῖν

"For the young, to be silent is better than speaking."
(Menander *Sententiae* 258 ed. Jaekel, 1964).

The construction is again different in **13** and **14**, where the sentential subject in the context is referred to not by a pronoun but by the demonstrative adverb ὡς. Since the infinitival clause or sentence is thus correlated with the adverb, we might regard the zero pronoun in θέσφατόν ἐστι and κέρδιον ἦεν as standing without any antecedent. Hence we could describe the construction of the verb here as "impersonal" with the subject position empty: *( ) is A*. But it must be stressed that this difference, though real, is purely formal and superficial: *So it is fated*, interpreted as an impersonal sentence, is a paraphrastic equivalent for *This is fated*, with τό referring to a sentential subject. The forms with demonstrative adverb and demonstrative pronoun are indistinguishable in meaning. And this equivalence is not limited to the copula construction.[18]

§7. CONCLUSION OF *Cop A*

Before passing to the cases where the predicate is a noun, I should point out that the construction examined so far, namely *N* is A* with *N** ranging over first-order nominals, abstract nouns and sentential subjects, is the most common form of the copula in Greek, and numerically the most conspicuous

---

[18] Thus we have precisely the same parallelism between ἐμοὶ δ᾽ ἐπιανδάνει οὕτως, with the content of what was pleasing specified by the context (at *Il.* 7.407), and οὐδ᾽ ἄρ᾽ ἔτ᾽ Αἴαντι ... ἥνδανε θυμῷ/ἐστάμεν ἔνθα with the content specified by the following infinitive (*Il.* 15.674).

of all uses of the verb εἰμί. As already remarked, the nominal copula accounts for between 50% and 85% of all occurrences of the verb in the texts which I have studied. Now within this mass of copula uses, the form *N* is A* is clearly predominant.[19] My figures for *N* is A* among all occurrences of εἰμί are: 43 to 46% for *Iliad* 1–12, 39 to 47% for two small samples from Lysias, and 32 to 36% for selected sections of the *Anabasis*. For *N* is N* over the same samples my figures are: *Iliad* 16 to 18%, Lysias 18 to 35%, Xenophon 13 to 22%.[20] Thus while *N* is N* ranges generally in the neighborhood of 15 to 20%, *N* is A* varies roughly from 35 to 45%. In a typical text, predicate adjectives are thus more than twice as numerous as predicate nouns. This is only natural since, as we shall see in the next section, adjectives are in principle restricted to predicate position.

This preponderance of *N is A* over all other uses of εἰμί in Greek may be brought into connection with the fact already observed that (in the texts studied) the most common subject form for the copula construction is a personal noun. On the one hand, we have as the most frequent use of the verb the copula construction with an adjectival predicate; on the other hand, we have as the most frequent subject term (in this and in other uses) a name or common noun designating a person. From a purely statistical point of view, then, Aristotle's paradigm for substance-accident attribution, ἄνθρωπος λευκός ἐστι "(A) man is pale," does in fact represent the most typical use of the verb *be* in Greek.

§8. THE DISTINCTION BETWEEN NOUNS AND ADJECTIVES

In many cases it is difficult to distinguish between predicate nouns and predicate adjectives, and hence between the sentence types *N is N* and *N is A*. It is no accident that substantives and adjectives were never systematically separated from one another in ancient grammar.[21] Even retrospectively it

---

[19] In the samples counted, the only case where *N is N* turned out to be more frequent than *N is A* is in Chapters 56–97 of Lysias XIII, where the two terms (οὐκ) ᾿Αθηναῖος and ἀνδρόφονος recur constantly as epithets of the accused. If I had counted these two words as adjectives instead of nouns – and such a choice could obviously be justified, at least for ᾿Αθηναῖος – the figures even for this brief sample would correspond to the results obtained elsewhere. I might add that the preponderance of *cop A* over *cop N* is really greater than my figures suggest, since I have for simplicity counted cases of *N is AN* (e.g. ἄναλκις ἔην θεός *Il.* 5.331) only as *cop N*, whereas in many instances they represent *N is A* (ἄναλκις ἔην) conjoined with *N is N* (θεὸς ἔην).

[20] For the unusual proportion of *N* is N* in my second Lysias sample, see the preceding note. For the identification of the samples, see n. 4 above, at the end of §1.

[21] For the ancient theory of adjectives as a special class of "apposed" nouns (ὀνόματα ἐπίθετα), see H. Steinthal, *Geschichte der Sprachwissenschaft bei den Griechen und Römern*, 2nd ed. Berlin 1891, II, 251ff. The ancient conception seems to be primarily syntactical, not morphological. For example, adjectives are said to be construed with nouns as adverbs

is not so easy to draw the distinction for ancient Greek. The most useful morphological criterion seems to be the existence of comparative and superlative forms for adjectives. Yet no one counts βασιλεύς "king" or κύων "dog" as adjectives, despite the fact that Homer has the forms βασιλεύτερος, βασιλεύτατος, κύντερος, κύντατος. This suggests that the existence of comparative and superlative forms is not a *sufficient* condition for classifying a word as an adjective. Even supposing that it is a necessary condition, this would scarcely help us decide the status of many nominal forms whose use is rare or restricted to certain formulas. For example, the form ἐπιτάρροθος "defender, supporter, master" occurs only half a dozen times in Homer, and once or twice in later literature. Is ἐπιτάρροθός ἐστι an instance of *N is A* or *N is N*? We simply do not know whether this word admits comparative and superlative forms. And as far as I can see, other morphological criteria fail completely; it is obvious for instance, that many proper names are formally indistinguishable from adjectives (e.g. Ἀρχεπτόλεμος, Νεοπτόλεμος and the Homeric adjective μενεπτόλεμος; so we have the use of διονύσιος as adjective and as name). [22]

The deeper criterion is syntactical. "Certain Nouns are mainly used as qualifying words in agreement with other Nouns; these are classed as Adjectives" (Munro, *Homeric Grammar* §165). That is to say, a nominally declined form which is typically construed as predicate or attribute for another nominal form is an adjective. Since in transformational grammar the attributive construction *AN* is usually derived from the predicate construction *N is A* (or, equivalently, from *N which is A*), these two conditions – attributive and predicative use – are in fact one. [23] Conversely, the noun

---

are with verbs (Steinthal, II, 256). Furthermore, agent nouns like ῥήτωρ and δρομεύς were counted as ἐπίθετα when they were *added to* the proper name to distinguish one bearer of the name from another. Thus an ancient grammarian construed names like *Antiphon the Orator, Antiphon the Sophist* as syntactically parallel to our formulas *Philippe le Bel, Charles the Bald.*

[22] Perhaps the most commonly used criterion is distributional: an adjective is a nominal form that is modified by an adverb, whereas a noun is modified by an adjective. But this does not work so smoothly for Greek, where we have expressions like μάλα φιλόσοφος, σφόδρα φιλία, σφόδρα γυναῖκες. In practice, the distinction between nouns and adjectives is drawn on the basis of a whole cluster of formal characteristics: adverbial modification, existence of comparative and superlative forms, existence of animate-neuter (or masculine-feminine-neuter) variation, existence of an adverbial derivative, and so forth. In the clearest cases, all criteria should give the same result. In fact this does not happen, as examples like κύντερος and σφόδρα γυναῖκες show. I suggest that when such anomalies arise, we in fact resolve them on the basis of the syntactic criterion proposed above: κύων and γυνή are clearly nouns because they can, and often do, stand in subject position. But when used as predicates they may be assimilated to adjectives and hence may take adverbial modifiers and comparative forms.

[23] The transformational analysis of attributive syntax is essentially that given by Kühner-Gerth, I, 260 §401, where τὸ καλὸν ῥόδον is derived syntactically from τὸ ῥόδον καλόν ἐστι.

or substantive may be recognized as the nominal form which typically takes *another* nominal form as predicate, attribute, or dependent genitive. The more general definition of the noun, from which this property follows, is that it is the nominal form that can stand alone as subject or object of the verb. Hence when an adjective like φίλος "dear, friendly" is used as subject of a sentence, or when it takes another adjective as attribute (φίλος πιστός "a reliable friend") we call this the *substantival use* of the adjective.[24] In the absence of other evidence, the substantival use of a nominal form may suffice to classify the form as a noun. And we may describe our problematic form ἐπιτάρροθος as a substantive, because of the construction τοῖος ... ἐπιτάρροθος "such ... a helper" which appears three times in the *Iliad* (out of seven occurrences of the word).[25]

§9. THE SUBSTANTIVAL COPULA (*cop N*)

In general the pattern of uses of εἰμί with predicate nouns is closely parallel to that with adjectives, which is what we would expect in view of the tenuous nature of the distinction between *N* and *A* in predicate position. As in the case of *N is A* we may analyze sentences of the form *N is N* with reference to two variables: the structure of the subject expression and that of the predicate. I shall consider the status of the predicate in a moment, but my classification is primarily based on the nature of the subject. Again as for the adjectival copula, we find that in ordinary or representative contexts a clear majority of *cop N* sentences take personal nouns as subject. (Thus personal subjects account for all 15 or 16 instances of *cop N* in *Iliad* 5; for 5 out of 11 instances in *Iliad* 9; for 12 out of 18 instances of *cop N* in my first Lysias sample; for 8 out of 11 in the first Xenophon sample.) Non-personal and abstract nouns, which do not occur frequently as subject for *cop A*, are even rarer for *cop N*, and particularly rare in Homer. (For examples see 36–37 in §10.) As a result, an example of *N is N* where the

---

[24] Compare Schwyzer-Debrunner II, 174. For an example, see 9 above in §5.

[25] Hence we must reject the otherwise attractive conclusion of Munro (*Homeric Grammar* §165) that "the use of a Nominative in the Predicate – as βασιλεύς ἐστι, *he is king* – is strictly speaking an adjectival use." The existence of sentences such as βασιλεύς ἀγαθός ἐστι, βασιλεύς ἐστι τῶν Περσῶν "He is a good king", "He is king of the Persians", shows that βασιλεύς in predicate position must still be considered a noun rather than an adjective, since it in turn takes an adjective (in attributive syntax) or a dependent noun (e.g. the "objective" genitive). Nominal forms which always or *usually* occur in predicate position are adjectives, for to that extent they lack the "substantival" capacity to stand alone as subject or object. But the occasional occurrence of a substantival form in predicate position does not show it has lost this capacity. It would be misleading to assign *man* to several different word classes in the following sentences: (1) *A man is at the door*, (2) *John is a man*, (3) *John is the man at the door*. Although *man* is subject in (1) and predicate in (2), its occurrence in (3) is derived from both (1) and (2).

subject is not a personal noun will nearly always have a sentential subject. We have practically to reckon with only two cases: *N is N* with personal subjects and *N* is N* with sentential subjects.

To illustrate the variety of predicates I list 12 examples of *N is N* for personal subjects.

22 *Il.* 1.338

τὼ δ᾽ αὐτὼ μάρτυροι ἔστων

"Let them (sc. the heralds Talthybius and Eurybates) be witness themselves"

23 *Il.* 2.26 (=63)

Διὸς δέ τοι ἄγγελός εἰμι

"I am a messenger to you from Zeus"

24 *Il.* 2.246

λιγύς περ ἐὼν ἀγορητής

"Fluent orator though you be (Thersites)"

(Lattimore)

25 *Il.* 2.485

ὑμεῖς γὰρ θεαί ἐστε

"For you (Muses) are goddesses"

26 *Il.* 2.760 (cf. 487)

οὗτοι ἄρ᾽ ἡγεμόνες Δαναῶν καὶ κοίρανοι ἦσαν

"These then were the leaders and princes among the Danaans"

(Lattimore)

27 *Il.* 3.229

οὗτος δ᾽ Αἴας ἐστὶ πελώριος, ἕρκος Ἀχαιῶν

"That one is gigantic Aias, wall of the Achaians"

(Lattimore)

28 *Il.* 3.429

ὃς ἐμὸς πρότερος πόσις ἦεν

"(Menelaos) who was once my husband"

29 *Il.* 4.266

μάλα μέν τοι ἐγὼν ἐρίηρος ἑταῖρος / ἔσσομαι

"I will be to you a staunch companion in arms"

(after Lattimore)

30 Lysias XIII.1

κηδεστὴς γάρ μοι ἦν Διονυσόδωρος καὶ ἀνεφιός

"For Dionysodorus was my brother-in-law and cousin"

31 *Ibid.* 33

ἔστι φονεὺς ἐκείνων

"He (Agoratus) is their murderer"

32 Xenophon *Anabasis* I.2.25

ἦσαν δ᾽ οὖν οὗτοι ἑκατὸν ὁπλῖται

"These (lost men) were 100 hoplites"

33 *Ibid.* I.3.6

νομίζω γὰρ ὑμᾶς ἐμοὶ εἶναι καὶ πατρίδα καὶ φίλους καὶ
συμμάχους

"I regard you as my country and my friends and my allies"

These examples of predicate nouns may be grouped as follows:

A. Classifier nouns (sortals)

  1. Classifying by intrinsic criteria (natural kinds)
     θεαί in **25**: *goddesses*

  2. Classifying by extrinsic criteria (artificial kinds)
     ὁπλῖται in **32**: *soldiers bearing heavy armor* (ὅπλα)

B. Relational nouns (with underlying sentence form *N is N of N*)

  1. Relations of birth
     ἀνεψιός in **30**: *cousin (of someone)*

  2. Relations established by marriage
     πόσις   in **28**: *husband (of someone)*
     κηδεστής in **30**: *brother-in-law*

  3. Political and military rule
     ἡγεμόνες, κοίρανοι in **26**: *leaders* and *princes*

  4. Other social ties
     ἑταῖρος   in **29**: *companion*
     cf. φίλοι, σύμμαχοι in **33**: *friends, allies*

C. Agent nouns related to corresponding verb

     μάρτυρος in **22**: *witness*   cf. μαρτυρέω
     ἄγγελος in **23**: *messenger* cf. ἀγγέλλω
     ἀγορητής in **24**: *orator*   cf. ἀγορεύω
     φονεύς   in **31**: *murderer* cf. φονεύω

D. Proper name

     Αἴας in **27**: *Ajax*

E. Metaphorical use of non-personal nouns as predicate of persons

     πατρίδα (sc. γῆν) in **33**: *country*
     cf. ἕρκος in **27**: *wall*

It is easy to see that many of these predicate nouns lend themselves to a
transformational analysis that would derive *N is N* from a sentence of a

different form. This is most obvious in the case of agent nouns under C. above, where the morphology of the word often reflects the underlying syntactic structure. Thus ἀγορητής in **24** bears its derivation on its face: *you are a fluent speaker* ← *you speak fluently* (λιγέως ἀγορεύεις; cf. *Il.* 3.214). If we were to undertake a transformational analysis of predicate nouns, we would describe the copula εἰμί in sentences of this type as a verb operator which helps to convert a *NV* (or *NVN*) sentence into *N is N* form. The same analysis applies in principle to ἄγγελος, μάρτυρος and φονεύς, though in the last two cases the verb is morphologically derivative. Syntactically, however, it is clear that ἐστὶ φονεὺς ἐκείνων is a transform of ἐφόνευσε ἐκείνους "He murdered them" (where the verb εἰμί does not appear), just as ἐστὶ νομεὺς ἵππων "He is herdsman of horses" is a transform of νέμει ἵππους, "He herds horses". In the case of νομεύς and ἀγορητής the corresponding verb is still current in such a form that the status of the noun as agent nominalization is immediately clear. In the case of φονεύς the underlying verbal root is preserved in early Greek but in an unrecognizable or scarcely recognizable form (in θείνω, ἔπεφνον, πέφαται); so that the action noun φόνος and the agent form φονεύς are left dangling, as it were, without verbal support. In this situation, it is easy to understand that a new verb φονεύω was formed from the stem of φονεύς.[26] Hence the morphological relationship between φονεύς and φονεύω is quite different from that between νομεύς and νέμω, or between γονεύς ("parent") and γίγνομαι/γείνομαι; yet the syntactical and functional connection between agent noun and verb is essentially the same in each case. When morphological and syntactical relations diverge in this way, we see that morphology reflects the history of the language but that it is the transformational relations which constitute its living structure at a given moment in time.

It is interesting to speculate as to which kinds of *N is N* sentences will resist a transformational derivation from one or more kernels without the verb *be*, as ἔστι φονεὺς ἐκείνων may be derived from ἐφόνευσε ἐκείνους "He murdered them." In other words, what are the non-derivative subclasses

---

[26] This is an instance of the general tendency in Greek to form special verbs corresponding to agent nouns in -εύς. Thus the formation νομεύω from νομεύς, as old as Homer, is apparently provoked by the great variety of senses associated with νέμω. The diversified use of νέμω makes it convenient to have a different verb meaning specifically "to pasture animals, to do the work of a herdsman."

Note that philologists speak of nouns in -εύς as "derived from action nouns," as φονεύς from φόνος, γονεύς from γόνος, etc. (So Chantraine, *La formation des noms*, p. 128.) The term "derivation" is of course ambiguous. In a purely formal sense γονεύς is derived from γόνος (i.e., a new suffix is added to the same stem). In a larger sense, both nouns are derived from an underlying verbal root *γεν- *to be born*, with causative forms meaning *to beget*. It is this verbal root which best represents the unity of form and meaning for the whole family of words in γεν- and γον-.

of predicate noun? The suggestion implied in Harris' list of kernel forms for English is that these will be of two kinds: N is N_{rel} of N, where "N_{rel} includes all relational nouns", and N is N_{cl}, where N_{cl} is a classifier noun and is can be interpreted is a member of or is a case of.[27] These two sentence types correspond roughly to groups A and B in my list above, though it must be noted that not all classifier and relational nouns will turn out to be elementary. In our example 32 the predicate ὁπλῖται is formally derivative from ὅπλα "weapons, heavy arms"; and it would be natural to derive the sentence They are hoplites as a transform of They bear ὅπλα. Similarly for a relational predicate like ἡγεμόνες "leaders" in 26: the sentence They are leaders represents an agent transformation of They lead (troops), with a verb form like ἡγοῦνται. In these sentences where we have a transformationally derived relational or classifier noun we also have a transformationally derived use of the copula, just as with the agent nouns of group C. (See the parallel remarks on predicate adjectives in Section 3 above). But there will be some cop N sentences with an elementary classifier noun, like You are goddesses in 25, and some with elementary relational nouns, like He was my husband in 28, He is my brother, and perhaps He was my cousin in 30.

In addition to the two elementary forms of N is N recognized by Harris, I am tempted to regard the nuncupative type He is Ajax in 27 as non-derivative. The only plausible derivation would be from the equivalent metalinguistic form His name is Ajax, which would be a special case of the "possessive" construction described in Chapter VI §12.[28] The alternative derivation from He is called Ajax (Αἴας καλεῖται) or better, from the active They call him Ajax (Αἴαν (αὐτὸν) καλοῦσι), is less attractive, since it leaves the proper name in predicate position; and this presupposes the copula form to be derived. I take it that They call him Ajax is related to He is (becomes) Ajax as They appoint him general to He is (becomes) general.[29]

---

[27] Mathematical Structures p. 171; cf. p. 166.

[28] The form is Homeric: e.g. Od. 24.306 ἐμοί γ' ὄνομ' ἐστὶν Ἐπήριτος; cf. Od. 7.54 and the formula for the naming of Odysseus, 19.409 τῷ δ' Ὀδυσεὺς ὄνομ' ἔστω ἐπώνυμον.

[29] William Kneale has recently argued, on philosophic grounds, that one should explain the meaning of proper names by referring to the use which I call nuncupative (his example is "This is Aristotle"), in order to avoid the metalinguistic complication involved in explaining "Aristotle" as equivalent to "the person called 'Aristotle'". (Proceedings of the Aristotelian Society, 68, 1967–68, pp. 265–7.) For the linguist who recognizes that "the metalanguage is included in the language," this might not be regarded as a crucial consideration. (See Harris, Math. Structures, p. 125.) But my reluctance to derive He is Ajax from His name is Ajax is based precisely upon the reluctance to derive a sentence which is not in the metalanguage from one which is. Harris (loc. cit. n. 10) suggests a derivation of We call Y (by the name) 'X' from The name is X, and ultimately from the kernel sentence X is a name. But the latter does not seem to me a natural source for He is Ajax. I agree with Harris in regarding We call him 'X' as non-elementary, but disagree as to the preferred form of the derivation.

In the case of the metaphorical use of non-personal *N* as a predicate for personal subjects (as πατρίς "country" is predicated of Clearchus' soldiers in **33** and ἕρκος "wall" is implicitly predicated of Ajax in **27**), it is easy to construct a transformational derivation that would throw some light on the literary function of the metaphor. The two examples given can be derived as comparisons: *Ajax protects the Achaeans like a wall, My soldiers are as precious to me as a fatherland (since I am in exile)*, or the like. We may also list here the use of an abstract noun as predicate of a person, which represents a metaphor of a different sort.

34 *Il.* 3.41

> καί κεν πολὺ κέρδιον ἦεν (sc. σὲ ἀπολέσθαι)
> ἢ οὕτω λώβην τ' ἔμεναι καὶ ὑπόψιον ἄλλων

> "It would be far better (for you to be dead)
> than to be our undignity thus, for others to sneer at."

> (after Lattimore)

Here the noun λώβη which normally designates an act or situation that provokes a sense of outrage or indignity, as in sentence **39** below, is predicated of Paris himself as personal cause or object of indignation. Such a transcategorical use of abstract predicate nouns for concrete subjects – as what may be called "reclassifiers" – is an essential feature of poetic and expressive language in every period. I cite one well-known example with a non-personal subject in Pericles' praise of Athens.

35 Thucydides II.41.1

> ξυνελών τε λέγω τήν τε πᾶσαν πόλιν τῆς Ἑλλάδος παίδευσιν εἶναι

> "In a word, the city as a whole is the education of Greece".

Here we may say that the unusual metaphorical effect results from the use of the action noun παίδευσις in a context where an agent noun or participle might be expected (e.g. παιδευτής or διδάσκαλος "teacher").

§10. COPULA WITH ABSTRACT *N* AS A PREDICATE: ABSTRACT AND SENTENTIAL SUBJECTS

There would be no point in cataloguing here the banal if relatively infrequent use of *cop N* with non-personal first-order nominals as subject, of the type *The trout is a fish* or *Epidamnus is a city, is the ally of Athens*. I shall briefly note the use of *N is N* with abstract nouns as subject. The latter is quite rare in Homer, and perhaps not very common in any period except in philosophical contexts where definitions are sought or offered.[30] I give two examples, one of them from Homer.

36 *Il.* 9.39

ἀλκὴν δ᾽ οὔ τοι δῶκεν, ὅ τε κράτος ἐστὶ μέγιστον

"Zeus did not give you valour, which is the greatest power of all"

The rarity of the construction is indicated by the fact that the second half-verse (which occurs only here and at *Iliad* 13.484) is a variant of a much more frequent formula where κράτος is subject rather than predicate in a sentence of the form *N is A*: τοῦ γὰρ κράτος ἐστὶ μέγιστον "for his power is greatest" (example **6** above, which occurs also at *Il.* 2.118, *Od.* 1.70, 5.4, with parallels at *Il.* 24.293, *Od.* 1.359 etc.).

37 Lysias XIII. 66

καὶ τούτου θάνατος ἡ ζημία ἐστίν

"And the punishment for this (sc. for adultery) is death"

In the more typical cases, abstract nouns are construed as predicates not with other abstract nouns but with sentential subjects:

38 *Il.* 4.322

ἀλλὰ καὶ ὧς ἱππεῦσι μετέσσομαι ἠδὲ κελεύσω
βουλῇ καὶ μύθοισι·τὸ γὰρ γέρας ἐστὶ γερόντων

"Yet even so I shall be among the riders, and command them with word and counsel; that is the privilege of old men"

(Lattimore, slightly adapted)

39 *Il.* 7.97

ἦ μὲν δὴ λώβη τάδε γ᾽ ἔσσεται αἰνόθεν αἰνῶς
εἰ μή τις Δαναῶν νῦν Ἕκτορος ἀντίος εἶσιν

"This will be an indignity upon us, shame upon shame,
if no one of the Danaans goes out to face Hector"

(Lattimore, adapted)

---

[30] The type is familiar from Plato, e.g. *Theaetetus* 147 B 10, (ἐρωτᾶν) ἐπιστήμη τί ἐστιν, 151 E 2 οὐκ ἄλλο τί ἐστιν ἐπιστήμη ἢ αἴσθησις. But even in Plato the abstract noun serves much less frequently than the nominalized adjective as subject of definitional questions and answers: *Euthyphro* 9 C 5 τί ποτ ἐστὶν τὸ ὅσιόν τε καὶ τὸ ἀνόσιον; 10 D 12 οὐκ ἄρα τὸ θεοφιλὲς ὅσιόν ἐστιν ... οὐδὲ τὸ ὅσιον θεοφιλές; *Rep.* 338 C 1 εἶναι τὸ δίκαιον οὐκ ἄλλο τι ἢ τὸ τοῦ κρείττονος συμφέρον etc.

The noun ἔργα "deeds" often serves as a general classifier or dummy predicate for sentential subjects.

40 *Il.* 1.573

> ἦ δὴ λοίγια ἔργα τάδ' ἔσσεται οὐδ' ἔτ' ἀνεκτά,
> εἰ δὴ σφὼ ἕνεκα θνητῶν ἐριδαίνετον ὧδε
> "This will be a disastrous matter and not endurable
> if you two are to quarrel thus for the sake of mortals"

(Lattimore)

The role of ἔργα as essentially a "filler" here is brought out by the parallel passages where λοίγια occurs alone as predicate (*Il.* 21.533, 23.310).

There is a class of abstract nouns meaning *what is right* or *what is inevitable* which regularly occur in Homer as subject or predicate of ἐστί in loose construction with an infinitive or a coordinate clause, or with another sentence in the context: θέμις, μοῖρα, αἶσα, δίκη. With these is associated a similar group whose construction differs from the first only in the fact that the verb ἐστί does not co-occur (in Homer): ἀνάγκη, νέμεσις, χρή, χρεώ. There is also a small group of nouns with different meanings, such as ἐλπωρή "(there is) hope" and ὥρη "(it is) time", which may take the same infinitival construction, generally without ἐστί. I do not recognize any distinction in principle – that is to say, in deep structure – between the cases where ἐστί does and does not appear. In Homer μοῖρα and αἶσα occur now with the verb, now without. With ἀνάγκη the verb *be* does not occur in Homer: we have ἔπλετ' ἀνάγκη in *Od.* 10.273, but never ἀνάγκη ἐστί. In Lysias and Xenophon, however, the latter is roughly as common as the verbless form. Whatever the stylistic and rhetorical interest of this phenomenon of verb omission, I do not believe it affects the problem of syntactic analysis. From the point of view of sentence structure, we may assume that an underlying occurrence of ἐστί (sometimes of ἦν) has been zeroed in every case where ἀνάγκη, νέμεσις or χρεώ appears without a verb. (The situation is slightly different for χρή which comes to be regarded as a verb form itself, as we shall see at the end of this section.) On the whole, however, I shall treat only examples where the verb in fact occurs. (For further discussion of the verbless sentence pattern, see Appendix B.)

In some cases the predicate construction of the abstract noun is unmistakable, but there are others where we may want to take it rather as the *subject* of ἐστί. It is clear that θέμις is predicate when a relative-demonstrative pronoun occurs as subject:

41 *Il.* 2.73

πρῶτα δ᾽ ἐγὼν ἔπεσιν πειρήσομαι, ἦ θέμις ἐστί [31]

"Yet first I will make trial of them by words, since that is the right way."

(Lattimore, adapted)

In **41** the pronoun ἦ functions (exactly like τό in the examples discussed above in §6) as a pro-word referring back to the preceding clause. In some cases the reference is to a sentence which lies at some distance in the text.

42 *Od.* 11.218

ἀλλ᾽ αὕτη δίκη ἐστὶ βροτῶν, ὅτε τίς κε θάνῃσιν

"But this is the way with mortals when they die."

(Palmer)

The ghost of Odysseus' mother is referring to her son's question in verse 210 ("My mother, why not stay for me who long to clasp you?"), and for the reader the ultimate reference is to the preceding description of Odysseus' fruitless attempts to embrace his mother, in verses 204–8. The true "antecedent" of αὕτη here is, in effect, the entire situation as described 10 verses earlier. In other cases the sentential subject is given by an immediately preceding infinitival clause:

43 *Il.* 9.275

μή ποτε τῆς εὐνῆς ἐπιβήμεναι ἠδὲ μιγῆναι,
ἦ θέμις ἐστίν, ἄναξ, ἥ τ᾽ ἀνδρῶν ἥ τε γυναικῶν

"(Agamemnon will swear a great oath)
that he never entered into her bed and never lay with her
as is the customary way between men and women."

(Lattimore, adapted)

More frequently, however, we have no pronoun expressed and the reference is specified by a *following* infinitival clause:

44 *Od.* 10.73

οὐ γάρ μοι θέμις ἐστὶ κομιζέμεν οὐδ᾽ ἀποπέμπειν

"It is not right for me to transport or send upon his way
(a man detested by the gods)."

---

[31] In earlier editions one finds ᾗ for ἦ, which would suggest a different construction. I take for granted here Allen's reading and Chantraine's identification of ἦ as "le pronoun démonstratif ou relatif sujet," i.e. the sentential pro-word which would normally occur as τό but is here attracted to the feminine form of its predicate. See Chantraine, *Grammaire homérique* II §26.

The infinitive may also occur before the *cop N* expression:

45 *Od.* 16.91

    ἐπεὶ θήν μοι καὶ ἀμείψασθαι θέμις ἐστίν

    "For surely I too have a right to answer."

                                 (Palmer)

Some authors have thought that the infinitive was more clearly the subject of ἐστί when it precedes, as in **45**, than when it follows, as in **44**.[32] Given the freedom of word order in Greek, however, it seems arbitrary to use this as the basis for a syntactic distinction between **44** and **45**: a single grammatical analysis should apply to both. The fact is that for these two cases, where no pronoun occurs, we are free to construe θέμις either as predicate or as subject of the verb. On the second construal we would not have a copula sentence of the form *N is N* at all, but an existential or possessive construction of μοὶ θέμις ἐστί (with epexegetical infinitives) as in Palmer's translation of **45**. The sentence would belong to a type discussed in Chapter VI §§ 12 and 15–16. The same ambiguity arises with other abstract nouns such as μοῖρα:

46 *Od.* 5.41

    ὣς γάρ οἱ μοῖρ᾽ ἐστὶ φίλους ἰδέειν καὶ ἱκέσθαι

    οἶκον ἐς ὑψόροφον

    "Thus it is his lot to see his friends and reach his high-roofed house."

                                   (Palmer)

Should we take μοῖρα here as predicate noun with the copula, as in Palmer's rendering of **46**, or as subject of an existential-possessive use of οἱ ἐστι as in the same author's translation of **45**? I call this the choice between the *predicative* (copulative) and the *subjective* (non-copulative) syntax of an abstract noun such as μοῖρα or θέμις in sentences like **44–46**.

In favor of taking μοῖρα as predicate and the infinitival clauses as underlying subject, we have the parallel sentence pattern in **41–43** above, where θέμις and δίκη must be taken predicatively. Similarly it is the predicative construction that is required for the equivalent sentence type with the corresponding adjective μόριμον or μόρσιμον.

47 *Il.* 20.302

    μόριμον δέ οἱ ἐστ᾽ ἀλέασθαι

    "It is fated for him (sc. for Aeneas) to escape."

47 belongs to a well-defined class of *cop A* sentences with sentential subjects

---

[32] So Hermann, "Subjektlose Sätze," p. 274 (See reference above, §6, n. 16.)

described in §6 above. This noun-adjective parallel between μοῖρα and μόριμον is duplicated for αἶσα/αἴσιμον: compare αἶσα γὰρ ἦν ἀπολέσθαι "It was destined (for Troy) to perish" (*Od.* 8.511), with ὡς οὔ τοι ποταμῷ γε δαμήμεναι αἴσιμόν ἐστιν "It is not your destiny to be conquered by the river" (*Il.* 21.291). Since the adjectives *must* be construed predicatively, it is natural to take the equivalent nouns in the same way. Hence for a great mass of sentences containing ἐστί with a noun like μοῖρα, αἶσα, θέμις and δίκη, we are led to prefer the predicative construction. In the interests of uniformity and generality, one would be inclined to adopt the same construction for the verbless sentences with ἀνάγκη, χρή, χρεώ, and the like.

However, there are serious objections to such a unified analysis. In the case of θέμις and δίκη, which do not occur in Homer as subjects of other verbs[33], there is no strong reason to construe them as subjects of ἐστί. But with μοῖρα and αἶσα the situation is different. Both occur frequently in "personified" form as agent-subjects for verbs of violent or decisive action. Thus we have standard formulas for the death of a hero in which "mighty Moira" (μοῖρα κραταιή) seizes him (ἔλλαβε *Il.* 5.83, etc.), covers him in darkness (*Il.* 12.116), chains him to the spot (πέδησεν *Il.* 22.5), and so forth. Similar subjective constructions are common for αἶσα as well (*Il.* 20.128, *Od.* 7.197, etc.), including locative-existential or possessive uses where the noun serves as subject for a verb of station (κακὴ Διὸς αἶσα παρέστη *Od.* 9.52), or subject of a verbless sentence with ἐστί understood (ἔτι γὰρ καὶ ἐλπίδος αἶσα *Od.* 16.101; ἐπεί νύ τοι αἶσα μίνυνθά περ, οὔ τι μάλα δήν "Since you have but a brief portion (of life) and not for long" *Il.* 1.416). Such uses of μοῖρα and αἶσα in the epic would lead us to expect that when these nouns occur in the nominative in a sentence with ἐστί they are to be construed as subject rather than predicate.

The subjective syntax is also characteristic of ἀνάγκη "necessity, compulsion" and χρεώ "need". Thus ανάγκη occurs as subject of the locative verb ἐπικείσεται ("mighty necessity will be laid upon you," *Il.* 6.458) and in the corresponding agent construction with ὑπό ("she completed it unwillingly, under compulsion" ὑπὸ ἀνάγκης *Od.* 2.110 etc.) whereas the variant ἀναγκαίη is subject of a verb meaning "to force" (ἐπείγει *Il.* 6.85; cf. *Od.* 19.73). The subjective construction with the suppletive verb ἔπλετο is at least plausible in *Od.* 10.273: κρατερὴ δέ μοι ἔπλετ' ἀνάγκη "for strong necessity is laid on me" (tr. Palmer). Similarly χρεώ is regularly subject of

---

[33] The only apparent exceptions are the occurrence of these nouns with suppletives of ἐστί, as in ἦ θέμις ... πέλει (*Il.* 9.134) and οὐχ ἧδε δίκη τὸ πάροιθε τέτυκτο (*Od.* 18.275); but in fact the predicative syntax is more natural in both cases, in view of the pronoun subject ἦ (ἧδε). I am not sure how far these grammatical considerations should be affected by the literal personification of Themis, e.g. at *Iliad* 15.87ff. and 20.4. For Dike compare *Il.* 16.388.

verbs of motion or of causing motion (ἱκάνεται *Il.* 10.118; cf. 10.142 etc. δεῦρ᾽ ἤγαγε *Od.* 4.312; cf. *Od.* 11.164). The variant χρειώ is subject of the suppletive verb γένηται in one passage:

48 *Il.* 1.340

εἴ ποτε δὴ αὖτε
χρειὼ ἐμεῖο γένηται ἀεικέα λοιγὸν ἀμῦναι
"If ever hereafter
there shall be need of me to beat back the shameful destruction".
(Lattimore)

Here we have a clear case of the abstract noun as subject of a verb of existence, with the infinitive construed as epexegetical or final. Similar constructions are attested for χρεώ as subject of γίγνεται and ἐστί, with a noun in the genitive in place of the infinitive clause:

49 *Od.* 9.136

ἐν δὲ λιμὴν εὔορμος, ἵν᾽ οὐ χρεὼ πείσματός ἐστιν
"Here is a quite harbor, where there is no need of mooring"
(Palmer, adapted)[34]

Examples **48** and **49** suggest that for χρεώ and χρειώ the subjective syntax is much more plausible than the predicative; and we have seen similar considerations in favor of the same construction for μοῖρά (ἐστι), αἶσά (ἐστι) and ἀνάγκη. The subjective construction is also *possible* for οἱ μοῖρ᾽ ἐστί in **46** and μοι θέμις ἐστί in **44–45**. It is excluded only for the special case in which θέμις or δίκη is preceded by a nominative pronoun ἥ or αὕτη as in **41–43**: here we have no choice but to construe the noun as predicative with copula ἐστί.

It is impossible to choose in general between these two constructions, and even for particular cases the choice is by no means clear. Thus for οἱ μοῖρ᾽ ἐστί φίλους ἰδέειν in **46** and αἶσα γὰρ ἦν ἀπολέσθαι in *Od.* 8.511

---

[34] So we have the curious construction with the accusative: *Od.* 4.634 ἐμὲ δὲ χρεὼ γίγνεται αὐτῆς (sc. νηός), *Il.* 21.322 οὐδέ τί μιν χρεὼ/ἔσται τυμβοχόης. The accusative ("of respect") is probably to be explained by the influence of the parallel formulas with a verb of motion where the accusative is normal: *Il.* 10.172 μεγάλη χρειὼ βεβίηκεν Ἀχαιούς, *Od.* 5.189 ὅτε με χρειὼ τόσον ἵκοι. The assimilation of χρειώ:χρεώ:χρή leads to the frequent construction of χρή with the accusative of person in need and the genitive of thing needed.

I note that Hermann ("Subjektlosen Sätze," p. 284) doubts this explanation of χρεώ (χρή) μέ τινος by analogy with χρειώ με ἱκάνεται (which had already been proposed by Brugmann) on the grounds that in the latter case χρειώ is subject whereas in the former the corresponding noun is predicate. But this argument simply begs the question against the syntactical ambiguity of χρεώ and χρή on which I am insisting.

the parallels in each direction tend to counterbalance one another, and we are left with an unstable ambiguity between two constructions. Under these circumstances it makes no sense to ask whether or not the noun was "felt" as predicate: it could be felt as predicate by a speaker with one set of parallels in mind, and as subject by a speaker who had in mind sentences like μοῖρα πέδησεν and αἶσα παρέστη. The mass of sentences under consideration in this section (whether verbless or with ἐστί) constitute an area of the language where two distinct sentence patterns tend to overlap and conflict with one another. The grammarian may, for convenience, divide this area in various ways.[35] But it is surely more important to see that the analogies with two distinct sentence patterns are equally real: the syntactic ambiguity is irreducible.

It is all the more striking, then, to observe that this ambiguity in the construction of ἐστί makes absolutely no difference in *meaning* for the sentence as a whole. Whether we render οἱ μοῖρ' ἐστὶ φίλους ἰδέειν in **46** by "It is his lot to see his friends", corresponding to the predicative syntax, or by "He has as his lot (="there is a destiny for him") to see his friends" with μοῖρα as subject of the verb, the sense of the sentence remains unchanged; for the alternative translations are acceptable as paraphrases of one another. The reason is simply that the difference here between subjective and predicative syntax is one of surface structure only, and the underlying syntax is the same in both cases. In sentences like **41–49** both the second-order copula and the existential use of ἐστί (comparable to Type V in Chapter VI §§15–16) are transformationally derived from an underlying structure where the verb *be* need not occur at all. This underlying syntax is most clearly revealed in an alternative formula with an impersonal verb as sentence operator on an infinitival clause:

50 *Il.* 21.281 (=*Od.* 5.312; cf. *Od.* 24.34)

νῦν δέ με λευγαλέῳ θανάτῳ εἵμαρτο ἁλῶναι

"But now it was fated for me to be caught in a wretched death".

In **50** also one might dispute the question whether εἵμαρτο is "really" impersonal or whether the infinitive clause is to be construed here as subject. But the dispute would be pointless, since there are no formal tests by which the distinction could be drawn and the meaning is in any case unchanged. The syntactic ambiguity which we have discussed in this section is trivial,

---

[35] Thus Guiraud, who recognizes the ambiguity for χρή, counts this form as predicate whenever an infinitive co-occurs as potential subject; otherwise he treats it as subject of an unexpressed verb of existence (*La phrase nominale en grec d'Homère à Euripide* (Paris, 1962), pp. 111–3). Hermann, on the other hand, counts χρή and our abstract nouns as predicate, and the verb as copula in every case ("Subjektlosen Sätze," pp. 272f.).

since the deep structure is unambiguous. In nearly every case, the kernel is a sentence or sentences represented by an infinitival clause or occurring independently in the context; the abstract noun (θέμις, μοῖρα, χρειώ, etc.) represents a lexical idea of right, fate, necessity, and the like, which governs this kernel as sentence operator. The underlying syntax is the same as in the English sentences *It is right (for me to go)*, *It is necessary (that I go)*, and *(I shall go;) that is my duty*, where the kernels are indicated by parenthesis. It is in terms of this transformational structure, and not in terms of subject, predicate, and copula in the surface syntax of the text, that we can give a unified account for all the locutions studied in this section. It makes no difference whether we describe ἐστί as copula or existential verb in these sentences, since in either case the verb and the abstract noun (or the latter alone) represent the "trace" of a modal sentence operator whose value is fixed by the choice of a particular noun (θέμις, μοῖρα, etc.).[36]

Thus the underlying syntax of sentences with μοῖρα, χρεώ and the like is the same as the impersonal verb construction in **50**. In classical prose the sentence forms with abstract noun and ἐστί (expressed or "understood") have nearly all disappeared. The Homeric forms χρεώ and χρειώ are preserved as χρεών (ἐστι) + *infinitive* in fifth-century prose and poetry; locutions like θέμις ἐστι survive only in poetical or archaic contexts. The Homeric δίκη ἐστί is supplanted by the "impersonal" sentence with the adjective (δίκαιόν ἐστι + *infinitive*, with a different meaning) or by the more common personal construction δίκαιός εἰμι "I am right (to do so-and-so)." Of the sentence types described here only ἀνάγκη (ἐστί) and χρή remain in current use. And in the case of ἀνάγκη the construction with abstract noun as modal sentence operator is rivalled by the adjectival form ἀναγκαῖον (ἐστί) unknown to Homer and by a new adverbial form ἀναγκαίως ἔχει (+ *infinitive*). The general decay of the sentence pattern with abstract noun – a decay which is perhaps due in part to the syntactic ambiguity which we have discussed – is illustrated by the new development of χρή. Although χρή + *infinitive* (without ἐστί) is quite common in Attic prose, the form has certainly ceased to be

---

[36] As far as I can see, the only exceptions to this general solution are the uses of χρειώ, χρεώ, and χρή with a concrete noun in the genitive, as in *Od.* 4.634

ἐμὲ δὲ χρεὼ γίγνεται αὐτῆς
Ἤλιδ' ἐς εὐρύχορον διαβήμεναι

"Now I need her (the ship) for crossing to broad Elis" (Palmer). Here the syntax is more complex, and the first member (*I need a ship*) cannot be properly described as a sentence-operator on the following infinitival clause.

Note that I exclude from my discussion here all examples where the abstract noun does not have a modal significance and the syntax of a sentence operator but represents the nominalization of an underlying kernel (as in τοι ... ἄχος ἔσσεται "You will grieve", and other examples cited by Hermann, p. 273). These constructions belong in Chapter VI §§15–16, under existential Type V.

an abstract noun, if it ever was one. In classical usage χρή is assimilated to a third person (impersonal) present indicative verb form, with a corresponding infinitive (χρῆναι), a future tense (χρῆσται), an imperfect (χρῆν or ἐχρῆν), and oblique moods.[37] The form of the endings shows that although χρή never actually co-occurs with ἐστί the latter was – in the fifth century at any rate – clearly "understood" as part of the underlying structure of sentences of this type.[38]

§11. COPULA WITH PRONOUNS AS PREDICATE

The use of εἰμί with pronouns as predicate raises a number of special problems concerning the theory of pronouns which will be briefly mentioned here. I shall also illustrate the pre-philosophic use of one particular sentence type that plays a major role in the philosophic career of the verb *be*: the interrogative form τίς (τί) ἐστι; *Who (what) is it?*

The forms traditionally described as pronouns can be divided into two syntactic groups: those which behave like nouns and those which behave like adjectives, i.e. those which normally appear as subject or object of a verb and those which normally appear as predicate or attribute for another nominal form. This latter group of adjectival pronouns (οἷος, τοῖος, ποῖος; ὅσος, τόσος, πόσος; τοιοῦτος) will not be discussed here. They are essentially correlative (comparative) or interrogative variants on ordinary adjectives of quality or quantity, and their use as predicates with εἰμί presupposes or implies a *N is A* sentence with the appropriate adjective. (For example, τοῖός ἐστι presupposes a sentence like ἄριστός ἐστι or κακός ἐστι, ὅσοι εἰσί presupposes πολλοί εἰσι, etc.) Nor will I discuss the possessive pronouns ἐμός, σός, etc., which are better described as adjectives. The cases of special interest for the verb *be* are the substantival pronouns, the pro-nouns in the strict sense, which can normally stand as subject of this or any other verb.

Pronouns in this narrow sense include personal pronouns (ἐγώ, σύ, etc.), demonstratives (ὅδε, οὗτος, ἐκεῖνος), and the interrogative τίς. Personal pronouns occur rather rarely in predicate position, as in English *It is I* or *The one I am looking for is you*. The corresponding sentence pattern is perhaps even rarer in Greek, and when it does occur, we can usually derive the sentence from a form with the pronoun as subject.

---

[37] For the details, see G. Redard, *Recherches sur ΧΡΗ, ΧΡΗΣΘΑΙ* (Paris, 1953), p. 48n.
[38] The sentence type *N* is N* with sentential subject and abstract noun as predicate does not disappear from classical prose. For the important post-Homeric development of ἔργον ἐστί+*infinitive* "It is (hard) work to do so" and ἔργον+*genitive*+ἐστι "It is the task of someone (to do so)", see LSJ s.v. ἔργον IV.1.

51 Sophocles *Ajax* 1157

> ὁρῶ δέ τοί νιν, κἄστιν, ὡς ἐμοὶ δοκεῖ,
> οὐδείς ποτ' ἄλλος ἢ σύ

> "I see him (sc. the man I have just described), and, it seems,
> he is no other than you."

Here we have, implicitly at least, a sentence of the form *The man I mentioned
is you*. But it is easy to see that we could derive this as an emphatic or
expressive transform of the more banal source: *You are the one I mentioned*.

In the case of first and second person pronouns, the difference between
subject and predicate syntax is marked, in English as in Greek, by the
personal ending of the verb. In the third person, however, the verb ending
gives no clue. In English the word order alone may suffice to establish the
distinction (except in interrogative sentences like *Who is the tallest boy in
the room?*), but this will not work for Greek. We generally suppose that the
article, when it occurs, picks out the subject term, but this is not always a
reliable guide, particularly not when the other term is a demonstrative
pronoun. And in the nominative form (which is what interests us here) the
third person pronoun exists in Greek only as a demonstrative. For this case,
where a demonstrative occurs in what might be regarded as predicate position, we may seriously doubt whether the syntactic distinction between
subject and predicate can be meaningfully drawn. [39]

52 Sophocles, *O.C.* 644

> εἴ μοι θέμις γ' ἦν. ἀλλ' ὁ χῶρός ἐσθ' ὅδε

> "(I would come to your palace) if it were permitted me.
> But the place for me is here" (literally, "is this").

53 Soph. *Electra* 1177

> Or. ἦ σὸν τὸ κλεινὸν εἶδος Ἠλέκτρας τόδε;
> El. τόδ' ἔστ' ἐκεῖνο

> "Is this (person) before me the famous form of Electra?"
> "This it is".

In examples **52** and **53** ὅδε (τόδε) serves for deictic identification of what
is immediately before the speaker and hearer and might be pointed at with
a gesture of the hand. (By contrast ἐκεῖνο in **53** signifies the girl Electra
as she has been heard of by Orestes, as κλεινὸν εἶδος. So the phrase ὁ χῶρος

---

[39] My examples here are taken from Guiraud, *La phrase nominale en grec*, pp. 142f.
For the ambiguity between subject and predicate in such sentences, see my remark in
Chapter II, pp. 39f.

in **52** indicates Colonos as the place known to Oedipus in advance, from the oracle.) We may call this situational deixis, since it depends upon the extra-linguistic environment of the speaker-hearer situation. The next example shows the use of the demonstratives for contextual deixis, where a relation is established to the preceding or following discourse. (For the distinction between speech situation and context, see Chapter III §5.)

54 Herodotus III.108.4

τὸ δὲ αἴτιον τούτου τόδε ἐστί

"The cause of this (namely, of the supposed fact that a lioness rejects her womb with her first cub) is as follows."

In **54** τούτου refers back to the preceding statement; τόδε refers forward to the coming explanation.

The special interest of **51–54** lies in the fact that ἐστί in such sentences represents the "is" of identity. This fact results here from the very character of deictic words, whose function it is to identify their reference uniquely (like first and second person pronouns). Hence demonstratives normally occur in subject (or object) position, where the identifying-referring function is normal. The cases where the demonstrative or personal pronoun appears in predicate position are just the cases where the identification of the subject has already been made by some other expression in the context. It is because the same subject is thus identified or uniquely referred to twice that the copula in such sentences has the logical value of an expression of identity. And since we have in effect two referring expressions with ἐστί, the distinction between subject and predicate of the copula has no logical significance here and perhaps no syntactical significance either, at least not in the third person. (As we have seen, the subject status of a first or second person pronoun is grammatically marked by agreement in the verb-ending.) What we do have in such cases is a psychological or rhetorical distinction between the "topic" and the "comment", between the term which is already familiar or expected and the new term which is only now discovered or announced. In **52–54** the deictic form ὅδε serves precisely as this novel term or comment. And it is perhaps only in this sense – namely as rhetorical *comment* – that demonstrative pronouns can be said to occur in predicative position. (For more remarks on the tenuous nature of the subject-predicate distinction for two nominal terms with the same extension, see the discussion of the articular participle below in §18.)

For a similar reason – namely, because it represents the new or unknown term – we may perhaps consider τίς the predicate in a question of the form *Who is he?* From a grammatical point of view the τίς ἐστι question could be properly studied only in the framework of a general analysis of interrogative forms. My motive for describing it here has to do not with syntax but with the history of ideas, and with the decisive role played by a question of the same form in the philosophical articulation of Greek concepts of Being. Plato's designation of the Forms as αὐτὸ τὸ ὃ ἔστι and Aristotle's designation of essence as τὸ τί ἐστι or τὸ τί ἦν εἶναι both reflect the Socratic question τί ἐστι which directs the search for a definition of courage, piety, or knowledge. The definitional answer that is sought for will be a statement of identity of a special type, and it will typically have the syntactic form of an N *is* N sentence.[40] Hence it will be interesting to note here, if only by way of contrast, the use and scope of questions of this form in Homer and in later non-philosophical literature, where this constitutes one of the characteristic uses of the verb εἰμί.

The typical sentence forms divide into two groups, which I label *questions of personal identity* and *interrogations of surprise and concern*.

§12. τίς ἐστι (GROUP 1): QUESTIONS OF PERSONAL IDENTITY

There is a well-defined set of literary formulae in Homer for dealing with an important typical situation, the meeting and recognition of strangers – a situation which in daily life seems to have been treated as a formalized moment in the socio-ritual institution of guest-friendship (ξενία). In this situation the question is naturally put in the second person: *Who are you?* The striking fact about the use of this question in the epic is that it is not interpreted primarily as a request for a proper name.

Take the famous episode in which Diomedes and Glaucus face one another and refuse combat when they discover that they are ancestral guest-friends (ξεῖνοι πατρώϊοι, *Il.* 6.231). Diomedes asks:

55 *Il.* 6.123

τίς δὲ σύ ἐσσι, φέριστε, καταϑνητῶν ἀνϑρώπων;

"Who among mortal men are you, good friend?"

(Lattimore)

Glaucus takes this to be a question concerning his family origins (τίη γενεὴν ἐρεείνεις 6.145) and answers with a genealogy in good form, mentioning the city of his ancestors (Ephyre in Argos) and the region in which his family is currently established (Lycia), and summarizing as follows:

---

[40] Except when the subject is expressed as a substantivized adjective. So the predicate too may be expressed in adjectival or participial form. For some typical examples of the τί ἐστι question in Plato, see n. 30 above, p.110.

56 *Il.* 6.211

> ταύτης τοι γενεῆς τε καὶ αἵματος εὔχομαι εἶναι

> "Such is my generation and the blood I claim to be born from."

> (Lattimore)

Personal identity is defined here exclusively in terms of family and local origin: Glaucus does not mention his own name, but only that of his forbears! Hence the τίς ἐστι question is answered not by a straight-forward nominal copula but by a predicative genitive in **56** and by a para-locative use of the genitive with ἐκ (6.206: Ἱππόλοχος δέ μ' ἔτικτε, καὶ ἐκ τοῦ φημι γενέσθαι). For these forms of the copula see below, §§24 and 26.

The pattern of **55–56** is a typical one, which recurs again and again. Thus when Achilles encounters Asteropaios son of Pelegon (*Il.* 21.140ff.) he asks

57 *Il.* 21.150

> τίς πόθεν εἰς ἀνδρῶν;

> "What man are you, and whence?"

> (Lattimore)

The doomed warrior answers by specifying his native land (εἴμ' ἐκ Παιονίης ἐριβώλου), his social and military role (Παίονας ἄνδρας ἄγων), the origin of his family from the river Axios (αὐτὰρ ἐμοὶ γενεὴ ἐξ Ἀξιοῦ εὐρὺ ῥέοντος) and his father's name (21.154–160). But the Paeonian hero dies without disclosing his own name, and Achilles boasts over the corpse by contrasting his descent from Zeus with his opponent's genealogy from the river (21.184ff.). Similarly, when Priam on his way to Achilles meets Hermes in disguise, he asks:

58 *Il.* 24.387

> τίς δὲ σύ ἐσσι, φέριστε, τέων δ' ἔξ ἐσσι τοκήων;

> "But who are you, good friend, and from what parents are you?"

Hermes' answer specifies a local group (Μυρμιδόνων δ' ἔξ εἰμι) and a fictitious family background (πατὴρ δέ μοί ἐστι Πολύκτωρ), but he does not bother to mention an assumed name.

Of course the same type of question may be answered by a personal name in the case of a god, whose genealogy and distinctive status are matters of common knowledge. Thus Apollo answers the *who are you?* question by giving simply his name and ritual title: Phoebus Apollo of the golden sword (*Il.* 15.256). But the personal name comes with special emphasis in Odysseus' self-disclosure to the Phaeacians:

59 *Od.* 9.19

εἴμ' Ὀδυσεὺς Λαερτιάδης, ὃς πᾶσι δόλοισιν
ἀνθρώποισι μέλω, καί μευ κλέος οὐρανὸν ἵκει.
ναιετάω δ' Ἰθάκην εὐδείελον

"I am Odysseus, son of Laertes, who for all craft am noted
among men, and my renown reaches to heaven. I live in Ithaca,
a land far seen."

(Palmer)

The patronymic and the local origin are here overshadowed by the fame of
the hero's own name; and curiosity concerning his name was at the center
of Alcinoos' query.[41] Recognition scenes and question of identity run
through the *Odyssey* like a *leitmotif*, from the visit of Athena disguised as
Mentes in the first book to the final and most moving recognition of all, when
Odysseus meets his father in Book 24 (compare verse 1.170 with 24.298).
But the pattern is generally the same as in the *Iliad*.[42] In the Homeric poems,
questions of personal identity are primarily questions of paternity and
genealogy, of local and social origins.

In classical times, and above all with the rise of the democratic polis, the
individual name assumes greater importance. The paradigm is Themistocles
whose own name was so much better known than that of his father. (See
Herodotus VII.143.1). It was presumably not his patronymic which
Themistocles in flight pronounced to inform his host or shipmaster *who he
was* (Thucydides I.136.4 δηλοῖ τε ὅς ἐστι; I.137.2 φράζει τῷ ναυκλήρῳ
ὅστις ἐστὶ καὶ δι᾽ ἃ φεύγει). The Sophists, as early cosmopolitans, are
regularly identified by name and city only: "Is there someone who is an
expert in virtue?" asks Socrates of Callias; "Who is he and where from and
how much does he charge?" "Euenus the Parian", he answered, "five mina."
(Plato *Apology* 20B τίς (ἐστι), ἦν δ᾽ ἐγώ, καὶ ποδαπός, καὶ πόσου διδάσκει;
Εὔηνος, ἔφη, ὦ Σώκρατες, Πάριος, πέντε μνῶν.) In Athens after Cleisthenes
the citizen was to be officially identified by proper name and deme, not by

---

41 See *Od.* 8.550ff.

εἴπ᾽ ὄνομ᾽ ὅττι σε κεῖθι κάλεον μήτηρ τε πατήρ τε
.../οὐ μὲν γάρ τις πάμπαν ἀνώνυμός ἐστ᾽ ἀνθρώπων
.../ἀλλ᾽ ἐπὶ πᾶσι τίθενται, ἐπεί κε τέκωσι, τοκῆες.

So Odysseus begins his response with the name νῦν δ᾽ ὄνομα πρῶτον μυθήσομαι (9.16).
42 See also *Od.* 10.325, 14.187, 15.264, and 19.105, where we have the same formula as
in 1.170 and 24.298: τίς πόθεν εἰς ἀνδρῶν; πόθι τοι πόλις ἠδὲ τοκῆες. Note that this full
form underlies Glaucus' answer to Diomedes' briefer question in **55** above. For other
variants in the *Odyssey*, see 3.71(= 9.252), 4.61, 4.138, 7.17, 7.238, 10.110, 15.423, 16.57,
17.368, 19.162. The proper name is perhaps more conspicuous in the responses here than
in the *Iliad* (see *Od.* 1.180 and 24.306), but it may still be omitted (14.199–204, 15.267,
16.425ff.).

patronymic.[43] But as we can see from Plato's dialogues, the personal identity in good Attic society was often established first of all by reference to the name of the father. Thus in the introduction of the title figure in the *Theaetetus*, Theodorus asks "Look whether you know him." "I know him," says Socrates; "he is the son of Euphronius of Sunium .... But I do not know the boy's name" (144C γιγνώσκω· ὁ τοῦ Σουνιῶς Εὐφρονίου ἐστίν .... τὸ δ᾽ ὄνομα οὐκ οἶδα τοῦ μειρακίου).

§13. τί ἐστι (GROUP 2): INTERROGATIONS OF SURPRISE OR CONCERN. THE BACKGROUND OF THE SOCRATIC QUESTION τί ἐστι

The questions of personal identity discussed in the last section are only a special case, even if a privileged one, of the interrogative form τίς ἐστι. The pronoun τίς can be used in agreement with a noun to ask *What place is this? What people?* (τίς γῆ, τίς δῆμος; *Od.* 13.233), *What would your plan or thought be?* (τίς ἂν δή τοι νόος εἴη; *Il.* 24.367), and so forth. And the neuter form can be used to query the identity of things unknown, such as the contents of the bag which Aiolus gave to Odysseus:

60 *Od.* 10.44

> ἀλλ᾽ ἄγε θᾶσσον ἰδώμεθα ὅττι τάδ᾽ ἐστίν,
> ὅσσος τις χρυσός τε καὶ ἄργυρος ἀσκῷ ἔνεστιν
> "Come, then, and let us quickly see what there is here,
> and how much gold and silver the sack holds."

> (Palmer)

In classical usage this generalized neuter interrogation takes an idiomatic turn which expresses not only curiosity but amazement and concern, as in Neoptolemus' response to Philoctetes' repeated cries of pain.

61 Sophocles *Philoctetes*

> 733 and 753 τί ἔστιν; "What's the matter?"
> 751 τί δ᾽ ἔστιν οὕτω νεοχμὸν ἐξαίφνης;
> "What's this, so strange and sudden?"

Or in a comic vein, in the face of an absurd spectacle:

62 Aristophanes *Acharnians* 156f.

> τουτὶ τί ἐστι τὸ κακόν;
> ...εἰπέ μοι τουτὶ τί ἦν;
> "What is this horror? .... Tell me what it means."

> *ibid.* 767

> τουτὶ τί ἦν τὸ πρᾶγμα;
> "What in the world is this?"

---

[43] Arist. *Ath. Pol.* 21.4.

Approximately the same form may serve more prosaically as a request for genuine information, as in Xenophon when scouts are sent to discover *what the situation is* beyond a hill to which the enemy has retreated. (*Anabasis* I.10.14 κελεύει κατιδόντας τὰ ὑπὲρ τοῦ λόφου τί ἐστιν ἀπαγγεῖλαι; compare II.1.22 τί οὖν ταῦτά ἐστιν; "What does this mean?" in reference to the noncommittal statement καὶ ἡμῖν ταῦτα δοκεῖ ἅπερ καὶ βασιλεῖ "Our view is the same as the King's.")

These banal or idiomatic uses of the τί ἐστι question bear only the most superficial resemblance to Socrates' request for definitions. There is, however, a more philosophical use of the question which is attested before Plato's dialogues.

63 Aristophanes *Clouds* 250
> βούλει τὰ θεῖα πράγματ' εἰδέναι σαφῶς
> ἅττ' ἐστὶν ὀρθῶς;
> "Do you wish to know divine matters precisely,
> What they truly are?"

In Aristophanes this question is the prelude not to a search for definitions but to a lecture on meteorology, and in this respect the poet is faithful to the major trends in early Greek natural philosophy. By the nature of the concepts under interrogation, and above all by the criteria used to test the response, the Socratic question as posed in Plato's dialogues represents something new in the history of Western thought. The remains of early Greek philosophical and Sophistic literature, from Heraclitus to the Hippocratic Corpus, do show a certain concern for conceptual definition as part of the investigation of the nature of things, and the verb *be* occasionally appears in this connection.[44] But the earlier investigation is dominated by an almost Homeric interest in the genetic background and origins of the item to be identified. The question as to *what X really is* is only gradually – and perhaps first by Socrates – distinguished from the question *how X originated, where it comes from*. The story of this intellectual innovation lies beyond the scope of the study of εἰμί undertaken here. I have cited the extra-philosophical examples of the τί ἐστι question only to show how certain current uses of the nominal copula provided the linguistic form for the Socratic interrogation, and to suggest how remote these uses are from the question which interested the philosophers from Socrates to Aristotle. The structure of the

---

[44] See for example Xenophanes fr. 29 γῆ καὶ ὕδωρ πάντ' ἐσθ' ὅσα γίνοντ(αι) ἠδὲ φύονται. A closer approximation to Socratic concerns may be seen in the definitions (with omitted ἐστί) assigned to Heraclitus as fragment 112: σωφρονεῖν ἀρετὴ μεγίστη, καὶ σοφίη ἀληθέα λέγειν καὶ ποιεῖν κατὰ φύσιν ἐπαΐοντας. Compare the remarks on "speculative predication" in Alexander P. D. Mourelatos, *The Route of Parmenides* (New Haven, 1970), pp. 57–61.

Greek language made possible the formulation of that question, with its multiple resonance with other uses of the verb, both veridical ("What a thing *truly* is," "what it is essentially"), and existential ("What is real, substantial, permanent, in any thing"). But the philosophical question itself is the work of one or two individual thinkers, not a product of the impersonal genius of the language.

§14. The periphrastic construction, with εἰμί as "auxiliary verb" and a participle as predicate: a syntactic definition of periphrasis

Having discussed the copula construction *N is Φ* for cases where the predicate *Φ* is an adjective or a noun and for a few cases where it is a pronoun, we come to the third major division, where the predicate is a participle. This is essentially the problem of the periphrastic construction, or the use of εἰμί as an auxiliary verb. At first sight it might seem that copula construction with participles is a wider phenomenon than periphrasis, and that we must distinguish between periphrastic and non-periphrastic uses of *N is Φ* for participial *Φ*. I shall argue, however, that the two phenomena should be regarded as identical, that periphrasis is best defined in purely syntactic terms, and that when it is so defined it coincides exactly with the copula construction for participles.

Before treating the problem I might call attention to the particular philosophical interest of this use. Since every verb has participial forms, every verb may (in theory, at least) provide periphrastic constructions with *be*. As a result, the verb *be* is, with the appropriate participle, in a position to replace every finite verb form in the language, and it is theoretically possible to transform every sentence into one that contains no finite verb except *be*. Hence the importance of the periphrastic construction for philosophical theories of *be* as the one universal or indispensable verb, from Aristotle to the present day.[45]

The periphrastic construction in Greek has been much studied by philologists in recent years, with curious results. On the one hand, there seems to be general agreement as to what is meant by a periphrastic construction of *be +participle*: English provides typical examples in *He is working, He is gone for the day*. On the other hand, a wide area of disagreement opens up as soon as we turn to specific cases in Greek. An example that is clearly periphrastic according to one interpreter is unrecognizable as such for the

---

[45] The relevant passages in Aristotle and the Port Royal *Logic* are cited above, Chapter I, n. 13 and below, Chapter V, n. 45.

next student of the subject.[46] Now we would in any case expect to find a zone of borderline cases on which opinions will differ; but in this instance the disagreement is so pervasive that even the existence of a solid core of clear cases is not beyond doubt. It seems that the general agreement as to what constitutes a periphrastic construction is only apparent, and that a more precise definition is required before the controversy over particular cases can be at all profitable.[47]

Let us follow Aerts in identifying the periphrastic construction with the use of εἰμί (and he includes ἔχω as well) as auxiliary verb. Like most of his predecessors, Aerts hesitates between two characterizations, one of them lexico-semantic and stylistic, the other properly syntactical:

(1) As auxiliary verbs, "*to have* and *to be* are used in an improper and weakened sense" (*Periphrastica*, p. 2). "Periphrasis is unlikely ... when the position of εἶναι ... suggests emphasis" (*ibid.* p. 12).

(2) Strictly speaking, "the terms periphrasis or periphrastic are only used when εἶναι or ἔχειν together with a participle express an elementary verbal conception, e.g. Koine ἦν διδάσκων = ἐδίδασκεν" (p. 2).

I suggest that, like the copula construction itself, periphrasis should be defined in purely syntactic terms without reference to the meaning of the verb, so that just as we admit the possibility of a copula construction with existential or possessive force, so we must accept the fact that in some periphrastic uses the verb is strong and emphatic.

I propose a syntactic definition of the following sort: the occurrence of εἰμί +*participle* in a given sentence is periphrastic whenever there is only one kernel sentence underlying both forms in the transformational source of the given sentence. In most cases this obviously coincides with Aerts' criterion of an "elementary verbal conception" or monolectic verb form, as when ἦν διδάσκων is derived from ἐδίδασκε, or *I am teaching* from *I teach*.[48] Discrepancies will arise above all in the case of so-called adjectivized participles, which will nearly always be periphrastic on my criterion, e.g.

[46] See the many points at which W. J. Aerts, in the latest and most comprehensive treatment of the subject (*Periphrastica*, Amsterdam, 1955), reverses the judgment of his predecessors on a given text; e.g. p. 31, where he says he must answer Björk's *Gewalt* with *Gewalt* in settling an old controversy over the construal of Thucydides IV.15.3. There are further dissents in K. J. Dover's review of Aerts in *Gnomon* 40 (1968), 87f. I myself am often inclined to reverse Aerts' judgment on the periphrastic character of a given text, and not only in those cases where he is disagreeing with some earlier interpreter.
[47] K. J. Dover replies (in a letter) that he believes there is a solid core of clear cases among Aerts' examples. If so, it must be my aim to capture these by my definition. In order to do so in a rational and coherent way, however, we will be obliged to include other cases which might not generally be regarded as periphrastic.
[48] So also in Dover's illustrative example, *Gnomon* 1968, p. 87: *Where John was baptizing* versus *Where John was, baptizing*. Since the latter is derived from two kernels (*John was there* and *John baptized*), it is non-periphrastic on my criterion.

ἀρέσκων ἐστί "He is pleasing (to someone)." Since here there is only one kernel for copula and participle (namely ἀρέσκει "He pleases"), we have a case of periphrasis.[49] It is another question whether ἀρέσκων ἐστί is strictly equivalent in meaning to its monolectic source ἀρέσκει. But this is not a question which we can easily answer, nor should we have to answer it in order to define periphrasis. Both morphologically and transformationally it is clear that every participle can be derived from a finite verb form (or from its stem), and in this sense we can say that a construction of ἐστί +*participle* is *always* formally and syntactically equivalent to a monolectic verb form.

It does not follow from my definition that every sentence containing both a copula use of εἰμί and a participial form in agreement with the subject of the copula will constitute an instance of periphrasis, since in many cases the copula and the participle are derived from distinct kernels. This is more easily seen if we begin with examples that do not involve the verb *be*.

64 *Il.* 11.612

> ὅν τινα τοῦτον ἄγει βεβλημένον ἐκ πολέμοιο
> "(Ask Nestor) who is this man he brings in wounded from the fighting."

(after Lattimore)

There is no suspicion of periphrasis here: βεβλημένον represents the typical participial transformation by which one sentence is reshaped for insertion into another. We have two distinct kernels: *Nestor carries this man from the battle* and *This man is wounded* (βέβληται). Let us call the kernel corresponding to the finite verb, i.e. to ἄγει in **64**, the "primary kernel", and use the term "secondary kernel" for the sentence underlying the participle βεβλημένον.[50]

We come closer to the phenomenon of an auxiliary verb in a much-discussed example with ἔχει.

65 *Il.* 1.356(=507, etc.)

> ἑλὼν γὰρ ἔχει γέρας, αὐτὸς ἀπούρας
> "(Agamemnon) has taken away my prize and keeps it."

(Lattimore)

"It is quite clear, and no one has ever challenged this, that ἔχει has an

---

[49] For this example, see **79** below. Contrast **69** where ἦν ... ἀρεσκόμενος is non-periphrastic, since ἦν represents a distinct kernel.
[50] For an equally clear case of non-periphrastic construction with εἰμί consider this sentence from the opening of the *Odyssey* (1.11): ἔνθ' ἄλλοι μὲν πάντες .../οἴκοι ἔσαν, πόλεμόν τε πεφευγότες ἠδὲ θάλασσαν. As the comma suggests, the participle πεφευγότες represents a conjoined sentence (*The others had escaped the battle and the sea*) which is distinct from the sentence with οἴκοι ἔσαν (*they were at home*).

independent meaning here and it is not an auxiliary to ἑλών."[51] How can we account for the unanimity in this case, when the criterion of "independent meaning" so often leads to divergent judgments? The solution is to replace *independent meaning* with *independent syntactic origin*, i.e. with my criterion of distinct kernels. A construction like **65** is felt to be non-periphrastic just because it is so obviously derived from the conjunction of two distinct sentences: *He has taken my prize* and *He keeps it*. These two kernels are tightly bound together in the resulting transform, where they share both subject and object. But the judgment that we have two distinct sentences here, corresponding to ἔχει and to the participle, is one on which all readers can agree.[52]

The tightness or looseness of the fusion of kernels in a sentence like **65** has no bearing on the non-periphrastic character of the result; nor does the latter depend upon the fact that the monolectic verb form ᾕρηκεν "He has seized it," was probably not available to Homer. This form occurs in the fifth century, yet the Homeric formula ἑλὼν ἔχει continues to be echoed by non-periphrastic phrases such as λαβὼν ἔχει.

66 Sophocles *Philoctetes* 1234

αἰσχρῶς γὰρ αὐτὰ κοὐ δίκῃ λαβὼν ἔχω

"I have and took (his bow) shamefully, unjustly"

Aerts (p. 137) speaks here of "a clearly periphrastic impression"; but impressions differ, and syntax is a better guide. *I hold (possess) his bow* is surely a kernel for **66**; i.e. it accounts for both the form and meaning of αὐτὰ ... ἔχω. And syntactically this is the *primary* kernel since it underlies

---

[51] Aerts, *Periphrastica*, p. 128.

[52] Strictly speaking, we have three kernels, since the participle ἀπούρας in **65** has essentially the same syntax as ἑλών, sharing both subject and object with ἔχει: There is a rhetorical difference, however, in that ἀπούρας is added as a kind of insistent after-thought, reinforced with its own subject expression in the intensive pronoun αὐτός; its separate status is indicated in the Oxford text by a comma. Notice that the occurrence of a comma or a normal pause between finite verb and participle will perhaps always show that the construction is non-periphrastic, but *not conversely*. We cannot put a comma between ἑλών and ἔχει in **65**.

My syntactic definition of periphrasis is compatible with Benveniste's study of the *have*-periphrasis in Hittite and in early Latin (*Hittite et Indo-Européen* (Paris, 1962), ch. III). Benveniste formulates three criteria to distinguish Hittite *hark-* as auxiliary verb from its use as "verbe autonome": (1) the independent verb has the lexical value *tenir* ("hold," "keep") whereas the auxiliary has the value *avoir* ("have"); (2) the tense of *hark-* alone determines that of the sentence in the independent case, whereas the *auxiliary + participle* together form a compound perfect tense, and (3) when *hark-* is independent, the participle is a "membre d'un syntagme prédicatif," i.e. it represents a distinct (secondary) kernel. Criteria (1) and (2) also follow from the fact that in the non-periphrastic construction it is the finite form of *hark-* which constitutes the elementary verb form in the primary kernel of the sentence.

the finite verb. The impression of a periphrastic construction, reinforced by Jebb's translation "I have gotten it basely and without right," is due to the syntactically irrelevant (but rhetorically essential) fact that the injustice of Philoctetes' possession of the bow is due precisely to the deceit by which it was obtained.

Truly periphrastic uses of ἔχω, in which the verb does not plausibly figure in one of the kernels in the underlying structure of the sentence, are much rarer in Greek than Aerts' discussion would lead one to believe. But the following may count as a clear case:

67 Euripides *Hippolytus* 932 (cited Aerts p. 143)

ἀλλ᾽ ἦ τις ἐς σὸν οὖς με διαβαλὼν ἔχει / φίλων

"Has one of your friends slandered me in your hearing?"

An underlying sentence of the form τις μὲ ἔχει; "Does someone possess (hold, control) me?" seems to play no part in the structure of **67**.

It would take us too far afield to consider further examples of ἔχω +*participle*. Judgments will naturally differ on particular texts, but at least such disagreements can be sharply formulated on the basis of my syntactical definition: ἔχω +*participle* is periphrastic in a given sentence if and only if there is in the transformational decomposition of that sentence no kernel with ἔχω distinct from the kernel for the participle. This definition cannot produce mechanical agreement, since the kernels which a reader is willing to recognize in transformational decomposition will depend upon his understanding of the sentence in the first place. What makes it plausible to pose a given kernel is just that it seems to contribute something to the meaning, and not only to the form, of the sentence under analysis. However, if my syntactical formulation of the problem is substituted for the vaguer notions of independent meaning (or "independent concept"), strong and weak sense, emphatic position and the like, I believe that the area of disagreement as to cases will be substantially reduced.

§15. Application of the definition to εἰμί +*participle*

The definition just formulated applies without any further change when εἰμί is substituted for ἔχω. I first consider some examples which are clearly non-periphrastic, in order to show that my definition does in fact specify that and why a given use is non-periphrastic. I shall then illustrate typical periphrastic constructions, and finally (§§16–17) discuss some problematic cases.

1. *Non-periphrastic Examples of Copula + Participle*

68 *Il.* 5.177 (Aerts p. 14)

εἰ μή τις θεός ἐστι κοτεσσάμενος Τρώεσσιν

"(Shoot at him,) unless this be some god enraged against the Trojans".

We clearly have two kernels: *This enemy is some god* and *He is enraged (κοτέσσεται) against the Trojans.*

69 Hdt. I.8.1 (Aerts, p. 10)

ἦν γάρ οἱ τῶν αἰχμοφόρων Γύγης ὁ Δασκύλου ἀρεσκόμενος μάλιστα

Here the two kernels are correctly given by Aerts in the course of his analysis: "He had in his bodyguard (a certain) Gyges. That man pleased him very well." Note that the use of ἦν in the primary kernel is existential-possessive, but of course this is not a necessary condition for the construction to be non-periphrastic. (We shall later see that it is not even a sufficient condition.) In **68** above the primary kernel has ἐστί as copula with a predicate noun; in **70** below the verb is a locative copula.

70 Xen. *Anabasis* 1.2.21 (Aerts p. 8)

ἐλέγετο δὲ καὶ Συέννεσις εἶναι ἐπὶ τῶν ἄκρων φυλάττων τὴν εἰσβολήν

"Syennesis was said to be on the heights, guarding the pass."

The comma in the translation indicates the division of the two kernels.

71 Hdt. VI. 65.2 (Aerts, p. 43)

ὁ δὲ Λευτυχίδης ἦν ἐχθρὸς τῷ Δημαρήτῳ μάλιστα γεγονὼς διὰ πρῆγμα τοιόνδε

Here we have a case of maximum fusion between two copula kernels, an identity of subject and predicate which is comparable to the identity of subject and object for ἔχω in **65** and **66**: *Leutychides was (ἦν) enemy of Demaretos* and *He became (γεγονώς) enemy of Demaretos above all because of the following incident.*

2. *Periphrastic Construction of Copula + Participle*

Periphrasis with the perfect participles is the oldest form and the only one unquestionably attested in Homer.

72 *Il.* 1.388

ἠπείλησεν μῦθον, ὁ δὴ τετελεσμένος ἐστί

"He uttered his threat, and now it is accomplished."

(after Lattimore)

Here the conjunction of ἐστί with the participle is formally equivalent to τελεῖται or ἐτελείετο except for the variation of tense and aspect. (For the same formula in the future with ἔσται, see *Il.* 1.212, 2.257, etc.) This may serve as a paradigm case of what I call "unitary periphrasis", where the construction εἰμί+*participle* serves as a single compound verb form, comparable in sense and syntax to monolectic forms of the underlying verb (in this case τελέω). I contrast this with "copulative periphrasis", where the surface syntax of *copula*+*participle* is analogous to that of *copula*+*adjective* (or, more rarely, to *copula*+*noun*). See below, §16.

Notice that the periphrasis with perfect middle participle in **72** is in effect passive, but this need not be the case.

73 *Il.* 6.488

μοῖραν δ᾽ οὔ τινά φημι πεφυγμένον ἔμμεναι ἀνδρῶν
"I say that no man has escaped his fate."

Here the participle is syntactically transitive, with μοῖραν as its direct object· Nevertheless, we do not have a *strong* transitive or "resultative" in Chantraine's sense, where the verb expresses "le resultat qui porte sur l'objet." [53] The typical use of the perfect in early Greek is to express the "fixation of a result or situation" which concerns the subject only or primarily, rather than a strongly transitive action affecting an external object.[54] The same value characterizes the perfect active participle in Homer.

74 *Il.* 5.873

αἰεί τοι ῥίγιστα θεοὶ τετληότες εἰμὲν / ἀλλήλων ἰότητι
"We gods have always to endure the most horrible hurts, by one another's hatred"

(after Lattimore)

The periphrasis here is again unitary, constituting an almost passive aspectual variant on the monolectic form τετλήκαμεν. (The latter might tend to have the more active or dynamic sense: "we have dared to, have had the boldness to *do* something". Compare *Il.* 1.227 οὔτε λόχονδ᾽ ἰέναι σὺν ἀριστήεσσιν Ἀχαιῶν/τέτληκας θυμῷ. Similarly in *Il.* 1.543. In *Od.* 19.347, however, the same stem is used with a passive sense: τέτληκε τόσα φρεσίν.) The inert or passive aspect of the perfect participles in Homer is naturally reinforced in periphrasis by what we may call the *static* value of the verb εἰμί, a value which we will discuss further in the next chapter. The transitive construction in **73** above may serve almost as the exception which proves the rule con-

---

[53] *Grammaire homérique* II, 199.
[54] For this characterization of the perfect, see Aerts, pp. 13ff. and 36ff., following Chantraine.

cerning the non-transitive or non-resultative character of the perfect. The participle πεφυγμένος is middle, i.e. typically intransitive; and the man who *fails* to escape his fate is in effect passive, not active, with regard to μοῖρα.[55] I cite one post-Homeric example to illustrate the development of the resultative perfect, i.e. of a periphrasis which is transitive not only in form but also in sense.

75 Hdt. IX. 115

Οἰόβαζος ἀνὴρ Πέρσης, ὃς τὰ ἐκ τῶν γεφυρέων ὅπλα ἐνθαῦτα ἦν κεκομικώς

"The Persian Oiobazus, who had brought the ropes there (to Sestus) from the bridge (on the Hellespont)."

§16. COPULATIVE PERIPHRASIS, WITH "ADJECTIVAL" PARTICIPLE

In **72–75** we have examples of unitary periphrasis, with little or no assimilation of the participle to an adjective. The following three cases **76–78** illustrate a tendency to what I call *copulative periphrasis*, where there is a surface analogy with an *N is A* sentence type rather than with an ordinary verbal (*NV*) form.

76 *Od.* 2.230 (=5.8; cf. 5.182) (Aerts, p. 13. n. 1).

μή τις ἔτι πρόφρων ἀγανὸς καὶ ἤπιος ἔστω
σκηπτοῦχος βασιλεύς, μηδὲ φρεσὶν αἴσιμα εἰδώς,
ἀλλ᾽ αἰεὶ χαλεπός τ᾽ εἴη καὶ αἴσυλα ῥέζοι

"Never again let sceptered king in all sincerity be kind and gentle, nor let him in his mind heed righteousness. Let him instead ever be stern, and work unrighteous deeds."

(Palmer)

There is here a syntactical parallel between the perfect participle (αἴσιμα) εἰδώς and the three adjectives (πρόφρων, ἀγανός, ἤπιος), which are construed with the same copula form (ἔστω) in the first verse of the quotation – a parallel which is underscored by the omission of the copula in the second verse. Yet the participial form has not been completely "adjectivized"; its verbal nature (brought out in Palmer's translation "heed righteousness") is utilized in the rhetorical contrast between αἴσιμα εἰδώς (ἔστω) and αἴσυλα ῥέζοι ("let him not think just thoughts but do evil deeds"). We thus have a

---

[55] It is perhaps no accident that Homer, who once uses the active participle πεφευγότες for those who *succeed* in escaping war and sea (*Od.* 1.12, cited above in n. 50), regularly uses the middle form in the negative (in the same context, *Od.* 1.18, in **73** above, in *Od.* 9.455, and in *Il.* 22.219; cf. *Hymn to Aphrodite* 34) for those who do not or cannot escape.

unitary as well as a copulative construction at work: the participle is treated both as a verb and as an adjective. (For the finite verbal form, see περὶ φρεσὶν αἴσιμα ᾔδη in *Od.* 14.433)

77 Sophocles *O.T.* 89f. (Aerts p. 34)

οὔτε γὰρ θρασὺς / οὔτ᾽ οὖν προδείσας εἰμὶ τῷ γε νῦν λόγῳ
"So far, thy words make me neither bold nor yet afraid."

(Jebb)

Here, again we have an unmistakable surface parallel between participle and adjective, so that a single copula form εἰμί serves for both. And yet the periphrasis has not ceased to be an equivalent for the monolectic form προὔδεισα "I shuddered in advance." [56]

78 *Ibid.* 747 (Aerts pp. 18f.)

δεινῶς ἀθυμῶ μὴ βλέπων ὁ μάντις ᾖ
"I fear the prophet may not be blind after all."

Once more the surface analogy with an *N is A* construction is unmistakable: the periphrasis is designed to bring out the contrasting parallel with τυφλὸς εἶναι, as my translation suggests. Literally, however, μὴ βλέπων ᾖ is roughly synonymous with μὴ βλέπῃ "I fear lest *he see* (the truth) after all."

In these cases **76–78** what has been called "adjectival periphrasis" is not an alternative but a complement to the monolectic construal of *copula + participle*. Copulative periphrasis is not a distinct construction but an added dimension of stylistic or expressive meaning made possible by an ambiguity in the surface syntax, a certain fluctuation between the *N is A* and the *NV* interpretation of periphrasis. In every case of periphrasis – by definition – *NV* represents the underlying structure, the transformational source. But because of the formal analogies between participles and adjectives, a *copula + participle* construction can always be treated as a parallel to the sentence form *N is A*. How far this possibility is exploited in any particular case will depend upon the author and the context. Since this is essentially a matter of style or rhetoric, it cannot serve as a basis for the grammatical classification of different types of periphrasis.[57]

---

[56] See Aerts' discussion of the value of the aorist here (p. 34), where he compares the use of a finite form ἔκλαυσα in Euripides.

[57] Hence the inevitably arbitrary nature of Aerts' decision in many cases, as to whether or not a given passage is to be interpreted as periphrastic. When this question is posed in syntactical terms, it admits a Yes or No answer (even where opinions will differ as to *which* answer to give), since it asks whether we recognize one or more than one kernel sentence underlying the *copula + participle* construction. But if the question is put in stylistic terms, as to whether the verb ἐστί or ἦν enjoys some "independence" from the participle or whether the latter is "adjectivized," it is a matter not only of degree but also of conflicting rhetorical tendencies within a given sentence, as in **76–78**. Under these circumstances, a Yes or No answer is not even possible *in principle*. It is in the very nature of a powerful

I distinguish, then, *unitary* and *copulative* periphrasis not as distinct kinds of construction but as distinct tendencies within a single construction. Theoretically, both tendencies are potentially present in every case of periphrasis, since the surface structure is copulative (ἐστί + *participle*) whereas the underlying structure or kernel is monolectic (μὴ βλέπων ᾖ ← μὴ βλέπῃ). It may be that there are some cases where, in practice, the copulative construal (which implies an analogy between participle and a predicate adjective or noun) seems simply irrelevant, and we might be tempted to speak of a purely unitary use of periphrasis. The extreme case is the more or less mechanical substitution of *perfect participle* + εἰμί for monolectic forms in the perfect subjunctive and optative and in the middle voice of the third person plural indicative (λελυκὼς ὦ for λελύκω, τεταγμένοι ἦσαν for ἐτετάχατο).[58] From this is derived the modern Greek use of the perfect middle participle in the passive construction: εἶναι γραμμένο *It is written* (where ancient Greek could have γέγραπται as well as γεγραμμένον ἐστί). But whether in any given case we can say that the periphrastic construction is felt as fully equivalent to a unitary verb form is not a question which I know how to answer – not even for *is written* or *was ordered* in English. As long as the two components of periphrasis are recognizably two, we do not have a completely unitary surface structure.

On the other hand, as long as we do have a recognizable participle we have the syntactical derivation from an underlying verb form and thus from a kernel in which ἐστί does not appear: in every case of periphrasis, by definition, the copula is transformationally derived as an aspectual or temporal verb operator on an underlying finite verb. The notion of a participle which is *completely* adjectivized seems to be a contradiction in terms. We do of course have some adjectives which resemble participles in form and are probably derived diachronically from some lost prehistoric verb, although they have no functioning syntactical connection with a current verb of the same stem. Such is the case for the adjectives ἑκών, ἄκων. And here it would make no sense to speak of periphrasis. Where it does make sense, that is, where there is a recognizable connection with finite verb forms from the same stem, it is not clear what criterion could be used to define complete adjectivization in Greek.[59]

---

style to achieve a maximum of effects with a minimum of means employed, to convey several different ideas or nuances with a single expression or construction. In such a case to ask *which* effect is intended – as if one of them excluded the others – is to mistake the nature of the stylistic phenomenon as such.

[58] See Aerts, pp. 39–51.

[59] For Aerts, p. 17 adjectivized participles "are characterized by frequent attributive and substantival application, with meaning-fixation derived from the impersonal or intransitive meaning of the verb." The second criterion is too vague to be useful; the first is a matter

For most of the examples on Aerts' list (pp. 14f.) it seems clear that the periphrastic construction is used and understood as a stylistically motivated transformation of the corresponding verb, e.g.

> πρέπον ἐστί   ← πρέπει
> "It is suitable"   "It suits"
> ἀρέσκων ἐστί   ← ἀρέσκει
> "he is pleasing"   "he pleases"

The only formal test I see for deciding when a participle acquires the syntax of an adjective or noun would be when it loses the verbal construction with accusative or dative object, as sometimes happens with the articular participle, e.g. οἱ προσέχοντες τούτου "his relatives". (But note that οἱ προσέχοντες τούτῳ – with verbal syntax – also occurs.) But in the case of an articular participle I would no longer speak of periphrasis, for quite other reasons which will be specified. (See §18). And in most of the so-called adjectivized participles the verbal construction is preserved; for example the dative is used with ἀρέσκων ἐστί as with ἀρέσκει:

79 Thucydides I.38.4

> εἰ τοῖς πλέοσιν ἀρέσκοντές ἐσμεν, τοῖσδ᾽ ἂν μόνοις οὐκ ὀρθῶς ἀπαρέσκοιμεν
> "If we are pleasing to most (of our colonies), it cannot be right that we displease them alone."

I do not claim that Greek participles never lose their verbal status, so that their construction with εἰμί would cease to be periphrastic in our sense. I do claim that the burden of proof lies on the other side, to define precisely what is meant by the loss of verbal status and to show that it in fact occurs for participles in Greek.[60]

---

of frequency, i.e. of degree (since every participle *can* take attributive position), and it does not specifically concern periphrasis, where the participle is in predicate position. The adjectival role of some participles is better indicated by the formation of adverbs from them, as K. J. Dover reminds me.

[60] What would be required in the way of evidence can be seen from some cases in English where we do indeed have occasional loss of participial status. For example, *interesting* has become an adjective in *This book is interesting to me*, where it no longer takes a direct object as in *This book interests me*. Periphrasis for the latter would be *This book is interesting me*, which is a possible but infrequent sentence form. (However, *interesting* is a very special case, and its separation from the verb *interest* is probably due to the direct influence of the French form *intéressant*.)

Note that some tests which show loss of verbal force for participles in English would be useless in Greek. Compare Jespersen's perceptive distinction between the two occurrences of *closed* in *When I came the door was closed* (German *war geschlossen*), *but I have no idea when it was closed* (*wurde geschlossen*). The second occurrence, but not the first, implies priority of time between *closed* and *came*; and only the second *was closed* is a finite form

§17. STATIC VALUE FOR PERIPHRASIS AND AFFINITY
WITH PERFECT PARTICIPLES.
SPECIAL CASES WITH EMPHATIC ἐστί

In the preceding section we illustrated the periphrastic construction of εἰμί with present (**78–79**) and aorist participles (**77**) as well as with perfect forms (**72–76**). The latter construction is the only one definitely attested in Homer. It is by far the most common in classic literature, and the only one preserved in current use in modern Greek (εἶναι γραμμένο "It is written"). There seems to be a natural connection between the perfect forms and the copula construction with εἰμί. This is recognized by Aerts in what he calls the situation-fixing character of periphrasis in the perfect. And he suggests that this value of the perfect has influenced the development of present periphrasis, which is not progressive-active as in English *I am building a house* but "static in character and usually intransitive in meaning." [61] This description seems to me correct, although Aerts' historical explanation is more doubtful. The same static-intransitive quality often attaches to periphrasis with an aorist participle as well.

80 Sophocles *O.T.* 1146 (Aerts p. 33)
> οὐ σιωπήσας ἔσῃ;
> "Be silent once for all!"
>
> (Jebb)

Even in the aorist, the stylistic effect of the construction with εἰμί is to present the action or attitude as a *state* or as a more or less durable property characterizing the subject. Only in very rare cases is this construction genuinely transitive in sense, describing an action that alters an external object, as in **75** above. More often the construction is only formally transitive, as in **73**, **74** and **76**: the periphrasis typically, and above all insofar as it is *copulative*, describes the subject's own condition or attitude. Hence even verbs that are formally transitive may be used periphrastically without an expressed object, precisely in order to focus attention on the subject as in the case of *see* (**77**) and *fear* (**78**).

How far this tendency in Greek periphrasis is due to the influence of the perfect forms, how far it is due to the very nature of the construction with εἰμί (where the surface structure suggests that the participle assigns a property

---

of the verb *close*. But the corresponding perfect forms in Greek indicate aspect only, not time sequence: ἀνεῳγμένη ἦν ἡ θύρα, corresponding to the first occurrence of *was closed*, is genuinely verbal and hence periphrastic (=ἀνέῳκτο), and the distinction would have to be made in Greek by shifting to the monolectic aorist passive (ἀνεῴχθη).

[61] Aerts, p. 14; cf. p. 51.

or quality to the subject, as an adjective does), I cannot say. What is worth mentioning, however, is the affinity between this "situation-fixing" effect of periphrasis and the general *stative* or *static* value of εἰμί as copula, in contrast to the mutative-kinetic value of the parallel copula verb γίγνομαι "become". This static-durative character of εἰμί will be discussed at length in the next chapter. Here I would only point out that the static aspect of the verb and the adjective-like predicate syntax of the participle reinforce one another, since a predicate adjective usually describes a lasting quality or state of the subject. I suggest that it is this convergence of static tendencies in the periphrastic construction which explains the preference for perfect periphrasis in Greek, from Homer to the present. This is in a way the converse of Aerts' historical hypothesis that the static character of present periphrasis comes (by contamination, as it were) from the influence of the older use of perfect periphrasis. But the latter use is itself left unexplained by Aerts' hypothesis.

The general aspectual characterization just given applies to periphrasis on any account, and not specifically to my definition. I should point out, however, that my definition leads in some cases to results which are systematically different from those of earlier interpreters. Thus on my view every case of adjectival periphrasis is *also* a case of periphrasis.[62]

81 *Od.* 18.327

σύ γέ τις φρένας ἐκπεπαταγμένος ἐσσί

"You are certainly some crack-brained person"

(Palmer)

We may say that ἐκπεπαταγμένος is treated here as a noun, insofar as it is nouns which are usually construed with τις. Hence we may properly speak of copulative (or "substantival") periphrasis. But the participle must also be construed as verb or adjective in order to account for the accusative of respect (φρένας): *"smitten in your wits"*. The form ἐκπεπαταγμένος does not occur elsewhere, but the compound verb ἐκπατάσσω is attested later in the relevant sense, and the simplex πατάσσω is common in Homer. Hence there is no doubt that we are dealing here with a participial transform of ἐκπεπατάξαι φρένας, *"you are knocked out (of your wits)."* Since the

---

[62] This might seem too obvious to mention, except that Aerts' statements on the matter lead me to doubt whether he would agree. On the one hand he describes "the combination of a copula with a participle that has been completely adjectivised" as "adjectival periphrasis" (p. 12: and so also for "substantival periphrasis", p. 3); on the other hand he says "There is no question of periphrasis if the participle is completely adjectivised" (p. 17). There is at least a regrettable confusion of terminology here; but there is also a real disagreement about specific cases, as in example **81**.

copula ἐσσί cannot represent a distinct kernel, we have an unmistakable case of periphrasis according to my definition.[63]

Another result of my definition is that the initial position of the verb is, by itself, no bar to a periphrastic interpretation.[64] Word order in Greek is a secondary feature of style or emphasis, but periphrasis is a question of syntax.

82 Herodotus IV. 32

ἀλλ᾽ Ἡσιόδῳ μέν ἐστι περὶ Ὑπερβορέων εἰρημένα, ἔστι δὲ καὶ Ὁμήρῳ ἐν Ἐπιγόνοισι

The syntax of ἐστι is the same in both clauses, but for stylistic reasons – perhaps, for sheer variety – it has been moved to the front in its second occurrence. But even in the first clause we can render the verb as existential: "There is something said about the Hyperboreans by Hesiod; there is also something by Homer in the *Epigoni*." Because of this strong value for ἐστι, perhaps no one has ever described this sentence as periphrastic. (Aerts does not even discuss it.) Yet it answers to my definition: ἐστὶ εἰρημένα is clearly a transform of εἴρηται, and Ἡσιόδῳ μέν ἐστι here cannot represent a kernel sentence distinct from the participle. In **82** we have a periphrastic use of ἐστι which is *also* existential in sense. In fact the point of the periphrasis – Herodotus' reason for saying ἐστὶ εἰρημένα instead of εἴρηται – is precisely to introduce the verb with its existential nuance.

Hence it is not the existential sense of the verb as such which prevents us from counting the following sentence as periphrastic:

83 Herodotus VII. 143.1 (Aerts, p. 7)

ἦν δὲ τῶν τις Ἀθηναίων ἀνὴρ ἐς πρώτους νεωστὶ παριών, τῷ οὔνομα μὲν ἦν Θεμιστοκλέης, παῖς δὲ Νεοκλέος ἐκαλέετο
"There was a man among the Athenians, having recently come to the fore, whose name was Themistocles, and he was called the son of Neocles."

As my translation suggests, ἐς πρώτους νεωστὶ παριών can be taken as a distinct clause (i.e. as derived from a distinct kernel) from the sentence introduced by ἦν: *There was a man among the Athenians whose name was Themistocles (and who had recently come to the fore)*. On this reading ἦν παριών is non-periphrastic, since the two forms are derived from separate

---

[63] Aerts' listing of this passage as "non-periphrastic" (p. 49 n. 3) is unexplained and, as far as I can see, unmotivated except by his general reluctance to recognize copulative periphrasis as periphrasis *tout court*. By contrast, the parallel he cites from *Il.* 13.681 (ἔνθ᾽ ἔσαν ... νέες ... εἰρυμέναι, *where the ships were, dragged up on the beach*) is plausibly derived from two distinct kernels, and hence really non-periphrastic.

[64] Contrast Aerts, pp. 11f.

kernels. On the other hand, with Hude's punctuation (reproduced above) it is more natural to take *whose name was Themistocles* as a secondary remark and to regard the primary sentence as *There was a man who had recently come to the fore among the Athenians*. On this reading it becomes plausible to describe the construction as periphrastic, since ἦν δὲ τῶν τις Ἀθηναίων ἀνήρ *(there was a man among the Athenians)* cannot stand alone as a complete sentence and calls out for its completion by παριών.[65]

Sentences with initial εἰμί are among those which have provoked most controversy in the discussion of periphrasis. Without going over the familiar list of disputed cases, let me point to one example which seems to me clearly periphrastic (**84**), and one (**85**) which raises interesting problems that will concern us in Chapter VI.

84 Xenophon *Anabasis* VI. 1.6. (Aerts, p. 47)

ἐξέφερον ὡς τεθνηκότα·ἦν δὲ οὐδὲν πεπονθώς

"They carried him off as dead (sc. the warrior fallen in a mock battle); but in fact he was not injured at all."

Aerts regards the participle here as adjectival, and renders, "but he was in-a-state-of-being-all-right." I agree with the judgment as to an adjectival-static nuance; but I repeat that adjectival periphrasis is still periphrasis. ἦν πεπονθώς is clearly a transform of πέπονθε (or ἐπέπονθε), and the verb cannot be derived from a separate kernel.[66] For the veridical force of the initial ἦν in **84**, see Chapter VII §5.

85 *Il*. 11.722

ἔστι δέ τις ποταμὸς Μινήϊος εἰς ἅλα βάλλων

ἐγγύθεν Ἀρήνης

"There is a river Minyeios, which empties its water in the sea beside Arene."

(Lattimore)

---

[65] In **83** the two constructions differ in syntax and emphasis, but not in sense. For an example where the ambiguity between a periphrastic and a non-periphrastic construal of initial ἔστι is significant, and surely intentional, see Aesch. *Agam*. 958

ἔστιν θάλασσα – τίς δέ νιν κατασβέσει; –
τρέφουσα πολλῆς πορφύρας ἰσάργυρον
κηκῖδα παγκαίνιστον, εἰμάτων βαφάς

These words, uttered by Clytemnestra as Agamennon walks the fatal carpet to his death, are open to two readings: (1) *The sea produces purple dye* (ἔστι τρέφουσα ← τρέφει), periphrastic, and (2) *There is a sea (of blood waiting for Agamemnon) in the house* (ἔστι sc. ἐν δόμοισι: cf. οἴκοις ὑπάρχει in verse 961), non-periphrastic, since here τρέφουσα ... βαφάς is a secondary kernel: *this sea will stain our garments red.*

[66] For similar reasons I must disagree with Aerts on many other cases of expressive periphrasis, above all in Herodotus, for example VI. 37 ἦν δὲ ὁ Μιλτιάδης Κροίσῳ τῷ Λυδῷ ἐν γνώμῃ γεγονώς. Aerts finds that "there is little question of periphrasis here" (p. 44); whereas on my definition there is no doubt that the construction ἦν ... γεγονώς is periphrastic for ἐν γνώμῃ ἐγέγονε.

In Chapter VI §7 we shall see that **85** is modelled on a standard existential sentence pattern in Homer (my Type II), where the initial ἔστι is in every case associated with a predicate of place, as here with ἐγγύθεν Ἀρήνης. But **85** is unique in that the local specification is construed not directly with ἔστι but with the conjoined participle βάλλων. We have as kernel *The river M. empties* (βάλλει) *into the sea near Arene*. As in **82** above, the finite verb is replaced by (i.e. transformed as) ἔστι +*participle* in order to play upon the value of initial ἔστι as existential sentence-operator, in a sense to be specified in Chapter VI. But a sentence-operator is not a kernel, and neither in English nor Greek does *There is a river Minyeios* represent a complete sentence. Hence **85** is periphrastic-existential in the same way as **82**; and we have a case of present periphrasis in Homer.

If this use of "periphrasis" seems to involve too gross a departure from the familiar connotations of the term, it would be easy enough to revise our definition in such a way as to exclude specifically the existential use of εἰμί. But the revision would be *ad hoc*, and I believe the interests of clarity and generality are better served by leaving the definition as it stands and by recognizing the fact of a periphrastic-existential use of εἰμί, just as we must recognize a copulative-existential use with predicate nouns and adjectives (below, §25).[67]

In conclusion, I must point out that although periphrasis is in principle applicable to all verbs, and hence εἰμί as auxiliary is capable of replacing any finite verb form, the actual use of the construction is much more restricted. If we set aside the expressive use of periphrasis by the poets and the even freer use of the same construction in Herodotus, we see that periphrasis in classical prose as in Homer is essentially a construction with perfect participles. The use with present participles is infrequent; with aorist

---

[67] My definition of periphrasis has the result of characterizing fewer cases of ἔχει +*participle* as periphrastic and more cases of ἐστί +*participle* then are admitted by Aerts. Thus I would recognize periphrasis in a whole series of cases where the derivation of ἐστί +*participle* from two distinct kernels seems to me an empty *jeu de l'esprit*. A typical example is Hdt. I. 146.3 ταῦτα δὲ ἦν γινόμενα ἐν Μιλήτῳ. (So Aerts, p. 23; cf. pp. 6 and 9 for parallels: Hdt. I. 152.1 κατὰ τάχος ἦν ταῦτα πρησσόμενα; I. 206.1 ἐς καιρὸν ἔσται ταῦτα τελεόμενα; similarly III. 134.4; IX 15.4 ἦν δὲ τὸ δεῖπνον ποιεύμενον ἐν Θήβῃσι). In such cases the participial phrase is added as a kind of stylistic afterthought, so that ἔστι +*participle* is not felt as an indissoluble unit. My definition could be applied in such a way as to characterize these sentences as non-periphrastic. However, a syntactic analysis that derives ἦν γινόμενα from two distinct kernels (*It happened* and *It took place in Miletus*) seems pointless, since the kernels are not significantly distinct: the first gives no information not also contained in the second. It is therefore more natural to regard such sentences as surface bifurcations (i.e. periphrasis) of a single underlying verbal sentence represented by the participle. Expressive periphrasis of this kind is a favorite stylistic device in Herodotus.

forms it is so rare as to be practically negligible.[68] The periphrastic passive
(ἐστὶ ἠδικημένος) is well established in the perfect; but the construction is
more common with active and middle-intransitive forms of the participle.

§18. THE ARTICULAR PARTICIPLE AS PREDICATE

As an appendix to the periphrastic construction we may consider one use
of the participle with εἰμί which I do not regard as periphrastic: when the
participle in predicate position is accompanied by the article. An articular
participle like οἱ ἄρχοντες "the rulers" is essentially a brief description;
that is to say, it represents a source sentence ἄρχουσι "they rule" that has
been reformulated as a noun phrase which refers to the (understood) subject
of the original sentence: οὗτοι "they", "these men", or τινες "some persons."
We might call this an *agent transformation*, in contrast with the *action
transformation* by which the same sentence is nominalized in terms of the
predicate: ἡ ἀρχὴ αὐτῶν or τὸ τούτους ἄρχειν "their rule". (The term *agent
transformation* points to the fact that this transformation is parallel to the
formation of *agent nouns*, which also refer to the subject of their source sen-
ence: οἱ ἄρχοντες like οἱ ἀρχοί "the rulers", from ἄρχουσι; ὁ ἐργαζόμενος
"the one who is working" like ὁ ἐργάτης "the workman," from ἐργάζεται
"he works.") A similar transformation of a sentence into a nominal description of its subject underlies the structure of the relative clause, by which
we usually translate the articular participle into English: *The one* (or *the
man) who is working in the field* from *He is working in the field*.

In the case of the articular participle, then, there is always some subject
understood from the underlying sentence, even if the subject is specified
only in the vaguest way as *someone* or *they*. We may even say that the
underlying subject is represented by the article as such, which is in origin
a demonstrative-anaphoric pronoun and which functions still in classic
Greek as a weak pro-word. In its typical use the articular participle reshapes
its source sentence for insertion into another sentence as a description of the
subject or object of the latter: λέγουσι τάδε οἱ ἄρχοντες *Some men rule,
and they say as follows*; πειθόμεθα τοῖς ἄρχουσι *Some men rule, and we
obey them*. The peculiarity of the construction of the articular participle with
εἰμί is not that it is periphrastic (it is not, for the kernel underlying the
participle will always be distinct from the sentence frame with εἰμί into

---

[68] In my samples from Lysias and Xenophon, representing 300 occurrences of the verb,
there are 10 or 12 periphrastic constructions of which 9 are in the perfect. There is only
one example of a present participle that is unquestionably periphrastic on my definition:
Anab. 2.2.13 ἦν δὲ αὕτη ἡ στρατηγία οὐδὲν ἄλλο δυναμένη ἢ ἀποδρᾶναι. In two other
cases, a periphrastic construal of the present participle can be defended: Lysias XIII.39
ἥ τις ἦν ἑκάστῳ αὐτῶν προσήκουσα; *ibid.* 91 ἀφείλετο ἃ ἦν ὑπάρχοντα ἐκείνῳ ἀγαθά.

which it is inserted), but that the sentence with εἰμί identifies its subject with that of the participial source. As in the case of "definite descriptions" in predicate position after *is*, copula sentences with articular participles represent the *is* of identity.

The article as such is at best incipient in Homer, and the articular participle is correspondingly rare. It is apparently never found in predicate or subject position with εἰμί.[69] Hence we must turn to classical examples.

86A Lysias I.16

ἔστι δ' ἔφη 'Ερατοσθένης 'Οῆθεν ὁ ταῦτα πράττων

"'The man who did this', she said, 'is Eratosthenes of Oa.'"

86B *Ibid.* 19

ἐμνήσθην 'Ερατοσθένους... καὶ εἶπον ὅτι οὗτος ὁ φοιτῶν εἴη πρὸς τὴν γυναῖκα

"I mentioned Eratosthenes ... and said it was he who was visiting my wife."

87 Xen. *Anab.* V.8.6

ἦ σὺ εἶ ὁ τὸν κάμνοντα ἀγαγών;

"Aren't you the one who carried the sick man?"

88 Aeschylus, *P.V.* 771 (see Aerts, p. 42)

τίς οὖν ὁ λύσων ἐστὶν ἄκοντος Διός;

"Who is the one who will free him against Zeus' will?"[70]

89 Plato, *Charmides* 166 D 8

θαρρῶν... ἀποκρινόμενος τὸ ἐρωτώμενον...ἔα χαίρειν εἴτε Κριτίας ἐστὶν εἴτε Σωκράτης ὁ ἐλεγχόμενος

"Go ahead and answer the question, and don't worry whether it is Critias or Socrates who is the one being examined."

In each case the articular participle represents an underlying sentence whose truth is presupposed by the form of the given sentence: *Someone is sleeping with the speaker's wife* in **86**, *Someone carried the sick man* (**87**), *Someone will free Prometheus* (**88**), *Someone is being examined* (in the Socratic exchange of question and answer) in **89**. There is no question of periphrasis, since the copula in the resulting sentence is never derived from this kernel which underlies the participle. What the copula does is to identify the subject of

---

[69] The article (or article-pronoun) does occur once even with the participle of εἰμί, but in object position: *Il.* 1.70 ὃς ἤδη τά τ' ἐόντα τά τ' ἐσσόμενα; cf. Chantraine, *Gramm. hom.* II 244.

[70] For this and other examples, see Aerts, p. 42. The sentence type is particularly frequent in Sophocles' *Oedipus Tyrannus*, where questions of identity constantly recur; see verses 139, 754, 819, etc.

this underlying sentence by specifying a proper name or a deictic reference (or in **88** to question the identity). In the resulting sentence we cannot easily say which term is subject, which predicate. And it makes no difference, since the sentence implies that the two terms are identical, i.e. that they refer to the same extra-linguistic subject. (From the point of view of logic, *both* terms are subject and the predicate is provided by the "is" of identity.) In a rhetorical analysis we can say that the "psychological" subject, or better the *topic* of the sentence is the term already familiar from the context and "present in the speaker's mind", whereas the psychological predicate or *comment* is the new or unknown term, like the proper name in **86A**, or *who?* in **88**. (But this criterion does not always give clear results. It apparently specifies the articular participle as comment or "predicate" in **87**; I doubt if it applies at all to **89**. Compare our earlier remarks on sentences of the form *This is that* with pronoun as "predicate" in §11.)

§19. PERIPHRASIS COMPARED WITH OTHER USES OF εἰμί AS VERB OPERATOR AND SENTENCE OPERATOR

In their periphrastic use εἰμί and ἔχω, like *be* and *have* in English, are known as auxiliary verbs, i.e., as secondary "helpers" with other verb forms (in this case, with participles) to constitute a sentence. In Harris' transformational grammar these auxiliary verbs appear as a special case of the more general concept of verb operator. A verb operator is a transformation that introduces a new verb or a verb phrase taking the original kernel verb as its "object" or, as I shall say, as its *operand*. Thus we have the elementary English sentence *He writes a letter* as operand or source for the *be-ing* and *have-en* transformations that yield *He is writing a letter, He has written a letter*, respectively.[71]

The general characteristics of a verb operator are (1) that it leaves the subject of the operand sentence unchanged, (2) it changes the form of the operand verb (*write → writing, written*), and (3) it is a unary transformation, that is, it does not conjoin two distinct kernels (e.g. it does not unite two independent verbs which happen to have a single subject), but represents only the transformational trace or difference between a single source sentence and its transform.

It is clear that the periphrastic uses of εἰμί and ἔχω, as defined above, correspond to this description of a verb operator; and indeed it was Harris' notion of verb operator that guided my own definition of periphrasis.

[71] See Z. Harris, "Transformational Theory", pp. 374f., where the two periphrastic operators (marked *Y*) are distinguished from other verb operators (marked *U*). In *Mathematical Structures* (pp. 66–8, 72f.) both classes are listed together (as *Φv*).

Thus between (μῦθος) τετελεσμένος ἐστί in **72** above, §15, and its non-periphrastic source, say μῦθος τελεῖται (1) the subject is unchanged, (2) the operand verb is changed to participial form, and (3) the verb ἐστί does not represent a distinct kernel but is simply the "trace" of periphrasis. What the more general formulation permits us to see is that the use of ἐστί here is strictly comparable to that with agent nouns and adjectives derived from underlying verbs. Syntactically, the relation between φονεύει "He murders" and φονεύς "murderer" is of the same general type as between φονεύει and φονεύων "murdering", φονεύσας "having murdered", etc., except for certain resulting differences in the treatment of objects of the source verb.

(1)   οὗτος φονεύει τὸν ἄνθρωπον → οὗτος ἐστὶ φονεύων τὸν
       ἄνθρωπον
       He murders the man → He is murdering the man

(2)   οὗτος φονεύει τὸν ἄνθρωπον → οὗτος ἐστὶ φονεὺς τοῦ ἀνθρώπου
       He murders the man → He is the murderer of the man.[72]

The difference in the case of the object in (1) and (2) corresponds to the fact that the participle φονεύων has kept its verbal character and thus takes the accusative just as its finite form does, whereas the agent noun φονεύς can preserve the underlying verbal object only in the genitive or (for some nouns) in the dative.[73] The same transformational relation holds between verbal sentences and a whole class of verbal adjectives, which we may call *agent adjectives*:

(3)   οὗτος φονεύει ἀνθρώπους → οὗτός ἐστι φονικὸς (ἀνθρώπων)
       He murders men → He is murderous (of men).
       οὗτος ἐργάζεταί τι → οὗτός ἐστι ἐργατικός τινος
       He produces something → He is productive of something.

There is of course a semantic or lexical difference between transformations (2) and (3), on the one hand, and the participial periphrasis in (1), a difference of meaning which corresponds to the fact that the latter is still verbal in character and therefore preserves not only its accusative syntax but also its temporal aspect. Hence, like the finite verb, the participial periphrasis describes as an action (murdering, producing) what the agent nouns and adjectives describe as a quality or characteristic of the subject (being murderous, being a murderer). As we have seen, copulative periphrasis

---

[72] It is unlikely that ἐστὶ φονεύων occurs as a periphrastic in classical Greek, but I cite it here to bring out the parallel. For actual examples of present periphrasis, see **78–79** in §16.
[73] For the exceptional cases where a nominal form is construed with the accusative like its underlying verb, see H. E. Smyth, *Greek Grammar* revised by G. N. Nessing (Cambridge, Mass. 1956) §§1598 and 1612; e.g. ἐξαρνός εἰμι (←ἐξαρνοῦμαι) τὰ ἐρωτώμενα.

represents a tendency towards the assimilation of the verbal participle to an ordinary nominal predicate, but this assimilation is never complete.

When the periphrastic construction is passive in form, its transformational structure is that of a sentence operator rather than a verb operator, since it effects a change of subject relative to the active form of its source.

Caesar was murdered by Brutus ← Brutus murdered Caesar.

The earliest unmistakable example of this passive periphrasis, with agent expressed, seems to be in Hesiod:

90 *Theogony* 415

ἀθανάτοις τε θεοῖσι τετιμένη ἐστὶ μάλιστα

"She (Hecate) is greatly honored by the immortal gods"

The agent represented here by the dative will appear as subject in the source sentence θεοὶ Ἑκάτην τιμῶσι "The gods honor Hecate." (A similar passive interpretation is possible for Homeric examples like μῦθος τετελεσμένος ἐστί if we assume that the subject has been zeroed: "The word is accomplished (by Agamemnon, by Zeus, etc.).") This use of εἰμί in passive periphrasis is largely restricted to the perfect forms, although it may occur with the present participle. (λυόμενός ἐστι as periphrasis for λύεται "He is being freed" is rare or marginal in comparison with λελυμένος ἐστί for λέλυται "He has been freed".) In the aorist and future passive only monolectic forms exist: ἐλύθης "He was freed", λυθήσεται "He will be freed."

Non-periphrastic uses of ἐστί with adjectives in -τός are frequently passive in sense. Their transformational structure is comparable to that of agent nouns and adjectives, except where there is a shift in subject:

(1) *non-passive adjectives in* -τός

θνητός ἐστι   ← θανεῖται

He is mortal   He will die

ἀναισχυντός ἐστι ← οὐχ αἰσχύνεται

He is shameless   He feels no shame

(2) *passive forms in* -τός

ἀμβατός ἐστι πόλις (*Il.* 6.434) ← ἀναβαίνουσι τὴν πόλιν

The citadel can be climbed   They climb the citadel

πιστός ἐστί (μοι)   ← πιστεύω αὐτῷ

He is trustworthy (for me)   I trust him

As these examples show, the sense of the adjectives in -τός need not be passive, but it is always or typically *potential* or *dispositional*. Unlike the cognate Latin forms in -*tus*, the Greek forms are not participles describing the action of a finite verb as such but true adjectives which characterize their subject. Thus a πιστὸς ἑταῖρος is not simply *a companion whom I trust* but *a trusty companion*, one who deserves or inspires trust.

Verbals in -τέος

There is a closely related class of quasi-adjectival forms which do not express possibility or dispositional tendency but rather obligation or necessity, and which remain essentially verbal rather than adjectival in their syntax. In their "personal" use in agreement with a subject, these adjectives are always passive. Their use is practically limited to predicate position with ἐστί (which is often omitted); they rarely occur in oblique cases and perhaps never in attributive position with a noun.[74]

91 Xenophon *Anab.* II.4.6

ποταμὸς δ' εἰ μέν τις καὶ ἄλλος ἄρα ἡμῖν ἐστι διαβατέος
"Whether some other river must be crossed by us (I do not know)"
←ποταμὸν διαβαίνομεν
"We cross a river."

92 Xen. *Memorabilia* III.6.3

ὠφελητέα σοι ἡ πόλις ἐστί
"You must benefit the city"

For the impersonal construction of these verbals see below, §30.

§20. The nominal copula concluded.
SUMMARY OF VERB AND SENTENCE OPERATOR USES OF εἰμί

We have considered six constructions in which εἰμί plays the role of verb or sentence operator, three of them involving a passive transformation with change of subject. The analysis of §19 can be summarized in the following outline.

I. Simple (active) transformations with εἰμί as verb operator

  A. Active periphrasis

    βλέπων ἐστί ← βλέπει (see **78** above, in §16)

  B. Agent transformations

    1. Agent noun

      φονεύς ἐστι ← φονεύει

      ἐργάτης ἐστί ← ἐργάζεται

---

[74] This is presumably why Chantraine (*Formation des noms*, p. 309) says that these forms "ont été durant toute l'histoire du grec ancien senties comme faisant partie de la conjugaison", like the passive periphrasis. Chantraine cites as the earliest example οὔ τι φατειόν "unspeakable" in Hesiod, *Theog.* 310. But this form is rather an adjective than a verbal (note the accent), and scarcely distinguishable in meaning from the corresponding form in -τός; cf. Γοργόνες ... οὐ φαταί in *Scutum* 230. For details on the forms in -τέος see Bishop, *AJP* 20 (1899), 1,121,241.

2. Agent adjective

φονικός ἐστι ← φονεύει
ἐργατικός ἐστι ← ἐργάζεται

II. Passive transformations with εἰμί as sentence operator

A. Passive periphrasis

ἠδικημένος ἦν (ἐγώ) ὑπὸ τούτου ← οὗτός με ἠδίκησε

B. Passive adjectival transformations

verbal adjective in -τός
ἀμβατός ἐστι πόλις ← ἀναβαίνουσι τὴν πόλιν

Compare other passive adjectives such as ἐργάσιμα (χωρία) *workable, tillable (land)* ← ἐργάζονται (τὰ χωρία) *They work the land.*

C. Verbal in -τέος

ποταμός τις ἡμῖν ἐστὶ διαβατέος ← διαβαίνομεν τὸν ποταμόν

In the periphrastic uses (IA and IIA) εἰμί is recognized as an auxiliary verb; in its construction with agent nouns and adjectives (IB1 and 2) it would probably be regarded as an ordinary copula (and so likewise for passive adjectives such as ἐργάσιμος under IIB). The construction with verbal adjectives in -τός and -τέος belongs somewhere in between: ἐστί construed with forms in -τός appears to be a normal copula, while with forms in -τέος it seems closer to an auxiliary verb. Despite these surface distinctions, however, there is a deep analogy between the syntactic status of the verb in all six cases, since it is introduced into the transformation of a verbal kernel which does not itself contain εἰμί. What all these transformations have in common is that they introduce no new words other than εἰμί but only add a morpheme to the stem of the underlying verb, namely a participial, agent noun, or adjectival suffix: -ων, -μένος, -εύς, -ικός, -τός, -τέος etc. (And in the passive forms we have the additional change of the underlying subject *N* from the nominative to the dative or the genitive with ὑπό.)

In this connection I must mention a small number of verb operators and a large class of sentence operators where εἰμί functions not alone but with a predicate adjective or noun. Some of the sentence operators have already been treated in the description of the *cop A* and *cop N* construction for sentential subjects. But the verb operators have a striking form of their own which recalls the periphrastic construction by its union of εἰμί with a participle: δηλός (φανερός) εἰμί τοῦτο ποιῶν, "I am clearly doing this, am plainly seen to be doing it."

93 Lysias XIII.92

εἰ τοίνυν τι ἐκεῖνοι ἀγαθὸν τὴν πόλιν ἢ τὸ πλῆθος τὸ ὑμέτερον φανεροί εἰσι πεποιηκότες

"If these men *have clearly rendered* some service to the city or to the people"

94 Xen. *Anab.* I.10.6

ἐν τούτῳ καὶ βασιλεὺς δῆλος ἦν προσιὼν πάλιν, ὡς ἐδόκει, ὄπισθεν

"At this point the King *was seen approaching* again, as they thought from the rear"[75]

Like the periphrastic, this construction has its kernel verb represented in the participle (πεποιηκότες, προσιών); the operand sentences are *They have rendered service, The king approached.* The *cop A* operator with δῆλος or φανερός is in effect an adverb: *plainly, in clear sight.*

The construction just illustrated is not peculiar to εἰμί. The *cop A* phrase functions here like many finite verb forms which are construed with a "supplementary" participle representing an operand kernel: the opposite of δῆλός εἰμι ποιῶν is λανθάνω ποιῶν "I escape notice doing it". Similarly adverbial in sense are τυγχάνω ποιῶν "I happen to do it", "I am doing it just now", φθάνω ποιῶν "I do it quickly (before someone else)." Other constructions of the same form correspond to standard verb operators in English: ἄρχομαι ποιῶν "I begin doing it", πειρῶμαι ποιῶν, "I try doing it", etc.[76] With some of these verbs εἰμί itself may appear as the kernel participle: ξένος ὢν ἐτύγχανεν αὐτῷ "He happened to be (="in fact was") Cyrus' guest-friend" (*Anab.* I.1.10). In this case the construction of εἰμί is an elementary example of *N is A* which undergoes the τυγχάνω +*participle* operator as does any other elementary sentence form. (So also with a locative use of

---

[75] The construction is frequent in classic prose, e.g. *Anab.* I.2.11, I.5.9 (δῆλος ἦν ὡς σπεύδων), I.9.11. So with γίγνομαι as suppletive in the perfect: *Anab.* I.6.8 ἐπιβουλεύων μοι φανερὸς γέγονας.

For similar constructions with other adjectives see κύριός εἰμι πράσσων, κρείττων ἦν μὴ λειτουργήσας, πόλλος ἦν λισσομένος, etc. cited by Schwyzer-Debrunner, p. 393.3.

[76] For a fuller list, see Smyth §§2089-105. For similar constructions with a "supplementary infinitive," *ibid.* §§1989-2000. The constructions with indirect discourse, verbs of perception, and verbs like κελεύω "command", πέμπω "send (to do)," belong in a different class, since they are all sentence operators. Some verbs function both ways, with or without a change in voice: παύομαι ποιῶν "I stop doing it" is a verb operator, but παύω σε ποιοῦντα "I stop you from doing it" is a sentence operator. As Harris points out, many verb operators can also be described as sentence operators of a special type, namely, where the subject of operator and operand verbs coincide. See *Mathematical Structures*, pp. 72-5.

εἰμί at *Anab.* II.1.7: ἐτύγχανε παρὰ Τισσαφέρνει ὤν ← παρὰ Τ. ἦν.)

In addition to the "personal" construction of δῆλος and φανερός as verb operator with the copula, we also have their "impersonal" construction as sentence operator: δῆλον (ἐστι) ὅτι..., φανερὸν (ἐστι) ὅτι... "It is clear that...." The impersonal construction as such is described below, §30. Here I note only that it is possible to construe the *that*-clause (ὅτι + *sentence*) as the subject of δῆλόν ἐστι, just as we can construe the infinitival clause as underlying subject of *cop A* in the use with sentential subjects described above in §6. From the transformational point of view, all second-order uses of the copula with sentential subjects are properly described as sentence operators, whether this copula construction has the form *N is A* (ἀργαλέον δὲ μοί ἐστι ... θέσθαι κέλευθον "It is hard for me to make a path" *Il.* 12.410) or *N is N* (ἀνάγκη δὲ ἦν στρατηγοῦ ἀκροᾶσθαι "It was necessary for them to obey the general" Lysias XIII.79). Thus the uses of *cop N* described in §10, like those of *cop A* in §6, may be grouped here with δηλός (φανερός) εἰμί as compound verb and sentence operator functions of εἰμί in conjunction with a special noun or adjective (generally of adverbial or modal meaning), as distinct from the similar functions of εἰμί alone which were summarized at the beginning of this section.

§21. COPULA CONSTRUCTIONS WITH ADVERBIAL "PREDICATE"
(cop adv)

The adverbial copula is listed here by way of transition between the nominal copula described in §§3–20 and the locative (and paralocative) copula to be treated in §§23–25. Hence I exclude from the present section all uses of the verb with local adverbs (including ἑκάς "far", ἐγγύς "near", χωρίς "apart"), as these belong below under the locative copula. I also exclude adverbs of time and duration, since I do not regard their construction with εἰμί as copulative but rather as adverbial in the usual sense. (For example οὐ δὴν ἦν "He did not live long", ἔτ' εἰσί "They are still alive"; for these uses see Chapter VI §6.) The forms to be considered here are certain adverbs of manner whose meaning in construction with εἰμί approximates to that of an adjectival predicate, so that the resulting sentence may be regarded as an instance of *N is Φ* and assimilated to the nominal copula.

One distinct class of *cop adv* with personal subjects consists of three or four terms for *silently, in silence*: ἀκήν, ἄνεῳ and in Attic σῖγα. (I omit the Homeric form ἀκέων ἦν (*Il.* 4.22), since its adverbial status is neither clear nor constant: elsewhere we have a feminine ending ἀκέουσα.) The first two adverbs occur in typical Homeric formulae; the last is used as predicate in a solemn and perhaps archaic turn of phrase.

95 *Il.* 9.29

ὣς ἔφαθ᾽, οἱ δ᾽ ἄρα πάντες ἀκὴν ἐγένοντο σιωπῇ.
δὴν δ᾽ ἄνεῳ ἦσαν τετιηότες υἷες Ἀχαιῶν·
ὀψὲ δὲ δὴ μετέειπε βοὴν ἀγαθὸς Διομήδης

"So he spoke, and all of them were stricken to silence;
For some time the sons of the Achaians were speechless in sorrow;
but at long last Diomedes of the great war cry addressed them."

(after Lattimore)

96 *Od.* 4.285 (cf. 2.82)

ἔνθ᾽ ἄλλοι μὲν πάντες ἀκὴν ἔσαν υἷες Ἀχαιῶν

"Then all other sons of the Achaians were silent."

97 Euripides *Hec.* 532

σῖγα πᾶς ἔστω λεώς

"Let all the folk be silent!"

cf. Ar. *Acharnians* 238: σῖγα πᾶς (sc. ἔστω)

Since the three expressions seem to be archaisms, it may help to consider their etymology. σῖγα is apparently an old adverbial form (like πύκα, λίπα, τάχα) from a root common to German *schweigen*; ἀκήν is said to be an accusative form of an unattested noun corresponding to the adverb ἦκα "gently, slowly"; ἄνεῳ was perhaps an instrumental form construed like the "comitative dative" σιωπῇ in the first verse of **95**, although some ancient commentators parsed it as a nominative plural.[77]

Grammarians have cited these and other adverbial constructions of εἰμί as indicating, in Munro's words, that "the verb is not a mere 'copula' but has a meaning which the Adverb qualifies."[78] Since the case illustrated in **95–97** is the most "concrete" of all adverbial uses of εἰμί (with personal subject and precise descriptive content), we may consider whether this can throw any light on the *Urbedeutung* of the verb. I offer the following remarks in a very tentative spirit, and I would not offer them at all if they did not seem to be confirmed by the purely synchronic analysis of the *be-become* system presented in Chapter V.

In **95** we have a clear contrast between ἀκὴν ἐγένοντο "they *fell silent*

---

[77] See J. B. Hofmann, *Etymologisches Wörterbuch des Griechischen*, s. v. v. ἀκέων, σιγή; Chantraine, *Grammaire homérique* I 249, 251. Other views in H. Frisk, *Griech. Etymol. Wörterbuch.*

[78] *Homeric Grammar*, p. 154. (Munro is actually referring to the construction with adverbs in -ως described below.) For similar comments, see Kühner-Gerth, II, 38; Chantraine, *Gramm. hom.* II 9: "Dans ces examples, le verbe εἶναι présente sa valeur pleine de verbe d'existence." This seems a considerable exaggeration in the case of most adverbial uses, though it may be true for οὐδὲ δὴν ἦν "He did not live long," which is one of Chantraine's examples.

then and there (ἄρα)", and δὴν ἄνεω ἦσαν "they *remained* speechless for a long time (until at last Diomedes spoke)." The lexical contrast between εἰμί and γίγνομαι tends to coincide here with the usual present stem/aorist stem contrast between the punctual-inceptive and the durative aspect, with γίγνομαι functioning as suppletive aorist for εἰμί. More exactly, as we shall see in the next chapter, the contrast can be characterized in terms of the general opposition of static-kinetic or stative-mutative aspect. If ἐγένοντο in such expressions indicates the entry into a new state, the passage from one condition to another, by the same token we can say that ἄνεω ἦσαν indicates the standing or remaining in a given state, the persevering in a certain condition. The verbal force of εἰμί, which the adverbs modify, can best be rendered by expressions like *stand* (in the metaphorical sense), *stay*, *persist* in a certain manner, as it were "frozen" in a certain state.

§22. THE COPULA WITH ADVERBS OF MANNER IN -ως

This construction is less suggestive for the meaning of εἰμί but more important as a productive syntactic device.

1. *With Personal Subjects*

98 *Od.* 11.336

> Φαίηκες, πῶς ὕμμιν ἀνὴρ ὅδε φαίνεται εἶναι
> εἶδός τε μέγεθός τε ἰδὲ φρένας ἔνδον ἐΐσας;
> "Phaeacians, how seems to you this man in beauty, height, and balanced mind?"

(Palmer)

99 *Il.* 4.318

> μάλα μέν τοι ἐγὼν ἐθέλοιμι καὶ αὐτὸς
> ὣς ἔμεν ὡς ὅτε δῖον Ἐρευθαλίωνα κατέκταν
> "Truly would I also wish to be so
> as I was when I cut down brilliant Ereuthalion."[79]

(after Lattimore)

Here πῶς and ὥς serve as interrogative and demonstrative pro-word for a description which might be given with the ordinary nominal copula or which need not use the verb *be* at all.

---

[79] See also *Il.* 11.762 ὣς ἔον, εἴ ποτ᾽ ἔον γε, μετ᾽ ἀνδράσιν discussed below as **39** in Chapter VII §6. Munro (*Homeric Grammar*. p. 154) compares the use of ὅμοια and ἴσα as adverbial predicates with εἰμί in Thuc. I.25.4 and III.14.1. There would be one Homeric example of this neuter pl. adverbial predicate if Allen's text for *Od.* 14.176 is accepted: καί μιν ἔφην ἔσσεσθαι ἐν ἀνδράσιν οὔ τι χέρεια/πατρὸς ἑοῖο φίλοιο, δέμας καὶ εἶδος ἀγητόν (note the parallel in sense to **98** above and to ὣς ἔον ... μετ᾽ ἀνδράσιν in *Il.* 11.762). However, χέρεια is the reading of Aristarchus; the MSS. have χερείω.

The only other examples I have found of adverbial predicates with personal subjects are the post-Homeric forms ἐκποδών and ἐμποδών, which may be mentioned here with other "concrete" uses of *cop adv* even though these are not adverbs of manner in -ως. They are in fact frozen monolectic forms of the locative (and paralocative) phrases ἐκ ποδῶν and ἐν ποσί. For the construction see e.g. Lysias XIII.7 ἡγοῦντο δὲ οὐδὲν ἄλλο σφίσιν ἐμποδὼν εἶναι ἢ ... τοὺς στρατηγοῦντας "They judged that there was nothing in their way except ... the generals"; cf. *ibid.* 90 οὐκ ἔστιν ἡμῖν ἐμποδὼν ⟨οὐδέν⟩; so ἐκποδὼν ποιήσασθαί τινα *ibid.* 24 and 43; Hdt. VI 35.3 Μιλτιάδεα ... βουλόμενον ἐκποδὼν εἶναι (sc. τῆς Πεισιστράτου ἀρχῆς) "Miltiades, wishing to be clear of the rule of Pisistratus."

One other isolated adverbial construction with εἰμί is represented by ἅλις, "in plenty" "enough", which is construed (1) as a quantifier word with concrete subjects and an existential-locative or possessive use of εἰμί (*Il.* 3.384 περὶ δὲ Τρῳαὶ ἅλις ἦσαν "There were Trojan women in a crowd around her;" *Il.* 14.122 ἅλις δέ οἱ ἦσαν ἄρουραι "He had fields in abundance"), where its syntax is like that of an undeclinable form of the adjectives ἀλής "crowded" or πολλοί "many"; and (2) as a sentence operator (with ἐστί understood): ἦ οὐχ ἅλις ὅττι... "Is it not enough that...?" (*Il.* 5.349). For further details, see LSJ s.v. ἅλις.

2. Adverbs of Manner in -ως with Abstract N

100 Hdt. IV.134.2

> βουλῆς ἀγαθῆς δεῖ ὅκως ἀσφαλέως ἡ κομιδὴ ἡμῖν ἔσται τὸ ὀπίσω
> "We need good counsel, so that our return may be safely carried out."

101 Thuc. IV.10.3

> καὶ τὸν πολέμιον δεινότερον ἕξομεν μὴ ῥᾳδίως αὐτῷ πάλιν οὔσης τῆς ἀναχωρήσεως, ἢν καὶ ὑφ᾽ ἡμῶν βιάζηται
> "Our enemy will become more formidable from the difficulty of his carrying out a retreat, even supposing that we repulse him"[80]
> (after Crawley)

So with γίγνομαι in the same construction.

102 Thuc. II.14.2

> χαλεπῶς δὲ αὐτοῖς διὰ τὸ αἰεὶ εἰωθέναι τοὺς πολλοὺς ἐν τοῖς ἀγροῖς διαιτᾶσθαι ἡ ἀνάστασις ἐγίγνετο
> "The removal (to the city) was hard for them, because most of them had always been used to live in the country."

---

[80] I give the traditional text, as in Kühner-Gerth I, 38. Stuart Jones in the O.C.T. prints the variant reading ῥᾳδίας ... οὔσης, which normalizes the copula construction – needlessly, as the parallels in **100** and **102** show.

In **100-102** εἰμί and γίγνομαι are not really copula verbs but "verbs of occurrence," with the lexical value *take place, occur, proceed*. This construction of the verb with action nouns as subject properly belongs with existential sentence Type V in Chapter VI §15. On the basis of the syntactical analysis given there, it will be seen that the adverbs ἀσφάλεως and ῥαδίως can be construed here with κομιδὴ ἔσται and ἀναχωρήσεως οὔσης because they are properly construed with κομίζονται and ἀναχώρουσι in the kernel sentences underlying **100** and **101**. Hence these examples are not structurally comparable to the other uses of *cop adv* illustrated in this section.[81]

3. *Adverbs in -ως with Sentential Subjects or Impersonal Construction*

One Homeric example with an infinitival clause as underlying subject is perhaps to be regarded as a parallel to **100-102**:

103 *Il*. 7.424

ἔνθα διαγνῶναι χαλεπῶς ἦν ἄνδρα ἕκαστον

"They found it hard to recognize each individual dead man"

(Lattimore)

Whether or not the infinitive is regarded as subject in the surface syntax, the construction of the adverb is certainly to be explained by an underlying χαλεπῶς διαγιγνώσκουσι, "They distinguish with difficulty."

In a quite distinct category we have a group of constructions with no specific subject expression provided by the context and with a predicate adverb indicating good or bad fortune.

104 *Il*. 9.551

τόφρα δὲ Κουρήτεσσι κακῶς ἦν

"(As long as Meleager was fighting) so long did things go ill with the Couretes."

Similarly with suppletives for εἰμί:

105 *Il*. 9.324

κακῶς δ' ἄρα οἱ πέλει αὐτῇ

"It goes badly for (the mother bird) herself".

106 Hdt. I.8.2

χρῆν γὰρ Κανδαύλῃ γενέσθαι κακῶς

"It was inevitable that disaster should befall Candaules."

[81] A more complex example of *cop adv* with abstract subject, for which I can cite no exact parallel, was pointed out to me by K. J. Dover: Aristophanes *Frogs* 953: οὐ σοὶ γάρ ἐστι περίπατος κάλλιστα περί γε τούτου "(Drop the question of democratic sympathies.) Conversation on this topic is not a good idea for you." Here ἐστι κάλλιστα functions as the superlative of ἐστι καλῶς (see below, sentence **108**); but the subject is an action noun equivalent in deep structure to *your talking about democracy*. The closest parallels are with unspecified sentential subjects below, **107-109**.

This single formula for misfortune is balanced by several expressions for a favorable outcome.

107 Euripides *Medea* 89

εὖ γὰρ ἔσται

"It will be well" (Compare εὖ γαρ εἴη "May it be well" in Aesch. *Ag.* 217.)

108 Ar. *Plutus* 1188

καλῶς ἔσται γάρ, ἢν θεὸς θέλῃ

"It will be well, if the god is willing." [82]

The polar contrast of good and evil fortune which characterizes the construction in **104–108** is clearly alluded to in **109** and probably explains the adverb in **110** as well:

109 Thuc. I.78.2

ὁποτέρως ἔσται ἐν ἀδήλῳ κινδυνεύεται

"The risk is uncertain, whether of success or misfortune."

110 *Il.* 5.218

πάρος δ᾽ οὐκ ἔσσεται ἄλλως,

πρίν γ᾽ ἐπὶ νὼ τῷδ᾽ ἀνδρὶ σὺν ἵπποισιν καὶ ὄχεσφιν

ἀντιβίην... πειρηθῆναι

"Our luck will be no better until you and I face this man in force with horses and chariot."

In **104–110** the subject of εἰμί and suppletives is vaguely *the situation, the course of affairs*, but since there is no specific sentential subject provided by a clause or sentence in the context we may describe these uses as "impersonal". The verb has its most general meaning of *(how) matters stand*, corresponding to the expression of state or condition for personal subjects in **95–99**. This general meaning is close to the sense of the verb in the veridical construction described in Chapter VII, where the most typical form involves an adverb in -ως: οὕτω πη τάδε γ᾽ ἐστί, ὡς ἀγορεύεις "These things are so, just as you say" (*Il.* 24.373). Further examples will be given in Chapter VII. The following instance is perhaps closer to the use as verb of occurrence in **100–101** and in Chapter VI §15:

---

[82] Comparable in sense but with a more definite sentential subject is a construction like ἡδέως ἂν αὐτοῖς εἴη "It would be pleasing to them" Demosthenes LIX.30. This is equivalent in meaning and comparable in structure to the idiomatic use of εἰμί with dative participle, which does not have a place in my classification (although it might perhaps be listed as "predicate dative" below, next to the predicate genitive): *Il.* 14.108 ἐμοὶ δέ κεν ἀσμένῳ εἴη, where Lattimore's translation specifies the sentential subject: "What he says will be to my liking." For the parallel Attic expression βουλομένοις εἴη, etc. see LSJ s.v. εἰμί C.III.3.

111 *Il.* 11.838

πῶς τ' ἄρ ἔοι τάδε ἔργα; τί ῥέξομεν, Εὐρύπολ' ἥρως;

"But how shall this be, my lord Eurypylos? What shall we do?"

(after Lattimore)

For the continuation of this topic, see Chapter VII §5.[83]

§23. THE LOCATIVE COPULA

Strangely enough the traditional discussions of the verb *be* either fail to recognize the syntactic parallel between the nominal and the locative copula or else fail to make any systematic distinction between them. Thus two of the most widely-used authorities in classical philology, the Liddell-Scott-Jones *Lexicon* and Kühner-Gerth's *Ausführliche Grammatik*, both restrict the term "copula" to the case of the nominal copula, with a predicate adjective or noun in agreement with the subject.[84] In comparative philology, on the contrary, the wider sense of copula is current but no difference in principle is recognized between the nominal and locative constructions. Thus in discussing the origin of the copula Brugmann cites sentences like *I am here* next to those of the form *N is A, N is N*: *The soldier is brave, He is a soldier*; and Meillet begins his classic article on the nominal sentence with the two examples *Pierre [est] savant, Pierre [est] dans la maison*.[85]

This contrast between the two points of view is understandable. The Greek grammarians are concerned with formulating rules for the agreement of predicate adjectives and nouns, and these rules have no application to sentences with a locative copula. The comparative philologists were interested in more general phenomena, such as the omission of the verb *be*, which affect both types of sentences to an equal extent. Above all since Meillet's study of the nominal sentence, the theory of the copula in I.-E. has been dominated by the example of languages like Russian and Arabic, where the verb *be* is lacking in the present indicative for both types. As a result,

---

[83] I mention here, since it is listed by the grammarians together with examples of *cop adv*, the use of the adverb of intensity μάλα with a construction of εἰμί, e.g. in statements of weather: μάλ' εὐημερίας οὔσης *It was very clear*, μάλα χειμῶνος ὄντος *It was very stormy* (cited by Kühner-Gerth, I.38 from Xen. *Hell.* II.4.2, V.4.14). If this is a copula use, it belongs below with the impersonal construction, §28. Alternatively, εἰμί may be taken as verb of occurrence with the noun as subject. In neither case does μάλα represent a predicate; it qualifies the adverb εὐ- or the verbal idea underlying the noun, as if we had μάλα χειμάζει "It is very stormy." Similarly for the adverb in Hdt. III. 152 δεινῶς ἦσαν ἐν φυλακῆσι, which is a paralocative transform of δεινῶς ἐφύλαττον as Kühner-Gerth recognize (*ibid.*).

[84] LSJ s.v. εἰμί B; Kühner-Gerth I, p. 42; cf. p. 3.

[85] K. Brugmann, *Kurze vergleichende Grammatik*, p. 627; Meillet, "La phrase nominale," p. 1.

the narrower notion of the copula in LSJ and Kühner-Gerth strikes us today as archaic. As far as the verb *be* is concerned, there would seem to be no formal distinction between these types other than the word class of the predicate. Even in Spanish, where the locative copula is provided only by *estar* (from *stare*) and never by *ser* (from *esse*), the distinction is not drawn in the distribution of the two verbs, since *estar* can also serve as copula with many adjectives and with participles.

But although the parallel between nominal and locative copula is undeniable, the distinction is equally important. This is clear from the consideration of other languages, such as Chinese, which have a distinct verb for the locative copula or which, like Hungarian, make use of a verbless sentence for nominal predication in a sentence like *Peter (is) a soldier* but normally require a verb for the locative construction *Peter is in the house.*[86] Even for English there is a significant formal difference between a sentence like *Peter is a soldier* or *Peter is wise*, on the one hand, and *Peter is here* or *Peter is in the house* on the other. In the first case the verb *is* can be replaced by only a very small number of other verbs (*becomes, is considered, is called*, perhaps *seems*), whereas in the second case it can be replaced by almost any verb in the language: *reads, works, plays, sleeps, dies, runs, jumps, sits*, etc.[87]

We have defined the locative copula as the verb *be* construed with an adverb or prepositional phrase of place, i.e. in sentences of the form N *is* D_{loc}, N *is PN*. The distinction between local adverb and prepositional phrase is a superficial one, and I shall neglect it in what follows. Thus I shall symbolize all locative sentences by the formula N *is PN*. Except in the limiting case of adverbs like *here* and *there*, whose meaning is implicitly given relative to the position of speaker and hearer, there is no such thing as an "absolute" use of local adverbs. Absolute location is as incoherent in grammar as in physics. Even for adverbs like *near* (ἐγγύς, σχεδόν, etc.) and *far* (τηλοῦ, ἑκάς) which are regularly used without further specification, there will always be some definite point of reference provided by the context or by the implicit position of the speaker.

---

[86] See F. Keifer in *The Verb 'Be' and its Synonyms*, Part 3, pp. 56f. Compare the situation in various Finno-Ugric languages described by R. Gauthiot *Mémoires de la Société de Linguistique de Paris* 15 (1908), 201ff., where in some cases the verb is required as in Hungarian, in other cases it is omitted when the sentence is *merely* locative: "Mais il suffit pour qu'il (le verbe) reparaisse que l'idée de *présence* se fasse jour même très discrètement, à côté de la simple indication de lieu" (p. 217).

[87] In terms of language learning, the locative *be* probably represents a more basic concept than the nominal copula and is apparently learned earlier. See the evidence cited in Chapter VIII n. 10.

112 *Il.* 10.113

τῶν γὰρ νῆες ἔασιν ἑκαστάτω, οὐδὲ μάλ᾽ ἐγγύς

"Their ships (sc. of Ajax and Idomeneus) lie farthest *from us*, and are not at all close."

(Lattimore, my italics)

In most cases, what is called an "absolute use" is an elliptical construction, in the strict sense of "ellipse, where the completion is required by meaning and syntax and is actually provided from the context.[88]

"Pure" examples of the locative construction, where the form *N is PN* serves only to indicate the position of the subject, are relatively rare. I count only about 40 examples in all (or 8%) in the 562 occurrences of the verb in *Iliad* 1–12, and only 5 examples in the third person present indicative (for 11 cases without the verb). Here are a few instances to add to **112** above:

113 *Il.* 5.360 ≈ 8.456

ὄφρ᾽ ἐς Ὄλυμπον ἵκωμαι, ἵν᾽ ἀθανάτων ἕδος ἐστί

"so I may come to Olympos, where is the seat of the immortals."

(after Lattimore)

114 *Il.* 8.16

τόσσον ἔνερθ᾽ Ἀΐδεω ὅσον οὐρανός ἐστ᾽ ἀπὸ γαίης

"(Tartaros), as far beneath the house of Hades as heaven is from earth."

The most common Homeric examples are in participial form, where the verb *be* is not always required in the English translation.

115 *Il.* 2.27

(Ζεὺς) ὅς σεῦ ἄνευθεν ἐὼν μέγα κήδεται

"Zeus, who although far away cares much for you"

(after Lattimore)

116 *Il.* 5.159

ἔνθ᾽ υἷας Πριάμοιο δύω λάβε Δαρδανίδαο
εἰν ἑνὶ δίφρῳ ἐόντας

"Next he killed two children of Dardanian Priam who were in a single chariot."

(Lattimore)

---

[88] Thus Chantraine cites *Il.* 3.45 καλὸν εἶδος ἐπί as an example of "l'emploi absolu" of ἐπί, but his own rendering makes clear that the form is to be construed as a preposition with an understood noun: "la beauté est répandue *sur ses membres*" (*Grammaire hom.* II, 105, my italics). In every case, as far as I can see, the absolute use of a preposition or preverb in Chantraine's account (pp. 82–149) could be better described as a zeroing of the "object" of the preposition. For some perceptive remarks on the superficial nature of the distinction between preposition, preverb, and adverb, see Chantraine, *ibid.* pp. 85 and 125 (§§117 and 181.)

I include among "pure" uses of the locative copula some cases where the preverb or proposition is joined to the verb:

117 *Il.* 10.357

ἀλλ᾽ ὅτε δή ῥ᾽ ἄπεσαν δουρηνεκὲς ἢ καὶ ἔλασσον

"But when they were a spear's throw away from him, or even less."

If we count the compound verb ἄπειμι in the expressions for *absence* or *distance* as purely locative, we should do the same for the symmetrical case of πάρειμι for *presence* and *proximity*.

118 *Il.* 2.485

ὑμεῖς γὰρ θεαί ἐστε, πάρεστέ τε, ἴστέ τε πάντα

"For you who are goddesses, *are there*, and you know all things"

(Lattimore, my italics)

Although in such uses the verb seems to have a stronger sense than the mere copula, that sense is itself purely locative.

§24. PARALOCATIVE USES OF *N is PN*

I employ the term "paralocative" to describe a variety of uses which are indistinguishable in form from the locative copula but where the meaning of the sentence is not primarily or exclusively locative. The chief types are (1) the pregnant locative, where the literal sense of place is appropriate but does not constitute the essential force of the expression (i.e. where the sentence is not adequately rendered as a mere statement of place), (2) the metaphorical paralocative, where the literal sense of place is no longer appropriate, and (3) the locative-existential, where we might render the construction by *there is* in English. Since these distinctions, and the contrast with pure locatives, depend primarily upon the meaning of the sentence in its context and not upon its syntactical form, there will be room for considerable difference of opinion in the classification of particular cases. Only in certain cases of the metaphorical use can we specify a syntactic criterion for distinguishing them from locatives in the literal sense.

1. *Pregnant Uses of the Locative*

When used literally as in **118**, πάρ-ειμι expresses *presence near* or *beside* a person, an object, or an event. In its pregnant uses the same compound verb indicates that the subject *stands on the side of, is a supporter of* the object in the dative. (Here "object" has the ambiguity already noted for "subject": it indicates both the noun in the dative and the person or thing to which the noun refers.)

119 *Il.* 3.440

πάρα γὰρ θεοί εἰσι καὶ ἡμῖν
"We too have gods on our side."

Similarly with the verb unexpressed:

120 *Il.* 1.174

πάρ' ἔμοιγε καὶ ἄλλοι
οἵ κέ με τιμήσουσι
"There are others with me, who will do me honor"

(Lattimore)

Note that in both **119** and **120** one might detect an existential nuance and
hence list these as examples under 3 below. When the subject is not a person
the sense of πάρ-εστι is rather *belongs to, is at his disposition.*

121 *Il.* 9.135 = 277

ταῦτα μὲν αὐτίκα πάντα παρέσσεται (sc. Ἀχιλῆϊ)
"See these gifts will be his at once."

(Lattimore)

The use of πάρειμι in **121** is clearly related to the standard construction
ἔστι μοι = "I have." Because of the frequent overlap between locative and
possessive constructions of εἰμί, the latter might be listed here among the
paralocative uses. Since in many possessive uses, however, no locative expression occurs, I treat this construction separately in Chapter VI §12.
(For other paralocative uses of πάρειμι, some of which are metaphorical,
see LSJ s.v.)

122 *Il.* 11.681

(συνελάσσαμεν ἵππους)
πάσας θηλείας, πολλῇσι δὲ πῶλοι ὑπῆσαν
"(We carried off 150 horses) mares all of them and many with
foals following underneath.

(Lattimore)

123 *Il.* 1.63

καὶ γάρ τ' ὄναρ ἐκ Διός ἐστιν
"A dream also comes from Zeus."

(Lattimore)

I count **122** as a pregnant use, since ὑπῆσαν indicates not only the position
of the foals but also their unweaned state. Similarly in **123** the construction
with ἐκ may be taken literally, but it expresses the idea that Zeus is the

guarantor or inspirer, not only the local source of dreams. So also in the usual phrases for parentage or ancestry:

124 *Il.* 21.189

ὁ δ' ἄρ' Αἰακὸς ἐκ Διὸς ἦεν

"But Aiakos was the son of Zeus."

We might list here as paralocative the parallel uses of the genitive of source alone, without ἐκ, on the grounds that the noun with oblique case-ending is in fact equivalent to a prepositional phrase: ταύτης τοι γενεῆς τε καὶ αἵματος εὔχομαι εἶναι "Of this race and blood do I claim to be" (*Il.* 6.211). On purely formal grounds, however, I treat this construction separately with other examples of the predicate genitive (below, §26).

As already mentioned, these pregnant uses are distinguished from the "pure" locative by the fact that they cannot generally be rendered by the English copula alone but call for some stronger expression like *come from, belong to, stand beside*. Observe that this stronger value for the verb is (paradoxically) compatible with its omission, as in **120**. As far as I can see, these pregnant uses are rather less common in classic prose than in Homer, and this may contribute to an impression that the strong uses of εἰμί tend to decline in favor of the "mere copula". However, the development of the next category points in the opposite direction.

2. *Metaphorical Uses of the Locative Construction*

Truly metaphorical uses in my sense, where the literal local value of the preposition is no longer appropriate to the context, are rather rare in Homer but extremely common in later Greek.

125 *Il.* 1.562

ἀλλ' ἀπὸ θυμοῦ / μᾶλλον ἐμοὶ ἔσεαι

"You (will) be more distant from my heart than ever."

(Lattimore)

Similar metaphorical uses of ἀπό in Homer can probably be counted on the fingers of one hand: I find only ἀπὸ δοξῆς in *Il.* 10.324 and a similar phrase at *Od.* 11.344. In Attic, however, we have an abundant series of metaphors built on the same pattern: ἀπὸ τρόπου, ἀπὸ καιροῦ, ἀπὸ γνώμης etc. (see LSJ s.v. ἀπό I.3).

126 *Il.* 9.116

ἀντί νυ πολλῶν

λαῶν ἐστιν ἀνὴρ ὅν τε Ζεὺς κῆρι φιλήσῃ

"Worth many fighters is that man whom Zeus in his heart loves."

(Lattimore)

The literal local sense of *position opposite, facing* is more frequent with the forms ἄντα, ἄντην, ἀντία (cf. ἀντικρύ, etc.), though it occurs also with ἀντί. From Homer on, however, the notion of *facing in battle* gives the construction with ἀντί its pregnant sense of *opponent, hostile to*, while the matching of items in barter and weighing one amount against another in the scales gives rise to the equally natural metaphor of *being a substitute (equivalent) for, being worth the price*, as in **126**.

Another preposition with a well-established metaphorical value in Homer is περί:

127 *Il.* 1.287

ἀλλ᾽ ὅδ᾽ ἀνὴρ ἐθέλει περὶ πάντων ἔμμεναι ἄλλων

"Yet here is a man who wishes to be above all others"

(Lattimore)

Lattimore has rendered περί (etymologically "beyond") by a different spatial metaphor ("above"). The etymological sense of περί-εἰμι ("lie beyond") is common in metaphorical uses in Homer, like **127**, as well as in the classic senses of the verb: *to be superior to, to survive, be left over*. When used literally in statements of place περι- means "around", "about", and this gives rise to a different metaphor, of which the beginnings are found in the Homeric use of compound verbs (see Chantraine, *Grammaire hom.* II, 125), and which is widely extended in classical and post-classical usage, e.g. for the title of treatises περὶ τῆς ψυχῆς "On the Soul", etc. One typical instance:

128 Lysias XIII.83

ὡς οὐ πεποίηκε περὶ ὧν ἐστιν ἡ αἰτία

"that he did not commit the acts concerning which he is accused."

The post-Homeric uses of *N is PN* in an "abstract" or metaphorical sense are too numerous and too diverse to catalogue here. In most cases there is an obvious analogy between the transferred or figurative sense and a strictly local use of the same preposition (or of its root: for περί "beyond" cf. πέραν, περάω). Thus in **128** the accusation "centers on" or comprehends certain acts just as a circumference or a surrounding wall encloses (περί-εχει) a certain space. The development of metaphorical or extended uses for expressions which also have a literal spatial sense is one of the most general and fruitful tendencies in all language, and the details belong rather to a study of the Greek prepositions and preverbs than to an investigation of the verb *be*. I note a few representative examples.

(a) εἰμί ἐν +*dative*: *I am in X's power*. Hesiod *Erga* 669 ἐν τοῖς γὰρ τέλος ἐστὶν ὁμῶς ἀγαθῶν τε κακῶν τε "On them (sc. the gods) depends the outcome of good and evil alike." Frequent in Attic prose, e.g. with a complex sentential subject: Lysias I.34 ἐν ὑμῖν δ᾽ ἐστὶ πότερον χρὴ τούτους (sc. τοὺς νόμους) ἰσχυροὺς ἢ μηδενὸς ἀξίους εἶναι "It is up to you whether these laws shall be binding or invalid." The figurative background of the construction can be seen in certain Homeric formulas, e.g. *Il.* 7.102 νίκης πείρατ᾽ ἔχονται ἐν ἀθανάτοισι θεοῖσιν "The threads of victory are held in the hands of the immortals" (Lattimore). This is presumably the sense of the much-discussed formula ταῦτα θεῶν ἐν γούνασι κεῖται "This lies on the knees of the gods" (*Il.* 17.514, 20.435, *Od.* 1.267, etc.).[89]

(b) The same construction is frequently used to specify the means or circumstances of an action or the state in which one stands. So without the verb: *Il.* 16.630 ἐν γὰρ χερσὶ τέλος πολέμου, ἐπέων δ᾽ ἐνὶ βουλῇ "Warfare's finality lies in the work of hands, that of words in council" (Lattimore); *Il.* 9.230 ἐν δοιῇ δὲ σαωσέμεν ἢ ἀπολέσθαι/νῆας "It is in doubt whether we save or lose our ships." With a suppletive of *be*: *Il.* 2.340 ἐν πυρὶ δὴ βουλαί τε γενοίατο "Let counsels be given to the flames" (Lattimore). Despite the vividness of the image, the metaphorical character of the expression can be defined syntactically here, since βουλή is not a first-order nominal but an action nominalization of βούλομαι/βουλεύομαι "to intend," "deliberate". The strength of the imagery depends upon the fact that a first-order (concrete) noun appears in the specification of place (ἐν πυρί, ἐν χερσί). This imagery is naturally weakened when the object of ἐν is itself no longer a concrete noun but a nominalization of the verbal predicate (as in ἐνὶ βουλῇ above). The verb *be* then figures as a verb operator, as in the English cases which we have described (in Chapter I §8) as morphological variants on the corresponding verb: *John is in love with Mary ← John loves Mary, John is in a hurry ← John hurries.* So in Greek:

οἱ ἐν ἀρχῇ ὄντες	← ἄρχουσι
"Those in power," "the rulers"	"They rule"
ἦσαν ἐν φυλακῇσι	← ἐφύλαττον
"They were on guard"	"They guarded"

Expressions of this type are about as common in Attic prose as in English: ἐν τούτῳ τῷ τρόπῳ μᾶλλον ἤδη ὄντες (Thuc. I.8.4) "being in this condition";

[89] I am unconvinced by the over-literal interpretation of R. B. Onians, *The Origins of European Thought* (2nd ed. 1954), e.g. p. 331 on the "mechanism of fate". Suggestive as his method is in many details, Onians' conclusions are vitiated by a naive primitivism. He forgets that the language of Homer is poetic, and that *all* language is metaphorical in that it works with analogies between visual spatial relations and abstract or intellectually perceived connections. Onians would reduce these analogies to identity, so that the Homeric gods cannot control the acts and fates of men unless they are holding on to the end of a lasso which is bound around the victim's bodies.

ἐν οὐδεμιᾷ πω τοιαύτῃ ἁμαρτίᾳ ὄντες (Thuc. I.78.4) "We are not yet in that error"; ἐν ἀσφαλεστάτῳ εἶναι (Xen. *Anab.* I.8.22) "be in the greatest safety"; ἐν τοιούτοις δὲ ὄντες πράγμασι (*ibid.* II.1.16) "since we are in such a situation"; ἤδη δὲ ἐν ὁρμῇ ὄντων (*Ibid.* II.1.3) "when they were already under way"; εἶναι ἐν ἀξιώματι, ἐν ταραχαῖς "be in esteem", "in trouble", etc. (see LSJ s.v. εἰμί C.IV.3).

(c) ἐπί + *dative*, with a sense close to (a) above: Xen. *Anab.* I.1.4 βουλεύεται ὅπως μήποτε ἔτι ἔσται ἐπὶ τῷ ἀδελφῷ "He resolved that he would never be again in his brother's power." Also with a wider variety of senses, as in (b) above: Lysias XIII.87 οὗτος ἐπ' αὐτοφώρῳ ἐστί "He is caught in the act"; εἶναι ἐπὶ τοῖς πράγμασιν "to be engaged in affairs", etc. (see LSJ, *ibid.* IV. 5).

(d) πάρ-εστι, ἔξ-εστι, and ἔν-εστι construed with infinitives in the sense "It is possible, permissible." (See the potential construction of ἔστι + *infinitive*, Chapter VI §17). Note that the metaphorical background is quite clear in the case of πάρεστι "It is at hand, at one's disposal" (cf. **121** above) and ἔνεστι (see (a) above), more obscure in the case of ἔξεστι. For metaphorical uses of παρά, πρός, etc. with εἰμί, see the Lexicon under the various prepositions.

§25. LOCATIVE-EXISTENTIAL USES.
NOMINAL COPULA WITH EXISTENTIAL SENSE

Since the pregnant uses of the locative described in the preceding section are those in which a literal statement of place is appropriate but insufficient as a rendering of the construction, it was pointed out that all locative-possessive uses of εἰμί – sentences in which, for a single occurrence of the verb, a statement of place overlaps or coincides with a statement of owner-ship – might be classified as pregnant locatives. The same is true for locative-existentials, where a construction of the form *N is PN* with a literal local sense has an additional nuance which we describe in terms of existence or render into English by our locution "There is a such-and-such". This nuance is discussed at length in Chapter VI. Here I only point out how common it is for statements of place to be accompanied by an "existential" suggestion which would justify the translation as "there is". We may say that, in general, when the subject *N* has not been mentioned or alluded to in the preceding context (or when the syntax of the subject is indefinite rather than definite), a statement of place of the form *N is PN* can always serve to *introduce* this subject into the discourse and thus to suggest or affirm its existence. This is particularly noticeable when the position of the subject noun is delayed, so that instead of N_1 *is* PN_2 the actual word order is PN_2 *is* N_1 or *is* PN_2 N_1.

129 *Od.* 12.80

μέσσῳ δ' ἐν σκοπέλῳ ἐστὶ σπέος ἠεροειδές

"About the middle of the crag is a dim cave."

(Palmer)

130 *Il.* 3.114

τεύχεά τ' ἐξεδύοντο· τὰ μὲν κατέθεντ' ἐπὶ γαίη
πλησίον ἀλλήλων, ὀλίγη δ' ἦν ἀμφὶς ἄρουρα

"They stripped off their armor and laid it on the ground/near to
one another, so there was little ground left between them."

(after Lattimore)

131 *Il.* 3.45

ἀλλ' οὐκ ἔστι βίη φρεσὶν οὐδέ τις ἀλκή

"But there is no strength in your heart, no courage."

(Lattimore)

132 *Il.* 1.300

τῶν δ' ἄλλων ἅ μοί ἐστι θοῇ παρὰ νηῒ μελαίνη

"But of all the other things that are mine beside my fast black
ship."

(Lattimore)

In the last two cases we have an overlap between the locative and possessive
construction (with dative of person, viz. σοι understood in **131**), in addition
to the existential nuance, which is perhaps weakest in **132** where it is not
rendered in Lattimore's translation. Only in **132** is there no delayed subject
N. Notice that the existential nuance of **129** is brought out in Palmer's
translation by imitating the Greek word order, without the formula "there
is." **129** may serve as the paradigm of a locative-existential construction which
is equally characteristic of classical prose:

133 Xen. *Anab.* I.2.7

ἐνταῦθα Κύρῳ βασίλεια ἦν καὶ παράδεισος μέγας

"In this place there was a palace and a great park belonging to
Cyrus."

134 *Ibid.* I.2.13

ἐνταῦθα ἦν παρὰ τὴν ὁδὸν κρήνη ἡ Μίδου καλουμένη

"Here there was by the roadside a spring called 'the spring of
Midas'."

In **133** we again have the convergence of locative and possessive constructions
with an existential nuance. The importance of this overlap between the
locative, possessive, and existential values of εἰμί has been noted in some

earlier studies of the verb.[90] Only recently, however, has the attempt been made to develop a theory of the verb *be* which takes account of this phenomenon.[91]

It is interesting to observe that the strong locative-existential sense is compatible with the omission of the verb:

135 *Il.* 1.156

> ἐπεὶ ἦ μάλα πολλὰ μεταξὺ
> οὔρεά τε σκιόεντα θάλασσά τε ἠχήεσσα
> "Since indeed there is much that lies between us,
> the shadowing mountains and the echoing sea"   (Lattimore)

The existential force is guaranteed in **135** not only by the delayed position of the subjects nouns (οὔρεα and θάλασσα spelling out πολλά) but above all by the quantifier-adjective πολλά "many", like ὀλίγη "little" in **130**. See parallel examples with πολλά and the verb expressed in the discussion of existential Type III, Chapter VI §11.

For completeness I illustrate here the overlap of the existential sense with instances of the *nominal* copula as well. The existential nuance is normally provided or confirmed by a quantifier adjective or pronoun like "someone", "no one", "all", "other", or a definite numeral.

136 *Il.* 1.144

> εἷς δέ τις ἀρχὸς ἀνὴρ βουληφόρος ἔστω
> "Let there be one responsible man in charge of her."
>   (Lattimore)

137 *Il.* 8.521

> φυλακὴ δέ τις ἔμπεδος ἔστω
> "Let there be a watch kept steadily"   (Lattimore)

138 *Il.* 1.271

> οὔ τις / τῶν οἳ νῦν βροτοί εἰσιν ἐπιχθόνιοι
> "No one of the mortals now alive upon earth"   (Lattimore)

139 *Il.* 5.877

> ἄλλοι μὲν γὰρ πάντες ὅσοι θεοί εἰσ' ἐν Ὀλύμπῳ
> "For all the rest, as many as are gods on Olympos"
>   (Lattimore)

---

[90] See Guiraud, *La phrase nominale en grec*, pp. 177ff. "existence locale", 188f. "existence possessive", 196ff. "existence locale possessive." Compare D. Barbelenet, *De la phrase à verbe être dans l'ionien d'Hérodote*, pp. 21–4.

[91] For the theoretical issues, see my brief remarks in "The Greek Verb 'to be'", pp. 257f. and above all J. Lyons, "A note on possessive, existential and locative sentences", *Foundations of Language* 4 (1967), pp. 390–6, *Introduction*, pp. 388–99, and "Existence, Location, Possession and Transitivity" in *Logic, Methodology and Philosophy of Science* III, ed. B. van Rootselaar and J. F. Staal (Amsterdam, 1968), pp. 495–503.

In **139** the translation might just as well read: "As many gods as (there) are on Olympos"; similarly in **138**: "those who are mortals on earth." In **139** the construction and in **138** the sense represents an overlap or ambiguity between nominal and locative copula. In **136** and **137** there is at best an implicit reference to place. The predicate construction as it stands is purely nominal, but the existential nuance is unmistakable.

This topic is continued in Chapter VI §13.

§26. THE PREDICATE GENITIVE

I mention here, for lack of a better place, the construction of εἰμί with a genitive, a construction which is not covered by our formal definition of the copula but whose similarity to the copula in a strict sense is intuitively clear. (For the possibility of regarding this construction as paralocative, and hence classifying it under the copula form *N is PN*, see above §24, p. 161 after sentence **124**.) The genitive case-ending serves in Greek to express a great number of different relations between its noun and another noun, verb, or adjective; and the same diversity – both syntactic and semantic – characterizes the predicate construction of the genitive with εἰμί. Attempts to classify these uses according to some systematic scheme tend to be arbitrary, and I simply list a few representative instances under four general headings. (For a fuller enumeration of examples and a rather unconvincing classification, see Schwyzer-Debrunner pp. 89–136.)

1. *Partitive Genitive (including what Schwyzer-Debrunner call "Zugehörigkeit zu einer Gruppe")*

> ἦν δὲ καί οὗτος καὶ ὁ Σωκράτης τῶν ἀμφὶ Μίλητον
> στρατευομένων
>
> "This man and Socrates were both among those who took part in the campaign against Miletus" (Xen. *Anab.* 1.2.3)
>
> ἐτύγχανε γὰρ καὶ βουλῆς ὤν
>
> "He happened to be a member of the council" (Thuc. III.70.5)
>
> ἡ γὰρ Ζέλειά ἐστιν τῆς Ἀσίας
>
> "Zeleia is (a city) of Asia Minor" (Demosthenes IX. 43)
>
> ἐστὶ τῶν χαλεπωτάτων λαβεῖν τινὰ πίστιν περὶ αὐτῆς
> (sc. ψυχῆς)
>
> "It is extremely difficult to come to a definite conclusion on this topic of the soul." (Aristotle *De Anima* 402ᵃ 10)

2. *Genitive of Source, Ancestry, Material (≈ Ablative-Genitive)*

πατρὸς δ' ἔιμ' ἀγαθοῖο
"I am of a good father" (*Il.* 21.109: cf. *Il.* 14.113 πατρὸς δ' ἐξ
ἀγαθοῦ ... εἶναι, which is a true paralocative)
ταύτης τοι γενεῆς τε καὶ αἵματος εὔχομαι εἶναι
"Of such a race and blood, I claim to be" (*Il.* 6.211: cf. *Il.* 19.111
σῆς ἐξ αἵματός εἰσι γενέθλης for paralocative parallel)
ἡ κρηπὶς μέν ἐστι λίθων μεγάλων
"The foundation is of large stones" (Hdt. I.93.2)
(στεφάνους), ὥσπερ ἴων ἢ ῥόδων ὄντας, ἀλλ᾽ οὐ χρυσίου
"As if the crowns were of violets or roses, but not of gold."
(Demosth. XXII.70)

3. *Genitive of Measure and Price*

(τὰ τείχη) ἦν δὲ σταδίων μάλιστα ὀκτώ
"The wall was of approximately eight stades" (Thuc. IV 66.3)
τοῦ δὲ Μαρσύου τὸ εὖρός ἐστιν εἴκοσι καὶ πέντε ποδῶν
"The width of the Marsyas (River) is 25 feet" (Xen. *Anab.* I.2.8)
τὸ τίμημ᾽ ἐστὶ τῆς χώρας ἐξακισχιλίων ταλάντων
"The valuation of the land is 6,000 talents" (Demosthenes XIV.19)

4. *Genitive of Belonging to (as Property or Distinctive Mark)*

Βοιωτῶν ἡ πόλις ἔσται
"The city will belong to the Boeotians" (Lysias XII.58)
τοῦ γὰρ κράτος ἐστι μέγιστον
"For to him (Zeus) does supreme power belong" (*Il.* 2.118, etc.)
τῶν γὰρ μάχην νικώντων καὶ τὸ ἄρχειν ἐστί
"For the rule belongs to those who are victorious in battle"
(Xen. *Anab.* II.1.4)
τὸ δὲ ναυτικὸν τέχνης ἐστίν
"Naval power is a matter for technical competence"
(Thuc. I.142.9)

When a particular example does not fit under any more definite category, it is often described as a "genitive of quality" or the like; e.g. Hdt. I.107.2 Καμβύσης, τὸν εὕρισκε οἰκίης μὲν ἐόντα ἀγαθῆς, τρόπου δὲ ἡσυχίου "Cambyses, whom he found to be of a good house and a quiet disposition". Note that the first genitive in this passage could be classified under 2 above, but not the second.

Unlike the construction of εἰμί+*dative*, most of these uses with the genitive seem to be essentially copulative; they are comparable to a metaphorical or abstract extension of the locative ideas involved in the partitive (*be among, be included in*) and in the ablative-genitive of source (*be from*). The case is slightly different for the genitive of possession, which would seem to be in competition with the dative construction if we judge from the English translations. According to Benveniste, however, εἰμί with the genitive does not express *possession* in the sense of the dative but rather *belonging to* (*appartenance*) as the predicate of some definite object determined as *his* or *mine*; whereas the dative construction expresses possession from the point of view of the person who does or does not possess something.[92] Hence, as Benveniste points out, the dative construction takes a (syntactically) indefinite object: ἔστι μοι χρυσός "I have gold", but not "I have *this* gold." The contrast is clearest in the negative, which with the dative means *I do not have any*: οὐκ ἔστι μοι χρήματα "I have no money"; while the negative form of the genitive construction means *It belongs not to him but to someone else*: Aesch. *Ag.* 940 οὔτοι γυναικός ἐστιν ἱμείρειν μάχης "It does not befit a woman to love battle" (though this may be a virtue in a man).

For the dative of possession, see Chapter VI §12.

§27. THE IMPERSONAL CONSTRUCTION

I have postponed to the end a discussion of the impersonal construction as such, since it involves some very general questions that are indifferent to the distinction between nominal and locative copula, indifferent even to the distinction between the copula and any ordinary verbal predicate.

As Edward Hermann remarked in 1926, the topic of impersonal verbs has probably been discussed more frequently than any other subject in traditional linguistics. The peculiar theoretical interest of this phenomenon lies in the challenge it poses to the classic analysis of the proposition into subject and predicate terms. It must be remembered that this traditional analysis has its roots not only in the syllogistic doctrine of terms but also in a coordinate theory of the intellect which is a common assumption of European philosophy from Aquinas to Kant. According to the post-Aristotelian doctrine of the "three operations of the intellect," a proposition or sentence is an expression of the second intellectual operation, namely *judgment* (*iudicium, Urteil*). The latter consists in the synthesis of two concepts (*intentiones, conceptus, Begriffe* or *Vorstellungen*), each of which is itself a product of the first, most elementary operation of the mind. Thus intuition or the apprehension of simples (*intuitio, apprehensio simplex, Anschauung*, etc.) furnishes the mind with ideas or concepts; the faculty of judgment combines and separates these concepts; combining them in affirmative judgments, separating them

[92] *Problèmes de linguistique générale*, pp. 196f.

in negative judgments. The third operation, or reason proper, moves from judgment to judgment, inferring conclusions from premises.[93]

We meet this doctrine briefly stated and applied to language in the first chapter on syntax in the Port Royal Grammar.

Le jugement que nous faisons des choses, comme quand je dis, *la terre est ronde*, s'appelle PROPOSITION; et ainsi toute proposition enferme nécessairement deux termes; l'un appelé *sujet*, qui est ce dont on affirme, comme *terre*; et l'autre appelé *attribut*, qui est ce qu'on affirme, comme *ronde*; et de plus la liaison entre ces deux termes, *est*.

The Port Royal authors observe that whereas terms are the object for the first operation of the mind, the link between them belongs to judgment, which is described as "the proper action of our mind and the manner in which we think." [94] Hence the fundamental importance of the verb *is*, as the expression of this essential action of the human mind in thinking and judging.

If our thinking consists in the linking of one concept (the subject) with another (the predicate), a judgment without a subject is properly unthinkable; and the Port Royal Grammar is at some pains to show that the "impersonal verbs" must in fact be analyzed into distinct subject and predicate terms.[95] Their analysis has not been generally adopted, but the theoretical tendency to reduce the impersonal construction to subject-predicate form has remained strong in classical grammar down to our own day. Not only does the 19th century Greek grammar of Kühner-Gerth announce that "unpersönliche Verben ... kennt die griechische Sprache nicht" (I, 36 Anm. 3), but the much more recent manual of Schwyzer, in the edition by Debrunner in 1950, continues to insist that "Nur für ein jüngeres Sprachempfinden und durch die Übersetzung in moderne Sprachen werden zu Impersonalien verba wie δεῖ, ἔξεστιν, πρέπει, δηλοῖ, μέλει..." (p. 621, Zusatz 2).

Nevertheless, the phenomenon exists, and it is not the invention of a modern *Sprachempfinden*. The term "impersonal verb" goes back to Priscian, and some of the typical examples were discussed by the Greek Stoics and grammarians.[96] The ancient term "impersonal" reflects the fact that such

[93] I do not know who is the true author of this vastly influential theory of the intellectual faculties. Its Aristotelian basis is neatly summarized and systematized by Alexander of Aphrodisias in his *De Anima*, in the early third century A.D.; but the completed doctrine is later, and perhaps Arabic in origin.

[94] "La liaison appartient à la seconde (opération), qu'on peut dire être proprement l'action de notre esprit, et la manière dont nous pensons." *Grammaire générale et raisonnée*, Seconde partie, ch. I, 3rd ed. 1769, p. 66.

[95] *Ibid.* ch. XIX; Des Verbes impersonels: "*Pudet me*; c'est-à-dire *pudor tenet*, ou *est tenens me* .... *Statur*, c'est-à-dire *statio fit*, ou *est facta*, ou *existit*."

[96] See Steinthal, *Geschichte der Sprachwissenschaft*, I, 306 for a Stoic description of (Σωκράτει) μεταμέλει as a παρασύμβαμα or παρακατηγόρημα, a deviant predicate. For an extended survey of the topic from Quintilian to Franz Brentano, see F. Miklosich, *Subjektlose Sätze*, 2nd ed. Vienna, 1883, pp. 7–23. It is only natural that defenders of the reality of the subjectless sentence at the end of the last century, in reaction against the

verbs occur only in the unmarked "third" person singular, and hence might properly be described as lacking any distinction of persons. The term "subjectless" has been preferred by modern authors who wish to emphasize the challenge to the classical subject-predicate dogma. I shall use the two terms as equivalent designations for a sentence type ( )$V\Omega$, occurring only in the third person singular, with no subject N.

The entire problem must be reformulated in the light of the contemporary distinction between surface grammar and deep structure. For on the one hand it is clear that, at the most superficial level, every English sentence must have a grammatical subject, if only the dummy pronoun *it*; whereas it is equally clear that in a case like *It is raining* the word *it* does not represent the subject or agent of the verb in any "deep" sense, i.e. is not a pro-word for some more specific N. Furthermore, the importance of the subjectless sentence pattern will vary greatly with the form assigned to deep structure in a given theory. In the case theory of Charles Fillmore, for example, one might say that the kernel of *every* sentence is provided by an impersonal verb that stands in various case relations to an array of nouns. The apparent subject position for a noun in any given sentence will represent only a superficial highlighting or emphasis on one of these realized case relations, and there is no reason why every sentence should prefer some noun in this particular way. (The only thing corresponding to the traditional notion of subject in Fillmore's deep structure is the category of *agent*, and many verbs will not require this category.)[97] In Fillmore's theory, an impersonal construction might well be regarded as the normal sentence form.

In the theory of sentence structure used here, we preserve the traditional subject-predicate pattern in our general formula $NV\Omega$ by the formal contrast between N on the one hand and $V\Omega$ on the other. (This is even more explicit in Chomsky's *noun phrase-verb phrase* terminology.) Hence the impersonal form ( )$V\Omega$, with an empty position for N in deep structure, must be recognized as a genuine anomaly – which does not mean that the anomaly cannot exist or that the theory must be false. It does mean that the theory may be inappropriate for the description of a language in which the most typical sentence types turn out to be without a subject N, for then the theory will describe *most* sentences as anomalous. In Chapter II we saw that there are languages such as Nootka for which this seems to be

---

classical theory of the intellect, were happy to invoke Brentano's alternative theory of judgment which takes as a basic judgmental form the simple, unitary recognition of a single object or concept. Besides Miklosich, p. 22, see a long series of articles by A. Marty, "Über subjektlose Sätze, etc." in the *Vierteljahrsschrift für wissenschaftliche Philosophie*, especially vol. 19 (1895), pp. 19–87, 263–334.

[97] See Fillmore, "The Case for Case", esp. pp. 24–51; above, p. 58 n. 33.

the case, and perhaps the same can be said for the so-called ergative languages.[98] It is to such languages that a theory like Fillmore's most naturally applies. But this is not the situation in Indo-European generally, and most decidedly not the case in Homeric Greek. For the latter we can say that a sentence without a subject nominal in deep structure is so rare – if it occurs at all – that we readily describe it as an anomaly. The situation is slightly different for classic Greek, where impersonal constructions become more conspicuous, at least in surface syntax. But the ease with which most of these can be derived from underlying $NV\Omega$ forms probably helps to explain the reluctance of the standard grammars to admit impersonal sentences as an authentic phenomenon in Greek.

In applying our transformational theory to the problem in hand we must distinguish at least three types of impersonal construction, in addition to a fourth type which has sometimes been mistakenly described as impersonal.

(1) An elementary construction for which there is no plausible subject N, such as Italian *piove*, Modern Greek βρέχει "it rains" and ξημερώνει "it dawns."

(2) An impersonal construction which has a paraphrastic ("synonymous") equivalent of the $NV\Omega$ type, so that it may be regarded as a stylistic variant or optional transform of the latter, for example μέλει μοι τούτων "It concerns me about these things," which can be analyzed as a secondary variant on μέλει μοι ταῦτα, "These things concern me."

(3) An impersonal construction that does not have a subject-predicate equivalent but which contains in its source a $NV\Omega$ kernel sentence that is recognizably "embedded" in the transform, as French *Il me faut partir* can be derived from a kernel *Je pars.*

(4) Finally, we distinguish a fourth class of pseudo-impersonals that must be excluded from the present discussion, where the subject of the verb is left vague or unexpressed but where it *could* be expressed without altering the structure of the sentence, e.g. λέγουσι "they (people) say", ἐσάλπιγξε, "(the soldier whose task it was) sounded the trumpet."[99]

Now the astronishing fact about Homeric Greek is that impersonal constructions of the first type are almost entirely absent, and there are only two or three instances of the second type. The only significant class of sentences in Homer which might be described as impersonal belongs to the third type, and here we can in most cases identify a sentential subject, as I have done in §§6 and 10 above. And whether we call this a sentential subject or simply

[98] For ergative languages, see Lyons, *Introduction*, 351–9, and Fillmore, "The Case for Case", pp. 54–60.
[99] See above, Chapter III §6, p. 75. The necessary distinction between type 4 and a true impersonal is made, e.g., by Miklosich, p. 2.

a kernel, this sentential component is itself of *NVΩ* form. We are left with only a very few cases where no definite sentential subject or kernel can be identified from the context.

Hence the *NVΩ* pattern, which is typical for Greek generally, is well-nigh universal in Homer. Although we find a considerable increase in the number and variety of impersonal constructions in classic Attic, this form still remains marginal in comparison, say, with the importance of impersonals like *es rauscht* or *es friert mich* in modern German. I illustrate the three types, with special reference to the use of εἰμί.

§28. IMPERSONAL CONSTRUCTIONS OF ELEMENTARY FORM (TYPE 1): EXPRESSIONS FOR WEATHER AND TIME

The privileged domain of elementary impersonals is the class of meteorological verbs, illustrated above by modern Greek βρέχει "It rains" and ξημερώνει "It dawns", "Day breaks". There are no examples of this type to be found in the Homeric corpus.[100] Statements concerning the weather are given either (a) with the name of a god as subject *N*, given in the sentence or specified by the context, as *Il.* 9.236 Ζεὺς ... ἀστράπτει "Zeus sends lightning", or (b) the weather event itself is expressed as noun with a verb of occurrence (*Od.* 14.476 χιὼν γένετ᾽ ἠΰτε πάχνη "Snow came like hoarfrost") or with an ordinary descriptive verb (*Il.* 12.278 ὥς τε νιφάδες χιόνος πίπτωσι θαμειαί "as flakes of snow fall thick").

Closely related to meteorological verbs are the locutions for time of day or season of the year. In Homer these are normally of form (b) above: *Il.* 9.474 ὅτε δὴ δεκάτη μοι ἐπήλυθε νύξ "when the tenth night came upon me", *Il.* 21.111 ἔσσεται ἢ ἠὼς ἢ δείλη ἢ μέσον ἦμαρ/ὁππότε ... There will be a dawn, an afternoon, or midday, when ...", γένετ᾽ ἠώς, ἐφάνη ἠώς "Dawn arose, appeared." These sentences with a verb of occurrence belong to a subclass of Type V existentials; see Chapter VI §§15 and 16. In post-Homeric Greek the verb of occurrence with nouns of time and weather is typically γίγνεται: Hdt. I.11.1 ὡς δὲ ἡμέρη τάχιστα ἐγεγόνεε "as soon as it was day", I.12.1 νυκτὸς γενομένης "when night had come".

The absence of impersonal constructions for weather and time in Homer is all the more striking in view of the contrast not only with Modern Greek ξημερώνει "it dawns" but with the probable existence of a corresponding impersonal verb in the etymological background of ἠώς (cf. Sanscrit *uccháti*, Lithuanian *aušta* "it dawns"). There is no reason to suppose that the

---

[100] See Hermann, "Subjektlose Sätze", pp. 275f. Cf. Chantraine, *Grammaire hom.* II, p. 7 §9, Remarque; Schwyzer-Debrunner p. 621.3.

Homeric situation is in any sense primitive: it represents a high point in the development of the personal or NVΩ sentence type for expressions which other languages, and other periods of Greek, render in impersonal form.[101] If we take into account the vivid pictorial value of ἠὼς ῥοδοδάκτυλος "Dawn the rosyfingered", like Zeus the Thunderer or Poseidon the Earth-shaker, we see that the suppression or repersonalizing of impersonal meteorological verbs in Homer corresponds to the dramatic anthropomorphism of Greek epic poetry, and to a certain descriptive vividness in Greek art and literature generally. In any case, the Homeric precedent remains influential. In classical prose a divine subject for a verb like ὕει need not be provided, but Ζεὺς ὕει remains possible, just as one may also say ὁ Θεὸς βρέχει "God rains" in Modern Greek.[102]

Nevertheless, even in Homer some expressions for time are open to an impersonal construal of ἐστί as copula or verb of occurrence. In most cases, I think, the NVΩ or N is Φ construction is far more natural, as in Il. 8.66 (=11.84), ὄφρα μὲν ἠὼς ἦν καὶ ἀέξετο ἱερὸν ἦμαρ, "As long as morning lasted and the sacred daylight was increasing", and Od. 23.371 ἤδη μὲν φάος ἦεν ἐπὶ χθόνα "Light was already (spread) over the earth."[103] But the surface syntax is no longer unambiguous in a sentence like the following:

140 *Od.* 3.180

τέτρατον ἦμαρ ἔην, ὅτε ...

"It was the fourth day, when (they landed their ships in Argos)."

The translation suggests an impersonal copula construction ( ) was AN, but we can also construe this as a normal N is A copula "The day was the fourth", or we can take ἦμαρ as subject of a verb of occurrence: "The fourth day was taking place, when", like ἠὼς ἦν and δεκάτη μοι ἐπήλυθε νύξ cited above. These parallels show that we *need* not take ἔην as impersonal or subjectless in **140**. However, we certainly *can* do so,[104] and this possibility is one which will later be exploited.

---

[101] Meillet believed that the personal weather expressions in Homer reflected a primitive I.-E. animism, but the more plausible view is that of Benveniste: "Les locutions Ζεὺς ὕει sont, à n'en pas douter, récentes et en quelque sorte rationalisées à rebours" (*Problèmes de linguistique générale*, p. 230).

[102] Hence some ancient grammarians described these meteorological verbs as θεῖα ῥήματα "divine verbs"; see Miklosich, *Subjektlose Sätze* p. 7.

[103] See the discussion of these two examples as sentences **103** and **111** in Chapter VI §§15–16.

[104] As Hermann proposes, p. 269. Some of his parallels seem to be less ambiguous. E.g. *Od.* 10.469 ὅτε δή ῥ' ἐνιαυτὸς ἔην "when the year end had come" seems to me syntactically equivalent to ὄφρα ἠὼς ἦν. For *Il.* 8.373 ἔσται μὰν ὅτε, see my discussion below of sentences **95** and **96** in Chapter VI §14.

141 *Od.* 12.312 (≈ 14.483)

ἦμος δὲ τρίχα νυκτὸς ἔην, μετὰ δ' ἄστρα βεβήκει

"When it was the third watch of the night, and the stars had moved across the sky."

(after Palmer)

It is again possible to take this as an impersonal (*it*) *is PN*, "'twas in the third watch of the night" (so LSJ s.v. τρίχα). The classical parallels cited in the next paragraph tell in favor of this construction. But it is also possible, within the context of Homeric usage, to preserve the *NV* form by taking τρίχα νυκτός as a nominalized phrase in military jargon for "the third watch", with ἔην as verb of occurrence. If we adopt this *NV* construction for **140** and **141**, there will be no impersonal expressions for time or weather in Homer.

This solution, which may be plausible in Homer because of the small number of cases involved, becomes absurdly artificial in classical prose, where similar formulas are so frequent that we are obliged to recognize an impersonal sentence form (*it*) *is* Φ, with adverbs and prepositional phrases of time as the values of Φ:

ἡνίκα δ' ἦν ἀμφὶ τὴν τελευταίαν φυλακήν
"it was about the last watch" (Xen. *Anab.* IV.1.5)

ἤδη μὲν ἀμφὶ ἡλίου δυσμὰς ἦν
"it was now about sunset" (*ibid.* VI.4.26)

ὀψὲ ἦν
"it was late" (*ibid.* II.2.16)

τῆς ἡμέρας ὀψὲ ἦν
"it was late in the day" (Thuc. IV.93.1)

To assume that we have in every case an understood subject *N* like *time* or *hour* (χρόνος, ὥρα), or to take these adverbial and prepositional phrases as subject, seems to me equally arbitrary.[105] Better to admit an impersonal construction here, competing with or replacing the *NV* construction that may still be recognized in ἡνίκα δὲ δείλη ἐγίγνετο, ἡνίκα δ' ἦν δείλη (*Anab.* I.8.8, III.4.34, etc. cf. ἀμφὶ δείλην *ibid.* II.2.14) "when afternoon came." The *NV* or "personal" construction remains dominant, however, as we can see from the examples with plural verb: μέσαι ἦσαν νύκτες (*Anab.* III. 1.33, cited as **16** in Chapter VII §3).

---

[105] The latter is proposed by Schwyzer-Debrunner, p. 622 Zusatz 3; the former is suggested by Kühner-Gerth I, 33 §352.C) β.

§29. IMPERSONAL VARIANTS ON *NVΩ* SENTENCES (TYPE 2)

Impersonal constructions which are roughly equivalent in sense to an ordinary *NVΩ* form may be regarded as transforms of the latter by an impersonal sentence operator. There are several variants on this transformation:

(A) μέλει μοι ταῦτα → μέλει μοι τούτων
    "This concerns me"

(B) δέω (δέομαι) τούτου → δεῖ (δεῖται) μοι τούτου
    "I need this"

In (A) the subject (which is not typically a personal *N*) is transformed to the genitive; in (B) the personal subject is shifted to the dative. In both cases only the left-hand form is represented in Homer, so in this instance the transformational derivation may also be interpreted as an historical development.[106] When the personal construction is copulative, the impersonal transform takes the neuter singular:

(C) οἷός τε εἰμί+infinitive → οἷόν τε ἐστί+infinitive
    "I am able to"   "It is possible to"

So in the periphrastic:

142 Lysias I.10
    οὕτως ἤδη συνειθισμένον ἦν
    "This had become the custom (in my house)"
    (On s'était ainsi habitué)

Note that in **142**, as generally in transformation (C), the verb εἰμί is not introduced by the impersonal construction but is present in the personal source: οὕτως συνειθισμένοι ἦμεν "Thus were we accustomed". The transformation simply restricts the verb to third person singular form. This contrasts with the situation in Latin, where the passive impersonal may introduce a periphrastic construction with *sum* as an aspectual transform of an active verb, e.g. *venerunt → ventum erat* "they came". This impersonal passive which is so characteristic of Latin is rare in Greek, and I have found no example involving the verb εἰμί.

---

[106] For the left-hand member of (B), see *Il.* 3.294 θυμοῦ δευομένους "deprived of breath", Attic δεῖσθαι τροφῆς "lack food". I find it strange that LSJ should list the right-hand member of B as a separate entry, the "impersonal verb" δεῖ, even stranger that they should derive it from "δέω (A) *bind, tie, fetter*" rather than from "δέω (B) *lack, miss, stand in need of*".

I note that the variant on δεῖ μοι τούτου with an infinitive in place of the genitive (and hence the possibility of με for μοι) does occur once in Homer: *Il.* 9.337 τί δὲ δεῖ πολεμιζέμεναι Τρώεσσιν/Ἀργείους "Why need the Argives fight against the Trojans?"

The use of the impersonal construction as an optional variant on the usual *NVΩ* sentence form, as illustrated in A–C and **142**, is attested in Homer but as far as I can see only in two examples: (1) *Il.* 22.319 ὡς αἰχμῆς ἀπέλαμπ' εὐήκεος "such was the shining from Achilles' lance", an expressive alternative for αἰχμὴ ἀπέλαμπε "the lance shone" (cf. the parallel simile *Il.* 6.295 ἀστὴρ δ' ὡς ἀπέλαμπεν, sc. πέπλος); and (2) *Od.* 9.143 οὐδὲ προὐφαίνετ' ἰδέσθαι "There was nothing to be seen of them", in contrast to the *NV* construction οὐδὲ σελήνη ... προὔφαινε "Nor did the moon shine forth", in the following verses.

One post-Homeric use of εἰμί that might be regarded as an impersonal transform is the initial occurrence of ἐστί or ἦν (also γίγνεται) followed by a "subject" *N* in the plural:

143 Hdt. VII.34
  ἔστι δὲ ἑπτὰ στάδιοι ἐξ Ἀβύδου ἐς τὴν ἀπαντίον
  "It is seven stades from Abydus to the other side (of the Hellespont)."

(For other examples see below, **92** in Chapter VI §14; also LSJ s.v. εἰμί A. V, Kühner-Gerth I, 68f., Schwyzer-Debrunner p. 608γ) 2.) Parallel uses of the copula construction are well attested in the same author: Hdt. VI. 36.2 εἰσὶ δὲ οὗτοι στάδιοι ἕξ τε καὶ τριήκοντα τοῦ ἰσθμοῦ (sc. ἐκ Καρδίης πόλιος ἐς Πακτύην)· ἀπὸ δὲ τοῦ ἰσθμοῦ τούτου ἡ Χερσόνησος ἔσω πᾶσά ἐστι σταδίων εἴκοσι καὶ τετρακοσίων τὸ μῆκος. (See also under genitive of measure, above §26.3.) But the initial ἔστι or ἦν tends to become fixed and formulaic (like a logical quantifier), and thus it need no longer agree with its "subject" in number. So ἔστι οἵ... "There are those who", where the verb is frequently singular before a relative clause in the plural. Since we would normally regard the agreement in number between *N* and *V* as evidence for their subject-predicate construction, we may regard the lack of agreement in **134** as a distinct weakening of this syntax. Should we explain the nominative case of στάδιοι by taking it as predicate *N*, as in my translation? This means construing an emphatic initial ἔστι as a copula with existential force. (Compare §25 above.) This is possible for **134**, but will not do for some examples where the plural noun cannot be predicate (e.g. it cannot be predicate in τῆς δ' ἦν τρεῖς κεφαλαί "The Chimaera had three heads" Hesiod *Theog.* 321). Hence I would regard the lack of agreement in **143** as idiomatic and the syntax of the noun as essentially ambiguous between subject, predicate, or "object" position. The ambiguity is trivial, since the copulative and existential constructions give the same sense. (Asyntactic initial *asti*, followed by plural subject, also occurs in Sanskrit, see Chapter VI §8, n. 25.)

§30. IMPERSONAL SENTENCE OPERATORS (TYPE 3)

The true home of the impersonal construction in Greek, and already in Homer, is the class of sentence operators. In the case of *cop A* and *cop N* construed with an infinitival clause, it seems to be only a question of terminology whether one describes this clause as the sentential subject of the copula verb (as I did in §§6 and 10) or whether one says it is an epexegetical-final infinitive to which the impersonal ἐστί is in some sense "bound", as Brugmann suggested.[107] In either case we have an *NVΩ* kernel (in the infinitival clause) and a modal sentence operator κέρδιόν ἐστι "it is better", ἀνάγκη (ἐστί) "it is necessary", etc. And similarly with a noun clause as "subject": δῆλον ὅτι "it is clear that."

As a special case of this syntax, where ἔστι appears *alone* as modal sentence operator without any predicate noun or adjective, we have what I call the potential construction of ἔστι + *infinitive* with the sense "it is possible, permissible to" (and in later Greek also πάρ-εστι, ἔξ-εστι + *infinitive*). This construction is discussed in Chapter VI §17. Here I point out only that the impersonal construal is even more natural for ἔστι + *infinitive* than in the case of *cop A* and *cop N*, since there is no direct analogy here with an elementary construction such as there is for *N is A* or *N is N* (i.e. no analogy comparable to that between *to die in battle is noble* and *Achilles is noble*). Furthermore, the sense is more clearly brought out if we take the infinitive as equivalent to a subordinate clause of purpose or result: "it is possible that you may do such-and-such." On the other hand, it is easy to see how this "impersonal" construction develops from the epexegetical-final use of the infinitive with a more elementary, personal construction for εἰμί:

144 *Il.* 13.814

χεῖρες ἀμύνειν εἰσὶ καὶ ἡμῖν
"We too have hands to defend ourselves"

145 *Il.* 11.339

οὐ δέ οἱ ἵπποι / ἐγγὺς ἔσαν προφυγεῖν
"Nor were his horses nearby for fleeing"

146 *Il.* 8.223 (=11.6)

ἥ ῥ' ἐν μεσσάτῳ ἔσκε γεγωνέμεν ἀμφοτέρωσε
"(Odysseus' ship) was in the middle (convenient) for shouting in both directions"

---

[107] See K. Brugmann, *Die Syntax des einfachen Satzes im Indogermanischen* (Beiheft zum. 43. Band der *Indogerm. Forschungen*) Berlin, 1925, pp. 22 and 33.

In **144** we have a possessive construction, in **145** and **146** a locative use of εἰμί. It is clear that whatever potential sense is present here attaches rather to the epexegetical infinitive than to the kernel sentence with the verb *be*.[108] But a point of ambiguity is reached when we cannot tell whether a given noun is to be construed as the subject of ἔστι or only as a constituent of the infinitival clause.

147 *Il.* 20.246

ἔστι γὰρ ἀμφοτέροισιν ὀνείδεα μυθήσασθαι
πολλὰ μάλα

"There are harsh things enough that could be spoken against us both."

(Lattimore)

Lattimore takes ὀνείδεα as subject of the verb, plausibly enough. But one can also take it simply as object of μυθήσασθαι: "it is possible for both of us to utter reproaches in abundance." In that case the initial ἔστι has become an independent impersonal formula, and we have a potential construction with no elementary syntax for εἰμί. For standard examples see Chapter VI §17.

Another use of ἐστί as impersonal sentence operator is the construction with the verbal in -έον. (For the personal construction of this verbal see above, §19). The impersonal construction – which, unlike the personal construction of the same form, is never passive in meaning – does not require any expression of the verb εἰμί.

148 Xen. *Anab.* II.2.12

πορευτέον δ᾽ ἡμῖν τοὺς πρώτους σταθμοὺς ὡς ἂν δυνώμεθα
μακροτάτους

"We must make our first marches as long as possible."

The personal pronoun in the dative represents the subject of the underlying source: πορευόμεθα τοὺς σταθμούς, "We make our marches." The addition of ἐστί in such a sentence is a stylistic option, just like the choice between neuter singular and plural forms for the verbal:

[108] This is perhaps as good a place as any to scotch the old view (repeated without criticism in Schwyzer-Debrunner, p. 358) that the Greek infinitive is a *dative* form, or that it has any case form at all that might be relevant to the interpretation of its syntax: "il est vain de chercher à retrouver dans les infinitifs grecs une désinence casuelle remontant a l'indo-européen" (Chantraine, *Grammaire hom.* II, 300; see also Meillet-Vendryès *Grammaire comparée* §868, and the literature cited by P. Burguière, *Histoire de l'infinitif en grec* (Paris, 1960), p. 24). For the force of the infinitive in the potential construction, see Chapter VI §17.

149 Thuc. I.86.3

> ἡμῖν δὲ ξύμμαχοι ἀγαθοί (sc. εἰσι), οὓς οὐ παραδοτέα τοῖς
> Ἀθηναίοις ἐστίν.
> "We have good allies, whom we must not abandon to the
> Athenians."

The introduction of ἐστί in **149** adds emphasis and perhaps sonority to the assertion. From the syntactic point of view, it also suggests that every Greek sentence can be regarded as containing or admitting a finite verb, so that ἐστί will always be expressed or understood if no other finite form is available. (The only exception seems to be the sentence operator χρή with which ἐστί never occurs; yet, as I pointed out in §10, the development of an infinitive χρῆναι, a future χρήσται, etc. points to an "understood" ἐστί in this case as well.) For an early parallel to **149** we can cite an example from Hesiod:

150 *Theog.* 732

> τοῖς οὐκ ἐξιτόν ἐστι
> "For the Titans there is no way out."

In **150** we do not have the verbal in -τέος (with its characteristic deontic force) but its historical antecedent, the neuter form in -τός (with potential force). Homer has an impersonal example of this with a suppletive of εἰμί and one without any expressed verb, though not (as it happens) with a form of εἰμί itself:

151 *Od.* 8.299 (≈ 14.489 ≈ *Il.* 16.128)

> καὶ τότε δή γίγνωσκον, ὅ τ᾽ οὐκέτι φυκτὰ πέλοντο
> "And then they realized, that it was no longer possible to flee."

152 *Od.* 11.456

> ἐπεὶ οὐκέτι πιστὰ γυναιξίν
> "For there is no more trust in women"

Note that the Homeric examples show the neuter plural, whereas the singular occurs in Hesiod, and both occur in classic Attic. (For the plural verb πέλοντο in **151**, see Chantraine, *Grammaire hom.* II, 18.) Like the classic examples, the impersonal construction in **150–152** is active, not passive in sense. The underlying kernels are, respectively, of the form *They go out* (ἐξέρχονται), *They escape* (φεύγουσι), and *They* (or *we*) *trust women* (πιστεύομεν γυναιξίν).

Where ἐστί or a suppletive appears in **149–151**, I would describe its surface syntax as that of an impersonal copula: ( ) *is Φ* with subject position empty. It is true that in an example like **151** we can, if we choose, say that "the real Subject ... is not a particular thing already mentioned or implied, but a vague notion – 'the case', 'the course of things'." [109] But it is probably better to say that there is no subject at all, even though there is certainly some sort of *reference* to a situation or course of affairs, just as in ὕει "it is raining" there is (in a similarly vague sense) some reference to the weather. As a rule of thumb in determining whether or not a sentence has an underlying grammatical subject, we can reframe it as a *what*-question: "what is raining?" "what is no longer φυκτά?" "what is no longer πιστὰ γυναιξίν?" In the first and third case the question seems unacceptable. In the case of φυκτά we hesitate, for a vague answer like "the situation" does seem possible. (This possibility may depend upon the erroneous construal of φυκτά as passive.) If so, I would take this to show not that 151 is less impersonal but that our rule of thumb is not a sure test. For a more formal definition of the impersonal construction I propose the following: a sentence lacks a subject in deep structure if there is no expression *provided by the context* – no word, phrase, or clause – which can be inserted in subject position in a plausible rewriting of the sentence. By this definition 150–152 remain impersonal, i.e. subjectless. (Note that 149 could be regarded as only superficially impersonal and assigned to type 2 in §29 above, if we accepted as its source the *passive* construction οἱ ξύμμαχοι οὐ παραδοτέοι εἰσίν, "Our allies must not be surrendered." But the derivation of an active form from a passive source is a dubious procedure, and 149 should probably be left as a true impersonal sentence operator.)

As a troublesome borderline case I mention 104 τόφρα δὲ Κουρήτεσσι κακῶς ἦν and the parallels with adverbial copula cited above in §22: 105–110. Here we do indeed have as vague subject "the situation" or "the course of events", but there seems to be no *expression* in the context that can plausibly be designated as subject. If we recognize these sentences as impersonal, as I think we should, we must admit they represent a special case. For, unlike 148–152, they do not contain a kernel of *NVΩ* form. Thus they seem to belong with the elementary impersonals of type 1 in §28 above.

As a kind of appendix to the impersonal construction I mention certain adverbial uses of the articular infinitive.

153 Lysias XIII.58

      καὶ τό γε ἐπ᾽ ἐκείνῳ εἶναι ἐσώθης

      "And insofar as it was up to him, you were saved"

---

[109] Munro, *Homeric Grammar* §161, who in this connection cites 151 and *Od.* 2.203 χρήματα δ᾽ αὖτε κακῶς βεβρώσεται, οὐδέ ποτ᾽ ἶσα/ἔσσεται "His substance shall be miserably devoured, and no return be made" (Palmer), where it is possible, but not necessary, to take χρήματα as subject of ἶσα.

154 Xen. *Anab.* I.6.9

(ἵνα) σχολὴ ᾖ ἡμῖν, τὸ κατὰ τοῦτον εἶναι, τοὺς ἐθελοντὰς τούτους εὖ ποιεῖν

"So that we shall be free, as far as he is concerned, to do good to those who are willing (to cooperate)."

155 *Ibid.* III.2.37

ὀπισθοφυλακοῖμεν δ' ἡμεῖς ... τὸ νῦν εἶναι

"Let us take the rear guard ... for the time being."

These and parallel examples are cited in LSJ (s.v. εἰμί E.1) as "redundant" uses of εἶναι. In the case of **153** at least we can see exactly where the infinitive comes from: it represents the nominalization of a sentence like Lysias I.6 ὥστε ... μήτε λίαν ἐπ' ἐκείνῃ εἶναι ὅ τι ἂν ἐθέλῃ ποιεῖν "so that it was not too much up to her to do as she pleased", where we have a paralocative construction *N* is PN* with sentential subject or with ποιεῖν as bound infinitive. (Compare Lysias I.34 and other examples of ἐστὶ ἐν + *dative* in §24 above, pp. 162f.) The source of the articular infinitive in **153** is a sentence of the form **153A**: ἐπ' ἐκείνῳ ἐστὶ πότερον σωθήσῃ σὺ ἢ μή "It is up to him whether or not you will be saved." In the nominalization of **153A** for insertion as adverbial modifier in the sentence ἐσώθης "You were saved", the clause with πότερον is zeroed (as truly redundant) but the copula is naturally preserved in infinitival form. Insofar as we recognize the πότερον clause as reconstructible here as sentential subject, the syntax of τὸ ἐπ' ἐκείνῳ εἶναι is not strictly impersonal.

In the case of **154** and **155** I do not see any underlying construction of the finite verb from which the infinitive can be derived. Perhaps we have here simply an extension of the articular infinitive in adverbial-restrictive syntax, by analogy with the regular transformational result in **153**. Equally obscure to me is the underlying syntax of the "redundant" infinitive with ἑκών, as in *Phaedo* 61 C 4 οὐδ' ὁπωστιοῦν σοι ἑκὼν εἶναι πείσεται "He will certainly not obey you, as far as it is up to him." In his note on this passage Burnet observes that ἑκὼν εἶναι is regularly used with a negative verb: "(He will not do it) if he can help it." Here again, then, the construction with a redundant εἶναι has the force of a conditional or restrictive clause; and it may be that the infinitive was added here because the verbal force of ἑκών was no longer felt.

By contrast, the redundant use of εἶναι with verbs of naming, choosing, and giving (illustrated in LSJ s.v. εἰμί E.2) poses no problem of syntactic analysis. In English as in Greek, *We chose him to be our ally* represents a normal factitive or causal operator on the kernel *He is our ally*, and σοφιστὴν ὀνομάζουσι τὸν ἄνδρα εἶναι "They call the man a sophist" (Plato, *Prot.* 311 E 4) has as its kernel (*They say:*) *He is a sophist.* For the use of *be* as possessive (or copula-possessive) verb in a factitive construction with verbs of giving, see below, Chapter V §7, p. 207.

THE THEORY OF THE COPULA

§1. SYNTACTIC AND SEMANTIC ROLES OF THE COPULA

In this chapter I shall attempt to clarify the traditional theory of the copula and, if possible, to put it on a sounder basis, both linguistic and philosophical.

As we have seen, the concept of the copula in medieval logic was reformulated as a grammatical theory by the time of the Port Royal Grammar, where the copula *be* appears under the rather antique title of "verbe substantif" (from Priscian). But perhaps the decisive statement as far as modern linguistics and logic are concerned is that of J. S. Mill:

A proposition is a portion of discourse in which a predicate is affirmed or denied of a subject.... As we cannot conclude from merely seeing two names put together, that they are a predicate and a subject, that is, that one of them is intended to be affirmed or denied of the other, it is necessary that there should be some mode of indicating that such is the intention; some sign to distinguish a predication from any other kind of discourse. This is sometimes done by a slight alteration of one of the words, called an *inflection*; as when we say, Fire burns; the change of the second word from *burn* to *burns* showing that we mean to affirm the predicate burn of the subject fire. But this function is more commonly fulfilled by the word *is*, when an affirmation is intended, *is not* when a negation; or by some other part of the verb *to be*. The word which thus serves the purpose of a sign of predication is called... the *copula*.

(*Logic* I. iv. 1)

We note in passing that Mill follows an ancient tradition in considering predication only in the case of sentences which have (or may have) truth values, that is, for what he calls propositions and I shall call *declarative sentences*; and in this connection he makes no distinction between sentences that are asserted and those that are not. Let us accept this simplification for the moment, and disregard questions, commands, and all "performative" functions of language other than statement-making. The essential point is that Mill, like the authors of Port Royal, takes the subject-predicate relation by which "something is affirmed or denied of something" to be the characteristic feature of declarative discourse, and that he thinks of this relation as properly expressed by a finite verb form. A similar view has been formulated by Quine:

Predication joins a general term and a singular term to form a sentence that is true or false according as the general term is true or false of the object, if any, to which the singular term refers....

Predication is illustrated indifferently by 'Mama is a woman,' 'Mama is big,' and

'Mama sings.' ... For predication the verb may even be looked on as the fundamental form, in that it enters the predication without the auxiliary apparatus 'is' or 'is an.'

The copula 'is' or 'is an' can accordingly be explained simply as a prefix serving to convert a general term from adjectival or substantival form to verbal form for predicative position. (*Word and Object*, pp. 96f.)

Like Mill, Quine has in mind the nominal copula only, and he overlooks the possibility of locative predicates like *here, in London, in the next room.* But we can easily generalize this doctrine as follows: the finite verb is the fundamental form for predication; and where a predicate expression is not a finite verb (whether it be a noun, adjective, adverb, participle, infinitive, or any longer phrase), a finite form of *be* is introduced as the sign of predication. This is precisely the "grammatical rule for the formation of the sentence" in English (and in many other languages) to which we alluded at the very beginning of this study.[1] But Quine's formulation calls attention to the fact that predication is here conceived at two levels, one syntactic and one semantic.

Syntactically, predication is a very general condition for sentencehood or grammaticality, and more particularly for declarative sentencehood. In order to describe it as *the* general condition for sentencehood we must add certain qualifications. Predication as described in the quotations from Mill and Quine is a structure consisting of two terms, the subject and the predicate. Now on the one hand, if we take into account the impersonal constructions described in Chapter IV §27, we must allow for a one-term sentence like ὕει "it-is-raining." And on the other hand, any theory of grammar must allow for three- or four-term sentences with transitive verbs, like *John gives the book to Mary.* The subject-predicate pattern strictly coincides with sentence structure only in two-term sentences with intransitive verbs, as in *John walks* or *Mama sings.* We can of course adapt the dyadic analysis to copula sentences like *John is tall* by agreeing not to count the copula as a term; and we can also extend it to sentences with direct and indirect objects by various other conventions.[2] But the result is to obscure some of the detail of the sentence structure in each case. In order to avoid this rather arbitrary procedure, let us abstract entirely from the dyadic subject-predicate structure and understand predication simply as identical with sentencehood. (This means that we temporarily abandon the traditional two-term scheme of S.-P. analysis; we shall return to it later as in some sense the privileged case.) When predication is understood in this wide sense, we can identify the *sign*

[1] See Chapter I, p. 2.

[2] Thus we can, in the style of Chomsky, identify the predicate with the entire verb phrase (or with $V\Omega$ in the general sentence form $NV\Omega$), in which case *gives the book to Mary* counts as a single complex predicate term; alternatively, we can take the line followed in logic and define a many-place predicate like "——— gives ——— to ———," with *John, book,* and *Mary* to be regarded as three subjects (i.e. arguments) of the sentence.

of predication in I.-E. with the finite verb form. For in English it is clear that a non-empty V in the general form $NV\Omega$ is a necessary condition for sentencehood. (Thus I count as elliptical or non-sentential such utterances as "Fire!" "Right on!" and "Ouch!") And in Greek, where we do encounter verbless sentences, we have agreed that these involve an "understood verb" in their deep structure. By contrast, in impersonal sentences the initial N (or subject position) is really empty. And the surface structure of many Greek sentences will consist of the finite verb alone. Thus the verb is in general a necessary condition for sentencehood, and in Greek surface structure it is often a sufficient condition.

So much for the syntactic function of the verb as sign of predication in the wide sense, for sentences generally. But declarative sentences are those which must be semantically interpreted in the light of their truth claim, i.e. by reference to conditions under which they are to count as true. This semantic perspective, which is explicit in Quine's description of predication, is also implied by Mill when he speaks of "affirming or denying one term of the other." Now when it functions as copula, the verb *be* serves as a sign of predication in both respects, syntactic and semantic: it provides the finite verb form required for sentencehood, and it also provides the signal of a truth claim in its indicative mood. However, in both respects it is the finite verb in general and not the copula as such that is properly described as a sign of predication.[3] The peculiar function of *to be* as copula is to perform this double role in sentences where the predicate in the narrow sense is not a finite verb form.

In using the term "truth claim" for the semantic aspect of predication I lay myself open to a serious misunderstanding, which I must try to dispel before proceding. I do not speak of truth claim in the sense of a *speech act* or intention implying a definite speaker and occasion, as when I utter the sentence "It is now precisely 3:00 P.M." with the intention of informing (or misinforming) my interlocutor as to the hour of day at the moment of utterance. (And similarly for a written sentence in a particular context.) What I have in mind is not such acts of *parole* (in Saussure's sense) but the

---

[3] After writing this, I discover what seems to be the same point made in Abelard's discussion of the copula function: "personalia verba...per se ipsa praedicantur et geminatim funguntur, quia vim praedicati habent et copulantis, ut simul et praedicentur et se ipsa copulent" (*Logica 'Ingredientibus'* ed. B. Geyer, *Beiträge z. Gesch. der Phil. des Mittelalters* XXI. 3 (1927), 359, 23–27). The advantage of rewriting *(A) man runs* as *(A) man is running* is that it separates these two functions of the finite verb, and assigns the copula role to *is* alone. In the post-Aristotelian tradition utilized by Abelard, the semantic aspect of the link-function is described as "affirmation" (as in Mill) and the syntactic function of the copula is described in terms of the completeness (the non-defective or non-elliptical form) of the proposition or of its sense. See my article "On the Terminology for *Copula* and *Existence*", in *Festschrift for Richard Walzer*, forthcoming.

structure of *langue* that makes them possible, i.e. the sentence type which is instantiated in such an utterance. Whether or not we want to say that sentences themselves "make statements" independently of the speakers who pronounce them on a given occasion, it is clear that there is something statement-like or declarative about the sentence form *It is now 3:00 P.M.* which distinguishes it from the question *Is it 3:00 P.M.?* or the exclamation *Would that it were!* Only the first form *can* have a truth value since it *does* have truth conditions; and this is all I mean by saying that the indicative-declarative sentence as such "makes a truth claim." [4] Of course one and the same sentence form can be used to announce a complete statement, to illustrate a grammatical rule, or to formulate an hypothesis, a conditional clause, or one member of a disjunction in a more complex statement. But the use of a declarative sentence to make a simple categorical statement is clearly the *primary* use of such a sentence, the use to which it is appointed by the system of grammatical contrasts that constitutes the formal structure of the language. Hence the utterance of such a sentence with normal declarative intonation by a speaker under normal circumstances (i.e. not in a play or an elocution lesson) will be taken by the hearer for a statement or assertion on the speaker's part. It is in this sense that the truth claim of sentences, at the level of general structure which constitutes the *langue*, makes possible the truth claims of particular speakers, at the level of *parole* or speech acts. [5]

§2. The Finite Verb as the Mark of Declarative Sentencehood

We can now pose the theoretical problem of the copula by way of two distinct questions. Why is a finite verb form required for declarative sen-

---

[4] Actually, this is not quite all. For a sentential form to carry a truth claim means something more than for it to have truth conditions and be a candidate for truth values, but this something more is very difficult to formulate. Compare a sentence with a map or a drawing. The map or drawing might be said to have truth conditions: it shows how things stand if it is a faithful representation. But it does not *claim* to be faithful: there is nothing in the picture that corresponds to the semantic function of the indicative mood. A declarative sentence, on the other hand, not only describes a possible state of affairs but says that it is realized. This is, I take it, the point of Wittgenstein's remark quoted below, p. 190 n. 9.
[5] In his article on "Assertion" (*Philosophical Review* 1965, pp. 449–65) Peter Geach points out that in written form a declarative sentence (or as he puts it, a sentence that "grammatically can be read as an assertion") is usually meant as an assertion when it is printed as an independent sentence with a full stop at the end (p. 456). He is mistaken, I believe, in holding that "there is no naturally used sign of assertion" (p. 457), because he thinks primarily of the written language. In spoken discourse, declarative sentence-intonation is just such a sign. Furthermore, in I.-E. languages the occurrence of an indicative verb in an independent clause (without a question mark or without interrogative intonation) is also a natural sign of assertion, although it is not a *universal* sign: unasserted declarative sentences and asserted sentences without a finite verb both occur, but they occur as exceptions to a more general rule.

tencehood? And why is it precisely the verb *to be* (Indo-European **es-* and its suppletives) that is introduced in the case of a non-verbal predicate?

The first question was answered in part long ago, in the classical discussions of the nominal sentence. As Meillet saw, the nominal or verbless sentence pattern is a very restricted form of utterance, limited in principle to the present indicative and in practice (in Greek and many other languages) nearly always to the third person. Alternatively, we can say that the nominal sentence is *unmarked* for tense and mood, and generally for person as well.[6] In I.-E., these marks for person, tense, and mood are carried primarily or exclusively by the verb. Hence in order to integrate the nominal sentence within the full range of variation for person, tense, and mood, it is necessary to introduce a finite verb form.[7] It is the peculiar power and efficiency of the I.-E. verb that it can specify *all* of these syntactic features – person, tense, mood, and also number and aspect – in a single form, and all but tense and aspect by means of a single complex morpheme, the personal ending. Thus a verb is generally required for sentencehood in Greek not because the verbless sentence form is impossible, but because it is a stiff and restricted syntactical device (which does not prevent it from retaining considerable expressive force just because of its laconic spareness).

So far I have been rehearsing the lesson of Meillet. But there is a more radical sense in which the finite verb is the characteristic mark of sentencehood in Indo-European, and specifically in Greek. In surface structure the verb *by itself* constitutes a sentence in the first and second persons, and within an appropriate context or situation it may do so in the third person form as well. (See Chapter III, §6). The conditions under which a single noun may represent a complete sentence – say, in the answer to a question – are far more restricted. Even the standard nominal sentence, which consists of at least two non-verbal expressions, is not formally distinguishable from a noun phrase that represents only a component of a sentence. For example, ἄριστον μὲν ὕδωρ constitutes a sentence in the opening verse of Pindar's First Olympic: "(The) best (of things is) water;" but the same words could represent the subject of a different sentence: "(the) best water (is found in

---

[6] The second formula reflects Benveniste's view that the nominal sentence is not *in* any particular tense, mood or person. See his "La phrase nominale" in *Problèmes de linguistique générale*, pp. 151–67. I think the difference between this and the usual view may be less significant than Benveniste suggests, since the present tense in I.-E. also serves as the unmarked tense, the indicative may be regarded as the unmarked mood, and the third person is properly unmarked for "person," as Benveniste himself has shown (*ibid.* p. 230).
[7] See Meillet, "La phrase nominale en indo-européen," pp. 19f.; Meillet-Vendryès. *Grammaire comparée* 2nd ed. § 873 (1st ed. § 839). For the relative rarity of verbless sentences in first and second person in Homer, and for examples in various persons, tenses and moods, see C. Guiraud, *La phrase nominale en grec*, pp. 281–327.

mountain springs)." In some languages this distinction between *N (is) A* "water is best" and *AN* "best water" is regularly drawn by a difference in word order; but not so in Greek. In pronunciation there was presumably no ambiguity, and verbless sentences have perhaps always been more common in spoken than in written discourse. (The relatively high frequency of nominal sentences in Homer probably has something to do with the oral style.) But apart from sentence intonation the distinction cannot be drawn in a systematic way, and the recognition of the nominal sentence *as a sentence* depends upon rather special circumstances. The introduction of a finite verb form immediately eliminates the ambiguity: we know that we are confronted with a sentence, or at least with a clause, and not with a noun phrase. Thus the finite verb, if not always necessary in Greek surface structure, is in general *sufficient* as a sign of sentencehood. And the indicative verb is in general a sufficient condition of declarative sentencehood.

This last remark calls for a qualification. The indicative mood ending, in its contrast with optative, subjunctive, and imperative, is the only formal mark of declarative force, aside from intonation. When associated with a characteristic intonation, the indicative signals a truth claim or assertion (in the sense specified in §1).[8] But the indicative mood as such represents the declarative register in general, since the same verb form is also used in questions, suppositions, quotation or ironical echoing of what someone else has said. Among these declarative-indicative uses in a wide sense, I suggest that the categorical or unqualified truth claim is to be regarded as the basic declarative form and as the primary use of the indicative mood. Let us call this the "unmarked" indicative. Interrogation, conjecture, conditional assumption and the like are best regarded as secondary modifications of this fundamental form, modifications in which the underlying statement form is subjected to various epistemic or intentional modalities, marked by contrasting intonation, interrogative particles, and other formal devices.

Insofar as these modifications take place according to fixed rules, they should be indicated in a complete grammar. Many of them are of course noted in traditional grammar, including those cases whether the modification is marked by a shift from the indicative to a different modal form. Thus in

---

[8] In speaking of a characteristic intonation for Ancient Greek we are of course guessing i.e. inferring on the basis of evidence from languages that are still spoken. But in this case the solid inductive base is so strongly reinforced by certain general ("a priori") considerations concerning the functional need for contrasting different kinds of utterances, that the conclusion with regard to Greek (or any other language) seems virtually certain. Still, it is an open question how much actual variation in sentence intonation was permitted by the Greek system of pitch accents associated with individual words and phrases. Perhaps the abundance of particles in Greek served to do much of the work normally performed by sentence intonation in other languages.

Greek the conditional modality is often expressed by an optative or subjunctive verb in the antecedent and sometimes by an optative with ἄν in the consequent. An assumption may be indicated by an imperative form, like ἔστω "let it be so" at the beginning of Euclid's proofs. But a conditional may also be expressed in the indicative. A question regularly takes the indicative, and is sometimes distinguished from the declarative form only by context and/or intonation. My suggestion is that in all such modifications, whether or not they are marked by a formal change of mood, the unqualified truth claim remains the immediate point of reference (for questioning, doubting, assuming), though it is not directly "tendered" or "posed". In Husserl's terminology, we may say that the indicative verb (as unmarked) is the distinctive sign for the primitive *Position* or *thesis* of making a statement, positing as true, but that the same sign (as marked indicative) also serves to express various secondary modifications of this elementary declarative posit.[9] If by predication in the widest sense we mean not only the formal condition of sentencehood but also the semantical dimension in which affirming and denying take place, and if the indicative mood is the proper sign for declarative discourse, both primary (when unmarked) and modified (marked), then we see even more clearly why the verb – and the indicative verb in particular – deserves to be called the sign of predication, and why some verb form is likely to be introduced into every sentence, declarative or otherwise. It is the declarative sentence form, with its indicative verb and its characteristic intonation, that makes possible the individual acts of assertion by a particular speaker. (Conversely, animals with some sort of "language" in which there are no declarative sentence forms as opposed to

---

[9] See *Ideen zu einer reinen Phänomenologie und phän. Philosophie*, I, §§ 103–14, for the doxic modalities as secondary modifications of the primitive *Setzung (Urdoxa)* of certain belief, with factual being-the-case (*schlichtes Sein*) as the correlative *Urform* on the side of the object posited. Husserl's careful analysis of *Setzung* and *Stellungnahme* should prove fruitful for the philosophy of language, if it can be disengaged from its specific background in Husserl's theory of "intentional acts of consciousness." I shall here make an analogical use of Husserl's concept of *Position*, assuming that his theory of doxic and epistemic modalities can be reinterpreted in properly linguistic terms. An appropriate device for this reinterpretation is perhaps provided by Lakoff's analysis of "performative verbs". See below, p. 193.

In his article "Assertion" (quoted above § 1, n. 5), Peter Geach follows Frege in taking as the basic sentential concept an unasserted *proposition*, or "a form of words in which something is propounded, put forward for consideration" (p. 449). My notion of sentential truth claim or *Position* differs from this only in (1) making explicit that "put forward for consideration" means "put forward for consideration *as to its truth*," and (2) taking as primary or primitive the case in which a declarative form of words is used to make an assertion, and as secondary or modified the case in which such a form is not asserted (for example when it is preceded by "if"). The first point is non-controversial; the second corresponds to Wittgenstein's criticism of Frege: "A proposition *shows* how things stand *if* it is true. And it *says that* they do so stand" (*Tractatus* 4.022).

imperatives, cannot be said to make statements as distinct from giving commands.) And this role of the declarative-indicative mood remains fundamental even if in some cases the verb is zeroed and the intonation alone suffices for assertion.

§2a. DIGRESSION ON THE GENERAL THEORY OF MOODS

So far we have considered the finite verb in general and not the verb *be*. In what follows we shall see how *be* figures as the verb *par excellence*, so that the verbal function as such comes to be characteristically represented by *be*, that is to say by ἐστί or εἶναι in Greek. I believe that it is the basic function of the finite verb as an expression of sentential truth claim that helps to make clear how this paradigm verb comes, in the veridical use, to serve as a general expression for fact or being-so. This truth-claiming function is of course most evident when εἰμί appears in the indicative. Yet the infinitive εἶναι or the participle ὄν may also serve to express this idea, as we shall see in Chapter VII. One might suppose that in this veridical use the infinitive and participle serve merely as a convenient nominalization of the indicative form ἐστί. I want to suggest, however, that the truth-claiming function belongs in a sense to all forms of the verb or to the verb as such, just insofar as the unmarked indicative use for statement-making is the basic or primitive sentential form, of which all other forms are secondary modifications. It is commonly assumed among linguists that the indicative is the fundamental form of the verb. I am extending this assumption to the sentential role of the unmarked indicative as expression of a truth claim. This extension involves us in a brief discussion of the theory of grammatical moods. The discussion is relevant here because, if my view of the indicative-declarative form is accepted, we will have a much tighter link between the copula function and the veridical use of εἰμί. Given that εἰμί plays the role of verb *par excellence*, if the function of a verb as such is first and foremost the expression of a truth claim, it follows naturally that εἰμί as a paradigm verb will express the veridical idea: "this is how things stand."

My remarks are formulated for the special case of I.-E. languages with their characteristic verb forms. But the suggestion that the declarative sentence form be taken as fundamental and primitive is a claim that should in principle hold good for any language whatsoever. For I.-E. my suggestion means that the unmarked use of the indicative verb (for unconditional statement) will be taken as the base upon which other moods, including marked uses of the indicative, can be defined as syntactic operations with the force of logical or intentional modalities – including conditional, interrogative, command, and wish, as well as other standard modalities such as possibility, necessity, and obligation ("one ought"). Which of these modalities are expressed by a verb-ending, which ones by a particle or phrase governing a sentence, will be determined by the grammar of a specific language. But if the formal description of moods within a given language is to be given a semantic interpretation, this description will unfold into a general (and possibly universal) theory of propositional "attitudes" – more exactly into a theory of logical, epistemic and intentional modalities, operating upon the basic statement form of the sentence.

It is within such a general theory of modalities that the modal peculiarities of a given language will be best described. In fact such a general theory is vaguely presupposed in any concrete description of moods. For example in Greek it must be pointed out that the particle εἰ "if" imposes a conditional mark on the following verb, regardless whether the verb form remains in the indicative or changes to the subjunctive or optative. These formal alternatives correspond to semantically distinct sub-species of the conditional, as the traditional grammars of Greek recognize. In other languages the general modalities may be more directly expressed in the verb form. Thus languages like Turkish have a distinct suffix (or family of suffixes) for the conditional as such. Furthermore, Turkish regularly derives the interrogative from the declarative form just as it derives the negative from the affirmative, by adding a particle or suffix in either case. The example of the Turkish verb is worth pondering in this as in other respects, since it suggests a general treatment of conditionalization, interrogation, and command as modifications of a declarative base, just as we treat negation as an operation on an underlying affirmative form. (Turkish also expresses the passive and causative transformations by suffixal modifications of the basic verb stem.) The epistemic force of certain Turkish suffixes is particularly interesting. A Turkish grammar illustrates as follows the difference in meaning between three ways of saying "my friend is waiting for me" which differ formally only in one syllable of the verb-ending. "The first states a fact; I can see him there at the corner. The second is based on hearsay; someone has seen him waiting and told me so. The third is a supposition – 'I'm sure he is waiting' – based on the knowledge that my friend is always punctual, that he said he would wait from five o'clock, and that it is now five past five."[10]

On my view, these three forms are to be interpreted as distinct epistemic operations on the universal primitive, the declarative sentential form represented in this case by "My friend is waiting for me." It would seem that the only systematic alternative to the view proposed here would be a

[10] G. I. Lewis, *Turkish Grammar*, (Oxford, 1967), p. 140. In addition to the conditional, the Turkish system of moods and tenses has forms whose function is naturally described as "inferential" and "necessitative" (="one ought to"); *ibid.* pp. 107–41.

quasi-Fregean analysis of the declarative form into a neutral, pre-sentential kernel ("my friend waiting for me") and a declarative operator ("it is so").[11] Whatever advantages such an analysis may have, they seem to be far outweighed by the disconcerting requirement that we define a declarative operation upon an operand that is not itself of sentential form. It is the essential principle of transformational theory as utilized here that all syntactical operations or transformations be defined as relations between sentence forms. It remains to be seen whether a coherent theory of language can be devised that does not respect this principle.

Beyond this principle, I have no proposal to make concerning an appropriate formal development for the general theory of epistemic and intentional modalities whose scope I have sketched. The most straight-forward solution is suggested by Harris' derivation of interrogative and imperative sentences from indicative-declarative form by what he calls "performative sentence-operators".[12] A more complex theory has recently been proposed by George Lakoff in a general analysis of "performative verbs" which includes the statement form as a special case. In Lakoff's theory the underlying structure of every surface sentence would be introduced by a performative verb in present tense with egocentric reference, and this verb would take as its object an embedded sentence S. The underlying structure of a declarative sentence would be of the form *I say to you that S*, with performative variants *I ask you (whether) S* and *I order you (to) S* for question and command. Thus Lakoff has generalized Harris' performative operators to include a statement-operator (though he would not describe it as such). When this statement-operator or performative clause of saying is zeroed, we are left with the declarative sentence represented by S.[13]

Lakoff's analysis of performative verbs is clearly only the beginning of a theory of moods, and it raises as many questions as it solves. But it does suggest an important distinction between epistemic and intentional modalities that are speaker-relative, and hence in his theory would be associated with the governing performative clause, and modes like conditionalization which are not speaker-relative and could be articulated within the embedded sentence S. (The three Turkish modalities illustrated above would presumably fit into the former category. The use of the Greek optative for wish would also belong there, whereas the Greek use of the "potential optative"

[11] For a recent statement of this type of analysis, see John Searle's distinction between the indicator of propositional content and the indicator of an illocutionary act, in *Speech Acts* (Cambridge, 1969), pp. 29–31.

[12] "Transformational Theory", pp. 39f.

[13] See George Lakoff, "Linguistics and Natural Logic," *Synthese* 22 (1970), pp. 165–75. Lakoff's analysis is perhaps acceptable to Searle, but it is much more carefully formulated from a linguistic point of view.

to express logical consequence would not.) In the belief that Lakoff's theory may furnish an interesting basis for further work on moods, I offer a few comments to relate it here to the preceding discussion of modalities.

In the first place Lakoff's analysis is free from the objection just raised against the quasi-Fregean notion of a statement-operator on a neutral kernel or pre-sentential content, since in this analysis the propositional content of the operand is represented by a *sentence*. In the second place this analysis would nonetheless seem to contradict my claim that the declarative form is more primitive than the interrogative or imperative, since statement, question and command are all generated by the same process. But this disagreement is more apparent than real. Lakoff's embedded sentence S, although unasserted, will be in declarative form, and this form is not altered either by the clause of saying or by the zeroing of this clause. (Contrast the treatment of S when the performative verb is *I order* or *I ask*.) The declarative form of S is clearly implied by Lakoff's proposal that truth conditions are associated directly with S: i.e., in my jargon S carries a truth claim. In fact Lakoff's analysis introduces *statement* or *assertion as a speech act* by way of a performative clause, but he takes the *declarative sentence form* as primitive for the universal operand represented by the embedded sentence S. If I have interpreted Lakoff correctly, then, his analysis is fully compatible with the view presented here of the logical and syntactic primacy of the declarative form underlying all modalities.

§3. *Is* VERSUS *becomes*, AND THE GENERAL ASPECTUAL OPPOSITION OF STATIC AND KINETIC (STATIVE-MUTATIVE)

So much for the function of the I.-E. verb as signal of sentence form and truth claim. We turn now to the second question raised at the beginning of § 2: where the predicate (in the narrow sense) is a non-verbal form such as an adjective or locative phrase, why is it precisely the verb *es-* that is introduced? This might seem to be the question of questions, the problem of the verb *be* as such. In fact the question is misleading, since it suggests that there was once a state of the Greek (or pre-Greek) language in which *es-* was not yet used as copula verb, whereas I shall argue that the copula use is primary. For the moment, however, I employ the convenient myth of the evolving copula sentence and ask "Why is the verb *es-* introduced as copula?" It will turn out that this is only a picturesque substitute for the more legitimate question: "What does the copula verb contribute to the sentence in which it occurs?"

First of all, it is remarkable that this question has so rarely been discussed. The closest thing to an answer in the traditional literature is perhaps

the suggestion of Meillet and Vendryès that, since it was necessary to introduce a verb into the nominal sentence as a purely grammatical device to
indicate person, tense, aspect, and mood, the verb chosen should be "as
insignificant as possible by itself." The root *es- was found appropriate for
the formal role since it originally expressed only "existence", and in its
secondary use as copula it soon lost what little meaning it had.[14] Like most
comparative linguists, Meillet and Vendryès take for granted an older sense
to exist for *es-, and offer no analysis of its assumed pre-copulative use.

A number of contemporary theorists have proposed a view of the verb be
that bears a striking analogy to Meillet's, except that they avoid any hypothesis concerning a development from some earlier state of the language. In
place of the myth of the primitive nominal sentence in Indo-European they
offer a theory of deep structure (or the "base component") in which the
verb be does not occur, and in place of the historical evolution of the copula
they propose a generative grammar in which be is introduced by various
transformations. Thus our verb is described by Lyons as "a semantically
empty 'dummy verb' generated by the grammatical rules" of a particular
language, "to 'carry' the markers of tense, mood, and aspect in the surface
structure of sentences" that do not contain another finite verb.[15] Lyons is
careful to point out that be is not entirely meaningless in this role, since it
does stand in contrast with certain other verbs such as become. But he sees
this as "a particular instance of a more general aspectual opposition which
might be called static and dynamic:…as locomotion is to location, so
acquisition is to possession, and 'becoming' to 'being'." [16] Thus we get the
following pairs of dynamic-static or, as I shall say, kinetic-static or mutative-
stative contrast:

(1)   John gets a book – John has a book

(2)   Mary becomes beautiful – Mary is beautiful

(3)   Richard goes/comes to San Francisco – Richard is in San Fran-
       cisco

[14] Meillet-Vendryès Traité de grammaire comparée des langues classiques, (2nd ed. § 873
=1st ed. § 839): "Mais pour indiquer dans la phrase nominale les diverses notions acces-
soires que les formes verbales expriment, il a fallu y introduire un verbe, aussi peu signi-
ficatif que possible par lui-même. La racine *es- qui signifiait "exister" (cf. εἴ που ζώει τε
καὶ ἔστιν, ω 236) s'est trouvée apte à ce rôle….Le verbe d'existence, perdant sa signification
propre, a été réduit peu à peu au rôle de simple copule."
[15] Lyons, Introduction, pp. 322f., 388. For other similar views, see below, § 9, n. 39.
[16] Ibid. p. 397. Jespersen had described the opposition of stability (state) and change (into or
out of a state) as one form of aspectual contrast in Philosophy of Grammar, pp. 287f. He
later proposed the terms static and kinetic (A Modern English Grammar III, 355). Lyons also
suggests the terms stative and mutative.

This suggests that what the nominal copula (2) and the locative copula (3) have in common – and what they share with that other "dummy-verb" *have* – is precisely the static or stative aspect by which they contrast with verbs of motion and change.

Lyons' analysis of the aspectual value of *be* applies even more neatly to Greek than to English. For in the first place it is εἰμί which provides the construction for static possession that corresponds to *have* in English (ἔστι μοι). And in the second place Greek has a *become* verb γίγνομαι which is not restricted to the role of the nominal copula (as *become* is in English) but functions in kinetic or mutative contrast to εἰμί in the locative and possessive constructions as well:

1   *Il.* 9.125 (=9.267)

οὔ κεν ἀλήϊος εἴη ἀνὴρ ᾧ τόσσα γένοιτο

"That man would not be poor in possessions, to whom so much *was given*"

(after Lattimore)

2   *Il.* 11.13

τοῖσι δ' ἄφαρ πόλεμος γλυκίων γένετ' ἠὲ νέεσθαι

"And now battle *became* sweeter to them than to go back (home)"

(Lattimore)

3   *Il.* 9.669

οἱ δ' ὅτε δὴ κλισίῃσιν ἐν Ἀτρεΐδαο γένοντο

"Now when these *had come back* to the shelters of Agamemnon"

(Lattimore)

This range of uses for γίγνομαι is preserved in classic Attic; furthermore (both in Homer and later) the same verb serves as kinetic or mutative pendant to εἰμί in most of the existential uses of εἰμί as well: e.g. γίγνομαι "I am born"/εἰμί "I am alive". Hence the *be-become* contrast in Greek is practically co-extensive with the static-kinetic aspectual opposition.

This analysis can be reformulated as a partial answer to our question: why is it precisely the verb *es-* or εἰμί that is introduced into sentences with non-verbal predicates? Whatever we take as the most fundamental or most characteristic uses of εἰμί, they must be such as to make it an appropriate expression for the static aspect in the sense defined by the contrasts in (1)–(3). This is in harmony with the fact that εἰμί in Greek has only durative (present and imperfect) forms, with no other "aspects" in the traditional sense (i.e. no aorist or perfect forms).[17] Since Lyons is discussing English rather than ancient Greek, he does not consider the relation between this static value

[17] In Ancient Greek generally (unlike Modern Greek) the future is not aspectually marked, but it is worth noting that the future forms of εἰμί are all derived from the durative stem ἐσ-. At the same time, it must be pointed out that there is no necessary agreement between

for the copula and the whole range of non-copulative uses of εἰμί which we discuss in the following chapters. He does suggest, however, that the existential and locative constructions are very generally connected with expressions for possession.[18] We postpone these larger questions, and restrict ourselves here to the copulative use of *es-.

Ignoring the suggestion of a theoretical level of deep structure without the verb *be* and considering only sentence forms in which the copula actually occurs, we can describe the situation in either of two ways: (1) In addition to its role as "carrier" for the verbal marks of tense, mood, etc., εἰμί has (a) the general aspectual value *static* as opposed to *kinetic*, i.e. it means *being (duratively) in a certain condition, standing in a certain state* (compare the static effect of periphrasis with εἰμί and the predilection of this construction for the "stative" perfect participles as remarked in Chapter IV, § 17); and (b) with locative predicates this general value is specified as *staying (being located) in a given place*. (2) Alternatively, we can proceed as dictionaries traditionally do, giving the most "concrete" use first and treating the others as derived or "extended" senses of the word: (a) εἰμί in the local sense, *be somewhere, be in a place*, and (b) in a wider or more abstract sense, *be in a given state, condition or relationship: be sick, be tall, be captain, be brother to*, etc. This second account is in part a simplified version of what we actually find as the conjectural history of the verb *be* in the Oxford English Dictionary.[19] We shall return, in Chapter VIII, to the hypothesis implied in (2),

---

the durative aspect as defined by Meillet and others (which concerns contrasting forms of *the same verb*, e.g. imperfect *contra* aorist) and Lyons' static aspect (which involves a contrast between different verbs). Thus the Greek verb εἶμι "I go" (in post-Homeric Greek "I will go") would in virtue of its meaning have to be counted as kinetic in Lyons' sense, yet (like its near-homonym εἰμί) this verb is conjugated only in durative forms: the aorist for "go" is provided by suppletive verbs (ἔβην, ἦλθον), just as in the case of ἐγενόμην ("I became") for εἰμί. Since the two oppositions are marked at different levels, one lexical and the other morphological, there is room within the *is-becomes* contrast in Greek for a further opposition between durative and non-durative expression for *becomes*: μέγαλος ἐγίγνετο, μέγαλος ἐγένετο. "He was becoming great," "He became great."

To some extent, then, the durative/non-durative and static/kinetic oppositions vary independently of one another. Yet the fact remains that there is no generally available non-durative expression for *is* or *was* in Greek, except precisely for those suppletive verbs like ἔπλετο and τέτυκται which would normally be rendered as kinetic ("it became" and "it has been made"), but which at the limit may provide simply an aorist or perfect for εἰμί (like ἔφυ and πέφυκα in Attic). When this limit is reached, the lexical contrast between *is* and *becomes* yields to an opposition which is aspectual in the narrower, traditional sense. For examples, see below § 7.

[18] Lyons, *Introduction* pp. 390–7; "A Note on Possessive, Existential, and Locative", *Foundations of Language* 3 (1967), 390–5.

[19] "The primary sense appears to have been that of branch II below, 'to occupy a place' (i.e. *to sit, stand, lie*, etc.) in some specified place; thence the more abstract branch I was derived by abstracting the notion of particular place, so as to emphasize that of actual existence, 'to be somewhere, no matter where, to be in the universe, or realm of fact, to

which takes the concrete local use of εἰμί as somehow basic or primitive. But on either view we see that the use of *be* as locative copula might be regarded as paradigmatic for its copula use generally, in the sense that *to stand* is paradigmatic for the notion of *state* in general, quite apart from etymological considerations.

§4. CRITICISM OF TRADITIONAL ACCOUNTS OF THE DEVELOPMENT OF THE COPULA

We may summarize the conclusion of the last section by describing εἰμί as a *verb of station* as opposed to a *verb of motion*, where *motion* is understood broadly to mean change of any sort, and *station* is similarly understood to mean any (at least temporarily) fixed state, quality, or relation. If we combine this with the result of § 2, we see that although *be* as a copula seems to have no "meaning of its own" in that it contributes no independent item of information, no distinct lexical idea, and hence may generally be reconstructed wherever it is omitted, nevertheless it is not altogether *meaningless* in that it does make some significant contribution to the sentence as a whole: (1) as finite verb in the indicative, *is* serves as distinctive sign of the truth-claim essential to declarative sentencehood, and (2) as verb of station *be* in any form represents the aspectual value *static* in contrast to *kinetic* (or *mutative*) represented by *become* (in Greek γίγνομαι, πέλομαι, τελέθω, τέτυγμαι etc.). Notice that while the first role could in principle be filled by any verb in the language, the second function defines a much narrower class of possible copula verbs, namely those meaning *stand, sit, lie, stay*, and the like. It is no surprise, then, to discover that forms derived from other verbs of this class have been incorporated into the conjugation of *es- in various I.-E. families: forms from *stare* in the Romance languages (*It. stato,* Fr. *été, étais*), forms from *ves- "to stay, dwell" in Germanic (Engl. *was,* Germ. *war*).[20]

---

have a place among existing things; to exist'. Branch III [sc. the copula] was derived from II by weakening the idea of actual presence, into the merely intellectual conception of 'having a place' in a class of notions or 'being identical with' another notion: 'centaurs are imaginary creatures' = 'centaurs have their place in the class of creatures of the imagination'." Note that the O.E.D. correctly situates *be* among verbs of station or position, but misses its distinctively static aspectual value.

[20] This is paralleled by a tendency for *become*-verbs also to lose their aspectual value and become assimilated to *es-. Thus I.-E. *bhū-, which originally figured as a *become*-copula (cf. Greek φύομαι, ἔφυ, where the mutative aspect is clear) has been integrated into the conjugation of Latin *sum* (*fui*) and English *am/is/are* (*be*), and has replaced *es- as primary copula in Russian (*byla,* etc.). On English *be,* see the O.E.D. *s.v.* B.I.2: "*To become, come about* was the Old English and early Middle English sense of *béon,* while still a distinct verb, before it became blended with *am, was.*" I am told, however, that this etymological sense is not at all common in old English texts.

With these observations in mind, we are in a position to judge more critically the standard historical accounts of the origin of the copula in I.-E. The aim of this and the next section will be primarily negative, since I wish to deny that the diachronic perspective can shed any light on the nature and function of *es- as copula verb. In particular I claim that the role of εἰμί as copula, illustrated in Chapter IV, must be taken for granted in any account of apposition and nominal predication with other verbs. And I shall suggest that the copula role is fundamental for εἰμί and that, if any, it is the existential uses (which are in every period much less frequent) that could more reasonably be regarded as secondary or "derived" – though in fact both copula and existential uses are attested in the earliest known state of Greek and of *every* I.-E. language, as far as I can tell.

The standard account of the copula begins with a hypothetical state of the I.-E. *Ursprache* in which there was no copula verb properly speaking, but where the functions of nominal and locative predication were performed by two other devices: (i) the nominal (verbless) sentence, and (ii) the construction of predicates in "apposition" with a verb of distinct meaning that might equally well be used alone, as in the English examples: *to go | first, to die | poor, to stand | still, to sit | at home.* In this primitive state of the language, the verb *es- was a verb like other verbs, meaning only *to exist* or perhaps having some more "concrete" sense which we cannot recover. Like many other verbs, it could be construed with nominal and locative predicates. The fading of the verb into a mere copula ("blosses Formwort," "Bindewort") occurred when the emphasis of the speaker and the attention of the hearer fell so strongly on the predicate that the content of the verb itself was no longer of any consequence. The verb thus lost its meaning, and the copula sentence with *es- emerged as a more flexible formal variant on the original nominal sentence.[21]

Since I am not a comparative philologist, I cannot undertake a general criticism of this view for I.-E. I simply note that neither of the conditions assumed by the developmental hypothesis – the original absence of a copula

---

[21] This is essentially the view of K. Brugmann, *Kurze vergleichende Grammatik* § 861, developed in greater detail by B. Delbrück, *Vergleichende Syntax der indogermanischen Sprachen* III (=Brugmann-Delbrück, *Grundriss* V), pp. 10–4; cf. p. 121. In his original article "La phrase nominale en indo-européen, *MSL* 14 (1906), 1–26, Meillet insisted that *es- served as copula in prehistoric I.-E., and that the nominal sentence was common only in the present indicative and above all in the third person. But his account in Meillet-Vendryès, *Grammaire comparée* (cited above, in § 3, n. 14) follows Brugmann and Delbrück in assuming that (1) *es- originally meant *to exist,* and (2) the copula use gradually becomes more important and leads to the loss of this original sense of the verb. Similar developmental assumptions underlie the account of the Greek copula in Kühner-Gerth I, 3 and 42; and Schwyzer-Debrunner pp. 623f. The latter claims explicitly that the nominal sentence pattern is older than the copula construction.

verb and the use of *es- as independent verb only – seems to be attested for any known form of I.-E.[22] And from the Greek point of view, neither assumption is at all plausible. The verbless sentence pattern occurs in Homer, of course, but it is more common than the copula form only in the third person singular present indicative, as we have seen.[23] Not only does the copulative construction occur for every form of the verb; it is overwhelmingly more frequent than the existential uses, or than all non-copulative uses combined. Let me recall the figures for εἰμί in the first 12 books of the *Iliad*: 451 copulative constructions against 111 other examples (and of these others, some 19 are mixed copulative uses). The distinctly existential uses scarcely number more than 45 or 55 out of 562 occurrences of the verb, i.e. about one case in 10.[24] The figures for the existential use in my Lysias and Xenophon samples are comparable (7%, 9%, 8%, 13%), and the frequency is perhaps not very different for the use of existential *there is* in Modern English.[25] The number and variety of non-copulative uses is greater in Homer than in Attic (and much greater in both than in modern English), and it is only reasonable to suppose that in some unknown earlier state of the language it was greater still. But when we consider the other side of the story, that the copula construction alone accounts for about 80% of the Homeric usage of the verb (as against 75–90% in Attic, perhaps 90–95% in modern English), it is perfectly arbitrary to assume that at some time in the remote past this figure stood at zero. A more likely guess is that the copula construction is as old as the verb *es-. And when we consider that the copula use of *gen- is also well-established in Homer (and in Vedic) and that the static-kinetic aspectual contrast is attested for *be-become* in most or all I.-E. languages (*esse/fieri* in Latin, *as-/bha-* or *as-/jan-* in Sanscrit, *sein/werden* in German, etc.) we may reasonably conclude that the copula sentence form, with its

---

[22] It has been suggested that in Russian *yest* (from *es-) represents an existential verb only. It is true that *yest* scarcely functions as nominal copula; and as locative copula it commonly has existential force ("there is"). But *yest* is at best the vestige of an I.-E. verb, having neither past nor future tense and no personal forms except the 3rd singular indicative (with its negative *niet*). The formal decadence of *yest* is presumably to be connected with two other facts: "en slave, les divers dialectes attestent que l'emploi constant de la phrase nominale pure est une innovation russe" (Meillet, "La phrase nominale," p. 15; other authors have thought differently); and the copula in past and future is provided by forms (*byl-*, etc.) derived from *bhū-, with loss of the original kinetic aspect. There is nothing here to suggest a primitive state of I.-E.

[23] See above, p. 188, n. 7; also below, Appendix B, pp. 438–40.

[24] The exact figure for the existential use depends upon whether or not the "vital" use (my Type I in Chapter VI) is counted as existential. The number of examples rises to 63 if we count the possessive construction as well, and to 75 if we add the veridical.

[25] I count seven examples of *there is/there are* in the first 100 occurrences of *be* in Ralph Ellison's *Invisible Man*, and the same number in the first 100 occurrences in Stevenson's *Treasure Island*.

characteristic aspectual opposition, is as old as the I.-E. language family. It is in any case as old as Greek.

Insofar as some versions of the developmental hypothesis admit that *es- has always been construed with nominal and locative predicates, my conclusion is not strictly incompatible with the traditional account. Insofar as it remains developmental, however, I reject the traditional view in any form. I see no reason to believe that the use of εἰμί in Homer has evolved from some earlier system that was fundamentally different in its construction of nominal and locative predicates.

§5. Transformational Derivation of Apposition and Quasi-Predication from Copula Sentences with *be*

The conclusion which I have been arguing empirically, on the basis of statistics from the *Iliad*, can be more directly established by a theoretical argument on transformational principles. The argument will go as follows. Of the two alleged alternatives to the copula construction, the first alternative, namely apposition, actually presupposes the copula, since the appositive form N_1, *the* N_2 or N_1, *a* N_2, (e.g. *Agamemnon son of Atreus*) is derived from the predicative form N_1 *is* N_2 (*Agamemnon is son of Atreus*), just as AN comes in general from N *is* A (e.g. *a bad boy* from *a boy (who) is bad*).[26] On the other hand the second alternative – the nominal sentence – is no alternative at all, since it must be regarded as containing the zero form of the verb *be*. The hypothesis of the primitive nominal sentence is, from the point of view of transformational theory, simply the conjecture that at some time in the I.-E. past the verb *to be* (as the static copula in N *is* A, N *is* PN, etc.) had only zero forms. For an account of the uses of εἰμί in Greek this conjecture is not very interesting, and I shall have no more to say about it.

The question of apposition is of direct interest, however, since we think of it as characteristic of the archaic "paratactic" style in Homer. Hence I want to make explicit the argument that appositional syntax cannot be primitive but presupposes a construction with *be*. This forms part of the more general claim that any predicative construction with verbs other than *be* or *become* presupposes at least one of these two basic copulas. The theoretical situation is the same for any I.-E. language, and we may more conveniently consider the case for English. Jespersen has summarized the data in his account of "predicatives of being." (Note that Jespersen uses the term "predicative" for what I call a predicate in the narrow sense.)

---

[26] For the derivation of appositive nouns, see B. L. Robbins, *The Definite Article in English Transformations*, pp. 204–6.

The phenomena to be dealt with here may be arranged in something like the following gradation: [27]

1. There he sat, *a giant among dwarfs.*
2. He came back *a changed being altogether.*
3. He married *young* and died *poor.*
4. The snow was falling *thick.*
5. The natives go *naked.*
6. The streets ran *parallel* with the beach.
7. She stood *godmother* to his little boy.
8. He seemed *anxious.*
9. It proved *true.*
10. It was *true.*
11. *The more fool* he!

All of Jespersen's examples involve nominal predicates, though we have a locative phrase as well in 1, and perhaps in 6. In order for locative and paralocative constructions to be fully represented, I add the following:

12. Suddenly I caught a glimpse of them, *half a mile away.*
13. John stays *in the same hotel* every summer.
14. He remained *in the Party* after the purge.
15. He seemed as much *in love with her* as ever.

Jespersen divides his samples into three groups: (A) extraposition, the limiting form of apposition in which the words are "added as a kind of afterthought after the sentence has been completed" (sentences 1 and 12), (B) quasi-predicatives, in which the sentence-nexus would be "wholly or nearly complete without the quasi-predicative" (sentences 2–5, 13–14), and (C) true predicatives, where the nexus (or, as we may say, the kernel) is incomplete without the predicative expression (sentences 8–11 and 15; note that there is only a difference of degree between (B) and (C) and that cases like 6 and 7, and perhaps 13–14, may be regarded as intermediate).

For extraposition, for ordinary apposition within the sentence, and for quasi-predicatives as well, Jespersen's own discussion makes clear that we have, in effect, the conjunction of two sentences: "Words in extraposition... form, as it were, a separate utterance, which might even be called a separate sentence" (*M.E.G.* III, 357); quasi-predicatives "admit of a circumscription [we would say, a paraphrase] in which the substantive or adjective appears as the predicative of a form of the verb *be*: *we parted the best of friends* = we were the best of friends when we parted | *they go naked* = they are naked as

---

[27] *Modern English Grammar* III, 356. I have added the sentence numbers for reference. Jespersen's general view is restated more briefly in *Essentials of English Grammar*, p. 124–31.

they go (about) | *he lay sick* = he was sick, and he was lying | *he died a beggar* = he died when he was a beggar, or, he was a beggar when he died" (*ibid.* 358). A transformational analysis will simply formalize this insight by defining the appropriate operations for sentence-connection, permutation, zeroing, and the like, so that the predicate constructions in italics will in each case be derived from a complex source in which one member is a copula sentence with *be*. In some cases the second component will be a sentence operator rather than a distinct sentence, e.g.

9.   *It proved true ← It proved to be true ← It was true* and *It proved so*,

where *It proved so* represents an operator which is comparable in meaning to *It became clear that*, but differs from the latter in that it transforms its operand sentence as an infinitive rather than as a *that*-clause. (Compare the Greek constructions of δῆλόν ἐστι with *that*-clause and δῆλός ἐστι with participle, in Chapter IV, § 20; also φαίνεται ὅτι with φαίνεται εἶναι, φαίνεται ὤν, etc.)

§6. *Be* MODIFIERS AND *be*-REPLACERS

In most of the examples just considered, the derivation of apposition and quasi-predication from a source of the form *N is Φ* raises no problems of principle, even if the detail of the analysis may offer some difficulty (for example, in deriving *The more fool he*! from a kernel of the form *He is a fool* or *He is foolish*). The situation is different for a sentence like 8, *He seemed anxious*, where we may be reluctant on principle to accept *He is anxious* as a source, for the obvious reason that 8 may be true where *He is anxious* is false. Can a given sentence be derived from a "source" which is not part of its meaning? Yet the derivation is surely correct, as we can see from

8A   He seemed to be anxious.

In 8A we have an explicit verb operator (*He*) *seemed* on a kernel *He is anxious*, just as in the case of *He began to be anxious, He wanted to be a painter*. We may describe such operators as *be*-modifiers to distinguish them from the *be*-replacers that do not admit *be* in the resulting transform. Examples of *be*-replacers are *stands (tall), lies (flat), stays (on the job), goes (naked)*. We find the same distinction in Greek between δοκεῖ, φαίνεται (εἶναι) καλός, νομίζεται (εἶναι) ἀγαθός on the one hand, and true *be*-replacers like πέλομαι, γίγνομαι, κεῖμαι etc. (In some cases of the "redundant" use of εἰμί the transformational structure of *be*-modifiers is clearer in Greek than in English: σοφιστὴν ὀνομάζουσι τὸν ἄνδρα εἶναι "They call the man a sophist"; σύμμαχόν μιν εἵλοντο εἶναι "They chose him as ally";

where the underlying *be* is zeroed in English but preserved in Greek. See L.S.J. *s.v.* εἰμί E.2.) In most cases these *be*-modifiers are general operators that can be construed with any verb: *He seemed to love her, He began to walk away, He wants to finish the job*. It is characteristic of many of these operators, particularly those which express intentional concepts, that they modify the truth claim of their operand sentence, just as a question, a dubitative utterance, or a conditional construction modifies the underlying truth claim of the indicative mood. (See above, § 2.) In this respect *He seems (to be) rich* behaves like *He wants to be rich*: neither sentence affirms their common kernel, *He is rich*.

Thus, accepting Jespersen's account of the parallels between apposition, quasi-predicatives, and true predicatives with or without *be*, a transformational grammarian will interpret these facts rather differently. Whereas Jespersen sees the verbless form *The more fool he*! as "the last link of a long series beginning with descriptions which stand really outside the sentence as an afterthought,"[28] we analyze them all, including the verbless form, as specified transforms of the basic copula sentence *N is Φ*. Only in the case of the *be*-replacers like *stays, stands*, etc. need we consider another possibility: namely, to treat these not as transforms of *is* but as genuine alternatives, that is to say, as elementary copulas. On this view, *be* will appear not as the unique kernel copula but only as the most important member of a small set of verbs occurring in elementary sentences of the form *NVA, NVN(nominative), NVPN*, etc., marked for static aspect. In contrast, we will have a similarly small group of "kinetic" copulas, with *become* as the major representative but also including *turn (green), grow (tall), fall (sick)*, etc. In the traditional diachronic theory of the development of copula *be*, these "copula-like" verbs are cited as evidence that "some verbs when connected with predicatives tend to lose their full meaning and approach the function of an empty link."[29] The verb **es-* would be the limiting case, where the loss of meaning is complete. Since we have abandoned the developmental perspective, however, we must reinterpret these facts synchronically. Shall we regard εἰμί among static *be*-replacers simply as first among equals? Or shall we derive the copula construction with other verbs from a single underlying form with *be*? The same question recurs in an even more funda-

---

[28] *Essentials of English Grammar*, p. 124.
[29] Jespersen, *MEG* III, 356. Compare Kühner–Gerth I, 42 on "Kopulaartige Verben": "Sie unterscheiden sich aber dadurch von der Kopula εἶναι, dass sie nicht zu einem rein abstrakten Begriffe herabsinken, sondern neben der kopulativen Kraft ihre konkrete Grundbedeutung festhalten." Kühner-Gerth's list includes not only *be*- and *become*-replacers like πέλω, ἔφυν, καθέστηκα, but also *be*-modifiers like φαίνομαι, νομίζομαι. Note that some verbs admit both constructions, with or without εἶναι (or ὤν): τυγχάνω, κυρῶ, ὀνομάζομαι. In principle, these are all *be*-modifiers.

mental form for the *be-become* opposition. Is this to be regarded as primitive? Or shall we derive *become* in turn from *be*?

§7. THE PRIORITY OF *be* TO *become*

These questions oblige us to clarify our theoretical concept of the verb *be*. In fact we seem to be dealing here not with a single notion but with a nested family of concepts on different levels of abstraction or theoretical generality. And a clearer view of these distinctions may help us to see what is at stake in the suggestion that the verb *be* can be eliminated from the deep structure of English and other languages.

Consider first the question whether we are to regard the opposition between *be* and *become* as primitive, or whether we derive *become* from *be*. The former view is suggested by the theory of aspects developed by Lyons, since the *be-become* contrast is presented there as a special case of a more general pattern of static-kinetic opposition. On the other hand, the conceptual derivation of *become* from *be* was explicitly proposed by Jespersen, who claimed that for "predicatives of becoming, the underlying notion is 'begin to be'."[30] Our answer to this question will determine the generality of our concept of the verb *be*. On the one hand we get a single copula form as source for *all* predicative constructions, both nominal and locative; on the other hand we accept an irreducible duality characterizing the copula in all its forms. Now the existence of this duality is a fact: the *be-become* contrast extends throughout the I.-E. languages and many others; and as we have seen, it may be correlated with a number of generalizations concerning the opposition between *have* and *get*, as well as between verbs of station (*is, stands, stays*) and verbs of motion (*goes broke* and *goes to town, runs dry* and *runs into trouble*). The kinetic aspect also characterizes another important class of predicative constructions, with causative or factitive verbs: *They made him king, they made him happy*.[31] Nevertheless, the derivation of *become* from *be* is philosophically deeper, and is probably also more useful for linguistic description. It is deeper in that *be* is "notionally" (i.e. conceptually) prior to *become*, as Jespersen saw: *X becomes Y* presupposes *X was not Y* and implies *X will be Y* or at least *X begins to be Y*. But the converse does not hold: *X is Y* does not presuppose or imply any sentence with *become*. Being is logically prior to becoming, just as location is prior

---

[30] *MEG* III, 383. Lyons might have some sympathy with this view, since he describes the stative forms as "unmarked", the mutative as "marked" (*Introduction* p. 398).

[31] Jespersen himself drew the parallel between "predicatives of becoming" and the proleptic object ("object of result") of factitive verbs like *He painted the fence green, He drove her mad*; and we may add the locative forms *He drove her to town, He ran his father into debt*. Compare Lyons, *Introduction* pp. 398f.

to motion and, in general, the concept of state is prior to the concept of a change of state. This priority is expressed in the mathematical form of the corresponding concepts in physics, where motion, for example, is defined in terms of position at different times.

This conceptual priority of *be* to *become* sheds light on a number of "empirical" facts. Thus the root for *is* (*es-) is common to all (or practically all) I.-E. languages, but there is no corresponding universality in the expression for the contrasting term. *Become, devenir, werden, fieri,* represent so many different roots, whose lexical function is in each case defined by their opposition to *es-. In Homer, where the aspect of *become* is expressed by four verbs, γίγνομαι, πέλω, τελέθω and τέτυγμαι, the four verbs *together* are considerably less frequent than εἰμί alone. (I count 13 forms of the former for 39 of εἰμί in *Odyssey* 13; the four verbs for *become* occupy a total of 2½–3 columns or less than 1½ pages in Gehring's *Index Homericus,* where the entries for εἰμί fill almost 8 columns or four pages.) Furthermore, in many of their occurrences these verbs tend to lose their aspectual contrast and to figure as more or less expressive substitutes for εἰμί, like *stand, lie,* etc. for *be.* For example, in the description of a scene on Achilles' shield, the verb τέτυκτο expresses the work of the craftsman: *Il.* 18.549 τὸ δὴ περὶ θαῦμα τέτυκτο "Such was the wonder of the shield's forging" (Lattimore), literally, "it was fashioned a marvel exceedingly". But in the description of Ithaca (*Od.* 13.243) οὐδ' εὐρεῖα τέτυκται "the island is not broad," the same verb is almost indistinguishable in meaning from ἐστί in the preceding verse (οὐχ ἱππήλατός ἐστιν "it is not good for driving horses"): there is at most a slight metaphorical suggestion of an analogy between the formation of the island and that of a work of art. Similarly ἔπλετο, which usually indicates a process or event (e.g. *Il.* 4.478 μινυνθάδιος δέ οἱ αἰὼν/ἔπλετο "His life became short, [as he was beaten down by the spear of Ajax]"), may be used with an aspectual value indistinguishable from εἰμί: *Il.* 6.434 ἔνθα/ἀμβατός ἐστι πόλις καὶ ἐπίδρομον ἔπλετο τεῖχος "where the city is openest to attack and the wall may be mounted" (Lattimore: the two copula-predicate phrases are so closely parallel here that they are actually transposed in this rendering). Thus πέλομαι in many passages in Homer tends to serve as an equivalent for εἰμί; and in the poem of Parmenides the two verbs are treated as strictly synonymous.[32] This is the same process of the assimilation of a kinetic verb to the meaning of its static counterpart which we find in the derivatives of *bhū-* that serve as suppletive or substitute for *es-* in Latin, in Russian, and in English *be.* (See § 4, n. 20.) But the opposite process, by which a form of *es-* acquires the meaning *become,* seems never to occur. The static copula represents the fixed point around which the predicative system

[32] See Parmenides fr. 6.8, fr. 8.11, 18, etc.

of the language revolves: it exerts a strong influence on other forms, including words for *become*, and thus it frequently draws them into its own position in the static center of the system.

Another striking testimony to the more fundamental role of *be* is provided by the case of factitive verbs, which are themselves kinetic in meaning but presuppose the static copula. Thus *John makes Mary happy* can be paraphrased by *John causes her to be* (not *to become*) *happy*; *We elected him president* has as a variant *We elected him to be president*. There is a parallel in the expressions for possession. As Lyons points out, "*Bill has given John a book* implies *John has a book*": *to give* is *to make to have*, not *to make to get*.[33] In Greek this relationship may be idiomatically expressed by the use of εἰμί in possessive (or copula-possessive) construction after the verb *to give*: *Il.* 10.269 Ἀμφιδάμας δὲ Μόλῳ δῶκε ξεινήϊον εἶναι "Amphadamas gave (the boar-tusk helmet) to Molos to be a gift of hospitality."

We see that we could, if we chose, eliminate *become and* γίγνομαι from the kernel forms of English and Greek and introduce them as an aspectual variant on *be* produced by some general verb operator like *begins (to be)* or *comes (to be)*, which operates on other verbs as well *(begins to rain, comes to prefer)*. But we cannot eliminate *be* from kernel forms without allowing for some other systematic marker of tense, mood and static aspect in sentences with non-verbal predicates.[34]

§8. THEORETICAL CONCEPT OF THE VERB *be* AS REQUIRED IN TRANSFORMATIONAL GRAMMAR

I have argued that both appositive syntax and *become*-copulas presuppose the copula *be*, as do other *be*-modifiers. But I have not yet dealt with the relation between *be* (or εἰμί) and the static *be*-replacers such as *stand, lie, sit*. Before turning to this question (in § 11) I wish to specify the theoretical level on which the verb *to be* is envisaged, when we say that it underlies an appositional construction or that it occurs in zero form in the nominal sentence.

It should be emphasized here that any concept of *be* involves a certain amount of theoretical abstraction: neither this nor any other verb is "given" to us in raw empirical form. We can see this clearly enough if we take what may be the closest thing to an empirical definition of the verb, as the sum of actual occurrences in a closed corpus. To be precise, let us define the verb

---

[33] *Introduction*, p. 399.
[34] Theoretically we do not need a marker for the static aspect if the predicative structure of the sentence is clear. Whereas tense and mood vary from sentence to sentence, the stative value is constant for every use of copula *be*. Hence we could leave this aspect unexpressed and introduce a verbal marker only for *become*. In a way, this theoretical possibility is realized in the nominal sentence.

εἰμί in the Homeric poems as the set of occurrences for all forms listed under this title in columns 249–257 of Gehring's *Index Homericus*. The individual occurrences (for example, the first occurrence of ἐστί in the poems, at *Iliad* 1.114) constitute specific *tokens*, each one identified by its position in the text, in contrast to the *type* ἐστί, the third singular present indicative form which is "instantiated" in each of these tokens. Corresponding to each type (ἐστί, ἐσμέν, εἶναι, etc.) there is a set of tokens, i.e. occurrences; and the verb εἰμί may be defined as the set whose members are these specific subsets. Thus the verb *be* in Greek, which we arbitrarily represent by one of its forms (namely, by εἰμί here, and elsewhere often by the infinitive εἶναι), is essentially a set of sets. Its constituent members are not the individual occurrences but their various type-classes, the different forms of the verb.[35] It is these subsets which have as their members the actual occurrences or tokens, classified by their shape and individuated by their position in the text.

Now this text itself – the Homeric corpus – is an abstract type or set of equivalent tokens, namely the set of all copies of the Homeric poems in existence, including any portions thereof which you or I may choose to write down, or read aloud. Your copy of ἐστί in *Iliad* 1.114 and my copy do not constitute distinct occurrences of the word, in the sense of "occurrence" which is relevant here: they are marked only once in Gehring's *Index*. Thus our empirical definition of the verb in terms of actual occurrences in a fixed text requires us to abstract from all particular marks on given sheets of paper and to specify a single general structure – the sequence of words and verses – which constitutes our theoretical object, *the Homeric text*. It is within this text that we identify individual occurrence-tokens for each of the forms (such as ἐστί) which we then group into a higher unity, the set of forms that constitutes the verb εἰμί.[36]

---

[35] This statement involves a major simplification, since several syntactic types are represented by alternative concrete forms or allomorphic variants. Thus the third plural present indicative εἰσί has in Homer a variant form ἔασι, the infinitive εἶναι has syntactical equivalents in ἔμμεναι, ἔμεναι, ἔμμεν, ἔμεν and so forth. The verb as a syntactical family is thus a third-order set of actual occurrences. Its subsets are the syntactical forms (infinitive, third plural present indicative, etc.), and these in turn are sets of morphologically distinct types of occurrences. If the morphological type is already an abstraction, the verb as such is a third-order abstraction.

[36] If we wished to reduce the theoretical element in our "empirical" concept of the verb εἰμί to a strict minimum, we could in principle avoid speaking of the text of Homer, or of any other specific works and authors, and refer more generally to all preserved documents and inscriptions from Ancient Greek. We could then identify the verb as the sum of occurrences of all the specified forms in the expanded corpus that would include all copies and reproductions of ancient texts (including future copies, if one wishes). These occurrences could be individuated by their material position on a particular stone, parchment, sheet of paper, black-board, etc., (or by their utterance by a given individual at a given time, if we include vocal occurrences). On this basis, what would normally be called the first Homeric occurrence of ἐστί (at *Il.* 1.114) would be an ill-defined multiplicity of occur-

I have insisted upon these various levels of abstraction presupposed by the ordinary notion of "the verb εἰμί" as used in traditional philology, because one source of resistance to transformational syntax lies in the suspicion that it deals in abstract theoretical concepts which have no direct basis in textual evidence. Indeed, transformational grammar does make use of theoretical abstractions; but so does historical morphology, lexicography, and comparative grammar. Transformational methods as used here simply go one step further. For our purpose we must recognize, in addition to the actual occurrences just defined, certain *theoretical occurrences* of invisible (zero) forms in derived sentences; or, what amounts to the same thing, we must reconstruct occurrences of the verb in the underlying source and specify that these forms have been zeroed or deleted in the course of transformation. Thus in so simple a transform as *I am hot and bothered* we must recognize the zeroing of a second *I am* in the source: *I am hot + I am bothered*. To refuse to admit a second invisible occurrence of *I am* in the syntax of *I am hot and bothered* is to refuse transformational grammar as such. And in this respect transformational theory simply makes explicit certain assumptions which underlie the traditional doctrine of syntax in our handbooks of Greek and Latin grammar. Let us take a comparable example from Homer:

4   *Il.* 4.534
      οἵ ἑ μέγαν περ ἐόντα καὶ ἴφθιμον καὶ ἀγαυὸν
      ὦσαν ἀπὸ σφείων
      "And though he was a mighty man and a strong and proud one
      (they) thrust him from them."

                                                              (Lattimore)

In traditional terms we would say that the three adjectives (μέγαν, ἴφθιμον, ἀγαυόν) are all construed with the single participle ἐόντα. But in transformational analysis every "construction" is interpreted by derivation from a distinct sentential form (or from a distinct operator on a sentence). Hence

---

rences: "the same passage" would be counted over and over again, indefinitely. In this way we could achieve the theoretical economy of eliminating *the text of Homer, the text of Herodotus*, etc.; but of course we would pay for this economy by an enormous expansion of our corpus with no real enrichment, and with the result that there could be no easy or uniform convention for referring to specific passages in the literature.

In fact, it seems that philology in its familiar form would be quite impossible on the basis of this sort of empiricist "nominalism" which attempts to define the linguistic data in terms of concrete *inscriptions* (in Goodman's sense). For example, the concept of a *hapax legomenon* would be undefined, since inscriptions of any given form can be multiplied as often as one pleases.

Note that, even on the basis of this fantastically "concrete" conception of an occurrence, the verb *to be* would still be defined as a set of sets of occurrences, with the subsets identified by their written or phonetic shape (or even as a third-order set, if we take into account the complications mentioned in the preceding note).

in transformational terms each of the adjectives in **4** represents a distinct source sentence of the form *N is A*. The subject *N* (or rather its pro-word ἑ "he") and the copula (ἐόντα) are expressed with the first adjective but elliptically omitted – i.e. zeroed – with the other two.

Hence if the concept of the verb *be* was already theory-laden in our empirical notion defined on actual occurrences in the text of Homer, this concept becomes doubly theoretical in transformational grammar. For we must now count not only the overt occurrences in the text but also the theoretical or zero occurrences reconstructed by transformational analysis: for example, the two unexpressed forms of ἐόντα in **4**. This reconstruction of zero forms follows from the general principles of transformational syntax and is of no special importance for the theory of the verb *to be*. Our verb happens to be very frequently zeroed, but so also is a pronoun like *he* (ἑ in **4**). The actual and the zero occurrences are equally present in deep structure, and the difference between them is accounted for by certain rules for the elimination of redundant forms from surface structure. In many cases zeroing is optional (or stylistic), as in the cases traditionally known as "ellipse."[37] For a study of *be*, the difference between actual and zero occurrences is of no significance in comparison, say, with the distinction between elementary and derived uses of the copula – between those surface forms which reflect a kernel use of *be* and those which represent a transformational operator. (See Chapter IV § 3.)

By "*be* as the copula in Greek", then, I mean the sum or set of occurrences of forms of εἰμί as elementary copula and operator, whether these occurrences are actually recorded in the text or have to be reconstructed in the transformational source of a given sentence. It is in this sense of "the verb *be*" that I have argued that appositional syntax presupposes a use of the verb as copula and that the nominal sentence represents a zero form of the verb. (Some of the considerations adduced in § 7 to show that *be* is more fundamental than *become* require the same theoretical definition of the verb; others rely only on the concept of actual occurrence: for example, when I cited the more frequent use of εἰμί than of its suppletives in Homer, and when I illustrated the assimilation of *become*-verbs to *be*. In general the methods of traditional philology require only the notion of surface occurrence; it is transformational syntax which insists upon the reconstruction of zero forms.) The nominal sentence in Greek is accounted for by an optional rule for zeroing the present indicative forms of εἰμί, above all in the third person. We may compare this to the rule in English which permits us to omit *that* in a sentence like *I know (that) he is at home*. The modalities of the rule

---

[37] On zeroing see Harris, "Transformational theory", pp. 387–96; *Mathematical Structures* pp. 78–83. For ellipse, see above, Chapter III § 4.

for omitting εἰμί will differ somewhat for Homer and for later Greek, and the proportion of zero occurrences may vary widely according to author, stylistic genre, and particular sentence type. But once we have introduced zero forms of the verb *be*, as we must do in any case for transformational grammar, there seems to be no reason to regard the nominal sentence as reflecting a different deep structure from the ordinary copula sentence with *be*.[38]

§9. ELIMINATION OF THE COPULA *be* FROM DEEP STRUCTURE: THE MORE FUNDAMENTAL NOTION OF THE *"is* OF PREDICATION"

The conclusion of the last section would be acceptable to a theorist who wishes to eliminate the verb *be* from deep structure. Accepting the basic structural equivalence of sentences with and without the copula verb, he can regard the verb as introduced by a transformation (which is optional in Greek, obligatory in English) of a sentential form that is already complete as far as its lexically "full" or meaningful elements are concerned. Unlike the full verbs represented in deep structure, the copula *be* thus appears as a "dummy verb" generated in surface structure to carry those markers of tense, mood and aspect which require a verb form for their expression.[39] In most of its recent formulations this view of *be* presupposes a distinction between an abstract base component and a transformational level of grammar, a distinction which is characteristic of generative grammars as developed by Chomsky but which is rather different from the Harris theory of syntax utilized here, where transformations operate only on actual sentences or sentence forms. It is not my intention to discuss the relative merits of these two types of transformational theory. And fortunately the description of *be* as a somewhat anomolous "dummy verb" is not in any way tied to the generative viewpoint. Harris himself has suggested a generalization of his system in which some transformations would operate not on sentences but on "infrasentences", and where in particular a rule for automatic insertion of *be* would operate on certain infrasentences that have precisely the form of the so-called nominal sentence: NA, ND_{1oc}, NN_{c1}, etc.[40] Now what is at stake in these various theoretical descriptions of *be* as automatically inserted, or

---

[38] For further discussion of the nominal sentence see Appendix B.

[39] See the quotation from Lyons in §3 above, p. 195. This view has been worked out systematically for English by E. Bach, in terms of a generative theory like Chomsky's; see his "*Have* and *be* in English Syntax," *Language* 43 (1967), pp. 462–85. A comparable treatment of *be* on the basis of a different conception of deep structure is suggested by Fillmore in "The Case for Case", *Universals in Linguistic Theory*, pp. 42–6, 75–9.

[40] See Harris, *Mathematical Structures*, pp. 170f. The insertion of *be* is compared to a morphophonemic operator φ_m (p. 180).

transformationally introduced or generated by the rules of the language, is just the fact that the verb *is* contributes no information content to copula sentences of the kind we associate with other verbs like *sleeps, swims, loves*. Without deciding whether or not it belongs in the base component of a generative grammar, we can certainly admit that *be* is not "a verb like other verbs". For indeed the recent discussions of *be* in the context of transformational theory only confirm the account of the copula given long ago by Meillet: a grammatical device for introducing the verbal markers of person, tense, mood, and aspect into a sentence which otherwise lacks a verb.

This formal role of the copula is perhaps most clearly seen in an abstract predicative system modelled on that of logic, where elementary sentences take the form *Fa, Fab*, and so on, with predicates construed as functions (F) and names or primitive nouns figuring as arguments (a, b, c, etc.).[41] In such a scheme there will be no distinct sign of predication, such as a copula or a finite verb form: predication is represented by the function-argument pattern as a whole. In rendering *Fa* into words, however, we may conveniently say "*a* is *F*"; and this rendering suggests an ultimate generalization of the concept of copula *be* which is illuminating in two respects. In the first place it indicates a predicative role for *be* which is much more general than the actual role of **es-* in I.-E. This by contrast sheds light on the specific nature of the copula in I.-E., and reminds us that its role there is in turn more general than that of copula verbs in some other languages. I shall briefly illustrate these two points by contrasting examples in both directions.

Consider first the very general notion of "the *is* of predication" as represented by the formal scheme for atomic sentences in modern logic. Leaving aside the question of many-placed functions or relations (*Fab, Fabc*, etc.) let us consider sentences of the simplest form, *Fa*. The vernacular rendering "*a* is *F*" corresponds roughly to the set-theoretical interpretation αεφ, "α is a member of the set φ", where the symbol "ε" for membership is actually derived from the initial letter of ἐστί. (Compare, in Chapter I §3, the interpretation of "ε" in Leśniewski's Ontology.) If we think of *Fa* as a schematic rendering of the simplest sentences in natural language, we see that *F* will correspond either (1) to verbs like *sleeps, sings*; (2) to adjectives and nouns in predicate position: (*is*) *hungry, (is a) man*; or (3) to locative and para-

---

[41] For a fully elaborated system of this sort, with transformational operators represented as second-order functions, see Harris, *Mathematical Structures*, Chapter 7. A programmatic suggestion along similar lines is made by Bach in his proposal to conceive "a system of universal base rules" modelled on first-order logic, with nouns, verbs and adjectives represented by a single category of "*contentives*...like the *predicates* of logic or the 'full words' of traditional Chinese grammar" (*Universals in Linguistic Theory*, pp. 115, 121). It is extremely doubtful, however, that the basic rules of any natural language can be formulated in first-order logic alone, though perhaps the elementary sentence forms may be so represented, as Harris suggests.

locative predicates: *(is) at home, (is) in a hurry*. The generalized *is* of predication, represented by the scheme *Fa*, is present in all three cases, whereas the actual use of **es-* in I.-E. is limited to 2 and 3, the nominal and locative copulas. The logical schema *Fa* thus ignores the grammatical differences between verbs, nouns, adjectives and adverbial phrases as counterparts of *F*, that is, as predicates in natural language, and gives a uniform representation for all these cases.

The uniformity for the expression of predication may be regarded either as an elimination or as a generalization of copula *be*. The copula is eliminated if we think of the general form of *F* as verbal, rendering *Fa* as "*a F's*". On the other hand, it is generalized if we think of *F* as nominal and of *is* as the predicate form as such: "*a is F*". Insofar as the latter is the more natural rendering of the logical scheme, modern logic formalizes a view of the copula which is essentially that of Port Royal, where *is* was conceived as the one true verb, the sign of affirmation that is present or latent in every sentence. Taking account of the actual limitations on the use of **es-* in I.-E., I said earlier that it was the finite verb form in general and not the copula as such which is properly described as the sign of predication (§1). However, the analysis of Port Royal reverses the situation by decomposing every finite verb into *is* plus a nominal form: thus *sleeps* or *loves* becomes *is sleeping, is loving*. But the verb *is* which is thus elevated to the status of universal verb is not the empirical **es-* of actual occurrences, not even the theoretically extended set which includes zero occurrences (where the zero occurrences are reconstructed by ordinary transformational techniques). The universal copula of Port Royal is a new theoretical entity introduced by the canonical rewriting of every simple sentence in the form *X is Y*. The copula or "substantive verb" of Port Royal is just the "*is* of predication" of modern logic insofar as the modern phrase is understood as coextensive with the predicative form *Fa*.[42] And it is obvious that the verb *be* or the copula *in this sense* will not be eliminated from the deep structure of any grammar for I.-E. languages. Nor will it be eliminated from any more general theory that wishes its basic sentence forms to be assimilated to, or intertranslatable with, the predicative forms of modern logic.[43] It is characteristic of *be* in

[42] This also applies to many-placed predicates like *Fab*, if we regard the first argument as "subject" in the traditional sense. I ignore here the *is* of identity. See below, p. 400 n. 33.
[43] Thus it is striking that E. Bach, who published in 1967 his proposal for eliminating *be* from the base component of English and other languages, published in 1968 a theory of "Nouns and Noun Phrases" which claims, in effect, that every occurrence of a noun in English will be derived from a sentential structure of the form *Someone (something) is N. (*See *Universals in Ling. Theory*, p. 104.) The apparent contradiction is resolved if we recognize that the *is* of the latter form is the generalized "*is* of predication," corresponding to the scheme *Fx*, and not the specific verb *be* as used in English sentences. Bach's presentation would have gained in lucidity if he had drawn attention to this distinction. In one sense,

this widest sense that it is indifferent to the superficial grammatical form of the predicate *F*. It is characteristic of *es-* as copula in I.-E., on the other hand, that it functions only where the predicate is a noun, adjective, or adverbial phrase; more precisely, only when the predicate does *not* contain a finite verb (outside of subordinate clauses).

The generalized copula of Port Royal goes far beyond the actual use of *es-* in I.-E., but it may have some closer approximations in other languages. The most favorable case known to me is the six copulative or predicative suffixes in Turkish, which correspond in distribution to the six personal forms of the I.-E. verb (without the dual).[44] Although there is a clear difference between verbal and non-verbal predicates in Turkish, there is a common underlying form for predication in either case, since the six personal suffixes which constitute finite verb forms are identical with the copulative suffixes that serve with predicate nouns, adjectives or locative phrases. I am told that the speaker of Turkish does not have the sentiment that the verb-endings are identical with the copula, i.e. that he does not perceive the verb form as the compound of a kind of nominal stem and a copulative suffix. Yet this is a correct description of the situation for a linguist. Hence, from a theoretical point of view we can say that the existence of these copulative suffixes, applicable to verbal and non-verbal stems alike, gives Turkish a natural parallel to the universal copula of Port Royal or to the uniform predicate scheme of modern logic.

In I.-E., where the opposition of verbal and non-verbal predicates remains fundamental, the copula *es-* never attains this universality as sign of predication. The possibility of a development in this direction was nevertheless suggested by the various uses of *be* as transformational operator, and in particular by the periphrastic construction with participles (Chapter IV, §§ 14–17). By generalizing this extension of *be* throughout the domain of verbal predication, the Greek philosophers were in effect able to formulate the notion of a universal copula which I have just illustrated from Turkish. Thus Aristotle could say, like the Port Royal theorists after him, that for any

---

even he leaves *be* in the deep structure of every sentence; only the *be* in question is the general predicative scheme of Port Royal and modern logic, not the empirical forms of *es-* in I.-E. languages.

[44] For the term "copulative suffix" see J. Nemeth, *Turkish Grammar*, English adaptation by T. Halasi-Kun (The Hague, 1962), pp. 67f. These enclitic suffixes are often referred to as "the present tense of 'to be'," for example in G. I. Lewis, *Turkish Grammar* (Oxford, 1967), p. 96. In the description given above I exaggerate the uniformity of the Turkish system by ignoring alternate forms of the personal suffixes in past and conditional, deviant forms in subjunctive and imperative, and the possibility of omitting the suffixes, above all in third-person singular. For a good summary, see Lewis, *op. cit.* pp. 98, 106–8.

verb *X*, *Socrates X's* is equivalent to *Socrates is Xing*.[45] It was of great importance for the theories of Being developed in Greek philosophy that this generalization was seen to be possible, and even natural. As we shall see in Chapter VII, it was all the easier for the Greek philosophers to widen the scope of εἰμί since the verb had, in its veridical use, actually achieved a greater generality still, independent of any subject-predicate structure. The copula of Port Royal, like the logical form *Fa*, presupposes a distinction between S. and P. term, between function and argument. The impersonal construction reminds us that a sentence in natural language need not have this dyadic complexity. In this respect the veridical ἔστι or εἶναι (like *p* or *q* in the sentential calculus, or like Wittgenstein's *Es verhält sich so und so*) is more general in form, since it expresses a sentential truth claim without any restrictions on the internal structure of the sentence. (See Chapter VII, § 8.) Assertion, affirmation, or "positing" (in the linguistic analogue to Husserl's epistemic sense of *Position* or *Setzung*) is more general than predication; and this is one function expressed by the verb *be* in *Greek*. But here we can no longer describe the verb as *copula*.

§10. COMPARISON WITH MORE RESTRICTED COPULA VERBS IN OTHER LANGUAGES: EWE AND CHINESE

Before returning to the specific features of the copula system in Greek, we may cast a glance at two other contrasting examples from outside I.-E. If the use of **es-* as copula in I.-E. is less general than the copulative suffixes in Turkish (since **es-* is restricted to non-verbal predicates), it is on the other hand more general than the copula verbs in some other languages. Whereas *be* as copula in I.-E. functions with predicate adjectives, nouns, and locative phrases alike, these three domains are variously distributed elsewhere. Thus in the West-African language Ewe we have a substantival copula *nyé*, used only with predicate nouns, and a locative-adjectival copula *le* (negative *no*), translated as "to be present", "to be located (somewhere)", "to be in a certain state or condition". The verb *le* also serves as operator in forming progressive and ingressive aspects: *mele yiyim*, "I am in the act of going", *mele yiyi gé*, "I am near going, am about to go". We may note that the same verb also serves as the expression for existence ("there is") and for possession: in Ewe "I have it" is *le asi-nye*, literally "it is in my hand." Thus *le*

---

[45] Arist. *De Int.* 21ᵇ9 οὐδὲν γὰρ διαφέρει εἰπεῖν ἄνθρωπον βαδίζειν ἢ ἄνθρωπον βαδίζοντα εἶναι. Similarly *Pr. An.* 51ᵇ13, *Met.* Δ7, 1017ᵃ27. At *Physics* 185ᵇ29 Aristotle rejects the opposite suggestion of Lycophron for eliminating copulative and periphrastic uses and putting every predicate into verbal form (without *is*): ὁ ἄνθρωπος οὐ λευκός ἐστιν ἀλλὰ λελεύκωται, οὐδὲ βαδίζων ἐστὶν ἀλλὰ βαδίζει.

tends to assume the general role of copula-existential verb which is familiar to us from I.-E. *es-. But its development as copula is blocked by the existence of a distinct form nyé used with predicate nouns, as well as by the occurrence of various stative or quality-verbs (in morphological connection with adjectives) and a few minor predicative forms.[46]

Thus Ewe presents us with a system where nominal predication is sharply split between two distinct forms, one of which is also the form for locative predication. Classical Chinese divides the territory in a different way. There is a distinct locative verb tsai, a substantival copula shih construed with predicate nouns, but no copula form for adjectives. The Chinese words which translate our adjectives are conjugated like verbs (the so-called stative verbs). And no part of this predicative system overlaps with the expression for existence-possession (yu/wu).[47]

Leaving aside the functions of *es- as verb of existence and possession in I.-E., we can see that the copulative use alone is already quite general in comparison with the more specialized copulas of Ewe and Chinese. Such a generalized copula is not uniquely characteristic of I.-E.; the copulative functions of *es- are closely paralleled by a single set of forms in a non-Indo-European language like Mundari.[48] The presence of such a flexible instrument of predication in Greek was surely not a sufficient condition for the general theories of Being developed in Greek philosophy, since there are other languages with equally flexible systems (and some systems, like Turkish, which seem to be even more flexible) but in which no such philosophic theories are developed. On the other hand, the I.-E. copula system might reasonably be regarded as a necessary condition for the creation of

---

[46] The interest of Ewe for a comparison with I.-E. was pointed out by Benveniste, "Catégories de pensée et catégories de langue", in Problèmes de linguistique générale, pp. 63–74. For the details, see D. Westermann, A Study of the Ewe Language transl. A. L. Bickford-Smith (Oxford, 1930), §§ 81, 90–91, 147 (b); and Westermann, Wörterbuch der Ewe-Sprache (Berlin, 1905). Westermann (A Study... § 90) lists five Ewe verbs "meaning to be", but the other three (di, du, wo) have very restricted uses as copula and might better be regarded as idiomatic variants (like French il fait beau for le temps est beau). I was told by an educated Ewe speaker that she regarded le and nyé as parallel or similar to one another (and this was not the case for di, du, wo). I am unable to guess how far this parallelism reflected her familiarity with be in English.

[47] See A. C. Graham, "'Being' in Western Philosophy compared with shih/fei and yu/wu in Chinese Philosophy", Asia Minor (N.S.) 7 (1959), 79–112, and the same author in The Verb 'be' and its Synonyms Part 1. I have simplified the situation in describing shih as substantival copula. From A. Y. Hashimoto's account of "The Verb 'to be' in Modern Chinese" (The Verb 'be' and its Synonyms, Part 4), I gather that the division between substantival copula (shi), locative verb (zai), and existential verb (you), with stative verbs for our adjectives, is roughly preserved in modern Chinese, though the substantival copula shi seems to overlap in some existential-locative-possessive constructions (ibid. pp. 78, 87, 89).

[48] See D. T. Langendoen in The Verb 'be' and its Synonyms, Part 1.

Greek ontology as we know it. It is not easy to see how Aristotle could have claimed that *being* has as many senses or uses as there are categories if εἰμί were a copula used only with predicate nouns or only with predicate adjectives.

§11. SURVEY OF THE *be-* AND *become*-REPLACERS IN HOMER

Before concluding our discussion of the copula, we must consider whether there is anything more to be said in answer to the question with which we began: why is it precisely the verb **es-* that is introduced in I.-E. as sign of predication, or as marker of person, tense and mood, in sentences which would otherwise lack a finite verb? As I have suggested, this question may be more accurately formulated as: What does the copula verb contribute to the sentence in which it occurs? We have seen that some functions of the copula – such as the marker of tense and the sign of truth claim in the indicative mood endings – could in principle be performed by *any* verb in the language, but that one role characterizes **es-* in particular: the stative aspect, by which it contrasts with verbs meaning *to become, arrive at, get,* and the like (§3). And we have seen that this static value of the copula in I.-E. – and indeed, of the basic copula (or copulas) in any language – is conceptually prior to, and in fact more fundamental than, the kinetic-mutative value of the contrasting *become*-verbs (§7). It remains for us to attempt to elucidate this value of **es-* in the context of the small class of static *be*-replacers mentioned earlier, and in contrast with the typical *become*-verbs in early Greek.

What I have to say about the static *be*-replacers in Greek is not very different from what Boyer and Spéranski have said concerning three common "substitutes for the verb *be*" in Russian, namely verbs which figure as alternatives to the nominal sentence in present tense. These verbs preserve their "concrete" sense in their use as *be*-replacers, though (I am told) their metaphorical force in Russian is weaker than that of the corresponding verbs in English. The three verbs are *sit, lie,* and *stand: sidet', ležat',* and *stojat'*. Boyer and Spéranski give examples of the following sort: *I am* (literally *sit*) *at home, The bag is (lies) in the corner, The book is (stands) on the shelf.*[49] These examples happen to be locative, but there are also common Russian expressions in which these verbs take adjectival predicates, e.g. *The weather stood fair for several days.* It would be easy to find parallels in English. What is more to the point here, in Homer too we frequently find the same

[49] See P. Boyer and N. Spéranski, *Manuel pour l'étude de la langue russe* (Paris, 1947), p. 250.

three verbs employed as vivid substitutes for *be* with predicate adjectives and nouns.

5 *Od.* 13.423

ἔκηλος / ἧσται ἐν Ἀτρεΐδαο δόμοις

"(Telemachus) sits at ease in the halls of Menelaus".

6 *Od.* 14.255

ἀσκηθέες καὶ ἄνουσοι / ἥμεθα

"We sat unscathed and unharmed (in our ships)"

7 *Od.* 13.234

ἤ πού τις νήσων εὐδείελος ἠέ τις ἀκτὴ
κεῖθ᾽ ἁλὶ κεκλιμένη ἐριβώλακος ἠπείροιο;

"(What land is this?) Is it some far-seen island or does it lie a tongue of fertile mainland stretching out to sea?"

(after Palmer)

8 *Il.* 22.318

ἕσπερος, ὃς κάλλιστος ἐν οὐρανῷ ἵσταται ἀστήρ

"Hesperus, who stands the fairest star in heaven."

So also στῆ ὀρθός "He stood upright", στῆ δὲ ταφών "He stood dazed", etc.[50]

A fuller study of what I here describe as *be*-replacers would have to distinguish several cases, of which the most important are (1) the construction with predicates that are nominal in form but adverbial in meaning, i.e. which state where or how one stands, sits, or lies ("upright" "opposite", "lowest of all"), and (2) the construction with nouns and adjectives that can be transformationally derived from a separate sentence with *be*, as in the examples of apposition and quasi-predication discussed above in §§5–6 (e.g. *He sits at ease in the halls ← He sits in the halls + He is at ease (there)*; *Hesperus stands the fairest star in heaven ← H. stands in heaven + H. is the fairest star*). In case (1) we have a properly locative or postural use of *sit, stand, lie,* and the copula form is merely a derivative feature of surface structure. In case (2) we have a locative verb that permits the zeroing of copula *be* in a second, conjoined sentence. Perhaps only the second case is correctly described as a *be*-replacer, if by *be* we mean the nominal copula. But of course *sit, stand,* and *lie* are *be*-replacers in every one of their uses, if we think of *be* as locative copula. And it is in the locative or paralocative

---

[50] Other examples of these verbs with nominal predicates in the early books of the *Iliad*: (*sit*) 1.415 ἀδάκρυτος ἧσθαι, 1.557 ἠερίη παρέζετο, 7.61 στίχες ἥατο πυκναί, 9.190 ἐναντίος ἧστο; (*stand*) 1.535 ἀντίοι ἔσταν, 7.136 πρόμος ἵστατο, 11.593 πλησίοι ἔστησαν; (*lie*) 4.144 βασιλῆϊ κεῖται ἄγαλμα, 6.295 ἔκειτο δὲ νείατος ἄλλων, 7.156 πολλὸς ἔκειτο παρήορος, 9.335 ἔμπεδα κεῖται.

uses that the assimilation of *es- and the be-replacers is most striking. Thus παρίσταμαί σοι "I stand by you" serves as a vivid synonym for πάρειμί σοι "I am with (by) you", so that one form can literally replace the other in a given context. (Compare Od. 13.393 with 387, where παρέσσομαι in Athena's answer corresponds to πὰρ...στῆϑι in Odysseus' request.)

In describing sit, lie, and stand as be-replacers in Russian, Boyer and Spéranski remark that "chacun de ces trois verbes comporte une idée de permanence, de durée et, dans certains cas, d'immobilité que ne possède pas le verbe 'être'." Now this idea of permanence, duration, and relative immobility is just what we have described as the static aspect of be in contrast to become. If verbs meaning lie, stand, sit have a stronger static value than être in French or be in English, it is not at all clear that this holds for the corresponding Greek verbs. In Greek almost alone among European languages, the stem *es- has remained rigorously durative, admitting no aorist or perfect forms like fui or been into the conjugation of εἰμί. My own impression is that the present and imperfect forms of this verb, and perhaps even the future, are every bit as durative-static in nuance as the corresponding forms of ἵσταμαι "stand" or κεῖμαι "lie". For example πάρειμί σοι "I am at your side" differs from παρίσταμαί σοι "I stand at your side" only in being slightly less vivid, insofar as it does not suggest any particular posture of the body. But the static aspect of the former expression in Greek is just as marked as that of the latter. And it is this strong static-durative value of the verb itself which explains the comparative rarity in Greek of be-replacers corresponding in sense to stay (young), remain (their leader), continue (friends).[51] Greek rarely needs a be-replacer with the sense stay, remain (so). For this is in effect the meaning of εἰμί itself.

Thus the three verbs of station ἧμαι (or ἕζομαι) "sit", κεῖμαι "lie", and ἵσταμαι "stand", together with their compounds, are almost the only be-replacers in Greek, if we except verbs with a kinetic-mutative value like γίγνομαι become. It should be noted that these three static be-replacers all apply properly to living things, and that stand and sit strictly understood can take as their subjects only animals with legs. Primarily, of course, all

---

[51] The only Homeric example of this kind which I have noted is Od. 13.364 (≈ Il. 24.382) ἵνα περ τάδε τοι σόα μίμνῃ "so that your goods may remain safe". LSJ, which cites this passage, cannot quote a second predicative construction for μίμνω in later Greek; and there are very few such constructions for the more common forms μένω and διαμένω. Note that the verb διατελέω "to continue (doing such and such)" is not a be-replacer but a general verb operator that may on occasion function as be-modifier: e.g. Hdt. VII.111.1 Σάτραι... διατελεῦσι τὸ μέχρι ἐμεῦ αἰεὶ ἐόντες ἐλεύθεροι μοῦναι Θρηίκων "The Satrai...alone among the Thracians have continued down to my time being always in a state of freedom". For the predicative construction of English verbs meaning be as it was, remain, see Jespersen, M.E.G. III, 369; for nominal predicates with sit, lie, and stand in English, ibid. 360f., 364.

three verbs apply to persons, that is to say, to human beings and gods. In the case of Greek verbs of movement or change corresponding to *become* in English, a similar biological or anthropomorphic tendency is often noticeable. The root **bhū-*, which supplies a verb for *become* in so many languages (including *béon* in Old English), has in its Greek form a frankly reproductive-vegetative sense: φύω "beget, put forth (leaves)", φύομαι "grow" (cf. φύλλα "leaves", φυτόν "plant"). The predicative construction of this verb (ἔφυ, πέφυκα) as *be-* or *become*-replacer is post-Homeric, and is perhaps never very common outside poetic and philosophical contexts. The chief *become-* verb in Greek, from Homer on, is γίγνομαι, with a literal sense "be born" (cf. γένος "family", γεννήτωρ "parent", "ancestor"). Like the static *be*-replacers, the verb is mostly used with personal subjects, though the literal sense applies in principle to any creature with recognizable ancestry. In the perfect, this verb means roughly "to be alive, to live, dwell (in a place)", whether for men or for animals: *Od.* 13.160 ἐς Σχερίην, ὅθι Φαίηκες γεγάασιν "(Poseidon hastened) to Scheria, where the Phaeacians live" (Palmer); *Od.* 9.118 ἐν δ' αἶγες ἀπειρέσιαι γεγάασιν/ἄγριαι "On (the island) innumerable wild goats breed" (so Palmer; "innumerable goats breed (*or* live) wild" is also defensible as a rendering).

Another verb of biological meaning which takes the predicative construction is τρέφω "to nourish", in the passive: *Il.* 1.266 κάρτιστοι δὴ κεῖνοι ἐπιχθονίων τράφεν ἀνδρῶν "These were the strongest generation of earth-born mortals" (Lattimore). For Attic parallels, see LSJ s.v. τρέφω A.V.[52] The more common Homeric copula τελέθω also admits a biological sense: *Od.* 4.85 Λιβύην, ἵνα τ' ἄρνες ἄφαρ κεραοὶ τελέθουσι. Palmer renders this "Libya, where the lambs are full-horned at their birth". A more literal translation would be "the lambs grow (become) full-horned right away". The verb seems to hesitate between static and kinetic aspect, between the values of *be* and *become*. Probably its aspectual value is more accurately described as "perfect" (=*having reached a state*), and the verb thus lies outside the *be-become* opposition. The etymology of **τελ-* has been much discussed, but from the point of view of Greek the relevant sense of the root is clearly "to accomplish, bring to completion" (cf.τέλος). τελέθω is an intransitive form with the corresponding sense, as we can see from the single non-copulative use in the epic: *Il.* 7.282 (=293) νὺξ δ' ἤδη τελέθει "night is now coming on".[53]

Let me complete this survey by a brief mention of the two other *be-*

---

[52] Compare Kühner-Gerth I, 43 for other Attic verbs meaning *grow* (*great*): μέγας ηὐξήθη, ἤρετο τὸ ὕψος τοῦ τείχους μέγα. Note that these verbs need not take animate subjects.
[53] On the derivation of τελέθω, see Benveniste, *Origines de la formation des noms* (1935), p. 195.

become suppletives in Homer.[54] πέλω, πέλομαι is not a biological verb, but it has a sound etymology as verb of motion in the literal sense: "move around", "turn about". (Compare περιπλόμενος, πωλέομαι, ἀμφίπολος, πόλος = "turning point", "axis", "circling vault of heaven".) For the sense we may compare the German copula *werden* with its Latin cognate *vertere* "to turn"; also the English idioms *turn pale, turn twenty*. As a copula πέλομαι is primarily a verb of process or kinesis in the wide sense. Both in present and in aorist the verb means properly *develop, come to be*, as we can see from the non-copulative uses: *Il.* 3.3 κλαγγὴ γεράνων πέλει οὐρανόθι πρό "the clamour of cranes goes high to the heavens" (Lattimore); *Il.* 11.737 ὅτε δὴ...ἔπλετο νεῖκος "when the battle came on" (Lattimore). In Homer the kinetic aspectual value associated with the etymological sense "turn" is nearly always preserved. But at the limit this value vanishes, and πέλω becomes a poetical synonym for εἰμί. (For examples of this in Homer and Parmenides, see above §7.)

The last common *become*-verb in Homer is ἐτύχθη, τέτυκται, whose lexical value is unusually clear. We have the middle-passive aorist and perfect of a verb τεύχω "to make, construct" in common use for the work of a carpenter or smith. Like εἰμί, γίγνομαι and the other members of this group, the passive of τεύχω can be used as existential verb: *Il.* 2.155 ἔνθα κεν ᾿Αργείοισιν ὑπέρμορα νόστος ἐτύχθη "Then for the Argives a homecoming beyond fate might have been accomplished" (Lattimore), i.e. "might have occurred". (Cf. Type V existentials in Chapter VI, §15). In the predicative construction the literal sense of *having been fashioned* or *built* is occasionally perceptible, as we have seen (§7, p. 206). More often the verb serves simply as a forceful equivalent to εἰμί with a perfect aspect: *Il.* 4.84 (=19.224) Ζεύς, ὅς τ᾽ ἀνθρώπων ταμίης πολέμοιο τέτυκται "Zeus, who is appointed lord of the wars of mortals" (Lattimore); *Il.* 5.402 (=901) οὐ μὲν γάρ τι καταθνητός γε τέτυκτο "for he was not made mortal at all".

In this connection we may mention τυγχάνω "meet", "hit the goal", "happen", whose forms are in part identified or confused with those of τεύχω. Τυγχάνω occasionally occurs as a *be*- and *become*-replacer, particularly in locative and possessive uses: *Il.*11.73 ῎Ερις ... οἴη...παρετύγχανε

---

[54] I omit consideration of the predicative construction with true verbs of motion, for this would take us too far from *be*, e.g. ἑσπέριοι ἀφίκοντο, χθιζὸς ἔβη, ὕπτιος ἔμπεσε, ὕστερος ἐλθών. See Munro, *Homeric Grammar*, 153; Chantraine *Grammaire hom*. II, 8f. The few examples which are neither verbs of station nor of motion would require a detailed analysis along the lines sketched in the discussion of appositional syntax in § 5. Note that in many cases the predicative construction is plausibly derived from an underlying adverb of time or manner: (οὐ) πρόφρων τέτληκας "you (do not) *willingly* dare", ἑσπέριοι ἀφίκοντο "They came *at evening*", εὗδον παννύχιοι "They slept *all night*". It is nevertheless suggestive that, besides the words for *be* and *become*, the construction occurs above all with verbs of station and motion.

μαρναμένοισιν "Strife alone of the immortals was among the fighters" (followed by ἄλλοι οὔ σφιν πάρεσαν θεοί); *Od.* 14.231 καί μοι μάλα τύγχανε πολλά "I gained much booty". The verb also occurs as operator with a participle prefiguring the Attic construction τυγχάνω ὤν: *Od.* 14.334 τύχησε γὰρ ἐρχομένη νηῦς "a ship happened to arrive". (For this construction see above, Chapter IV §20, pp. 149f.)

§12. THE VALUE OF εἰμί AS CENTER OF THE COPULATIVE SYSTEM: GENERAL AND SPECIFIC FEATURES OF THE GREEK COPULA

This is not the place for a systematic study of all the copula verbs in post-Homeric Greek; our aim is to situate εἰμί within a nuclear group of *be-* and *become*-replacers. From our survey of the Homeric data two conclusions emerge. (1) The true *be*-replacers are all verbs of station, and literally verbs of *posture*; they indicate a specific position of the body: *sit, stand, lie*. (2) The *become*-verbs form a more heterogeneous group, but the chief representative γίγνομαι/ἐγενόμην (which is the only one with an important use as copula in Attic prose) has the literal sense of biological birth. The biological sense is scarcely accidental, since the corresponding *become*-verb in many or most I.-E. languages is derived from a root **bhū-* which has an etymological connection with vegetative growth or reproduction (as in Greek φύομαι). The *become*-verbs in Homer whose literal meaning is not essentially biological (πέλομαι, τέτυγμαι, τελέθω) may perhaps be regarded as poetic variations; at all events they scarcely occur as copula in Attic prose.

If one bears in mind that the verbs of posture under (1) apply strictly only to animals with legs, one sees that the static and biological features of this system reinforce one another: εἰμί (and to some extent **es-* in I.-E. generally) is situated at the center of a group of copula verbs whose chief representatives have collateral uses indicating birth or growth and animal or anthropomorphic posture. If we are to define εἰμί by its place within this system we can say that the verb properly indicates a state or position for an animal – above all, for a person – which is independent of, or more general than, the specific postures of sitting, standing, lying; that this state contrasts with, or abstracts from, the processes of birth, growth and change in general, but that it does not contrast with the notion of *being alive* which is usually implied by the other principal members of the group. Considering that the grammatical aspect of εἰμί is not only static (in contrast to mutative-kinetic) but also durative (in contrast to aorist or punctual), we may be inclined to paraphrase the value of εἰμί within this system as *to stay alive, live, dwell, persevere* (*in a place, state, or condition*).

In thus focussing on the cases where εἰμί takes a living animal or person as subject, I am simply calling attention to the nuclear, predominant uses of the verb and its replacers in Homer, and probably in the language as a whole. I do not mean to suggest that there was once a time when *es- was not also used in a broader way for inanimate subjects, any more than there was a time when *stand* (*sta-*) could not be used for beings without feet. And indeed, the word *foot* itself (*pod-*) must have been applied "from the beginning" to inanimate props, as to the legs of a *tripod* for example. The vivid, anthropomorphic use of language is not older than the extended, metaphorical, or "abstract" uses, but it is inevitably central and more basic. For the speakers of the language are themselves persons, and the existence of first- and second-person forms, referring to speaker and hearer, guarantees the primordial role of persons as paradigm subjects. (See Chapter IV, §4.)

In thus reconstructing a nuclear sense for *es- or εἰμί within the system of copula verbs I have in a way begged the question against Meillet, who suggested that *es- was selected as copula just because it was so insignificant, having only the vague and general meaning "exists". For it is only if we assume that the group of *be-* and *become*-replacers in early Greek (or in I.-E.) is *significant as a system* that we are justified in using the familiar meanings of the other verbs in this group in order to specify the more elusive value of *es- at the center of the system. In general, such an assumption can itself be justified only by the results which are obtained from it. We have refuted Meillet on this point only insofar as the vital-static-locative value just proposed for the verb is fruitful in giving a unified account of a large number of linguistic facts. Others will have to judge how far this is actually the case. But I will point out that the vital-biological bias of this hypothetical value shows up in the curious Homeric use of εἰμί as "I am alive" (Chapter VI §6). On the other hand, the vital-static value is reflected in the root *wes- which provides the past suppletive for *be* in Germanic (English *was*, German *war*): the underlying sense of this root is indicated by Sanskrit *vasati* "he stays", "he dwells", "he passes the night (somewhere)". Looking in another direction we find that the static-locative connections with verbs of posture is confirmed by a continuous interaction of *be* with verbs for *stand* and *sit*, for example in the Romance languages, where Latin *status* provides a perfect participle for the derivatives of *esse* (Italian *stato*, French *été*), while in Spanish and Portugese the verb *sit* (*sedere*) becomes in part indistinguishable from the verb *be* (*ser*, from late Latin *essere*).[55] Of the two

---

[55] According to W. Meyer-Lübke *Grammaire des langues romanes*, French transl. by A. and G. Doutrepont (Paris, 1895) II, § 218, the Portuguese first sing. subj. *seja* (cf. Spanish *sea*) is the only form derived from *sedere* which has entered the conjugation of the verb *be*. Some scholars claim an influence on the future forms as well. On any view known to me, Heidegger's statement that Spanish *ser* "leitet sich her von sedere, sitzen" is simply a mistake. (See *Kants These über das Sein*, p. 32.)

Spanish verbs for *be*, *ser* and *estar*, not only are the forms of the first contaminated with Latin *sedere* "to sit": the second verb is entirely derived from *stare* "to stand". And this connection between the copula and verbs of posture or position seems to have some basis in the nature of things – or in the nature of language – since it is not limited to I.-E. For example in Turkish the verb stem *dir-* "stand" provides the third person forms for the general system of copulative suffixes mentioned in §9. And we have seen that many copula functions in Ewe are performed by a verb *le* which has the literal sense *is present, is located (there)*. I would explain these striking parallels to the I.-E. facts by pointing to a necessary or at a least natural connection between the basic function of predication and what we have called the static aspect; for the latter is of course most directly expressed by terms for station or position. On the nature of this connection I shall have more to say in Chapter VIII §8. But first let me point out what paradigm of predication is suggested by my hypothetical value for εἰμί as the core copula.

If we regard εἰμί as the generalized form of the verbs of posture *sit, stand, lie*, we may say that the typical or primordial use of the verb is for a living creature and more specifically a person as subject (as is always the case in the first- and second-person forms); and that the verb itself indicates a station or position for that person's body at a given moment or over a certain stretch of time. Whereas the three *be*-replacers specify the posture of the person, that is, the relative location of the parts of his body to one another and to their immediate ground (seat, etc.), the verb **es-* abstracts from this internal disposition of the body (though not from its being alive, i.e. from its being the body of a person) and indicates the extrinsic position or presence of the person in a given place. If no place is specified, the verb alone may indicate simply that the person *is present* somewhere or other, i.e. *is alive* (at a given time). If the place is given but the emphasis falls on the verb and its subject (i.e. if the locative expression is the "topic", or the element given by the preceding context, and the verb with its subject is the novel element or "comment"), we can render εἰμί by *lives, dwells* (in the place specified). In neither case can we describe the verb as a copula; and hence these uses are discussed in the next chapter (VI §6). But the difference between *He lives in Athens*, which is non-copulative, and *He is in Athens*, where we recognize the copula, is after all a difference in degree. From the point of view of the meaning, it is a question of how frequently and continuously the person remains in one place; from the point of view of Homeric usage it is a question of how much interest and emphasis is connected with the verb in a particular context, since ἐστί (or at least the imperfect ἦν or ἔσκε) may be translated in either way. The typical examples of a locative copula arise when the identity of the subject is familiar or assumed, and the interest of the sentence lies in its locating the subject in this or that place.[56]

Thus I tentatively propose that the use of εἰμί as locative copula, though not the most frequent, may be regarded as the central predicative use in that it corresponds to the locative sense of the *be*-replacers and also connects in a natural way with certain non-copulative uses of the verb for "is alive", "is present", "dwells". And this paradigm case of predication with εἰμί obviously fits the Aristotelian notion of an *attribute* as that which can change radically – "into its opposite" – while the subject remains one and the same. A person can shift his position or his dwelling-place as he can change his posture, without ceasing to be the same individual. In insisting that an attribute can change into its *opposite*, however, Aristotle has in mind a different case, namely the predominant use of εἰμί with predicate adjectives, as in *Socrates is pale, Socrates is ignorant*. This use of the verb as nominal copula (which is also "typical" for εἰμί, but in a rather different sense) departs from our paradigm. The language *needs* a copula verb for predicate nouns and adjectives; more specifically, it needs a predicative verb with static aspect. According to our hypothetical paradigm, I.-E. possesses a verb with vital-static-locative value that is naturally used with predicates or complements of place. Our paradigm is designed to explain – in a synchronic, non-developmental perspective – why it is just *this* verb that is introduced as copula with nominal predicates as well. There is no direct or obvious connection between the proposed primitive value for *es-* and the copula use with predicate nouns and adjectives. But there are several important indirect connections, of which we can recognize two: (1) εἰμί as vital-locative verb has the static aspect which is required of the fundamental copula, and (2) εἰμί with this value is naturally used as copula in statements of place. By contrast, the same considerations shed light on the frequent construction of verbs of motion with nominal predicates: *He came first, He goes blind*, etc.[57] The verbs of motion have the appropriate mutative aspect and are naturally construed with locative adjuncts or "complements". Just as the static use of εἰμί, ἵσταμαι, etc. with nominal predicates implies a syntactical parallel between nominal and locative expressions, so also in the corresponding construction with verbs of motion. My hypothesis of a vital-static-locative value for *be* provides us with a systematic connection between *be* (εἰμί) and *go* (εἶμι) that makes perfect sense of this formally parallel but lexically contrasting use of the two verbs (and their respective

---

[56] Thus we return to a view of the copula not unlike that of Brugmann (see § 4 above, n. 21), except that we do not presuppose a vague existential sense for the verb and do not envisage any chronological development.

[57] For Greek examples see above, § 11, n. 54.

replacers) as copula with nominal predicates. In terms of the myth of development we could say that the language adopted the old locative verb *es- for nominal predication with stative aspect, just as it adopted various verbs of motion for predication with a kinetic aspect. In more sober synchronic terms we can say that the system of predication associated with copula and semi-copula verbs, both static and kinetic, has as its vivid focus the spatial ideas of location and movement.

This is as far as we can now go in elucidating the use of εἰμί (and of *es-, insofar as our remarks apply generally to I.-E.) as copula verb. The discussion will be continued in Chapter VIII. By way of summary here, let me recall the three distinct levels of generality at which we have been discussing the concept of predication.

(1) At the most general level, the concept of predication is simply the concept of sentencehood, and in the first place of declarative sentencehood. This is the notion of statement or truth claim – in Husserl's language, *Position* or *Setzung* – for a sentential structure of arbitrary form and content. If we look for a universal or necessary *sign of predication* in this sense, perhaps all we find is the declarative intonation by which the utterance of statements in every language is contrasted with questions, commands, suppositions, and the like. (What is universal is the central position of declarative intonation within a system of contrasts, though of course no *particular* declarative intonation is common to all languages.) In I.-E., however, the finite verb form also generally serves as sign of predication in this sense: as the mark of sentencehood and (with its indicative mood) as the basic signal of truth claim. In Greek, as we shall see in Chapter VII, the verb ἐστί or εἶναι *alone* may serve as sentential variable in this respect, as an expression for the truth claim of an arbitrary sentence. But this use of εἰμί, and this notion of predication, is not necessarily that of a copula.

(2) In the traditional notion of predication this truth claim is particularized for a two-term sentential structure of the form *Fa* in modern logic or *X is Y* in traditional syllogistic analysis. In the latter form, the copula *is* serves as the sign or signal of declarative sentencehood, affirming one term of another, as *is not* denies one term of another. Insofar as the *X is Y* analysis is extended in principle to all sentences, the copula is taken as the universal sign of predication in the sense of (1) above. As we have seen (in §9), this concept of the copula is a theoretical generalization which goes far beyond the actual use of *es- in I.-E. But this generalization is prepared by the treatment of εἰμί in Greek philosophy, and in particular by Aristotle's doctrine that there are as many distinct uses for εἰμί as there are categories – i.e. as there are distinct types of simple propositions for singular subjects, corresponding to different classes of *F* for the sentence form *Fa* in the modern scheme.

This identification of the two-term subject-predicate pattern with the underlying form of sentences in general is open to many objections. And in Greek philosophy it leads to some confusion between the special use of εἰμί as copula and the more general sign of sentential truth claim described under (1). In linguistic fact, the copula is simply the finite verb in a special type of sentence – namely, in copula sentences. But insofar as the form of the copula sentence is taken as the form of the sentence in general, it is no longer easy to distinguish the role of ἐστί as a sentential variable (with truth claim) from ἐστί as copula. This confusion is regrettable; and yet we can recognize its underlying motivation. As I have suggested, the deep fascination of subject-predicate analysis for philosophers from the Greeks to the present day is ultimately due to the fact that the subject-predicate construction of sentences mirrors within the language that semantic or extra-linguistic relationship between language and the world (expressed in logic as *satisfaction* or *is true of*) on which not only declarative sentences but all descriptive discourse – whether in questions, commands, wishes or what not – is grounded.[58]

(3) Finally, we have the specific features of the copula in I.-E. and in Greek in particular. Here the copula is characterized formally by the construction with predicate adjectives, nouns and locatives in elementary sentences, and by various transformational roles including the periphrastic construction with participles. Both in the elementary and derived uses, these copula sentences are formally contrasted with those containing ordinary "full "verbs. Systematically, copula *be* is contrasted with *become*, as static to kinetic; and its use is to some extent paralleled by the verbs of posture: *sit, stand, lie*. Materially, the static copula is provided by a root *es-* which in its Greek form εἰμί is characterized by various non-copulative uses, generally described as *existential*. Of these we have here emphasized the vital sense when the subject is a person: "I am alive, live, dwell (in a place)". I have suggested that the locative idea involved here might tentatively be regarded as the central core of the predicate construction. But it is above all the static-durative aspect of the verb (as implied in the vital sense just mentioned) which made it appropriate as the sign of predication and the expression of truth claim in the more general functions described under (1) and (2).

[58] See Chapter II, pp. 52f. Cf. p. 60.

CHAPTER VI

THE VERB OF EXISTENCE

§1. Existential and Non-copulative Uses

The uses of εἰμί which remain to be described are distinguished by a negative criterion: they represent constructions which are non-copulative according to the syntactic definition of the copula given in Chapter IV §§ 1–2. It is often supposed that these uses can also be positively characterized as *existential*. But in addition to the existential use (or uses) the non-copulative constructions of εἰμί include the following:

Possessive: ἔστι μοι χρήματα "I have money"

Potential: ἔστι + *infinitive* "It is possible, permissible (to do so-and-so)"

Veridical: ἔστι ταῦτα, ἔστι οὕτω "That is so."[1] For reasons which will become clear, I treat the possessive and potential constructions in this chapter together with the existential verb. The veridical use is postponed to Chapter VII.

The description of existential uses of εἰμί raises a number of fundamental problems which are different in kind from those encountered in the description of the copula. The copula is essentially a syntactic concept, and it has proved relatively easy to adapt the techniques of modern syntactic analysis to an account of the Greek data. Much the same is true for the possessive, potential, and veridical uses, which, although they are characterized by distinct meanings, are closely associated with well-defined syntactic structures. But the situation is entirely different for the mass of uses generally regarded as *existential*. This was from the beginning a lexical or semantic concept, designating those cases where the verb "has a meaning of its own", namely "when it signifies *to exist*" (Mill). Now there is no available method of lexical or semantic description which is even remotely comparable in clarity and precision to the syntactic analysis of transformational grammar. Whereas our description of the copula consisted largely in the application to Greek of an existing theory for English, in dealing with the existential verb we are

---

[1] Strictly speaking, we might also regard the predicate genitive of Chapter IV § 26 as non-copulative, i.e. as syntactically parallel to the "predicate dative" of the possessive construction. For discussion of this point, see Chapter IV, p. 161. The adverbial copula of Chapter IV § 21 also represents an extension of the formal definition of the copula, since the original definition applied only to nominal and locative (or paralocative) predicates.

obliged to forge our own tools. Not only do we have no theory of the existential verb to start with; we do not even have a method that determines what *kind* of theory we need. Hence our procedure must be tentative and exploratory; and I shall be happy if I succeed in bringing some semblance of order and precision into an area that has hitherto been left in vagueness and confusion.

As a first approximation, we can identify an existential use of εἰμί as one that is rendered by *there is* in English, by *il y a* in French, by *es gibt* in German, and so on. As we shall see, however, this is unsatisfactory not only as a definition but even as a delimitation of the data generally covered by the concept of the existential verb in Greek. In search of a more adequate account I shall follow a method to be developed in three successive stages of analysis, the first of which is essentially preliminary to and will eventually be replaced by the other two. These stages are (1) *lexical* or philological, (2) *syntactic* or transformational, and (3) *semantic* in a narrow sense, comparable to the use of the term "semantics" in logic for the interpretation of a formal system. In the first stage (§§ 3–4) I catalogue the "meaning" of the existential verb in the traditional dictionary style, where the various senses of a term are rendered by alternative paraphrases or translations, that is, by other expressions with approximately "the same meaning" as the sense or use to be specified. In the second stage I define a small number of sentence types to account for the bulk of uses commonly regarded as existential, and indicate some connections between these syntactic structures and the lexical concepts (or "nuances") described in stage one. In the third stage I attempt to give a deeper analysis of the significance and function of the key existential sentence types, in terms of basic logical concepts such as truth, reference and implication (or presupposition). Thus the third stage, which is semantic in a strict sense, corresponds to what Henry Hiż has called "strong semantics", in contrast to the lexical and philological account of meaning in stage one, which corresponds (in an informal way) to the treatment of meaning in terms of paraphrase relations or "weak semantics".[2] Hence I shall generally use the term "lexical" to refer to an analysis of meaning in terms of translation or paraphrase value, and reserve the term "semantical" for the concepts used in stage 3.

Our method is thus to proceed from lexical philology to syntax, and from syntax to semantics in a strong sense. The three stages of the analysis are clearly distinct in principle, but in practice the syntactic and semantic analysis often go hand in hand. (The primarily syntactic description of sentence types is given in §§ 5–17; the semantic analysis proper comes in §§ 18–20.) We begin with an amorphous mass of uses intuitively classified as

---

[2] See H. Hiż, "The Role of Paraphrase in Grammar," *Monograph Series in Languages and Linguistics*, No. 17, ed. by C. I. J. M. Stuart (1964), 97–104.

existential. We first attempt to distinguish various aspects or nuances in the lexical concept of existence as expressed in this mass. This gives us a preliminary survey of the material to be analyzed (§§ 3–4). The analysis proper consists in sorting the material into manageable units, namely, into the five or six existential sentence types. (Notice that this process of sorting out or chipping off sections of the primitive mass has already begun with my recognition of the possessive, potential, and veridical constructions as distinct non-copulative types. In more generous conceptions of the existential use, some or all of these types have been classified indiscriminately as instances of the existential verb.) I shall suggest that all uses of εἰμί intuitively recognized as existential can be analyzed as examples of these types, either taken singly, in combination with one another, or in contamination with a copulative or possessive (more rarely, with a potential or veridical) construction.

§2. Difficulty of any general description of existential uses

We begin, then, with a lexical survey of the existential uses. I assume that we have, on the whole, reliable intuitions as to when the Greek verb is used in what is loosely called the existential sense but that, if challenged, we are not able to say just what this sense *is*.[3] Is there one basic idea expressed by the verb, some paraphrase formula which might replace it in every case? This is a question that we must face. We cannot suppose that an adequate answer is provided by the simple expedient of offering the English verb "to exist" or the locution "there is…" as an explication of the existential use. For any serious attempt to list the uses which we normally recognize as existential will show that they form a heterogeneous conglomerate, not all specimens of which can properly be rendered by "exists" or even "there is." Thus we would certainly consider ἔτ᾽ εἰσί "(your parents) are still alive" (*Od.* 15.433), or ἔνθα δὲ Σίσυφος ἔσκεν "there dwelt Sisyphus" (*Il.* 6.153) as examples of the strong or existential use, but the verb here cannot be translated as "exist" or "there is." Nor can it be so translated in ὄφρα μὲν ἠὼς ἦν "while dawn lasted" (*Il.* 8.66).

---

[3] By reliable intuitions, I mean that competent Hellenists will tend to agree in their answer to the question whether or not εἰμί in a given passage is or is not being used with existential sense or force. This unanimity is of course limited by (1) the hesitation mentioned above as to whether the possessive, potential, and verdical uses are to be described as existential, and (2) the problem of the mixed cases, where copulative construction and existential meaning coincide (Chapter IV § 25; below § 13). Those scholars – if any there be – who feel that a given use of εἰμί must be *either* copulative *or* existential will be obliged to determine the mixed cases in an arbitrary way.

Even in the case of sentences which can be so rendered, the rendering may not be very informative. In καναχὴ δ' ἦν ἡμιόνοιῖν "there was a clatter of mules (as Nausicaä cracked the whip to start for the river)" (*Od.* 6.82), the existential sense seems clearly different from ἔστι πόλις Ἐφύρη μυχῷ Ἄργεος ἱπποβότοιο "there is a city Ephyre in the corner of Argos" (*Il.* 6.152). To say that all these examples are existential is to state the problem, not to solve it.

Since we are obliged to make use of the term "existence" at every point, I might say a word about the dangers which are latent in this terminology. The colloquial uses of the verb "to exist" and its cognates differ somewhat from language to language. For example, *exister* seems to be more frequently and idiomatically used in French than "exists" in English. *Est-ce qu'une telle chose existe*? is normal usage where we would say "is there such a thing?" But all contemporary uses are conditioned by the discussion of existence in medieval and modern philosophy, and in particular by the systematic treatment of the questions "Does God exist?" and "How can His existence be proved?" or, (since Descartes) by the debate which begins: "I know that I exist; but how can I tell that anyone else does, or that there is an external world?" This theoretical framework for questions of existence tends to make the term relevant above all when we are discussing the problem *whether x exists or not*: when we are denying the existence of some subject or asserting it in the face of possible denials. The idea that talk of existence is always talk of something problematic, subject to doubt and requiring justification, casts its shadow over contemporary uses of the term which in other respects differ as widely as one could wish: in existential quantification in logic, on the one hand, and in "existentialism" on the other. Thus Heidegger asks: "Warum ist überhaupt Seiendes und nicht vielmehr Nichts? Das ist die Frage" (*Einführung in die Metaphysik*, p. 1). Now this speculative, controversial background, which still characterizes the idiomatic usage of "exists" in English and perhaps in most modern languages, is generally irrelevant to the normal use of εἰμί in Greek, as the examples cited in the preceding paragraph should show. Even in the case of such a distinctly "existential" use as ἔστι πόλις Ἐφύρη, no one is expected to *deny* the existence of the Argive town, and it would therefore be quite unidiomatic to translate as "there exists a city Ephyre." From the point of view of the modern usage of "exists," the term *existential use* of εἰμί is a misnomer.[4]

---

[4] Another way of making this point is to say that certain standard sentence types for existential εἰμί in the affirmative do not have a corresponding negative or interrogative form. (See Types II and III in §§ 7–11.) The negative existential and the interrogative are expressed in a different form (Type IV), which does indeed point in the direction of the modern logical quantifier. The modern use of "exists" in the affirmative suggests an answer to the question, "Does it exist?" whereas (except for Type IV and the post-Homeric Type VI) the ancient affirmative forms suggest no such question at all.

Nor do the linguistic origins of "existence" qualify it in any special way to explicate the characteristic features of the Greek usage. "Exist" is a derivative of *ex-sisto* "to step out, emerge." The metaphor latent in the Latin verb is quite irrelevant as a direct rendering of the Greek expressions quoted. The aspectual value of the Greek verb is durative (as in ὄφρα μὲν ἠὼς ἦν "while dawn lasted"), whereas the aspect of the Latin compound verb is essentially punctual and emergent. Hence where ἔστι suggests constancy, stability, and rest, *exsistit* points rather to the appearance of novelty set in relief against the darker background out of which things come. As I have noted elsewhere, the original connotations of *exsisto* are actually much closer to those of γίγνομαι than to εἰμί, and the use of the verb as a substitute for *esse* first became frequent in the perfect tense: "what is" was thus represented as *id quod exstitit*, "what has emerged."[5] Since Cicero and Lucretius, *exsistere* (like other compounds of *stare*) had been employed as a literary and poetic substitute for *esse* in all its uses, including the copula construction. It is an historical problem, which remains largely unsolved, why this particular verb was singled out in the late medieval period to distinguish what we must now call the existential value of *to be*.[6]

§3. FOUR LEXICAL NUANCES OF THE EXISTENTIAL VERB

How are we to specify this value? How are we to describe the existential use of εἰμί, first of all by an English paraphrase or translation? (For present purposes I ignore the distinction between paraphrase *within* a language, as illustrated in the Oxford English Dictionary, and translation from Greek to English, as exemplified in Liddell and Scott. For a bilingual subject, translation can be regarded as a special case of paraphrase or "saying the same thing in different words", where the special condition is that the different words be in a different language.) We have just seen that we cannot provide a single idiomatic paraphrase for the verb in all of the instances for which we wish to account. The most generally available rendering will be "there is." But the existential use of the verb in Greek is wider and freer than the use of *there is* in English, and in any case glossing ἔστι by *there is* will not do much to advance our analysis. I propose the following list of four nuances or paraphrase

---

[5] See my article, "The Greek Verb 'to be' and the Concept of Being," *Foundations of Language* 2 (1966), p. 256. Compare Gilson, *L'être et l'essence*, p. 14: "*Ex-sistere* signifie donc...moins le fait même d'être que son rapport à quelque origine."

[6] For the original use of *exsistere*, together with *stare, constare*, etc. as a synonym for *esse* in both the copulative and existential uses, see A. Ernout, "*Exsto* et les composés latins en *ex-*," *BSL* 50 (1954), 18. For the development of the terminology for "existence", see my article in the *Festschrift for Richard Walzer* (forthcoming).

values as a preliminary sketch of the lexical value of εἰμί in the uses which might be recognized as typically existential:

A. The vital nuance: being *alive* in contrast to being *dead* (which is expressed by the verb when negated).
B. The locative nuance: being here, there or in some definite place, in contrast to being absent from the place specified: not being there. When the sentence itself contains no specification of place, the value of the verb is *being present, being there* (in the situation indicated by the context).
C. The durative nuance, which can be further analyzed into
   C_1, the idea of *occurrence*, as opposed to non-occurrence, and
   C_2, the idea of static or *lasting* occurrence, of *continuing to be so*, in contrast to punctual emergence of a new situation or event (as expressed by the Greek aorist).[7]
D. The nuance associated with the pronouns *some (someone)*, *none (no one)*, and approximately rendered by the existential quantifier: $(\exists x)Fx$. This might be called the existential idea *sensu stricto*: there being *some* (who are such and such) as opposed to there being *none*.

This list is intended to suggest that, instead of postulating some single, fixed lexical value for existential εἰμί that is capable of being rendered by a single formula or paraphrase, we should be prepared to analyze its meaning as a variable cluster of constituent nuances or notions or ideas, not all of which need be presented by any particular example of the verb. It should be clear that when I speak of "ideas" or "notions" here in an account of the lexical value of a word, these terms are not to be taken in a psychological sense as when we speak of "the association of ideas." The ideas to which I refer are not to be understood as quasi-perceptual images present in consciousness nor as items of mental experience in any sense. By "ideas" I mean statable concepts like dictionary entries, i.e. explanatory paraphrases. Similarly, to say that an idea is *expressed* or *presented* by an instance of εἰμί is just to say that we would feel justified in rendering or explicating the verb here by the corresponding paraphrase.

I speak of distinct nuances or notions which may be found together in a single instance of the verb, not of different senses which would exclude one another or produce ambiguity. The problem of lexical ambiguity, and the equivalent problem of distinct senses of a word, is full of difficulties, and I shall not propose any general solution. As Quine has shown, we must

---

[7] For the connections between this durative aspect of εἰμί and the more general "static aspect" of *be* versus *become*, see Chapter V § 3, n. 17. For vital and locative values in the paradigm copula uses, *ibid.* § 12.

distinguish between cases of strong ambiguity, when the same word in different senses can be both true and false of the same subject – as in *The feather is light* (in weight) *but not light* (in color), and cases of weak ambiguity, where differences in sense are correlated with differences in extra-linguistic application in such a way that contradiction can scarcely arise, as in Quine's example of *hard chairs* and *hard questions* (*Word and Object*, p. 130). The more interesting cases of word play involve ambiguity of the latter sort: "The Germans are separated from the Dacians by mountains, rivers, and mutual fear." My distinction of nuances involves a weaker contrast still, for these nuances may occur together in a single example of the verb without any effect of ambiguity. Nevertheless, in some case we do get a weak (non-contradictory) difference of sense or paraphrase value corresponding to a difference in subject. Thus ἦν said of a man may mean "was alive", but when said of an event it means "occurred, took place." At the limit, we may even have a strong, contradictory form of ambiguity between the vital nuance (A) and the timeless existential use corresponding to the quantifier (D): *Socrates the philosopher is no longer alive* (οὐκέτι ἔστι), but *There is a philosopher Socrates who speaks in the dialogues of Plato* (ἔστι Σωκράτης φιλόσοφος ὅστις...).

At the limit, then, what I call the vital nuance might be counted as a distinct sense of εἰμί. In general, however, there is a kind of logical connection between this and the other nuances that can be described as an order of entailment. Thus the vital notion (A) entails the other three (but not conversely): a living person must be (D) someone, (B) somewhere, (C) for some time. Similarly, the locative nuance (B) entails the other two: what is somewhere is something, and if its location is expressed by εἰμί the item localized is presented as lasting or persisting (statically). Whether the converse holds in this case is not so easy to say. We might want to deny that everything which is at all is *somewhere,* in order to leave open the possibility of non-spatial entities. Greek common sense, however, tends to insist that what is nowhere is nothing at all.[8] From the Greek point of view, the locative idea (B) seems to be entailed by every existential use of the verb, i.e. by the other nuances wherever they occur.

The fact that an idea is logically entailed by any given instance of the verb does not mean that it is actually *expressed* there. The sentences in which the verb occurs with a predominantly vital nuance (A) generally do not contain any indications of place at all, nor does their context necessarily specify a definite location. (In fact, when a vital and a locative use occur together, we seem to have a case either of ambiguity or of the fading of the vital sense *is*

---

[8] See the passages quoted in my article, *Foundations of Language* 2 (1966), p. 258 with n. 14.

alive into the semi-locative sense *dwells*; see below § 6, on sentences **24–26**.) We frequently find, however, that an expression of place *does* accompany the verb when it presents nuance (D), the idea that there is *something* (someone) rather than nothing (no one). (See below, examples **2–6**.) Finally the durative notion (C) is generally entailed by all uses of the verb, not for logical but for morpho-semantic reasons, because of the durative aspect which is inseparable from the stem of εἰμί.[9]

§4. EXAMPLES OF THE FOUR NUANCES

The following passages illustrate the expression of these four nuances, either singly or in clusters of two or more.

(A) *The Vital Nuance*

1 *Od.* 15.433

> ἦ γὰρ ἔτ᾽ εἰσὶ καὶ ἀφνειοὶ καλέονται

> "(Your parents) are living still and still accounted rich."[10]

(Palmer)

This nuance (or sense) of the verb is illustrated more fully in the discussion of sentence type I below, § 6.

(B) *The Locative Nuance*

The idea of being present in a place is obviously associated with the use of the verb as locative copula. But the cases of interest to us here belong rather to the mixed locative-existential use illustrated in Chapter IV § 25. These sentences do not simply specify the location for a given subject, but rather insist upon the fact that something (i.e. a subject of a given kind) is or is not *present, to be found* in the place indicated.

2 *Il.* 16.750

> ἦ ῥα καὶ ἐν Τρώεσσι κυβιστητῆρες ἔασιν

> "So, to be sure, in Troy also they have their acrobats"

(Lattimore)

---

[9] See above, Chapter V § 3, n. 17. In Greek the future is generally unmarked for aspect, but in the case of εἰμί the durative aspect may also characterize the future forms, as in example **7** below. There is a complication for the imperfect form ἔσκον, which sometimes lends itself to an interpretation as iterative (or durative-iterative): ἔνθα δὲ Σίσυφος ἔσκε, "There dwelt Sisyphys" (=**24** below). In most cases, however, the form seems to have no iterative valve and "à vrai dire ne se distingue pas toujours nettement de ἦν" (Chantraine, *Grammaire hom.* I, 290).

[10] For the translations used, see n. 14 in Chapter IV § 5.

3 *Il.* 7.446

Ζεῦ πάτερ, ἦ ῥά τίς ἐστι βροτῶν ἐπ᾽ ἀπείρονα γαῖαν
ὅς τις ἔτ᾽ ἀθανάτοισι νόον καὶ μῆτιν ἐνίψει;

"Father Zeus, is there any mortal left on the wide earth who will still declare to the immortals his mind and purpose?"

(Lattimore)

4 *Od.* 21.107

οἵη νῦν οὐκ ἔστι γυνὴ κατ᾽ Ἀχαιΐδα γαῖαν

"(Penelope) a lady whose like cannot be found throughout Achaean land."

(Palmer)

5 *Il.* 13.789

βὰν δ᾽ ἴμεν ἔνθα μάλιστα μάχη καὶ φύλοπις ἦεν

"They went on, to where there was most fighting and clamor."

(after Lattimore)

One striking post-Homeric example:

6 Hesiod, *Works and Days* 11

οὐκ ἄρα μοῦνον ἔην Ἐρίδων γένος, ἀλλ᾽ ἐπὶ γαῖαν
εἰσὶ δύω

"There was not only one kind of strife; there have always been two on earth." [11]

(after Lattimore)

The idea of locative existence, or of there being such-and-such somewhere, is here expressed in various connections: with nuance (D), that there is *someone* (something) as opposed to no one (nothing) in **3** and **4**; with numerical quantifiers (*two* rather than one only) in **6**; and elsewhere with the idea of there being *many* as opposed to few. (See below § 11.) In general, we can say that the existential as distinct from merely locative force of the verb (or of the sentence as a whole) is guaranteed by the presence of a quantifier pronoun.

---

[11] I am not concerned here with the idiomatic use of the past tense illustrated in **6**. This is often grouped with the "philosophical imperfect", but the latter in turn calls for careful definition. In the typical philosophical uses of the imperfect (in Plato and Aristotle) the past tense refers back to some previous statement in the larger context: ἀλλ᾽ ἦν ἐκείνη (sc. μουσικὴ) ἀντίστροφος τῆς γυμναστικῆς, εἰ μέμνησαι "But music has been shown to be the counterpart of gymnastics, if you remember" (Plato *Rep.* 522 A3, referring back to 410C–412A). On the other hand, there is a looser use of the imperfect to "express a *fact* which is just recognized as such by the speaker or writer, having previously been denied, overlooked, or not understood" (W. W. Goodwin, *Syntax of the Moods and Tenses of the Greek Verb* (Boston, 1897), p. 11, § 39). Goodwin counts our sentence **6** as an example of the latter. I am inclined to agree rather with those scholars who regard this as a reference back to (and correction of) *Theogony* 225, where only *one* Strife was mentioned.

But this is not a necessary condition for the strong locative-existential nuance, as we can see from 2 and 5.

It is a striking fact, which we will find abundantly confirmed in the description of Types II and III in §§ 7ff., that the Homeric use of εἰμί which we may render by "there is" is very frequently completed by a specification of place. The Greek notion that whatever is at all is *somewhere* is firmly grounded in the idiomatic expression of existence.

(C) *The Durative Notion*

Like all verbs εἰμί expresses occurrence, in the very general sense of something being the case at a given time. Like a few other verbs in Greek with no aorist or perfect forms, it expresses occurrence only under the durative or static aspect as something which *lasts*, *prevails* or *obtains* (whether for an indefinite or for a specified time).[12] In some cases the durative aspect is conspicuous and will find expression in the translation:

7 *Il.* 7.458 (≈451)

> σὸν δ' ἤτοι κλέος ἔσται ὅσον τ' ἐπικίδναται ἠώς
> "But the fame of you shall last as long as dawnlight is scattered."
>
> (Lattimore)

8 Thucydides 1.58.2

> τῆς ἑαυτοῦ γῆς... ἔδωκε νέμεσθαι, ἕως ἂν ὁ πρὸς Ἀθηναίους πόλεμος ᾖ
> "(Perdiccas) gave them a part of his territory...as a place of abode while the war against the Athenians should last."
>
> (trans. Crawley)

In other cases the aspect is clearly discerned only by contrast and comparison.

9 *Od.* 11.605

> ἀμφὶ δέ μιν κλαγγὴ νεκύων ἦν οἰωνῶν ὥς
> "Around him rose a clamor of the dead, like that of birds."
>
> (Palmer)

There is no emphasis on duration here; but the relevance of the aspect is clear if we compare such a case with

10 *Il.* 1.49

> δεινὴ δὲ κλαγγὴ γένετ' ἀργυρέοιο βιοῖο
> "Terrible was the clash that rose from the bow of silver."
>
> (Lattimore)

---

[12] The absence of the aorist is generally characteristic of the I.-E. root *es-. Whether the absence of a perfect is also inherited or an innovation in Greek is a matter of dispute. According to Chantraine, "l'existence d'un parfait ancien de la racine durative *es- ne semble pas probable" (*Grammaire hom.* I, 287).

The translations do not render the difference in aspect (although it is here reinforced by the lexical contrast between ἦν and γένετο), for there is no convenient expression for it in English. But an analysis of the context in each case shows that the contrast is a real one. In **10** the action noun κλαγγή has just been preceded by ἔκλαγξαν and ἧκε in the aorist, and the description portrays the suddenness of Apollo's assault. **9**, on the other hand, forms part of a static description of the shade of Heracles in Hades, where he appears as a Dantesque *figura* frozen in the act of perpetually drawing his bow. The durative value is similar in

11 *Od.* 6.82

    μάστιξεν δ' ἐλάαν· καναχὴ δ' ἦν ἡμιόνοιϊν

    "(Nausicaa) cracked the whip to start. There was a clatter of the mules and steadily they pulled..."

                                                    (Palmer)

The initial whip-crack (like the bow-twang above) is rendered by an aorist; the clatter of the mules, however, is part of a lasting occurrence, immediately rendered by two other imperfect verbs which express the movement of the mules towards the shore (τανύοντο, φέρον).[13]

(D) *The Idea of the Existential Quantifier*

When the idea of *there being some* rather than none (who are such and such) predominates, the verb is often accompanied by an indefinite pronoun:

12 *Od.* 12.120

    οὐδέ τίς ἐστ' ἀλκή· φυγέειν κάρτιστον ἀπ' αὐτῆς

    "There's no defence (against Scylla): the best thing is to flee from her."

As we have seen in commenting on **6** above, the indefinite pronoun may be replaced by other quantifier words such as *many* or *two*; and much the same nuance can be detected in uses of εἰμί without any quantifier word, as in **2** and **5**. This strictly existential nuance is most typically expressed in sentence Type IV, ἔστι ὅστις..., illustrated below in § 14.

We have noted the general tendency for these four nuances to occur together in clusters of two or more. Thus the vital and the durative ideas

---

[13] As we have seen in Chapter V (n. 17), the durative-aorist contrast often coincides with the static-kinetic opposition, but the two may also vary independently. Thus we can have a static-kinetic contrast between a *be-* and a *become*-verb even where both are in present-durative form: Compare πάντων μὲν κόρος ἐστί, καὶ ὕπνου καὶ φιλότητος (*Il.* 13.636) with αἶψά τε φυλόπιδος πέλεται κόρος ἀνθρώποισιν (*Il.* 19.221). Here "there is satiety in all things" (Lattimore) contrasts with "men quickly get their fill of battle" as static with kinetic.

strictly coincide when the subject is a person, since for a person *to last* or *to endure* is just for him *to remain alive*. A combination of vital and existential ideas is illustrated in the following sentence (which follows the general pattern of Type IV):

13 *Od.* 6.201

οὐκ ἔσθ᾽ οὗτος ἀνὴρ διερὸς βροτὸς οὐδὲ γένηται,
ὅς κεν Φαιήκων ἀνδρῶν ἐς γαῖαν ἵκηται
δηϊοτῆτα φέρων
"The man is not alive and never will be born, who can come and offer harm to the Phaeacian land."[14]

(Palmer)

§5. PRELIMINARY SKETCH OF SIX EXISTENTIAL SENTENCE TYPES WITH εἰμί

So far we have canvassed the range of meaning of the existential verb in the traditional manner of lexical philology. My only innovations were to distinguish constituent nuances in variable combinations instead of alternative *senses* for a given word, and to make somewhat more explicit the methodology (which every dictionary practices) of defining meaning by paraphrase. But dictionaries also recognize variations in the meaning of a word in different syntactical constructions, and this is a factor to which we must now turn.

As a basis for the syntactic analysis of the existential verb in Homer I propose five sentence types, illustrated by the following specimens:

I. 1   ἦ γὰρ ἔτ᾽ εἰσὶ (πατὴρ καὶ μήτηρ)
         "Your parents are still alive."

II. 27   ἔστι πόλις Ἐφύρη μυχῷ Ἄργεος ἱπποβότοιο
         "There is a city, Ephyre, in the corner of horse-pasturing Argos."

III. 51 πολλαὶ γὰρ ἀνὰ στρατόν εἰσι κέλευθοι
         "There are many paths up and down the encampment."

IV. 84   νῦν δ᾽ οὐκ ἔσθ᾽ ὅς τις θάνατον φύγῃ
         "Now there is not one who can escape death."

---

[14] I assume that διερὸς βροτός is construed here in apposition with ἀνήρ and not as direct predicate with ἐστί, which is the existential verb here (in vital sense), not the copula. Such an emphatic position for the copula would be almost unparalleled in Homer. For the general form of **13**, compare *Od.* 16.437 οὐκ ἔσθ᾽ οὗτος ἀνὴρ οὐδ᾽ ἔσσεται οὐδὲ γένηται,/ὅς κεν Τηλεμάχῳ ... χεῖρας ἐποίσει, which Palmer translates in the same way: "The man is not alive and never will be born, who...." In Lattimore's new version of the *Odyssey* we have for 16.437 "The man is not living, nor will there be one, nor can there ever/be one, who...."

V. 9   ἀμφὶ δέ μιν κλαγγὴ νεκύων ἦν
         "Around him rose a clamor of the dead."[15]

In addition we must recognize one post-Homeric type:

VI. 121   οὐδ᾽ ἔστι Ζεύς
          "There is *no* Zeus" (or "Zeus doesn't even exist")

These six sentence types may be briefly described as follows. Type I is an absolute construction of the verb with personal subjects. (By an absolute construction I mean that there is no nominal or locative predicate and no other complement such as the possessive dative, nor even an adverb of manner. An absolute construction may, however, admit adverbs of time.) This sentence type corresponds exactly with the vital nuance mentioned in §§ 3–4; that is, in every sentence of this type, εἰμί can be translated "am alive". Type IV is the natural analogue to a formal statement of existence (with nuance D): "There is someone (no one) who..." Type V is existential in a different sense, since the subject expression is not a first-order nominal but an abstract noun (i.e. the nominalization of an underlying predicate or sentence). εἰμί functions here as a kind of dummy verb or verb of occurrence; it can be translated by "arises", "takes place," "lasts", as well as by "there is". (I shall call the verb in Type V a *surface predicate*.) The post-Homeric Type VI is the traditional philosophical model of a statement of existence: *There is a God, There are no unicorns.*

Types II and III are more difficult to define, although they are easy enough to identify in Homer. We may say tentatively that they represent mixed cases in which a strictly existential use of Type IV has been fused with a locative construction (or, less frequently, with a nominal copula).

In illustrating Types I to V I shall deal primarily with the Homeric data and attempt to give something like an exhaustive account, since it is in these early texts if anywhere that we should find the "original" use of the verb *be* in Greek. As we shall see, Types IV and V occur very frequently in later Greek as well, where there are also some analogues to Type II. Type I survives in Attic tragedy and prose, but perhaps only as an archaism. It should be noted that only Type I occurs with the verb in first or second person; Types II–VI are essentially restricted to a third person form, for reasons to be discussed later.

§6. TYPE I (THE VITAL USE)

The subject expression (whether given in the sentence or reconstructed from

---

[15] The specimens for I and V have been cited above, with full references. For sentences 27, 51, and 84, see below §§ 7, 11, and 14; for sentence 121 see § 18.

the context) is a personal noun; that is to say, the extra-linguistic subjects of Type I sentences are members of the class of *persons* (human or divine) who populate the world of the poems – including not only the *dramatis personae*, who play a role as actors and speakers, but also those who are simply mentioned as off-stage characters. In this type the construction of εἰμί is "absolute" in the sense just specified: namely, the verb takes no complement or modifier except for adverbs of time and duration (*now, still, always*). The form can be schematized as N_{pers} *be* (D_{temp}), where the parenthesis indicates an optional component. I repeat the specimen sentence given in § 4:

1 *Od.* 15.433

  ἦ γὰρ ἔτ᾽ εἰσὶ καὶ ἀφνειοὶ καλέονται
  "(Your parents) are living still and still accounted rich."

(transl. Palmer)

14 *Il.* 2.641

  οὐ γὰρ ἔτ᾽ Οἰνῆος μεγαλήτορος υἱέες ἦσαν,
  οὐδ᾽ ἄρ᾽ ἔτ᾽ αὐτὸς ἔην, θάνε δὲ ξανθὸς Μελέαγρος
  "Since no longer were the sons of high-hearted Oineus living, nor Oineus himself, and fair-haired Meleagros had perished."

(Lattimore)

15 *Il.* 6.130 (cf. 139f.)

  οὐδὲ γὰρ οὐδὲ Δρύαντος υἱός, κρατερὸς Λυκόοργος,
  δὴν ἦν
  "Since even the son of Dryas, Lykourgos the powerful, did not live long."

(Lattimore)

This type, alone among the existential uses, takes all the usual transformations of person, mood, and participle.

16 *Od.* 18.79

  νῦν μὲν μήτ᾽ εἴης, βουγάϊε, μήτε γένοιο
  "Better you were not living, and never had been born."

(Palmer)

17 *Od.* 8.147

  οὐ μὲν γὰρ μεῖζον κλέος ἀνέρος ὄφρα κεν ᾖσιν
  "There is no greater glory for a men in all his life."[16]

(Palmer)

18 *Od.* 6.287

  πατρὸς καὶ μητρὸς ἐόντων
  "While father and mother were alive"

(Palmer)

---

[16] Note here the omission of an existential verb (ἔστι, γίγνεται) in a Type V construction with κλέος, and also the strong durative value of this vital use of ᾖσιν: "as long as he lives."

19 *Il.* 22.384

καὶ ῞Εκτορος οὐκέτ᾽ ἐόντος

"though Hector lives no longer"

(Lattimore)

20 *Il.* 1.290, 494, etc.

θεοὶ αἰὲν ἐόντες

"the everlasting gods", "the gods who live forever"[17]

(Lattimore)

The obvious translation "live, is alive" causes a difficulty only in the rare cases where ἐστί occurs in conjunction with ζώει:

21 *Od.* 24.262

ὡς ἐρέεινον

ἀμφὶ ξείνῳ ἐμῷ, ἤ που ζώει τε καὶ ἔστιν,

ἤ ἤδη τέθνηκε καὶ εἰν ᾽Αΐδαο δόμοισιν

"When I inquired for my friend, and asked if he were living still or if he were already dead and in the house of Hades".

(Palmer)

Note that Palmer has, in effect, left ἔστιν untranslated, as if it were indistinguishable in meaning from ζώει; Lattimore now renders the verse "whether he still lives and *is somewhere here.*"[18] I shall return to this question of lexical value for ἔστι in a moment. First we observe that sentences of Type I occur frequently enough in Attic tragedy but only rarely in prose.

22 Sophocles *Ajax* 778 ἀλλ᾽ εἴπερ ἔστι τῇδε θἠμέρα

783 οὐκ ἔστιν ἀνὴρ κεῖνος, εἰ Κάλχας σοφός

"If he lives through this day"

"The man is doomed, if Calchas knows his trade."

23 Euripides *Hecuba* 284

κἀγὼ γὰρ ἦ ποτ᾽, ἀλλὰ νῦν οὐκ εἴμ᾽ ἔτι

"I was alive once, but now I'm as good as dead."

Sophocles is particularly fond of this Homerism (see *Antigone* 871, *O.T.* 1368, *O.C.* 392, *Philoctetes* 422, 445, etc.). By contrast, I note only one example in Herodotus (1.120.2 ἔστι τε ὁ παῖς καὶ περίεστι in answer to the

---

[17] Compare the frequent use of the future participle ἐσσομένοισι "for men to come", e.g. *Il.* 2.119 αἰσχρὸν γὰρ τόδε γ᾽ ἐστὶ καὶ ἐσσομένοισι πυθέσθαι. For a fuller list of examples, see Ebeling's *Lexicon Homericum*, I, p. 359, s.v. εἰμί 1 "vivo et vigeo".

[18] Compare Demosthenes 18.72 ζώντων καὶ ὄντων ᾽Αθηναίων, where the coupling of the two verbs is perhaps an echo of the Homeric verse in **21**. For further discussion of **21** see Chapter VIII p. 378.

question εἰ ἐπέζωσε). There are two participial instances in the Funeral Oration (Thucydides 2.44.3 τῶν οὐκ ὄντων λήθη οἱ ἐπιγιγνόμενοί τισιν ἔσονται, 2.45.1 τὸν γὰρ οὐκ ὄντα ἅπας εἴωθεν ἐπαινεῖν), and perhaps a few examples in Xenophon.[19]

As defined here, Type I requires a personal subject. But we may recognize a poetical extension of this type to cities, for example, with a literary effect of personification: Euripides *Troades* 1292 ὄλωλεν οὐδ᾽ ἔτ᾽ ἔστι Τροία "Troy has perished, and is no more" (cited LSJ s.v. εἰμί A.I, with parallels). Although the vital nuance would seem to apply literally to animals and plants as well, I have found no good parallels to Type I with animal subjects. However, Aristotle sometimes plays upon this vital sense in an absolute "existential" use of the verb with non-personal subjects which we might regard as a contamination of Types I and VI: *De Anima* 416^{b}19 διὸ στερηθὲν τροφῆς οὐ δύναται εἶναι "Therefore it (sc. an organism) cannot live when deprived of nutriment" (tr. Hicks). Similarly in the contrast between τὸ εἶναι "mere survival," and τὸ εὖ (ζῆν) "a good life", *ibid.* 435^{b}20. Compare *Eudemian Ethics* 1215^{b}26 where τὸ μὴ εἶναι is used for τὸ μὴ ζῆν (but the reference is to men).

The strong vital sense which is characteristic of the verb in Type I is noticeably weakened when the verb is construed with a locative. Hence the following may be considered as marginal or transitional cases between Type I and the ordinary locative copula:

24 *Il.* 6.153 (for the context, see **27** in § 7)
　　ἔνθα δὲ Σίσυφος ἔσκεν
　　"There lived Sisyphus"

(Lattimore)

25 *Od.* 9.508
　　ἔσκε τις ἐνθάδε μάντις ἀνήρ
　　"Here once a prophet lived"

(Palmer)

In both cases we might also render the verb by "dwelt", in neither case by "was alive", for there is no special emphasis on the idea of life as opposed to death. In other cases we may reasonably hesitate between alternative renderings, since we cannot be sure whether the poet intended the rhetorical stress to fall upon the verb as predicate or upon the local adverb:

---

[19] Thus *Anabasis* III. 2.29 ὄντων μὲν τῶν ἀρχόντων may be rendered "while the generals were alive," although a possessive-existential construction with ἡμῖν from the preceding context is also possible. Compare Aeschines 1.102 Ἀρίγνωτος, ὃς ἔτι καὶ νῦν ἔστι, 3.132 τοῖς ἐσομένοις μεθ᾽ ἡμᾶς, where the latter clearly represents an Homeric echo.

26 *Od.* 24.351

ἦ ῥα ἔτ' ἐστὲ θεοὶ κατὰ μακρὸν Ὄλυμπον

"Surely you gods still live on high Olympus" (Palmer)

"Verily ye gods yet bear sway on high Olympus" (tr. Lang,

Leaf, Myers)

To bring out both local and vital nuances, we would be obliged to over-translate:

> "You gods are still alive (still immortal, i.e. still gods) and still dwell on Olympus (i.e. still occupy the seat of power)."

The ambiguity might be partially resolved in the actual utterance of such a sentence.

The point is not that the ideas of being alive and dwelling somewhere are incompatible – they obviously are not – but that their simultaneous expression in a given occurrence of εἰμί is difficult or impossible: one cannot at one time, with a single word in a single context, contrast life with death and living *here* with living *there*.[20] Hence there is an inevitable weakening of the vital sense of εἰμί whenever the verb is construed with a locative predicate in the same kernel structure.

It should be noted that the vital sense in Type I, with its weaker variant *dwell* in **24** and **25**, represents the case when εἰμί comes closest to having the lexical status of an ordinary verb. Its syntax in Type I is indeed that of an elementary sentence, with a first-order nominal as subject and no transformational derivation in the predicate. Hence it is only natural that some nineteenth century etymologies regarded this as the "original" sense of the verb; and it is no accident that this sense coincides with the nuclear value I have reconstructed for εἰμί within the system of *be*-replacers: to stay alive, to live or remain (*in a place, state, or condition*). (Chapter V § 12.) In contrast to its "empty" or formal role as copula, εἰμί in a Type I sentence has the full lexical force of an ordinary verb, in the following sense. Whereas in a sentence of the form *Socrates ——— in Athens*, the copula *is* represents the minimal or "dummy" filler for the blank, the one verb which can often be omitted and which we automatically reconstruct (in zero form) if no verb occurs, the insertion of *dwells* or *lives* on the other hand is not automatic and a verb of this meaning will scarcely be omitted. *A fortiori*, if there is no locative phrase but only a sentence pattern of the form *Socrates ——— no longer or*

---

[20] If this can be done, it is only in exceptional uses like *John really LIVED in Paris in 1935*, meaning he had a good life there. Normally we could say either *He was living (=dwelling) there in 1935* or *He was alive – and there – in 1935*, but not *He was alive there in 1935*. The incompatibility is not a vagary of English idiom. In French, *Il vivait encore en 1935* means *He was still alive (était vivant)*, but *Il vivait encore là en 1935* means *He was still living there (habitait là)*. The reason for this incompatibility is given in the text.

Your parents ——— still, we would in general have no grounds for reconstructing εἰμί in the sense *is alive*. Unless there is some special clue from the context, εἰμί in the vital use will not be omitted since it could not be reconstructed by the hearer. The verb carries its own distinct item of information, like any elementary verb in the language. Thus even if we are prepared to admit some difference of lexical meaning between ζώει and ἔστιν in **21** ,there is no reason to suppose any fundamental difference in their syntactic role or in the relative fullness of their meaning.[21]

§7. TYPE II. MIXED ASSERTIONS OF EXISTENCE FOR SINGULAR SUBJECTS

I call these *mixed* assertions since the existential use of εἰμί is not easily separated here from the copulative constructions of the verb (locative, nominal or both) in the same sentence. Because of this difficulty, I postpone the syntactic analysis until the type has been fully illustrated. It turns out that although Type II is the most *conspicuous* existential use of εἰμί in Homer, it cannot be regarded as the most typical or the most distinctively existential.

There are two subtypes corresponding to two different metrical formulas in Homer. In the most common of these, which I call Type IIA, the subject is a city, hill, cave or other topographical item. In the second subtype (Type IIB) the subject is a man. In both patterns the verb ἔστι usually occurs in strong initial position, as first word in the sentence and also in the verse. In four instances of Type IIA the position of the verb is non-initial; and from the strictly formulaic point of view these examples **34–37** do not represent the same pattern, since they contain no word in the same metrical position as in **27–33**. From the point of view of sense and syntax, however, it would be

---

[21] As mentioned above (Chapter I, n. 41), I cannot follow Lyons' argument to the effect that *live* and *exist* in sentences like *Socrates lived in the fifth century B.C.* and *This building has existed for thirty years* are "temporal copulas", "purely grammatical 'dummies'", like the surface predicate *occurred* in *The demonstration occurred on Sunday* (*Introduction*, p. 349). The verb *exist* presents problems of its own, and I would agree that it is not an elementary verb. But I do not find this thesis plausible for *live*. Presumably a grammatical dummy is a word which contributes no non-redundant information (apart from purely formal indications, such as tense and aspect), no information which could not be reconstructed if that word was omitted (unlike *occurred*, which is easily reconstructed from the compressed sentence *The demonstration on Sunday*). But I do not see how the verbs *live* and *die* – any more than the adjectives *alive* and *dead* – can be regarded as redundant in this sense. If the parenthesized words are omitted in the following sentences, there seem to be no other linguistic devices to give us the corresponding information: *Socrates (was alive) in 400 B.C., Socrates (lived) in the time of Pericles, Socrates (died) in 399 B.C.* To specify that *Socrates* is an animate or personal noun is not enough, since that will not discriminate between *is born, lives* and *dies* (not to mention other possibilities like *was famous, was a soldier*) as relevant predicates with temporal adjuncts.

misleading to separate these four from the more compact group constituted by **27–33**.

Note that passage **27**, which provides our specimen of Type II, also includes sentence **24**, which was quoted in the last section as a vital-locative variant on Type I.

Type IIA

27 *Il.* 6.152

ἔστι πόλις Ἐφύρη μυχῷ Ἄργεος ἱπποβότοιο,
ἔνθα δὲ Σίσυφος ἔσκεν, ὃ κέρδιστος γένετ' ἀνδρῶν,
Σίσυφος Αἰολίδης· ὁ δ' ἄρα Γλαῦκον τέκεθ' υἱόν
"There is a city, Ephyre, in the corner of horse-pasturing
Argos; there lived Sisyphos, that sharpest of men,
Sisyphos, Aiolos' son, and he had a son named Glaukos,
(and Glaukos in turn sired Bellerophontes the blameless)."

(Lattimore)

Glaukos, son of Hippolochos, is responding to Diomedes' question, τίς δὲ σύ ἐσσι; "who among mortal men are you?" He begins with a genealogy in good form, tracing his family from Sisyphus to his grandfather Bellerophon and finally to his father Hippolochos. It is clear that, just as ἔσκεν serves to introduce Sisyphus in a relatively unemphatic way, ἔστι serves to present Ephyre with greater emphasis, since it is by reference to this city that the ancestor is located and with it the fame of the family is connected. (See the echo of **27** at the end of the passage, 6.209: πατέρων... οἳ μέγ' ἄριστοι / ἔν τ' Ἐφύρῃ ἐγένοντο καὶ ἐν Λυκίῃ εὐρείῃ.) Ancestry and place of origin provide the normal answer to a question of personal identity in Homer, as we have seen (Chapter IV § 12). The rhetorical function of Type IIA in this example is clear and typical: it introduces a local item as point of reference for the following narrative. This sentence type is so well established in Homer that it might be regarded as the existential use par excellence. Because of its importance, I give the parallels in full.

28 *Il.* 2.811

ἔστι δέ τις προπάροιθε πόλιος αἰπεῖα κολώνη,
ἐν πεδίῳ ἀπάνευθε, περίδρομος ἔνθα καὶ ἔνθα,
....
ἔνθα τότε Τρῶές τε διέκριθεν ἠδ' ἐπίκουροι
"Near the city but apart from it there is a steep hill
in the plain by itself, so you pass one side or the other.
(This men call the Hill of the Thicket, but the immortal
gods have named it the burial mound of dancing Myrina.)

There the Trojans and their companions were marshalled in order."

(Lattimore)

29 *Il.* 11.711

ἔστι δέ τις Θρυόεσσα πόλις, αἰπεῖα κολώνη,
τηλοῦ ἐπ᾽ Ἀλφειῷ, νεάτη Πύλου ἠμαθόεντος·
τὴν ἀμφεστρατόωντο

"There is a city, Thryoessa, a headlong hill town
far away by the Alpheios at the bottom of sandy Pylos.
They had thrown their encampment about that place."

(Lattimore)

30 *Il.* 11.722

ἔστι δέ τις ποταμὸς Μινυήϊος εἰς ἅλα βάλλων
ἐγγύθεν Ἀρήνης, ὅθι μείναμεν Ἠῶ δῖαν

"There is a river, Minyeios, which empties its water
in the sea beside Arene. There we waited for the divine Dawn."

(Lattimore)

31 *Il.* 13.32

ἔστι δέ τι σπέος εὐρὺ βαθείης βένθεσι λίμνης,
μεσσηγὺς Τενέδοιο καὶ Ἴμβρου παιπαλοέσσης·
ἔνθ᾽ ἵππους ἔστησε Ποσειδάων ἐνοσίχθων

"There is a cave, broad and deep down in the gloom of the water,
lying midway between Tenedos and Imbros of the high cliffs,
There Poseidon the shaker of the earth reined in his horses."

(Lattimore)

32 *Od.* 3.293

ἔστι δέ τις λισσὴ αἰπεῖά τε εἰς ἅλα πέτρη
ἐσχατιῇ Γόρτυνος, ἐν ἠεροειδέϊ πόντῳ,
ἔνθα Νότος μέγα κῦμα ποτὶ σκαιὸν ῥίον ὠθεῖ,
ἐς Φαιστόν....
αἱ μὲν ἄρ᾽ ἔνθ᾽ ἦλθον

"Here is a cliff, smooth and steep toward the water, at the border
land of Gortyn, on the misty sea, where the south wind drives in
the heavy waves on the western point toward Phaestus.... Some
(ships) came in here."

(Palmer)

33 *Od.* 4.844

ἔστι δέ τις νῆσος μέσσῃ ἁλὶ πετρήεσσα,
μεσσηγὺς Ἰθάκης τε Σάμοιό τε παιπαλοέσσης,
Ἀστερίς, οὐ μεγάλη· λιμένες δ᾽ ἔνι ναύλοχοι αὐτῇ
ἀμφίδυμοι· τῇ τόν γε μένον λοχόωντες Ἀχαιοί

"Now in mid-sea there is a rocky island, midway from Ithaca to rugged Samos – Star Islet called – of no great size.... And here it was the Achaeans waited, watching."

(Palmer)

In these seven examples, ἔστι takes initial position. In four others (all from the *Odyssey*) its occurrence is delayed:

34 *Od.* 4.354–360

νῆσος ἔπειτά τις ἔστι πολυκλύστῳ ἐνὶ πόντῳ
Αἰγύπτου προπάροιθε, Φάρον δέ ἑ κικλήσκουσι,
....(4 verses omitted)
ἔνθα μ᾽ ἐείκοσιν ἤματ᾽ ἔχον θεοί

"Now in the surging sea an island lies off Egypt – Pharos they call it.... Here the gods kept me twenty days."

(after Palmer)

35 *Od.* 13.96–113

Φόρκυνος δέ τίς ἐστι λιμήν, ἁλίοιο γέροντος,
ἐν δήμῳ ᾽Ιθάκης
....(15 verses omitted)
ἔνθ᾽ οἵ γ᾽ εἰσέλασαν πρὶν εἰδότες

"Now in the land of Ithaca there is a certain harbor sacred to Phorcys, the old man of the sea.... Here they rowed in, knowing the place of old."

(Palmer)

36 *Od.* 19.172–180

Κρήτη τις γαῖ᾽ ἔστι, μέσῳ ἐνὶ οἴνοπι πόντῳ,
καλὴ καὶ πίειρα, περίρρυτος· ἐν δ᾽ ἄνθρωποι
πολλοί, ἀπειρέσιοι, καὶ ἐννήκοντα πόληες
....(3 verses omitted)
τῇσι δ᾽ ἐνὶ Κνωσός, μεγάλη πόλις, ἔνθα τε Μίνως
ἐννέωρος βασίλευε Διὸς μεγάλου ὀαριστής,
πατρὸς ἐμοῖο πατήρ

"There is a country, Crete, in the midst of the wine-dark sea, a fair land and a rich, begirt with water. The people there are many, innumerable indeed, and they have ninety cities.... Of all their towns the capital is Cnosus, where Minos became king when nine years old – Minos, the friend of mighty Zeus and father of my father."

(Palmer)

One rather deviant example in past tense illustrates the same general form:

37 *Od.* 22.126

 ὀρσοθύρη δέ τις ἔσκεν ἐϋδμήτῳ ἐνὶ τοίχῳ,

 ....(2 verses omitted)

 τὴν δ᾽ Ὀδυσεὺς φράζεσθαι ἀνώγει δῖον ὑφορβόν

 "Now in the solid wall there was a postern-door.... Odysseus
 ordered the noble swineherd to guard this."

(Palmer)

For a study of the artistic use and expansion of formulaic material in Homer, these ten passages provide a most instructive group. In every case a geographic or topographic feature, which has not been mentioned before or not in the relevant context, is introduced into the narrative by an existential ἔστι (which may in every case be rendered by "there is") in order to serve as a point of localizing reference for the following narrative episode. In every case this localization is indicated by some form of deictic or anaphoric reference – by a relative-demonstrative pronoun or local adverb – at the point where the new episode begins (ἔνθα, τῇ "there", ὅθι "where", τήν "it"). It is characteristic of Homeric technique that a relatively simple form of words, which in **27** scarcely occupies more than a single verse, is capable of almost indefinite expansion and elaboration without loss of its distinctive linguistic and rhetorical structure. Thus in **35** we have 16 verses intervening between the existential ἔστι and the demonstrative ἔνθα which marks the end of the formulaic episode.[22] But in every case the narrative function of the sentence with ἔστι is in principle the same: to introduce a new topographical item as a basis for local reference in the following story.

The rhetorical role of ἔστι in Type IIA is thus clear; less clear its syntactic role. This will be easier to specify for the second subtype IIB, where the pattern is more uniform.

Type IIB

38 *Il.* 5.9

 ἦν δέ τις ἐν Τρώεσσι Δάρης, ἀφνειὸς ἀμύμων,

 ἱρεὺς Ἡφαίστοιο· δύω δέ οἱ υἱέες ἤστην,

 .../τώ....

---

[22] It is also characteristic that the more elaborate variants, including all cases of non-initial ἐστί, occur in the *Odyssey*. For an interesting variant which serves exactly the same narrative function, but where the role of εἰμί is taken by a nuncupative construction of κικλήσκομαι (=καλέομαι) as *be*-replacer, see *Od.* 15.403ff. νῆσός τις Συρίη κικλήσκεται, εἴ που ἀκούεις / Ὀρτυγίης καθύπερθεν, ὅθι τροπαὶ ἠελίοιο, ... ἔνθα δέ (415). (For other examples where καλέομαι is used as a substitute for εἰμί, see LSJ s.v. καλέω II.2 and 3.a.) Note that τῇσι δ᾽ ἐνὶ Κνωσός in **36** represents another variant on Type IIA with the existential-locative verb ἔστι *omitted*.

"There was a man of the Trojans, Dares, blameless and bountiful,
priest consecrated to Hephaistos, and he had two sons, /..../
These two (breaking from the ranks charged against Diomedes)."

(Lattimore)

39 *Il.* 10.314–318

ἦν δέ τις ἐν Τρώεσσι Δόλων, Εὐμήδεος υἱὸς
κήρυκος θείοιο, πολύχρυσος πολύχαλκος,
....(2 verses omitted),
ὅς... μῦθον ἔειπεν

"But there was one among the Trojans, Dolon, Eumedes'
son, the sacred herald's, a man of much gold and bronze,
....
This man now spoke his word."

(Lattimore)

40 *Il.* 13.663

ἦν δέ τις Εὐχήνωρ, Πολυΐδου μάντιος υἱός,
ἀφνειός τ' ἀγαθός τε, Κορινθόθι οἰκία ναίων, /.../
τὸν βάλε (Πάρις)

"There was a man, Euchenor, son of the seer Polyidos,
a rich man and good, who lived in his house at Korinth,
(who knew well that it was his death....)
Paris struck him."

(Lattimore)

41 *Il.* 17.575

ἔσκε δ' ἐνὶ Τρώεσσι Ποδῆς, υἱὸς Ἠετίωνος,
ἀφνειός τ' ἀγαθός τε...
τόν ῥα... βάλε... Μενέλαος

"There was one among the Trojans, Podes, Eetion's son,
a rich man and good...
Now Menelaos struck this man."

(Lattimore)

42 *Od.* 9.508

ἔσκε τις ἐνθάδε μάντις ἀνὴρ ἠΰς τε μέγας τε,
Τήλεμος Εὐρυμίδης.../...
ὅς μοι ἔφη τάδε πάντα τελευτήσεσθαι ὀπίσσω

"Here once a prophet lived, a prophet brave and tall, Telemus,
son of Eurymus,.... He told me it should come to pass in after-
time."

(Palmer)

The *Odyssey* contains two other examples of this subtype (15.417 and 20.287)
with minor variations to be noted in the next section.

§8. Syntactic Analysis of Type IIB

A simple examination of **38–42** shows that the rhetorical function of Type IIB is exactly parallel to that of IIA. The only difference is that whereas the latter introduces a topographical item such as a city or hill, the former introduces a person: a particular individual not previously mentioned, who plays a role in the narrative which follows.

A syntactical analysis of these sentences is more delicate. After much hesitation, I have come to the conclusion that Types IIA and IIB cannot be adequately defined in transformational terms. The intuitive value and rhetorical force of εἰμί in these sentences is unmistakable, but it is not correlated with a definite syntactic form. What the transformational analysis does show is that εἰμί occurs as copula (and usually as locative copula) in the underlying structure of these sentences. But the formal analysis cannot make clear just why or how εἰμί functions here as *more* than the copula. That is to say, we cannot specify the formal conditions under which the copula verb in such sentences always has existential force, and without which it never does. In this respect our strategy of analysis is a failure, at least in part. For we had hoped to correlate every intuitive difference of meaning in the use of εἰμί with a formal description of the corresponding sentence type.

Now in many cases we can in fact correlate the intuitive existential value of εἰμί in Types IIA and IIB with initial position for the verb, with the presence of an indefinite pronoun τις, or with both. Taken together, initial position and the pronoun τις may be *sufficient* conditions for the existential value of the verb. But neither alone is necessary. (And neither alone is sufficient, as we shall see in a moment.) No τις occurs in our specimen for Type IIA, sentence **27**; nor is there a τις in sentence **41** under Type IIB. The verb is non-initial in **34–37**. I doubt that these sentences can be regarded as any less existential than those in which both conditions are satisfied. All we can say is that the existential function illustrated in these Types *tends* to be expressed by a sentence form with initial verb and pronoun τις. But the exceptions just cited show that this function does not depend upon either one of these formal conditions. (It may depend upon at least *one* of these conditions being satisfied. But this does not provide us with the desired definition, since either condition may also be satisfied in a non-existential sentence.)

There is a tendency, then, for the existential force of the verb in such sentences to be associated with a certain formal structure, just as the existential force of *be* in English is regularly expressed by the form with quasi-initial verb, *there is*. But unlike the situation in English, the existential force of the verb in Greek does not depend upon this formal structure. On what, then, does it depend? We touch here on the most fundamental question concerning the verb *be* in I.-E.: the underlying connection between the copula and the existential uses of *be*. I give my answer briefly at this point, before spelling it out more fully in what follows.

The copula verb, whose elementary function is to affirm (as that of its negation is to deny) that a given predicate belongs to a given subject – or to put it in less Aristotelian terms, to affirm that a given subject is *characterized* in a certain way – can have as its secondary function to affirm, present, or introduce the subject itself. This is a fact about the I.-E. verb which we must recognize and can try to understand. In the first instance, this secondary function is based upon the use of the verb as locative copula. As copula in elementary locative sentences, the verb εἰμί carries the mark of affirmation or truth-claim that an individual subject, such as a person or a city, is located in a particular place. But the same verb, in almost the same sentence with a slightly different context, can affirm or present the subject itself, as localized in that place. In such a case, the verb does not cease to function as locative copula; but in addition it introduces the subject into the narrative or into the discourse. It is this rhetorical function of *introducing its subject*, and not any fixed syntactic form, that is regularly correlated with existential force for the verb (as measured by our temptation to translate it by "there is").[23] But since its function is to introduce its subject into the context, the verb naturally tends to precede this subject and thus to move to the head of the sentence.

This subject-introducing or existence-asserting function of the verb is most naturally associated with the locative copula. (For the primary role of locative ideas in this connection see above, Chapter V §12 and below, Chapter VIII §4.) But it may also be associated with the nominal copula, or with the copula function as such. The verb which serves to assign predicates to subjects, or to characterize subjects in various ways, may also serve to present the subject itself – to introduce it into the discourse or to assert its existence, precisely as a subject for further predication. In certain variants on Type II we find the nominal copula playing this role, with no predication of place or location. (See sentence **40** above, **45** and above all **46** in §10; compare **128** and **129** in §22.) And in Type IV we will find the verb playing this role *alone*, without serving at the same time as copula. Since it is this function of providing, presenting, or asserting a subject for further predication which is the existential function proper, it is in Type IV that we find the existential verb in its purest form. What we have in Type II (and also in Type III) is a mixed case where the verb functions both as copula and as sign of existence, that is, where it serves both to characterize

---

[23] Even this may be an overstatement. See below on sentence **48**.

or localize the subject and also to present it *as a subject*. I shall suggest in a moment (below, p. 257) why the locative copula is suited to perform this double role. My suggestion as to why the copula verb *as such*, that is, the nominal copula as well, is able to do so – or, more generally, why the same verb can serve both as copula and sign of existence – will be given later, in Chapter VIII §7 (see especially pp. 409–11). In a word, the most general explanation is that the verb *be*, which is the primary instrument for first-order predication and which agrees with its subject in person and in number, may naturally serve to express a presupposition of such predication: the existence of a first-order subject.

Whatever the explanation, there is no doubt as to the facts. A form of εἰμί which has the underlying syntax of the copula (and in most cases, that of the locative copula) is typically used to introduce a person or place into the narrative situation at the beginning of a tale or episode. This function, which is familiar from other I.-E. languages as well, is illustrated for Greek by Types IIA and IIB. In this use the verb occurs very frequently (but not necessarily) in initial position. We turn now to the syntactic analysis of the two Types and to a description of the formal variants.

In the case of IIB the analysis is simple. In every example except 40 we have a locative kernel in which εἰμί would occur as ordinary locative copula: **38K** *Dares was among the Trojans,* **39K** *Dolon was among the Trojans,* **42K** *A prophet was here,* etc. (Here the symbol "38K" is an abbreviation for "kernel structure of **38**".) We can assign the same kernel form to **40** if we are willing to reconstruct the corresponding locative from the general context: "There was ⟨among the Acheans⟩ a certain Euchenor.... Him Paris struck." It is characteristic of Types II and III that we can in every case assume a kernel form in which εἰμί will occur as copula. (Thus if we prefer not to reconstruct a locative form for **40**, we can derive it – less plausibly – from the *cop N* sentence *Euchenor was son of Polyidos* or from the *cop A* sentence *Euchenor was rich and good.*) In the underlying locative sentences which I pose for Type IIB, the subject expression is a proper name, except that in **42** the name is given in apposition (i.e. as a transformed nuncupative *the prophet (is) Telemus*) after the general designation of the subject as a prophet (μάντις ἀνήρ). Similarly in *Od.* 15.417, where the subject of initial ἔσκε is a slave girl, her name is not given at all; and in 20.287 the name is added in a separate sentence: ἦν δέ τις ἐν μνηστῆρσιν ἀνὴρ ἀθεμίστια εἰδώς,/ Κτήσιππος δ᾽ ὄνομ᾽ ἔσκε ("There was among the suitors a man of lawless mind; Ctesippus was his name.") To cover all cases, we may say that the subject of εἰμί is given either as a common (sortal) noun or as a proper name, but in either case as the designation of a *person*. In five out of seven cases, we have the indefinite pronoun τις agreeing with the subject. Perhaps we should take the occurrence of τις as standard for this type, and regard the other two examples as variant, viz. **41** and the slave-girl in *Od.* 15.417: ἔσκε δὲ πατρὸς ἐμοῖο γυνὴ Φοίνισσ᾽ ἐνὶ οἴκῳ, "Now in my father's house lived a Phoenician woman" (Palmer). In every case the verb *be* occurs in the past tense (ἦν, ἔσκε). And in every case the kernel structure is followed by descriptive adjectives in apposition: *rich and good, brave and tall,* etc.; while this description is in turn followed by a demonstrative-anaphoric pronoun (τώ, ὅς, τόν, etc.) by means of which the person previously introduced and described is then taken up into the following narrative.

We may generalize our account of IIB as follows. We have in each case a particular individual who is (i) located among the participants or within the landscape of the story (*among the Trojans, here, in my father's house*), (ii) described by various nominal predicates, and (iii) in most cases, identified by name. The verb εἰμί must be regarded as present as copula in the underlying structure, that is, in the constituent kernels which correspond to (i)–(iii). In the kernels for (i) we have the locative copula; in those for (ii) and occasionally for (iii) we have the nominal copula.

Despite these underlying copula uses, in the resulting sentences **38–42** we do not intuitively regard εἰμί as copula – certainly not as "mere copula" – but rather as existential verb. This existential force is clearly connected with the fact that sentences of Type IIB serve to introduce their subjects into the narrative. But from the formal point of view, the only distinction between ἦν or ἔσκε in these sentences and the ordinary locative copula is (i) the verb occurs in initial position, and (ii) the subject expression is usually accompanied by τις ("someone", "a certain"). Now the presence of such an indefinite pronoun may confirm or reinforce the existential value of the sentence, but it cannot be regarded as the source or even as the formal criterion of this value. For on the one hand τις occurs very often with other verbs, or even with copula εἰμί, where we do not wish to speak of an existential use. (See e.g. **68** in Chapter IV §15.) On the other hand τις is absent from some examples of Type IIB – and from the paradigm of Type IIA – without any noticeable loss of existential value for the sentence as a whole.

It might seem then, that it is the initial position of εἰμί which – alone, or in conjunction with the rhetorical function of introducing its subject – accounts for the existential value of the verb. We may be tempted to describe this as a regular syntactic transformation of the locative copula, just as in English we have described *There is a man at the door* as the existential transform of *A man is at the door.* (See Chapter I §9.) Indeed, Jespersen long ago called attention to this function of "preposed ἐστί" in Homer, and to the parallel position of the verb in English *there is* and in similarly existential constructions in Danish and Russian.[24] However, in ancient Greek the word order is so flexible and so sensitive to rhetorical features of the context such as contrast, emphasis, repetition, and novelty, that it is difficult to believe that a mere change in the position of the verb can ever have functioned as the regular mark of a distinct sentence type, in the sense defined in transformational grammar. And in fact, even in Homer we find the verb εἰμί occurring in initial position in sentences with no existential force. In later Greek, where initial position for the copula is much more frequent, it is only in a minority of cases that this position can be correlated with an existential value for the verb. (For examples and further discussion, see Appendix A.3, pp. 424–33.) What we have here is not a regular transformation involving a standard shift in word order (what Harris calls a permutation), but only a natural affinity between the existential function of Type II and initial position, an affinity which springs from the rhetorical role of introducing the subject of the verb into the narrative by localizing it. For this purpose the mention of the subject expression is normally delayed until the localization has been given or begun. Hence it is either the copula verb or the locative expression (or both) which comes first. Now if the locative phrase precedes, the verb is less conspicuous and may be rendered by the copula in English. Compare **129** in Chapter IV §25: μέσσῳ δ'ἐν σκοπέλῳ ἐστὶ σπέος "In the middle of the crag is a cave." (And see below, §11, sentences **56–58**.) But if the verb comes first, it seems to carry the whole weight of the sentence, and hence to embody its introductory-existential role: ἔστι δέ τι σπέος...βένθεσι λίμνης "There is a cave in the depths of the water" **31**. Here we may say that the appearance of an existential verb in Type II as distinct from the copula εἰμί arises as a special case of a more general phenomenon: the use of copula (and particularly of locative) sentences as a device for identifying an unfamiliar subject and introducing it into the narrative.

§9. ANALYSIS OF TYPE IIA

The conclusion of the last section suggests the following analysis for our more complex subtype IIA. We have in every case an underlying kernel sentence of the form *N is PN*, with εἰμί as locative copula. In its context, however, a sentence of Type II serves not to specify the location of a subject whose identity is assumed as already familiar (as in the case of the "mere copula"), but to *introduce* the subject of εἰμί by localizing it. This may be done by beginning the sentence with the locative expression, and in this case the verb can be delayed or even omitted: τῇσι δ' ἐνὶ Κνωσός "among

---

[24] *Philosophy of Grammar*, pp. 155f.

these cities (is) Cnossus" (in **36** above). On the other hand, the same effect is obtained with somewhat greater emphasis by putting the verb first: ἔστι πόλις Ἐφύρη μυχῷ Ἄργεος, "There is a city Ephyre in a corner of Argos." In either case what we have is a locative-existential sentence. But in the first case we seem closer to the copula construction, whereas in the second case the verb is so prominent and the introduction of the subject so emphatic that we are obliged to translate the verb by "there is" and hence to describe it as existential. From the point of view of deep structure, however, (i.e. in the underlying source sentence) the verb ἔστι is simply the locative copula, and its special value here consists not in a proper assertion of existence but in a certain impressive, formulaic beginning for a localizing introduction, as in the rather similar formula in story-telling; "Once upon a time in a far-away kingdom there lived...." This emphatic presenting to us of an unknown subject ("There is somewhere a city Ephyre, namely in Argos") can perhaps be described as an assertion of existence for the city in question. But insofar as the initial ἔστι of this type asserts existence, it does so only within a definite local context. Hence the negation of a Type II sentence – if it occurred – would never be a general denial of existence ("There is no such thing") but a clearly locative or locative-existential sentence "The city Ephyre is not in Argos" or "There is no such city in Argos", "There is no hill by the city in this place", and so forth. (See further §13 below on the negative sentence forms.)

The underlying locative kernel of Type IIA may be expanded in various ways comparable to those mentioned for Type IIB. The subject noun is generally a sortal term or classifier (*city, hill, island*, etc.). Where a proper name is given, it usually follows in immediate apposition to the subject (sortal) noun; in **34**, however, the name is provided in a separate nuncupative clause ("They call it Pharos"). In every case of IIA except for our paradigm **27**, the subject expression is accompanied by the pronoun τις. In nearly every case the locative kernel is expanded by descriptive nouns and adjectives in predicate or appositive construction (thus implying an underlying nominal copula), and often by further locative predicates as well. A special case is presented by **30**, where the descriptive expression is a participial phrase εἰς ἅλα βάλλων. (For the periphrastic interpretation of **30**, see above, pp. 140f.) Finally, in every case the subject introduced by our locative kernel is taken up into the narrative by demonstrative or anaphoric reference (ἔνθα, τῇ, τήν, etc.)

In seven cases out of eleven, the verb ἔστι occurs at the head of the sentence. But intuitively speaking, the other four cases **34–37** are scarcely less existential, and the post-initial verb could not be rendered in English as a simple copula. It might be possible to argue that the existential force is preserved in these sentences by the presence of τις or by the non-final position of the verb. But the only factor which is common to *all* examples of Types IIA and IIB, and which distinguishes them from a simple copula construction, is the rhetorical or contextual function of introducing their subjects into the narrative.

Anticipating for a moment the semantic analysis which belongs to the next stage of the discussion (§§19–21), I suggest that the verb in Type II (as well as in the related examples of Type III, and in those of Type I where it has a locative complement) serves to introduce its subject into the narrative because it serves to *locate* (in Kantian terms, to *pose*) an extra-linguistic subject within the realm of actors, actions, and landscape which the narrative describes, and which constitutes the "universe" or domain of interpretation for the poem. It is precisely because, in logical terms, εἰμί locates the subject within the world to which the narrative refers, that it can, in stylistic or rhetorical terms, introduce the subject into the narrative. My analysis claims that this stylistic function of sentences with εἰμί, which is unmistakable, corresponds to the logical function that has just been mentioned; and that both functions rest on, and are made possible by, the locative use of the verb in elementary statements of place.[25]

---

[25] George Cardona informs me that the typical narrative opening in Sanskrit stories has the following structure: initial *asti* (=ἔστι) followed by a locative ("on the bank of the river X", "in the area of Y"), followed by the subject noun; and this subject, or the whole localization, is taken up in the following clause by a demonstrative pronoun or adverb ("there", "in its hollow", "by him", etc.). For example, the first story in the collection known as *Hitopadeśa* begins: *asti bhāgirithītīre pāṭaliputranāmadheyaṃ nagaram. tatra ... āsīt.* "There is on the bank of the Bhagirathi a city named Pataliputra. There there was (a king by the name of Sudarsena)." This sentence form is syntactically identical with my Type II as illustrated in 27, although (except for initial ἔστι) the Greek word order happens to be different, with subject noun preceding the locative predicate. (For the Sanscrit order, compare sentence 28.) As in the Greek, the specification of a proper name for the localized subject is optional. Cardona's second example (*ibid.* p. 7. 13–4) is "There is (*asti*) on the bank of the Godavari a broad salmali tree. There...." Note that *salmali* is a classifier or sortal noun, not a proper name. This is roughly the form of 28, 31 or 32, without the indefinite pronoun that occurs here in the Greek. The corresponding pronoun may also occur in Sanskrit, e.g. "There is (initial *asti*) a certain (*kaścid*) merchant; by him was made a temple near the town" (*Tantrākhyāyika* Book I.1, ed. Hertel p. 5). This approximates to the form of 128–129 below, in § 22, where εἰμί + *subject N* is syntactically articulated as a separate clause, prefiguring Type VI. Sanskrit provides other variants, including an asyntactic initial *asti* ("There is" or "It is true [that]"), followed immediately by a clause with finite verb which may even be in the plural. (Compare the semi-formulaic use in Greek prose of initial ἔστι with plural subject, Ch. IV § 29, p. 177.)

These secondary variants in Sanskrit are only roughly comparable to Greek sentence forms, but the primary form given in the first example quoted in this note is exactly parallel to Type II. I take this to show that if Type II is not an inherited I.-E. form, it is at least a perfectly natural development of the inherited uses of *es-*, and above all of the use of *es-* as locative verb. The Sanskrit parallels seem to confirm my analysis of the basic structure of II as ἔστι + *subject N* + *locative* where *N* is a common (sortal) noun, with proper name and

Nevertheless, this logical or semantic function, which is that of the existential verb in the strict sense, is most clearly and typically represented not by the semi-locative pattern just described but by Type IV, where the verb is neither construed as nor clearly derived from a locative or nominal copula. In Type IV (and also in Type V) the existential verb has the distinct second-order syntax of a sentence operator. In Type II, by contrast, we have an ambiguous or intermediate situation where the verb can on the one hand be construed as elementary (*Ephyre is in Argos, Dares is among the Trojans*), but on the other hand has an existential value which is properly that of a sentence operator. A similar ambiguity characterizes the syntax of the verb in Type III.

§10. POST-HOMERIC PARALLELS TO TYPE II

As formulaic patterns, Types IIA and IIB are closely bound to the hexameter, and they naturally reappear in later uses of epic verse.[26] We occasionally find the pattern of IIB in prose, with freer variation:

43 Xen. *Anab*. III.1.4

ἦν δέ τις ἐν τῇ στρατιᾷ Ξενοφῶν Ἀθηναῖος, ὃς οὔτε στρατηγὸς οὔτε λοχαγὸς οὔτε στρατιώτης ὢν συνηκολούθει

"There was in the army a certain Xenophon of Athens, who came along neither as general nor as captain nor as common soldier."

44 Hdt. IV.141

ἦν δὲ περὶ Δαρεῖον ἀνὴρ Αἰγύπτιος φωνέων μέγιστον ἀνθρώπων

"There was in the company of Darius an Egyptian who could shout exceptionally loud."

---

indefinite pronoun (τις) as optional additions. I should mention that the analysis given above was worked out on the basis of the Homeric material alone, before I was familiar with the Sanskrit parallels.

See further A. Bloch's discussion of some of our examples under the concept of "erläuternder Einschub", in *Museum Helveticum* I (1944) pp. 243ff. Block refers (p. 246) to Wackernagel's observation of the parallel narrative beginnings in early Greek and Sanskrit literature, in his "Vortrag über die indogermanische Dichtersprache", *Philologus* 95, p. 18.

[26] See for example the oracle cited in Hdt. I.67.4 ἔστι τις Ἀρκαδίης Τεγέη λευρῷ ἐνὶ χώρῳ, which is a slight variant on IIA, (without a sortal noun as subject). For an example of IIB see Empedocles fr. 129 ἦν δέ τις ἐν κείνοισιν ἀνὴρ περιώσια εἰδώς (a variant on *Od*. 20.287, cited above, p. 253). Metrically parallel but grammatically divergent is the negative form in Emped. 128.1 οὐδέ τις ἦν κείνοισιν Ἄρης θεός where the construction with dative is possessive rather than locative.

45 Xen. *Anab*. III.1.26

ἐκέλευον πάντες, πλὴν Ἀπολλωνίδης τις ἦν βοιωτιάζων τῇ φωνῇ· οὗτος δ᾽ εἶπεν....

"All approved, except for a certain Apollonides there was who spoke with a Boeotian accent. He declared...."

46 Plato *Apology* 18 B 6

κατηγόρουν ἐμοῦ... ὡς ἔστιν τις Σωκράτης σοφὸς ἀνήρ, τά τε μετέωρα φροντιστὴς καὶ τὰ ὑπὸ γῆς πάντα ἀνεζητηκὼς καὶ τὸν ἥττω λόγον κρείττω ποιῶν

"They accused me... (claiming) that there is a certain Socrates, a wise man, a student of things aloft and a searcher into all things under the earth, who makes the weaker argument the stronger."

In **43** and **44** we have an underlying locative copula, as in the Homeric examples. In **45** it is possible to reconstruct a locative or paralocative source ("among them was a certain Apollonides") which accounts for the apparently periphrastic construction ἦν βοιωτιάζων.[27] In **46** we have as kernel a purely nominal copula *Socrates is a wise man*, with adjoined predicate nouns and participles. This represents a deviation from the locative pattern of Type II in Homer; yet **46** still illustrates the same general form and function: a copulative ἐστί transposed to initial position serves to introduce a subject with emphasis.

We also find classical parallels to Type IIA, where the subject is a place rather than a person:

47 Aesch. *P.V.* 846

ἔστιν πόλις Κάνωβος ἐσχάτη χθονός,
Νείλου πρὸς αὐτῷ στόματι καὶ προσχώματι·
ἐνταῦθα δή σε Ζεὺς τίθησιν ἔμφρονα

"There is a city Canobus at the end of the earth, by the very mouth and delta of the Nile; in this place will Zeus make you sound again in mind."

In prose, curiously enough, the corresponding function of introducing places as points of narrative reference seems to be normally performed by ordinary

---

[27] If we reconstruct the locative or partitive source as suggested, we no longer have a true periphrastic in **45**, since ἦν and βοιωτιάζων are then derived from distinct kernels: *Apollonides was among them* and *He spoke with a Boeotian accent*. This is clearly the (non-periphrastic) structure of **44**. In **30** above, however, we seem to have a true periphrastic-existential, as in other cases discussed in Chapter IV § 17.

copula constructions, with the sortal noun as predicate (rather than subject as in IIA) and with a locative specification as secondary predicate:

48 Thuc. I.24.1

Ἐπίδαμνός ἐστι πόλις ἐν δεξιᾷ ἐσπλέοντι ἐς τὸν Ἰόνιον
κόλπον·... ταύτην ἀπῴκισαν μὲν Κερκυραῖοι
"Epidamnus is a city on the right side as one sails into the
Ionian gulf.... It was founded as a colony by Corcyra."

The literary or rhetorical function of **48** is roughly the same as in Type IIA, but in narrative prose this function seems more often to be performed by a standard copula sentence. In the absence of both the pronoun τις and initial position for the verb, we are not inclined to translate ἐστί by "there is." Logically speaking, however, **48** is scarcely less existential than ἔστι πόλις Ἐφύρη in **27**.[28]

Similarly, a copula sentence with εἰμί immediately following the proper name serves in classic prose for introducing personal subjects, instead of the more "existential" Type IIB in Homer:

49 Lysias I.22

Σώστρατος ἦν μοι ἐπιτήδειος καὶ φίλος. τούτῳ... ἀπήντησα
"Sostratus was my friend and acquaintance. Him... I met."

50 Xen. *Anab*. VII.4.7

Ἐπισθένης δ' ἦν τις Ὀλύνθιος παιδεραστής, ὅς... Ξενοφῶντα
ἱκέτευε βοηθῆσαι παιδὶ καλῷ
"Episthenes was an Olynthian, a lover of boys, who... begged
Xenophon to come to the aid of a handsome youth."[29]

We note again that in these examples the verb does not take final position: we have the word order *N is Φ* which is normal in English but not particularly common in Greek.[30] The language of classic prose thus provides a rather distinctive (but not "existential") form for the same general function as Type IIB, namely, to identify and introduce a personal subject not previously mentioned.

---

[28] For copula sentences of similar form with the same rhetorical function as **48** compare Hdt. I. 148.1 τὸ δὲ Πανιώνιόν ἐστι τῆς Μυκάλης χῶρος ἱρός, πρὸς ἄρκτον τετραμμένος ... ἡ δὲ Μυκάλη ἐστὶ τῆς ἠπείρου ἄκρη πρὸς ζέφυρον ἄνεμον κατήκουσα Σάμῳ, ἐς τὴν συλλεγόμενοι... Ἴωνες ἄγεσκον ὀρτήν.

[29] So also Lysias XIII.55 Ἀγνόδωρος δ' ἦν Ἀμφιτροπαιεύς.... οὗτος οὖν.... Similarly in Hdt. I.6.1 Κροῖσος ἦν Λυδός.... οὗτος ὁ Κροῖσος etc.; I.7.2–8.1 ἦν Κανδαύλης... τύραννος Σαρδίων.... οὗτος δὴ ὦν ὁ Κανδαύλης. Note that the initial position of ἦν in the last example encourages Rawlinson to translate the verb as existential, although both syntax and rhetorical function are the same as in the preceding examples: "There was a certain king of Sardis, Candaules by name."

[30] See the figures in Appendix A, pp. 427–33.

§11. Sentence type III and the locative-existential use in
general

There seem to be no negative sentences which illustrate Type II; and this
is what we would expect if the function of the type is to introduce its subject
into the discourse. (For certain negative sentences which might be regarded
as parallel in form but not in function to Type II, see below §13.) The only
appropriate form is the third person indicative affirmative, past or present.
Furthermore, all the examples cited so far are in the singular. When the
corresponding form occurs in the plural, it no longer seems to introduce or
to "present" its subject in such a characteristic way. I list this plural version
separately as Type III, since neither in form nor in function is it as sharply
defined as Type II. Type III has close connections with locative and also
with possessive constructions; and it may be regarded as a bridge between
the formulaic Type II and a wide variety of sentences (with first-order nominals as subject) that are in a still looser sense "existential".

Type III is generally characterized by a locative kernel, a plural indefinite
quantifier such as πολλοί "many" or ἄλλοι "others", and often by initial
or at least non-final position for the verb.

51 *Il.* 10.66

πολλαὶ γὰρ ἀνὰ στρατόν εἰσι κέλευθοι
"There are many paths up and down the encampment" (so we
must be careful not to miss one another).

(Lattimore)

52 *Il.* 9.395

πολλαὶ Ἀχαιΐδες εἰσὶν ἀν' Ἑλλάδα τε Φθίην τε
"There are many Achaian girls in the land of Hellas and Phthia"
(any one of whom I might take as wife).

(Lattimore)

53 *Od.* 21.251

εἰσὶ καὶ ἄλλαι πολλαὶ Ἀχαιΐδες, αἱ μὲν ἐν αὐτῇ
ἀμφιάλῳ Ἰθάκῃ, αἱ δ' ἄλλῃσιν πολίεσσιν
"There are enough more women of Achaea, both here in Ithaca
and in the other cities."

(Palmer)

54 *Od.* 2.292

εἰσὶ δὲ νῆες
πολλαὶ ἐν ἀμφιάλῳ Ἰθάκῃ νέαι ἠδὲ παλαιαί
"The ships are many in sea-girt Ithaca, ships new and old"

(Palmer)

In three out of four of these examples the primary kernel is clearly of the locative form *N is PN*: *paths are in the camp, girls are in Hellas, ships are in Ithaca*. In **53** the locative phrases are added in apposition, i.e. as secondary adjoined kernels (with zeroing of the copula verb after εἰσί in the first clause). The form of the primary kernel in **53** is not clear. A similar obscurity characterizes the following example, where the locative specification is left implicit:

55 *Od.* 20.182

εἰσὶν δὲ καὶ ἄλλαι δαῖτες ᾿Αχαιῶν

"Surely there are Achaean feasts elsewhere." (So why always beg here?)

(Palmer)

Here Palmer's translation of ἄλλαι by "elsewhere" is justified by the contrast with ἐνθάδε...κατὰ δῶμα "here in the house" in the preceding context (*Od.* 20.178). In general, the intuitively existential value of εἰσί in this type, like that of ἐστί and ἦν in Type II, is closely associated with the construction of the verb as locative copula in an underlying kernel. Hence we can interpret this general value by the paraphrase "Here, there, somewhere or other, are X's." In effect, whenever a locative construction for εἰμί is given or easily reconstructible as in **55**, we may regard Types II and III as special cases of the locative-existential use. In the few examples of Types II and III where a locative kernel is lacking, as in **46** above, we can recognize an underlying nominal copula. Hence instead of listing Types II and III as distinct existential sentence forms, as I have done, one might reasonably describe them as the most conspicuous examples of a mixed class, namely of the very numerous class of sentences in which some existential value for εἰμί is superimposed upon a copula construction. (See IV §25, and below §13.) If I have not followed this course, it is because sentences of Type II and III are normally cited as examples par excellence of the existential use of the verb.

The general description of Type III as a mixed existential-copulative form seems unproblematic. But any more detailed syntactic analysis of Type III raises several difficult problems which can only be mentioned here. The most serious difficulty is the analysis of the quantifier-adjectives πολλοί "many" and ἄλλοι "others". On the one hand, it is possible to construe an adjective like πολλοί as predicate in surface structure: *The girls are many (in number), The ships are many*. We can often construe definite numerals in the same way: ἔπτ᾿ ἔσαν ἡγεμόνες φυλάκων (*Il.* 9.85) "The captains of the watch were seven." On the other hand, it is clear that words like *many* or *seven* function as (indefinite or definite) plural forms of the indefinite pronoun τις "someone", "a certain", which occurs regularly in Type II: *There are many (seven) cities in Argos* is a plural of *There is a city in Argos*. What is needed for an analysis of sentences like **51–55** is a general theory of quantifier-words that would apply not only to numerals but also to indefinite forms like *some, others*, and *many*. A satisfactory syntactic analysis should account for the well-known logical peculiarities of these adjectives. For example, quantifier adjectives are distinguished from ordinary descriptive adjectives by the fact that one cannot pass from the plural to the singular form, i.e. that they apply to their subjects collectively. Whereas for an ordinary predicate like *The (twelve) Apostles are pious* it follows that *Each Apostle is pious*, from *The Apostles are twelve*, or *The Apostles are numerous* it does not follow – and it is even false or senseless to claim – for any particular Apostle that *He is twelve* or *He is numerous*. I suppose that these quantifier-words must be interpreted not as elementary predicates but as a kind of adnominal sentence-operator, operating on the subject (in other cases, on the object) noun within the framework of a given elementary sentence form.[31] These quantifier-operators have a definite existential role: they assert or imply the existence of one, two, or more entities described by the noun to which they are attached (*some man, many girls, seven captains*, etc.). Hence an adequate theory of such adjectives would certainly shed light on the existential uses of εἰμί. On the other hand, the role of such adjectives is entirely independent of the use of the verb *be*: the existential force of *many* is the same in *(The) ships in Ithaca are many* and in *Many ships sail to Ithaca*. Hence the absence here of an adequate theory of quantifier words, although it prevents us from giving a full analysis of sentences like **51–55**, should not affect our central project which is to examine the uses of εἰμί as such.

In three of our five examples of Type III the verb occurs in initial position; in the other two cases it occurs in second position, before the subject in **51** and before the locative predicate in **52**. (These forms can be paralleled from classic prose. For an example of Type III with initial verb see Plato *Phaedo* 108 C 5 εἰσὶν δὲ πολλοὶ καὶ θαυμαστοὶ τῆς γῆς τόποι 'There are many (and) marvellous regions of the earth.'') However, in cases where we find neither an initial verb nor a quantifier adjective we no longer have a clear example of Type III, even if the sentence remains vaguely existential:

56 *Il.* 7.73
> ὑμῖν δ' ἐν γὰρ ἔασιν ἀριστῆες Παναχαιῶν
> "Among you are the bravest of all the Achaians."
>
> (Lattimore)

---

[31] Compare Harris' remark (*Mathematical Structures*, p. 72) that in *Some boy saw a dog* the transformation represented by *some* "operates not simply on *boy* but on *boy* in a particular sentence position."

We may compare **2**, quoted above in §4: ἦ ῥα καὶ ἐν Τρώεσσι κυβιστητῆρες ἔασιν "So among the Trojans too there are acrobats." With such examples we move into the larger class of locative-existential sentences.

57 *Od.* 13.105

    ἐν δὲ κρητῆρές τε καὶ ἀμφιφορῆες ἔασι / λάϊνοι

    "Within (the cave) are bowls and jars of stone."

                                                 (Palmer)

58 *Il.* 22.153

    ἔνθα δ' ἐπ' αὐτάων πλυνοὶ εὐρέες ἐγγὺς ἔασι

    καλοὶ λαΐνεοι

    "Beside these springs in this place, and close to them, are (the) washing hollows of stone, and magnificient."

                                          (Lattimore)

We stand here on the borderline between the locative copula and existential sentences of Type III. In **57** and **58** where the subject is vaguely "indefinite" in syntax, we may say that the sentence serves to introduce the jars or washing hollows (and to this extent these sentences are more "existential"). In **56**, where the identity of the "bravest of the Achaeans" is perhaps presupposed, this introductory function is more dubious. But it is less profitable to weigh the existential value of the verb in any particular sentence than to recognize the general similarity between these cases and the wider class of locative-existentials illustrated in Chapter IV §25.[32]

---

[32] For any reader who wishes to observe the detailed interplay of locative and nominal copulas with existential force, and at the same time to note the syntactic and semantic irrelevance of the (stylistically motivated) omission of the verb, I recommend a comparison of two sustained descriptive passages: (1) the description of Agamemnon's armor at *Il.* 11.30–38, and (2) the account of the harbor at Ithaca in *Od.* 13.96–112. In (1) we find five distinct occurrences of locative-existential *be* (περὶ κουλεὸν ἦεν, ἦν πέρι μὲν κύκλοι δέκα χάλκεοι ἦσαν, ἐν δέ οἱ ὀμφαλοὶ ἦσαν, etc.), each one of which is accompanied by a descriptive or quantifier adjective, or both. (In 11.35 the descriptive adjective is replaced by a predicate genitive: ἐν δὲ μέσοισιν ἔην μέλανος κυάνοιο.) In this passage we have only one elliptical omission of the verb (11.37 περὶ δὲ Δεῖμός τε Φόβος τε). In the description of the harbor of Ithaca, on the other hand, we have two elliptical omissions (*Od.* 13.107 and 109), together with three zero occurrences of the locative-existential verb in what would traditionally be described as a nominal sentence (*ibid.* 97: δύο δὲ προβλῆτες ἐν αὐτῷ/ἀκταί; similarly 102 and 103). In this passage in the *Odyssey*, then, we find five verbless sentences in the context of our example **35** above, Φόρκυνος δέ τίς ἐστι λιμήν (which introduces the description by a variant on Type II with non-initial verb). The two elliptical omissions of the verb follow directly on its occurrence in **57**, which we have just cited as an example of the locative-existential use of εἰμί. The description closes with a possessive-existential use (v. 109 δύω δέ τέ οἱ θύραι εἰσίν) followed by two occurrences of the verb as nominal copula (vv. 111–2) and one omission of the same (verse 110). In these two cases where the verb actually occurs as nominal copula we have the same oscillation between non-initial and final position for the verb as in the three semi-existential constructions with a locative or possessive kernel. In a passage like this it seems impossible to

For reasons which will become apparent, in the next two sections I discuss the possessive construction and certain mixed or borderline cases as an appendix to Types II and III, before continuing with Type IV in §14.

§12. THE POSSESSIVE CONSTRUCTION

The term "possessive" is here used to designate a purely formal or syntactic phenomenon: the construction of εἰμί with a personal noun or pronoun in the dative, or more generally with any dative form. (The use of this dative of possession with non-personal nouns, or with pronouns replacing non-personal nouns, is comparatively rare, but an example was cited in the preceding note: δύω δέ τέ οἱ θύραι εἰσί "And the cave has two doors.") Such a construction will generally be translated into English by the verb "have," where the dative form in Greek is rendered by the subject of the English verb: ἔστι μοι = "I have." As we shall see, the possessive construction in this formal sense is a phenomenon of surface structure in Greek (and in Indo-European), derived from several distinct syntactic sources corresponding to distinct meanings or distinct relations of *having*. Perhaps the most fundamental concept here is that of legal or socially recognized ownership: having in one's possession, as property or chattel.[33]

(i) In this paradigm use of the possessive construction for *ownership* or possession of *property*, there is an obvious connection with the idea of location: to own something is to "have it in one's possession," to hold it in one's hand, in one's house, or in one's power. And "to hold" in this sense is the basic meaning of ἔχω, the Greek verb we usually render as "have." The ownership of moveable goods generally determines where they are stored and guarded (unless it is the converse which is true), and this connection between the ideas of possession and location is particularly important in an archaic economy with no bank deposits and no property titles protected by the state. Hence it is natural that the expressions for location and possession should be associated in many or most languages. In Greek this shows up as a frequent overlap between the formally possessive and formally locative constructions. In particular we find a regular convergence of the possessive

---

correlate any variation of sense or syntax either with the position or with the omission of the verb. It is evidence of this kind which leads me to conclude that neither word order nor omission is directly dependent upon the syntactic form or semantic (i.e. lexical) content of the sentence. Position and omission alike are more easily correlated with stylistic factors such as emphasis, contrast, variety, and brevity. For further discussion, see Appendix A.3 on word order and Appendix B on omission of the verb.

[33] I ignore here the construction of εἰμί with a possessive genitive, which has been described and distinguished from the dative construction in Chapter IV § 26.

with the locative-existential uses just illustrated.[34] Where the existential nuance is noticeable, the verb is frequently (but not always) in initial position.

59 *Il.* 23.549

> ἔστι τοι ἐν κλισίῃ χρυσὸς πολύς, ἔστι δὲ χαλκὸς
> καὶ πρόβατ', εἰσὶ δέ τοι δμῳαὶ καὶ μώνυχες ἵπποι
> "There is abundant gold in your shelter, and there is bronze there
> and animals, and there are handmaidens and single-foot horses."
>
> (Lattimore)

Here the first occurrence of ἔστι represents a locative-existential sentence parallel in form to Type IIA, with a superimposed possessive construction of the verb with τοι. We might also take the possessive idea as primary and translate as "You have plenty of gold in your hut." In the second verse the plural εἰσί suggests a variant of Type III where the locative construction has disappeared and only the possessive (or possessive-existential) remains. But this omission of the locative specification is partial and superficial, since *in your shelter* is elliptically understood as predicate with *handmaidens* (as with *bronze* in the preceding clause), while the horses and flocks are also assumed to be situated nearby. Even where locative and possessive constructions do not explicitly coincide in a single occurrence of εἰμί, the connection of ideas is often clear:

60 *Il.* 9.364

> ἔστι δέ μοι μάλα πολλά, τὰ κάλλιπον ἐνθάδε ἔρρων
> "I have many possessions there (sc. in Phthia) that I left behind
> when I came here."
>
> (Lattimore)

61 *Il.* 10.378

> ζωγρεῖτ', αὐτὰρ ἐγὼν ἐμὲ λύσομαι· ἔστι γὰρ ἔνδον
> χαλκός τε χρυσός τε πολύκμητός τε σίδηρος
> "Take me alive, and I will pay my ransom: in my house
> there is bronze, and gold, and difficultly wrought iron"[35]
>
> (Lattimore)

---

[34] Compare the sentences listed by Guiraud under the title "existence locale possessive" (*La phrase nominale en grec*, pp. 196–8). For the same connection in other languages, see Lyons, "Note on Possessive, Existential and Locative Sentences", *Foundations of Language* 3 (1967), 390–6.

[35] For examples of possessive-locative-existential with the verb in non-initial position, see *Il.* 1.300 ἅ μοί ἐστι θοῇ παρὰ νηΐ (cited as **132** in Ch. IV § 25), 2.226 πολλαὶ δὲ γυναῖκες/ εἰσὶν (sc. τοι) ἐνὶ κλισίης, etc. With πάρ-ειμι the paralocative construction is often equivalent to the possessive in meaning and nearly indistinguishable in form, e.g. *Il.* 1.213 τοι... παρέσσεται... δῶρα. See also example **121** in Ch. IV § 24.

(ii) Our examples so far illustrate the idea of possession in the literal sense of ownership, where the subject of the verb is an item of property or chattel. The language makes no formal distinction between this and what linguists rather misleadingly call "inalienable possession", which may be subdivided into two notionally distinct categories: (a) kinship relations between persons, and (b) whole-part relations between a person or object and its body parts (eye of a person, door of a house or cave, etc.). In (a), when *having* refers to kinship relations, the locative specification often lapses; but it need not do so:

62 *Il.* 6.413

οὐδέ μοι ἔστι πατὴρ καὶ πότνια μήτηρ
"I have no father, no honored mother"

(Lattimore)

63 *Il.* 9.144

τρεῖς δέ μοί εἰσι θύγατρες ἐνὶ μεγάρῳ εὐπήκτῳ
"I have three daughters there in my strong-built castle."

(Lattimore)

62 shows how ill-suited the term "inalienable possession" is for kinship relations: Andromache means that her parents are dead; and ἔστι here could in fact be given the vital sense "are (not) alive". **63** illustrates the locative expression with kinship relations. The only formal distinction between sentences of kinship-possession such as **62–63** and sentences of *ownership*, as in **59–61**, is that the subject in the former case must be a personal noun; and even this point cannot distinguish *having a husband* or *father* from *having (owning) servants* (e.g. δμῳαί in **59**). The relevant distinctions can be drawn in Greek, of course, but they are not drawn by any surface variation in the expressions for possession.[36]

(iii) The second category of what is called inalienable possession is illustrated by the possessive construction with *body parts* as subject of εἰμί.

64 *Il.* 2.489

οὐδ᾽ εἴ μοι δέκα μὲν γλῶσσαι, δέκα δὲ στόματ᾽ εἶεν,
φωνὴ δ᾽ ἄρρηκτος, χάλκεον δέ μοι ἦτορ ἐνείη

---

[36] However, we could distinguish kinship-possessive sentences in deep structure from property possession by deriving the former from copula sentences with a relative noun: N_1 is N_2 of N_3, πατὴρ δέ μοί ἐστιν Ὀδυσσεύς "Odysseus is my father" (*Od.* 15.267). The existential-possessive *I have a father*, as in **62** above, would then represent a zeroing of the proper name (N_1) and hence a superficial reconstruing of the sortal predicate (N_2) as subject. Interpreted in terms of its deep structure, *I have a husband* (ἔστι μοι πόσις) would thus mean *Someone is my husband* (cf. ἥ μέν μοι πόσις ἐστὶν Ἀλέξανδρος *Il.* 24.763). On this view, existential-possessive sentences of kinship, as in **62–63**, would be regarded as an elliptical transform of a copula sentence with εἰμί.

"Not if I had ten tongues and ten mouths, not if I had
a voice never to be broken and a heart of bronze within me."
(Lattimore)

Here we have four distinct subject expressions, three of which are recognizable
as body parts (*tongue, mouth, heart*). But the fourth case, φωνή "voice",
represents a faculty or disposition rather than a physical part of the body;
and indeed ἦτορ "heart" is here almost equivalent with "strength" or "force
of breath". In Homer we can make no very sharp distinction between body
parts and psychical or physiological functions of this kind. Emotions like
anger as well as dispositions like fury and strength are generally spoken of
as located in the φρένες ("lungs") or in other parts of the body, as if they
were vital fluids secreted by the internal organs or injected into the body
by the gods.[37] Hence the presence or absence of such strength or passion
in a given person is naturally expressed by a locative-possessive construction
with existential force. Note that although the verb in this construction may
take initial position (65), it may also be omitted altogether (66).

66 *Il.* 3.45

ἀλλ' οὐκ ἔστι βίη φρεσὶν οὐδέ τις ἀλκή
"But there is no strength in your heart, no courage"
(Lattimore)

66 *Il.* 2.241

ἀλλὰ μάλ' οὐκ Ἀχιλῆϊ χόλος φρεσίν, ἀλλὰ μεθήμων
"But there is no gall in Achilles' heart, and he is forgiving."
(Lattimore)

(As Lattimore's version shows, in 65 we must reconstruct the second person
dative pronoun – i.e. τοι in zero form – from other second person references
in the same speech.) From the point of view both of grammar and Homeric
psycho-physiology, there is practically no distinction to be drawn between
the "possession" of powers or emotions in 65–66 and that of body parts
in 64. Or rather, the distinctions which can be drawn – e.g. that the body
parts are relatively constant, while strength and passion vary greatly from
time to time and from individual to individual – are apparently of no importance for the linguistic analysis.

(iv) Finally, we have the case where, although the possessor is (or may be)
still a person or persons referred to by the dative noun, the subject possessed
(i.e. the subject of εἰμί) is neither a person, a physical object, nor a psycho-

---

[37] See the classic description of the "dark φρένες" of Agamemnon filling with μένος
("passion", "rage") at *Il.* 1.103, and also the formula for μένος "breathed into" a warrior
by a favorable god at *Il.* 15.262 (= 20.110), etc.

somatic disposition conceived as an object, but rather an action, an event, or a state. In formal terms, the subject of εἰμί in this case is an abstract "action noun" and not a first-order nominal. (For the basic distinction between abstract nouns and first-order nominals, see Chapter III §7 and Chapter IV §4.) Hence these examples properly belong below, under existential Type V in §15, which is characterized precisely by the fact that the subject of εἰμί is an action noun. By contrast, in almost every case of the existential verb so far discussed, and for most cases of Type IV to be analyzed in §14, the subject of the verb is a first-order nominal.[38] In terms of meaning and deep structure, this category is not properly described as possessive. However, I list these sentences here since their surface syntax conforms to the possessive construction.

67 *Il.* 2.379

οὐκέτ' ἔπειτα
Τρωσὶν ἀνάβλησις κακοῦ ἔσσεται
"Then no longer shall the Trojans' evil be put aside"

(Lattimore)

We may render more literally: "No longer will there be for the Trojans a postponement of evil." The source sentence for **67** is of the form Τρωσὶν ἀναβάλλουσι κακόν "They postpone the evil for the Trojans." Here we recognize Τρωσίν as the ordinary dative with verbs of interest or benefit, and there is no question of a possessive construction. But when the verb *be* is introduced as sentence operator or verb of occurrence (according to the normal transformation of Type V), an ambiguous structure results. The dative can now be taken with εἰμί as well as with the underlying verb ἀναβάλλω (κακόν), and on the former construal we have a surface analogy to the possessive construction. Hence Lattimore's translation, "the Trojan's evil." In other cases the same surface construction results from an entirely different source sentence, in which no dative occurs:

68 *Il.* 11.443

σοὶ δ' ἐγὼ ἐνθάδε φημὶ φόνον καὶ κῆρα μέλαιναν
ἤματι τῷδ' ἔσσεσθαι, ἐμῷ δ' ὑπὸ δουρὶ δαμέντα
"But I declare that here and now dark death and slaughter
will come upon you this day,... beaten down under my spear."

(Lattimore)

---

[38] The exceptions so far are (i) the possessive constructions **65–66**, where βίη, ἀλκή and χόλος would not normally be regarded as first-order nominals, and similarly for φωνή in **64** (as we have seen, in the psychosomatic Homeric view the ontological status of these items is dubious); and (ii) δαῖτες in **55** might be analyzed as the action noun ("feasting") corresponding to the verb δαίνυμι "to feast". An interpretation of δαῖτες as first-order nominal ("these men feasting") would be compatible with the concrete construal of action nouns illustrated below in §16.

The personal object which would appear as an accusative in the underlying sentence *I shall kill you* is reshaped as a dative form in the Type V transformation of **68**, so that we again have a surface possessive σοί... φόνον... ἔσσεσθαι "Death will be yours." (We find the same construction with suppletive verbs in place of the Type V use of εἰμί: *Od.* 4.771 οἱ φόνος υἷι τέτυκται "(She does not know that) death is prepared for her son"; compare *Il.* 12.392 etc. Σαρπήδοντι δ' ἄχος γένετο "Grief came to Sarpedon", where the dative reflects the nominative subject of a verb like ἄχομαι "to grieve" in the underlying source.)

Type V possessives of this kind are extremely frequent in classic Greek: I suspect that they represent the most common of all existential uses of the verb εἰμί in post-Homeric literature. I list a few later samples, including some where the abstract noun that is subject of a Type V use of εἰμί can be derived from an adjectival as well as from a verbal source (thus ἔχθρα from ἐχθρός "hostile", ἀφθονία from ἄφθονος "plentiful").

69 Lysias I.4

οὔτε ἔχθρα ἐμοὶ καὶ ἐκείνῳ οὐδεμία ἦν πλὴν ταύτης
"There was no other enmity between him and me."

70 Xen. *Anab.* I.9.14

ἦν αὐτῷ πόλεμος πρὸς Πισίδας καὶ Μυσούς
"(Cyrus) had a war with the Pisidae and Mysians."

71 Xen. *Anab.* I.9.15

πολλὴ ἦν ἀφθονία αὐτῷ τῶν ἐθελόντων κινδυνεύειν
"He had no lack of men willing to risk their lives."

72 *Ibid.* II.2.10

ἐπείπερ ὁ αὐτὸς ὑμῖν στόλος ἐστὶ καὶ ἡμῖν
"Since you and we both have the same journey (to make)."

The detailed syntactic analysis of **69–72** would involve complexities that do not concern us here. For a theory of the possessive construction in Greek we need only note that ἦν or ἐστί in these examples is introduced as a sentence operator as in Type V, where the verb takes as its subject the nominalized predicate (verb or adjective) of the more elementary operand. The dative forms in **69–72** represent either the nominative subject of this operand sentence ("*He and I* were not enemies", "*He* was fighting against the Pisidae", "*You* and *we* will travel the same path") or some other noun case that is *not* construed with εἰμί in the source. (Thus the dative in **71** may represent a dative of interest in the source: *Many men were willing to risk their lives for him*, κινδυνεύειν αὐτῷ). In every case, the possessive construction of εἰμί with dative is the result of a transformational derivation.

We have thus distinguished four categories of the possessive construction of εἰμί:

  (i) possession of property or *ownership*: **59–60** above,
  (ii) kinship relations: **62–63**,
  (iii) whole-part relations (especially body-parts): **64**,
  (iv) surface possession with abstract subjects for εἰμί as sentence operator: **67–72**.

(Note that examples **65–66** are ambiguous between (iii) and (iv), depending upon whether or not βίη, ἀλκή and χόλος are interpreted as first-order nominals designating bodily objects.) Categories (ii)–(iii) correspond to what is generally called "inalienable possession". From the point of view of Greek, the verb εἰμί is required in the *elementary* expression of the first three categories; whereas in constructions of type (iv) the verb is transformationally introduced. Thus the possessive construction with εἰμί represents the simplest or the only way to say "You have much gold", "I have three daughters", and "if I had ten tongues". But for surface possession in category (iv) there is always a simpler expression that is roughly equivalent in meaning: namely, the underlying operand sentence in which εἰμί does not occur at all (or at least not in the possessive construction).[39] Hence the verb εἰμί – and the possessive construction as such – is "eliminable" in an obvious way from sentences of category (iv), but not from (i)–(iii). It might be urged as an objection to recent proposals to eliminate *be* and *have* from deep structure (of English, or of I.-E.) that they have the regrettable consequence of obliterating this distinction between elementary and derivative forms of the possessive construction.[40]

§ 13. INDEFINITE DENIALS AND AFFIRMATION OF LOCATION IN A GIVEN PLACE, AND OTHER MIXED OR BORDERLINE COPULA-EXISTENTIAL USES RELATED TO TYPES II-III

Most of the examples of Types II–III considered above, as well as the locative-existentials mentioned in § 11, are existential in the following sense: they assert that a certain individual or a certain kind of thing *is present* or is to be found in a given place or environment ("in Argos", "among the Trojans", "in the camp", etc.) What would be the corresponding negative form? To an assertion of presence for a given subject in a given place will

---

[39] In some samples of category (iv) εἰμί may appear in the operand as ordinary copula: e.g. "We were not enemies" (οὐκ ἦμεν ἐχθροί) in the source of **69**.
[40] See the works of Lyons, Bach and Fillmore cited in Chapter V §9 n. 39. None of them distinguishes the four categories described above, although Fillmore does give a careful analysis of "inalienable possession."

correspond a denial of presence – or an assertion of absence – for the same subject and the same place. But here it makes a great deal of difference whether the syntax of the subject expression is definite or indefinite, that is, whether the subject is identified as a definite individual (or individuals), or only as a distinct *kind* of thing. For only in the second case will the negative sentence bear an existential nuance. To *John is present here* corresponds the denial *John is not present here*; and the latter is not in the least existential. But to *(Some) ships are present in the harbor* corresponds the denial *Ships are not present in the harbor* or *No ships are in the harbor*; and this can easily be given an existential turn: *There are no ships in the harbor*. We might describe this latter form, the denial of presence for a given kind of thing in a given place, as a "relative denial of existence" since the existence involved is relative to the place specified. Notice that the difference between an ordinary negative statement of location (in other words, an assertion of absence) and a relative denial of existence does not depend in the least upon the difference between singular and plural subjects but only upon the question whether the subject is definitely identified (by name, previous mention, or deictic reference) or whether it is identified only by kind, i.e. by a common noun with no deictic or anaphoric indications. Since there is often no formal indication of definiteness-indefiniteness in Greek, ambiguity may arise:

73 *Il*. 14.299

  ἵπποι δ' οὐ παρέασι καὶ ἄρματα, τῶν κ' ἐπιβαίης
  "And your horses are not here, nor your chariot, which you
  would ride in."

                 (Lattimore)

If we follow Lattimore in seeing this as a reference to particular horses and chariot (the personal *équipage* of Hera), we have only an assertion of their absence. Taken out of context, however, **73** might just as well bear the indefinite reading "There are no horses and chariot here." We do have such a relative denial of existence in the next case:

74 *Il*. 15.737

  οὐ μέν τι σχεδόν ἐστι πόλις πύργοις ἀραρυῖα
  "We have no city built strong with towers lying near us."

                 (Lattimore)

  "Verily there is not hard by any city arrayed with towers."

             (Lang, Leaf, Myers)

It would be difficult to count this as a negative example of Type II: it has neither the initial verb nor the pronoun τις agreeing with the subject. But **74** may reasonably be regarded as the general denial corresponding to a locative-existential sentence like **57** in § 11: "Within the cave are bowls and jars," where again the subject is syntactically (and semantically) indefinite. Since the indefinite sentence affirms the presence or location of *some* (one or more) individuals of a given sort, the denial must affirm the absence of *all* individuals of the same sort: "There are no X's there".

The distinction between the definite and indefinite syntax of nouns varies from language to language, and even from period to period. Greek has no indefinite article; and the definite article, which in Homer is almost indistinguishable from a demonstrative pronoun, is used in classic Greek with considerable freedom (from our point of view). Thus the difference between definite and indefinite syntax is even less marked in Homer than in classic Greek, and less marked in the latter than in English. As a result, the distinction we wish to draw will often be based on the context as a whole rather than on any specific formal indications of definite and definite syntax for nouns. Of course such formal indications are not altogether lacking, even in Homer: the demonstrative ὁ "he", "this" (which was to become the definite article) naturally serves for definite reference, whereas the indefinite singular is often marked by the pronoun τις. We have seen how this indefinite pronoun regularly accompanies affirmative examples of existential statements in Type II, even when the subject is identified by name: ἦν δέ τις Δόλων, ἔστι Σωκράτης τις. This curious device for introducing *a man* and his name at the same time makes one wonder whether the syntax of a proper name can always be counted as "definite", even when the name refers to a single individual. But I shall not pursue the question further.

In the relative or restricted denials of presence for indefinite subjects, the more general the local restriction the more it suggests a denial of existence as such.

75 Hdt. IV. 129.2

οὐδὲ ἔστι ἐν τῇ Σκυθικῇ πάσῃ χώρῃ τὸ παράπαν οὔτε ὄνος οὔτε ἡμίονος διὰ τὰ ψύχεα

"There is in the whole land of the Scythians neither ass nor mule, none at all, because of the cold."

76 Hdt. III. 113.1

δύο δὲ γένεα ὀΐων σφι ⟨sc. Ἀραβίοισι⟩ ἔστι θώματος ἄξια, τὰ οὐδαμόθι ἑτέρωθι ἔστι

"The Arabians have two kinds of sheep worthy of note, which are found nowhere else."

In **76** the first occurrence of ἔστι is possessive-copulative, with ἄξια as predicate adjective. Notice that the possessive construction can be taken not as an elementary expression for ownership but as a derived form of locative-

existential: *There are in the land of the Arabians (two kinds of) sheep ← Sheep
are in this land*. The second occurrence of ἔστι in **76**, like that in **75**, illustrates
this relative-existential use in its clearest form. (Note that the verb may be
initial, as in the first case, but also final as in **76** or omitted as in the second
verse of **77** below.) Example **75** seems to differ from a general denial of existence ("there are no unicorns, none at all") merely by the limitation to Scythia.
The assumption in **75** is that mules and asses *are* found elsewhere. We would
have the general denial of existence if this limitation were dropped: "There
are no mules in Scythia, nor anywhere else." But the dropping of the local
limitation should be regarded as a difference of kind rather than of degree.
Whereas locally restricted existential statements such as **75** and **76** are common in a lay writer like Herodotus (cf. IV. 185.3, 191.4–192 *passim*), the
corresponding unrestricted assertions of existence or non-existence seem to
appear only in the language of the philosophers, as we shall see when we
illustrate Type VI in § 18.

There is one striking Homeric example which at first sight suggests the
familiar later pattern of Type VI: (οὐκ) ἔστι κένταυρος "There are (no)
centaurs."

77 *Il.* 23.103

> ὦ πόποι, ἦ ῥά τίς ἐστι καὶ εἰν Ἀΐδαο δόμοισι
> ψυχὴ καὶ εἴδωλον, ἀτὰρ φρένες οὐκ ἔνι πάμπαν
> "Oh, wonder! Even in the house of Hades there is left something
> a soul and an image, but there is no real heart of life in it."

(Lattimore)

This is perhaps the most "philosophical" use of εἰμί in Homer, a general
assertion of *presence* or *persistence* which resembles a general assertion of
existence. This is probably as close as Homer ever comes to a statement of
the form "Pygmies exist" or "There are no centaurs." But the difference is
conspicuous. Where we speak simply of the existence of the soul after death,
Homer speaks of its presence or location in the house of Hades. To a
surprising extent, this locative turn of speech still prevails in Plato's formulation of the question of immortality.[41]

---

[41] See *Phaedo* 70 C 4 εἴτ᾽ ἄρα ἐν Ἅιδου εἰσὶν αἱ ψυχαὶ τελευτησάντων τῶν ἀνθρώπων
εἴτε καὶ οὔ.70 A 2–6 ἀπιστίαν παρέχει τοῖς ἀνθρώποις μή, ἐπειδὰν ἀπαλλαγῇ τοῦ σώματος,
οὐδαμοῦ ἔτι ᾖ... καὶ οὐδὲν ἔτι οὐδαμοῦ ᾖ, with the remarks of Gregory Vlastos,
in *New Essays on Plato and Aristotle* (1965), p. 8 n. 5. In the same context, however, Plato
does make use of the absolute construction corresponding to the existential predicate
of our Type VI: 70 B 2 ὡς ἔστι τε ψυχὴ ἀποθανόντος τοῦ ἀνθρώπου καί τινα δύναμιν
ἔχει καὶ φρόνησιν; 77 A 10 πεπεῖσθαι αὐτόν, ὅτι πρὶν γενέσθαι ἡμᾶς ἦν ἡμῶν ἡ ψυχή·
εἰ μέντοι καὶ ἐπειδὰν ἀποθάνωμεν ἔτι ἔσται, οὐδὲ αὐτῷ μοι δοκεῖ... ἀποδεδεῖχθαι.
Plato's oscillation here between the generalized existential form of Type VI and the locally
restricted form of **75–77** confirms the intuitive affinity between the two types; but it would
not justify our reducing one type to (or even deriving it from) the other.

Essentially the same pattern of emphatic assertion of presence occurs in sentences where the local reference is elliptically "understood" from the context:

78 *Od.* 13.244

ἐν μὲν γάρ οἱ σῖτος ἀθέσφατος, ἐν δέ τε οἶνος
γίγνεται .../... ἔστι μὲν ὕλη
παντοίη, ἐν δ᾽ ἀρδμοὶ ἐπηετανοὶ πάρεασι
"(In Ithaca) grain grows abundantly and wine as well...; trees
of all kinds are here, and neverfailing springs."

(Palmer)

In other cases where an existential nuance is present, the locative construction overlaps with a copula use of εἰμί with comparative adjectives:

79 *Od.* 15.533

ὑμετέρου δ᾽ οὐκ ἔστι γένεος βασιλεύτερον ἄλλο
ἐν δήμῳ Ἰθάκης
"There is no house in Ithaca more kingly than your own."

Compare **4** above, cited in § 4:

οἵη νῦν οὐκ ἔστι γυνὴ κατ᾽ Ἀχαιΐδα γαῖαν
"(Penelope) a lady whose like cannot be found throughout
Achaean land."

(Palmer)

The syntax of comparative adjectives is complex, and I shall undertake no analysis. I simply point out a certain logical similarity between comparatives and quantifier adjectives like *many* or *other*. Like the quantifiers, the comparative adjective alone (in negative sentences) can convey existential force, even without the locative construction or even where the verb is omitted.

80 *Il.* 17.446

οὐ μὲν γάρ τί πού ἐστιν ὀϊζυρώτερον ἀνδρὸς
πάντων ὅσσα τε γαῖαν ἔπι πνείει τε καὶ ἕρπει
"Since among all creatures that breathe on earth and crawl on it
there is not anywhere a thing more dismal than man is."

(Lattimore)

81 *Il.* 23.439 (≈ 3.365)

Ἀντίλοχ᾽, οὔ τις σεῖο βροτῶν ὀλοώτερος ἄλλος
"Antilochus, there is no other man more cursed than you are"

(Lattimore)

Note that Lattimore's rendering of που as "anywhere" in **80** is not required; we might equally well translate the phrase as "there is not *at all* a thing more dismal than man." With sentences like **79–81** we have reached a neutral border zone between the copula and the existential verb.[42] More exactly, we have reached the area of overlap between the syntax of the nominal copula and the lexical value of existence as indicated by our translation "there is". Some examples of this were given in Chapter IV § 25, **136–138**. One of the most typical forms is the subordinate clause οἷοι (or ὅσσοι) νῦν βροτοί εἰσι, which can be rendered "such (so many) as mortals are now", which suggests only the copula, but also as "such (as many) mortals as there are now" with an existential flavor. (See *Il.* 5.304 = 12.449 = 20.287; compare 12.383. For ὅσοι see *Od.* 8.222; Il. 2.125 5.267, 5.877, 8.451, 18.429, etc.) Another typical form already noted is the construction with definite numerals:

82 *Il.* 2.618

   τῶν αὖ τέσσαρες ἀρχοὶ ἔσαν
   "Of these there were four chieftains"

(Lattimore)

Of course we might equally well render τέσσαρες as predicate adjective: "Their chiefs were four in number".[43]

I conclude this discussion of mixed or borderline case related to Types II–III with an example where the existential value "there is" coincides both with a possessive construction and also with a use of εἰμί as nominal copula:

83 *Il.* 4.51

   ἤτοι ἐμοὶ τρεῖς μὲν πολὺ φίλταταί εἰσι πόληες
   "Of all cities there are three that are dearest to my own heart."

(Lattimore)

The translation construes ἐμοί with φίλταται only: "dearest to me". But it can also be taken as surface possessive with εἰσι: "I have three dearest cities."

---

[42] J. Marouzeau (*La phrase à verbe "être" en latin*, pp. 40 f.) noted this indifference for *nihil est hac docta doctius* in Latin, but erroneously believed that it was "resolved in Greek by a difference in accent." He had in mind the contrast between enclitic ἐστιν in **80** above and the accented form in *Od.* 15.343 πλαγκτοσύνης δ᾽ οὐκ ἔστι κακώτερον ἄλλο βροτοῖσιν "There is nothing worse for mortal men than the vagrant life" (Lattimore). However, the accent of ἔστι in the second case is determined by the immediately preceding negation: οὐκ ἔστι is regularly so accented, whereas the distance between verb and negative particle in **80** allows the verb there to have its normal enclitic accent.

For the incorrect theory of the accent on which Marouzeau and many others have relied, see Appendix A.

[43] See the discussion of quantifier adjectives above in §11. For a celebrated example of the same form as **82** except for zeroing of the partitive genitive, see *Il.* 2.204 εἷς κοίρανος ἔστω,/εἷς βασιλεύς "Let there be one leader (for us), one king."

(Compare **63** above, "I have three daughters", and also *Il.* 2.372 τοιοῦτοι δέκα μοι συμφράδμονες εἶεν Ἀχαιῶν "Would that among the Achaeans I had ten such counsellors," Lattimore). Alternatively, the numerical adjective can be taken as predicate: "the cities dearest to me are three." A sentence like **83** is the transformational product or fusion of three different underlying constructions: (i) *Cities are three*, (ii) *Cities are dear to me*, (iii) *I have three cities = There are three cities for me.*

In cases such as **79–83**, where the occurrence of a comparative or quantifier adjective with εἰμί gives us both a copulative construction and an existential sense, there would appear to be no real ambiguity in the Greek. We are obliged to choose between different but essentially equivalent English translations. Perhaps we may say that whereas English has institutionalized the existential value in the set phrase *there is*, Greek lets this value wander freely over various copulative and possessive constructions, including the Homeric sentence patterns listed as Types II and III. For these types are, as I have suggested, only stylistically favored representatives of the wider class of copula-existential sentences, that is to say, of sentences with existential force where εἰμί has the underlying syntax of the copula. For the distinctly and exclusively existential uses of the verb we must turn to Types IV and V.

§14. TYPE IV: THE EXISTENTIAL SENTENCE OPERATOR
(οὐκ) ἔστι ὅς (τις) + *relative clause*

This has a good claim to be considered the existential type proper, the expression of the existential nuance strictly so-called (there being *some* as opposed to there being *none* who are such-and-such), and the idiomatic Greek sentence form that corresponds most closely to the pattern of existential quantification in logic, (∃x) (Fx). As a sentence form in natural language, Type IV differs from this generalized logical scheme primarily in the fact that the range of the variable *x* is in most cases restricted to persons: *There is someone who* (ὅς τις)....

Type IV is well established in Homer and is likely to have been inherited from earlier Indo-European. (The same type exists in Latin, and apparently also in Sanskrit.) As we shall see, there are some mixed or borderline constructions of Type IV with a vital or locative use. But in the standard cases the syntax of the verb is unambiguously non-copulative and non-elementary. ἔστι in Type IV functions as an operator, and its operand sentence appears as a relative clause that shares its subject with ἔστι. Anticipating the semantic interpretation, we say that the verb in this type asserts or denies the existence of an extra-linguistic subject – normally a person – that satisfies the condition stated in the relative clause.

Like all existential uses of εἰμί except Type I, Type IV occurs only in the third person. The most frequent form is negative, singular, present indicative; but affirmative and plural are attested, as well as other tenses and moods.

84 *Il.* 21.103

> νῦν δ᾽ οὐκ ἔσθ᾽ ὅς τις θάνατον φύγῃ, ὅν κε θεός γε
> Ἰλίου προπάροιθεν ἐμῇς ἐν χερσὶ βάλῃσι,
> καὶ πάντων Τρώων, πέρι δ᾽ αὖ Πριάμοιό γε παίδων
> "Now there is not one who can escape death, if the gods send
> him against my hands in front of Ilion, not one
> of all the Trojans and beyond others the children of Priam"

(Lattimore)

85 *Il.* 2.687

> οὐ γὰρ ἔην ὅς τίς σφιν ἐπὶ στίχας ἡγήσαιτο
> (The Myrmidons did not join the battle array) "since there was
> no one who could guide them into close order."

(Lattimore)

So in the optative (affirmative):

86 *Il.* 14.107

> νῦν δ᾽ εἴη ὅς τῆσδέ γ᾽ ἀμείνονα μῆτιν ἐνίσποι
> "Let there be someone who will speak wiser counsel than this."

87 *Il.* 17.640

> εἴη δ᾽ ὅς τις ἑταῖρος ἀπαγγείλειε τάχιστα
> Πηλεΐδῃ
> "But there should be some companion who could carry the
> message
> quickly to Peleus' son."

(Lattimore)

Notice that the presence of ἑταῖρος in **87** in the relative clause introduced by ὅς τις in effect restricts the range of subjects from persons generally to companions of Achilles, or Myrmidons. A similar restriction is in most cases implied by the context and sometimes specified expressly, as by the partitive genitives ("of all the Trojans, and above all the children of Priam") in our paradigm **84**.

For an example in interrogative form we cite again a passage given earlier in § 4:

3

> ἦ ῥά τίς ἐστι βροτῶν ἐπ᾽ ἀπείρονα γαῖαν
> ὅς τις ἔτ᾽ ἀθανάτοισι νόον καὶ μῆτιν ἐνίψει;
> "Is there any mortal left on the wide earth who
> will still declare to the immortals his mind and purpose?"

This is not a pure case of Type IV, since the restriction on the subject (ὅς τις) is expressed not only by a partitive genitive as in **84** but also by a locative phrase ("on the earth") construed with ἐστί, which thus figures as copula as well as existential verb.

I have not found affirmative or plural examples of IV in Homer, but both occur in classic Greek:

88 Sophocles *Philoctetes* 1241

ἔστιν τις ἔστιν ὅς σε κωλύσει τὸ δρᾶν

"There is someone, there is, who will prevent you from doing it".

89 Herodotus I.201

εἰσὶ δὲ οἵτινες καὶ Σκυθικὸν λέγουσι τοῦτο τὸ ἔθνος εἶναι

"There are those who say this tribe is Scythian."

(Compare *sunt qui* in Latin; and see further LSJ s.v. εἰμί A.IV.) As a variant on IV, we note the case where the operand sentence appears in infinitival form rather than a relative clause.

90 *Il.* 24.489

οὐδέ τίς ἐστιν ἀρὴν καὶ λοιγὸν ἀμῦναι

(Your father Peleus is old and alone) "nor is there any to defend him against the wrath, the destruction".[44]

(Lattimore)

In every example of Type IV quoted so far the subject of ἐστί is a person (or persons) who is *also* subject of the operand clause. Variants occur in later Greek where the subject of ἐστί is either (i) not a person, (ii) not the subject of the relative clause, or (iii) neither person nor subject.

91 Aesch. *P.V.* 291

οὐκ ἔστιν ὅτῳ / μείζονα μοῖραν νείμαιμ' ἢ σοί

"There is no one to whom I pay greater respect than to you."

92 Xen. *Anab.* I. 5.7

ἦν δὲ τούτων τῶν σταθμῶν οὓς πάνυ μακροὺς ἤλαυνεν

"There were some of these marches which he made very long."[45]

---

[44] We have similar infinitival variants on IV overlapping with the locative construction in *Il.* 13.312 νηυσὶ μὲν ἐν μέσσῃσιν ἀμύνειν εἰσὶ καὶ ἄλλοι "There are others (beside us) to defend the ships in the centre" (Lattimore); and *Il.* 9.688 εἰσὶ καὶ οἵδε τάδ' εἰπέμεν, where the locative idea is conveyed by the demonstrative οἵδε: "There are also these here to tell of it."

[45] For the idiomatic use of initial ἦν followed by a plural pronoun see Chapter IV §29, p. 177 with **143**. The idiom is probably explained in this case by the predominance of the singular form in Type IV.

93 *Ibid.* I. 6.6

> ἔστιν ὅ τι σε ἠδίκησα;
>
> "Is there some wrong that I have done you?"

94 Lysias 13.28

> σοὶ... ἐκπλεῦσαι συνέφερεν, εἰ μή τι ἦν ᾧ ἐπίστευες
>
> "It would have been to your advantage to sail away, if there had not been something on which you were relying."

Such variations lead to a generalization of Type IV which is at best incipient in Homer:

95 *Il.* 8.373

> ἔσται μὰν ὅτ᾽ ἂν αὖτε φίλην γλαυκῶπιδα εἴπῃ
>
> "(Now Zeus hates me....) Yet time shall be when he calls me again his dear girl of the grey eyes."[46]

> (Lattimore)

In fifth-century prose and poetry we find the generalized forms ἔστι ὅτε, ἔστι ὅπου, ἔστι ὅπῃ, etc., which can be used parenthetically or adverbially for *sometimes, somewhere, somehow*, etc. (Even in their parenthetical use, these constructions are still *sentential* adverbs, i.e. sentence operators in compressed form – just like *possibly, apparently*, which represent compressed forms of *it is possible that* and *it seems that*.) In Homer, where a construction like **95** is quite isolated, it is most naturally derived (by zeroing of the subject noun) from the following long form:

96 *Il.* 21.111

> ἔσσεται ἢ ἠὼς ἢ δείλη ἢ μέσον ἦμαρ,
>
> ὁππότε τις καὶ ἐμεῖο Ἄρη ἐκ θυμὸν ἕληται
>
> "And there shall be a dawn or an afternoon or a noontime
>
> when some man in the fighting will take the life from me also."

> (Lattimore)

Here we do not have a clear-cut specimen of Type IV but rather a Type V use of ἔσσεται (on my construal of "dawn" and "afternoon" as abstract nouns: see below § 16), which is conjoined with a restrictive relative clause of time in a form that parallels the ἔστι + *relative clause* structure of Type IV. Thus **96** represents an intermediate or overlap case between Types V and IV. The shorter form **95** may be regarded as a further transitional case between

---

[46] For a construction like **95** in indirect discourse, with the addition of a locative- temporal adverb σχεδόν, see *Il.* 13.817: σοὶ δ᾽ αὐτῷ φημὶ σχεδὸν ἔμμεναι, ὁππότε φεύγων/ἀρήσῃ Διὶ πατρί "I say that (the time) is close, when...".

96 and the classic construction ἔστι ὅτε, which in turn stands closer to Type IV.

In standard forms of Type IV like **84–89**, the subject of ἔστι is a person and the construction is "absolute" (in the sense that there is no nominal or locative predicate and no "complement" such as the possessive dative or the predicate genitive, although there may be a temporal modifier like νῦν "now"). In both respects Type IV resembles Type I; and in fact we find an occasional fusion of the two types, as in an example cited in § 4:

13   οὐκ ἔσθ᾽ οὗτος ἀνὴρ διερὸς βροτὸς οὐδὲ γένηται,
ὅς κεν Φαιήκων ἀνδρῶν ἐς γαῖαν ἵκηται
δηϊοτῆτα φέρων
"The man is not alive and never will be born, who can come and offer harm to the Phaeacian land."

(Palmer)

As **96** presented us with a Type V use of εἰμί assimilated to a Type IV construction with relative clause, in **13** we have a Type I use incorporated into the general pattern of Type IV. It is characteristic of Type I uses of εἰμί that they can stand alone as independent sentences, and here we might reconstruct a kernel of this type: *a man is alive*. But οὗτος in **13** points to the restrictive relative clause: *a man who can offer harm*. Thus we have an intermediate or mixed construction of ἔστι. In the pure examples of Type IV the syntax of ἔστι is absolute but *not* independent, for the clause with ἔστι does not represent an elementary sentence or kernel. In true cases of Type IV the verb serves only to posit or reject a subject (or in the variants, an object, time, etc.) for the associated relative clause. Thus in Type IV the verb ἔστι without its relative clause is not a sentential whole, any more than $\exists x$ alone is well-formed as a sentence in logic.

In summary, I repeat that the existential verb of Type IV is a sentence operator and the associated relative clause is its operand. It is characteristic of Type IV that εἰμί occurs *only* as existential operator, and not again as copula in the relative clause. We never – or hardly ever – find a Greek sentence which is literally of the form "There is an x which is F", where the verb occurs first as existential operator and then as copula.[47] In Type IV

---

[47] I have looked hard for an exception to this generalization. There seems to be one in Sturz's *Lexicon Xenophonteum* (published 1802), s.v. εἶναι: *Hell.* VI. 5.39 ἔτι εἰσὶν, οἳ σύμμαχοι εἶεν ἄν. But this reading turns out to be an old (and inelegant) conjecture. The MSS. generally have οἱ σύμμαχοι ἄν; Marchant in the O.C.T. gives Dindorf's emendation οἳ συμμαχοῖεν ἄν. In Hdt. III. 155.2 we do have an example of a variant of Type IV with ἐστί repeated in the relative clause, but in this case the construction is possessive and not copulative: οὐκ ἔστι οὗτος ἀνὴρ ὅτι μὴ σύ, τῷ ἐστι δύναμις τοσαύτη ἐμὲ δὴ ὧδε διαθεῖναι. (For translation and discussion of this example see below p.327, **134**.) In another Herodotean variant on IV the verb εἰμί recurs, but not in the primary operand clause:

the language has rendered perspicuous the role of ἔστι as existential sentence operator by articulating operator and operand in distinct clauses, and by generally refraining from using the same verb again in the second clause. (Types II–III and the copula-existential use in general represent the case where the operator and operand roles of εἰμί are not sharply distinguished from one another in this way.) Hence it seems correct to regard Type IV as a true analogue to the scheme for existential quantification in logic. But of course there are differences. The stylistic function of this sentence type is not directly accounted for by the logical analysis: the speaker in Homer (or the poet himself) is not interested in choosing a sentence form whose logical syntax is transparent, but one whose rhetorical weight is impressive. Above all, the ordinary uses of Type IV are much less general and at the same time more flexible than their formal analogues in logic. And this is just what we would expect for the logical devices of a natural language. Thus the greater flexibility of the Greek existential forms shows up in the mood and tense of the verb. Their more limited generality is marked by the typical restriction to personal subjects (indicated by the "animate" – and usually masculine – form of ὅς τις), as well as by narrower restrictions such as the partitive genitives that determine the range of the relative pronoun in our specimen **84**. Thus the existential sentence operator in idiomatic Greek carries as it were a sortal quantifier (expressed by personal pronoun, partitive genitive and the like) which limits the class of possible extra-linguistic subjects or "values" for its variable, so that in any given sentence the latter ranges not over the universe as a whole but over some definite set or kind of individuals: mortals, Trojans, sons of Priam.

§15. Type v: εἰμί as surface predicate or verb of occurrence

In this type the verb *be* takes as its subject not a first-order nominal like *man*

Hdt. VIII. 98.1 τούτων δὲ τῶν ἀγγέλων ἔστι οὐδὲν ὅ τι θᾶσσον παραγίνεται θνητὸν ἐόν "There is nothing mortal which arrives faster than these messengers." Similarly in **89** above εἶναι occurs in indirect discourse embedded *within* the operand clause, whose principal verb is λέγουσι.

Perhaps my only true example of Type IV with copula ἐστί in the operand is Plato, *Cratylus* 396 A 6 οὐ γὰρ ἔστιν ἡμῖν καὶ τοῖς ἄλλοις πᾶσιν ὅστις ἐστὶν αἴτιος μᾶλλον τοῦ ζῆν ἢ ⟨Ζεύς⟩ "There is no one more responsible for our life and that of all other things than Zeus." Here the repetition of ἐστίν seems to be made acceptable by the delay due to the intervening datives. Note that these datives *suggest* a possessive construction for the first ἔστιν which would make it an impure example of the Type IV operator. In fact, however, the datives are to be construed with αἴτιος τοῦ ζῆν (ἡμῖν = τοῦ ἡμᾶς ζῆν), and the example is authentically Type IV. For an explanation of the fact that this form with repeated ἐστί is so rare, see below, p. 299 n. 61.

or *city* but an abstract noun, and in the most typical cases a verbal (action) noun like *shouting, murder, defence*. As in Type IV the underlying syntax of the εἰμί is that of a sentence operator, but one of an entirely different form. Whereas in the standard examples of IV the existential verb shares its subject with the operand clause, in Type V we may say that the verb takes as its subject *the operand sentence as a whole* as nominalized in the abstract verbal noun. In semantic terms, while the role of εἰμί as operator in Type IV is to assert that there is a subject for the operand clause, its role in Type V is to assert that the action (event, situation) described by the underlying sentence *occurs* or *fails to occur*.

We take as our specimen an example already quoted in §4:

9 *Od.* 11.605

   ἀμφὶ δέ μιν κλαγγὴ νεκύων ἦν οἰωνῶν ὥς

   "Around him rose a clamor of the dead, like that of birds."

(Palmer)

In the surface structure of **9** the subject is κλαγγή, the action noun of κλάζω "to clamor, shriek". In transformational terms this noun is derived from the verb of the operand kernel **9K** ἀμφί μιν νέκυες ἔκλαγξαν (οἰωνοὶ ὥς) "The dead clamored around him (like birds)." The transformation which derives **9** from **9K** is of the general form

$$NV \rightarrow V_n \text{ of } N + be$$

where V_n stands for the nominalized form of V. (Compare in English *The leaves rustled → There was a rustling of the leaves*.) In our example *NV* is νέκυες ἔκλαγξαν; the transformation replaces ἔκλαγξαν by its nominalized form κλαγγή, νέκυες by the genitive νεκύων, and introduces ἐστί as finite verb in the transform (which here appears as ἦν, reflecting the past tense of the underlying *V*). Thus the form of *N* and *V* is changed; but other elements of the source sentence, such as the locative phrase ἀμφί μιν "around him", may be left unaltered. As a result, this locative phrase which is construed adverbially with κλάζω in the source may be reconstrued as adverbial of place with ἦν in the derived sentence: we have a surface ambiguity between *A clamor around him occurred* and *A clamor occurred (was) around him*. But there is no real ambiguity, since in either case the underlying syntax of ἀμφί μιν connects it with the operand verb κλάζω.

In simpler cases we have no modifier of *V* in the source sentence, and even the subject of this underlying verb may be zeroed in the Type V transform:

97 *Il.* 2.95

   τετρήχει δ᾽ ἀγορή, ὑπὸ δὲ στεναχίζετο γαῖα

   λαῶν ἱζόντων, ὅμαδος δ᾽ ἦν

"The place of their assembly was shaken and the earth groaned
as the people took their positions and there was tumult."

(Lattimore)

98 *Il.* 22.401

τοῦ δ' ἦν ἑλκομένοιο κονίσαλος

"A cloud of dust arose where Hector was dragged"

(Lattimore)

Here ὅμαδος and κονίσαλος describe events which would be expressed in
the operand sentence by the finite verbs ὁμαδέω and κονίω, whose subjects
("the Achaean host", "Achilles") have been zeroed in **97–98** but are easily
reconstructed from the context. The object of the transitive κονίω "cover
with dust" (or the subject of the corresponding medio-passive form) is
indicated by the genitive τοῦ in **98**. (For the underlying form with finite
verb, compare ὡς τοῦ μὲν κεκόνιτο κάρη ἅπαν a few verses later, *Il.* 22.405.)
When the tense of the underlying verb is future, this mark is preserved in
the tense of εἰμί as verb of occurrence:

99 *Od.* 1.40

ἐκ γὰρ Ὀρέσταο τίσις ἔσσεται

"Vengeance shall come from Orestes."

100 *Od.* 11.444

ἀλλ' οὐ σοί γ', Ὀδυσεῦ, φόνος ἔσσεται ἔκ γε γυναικός

"On you no violent death shall ever fall from your wife's hand."

(Palmer)

The form of the underlying sentences is *Orestes will take vengeance (on
Aegisthus)*, with τίνω, τίνυμαι, and *Your wife will not kill you*, with θείνω/
ἔπεφνον. As we have pointed out (in Chapter III §7), it makes no difference
for the transformational analysis whether the action noun is morphologically
derived from the stem of the corresponding verb (κλαγγή from κλάζω),
whether conversely the verb is derived from the noun (ὁμαδέω from ὅμαδος),
or whether both are derived from some common root (τίσις and τίνω,
φόνος and ἔπεφνον).

100 illustrates a variant on Type V already mentioned in §12, where the
occurrence of a personal dative (σοι) has the effect of making the use of
εἰμί as sentence operator or verb of occurrence coincide with the surface
syntax of the possessive construction. In **100** the dative corresponds to
the object of the underlying verb *kill*, but in most cases the dative represents
the underlying subject, like the genitive in **9** above and ἐκ +*genitive* in **99**:

Il. 4.169

ἀλλά μοι αἰνὸν ἄχος σέθεν ἔσσεται ← (ἐγὼ) ἄχνυμαι

"But I shall have terrible grief for you." "I grieve"

Il. 6.462

σοὶ δ' αὖ νέον ἔσσεται ἄλγος ← (σύ) ἀλγεῖς

"For you it will be a fresh pain"   "You suffer pain"

With or without this dative construction, Type V is probably the most frequent of all existential uses of εἰμί; and it is also widely attested with various suppletive verbs:

Il. 1.188

Πηλεΐωνι δ' ἄχος γένετο

"Grief came to the son of Peleus"

Il. 3.3

κλαγγὴ γεράνων πέλει οὐρανόθι πρό

"The clamor of cranes goes high to the heavens"

(Lattimore)

Il. 12.471

ὅμαδος δ' ἀλίαστος ἐτύχθη

"Clamor incessant rose up"

(Lattimore)

Il. 9.573

τῶν δὲ τάχ' ἀμφὶ πύλας ὅμαδος καὶ δοῦπος ὀρώρει

"Presently there was thunder (sc. of the foe) about the gates, and the sound rose (of towers under assault)"[48].

(Lattimore)

Type V is also frequent in classic prose with εἰμί and γίγνομαι:

Xen. *Anab.* II. 2.21

ὅτε ἦν ἡ μάχη   "when the battle took place"

Ibid. II. 2.19

θόρυβος καὶ δοῦπος ἦν (sc. τοῖς Ἕλλησι)

"There was noise and disorder (among the Greeks)"

Ibid. II. 1.21

ἡμῖν ... σπονδαί εἰσιν   "a truce is in effect (for us and you)"

Ibid. I. 8.25

ὡς δ' ἡ τροπὴ ἐγένετο   "when the rout occurred"

Lysias XIII. 16

ἐπιθυμοῦντες εἰρήνην γίγνεσθαι

"desiring that there be peace"

---

[48] ὀρώρει does not serve as a *be*-replacer for copulative εἰμί, but it occurs frequently in Type V sentences with action nouns as subject, above all with nouns signifying noise or quarrel: *Il.* 2.810 (4.449, 8.59, etc.) ὀρυμαγδὸς ὀρώρει, 11.500 βοὴ δ' ἄσβεστος ὀρώρει, 17.384 νεῖκος ὀρώρει (cf. 3.87, 7.374, etc.).

Ibid. 71

κραυγὴ γίγνεται   "shouting took place"

Ibid. 80

διαλλαγαὶ πρὸς ἀλλήλους ἐγένοντο

"a reconciliation was arranged between them"

In the typical cases of Type V, there is a transparent resemblance of form and meaning between the action noun and its corresponding verb. In other cases where there happens to be no verb (as for εἰρήνη "peace" in the example just quoted from Lysias XIII. 16), the points of analogy are so clear that we do not hesitate to list the construction in the same category. But some cases may give pause. For example, an action noun may have developed meanings of its own, not reflected in the use of the verb.

101 *Od.* 4.695 (≈22.319; cf. *Il.* 9.316=17.147)

οὐδέ τίς ἐστι χάρις μετόπισθ' εὐεργέων

"There is no gratitude for good deeds done"

(Palmer)

χάρις might be regarded as a verbal noun corresponding to χαίρω "rejoice," "take pleasure in" and χαρίζομαι "make oneself agreeable to," "do (someone) a favor." But it is perhaps more accurately seen as a noun of quality connected with the adjective χαρίεις "grateful", "beautiful", "giving pleasure (to the beholder)." On this analysis **101** represents the rare case in Homer of an existential use of εἰμί with a quality noun as subject. However, neither the cognate adjective nor the verbs suggest the idea of gratitude (or *reciprocal* showing of favor) which is required for χάρις in uses like **101**. Instead the verbal or adjectival idea "(to be) grateful" is expressed by means of this very noun: χάριν εἰδέναι "to be conscious of favor", i.e. of favor shown and favor due. Hence we cannot derive **101** by a Type V transformation $NV \to V_n$ of $N+be$ or even from N is $\Phi \to \Phi_n$ of $N+be$, as in English we can derive *There is no gratitude on their part* from *They are not grateful.* For in Greek there is no corresponding elementary form.

This is the kind of irregularity which distinguishes a natural language from a formal system and sets limits to the application of formalized syntax. Yet there seems to be no real problem of principle here. χάρις is clearly an abstract noun, even if the cognate adjective and verbs do not have the exactly corresponding sense in this case.

I am inclined to extend the Type V analysis to all sentences where existential εἰμί takes an abstract or sentential subject, that is, where the subject noun has the syntactical complexity of a nominalized sentence or predicate rather than the syntactic simplicity of a name or first-order nominal, and where the verb can accordingly be translated as "occurs", "takes place", "prevails", "lasts", or the like. I list a few examples of this theoretical extension of the type to sentences with abstract nouns where we cannot give a straightforward derivation of the sort suggested for **9** and **97–100**.

102 *Od.* 10.192

ἀλλὰ φραζώμεθα θᾶσσον
εἴ τις ἔτ᾽ ἔσται μῆτις· ἐγὼ δ᾽ οὐκ οἴομαι εἶναι
"Let us at once consider if a wise course is left. I do not think there is."

(Palmer)

The prehistoric verb underlying μῆτις is no longer represented in Greek, but the form belongs to "un système de noms d'actions tirés de racines verbales" (Chantraine, *Formation des noms*, p. 275); and the verbal connections of μῆτις are recreated in the derivative verb μητίαω.

103 *Il.* 8.66 (=11.84)

ὄφρα μὲν ἠὼς ἦν καὶ ἀέξετο ἱερὸν ἦμαρ
"As long as morning lasted and the sacred daylight was increasing"

(after Lattimore)

The old noun ἠώς must once have had its corresponding verb, like *to dawn* in English. (Compare *ucchati* "it dawns" in Sanskrit, which is cognate with ἠώς and Latin *aurora*.) But there is no trace of such a verb in Greek, and instead of "it dawned" Homer must say "it was dawn" or "dawn appeared" (γένετο, ἐφάνη ἠώς).

104 *Il.* 9.415

ἐπὶ δηρὸν δέ μοι αἰὼν / ἔσσεται
"There will be a long life left for me."

(Lattimore)

105 *Il.* 19.157

οὐκ ὀλίγον χρόνον ἔσται / φύλοπις
"Not for a short time will the battle last."

In classic prose we find a frequent use of Type V sentences with abstract nouns of state or condition that are more naturally derived from adjectives than from underlying verbs. Thus the derivation is of the form *N (is) A →* A_n *(of N) +be*:

106 Xen. *Anab.* III. 1.11

ἐπεὶ δὲ ἀπορία ἦν
"Now that there was a desperate situation"

107 *Ibid.* III. 3.11

     ἔνθα δὴ πάλιν ἀθυμία ἦν

     "Here again there was much despondency"

                              (tr. R. Warner)

So also in the case of ἔχθρα and ἀφθονία in sentences **69** and **71**, cited above in §12. The obvious operand sentence here contains a predicate adjective: ἄποροι, ἄθυμοι, ἐχθροί, ἄφθονοι (εἰσί). (Note, however, that the corresponding verbal forms also occur: ἀπορέω, ἀθυμέω, ἐχθαίρω; and cf. φθονέω.) In each case we have a rather complex derivation, which I shall not pursue in detail. It is interesting, however, that we do not ordinarily find such Type V sentences in the case of abstract nouns corresponding to *simple*, more or less elementary adjectives like κάλλος "beauty", ἀρετή (from the root of ἄριστος) "excellence", or μέγεθος "size", "grandeur". Sentences like ἔστιν ἀρετή "Virtue exists" scarcely appear outside of philosophic contexts; but when they do occur we may classify them with Type VI.

§16. Concrete uses of abstract nouns, and other problem cases connected with Type V[49]

It is well known that words with the formal suffixes of action nouns are not always used with their abstract syntactical value. Certain *nomina actionis* are regularly employed like first-order nominals to designate the means or product of an action rather than the activity as such. Thus *invention* in English once meant "the action of coming upon or finding", and it may still be used for the act or faculty of inventing; but the noun is most frequently applied to the resulting object, i.e., to "the thing invented.... Something devised or produced by original contrivance;... an original contrivance or device."[50] This built-in ambiguity, which seems to characterize action nouns in all I.-E. languages, is clearly exemplified in Homer.

108 *Od.* 12.320

     ὦ φίλοι, ἐν γὰρ νηῒ θοῇ βρῶσίς τε πόσις τε

     ἔστιν

     "Friends, there is food and drink enough on the swift ship."

                                  (Palmer)

108 is a normal example of the locative-existential use paralleling Type II (except for the unusual position of a sentence-final ἔστιν at the beginning

---

[49] This section is concerned with certain problems of detail in applying my analysis of Type V to particular sentences. The section may be skipped without loss of continuity.

[50] *Oxford English Dictionary.* Note that the definientia here, namely *device* and *contrivance*, illustrate the same phenomena of action nouns with concrete applications.

of the verse, instead of the more common position at or near the head of the
sentence). It is not an example of Type V, although βρῶσις and πόσις
are formally classified as action nouns.

109 *Od.* 5.483

> φύλλων γὰρ ἔην χύσις ἤλιθα πολλή,
> ... (2 verses omitted)
> τὴν μὲν ἰδὼν γήθησε....
> ἐν δ᾽ ἄρα μέσσῃ λέκτο
> "For a thick fall of leaves was there.... This Odysseus saw with
> joy, and lay down in their midst."

(Palmer)

Here we have the introduction of a topographical item with exactly the same
narrative function as in sentences of Type IIA. Hence we must follow Palmer
in construing ἔην as locative-existential, with the value "was present, was
found there", i.e. with an adverb like *here* or *there* understood. (Lattimore
has "since there was a great store of fallen leaves there.")

110 *Il.* 23.420

> ῥωχμὸς ἔην γαίης, ᾗ χειμέριον ἀλὲν ὕδωρ
> ἐξέρρηξεν ὁδοῖο, βάθυνε δὲ χῶρον ἅπαντα·
> τῇ ῥ᾽ εἶχεν Μενέλαος
> "There was a break in the ground where the winter water had
> gathered and broken out of the road, and made a sunken place
> all about. Menelaos... steered there."

(Lattimore)

110 is exactly parallel in form and function to **109**.[51] Although ῥωχμός,
χύσις, βρῶσις and πόσις are, from the morphological point of view, action
nouns for the corresponding verbs (ῥήγνυμι "break", χέω "pour", "fall",
βιβρώσκω "eat", πίνω "drink"), the use of such a noun as an item of
topographical reference makes clear that it is the product (and in **108** the
instrument or means) of the activity which is denoted by the noun, and not
the activity of *breaking, falling, eating*. Hence the use of εἰμί in **108–110** does
not represent a Type V sentence, despite the morphological structure of the
subject as an action noun. I call this the "concrete use" of an abstract
(action) noun, where such a noun is in fact used like a first-order nominal
and might be replaced by an elementary noun like *bread* in **108**, *bush* or *hill*
in **109–110**. Note that the syntactic and semantic criteria for distinguishing
abstract and concrete uses give exactly the same results in such a case,

---

[51] For the suffix -μός as mark of action nouns, see Chantraine, *La formation des noms*,
p. 135.

whereas there is no corresponding distinction to be drawn in morphological terms. Semantically, we define the concrete use of a noun in **108–110** as one which designates one or more individuals (localizable, enduring objects), whereas an abstract use (as in Type V) is one in which the noun does not designate either an individual or a group of individuals. Syntactically, a concrete use is one in which the noun functions as a first-order nominal, i.e. can replace and be replaced by an elementary noun; whereas an abstract use is one in which the noun functions as nominalization of a verb, an adjective, or a predicate noun. This pre-established harmony between syntactic and semantic criteria results from the semantic intuition that conditions our definition of elementary sentence forms, and hence of first-order nominals (Chapter II §7). In morphological terms, we can describe the class of nouns determined by a suffix like -σις as abstract, or more specifically as action nouns, *only* by reference to the syntactical or semantical criteria. That is to say, a formal word-class of this kind is recognized as a class of action nouns precisely because most members of the class are generally used as abstract in the syntactic and semantic sense. In principle, however, every formally abstract noun (i.e. every action and quality noun) is capable of being used concretely.

In **108–110** we have a construction where the form of the noun admits an ambiguity between Type V and the concrete locative-existential use with first-order nominal. There is no ambiguity for these sentences in their context; but in other circumstances we recognize that βρῶσις παίδων ἔσται ἐν δώμασι would mean "There will be (=occur) eating of children in the halls", where ἔσται is a sentence operator of Type V.[52] In other cases we are confronted with a more radical form of ambiguity, because we do not know whether to classify a given form as action noun or first-order nominal, even in a specific context:

111 *Od.* 23.371

ἤδη μὲν φάος ἦεν ἐπὶ χθόνα
"Light was already over the land."

The presence here of a locative specification does not prevent us from construing φάος as action noun for φαίνομαι, as we see from the corresponding construction of ἀμφί μιν κλαγγή in **9** above. On this view **111** will be a Type V use of εἰμί. The relevant translations "The shining was taking place" or "Sunshine prevailed over the land" sound clumsy in English, but they are certainly defensible as interpretations of the underlying syntax.

---

[52] I have changed the tense of βρῶσις ἔστι to future, since Type V uses of εἰμί with action nouns are generally past or future. The corresponding sentence in present tense is likely to have a *be*-replacer like γίγνομαι, πέλομαι or the like. For samples with εἰμί in present tense, see **101** above and **112–114** in the next section.

On the other hand, there is a natural tendency to speak of light as a kind of object or individual, as if *Daylight was over the land* were a sentence of the same form as *Clouds were over the land* or *The sun was overhead*. The syntactical ambiguity here between verbal noun and first-order nominal reflects a genuine conceptual hesitation as to whether light is to be counted as a thing or a process.[53]

In 103 in §15 there was no such ambiguity in the analysis of ἠώς, since "dawn" there must be understood as a process or state lasting over a certain time. But in other contexts we find a similar problem, when the "rosy-fingered Dawn" seems to be personified and editors are inclined to write her name with a capital letter. If Dawn is regarded as a person, the noun ἠώς is a first-order nominal. It turns out that none of our sentences with εἰμί involve this problem, but I mention it nevertheless since it points to a certain border region or no man's land between our basic concepts of first-order nominal and abstract noun. Although there are many clear-cut examples of both categories in Homer, the mythopoetic tendencies of archaic language and literature will not admit any sharp and general distinction between persons and objects on the one hand and powers, qualities, and activities on the other. Poetry and myth often require us to take the surface syntax of our sentences quite literally. Thus in our specimen 9 of Type V, the outcry of the dead (κλαγγή) is localized just as if the noun referred to an individual subject or topographical feature. If we consider only the surface structure of ἀμφὶ δέ μιν κλαγγὴ ἦν, we may be inclined to regard this sentence as localizing and indeed hypostasizing a *clamor* as a kind of entity. A mild hypostasization of this sort is characteristic of the surface syntax of nominalized predicates in Homer, and not only with εἰμί. As a result, such sentences often suggest the personification of important powers or states. For example, in a phrase like ἦρχε φόβοιο "He led (the) rout", φόβος is easily recognizable as a nominalized verb: the phrase is roughly equivalent to ἦρχε φέβεσθαι "He was the first to flee". But in Δαναῶν γένετο ἰαχή τε φόβος τε (*Il.* 15.396), "The outcry and (the noise of) terror rose from the Danaans" (Lattimore), the syntactical status of φόβος is slightly more ambiguous. And elsewhere Φόβος is personified as the son of Ares (*Il.* 13.299; cf. 11.37 etc.). Similarly, μοῖρα "share", "portion," is often recognizable as the nominal form corresponding to μείρομαι "receive as one's portion". The typical epic use for the noun reflects the verbal idea of receiving one's portion of life, terminated by death (cf. νῦν δέ με λευγαλέῳ θανάτῳ εἷμαρτο ἀλῶναι, *Il.* 21.281). Hence the noun frequently occurs as subject

---

[53] Kenneth Dover expresses to me his doubts whether the Greeks were aware of the etymological connection between φάος and φαίνομαι. If they were not, the difficulty in categorizing φάος will have been all the greater.

in such figurative or expressive transformations as Ἕκτορα... μοῖρα πέδησεν (*Il.* 22.5), "(his) fate shackled Hector," where μοῖρα is cast in the active role of determining the moment of death, a role which properly belongs to Zeus and other gods. (Compare *Il.* 2.111 Ζεύς με... ἄτη ἐνέδησε βαρείη, *Od.* 23.353 ἐμὲ Ζεὺς ἄλγεσι καὶ θεοὶ ἄλλοι/πεδάασκον). Such parallel formulae lead to the explicit personification of Moira as a divinity standing next to Zeus (*Il.* 19.87 Ζεὺς καὶ Μοῖρα καὶ ἠεροφοῖτις Ἐρινύς). Later poets, such as Hesiod, will specify the number of Moirae and establish their genealogy and eventually set them up as a power superior to Zeus (cf. Aesch. *P.V.* 515–8).

Confronted with such a development from verbal noun to deity, who can assess the respective contributions of misunderstood nominalizations, genuine religious feeling, and the essentially poetic delight in expressive language and vivid personification? Most studies of ancient personification (from Usener to Onians) seem to underestimate the complex interaction of syntax, piety, and poetry in producing such figures as Phobos and Moira. In attempting to analyze a verse like ἠὼς (Ἠὼς?) μὲν κροκόπεπλος ἐκίδνατο πᾶσαν ἐπ' αἶαν "saffron-robed dawn was scattered over all the earth" (*Il.* 8.1) we cannot distinguish the element of sheer imagery from a more intimate or official personification of the morning light.[54]

But the existence of borderline cases does not legitimately call into doubt the distinction itself between first-order nominals and abstract nouns. *Men, ships,* and *hill* are perfectly clear examples of the former, and *murder, shouting,* and *vengeance* of the latter, in Greek as in English.

§17. THE POTENTIAL CONSTRUCTION: ἔστι +*infinitive*[55]

This construction was briefly illustrated in Chapter IV §30, in our discussion of the impersonal use of ἐστί as sentence operator. In commenting there on examples **144–147**, I pointed out that the force of the infinitive is roughly that of the epexegetical or final infinitive with nouns, adjectives or other constructions, including the use with more elementary (and "personal") constructions of εἰμί; for example, in χεῖρες ἀμύνειν εἰσὶ καὶ ἡμῖν "we too have hands to defend ourselves" (above, pp. 178f). If I return to the construction in this chapter, it is not only because the strong value of ἔστι suggests

---

[54] Here again, in the imagery of *scattering* or *spreading* we have a kind of naive solution to the problem familiar to modern physics, whether light is to be conceived as process or thing. Compare Plato's tentative comparison of daylight to an awning stretched over men's heads, *Parmenides* 131 B.

[55] See Ebeling, *Lexicon Homericum* I, 360 under εἰμί 4; LSJ s.v. εἰμί A.VI. Compare also ἐξ-εστι and πάρ-εστι in classic prose and poetry. Two related forms are (1) ἔστι ὅπως + *optative,* a variant on Type IV (cf. above, p. 280), and (2) ἔστι ὥστε + *infinitive* "it is the case that" (below, p. 370 n.).

a connection with the existential uses, but also because the construction itself has several points of resemblance with Type V. In Type V the subject of the verb is normally an abstract verbal noun; in the potential construction a specious subject for ἔστι is provided by the infinitive, which is itself a kind of verbal noun. In both cases the deep structure of εἰμί is that of a sentence operator, whose operand is represented by the verbal noun or infinitival clause.

In illustrating Type V in § 15 I largely neglected examples with *be* in present tense. The connections with the potential construction will be clearer if we consider now a few instances of this form.

112 *Il.* 13.636

> πάντων μὲν κόρος ἐστί, καὶ ὕπνου καὶ φιλότητος
> "There is satiety in all things, in sleep and in lovemaking."
>
> (Lattimore)

113 *Od.* 12.120

> οὐδέ τίς ἐστ' ἀλκή· φυγέειν κάρτιστον ἀπ' αὐτῆς
> "There's no defence (against Scylla): the best is to flee from her."

114 *Il.* 11.648

> οὐχ ἕδος ἐστί, γεραιὲ διοτρεφές, οὐδέ με πείσεις
> (after κατὰ δ' ἑδριάασθαι ἄνωγε, 646)
> "There's no sitting down, aged sir. You will not persuade me."
>
> (after Lattimore)

Whereas in the past and future forms of Type V we may describe εἰμί as a *verb of occurrence* (since it asserts that an event has taken or will take place), in these examples we might almost call it a verb of *possibility*, since the sentence asserts that such things generally take place (**112**), or in the negative, that there is no prospect of their occurring, in other words, that they *cannot* occur (**113–114**). In its context, **114** οὐχ ἕδος ἐστι is a paraphrase equivalent of οὐκ ἔστι ἑδριάασθαι "It is impossible (for me) to sit down", which would be a case of the potential construction.

In these three examples of Type V, the subject of the underlying sentence or operand has been zeroed. In **112–113** this omission of the subject expression is a mark of generality: the sentence is true for any living or at least any mortal subject. In **114**, on the other hand, the understood subject (*I, Patroclus*) is unambiguously specified by με in the following clause.

The situation is exactly similar with regard to the omission of the underlying subject of the infinitive in potential constructions. The subject may be expressed in the usual accusative form as in **116**, or it may be omitted to suggest generality as in our paradigm **115**, or it may be zeroed but clearly specified by the context as in **117**.

115 *Il.* 21.193

ἀλλ᾽ οὐκ ἔστι Διὶ Κρονίωνι μάχεσθαι

"But it is not possible to fight Zeus son of Kronos."

116 *Il.* 13.114

ἡμέας γ᾽ οὔ πως ἔστι μεθιέμεναι πολέμοιο

"There is no way for us now to hang back from the fighting."

(Lattimore)

117 *Od.* 8.298

οὐδέ τι κινῆσαι μελέων ἦν οὐδ᾽ ἀναεῖραι

"It was not in their power (for Ares and Aphrodite) to move or raise a limb."[56]

(Palmer)

Like Type V, the potential construction of εἰμί is found in past and future tense but rarely in oblique (i.e. non-indicative) moods. For the past tense, see **117** above; for the future see *Il.* 21.565 οὐκέτ᾽ ἔπειτ᾽ ἔσται θάνατον καὶ κῆρας ἀλύξαι. For an Homeric example that might be regarded as the optative of the potential construction see *Od.* 1.261 φάρμακον ἀνδροφόνον διζήμενος, ὄφρα οἱ εἴη/ἰοὺς χρίεσθαι χαλκήρεας. In classic Greek, the oblique moods of the compound ἐξέστω, ἔξῃ and ἐξέσοιτο are well attested, together with the participial and infinitival forms (ἐξόν, ἐξεσόμενον, ἐξεῖναι). I have not found examples of non-indicative moods for the simplex εἰμί in the potential construction, and in later Greek the existence of the compound makes their occurrence unlikely. In oblique moods as well as in the case of participle and infinitive, a potential construction of εἰμί is difficult to recognize as such, and this may help to explain the development of ἔξεστι with its complete conjugation (in the 3rd singular). ἔξεστι represents the potential construction in unambiguous form.[57]

The negative form is predominant in Homer (and apparently in later Greek as well), but the affirmative is also attested:

---

[56] In a small minority of cases the subject of the infinitive in a potential construction appears in the dative, apparently only once in some 20 examples of this construction in the *Iliad*: 22.219 οὔ οἱ νῦν ἔτι γ᾽ ἔστι πεφυγμένον ἄμμε γενέσθαι, where the dative form for the subject is motivated by the contrast with the accusative object ἄμμε. Note, however, that the predicate participle πεφυγμένον takes the usual accusative form.

[57] In classic Greek the potential construction with the infinitive εἶναι does occur, but I have found no convincing examples with the participle ὄν (or ἐόν). This has a direct bearing on the interpretation of a difficult passage in Parmenides, fr. 6.1: χρὴ τὸ λέγειν τε νοεῖν τ᾽ ἐὸν ἔμμεναι, where it is often assumed (e.g. by Burnet and Kirk and Raven) that τὸ ... ἐόν can mean "what can be spoken and thought." I would want to see a non-controversial example of the potential construction in participial form before admitting that this is even a marginally possible interpretation of the verse.

118 *Il.* 14.313

> Ἥρη, κεῖσε μὲν ἔστι καὶ ὕστερον ὁρμηθῆναι

"Hera, there will be a time afterwards when you can go there (but now let us go to bed)."

(Lattimore)

119 Xen. *Anab.* I.5.3

> τὰς δὲ ὠτίδας ἄν τις ταχὺ ἀνιστῇ ἔστι λαμβάνειν

"(No one caught an ostrich.) But it is possible to catch bustards if one flushes them quickly."

How can we explain this idiomatic use of ἔστι with an infinitival clause to express the idea "it is possible (to do so-and-so)"? If by an explanation we mean a subsumption under more general laws or rules, then idioms are by definition inexplicable. And this potential construction is in a very definite sense idiomatic: it is perhaps the only major use of εἰμί in Homeric Greek that is not directly paralleled by similar constructions of *es-* in other I.-E. languages. (And this presumably hangs together with the fact that the infinitive as such is not an inherited I.-E. form.) But if we cannot *explain* the peculiar lexical value of ἔστι in this construction, we can certainly *understand* it, by considering the general function of the infinitive. In Greek (and not only in Homer) the infinitive serves to express an action in the form of a goal or project, a course of action as envisaged or desired. Hence the regular construction of this form as "object" with verbs of willing, intending, knowing-how (to do such-and-such).[58]

Like the action nouns which figure in Type V, the infinitive expresses the verbal idea in general, in abstraction from the personal, modal, and to some extent also from the temporal marks of the finite verb form. But whereas the structure of the *nomen actionis*, as a noun with singular-plural and case forms, tends to present the action (or the verbal idea, whatever it may be) as a kind of entity, as a second-order "thing", the infinitive presents the same idea as a project or intention, a course of action desired, undertaken, or reported (e.g. in indirect discourse). In Type V, with an action noun as subject, the verb εἰμί asserts that the act itself is given as a fact – a second-order thing – that is (was, will be) present "in reality". In the construction with infinitive, what the same verb asserts as present and given is not this action as a fact but as a goal or project to be carried out. Thus the sharp lexical difference between the uses of the verb in Type V and in the potential construction seems to depend upon a contrast between the reifying suggestions of the noun form in one case and the *intentional*

---

[58] See, e.g. Chantraine, *Grammaire hom.* II, 304.

connotations of the infinitive in the other. And this tendency for the infinitive to be used as the expression of an intention, a tendency that is suggested or reinforced by the regular occurrence of the form in indirect discourse as well as in clauses of purpose or finality, can be readily seen in an example where we have an elliptical version of the potential construction:

120 *Il.* 24.71

ἀλλ' ἤτοι κλέψαι μὲν ἐάσομεν – οὐδέ πη ἔστι –
λάθρη Ἀχιλλῆος θρασὺν Ἕκτορα
"The stealing of him we will dismiss, for it is not possible
to take bold Hector secretly from Achilleus."

(Lattimore)

The infinitive κλέψαι was introduced as complement of ὀτρύνεσκον in the upper context (in verse 24), where the gods in pity urge Hermes to steal Hector's corpse in order to save it from further mistreatment. What οὐδέ πη ἔστι denies is the *availability* (or "presence at hand") of this projected course of action.

We need not return to the question whether or not the infinitive is in some sense to be regarded as the subject of ἔστι in this construction, as the parallel to the action noun in Type V might suggest. Here if anywhere the verb is used "impersonally", i.e. the surface syntax of εἰμί cannot be characterized in subject-predicate terms. (Thus the potential construction does not admit the articular infinitive.) The only satisfactory description of the syntax of the verb in this construction is in terms of deep structure: it is a (modal) sentence operator on the underlying sentence represented by the infinitival clause.[59]

§18. DESCRIPTION OF THE POST-HOMERIC TYPE VI

I have now completed my survey of the uses of εἰμί in Homer, except for the veridical sentence type (ἔστι ταῦτα, ἔστι οὕτω "it is so") which is postponed to Chapter VII. At the same time I hope to have accounted for the great mass of uses of the verb in post-Homeric Greek as well. Of course any detailed consideration of particular occurrences of εἰμί, in Homer as

[59] See above, Chapter IV §30. I think it is misleading to cite this construction as an example of the "infinitif sujet", with Chantraine, *Grammaire hom.* II §446, pp. 304f. (who however also describes the verb ἔστι here as "impersonal", which seems correct, but incompatible with the notion of the infinitive as subject). Even Brugmann's terminology of "bound impersonals" with attached infinitives, as in *It is a pleasure to see you here,* is not applicable to ἔστι λαμβάνειν, since in the typical English and German examples of bound infinitives we have a superficial assimilation to S.-P. form ("*It* is a pleasure", "*Es* freut mich") of which there is no trace in the Greek potential construction.

in the later literature, will reveal many cases of mixed or borderline use between the various types distinguished. Some cases of regular overlapping (as between existential and locative or locative and possessive) have been mentioned; a few more complex cases will be illustrated in §23. But these mixed cases are in turn to be analyzed by reference to the principal types already defined. Taken together with the various copula uses of Chapter IV and with the veridical of Chapter VII, the five existential types and the possessive and potential constructions illustrated in this chapter not only provide the basis for a complete theoretical description of the uses of εἰμί in Homer and, to a large extent, in classic Greek as well: they also specify the uses of *es-* which Greek has inherited from Indo-European.[60]

There remains one sentence type which is not actually attested in Homer but which appears in literary Greek of the late fifth century and is of considerable importance for the use of the verb in philosophical texts. Curiously enough, this post-Homeric form seems to have an exact analogue outside Greek in other early I.-E. languages. This is my Type VI, the absolute use of εἰμί as *existential predicate* in sentences like (οὐκ) εἰσὶ θεοί, "The gods (do not) exist," in the construction which is sometimes regarded by philosophers as "systematically misleading" but which is often taken by philologists as representing the fundamental and original use of *es-*. I cannot pass judgment on the I.-E. situation as a whole. Judging from the Greek evidence, however, the standard view of this type as an inherited I.-E. form seems to rest upon an inadequate analysis of sentence types which are only superficially parallel to one another.

In order to define the originality of Type VI I must first review the existential and related types recognized thus far, in the light of a syntactical distinction between *first-order* and *second-order* uses of εἰμί. This represents a generalization of the distinction between *elementary* and *transformationally derived* uses first drawn for the copula in Chapter IV §3. What I call the second-order uses of εἰμί are those in which the verb serves as transformational operator on an operand sentence which does not (or at any rate need not) itself contain a form of εἰμί. The first-order uses of εἰμί, on the other hand, are those which either (i) occur in elementary sentences, or (ii) occur in a non-elementary sentence but may be derived from an elementary occur-

---

[60] Since I am not a comparative grammarian, this claim is presented as an hypothesis to be confirmed or corrected by comparative studies in I.-E. syntax. In any case, one must certainly make an exception for the potential construction of §17, which is in this form peculiarly Greek. With certain qualifications, the same seems to be true for the use of ἐστί as sentence operator with verbals in -έος (Chapter IV §§19 and 30), though there are analogies in other languages. Among the existential uses, Type I (where the verb has the value "is alive") may also be unattested for any language that has not been influenced by Greek.

rence of εἰμί in the source. For an illustration of (ii) consider sentences of the form *The teacher is sick*, to be derived from *N teaches* and *N is sick*. In the second kernel the copula is elementary; and hence in the resulting sentence *The teacher is sick* the construction of *is* is still first-order, though no longer strictly elementary. We might call this a near-elementary use of the copula.

The connection between this distinction between two uses of εἰμί and the earlier distinction between first- and second-order nominals is simply that in a first-order use of εἰμί the subject must be a first-order nominal. For if the subject is a second-order nominal (i.e. an abstract noun or a sentence-nominalization), then εἰμί will always be a sentence operator. But the converse is not true. Some second-order uses of the verb have first-order nominals as subject, for example in the periphrastic use of the copula (Chapter IV §§14–17) and in existential Type IV for personal or individual subjects (above §14). Among the first-order uses of εἰμί we have the following:

(1) elementary and near-elementary uses of the copula (nominal, locative, adverbial)

(2) possessive construction with first-order *N* as subject

(3) existential Type I (εἰμί = "I am alive").

Among second-order uses:

(4) transformationally derived uses of the copula, as verb operator or sentence operator (Chapter IV §§19–20)

(5) Type IV, the existential sentence operator ("There is (no) one who")

(6) Type V, εἰμί as surface predicate or operator of occurrence (κλαγγὴ ἦν)

(7) Potential construction (ἔστι + *infinitive*).

And from the next chapter we add:

(8) Veridical use, with sentential subject ("It is so").

It is not easy to classify Types II–III from this point of view. Together with the wider class of copula-existentials, the use of ἔστι in Type II may be regarded as first-order insofar as it can be derived from an elementary construction of the copula (whether locative or nominal) in the underlying kernel, with person or topographical item as subject. But from another point of view, the syntax of the verb in Type II can be described as second-order insofar as its existential function is *to provide a subject for the copula kernel*. For to provide or claim an (extra-linguistic) subject for a given sentence is precisely the function of the existential sentence-operator of Type IV. In Types II–III, as generally in the copula-existential uses and also in the possessive-existentials, we have a kind of intermediate or ambiguous case between a first-order and a second-order use of the verb. To the extent that εἰμί in these sentences is still the copula or the expression of possession, its syntax is first-order. But to the extent that it is *also* an existential verb, its syntactic role seems to be second-order. Theoretically we might derive Types II–III and copula-existential uses generally from a combination of one or more copula-sentences with an existential sentence operator of Type IV.[61]

What this analysis suggests is that every existential use of εἰμί is second-order, *precisely to the extent that it is existential.* The apparent exception to this rule, our Type I, is not existential in any proper sense. What is asserted in a sentence like **1** ἦ γὰρ ἔτ᾿ εἰσί is not that there is (or is not) a certain individual, or an individual of a certain kind, but that a definite individual (in this case, the father and the mother of the Phoenician slave-girl) is or is not alive. Like any elementary verb, εἰμί in this vital use normally takes for granted the (untensed) existence of the subject, as a person who *was* alive at some previous time, and goes on to assert that this person is or is not still living. Thus *is alive*, as an elementary predicate expression, is affirmed or denied of a definitely identified subject. A difficulty arises, as far as I can see, only for the formalized Type I uses in the future tense, which perhaps occur only in the participle ἐσσομένοισι "for men to come." We seem to have here the limiting case of an apparently first-order use of εἰμί that is in effect existential, in virtue of its indefinite plural form and future tense. (To say *men who will be alive* is scarcely different from saying *men who will exist.*) Perhaps in this marginal case of the indefinite future plural, we can say that the Homeric Type I anticipates the later Type VI. In general, however, it seems intuitively clear that εἰμί in its first-order uses does not express the idea of existence as such. And this is just what we would expect if, as Frege and others have maintained, existence is a second-order concept and cannot form the content of an elementary predicate, i.e. it does not characterize individuals. In Homeric Greek, at any rate, the idea of existence in the strict

---

[61] For example, we can derive our paradigm of Type II **27** ἔστι πόλις Ἐφύρη μυχῷ ῎Αργεος from (i) an existential operator on the model of Type IV ἔστι πόλις ἥτις... "There is a city which..." (ii) a locative kernel πόλις ἐστὶ ἐν ῎Αργει "(A) city is in Argos", and (iii) an adjoined nuncupative kernel with nominal copula πόλις ἐστὶ Ἐφύρη "(A) city is (= is called) Ephyre." We then explain the non-occurrence of *ἔστι πόλις ἥτις ἐν ῎Αργει ἐστί or *ἔστι πόλις ἥτις Ἐφύρη ἐστί by normal operations of zeroing. Thus, beginning with the transformation of (ii) and (iii) by the operator in (i) we have the following resultants: ἔστι πόλις ἥτις Ἐφύρη ἐστί (καὶ) ἥτις ἐν ῎Αργει ἐστί→ἔστι πόλις ἥτις Ἐφύρη (καὶ) ἥτις ἐν ῎Αργει→ἔστι πόλις Ἐφύρη ἐν ῎Αργει. The first result in this series is the conjoined transform of (ii) and (iii) by (i), without zeroing. The second transform involves deletion of repeated ἐστί. The third transform results from zeroing of ἥτις, i.e. from the reduction of the relative clauses to appositive (Ἐφύρη) and locative-adverbial form (ἐν ῎Αργει). This gives us a sentence of Type II, a slightly simplified version of **27**.

Note that these zeroings explain why copula ἐστί rarely if ever occurs in the relative clause of Type IV: in a sentence of the form *There is an X which is Y* or *There are many X's which are Y*, zeroing of the repeated ἐστί (or εἰσί) in Greek automatically results in a sentence of Type II or Type III. For the rare exceptions see above, pp. 281f. n. 47.

sense (there being *some*, or someone, or something, as opposed to there being *none*, or no one or nothing) is properly expressed by the second-order use of εἰμί in Type IV and by the operator of occurrence in Type V.

This syntactical analysis will be clarified and supported by the semantical considerations of the next section. For the moment it permits us to specify the peculiarity of Type VI. In sentences of the form οὐδ' ἔστι Ζεύς or εἰσὶ θεοί the verb *seems* to have first-order syntax, since the subject is a first-order nominal and there is no trace of syntactic complexity in the construction of the verb. And yet the sense is unmistakably existential: *There is no Zeus, There are gods.* On logical and syntactical grounds, we expect a second-order syntax to accompany this strictly existential sense. But here we find no trace of the underlying operand or "embedded" sentence. It is this fact which makes Type VI the most problematic of all uses of εἰμί.[62]

The earliest examples of Type VI known to me are from Protagoras, Melissus, and Aristophanes, in the second half of the fifth century. The type seems to arise almost as a technical novelty. As we shall see (in §23) there are apparently no sentences of this form in the work of Herodotus, who is approximately contemporary with Protagoras but whose language is largely free of Sophistic or philosophic influence.

I distinguish three sub-types, according as the subject is (A) a proper name or definite singular term, (B) a plural noun, or (C) a generic singular.

VI A. οὐδ' ἔστι Ζεύς   "There *is* no Zeus" or "Zeus doesn't even exist"

VI B. εἰσὶ θεοί   "There are gods"

VI C. οὐκ ἔστι κένταυρος   "There is no centaur."

The only examples of VIA that I have noted occur in a comedy of Aristophanes produced in 423 B.C.

121 *Clouds* 366

> (Στρ.) ὁ Ζεὺς δ' ἡμῖν, φέρε πρὸς τῆς γῆς, οὐλύμπιος οὐ θεός ἐστιν;
> (Σωκ.) ποῖος Ζεύς; οὐ μὴ ληρήσεις· οὐδ' ἔστι Ζεύς
> "(Strepsiades) But Zeus on Olympus, by Earth, is he no god?
> (Socrates) What Zeus? Don't be silly; there is no Zeus."[63]

(trans. Moses Hadas)

The exchange between Strepsiades and the Aristophanic Socrates neatly reveals the role of the existential ἔστι in formulating a *presupposition* of the

---

[62] This is essentially a restatement in modern syntactic terms of Russell's and Ryle's observation that the corresponding English sentences (e.g. with *exist*) are systematically misleading.

[63] In the repetition of this question at the end of the *Clouds* ἔστιν occurs in final position, but its existential force is then supported by τις:

first-order copula use of the same verb. According to our speaker a sentence like *Zeus is a god* is absurd (or absurdly false) because the grammatical subject does not refer to anything – in other words, because Zeus does not even (οὐδέ) exist. This strictly absolute and independent use of the verb in Type VI may be regarded as a kind of generalization of the more limited existential uses in Types II–IV, where the assertion of existence for a subject was *relativized* to the following predicates, for example, to the relative clause in Type IV. These Homeric types do not affirm or deny the existence of a subject taken *in abstracto*, but the existence of a subject of a given sort *for given predicates*. In sentences of Type VI, however, these further predicates have vanished, and we are left with a bare assertion of existence no longer relativized to a given operand sentence.

This peculiarity will emerge more clearly if we contrast **121** with a normal variant on Type IIB where the subject is also identified by name, sentence **46** already cited in § 10: ὡς ἔστιν τις Σωκράτης σοφὸς ἀνήρ, τά τε μετέωρα φροντιστὴς...καὶ τὸν ἥττω λόγον κρείττω ποιῶν. Here the existence of Socrates is asserted not in general or absolutely but precisely as subject for the following predications, i.e. as subject for the operand sentences that are here condensed into appositive and participial form: *a man who is wise, who studies things aloft and makes the weaker argument the stronger*. If **46** were interrupted after the word Σωκράτης it would be grammatically incomplete. Anticipating the semantic terminology of the next section, we can say that in **46**, as in Types II–IV generally, the logical function of the verb ἔστι is to pose an extra-linguistic subject of a given sort that satisfies certain descriptive conditions, namely, those which are formulated in the following phrases or clauses (i.e. in the operands of the existential operator). The originality of Type VI consists in the fact that such descriptive conditions are omitted and the verb serves *to pose the extra-linguistic subject as such*, identified simply by name or sortal noun.

Another example of Type VI from non-technical literature of the late fifth century will illustrate the proper function of this sentence form in a natural context, where it serves to formulate the existential presupposition of a first-order use of the same verb. (This example is intermediate between subtypes A and C, since the singular noun τάφος shifts here from individual to generic reference.)

Clouds 1470
> Ζεὺς γάρ τις ἔστιν; Στ. ἔστιν. Φε. οὐκ ἔστ᾽, οὔκ, ἐπεὶ
> Δῖνος βασιλεύει τὸν Δί᾽ ἐξεληλακώς
> "(Pheidippides) Is there a Zeus?
> (Strepsiades) There is.
> (Pheidippides) There is not. Vortex turned Zeus out and is now king."
> (trans. by Hadas)

122 Sophocles *Electra* 1218

(Ηλ.) ποῦ δ᾽ ἔστ᾽ ἐκείνου τοῦ ταλαιπώρου τάφος;

(Ορ.) οὐκ ἔστι· τοῦ γὰρ ζῶντος οὐκ ἔστιν τάφος

"Electra: Where is the tomb of that wretched man (sc. Orestes)?
Orestes: There is none; for the living has no tomb."

Here Sophocles' use of Type VI hovers close to more idiomatic or traditional uses: to the locative on the one hand and the possessive-existential on the other. If we were to develop the possessive idea by filling out οὐκ ἔστι as οὐκ ἔστ᾽ ἐκείνῳ τάφος, "That man has no tomb," **122** would no longer be an example of Type VI. But the context does not provide a dative, and by his use of the genitive instead the poet has allowed οὐκ ἔστι (τάφος ἐκείνου) to stand in its more striking, general form, as an implicit denial of all possible answers to the question *Where is his tomb?*, just as οὐδ᾽ ἔστι Ζεύς in **121** denies all possible statements of the form *Zeus is a god on Olympus*. The influence of quasi-philosophic reasoning is even more obvious in **122** than in **121**, since Sophocles' verses present an enthymeme that is almost Sophistic in its condensed elegance: There is no tomb of Orestes, for (Orestes is alive and) there is no tomb of the living.

Like **121**, most early examples of VIB are concerned with the existence of the gods.

123 Protagoras fr. 4 (Diels-Kranz)

περὶ μὲν θεῶν οὐκ ἔχω εἰδέναι, οὔθ᾽ ὡς εἰσὶν οὔθ᾽ ὡς οὐκ εἰσὶν οὔθ᾽ ὁποῖοί τινες ἰδέαν

"Concerning the gods I am unable to know whether they exist or whether they do not exist or what they are like in form."

Here in what is perhaps the earliest surviving "technical" use of εἰμί as existential predicate we see that questions of existence are explicitly distinguished from what will later be called questions of essence. And we see also that the latter would typically be formulated by sentences with *be* as copula: ὁποῖοί εἰσι ἰδέαν. (Compare the standard Hellenistic doctrine which asserts that we can know *that* the gods are but not *what* or *what sort* they are.) This distinction between the existence and the essence or nature of the gods corresponds in logical terms to the syntactic contrast between ἔστι as existential sentence operator and as first-order copula. A comparable distinction seems to be latent in another fifth-century example that may not be much later than Protagoras:

124 Hippocrates, *The Sacred Disease* ch. 4 (Loeb ed. II, 146) = 1.30 ed. Grensemann

οἱ ταῦτ᾽ ἐπιτηδεύοντες δυσσεβεῖν ἔμοιγε δοκέουσι καὶ θεοὺς οὔτε εἶναι νομίζειν οὔτε ἰσχύειν οὐδέν

"Men who practice such arts (claiming magic control over moon sun, storm, land, and sea) are in my opinion guilty of impiety and they do not believe either *that the gods exist* or that they have any power."

123 and **124** fall under VIB, with plural subject. **125** and **126** belong under VIC, since the subject of εἶναι is a generic singular rather than a plural noun. But this is in fact only a stylistic variant on VIB, as we can see from the use of plural forms (θεούς, δαιμόνων) in the continuation of **125**:

125 Critias, *Sisyphus* (Diels-Kranz 88 B 25, 16–42)

ἐντεῦθεν οὖν τὸ θεῖον εἰσηγήσατο,
ὡς ἔστι δαίμων ἀφθίτῳ θάλλων βίῳ,
νόῳ τ' ἀκούων καὶ βλέπων, .../...
ὃς πᾶν τὸ λεχθὲν ἐν βροτοῖς ἀκούσεται...(2 verses omitted)
τοῦτ' οὐχὶ λήσει τοὺς θεούς...(long omission)
οὕτω δὲ πρῶτον οἶομαι πεῖσαί τινα
θνητοὺς νομίζειν δαιμόνων εἶναι γένος

"For this reason (some clever man) introduced the divine, (teaching) that *there is a spirit* (=*there are gods*) flourishing with eternal life, hearing and seeing with the mind..., who will hear whatever is said among men.... This will not escape the gods.... In this way, I think, someone first persuaded mortals to believe that *the race of gods exists*."

The initial assertion ὡς ἔστι δαίμων is syntactically bound (as sentence operator) to the following predicates, beginning with the copula-periphrastic constructions δαίμων (ἐστὶ) θάλλων, ἀκούων, etc. The statement *that* the gods are is thus expressed as a kind of existential operator on the statement of *what* they are, with a single use of the verb for operator and operand, as in Types II and III or as in **46** above (requoted on p. 301). But the author clearly has in mind the more general assertion of Type VI as in **123–124**, and hence the link between ἔστι δαίμων and the descriptive predicates is dropped in the summary formula of the last verse, where the existence of the race of gods is posed in absolute and independent form: δαιμόνων εἶναι γένος.

It is surely no accident that most of these early examples concern the existence of the gods. So in Aristotle's sample question of Type VIC gods and mythological creatures figure side by side:

126 Arist. *Post. Anal.* II.1, 89ᵇ32

εἰ ἔστιν ἢ μὴ ἔστι κένταυρος ἢ θεός
"Whether there is or is not (a) centaur or (a) god".

Sentences of Type VI, which have the effect of isolating the existential presupposition of any and all first-order statements for a given subject, are the

natural expression for a certain kind of critical doubt that first arises in
connection with theological speculation. These new doubts are concerned
not with the truth of particular assertions (for doubts of that kind must be as
old as language) but with the validity of an entire tradition. In Greece the
first stage of such criticism is represented by Xenophanes, who rejects the
Homeric and Hesiodic account of the gods as a pack of shameful lies, but
does not question the concept of divinity as such. The next stage attacks the
tradition at its roots, by doubting or denying not only the assertions of the
poets but the very existence of a divine subject about which anything might
be truly said. It is this more radical form of theological criticism, or "atheism"
proper, which is reflected in **121** and **123–126**. There seems to be no trace of
this in Greece before the middle of the fifth century B.C. Yet we must
scarcely be surprised to discover that in other lands, for example in India,
both theological speculation and radical scepticism concerning the gods
developed earlier than in Greece. And in fact we find the absolute existential
sentence of Type VI in the *Rigveda*, in the statement of an atheistic position:

Bring forth a true hymn of praise for Indra, if he truly exists (*yadi satyam asti*). "Indra
is not" (*nēndrō astīti*): this is what someone has said. Who has seen him? Whom shall
we praise? "Here I am (or "This one I am", *ayamasmi*), singer: see me here (*iha*). I
encompass all beings (*jatani*) with my might." [64]

The passage is cited by Delbrück as an example of the oldest known meaning
of **es-* in Indo-European. [65] But if the Greek parallels are to be trusted, we
are dealing here not with a prehistoric sentence type but with a generically
new form of expression reflecting a cultural development that took place in
different religious traditions at different times. It would be interesting to
know when Near Eastern literature first recorded the thoughts of the fool who
says in his heart "There is no God".

In Indo-European this thought is typically expressed by a sentence form
in which ἔστι as existential operator has been isolated from the operand
sentences to which it is normally bound. It is as if the relative clause in Type
IV ("There is someone who...") had been struck away, leaving only an
initial ἔστι to which a name or noun can be attached as subject. Alternatively,
this form could be seen as the initial fragment of a Type II sentence, ἔστι
πόλις "There is a city", from which the following predicates have been
removed. But on our view the existential function of the verb in Type II is
itself only a less clear articulation of the existential operator of Type IV.
Hence it is the latter, and not Types II-III, which provides the proper basis
for a syntactical analysis of Type VI. Speaking more loosely for the moment,
however, we may describe the absolute use of εἰμί in Type VI as a generaliza-

---

[64] *Rigveda* VIII. 100.3–4. I am indebted to George Cardona for the translation.
[65] Delbrück *Vergleichende Syntax*, III (= Brugmann-Delbrück, *Grundriss*, V), p. 13.

tion of all relative existentials of Types II–IV. *There is no (god) Zeus* means that all sentences of the form *There is a god Zeus who does such-and-such* – and indeed, all sentences of the form *Zeus is (or does) such-and-such* – are false. To deny the existence of someone or something is to deny its availability as subject for any first-order predication whatsoever. Russell once proposed to interpret affirmations of existence as asserting that some instances of a given sentence form were true, and denials of existence as asserting that all instances of this form were false. Whatever its merits in philosophical logic, this suggestion seems intuitively correct as a phenomenological account of the pre- or proto-philosophical understanding of existence statements of Type VI. To deny the existence of Zeus is not to reject this or that particular assertion but rather to deny the truth of the whole religious, poetic, and ritual tradition in which statements refer to Zeus and in which actions and prayers are addressed to him. Similarly, to deny the existence of centaurs is to deny the truth of all stories told about them, to deny, for example, all sentences of the form *A centaur taught Achilles* or *Hercules shot a centaur*.

This link between the concepts of truth and existence is brought out in a striking way in a passage which, with **123**, represents the earliest attested use of the existential predicate of Type VI in philosophical prose.

127 Melissus fr. 8.2 (Diels-Kranz)

> εἰ γὰρ ἔστι γῆ καὶ ὕδωρ καὶ ἀὴρ καὶ πῦρ καὶ σίδηρος καὶ χρυσός, καὶ τὸ μὲν ζῶον τὸ δὲ τεθνηκός, καὶ μέλαν καὶ λευκὸν καὶ τὰ ἄλλα, ὅσα φασὶν οἱ ἄνθρωποι εἶναι ἀληθῆ, εἰ δὴ ταῦτα ἔστι, καὶ ἡμεῖς ὀρθῶς ὁρῶμεν καὶ ἀκούομεν
>
> "If earth exists and water and air and fire and iron and gold, and living and dead and black and white and all the other things which men say are true (= "real"), if these exist ("are so"?) and we see and hear rightly...."

Whereas the initial clause contains a clear example of Type VI, the second use of εἶναι is copulative with ἀληθῆ "true" as predicate, and the third use of the verb in ταῦτα ἔστι is really ambiguous between an existential construction of Type VI and a veridical use (ἔστι ταῦτα "This is so"). It is the notion of truth as cognitive correctness (ὀρθῶς) which is taken up in the next clause. Just as ἀληθῆ means not only "true" (of a statement) but also "genuine", "real" (of a thing or object), so also ταῦτα ἔστι is ambiguous here between "such things are real" and "What men say (about them) is so".

This ambiguity between the truth of statements and the real existence of things is characteristic of much Greek discussion of "being"; but it is certainly not limited to that language.[66] Such ambiguity cannot be discounted

---

[66] Compare the ambiguous formula used by Prospero's recently disenchanted victims

as mere confusion, since it reflects a deep connection between the two concepts of truth and existence. From the beginning, that is to say from Protagoras and Melissus to Plato and Aristotle (and down to existential quantification in our own day), existential sentences of Type VI are designed to transport us from the words of mankind and the lies of the poets to the truth of things; their function is to show or claim (or to deny) that the language we are using has been anchored securely in the world. In this respect, the logical function of Type VI uses of εἰμί is analogous, and in a sense subordinate, to the veridical use of Chapter VII. But whereas the veridical is a basic, inherited I.-E. use of *es-, the existential Type VI seems to be a late and problematic development that has no role to play in ordinary language before the rise of theological scepticism, philosophic speculation, and the popularization of both by the Sophists.[67]

---

in response to his sudden appearance and identification of himself as Duke of Milan: "An if this be at all"; "Whether this be / Or be not, I'll not swear" (*The Tempest* V. 1.117, 122). What they question is at once the truth of Prospero's words and the reality of his appearance after so many phantoms.

[67] These historical conclusions are based upon the Greek evidence alone, but they seem to be confirmed by what little I have learned concerning existential uses of *es- in early Indo-Iranian. Professor Benveniste called my attention to several passages in Bartholomae's *Altiranisches Wörterbuch* which bear a superficial resemblance to (and have often been translated as) examples of the philosophic use of *es- in the post-Homeric Type VI. However, upon closer inspection of the context (which was made possible by the generous help of George Cardona), I find that most of these passages belong with Types I or V, which have a similarly "absolute" construction but do not explicitly involve the notion of existence in contrast with non-existence, as does Type VI. Thus in Yasna 33.10: "may all the good things of life be at your disposal, those that were, that are, (*hanti*), and that will be". Since the subject *hujiti* ("life", "living") is the action nominalization of the verb "to live", we might have a familiar case of Type V, with *es- as verb of occurrence; but this seems to be overlaid by a possessive-existential construction, if the "abstract" subject noun is taken concretely as applying to particular objects or possessions. (Compare βρῶσις and πόσις in **108** above, §16.) Most of the other examples are closely parallel to the Type I vital use of εἰμί in ἔτ᾽ εἰσί "they are still alive", θεοὶ αἰὲν ἐόντες "the gods who live forever", or ἐσσομένοισι "for men to come". Thus in Yasna 45.6, the great god is "beneficent (towards) those who are" ("von guter Gabe für die Lebenden" H. Humbach, *Die Gathas des Zarathustra*, Heidelberg, 1959, p. 126). In the opposite formula of 51.10 the meaning of *es- must be the same: the evil man, who seeks to harm me, is "maleficent (towards) those who are" ("von übler Gabe für die Seienden", Humbach p. 153). In Yašt 13.150 we have a symmetrical formula for "the teacher (or "the pious") who were, who will be (lit. "have become"?), and who are." (We have the same triadic formula in *Od.* 16.437, cited above in n. 14 to sentence **13**: οὐκ ἔσθ᾽ οὗτος ἀνὴρ οὐδ᾽ ἔσσεται οὐδὲ γένηται. Compare **16** above for the contrast μήτ᾽ εἴης μήτε γένοιο "Better you were not living and never had been born.") Finally, in the inscriptions of Darius we have a reference to "Ahura Mazda and the other gods who are" (*ha(n)tiy*, R. Kent *Old Persian Texts*, p. 129, 61). There seems to be no suggestion here of a contrast with fictitious or "non-existent" gods, as in the standard examples of Type VI (and in the *Rigveda* passage quoted on p. 304). Whether the sense is properly "the living gods" or rather "the gods who are effectively there, who make their presence felt in the world," I would not dare to say. It may be that we have simply a generalizing relative clause, like ἄλλοι μὲν γὰρ πάντες, ὅσοι θεοί εἰσ᾽

§19. THE DISTINCTION BETWEEN EXISTENCE₁ (FOR INDIVIDUALS)
AND EXISTENCE₂ (FOR EVENTS, PROPERTIES, STATES OF AFFAIRS)

We are now in a position to complete the third and final phase of our description. After the initial lexical survey of existential nuances for the verb (§§ 2–4) we have given a syntactic analysis of five Homeric and one post-Homeric sentence type which may be loosely called "existential" (§§ 5–11, 14–15, 18), together with the possessive (§ 12) and potential constructions (§ 17) and various mixed or borderline cases (§§ 13 and 16). We have observed that in only two of the Homeric sentence forms, in Types IV and V, is the use of εἰμί strictly and properly existential; and to these two we may now add the post-Homeric Type VI. It is for these three types, then, that I shall propose a semantic analysis of the existential verb. But my analysis will also apply to Types I–III, and to the copula-existential and possessive-existential uses as well, precisely to the extent that these other sentence forms are correctly construed as assertions or denials of existence.

I begin with Types IV and V, the two existential forms that clearly have a role to play in the natural language prior to, or independent of, philosophical speculation. In the next section I shall define a semantic role which is common to these two types, in virtue of which they are both properly described as "existential." But first we consider the differences between the two forms. For these differences are so marked that one might almost be inclined to say that the two sentence types illustrate distinct senses of "existence."

In Type IV the subject is typically a noun referring to persons or places; in Type V it is an abstract action noun. In both cases we can translate ἔστι by *there is*, but in the first case (and not in the second) we can often render the verb as *there is found*, *there is located*, or as *exists*; and in the second case (but not in the first) we may naturally render it as *arises*, *occurs*, *takes place*, or *lasts*. This difference in lexical value for the verb is of course correlated with the difference in syntactic category for the subject: in one case a first-order nominal, in the other case an abstract noun (more precisely, in the examples which interest us, an action nominalization of a verb). Translating this lexical and syntactic contrast into more philosophical language, we may say that in Type IV ἔστι expresses the existence of individuals (persons, things) as relatively stable items in the landscape or in the narrative, while in Type V it expresses the temporal existence or occurrence of events and states of affairs. Let us distinguish these two concepts as existence₁ and existence₂ respectively.

ἐν Ὀλύμπῳ (*Il.* 5.877; cf. 1.566, etc.): "all the gods that there are, however many they may be."

The question whether "exists" in English admits of different senses has been much discussed. On the one hand there is the position of Quine who denies that the word has distinct meanings; he holds that "exists," like "true," is "unambiguous but very general."[68] On the other hand several British philosophers have distinguished two senses or uses of "exists" that closely parallel the syntactic-lexical distinction just drawn. These authors contrast a non-predicative or non-propositional use of "exists", where the subject is a definite individual, with a predicative or propositional use where the subject is a concept or property and *to exist* means *to be instantiated*. This corresponds to my distinction between Types IV and V, and between existence$_1$ and existence$_2$, with one important difference. Whereas in my discussion the typical examples of subject-expressions for existence$_2$ are verbal nouns like *clamor, uproar, murder* (κλαγγή, ὅμαδος, φόνος), the philosophers in question conceive of properties as expressed by predicate nouns (the property of *being a unicorn*) or by the nominalizations of predicate adjectives (*virtue* ← *X is virtuous*).[69] As was pointed our earlier, these two cases are syntactically parallel in that they both have second-order nominals as subjects. Philosophers have often overlooked this parallel, apparently because we do not ordinarily speak of actions and events as "existing" but rather as "taking place" or "occurring". But this seems to be only an accident of idiom. In pre-philosophic Greek, on the other hand, existential sentences of Type V are found almost exclusively with verbal nouns (i.e. state- or event-words) as subject of εἰμί, so that I shall ignore the problem of existence statements with quality nouns, numbers and the like as subject. (Existential sentences with concrete sortal nouns like "gods" or "centaurs" as subject of εἰμί fall below under Type VI.) For our purposes there is no need to decide whether the distinction in question represents two different senses of "exists"

---

[68] *Word and Object*, p. 131; cf. *Methods of Logic*, p. 198.

[69] See Eric Toms, *Being, Negation and Logic* (Oxford, 1962) p. 28, who distinguishes between (1) "a basic, trivial, and non-propositional sense of 'exists'... [in which we] truly assert of a given individual subject that it 'exists,' but this assertion is trivial since the word 'exists' only repeats what is already presupposed by the fact that it is predicated of *something*, i.e. of an *existing thing*;" and (2) a derivative and "significant" sense of "exists" or "there is" in so-called existential propositions, which "say, in effect,... that a certain idea, universal, or property (e.g. the property of being a unicorn) has instances or has no instances." Toms insists that sense (2) presupposes sense (1), presumably because the instances in question must "exist" in sense (1), i.e. as *given, individual subjects*. Strawson has drawn a somewhat similar distinction between what he calls the non-predicative use of "exists," which applies primarily to particulars as the paradigm case of logical (extra-linguistic) subjects, i.e. as items to which reference can be made, and (2) a predicative use, which applies only to "concepts or properties," and where the use of "exists" serves to declare, or deny, that the concept or property is instantiated (*Individuals*, p. 241). Strawson also generalizes the non-predicative use (1) so that it may apply to "any type of thing whatsoever"; but this generalization has the effect of eliminating the distinction which concerns us here.

or merely two applications of the same sense. I suggest, however, that those who would distinguish two senses of "exist" have in mind syntactical and lexical differences of the sort mentioned in the preceding paragraph; whereas those who insist upon a single sense for "exists" wish to emphasize the semantical role which (as we shall see) is the same in both types. If this is correct, the debate about difference of sense for "exists" is not properly a debate about "exists" but about the sense of the word "sense" and about the criteria for sameness of sense. And this is not a question which needs to be discussed here.

Thus I distinguish existence$_1$ (for individual subjects) and existence$_2$ (for abstract subjects, as expressed by action nouns) merely to call attention to the syntactical and lexical contrasts which have been described. We may say, then, that the existence which is affirmed or denied in a Type IV use of εἰμί is existence$_1$, the presence or being-there for persons and objects in the world. And this is the existence which is always taken for granted for the subjects of true elementary sentences – including elementary sentences with copula be. Thus the existence$_1$ which is expressed by εἰμί in Type IV is the existence which is *presupposed* or implied by any elementary (or near-elementary) use of any verb, including any elementary use of εἰμί.[70] This connection between the role of εἰμί as existential operator in Type IV and the elementary or first-order uses of the same verb will be of some importance when we consider the whole system of uses for the verb. For the moment I simply note that it is this same existence$_1$ for individual persons or things that is expressed in Types II–III, in the copula- or locative-existential, and in the possessive-existential – whenever the subject is a first-order nominal and insofar as the use of the verb is properly existential.

The expression of existence$_2$, on the other hand, seems almost to be limited to Type V uses of εἰμί. (The only apparent exception is provided by the mixed cases where Type V overlaps with the possessive construction: above, § 12 sentences 67–72.) In fact the lexical and syntactical features of Type V are not quite as isolated as they seem: we shall find something similar in the case of the veridical construction, where εἰμί takes a sentential subject. As it turns out, the borderline between existence$_2$ and the veridical value *is true, is a fact* is not always easy to draw. However, the contrast between existence$_1$ and existence$_2$ is just as clear as the difference between the subject of the verb in the two cases. In grammatical terms it is as clear as the dis-

---

[70] This is merely the reformulation in linguistic terms of the logical law $Fy \rightarrow (\exists x) Fx$. See, for example, the discussion in Strawson's *Individuals*, pp. 234f. I am assuming that the quantifier is interpreted (with Quine and most logicians) as a genuine existence claim, and not with the wider value proposed by Leśniewski. For the latter view, see C. Lejewski, "Logic and Existence", *British Journal for the Philosophy of Science* 5 (1954), 104ff.

tinction between first-order nominals and nominalized verbs or sentences. In philosophical terms it is as clear as the distinction between individuals and events or between individuals and states of affairs. When the distinction is formulated in this way, we need not hesitate to describe Type VI also as an expression of existence$_1$, the existence of individuals: *There is no Zeus*; *The gods exist*.

§20. THE SEMANTIC ROLE OF THE EXISTENTIAL VERB

Having distinguished the two kinds (or senses) of existence expressed in Types IV and V, we must now give an account of the semantic function which the two types have in common. It turns out that this function is not essentially different from that of the veridical use of εἰμί.

We may take as our clue the fact that both in Type IV and Type V the verb εἰμί has the syntactic status of a sentence operator. This means that the verb in each case is construed with an embedded sentence or operand. It is natural to conclude that, just as at the level of syntax we analyze an existential sentence into two components, we must do likewise at the level of logical function or semantics. In the syntactical analysis we have distinguished (1) one or more underlying operand sentences (which, for simplicity, I here assume to be elementary sentences, requiring no further decomposition), and (2) a sentence operator represented by εἰμί. In the logical analysis I propose to make a corresponding distinction between (1) the descriptive content of the sentence and (2) the semantic component, where "semantic" is intended in the strong sense to indicate a use of the extra-linguistic concepts of truth and reference. Speaking somewhat loosely we may say that the descriptive content of a sentence says something about the world; the semantic component says something about the relation *between* this descriptive content and the world to which it refers or which it purports to describe. The descriptive content may be of unlimited variety; but the semantic component is uniformly two-valued: positive and negative, yes and no. In Greek, ἔστι poses the semantic relation as actually obtaining, i.e. it poses the descriptive content as present in the world; οὐκ ἔστι denies this posit. We might compare the descriptive content with Wittgenstein's *Sinn*, what a proposition "shows" in each particular case (*Tractatus* 4.022). The semantic component, on the other hand, is what the proposition "says" in every case: "This is how things stand" (*Es verhält sich so und so*, 4.5). Thus the proposition restricts reality to a yes or no answer (4.023).[71]

---

[71] My own distinction between descriptive content and semantic component was directly inspired not by Wittgenstein's remarks but by Arthur Danto's development of this insight in his theory of *semantic vehicles* and *semantic values*. (See his *Analytical Philosophy of Knowledge*, Cambridge University Press, 1968, Chapter Seven.) A semantical vehicle is

The semantic component envisaged by Wittgenstein's remarks is just the truth claim implicit in every declarative sentence. But in a sentence of the form *That is true* or *That is a fact*, this component is articulated separately as a sentence operator *is true*, *is a fact* – an operator which may be expressed in Greek by a veridical use of ἔστι. In the typical forms of the veridical construction (as we shall see in detail in the next chapter), the descriptive content is formulated separately in one or more distinct sentences, which may be referred to by a pro-word like *that* in the examples just given. In such a case, the descriptive component will appear as underlying subject, the semantic component as surface predicate. But this veridical use is merely the overt expression of a general duality of logical function between semantic value and descriptive content which we find reflected in the operator-operand structure of all existential sentences of Types IV and V. As in the veridical construction so also in these two types: the semantic component, the Yes or No claim, is expressed by ἔστι or οὐκ ἔστι. Note that both in the veridical and in Types IV and V the verb εἰμί occurs only in the third person singular. From the purely syntactic point of view we may regard this restriction as a natural consequence of the fact that such sentences have either a sentential structure (in the veridical), an abstract noun (in Type V), or an indefinite pronoun (in Type IV) as subject. But from the logical point of view the occurrence of only two forms, one affirmative and one negative, is just what we would expect for an expression of the positive and negative semantic values: *true, false*; *exists, does not exist*; *occurs, fails to occur*.[72]

This dual structure is most fully articulated in the case of Type IV, where the descriptive operand and the existential operator ἔστι occur as two distinct clauses in the surface syntax of a single sentence. For example in our specimen sentence **84** for Type IV (νῦν δ᾽ οὐκ ἔσθ᾽ ὅς τις θάνατον φύγῃ),

---

anything which bears (or can bear) a plus or a minus semantic value, e.g. *true* and *false* in the case of a (declarative) sentence. Other semantic vehicles in Danto's analysis are concepts (with the values *instantiated, not instantiated*), terms (which *refer* or *fail to refer*), and pictures (which *represent* or *fail to represent*). In my version, the semantic vehicle is represented by the operand sentence (or sentences) with its descriptive content; Danto's semantic values, plus and minus, correspond to my *semantic component* as expressed by the sentence operators ἔστι and οὐκ ἔστι respectively.

[72] My remarks apply without qualification only to the declarative forms in present tense, where the semantic operator can appear only as ἔστι or οὐκ ἔστι. As we have seen, past and future tenses of εἰμί in Types IV and V will reflect the tense of the underlying operand sentence, and to this extent the function of the verb is not limited to the expression of a semantic value. Furthermore, to take account of interrogative and optative forms of IV and V we would have to qualify the notion of semantic component in certain obvious ways, recognizing the possibility of secondary modifications in which the primary semantic value or posit (yes or no, ἔστι or οὐκ ἔστι) in turn becomes the object of doubt or question, wish or desire. Compare our remarks above on modalities and my own development of this doctrine in Chapter V §§2–2a.

the descriptive content is given in the operand sentence that underlies the relative clause: (*Someone*) *will escape death*, (τις) θάνατον φεύξεται. The semantic component, on the other hand, is provided by the existential operator that imposes the form of a relative clause upon this operand: *There is (no) one who* (οὐκ) ἔστι ὅς (τις). If we analyze **84** within its full context, we see that the descriptive content is further specified by partitive genitives restricting the range of the subject term ὅς τις and by another relative clause: ὅν κε θεός γε/... ἐμῆς ἐν χερσὶ βάλῃσι "whom the gods cast into my hands." (See above, p. VI-78.) Now relative clauses, as Quine has remarked, "afford admirably flexible means of formulating conditions for objects to fulfill."[73] Thus the full descriptive content of **84** may be given as follows: (*There is no one*) *who will escape death, whom the gods place in my hands, of all the Trojans, but above all of the sons of Priam.* Ignoring the last *a fortiori* refinement, the descriptive content can be reformulated as a set of conditions on an extra-linguistic subject *x*: (i) *x* is a Trojan warrior, (ii) the gods place *x* in Achilles' hands, (iii) *x* will escape death. The semantic component represented by the sentence operator οὐκ ἔστι (ὅστις) asserts that *there is no such (extra-linguistic) subject*, i.e. that the conditions (i)–(iii) are not jointly satisfied for any value of *x*. Thus we can say that the logical function of the sentence operator ἔστι in Type IV is to posit an extra-linguistic subject for one or more elementary sentences, while the function of οὐκ ἔστι is to deny such a posit. (Note that the extra-linguistic subject may be represented not only by a grammatical subject but also by the *object* of the verb, as in the operand sentence corresponding to (ii).)

Whether we speak here of the *existence* of an appropriate individual or of the satisfaction of a condition (as formulated in an open sentence), we may in either case describe the general function of ἔστι as the assignment of the positive semantic value. Thus the semantic function of ἔστι/οὐκ ἔστι corresponds to that of such English pairs as *there is/there is not, occurs/does not occur, true/false*. So generalized, this account of the semantic function applies not only to the existential operator of Type IV but also to the veridical use and to the use of ἔστι as surface predicate or verb of occurrence in Type V. Thus in our specimen **9** of Type V in § 15, ἀμφὶ δέ μιν κλαγγὴ νεκύων ἦν, we have a descriptive content formulated by the underlying sentence ἀμφί μιν νέκυες ἔκλαγξαν "Around him the dead clamored." The transformation represented by ἦν as surface predicate involves a nominalization of the operand verb (ἔκλαγξαν→κλαγγή + *past tense*, the latter reflected in the tense of ἦν) with a secondary inflection of the operand subject (νέκυες → νεκύων). The operator ἔστι (now appearing as ἦν) assigns the positive

[73] *Word and Object*, p. 110.

semantic value *it occurs (that ...)*. As semantic operator in Type V ἔστι thus asserts that the action of the operand sentence *takes place*; in other words, it asserts the truth of this operand sentence in a particularly expressive or emphatic form.

In Type V the semantic transformation really affects the operand sentence as a whole, but its direct target in surface structure is the underlying verb which it nominalizes. In this respect, and in this respect only, the verb of occurrence in Type V differs from the veridical use of εἰμί described in the next chapter. For in the veridical use it is the operand sentence as a whole which is construed as grammatical subject for ἔστι (e.g. as antecedent for ταῦτα in ἔστι ταῦτα). Hence the particularly close connection between the use of ἔστι as verb of occurrence in Type V, expressing existence$_2$, and the veridical use of the verb where it expresses truth or fact.[74] In Type IV, on the other hand, the operand verb remains as a finite form in third person, and the surface focus of the semantic operator is on the (generalized) operand subject which also serves as subject for ἔστι. Since in Type IV this subject is typically an individual object, and most typically a person, the operator ἔστι expresses existence$_1$. Thus we see that the lexical and conceptual differences between existence$_1$, existence$_2$, and the notion of truth correspond exactly to the syntactical differences between sentences of Type IV, Type V, and the veridical construction. But the logical function of ἔστι and οὐκ ἔστι in the assignment of a positive or negative semantic value is the same in all three cases. We may bring out this parallelism by three English sentence forms which correspond roughly in meaning to the sentence operators of Types IV, V and the veridical, in that order: (a) *There is someone (something) such that he (it) ...*, (b) *It happened (occurred, took place) that ...*, and (c) *It is the case that ....*

In attempting to elucidate the notion of a positive semantic value we may say that ἔστι as operator poses a relation between a given descriptive content and the world to which it refers or which it purports to describe, or, more specifically, that it *poses the descriptive content as actually present in the world*. This is an essentially metaphorical mode of speech; but there seems to be no other mode available if we are to give anything beyond a formal account of the concepts of existence and truth. In formal terms we might say that the positive semantic value means that certain truth conditions are satisfied. The specifically existential idea could be made more precise but scarcely clarified

[74] For the underlying equivalence between *(The event of) Socrates running took place* and *That Socrates ran is true*, see the remarks of Wilfrid Sellars in *The Logical Way of Doing Things*, ed. K. Lambert (1969), p. 229. In the full veridical construction, however, the clause with εἰμί is correlated with a verb of speaking or thinking that has no counterpart in a Type V construction. The parallel drawn in the text applies only between Type V and what I call the *essive* clause of the veridical. See Chapter VII §3.

by saying that a sentence form containing a variable *x* is satisfied for some values of the variable. Perhaps the best formal analogue to the intuitive notion of existence as *presence in the world* is the notion in model theory of *membership in a model*, where a model is a set-theoretical structure consisting of a class of individuals, a class of sub-classes of these individuals, a class of ordered pairs of individuals, and so on. This analogy has its limits, of course, but there does seem to be a similar basic spatial intuition which helps to give meaning to the primitive relation of membership in set theory.[75]

If we accept this metaphor of *presence in the world* for a given individual and more generally for a given descriptive content as offering a natural account of our intuitive notion of a positive semantic value, we can see an obvious connection between the semantic function of εἰμί and the more elementary, descriptive value *to be located (somewhere), to be present (in a place, near a person)* which is characteristic of the locative copula as well as of various locative-existential uses. For example in analyzing Type II in §§ 8–9 we saw that the rhetorical function of this type, namely to introduce its subject into the narrative, can be understood in the light of its logical function as posing or locating the subject in the universe of discourse to which the narrative refers. I suggested that both the rhetorical and the logical functions are made possible by – at least they are often connected with – the elementary use of the verb in statements of place. Although I do not claim that this is the only way in which the semantic function of the verb in Types IV and V is connected with other, more elementary uses of εἰμί, it does seem that some such privileged link between the locative copula and the verb of existence is confirmed not only by the importance of the locative component in Types II and III but also by the intuitive conviction in Greek thought that *being something* entails *being somewhere*, so that what is nowhere is nothing at all.[76]

---

[75] Compare A.A. Fraenkel's remark on the membership relation: "*x* ε *y* may be read '*x* is a *member* (or element) of *y*' or '*x* is contained in *y*' or '*x* belongs to *y*' or '*y* contains *x* (as a member)'" (*Abstract Set Theory*, p. 12). Some logicians like to describe a set in picturesque terms as a group of arbitrary objects surrounded by a kind of lasso. And of course the standard representation for a set shows a pair of brackets {....}, within which lie the members (or rather their symbols).

[76] In view of the apparently Heideggerian flavor of some of my conclusions, I ought to point out that my use of the expression *to be present in the world* is intended to suggest something much more like Wittgenstein's notion of the world as "the totality of facts" (and, I would add, of persons and things), just as my idea of the semantic component is dependent upon Wittgenstein's notion of the pictorial or projective relation between a sentence and the world. Whether any deep connection can be established between these notions and Heidegger's concepts of *in-der-Welt-sein* and *innerweltlich Seiendes* is an important question to which I do not pretend to offer an answer.

There is also something in common between my spatial metaphors of *posing* and *being present in the world* and Husserl's characterization of the "natural standpoint" (*natürliche*

§21. THE PROBLEM OF AN ANALYSIS FOR TYPE VI

My distinction between descriptive content and semantic component encounters an obvious difficulty in the case of Type VI. Whereas the descriptive content of Types IV and V is represented in the syntactic analysis by an operand *sentence*, the analysis of VI yields only a proper name (like *Zeus*) or a common noun (like *the gods*) as representative of the underlying content to which a positive or negative semantic value is to be attached. If, as I have claimed, the properly existential uses of εἰμί must have the second-order syntax of a sentence operator, what is the form of the underlying sentential operand in Type VI: *There is no Zeus, The gods exist*?

Modern logic tends to answer this question differently in the case of Type VI A, where the subject is a proper name like *Zeus*, and in Types VI B and C, where it is a common noun or general term like *gods* or *centaur*. In the second case the subject noun is reconstrued as predicate, so that *The gods exist* is analyzed in the form *There is something which is a god*, i.e. $(\exists x) Fx$. In the case of proper nouns, however, the most common analysis of existential statements takes the form $(\exists x) (x=a)$. Thus *Zeus exists* means *there is something which is identical with Zeus*. Quine's proposal for the elimination of proper names from canonical notation is essentially a proposal to assimilate the latter case to the former, by construing *is Zeus* as formally equivalent to *is a god*. In linguistic terms, this means regarding the nuncupative *I am Charles* as a case of the ordinary nominal copula, like *I am (a) professor*. In every case, and on either reading of *Zeus exists*, the logical transcription gives us an open sentence (with variable *x*) as the descriptive content that is "closed" by the existential quantifier, which assigns to this open sentence a positive or negative semantic value. If we draw the obvious parallel between these formulae and our own syntactic types, we see that the logical construal of Type VI existentials gives them the underlying form of Type IV.

In the long run we need not quarrel with this familiar logical analysis of the deep structure of Type VI. But it has the short-run disadvantage of concealing the genuine oddity of this Type VI use of εἰμί as a sentence form in surface structure. For the logical transcription has the effect of eliminating

---

Einstellung) as an acceptance of the world of objects and persons as *da-seiend, vorhanden* (*Ideen* §§29–31). But for Husserl as for Heidegger the world is relativized to an individual subject, as *there* or *present for me* in experience. By contrast, when I speak of posing objects or contents in the world, I do not mean locating them in *my* world or in that of any particular subject. I mean their presence or location in the intersubjective world of a unified spatio-temporal system, the system we presuppose as the universe of discourse for an interpretation of the texts under discussion.

For further remarks on the connection between the ideas of existence and location, see Chapter VIII §4.

a significant discrepancy between Types IV and VI as they actually occur in Greek. It is characteristic of Type IV uses of εἰμί that the verb does *not* appear as copula in the operand sentence underlying the relative clause: for example, it does not occur in the source of either of the two relative clauses in our sample sentence "(There is no one) who will escape death now, whom the god puts into my hands." The identification of the extra-linguistic subject as a *person* (or, to put it more precisely, the specification of the range of appropriate extra-linguistic subjects as *persons*) is not given by a predicate expression but by the personal pronoun "who" or "whom" (ὅς, ὅν). In the logical rewriting of such a sentence, however, these pronouns will be replaced by a neutral referential *x*, and the specification of this *x* as a *person* can be given only by a predicate expression: "There is no *x*, such that *x* is a man (a Trojan warrior, etc.) and *x* will escape death." By this means *every* example of Type IV comes to have a copula use of *be* or a formal equivalent thereof in its logical transcription. Hence no essential gap appears between such sentences and Type VI existentials: "There is no *x* (some *x*) such that *x* is a god." The latter is simply shorter than the former: its elementary component consists of only one predicate construction (*Fx*), whereas several are present in the formulae corresponding to Type IV. But in the actual use of εἰμί in Greek, the difference between Types VI and IV is not a difference of length or complexity but a difference of syntactic *form*: in Type IV the verb ἔστι serves once only, as semantic operator; in Type VI it seems to serve twice, both as semantic operator and as predicative verb in the underlying operand, if we reconstruct this operand in the way just suggested: "*there is* something such that it *is* a god."

I propose to follow the logical analysis of Type VI sentences in quantification theory to the extent of admitting that every properly existential use of εἰμί must be syntactically second-order.[77] But I shall not follow the logical transcription insofar as it suggests that *every* existential use of εἰμί has a copula *be* in its operand, or insofar as it implies that there is no difference in syntactic form between a copula operand and one with an elementary verb (since both will be represented in logic as *Fx*). In the analysis which I propose for Type VI existentials, we recognize (i) a use of εἰμί as existential sentence

[77] This implies, of course, that *exists* in English is also a complex, second-order predicate and not an elementary verb. The syntactic analysis of *Electrons exist* or *Unicorns do not exist* should in principle be the same as for Type VI sentences in Greek. However, this fact is obscured in English and in other modern languages by the presence of a "technical" verb *exist*, derived from the philosophical vocabulary of medieval Latin, with no living connections either with the copula or with any other forms of be. Far from being a logical advance (as many seem to think it is), the introduction of pseudo-elementary sentences like *Electrons exist* is simply a more misleading way to say *There are electrons*. In the latter case, but not in the former, we recognize an obvious parallel to the sentence-operator use in *There are electrons which....*

operator, as in Type IV, and (ii) a degenerate operand sentence represented by the subject noun in sentences **121–127** in § 18. By describing this operand sentence as degenerate I mean to say that its underlying form cannot be reconstructed with any assurance. We may recognize three or four possible derivations, each of which has something to be said in its favor.

(1) We might assume that the operand is an underlying copula sentence in which the surface subject of ἔστι is construed as predicate, just as in the logical transcription of *F's exist as* (∃x) *Fx*. Thus εἰσὶ θεοί "There are gods" would be decomposed as * ἔστι ὅ τι θεός ἔστι "There is something which is a god." This solution has the advantage of not assuming the presence of any word in the source which is not reconstructible from the product alone. But unfortunately this source does not seem to be a possible sentence in Greek. Hence this analysis, although directly modelled on the logical formula for existence statements, is perhaps the least plausible account of Type VI from the point of view of a theory of Greek syntax (at least on the system used here, which seeks to derive acceptable sentences from acceptable sentences).

(2) Alternatively, we may assume that the operand contains the nominal copula as in the first case, but that the surface subject of εἰμί is also subject (and not predicate) in the underlying operand sentence. The *predicate* of this operand sentence will be suggested somehow by the context or simply left unspecified. Thus in our sample **121**, quoted above in § 18, the Type VI sentence οὐδ' ἔστι Ζεύς "There *is* no Zeus" is immediately preceded by a construction of the same subject noun with *cop N*: ὁ Ζεὺς ... οὐ θεός ἐστιν; "Isn't Zeus a god?" The analysis suggested by this context is: *There is no Zeus such that he (Zeus) is a god.* Unlike solution (1) (which it otherwise resembles), this analysis has the merit of posing as operand for **121** a form like ὁ Ζεὺς θεός ἐστι (or θεός ἐστιν ὁ Ζεύς) that is clearly an acceptable sentence in Greek. And the transformation of this sentence under the existential operator leads to a Type II form like ἔστι Σωκράτης τις σοφὸς ἀνήρ. (See above § 10, sentence **46**.) We could thus derive our sample (οὐδ') ἔστι Ζεύς by deletion from the corresponding Type II form: ἔστι Ζεὺς θεός τις. Similarly for the plural version of VI: εἰσὶ θεοί would be construed as an abridged or deleted form of εἰσὶ θεοί οἱ – εἰσί "There are gods who are (something or other)."

(3) The third possibility is to posit εἰμί in the underlying kernel as a *locative* rather than a nominal copula; that is to say, we assume that the existential ἔστι operates on *N is PN* rather than on *N is A* or *N is N*. This hypothesis would serve to account for – or at least to take account of – the widespread connections between the existential and locative uses of εἰμί. For on this view we would, in effect, interpret Type VI existentials as locative-

existentials, but with the local specification omitted or generalized. *There are gods* would mean *There are gods here, there, or somewhere.* There is a good deal to be said for this suggestion both from the intuitive and from the historical point of view. We have already noted the regular connection between existence and location. Here I simply cite a few indications that help to make it plausible to construe *X is (exists)* as *There is an x which is somewhere.*[78] For example, we seem to have a Type VI existential *fused* with a locative use in an example already quoted in § 6:

26

ἦ ῥα ἔτ᾽ ἐστὲ θεοὶ κατὰ μακρὸν ᾽Ολυμπον
"Surely you gods are still there on high Olympus."

Everywhere one looks one finds evidence in Greek for a smooth and natural transition between the idea of existence and that of location. Thus Critias, in the passage cited as sentence **125** above, after explaining how some cunning innovator introduced the belief that "there is a deity flourishing with imperishable life" (ὡς ἔστι δαίμων ἀφθίτῳ θάλλων βίῳ, a periphrastic variant on Type VI or Type IV), immediately goes on to specify the place in which the gods are said to dwell.[79]

(4) Finally, we might construe the deep structure of Type VI on the assumption that the operand is to be regarded as completely general in form, with the subject expression specified but its predicate left totally undetermined. On this view *There are gods* is to be interpreted as *There are gods who...*, admitting any appropriate relative clause as a possible completion. Thus we leave open the question whether or not εἰμί occurs as copula in the underlying operand clause. If it does occur, then we get interpretations (2) and (3) above as special cases of (4), depending upon whether the verb is nominal or locative copula. But of course hypothesis (4) is much more general, since it need not imply an operand copula at all. According to hypothesis (4) the operand may be of the form *N is A* or *N is PN*; but it may also be of *any* form *NVΩ*. Thus a possible source for εἰσὶ θεοί "There are gods" is εἰσὶ θεοί οἳ πάντα ἴσασι "There are gods who know everything." On this view we simply interpret Type VI as a generalized schema for Type IV, a schema which specifies only the subject expression for the relative clause, but leaves the form of the predicate undetermined – in other words, which specifies a range of values for the extra-linguistic subject that is to

[78] See, e.g. Arist. *Physics* IV.1, 208ᵃ29: τά τε γὰρ ὄντα πάντες ὑπολαμβάνουσιν εἶναί που (τὸ γὰρ μὴ ὂν οὐδαμοῦ εἶναι· ποῦ γάρ ἐστι τραγέλαφος ἢ σφίγξ;)
[79] Critias fr. 25 ναίειν δ᾽ ἔφασκε τοὺς θεοὺς ἐνταῦθ᾽, ἵνα/μάλιστ᾽ ἂν ἐξέπληξεν ἀνθρώπους λέγων/...καλῶς τε τῷ λόγῳ κατῴκισεν/τὸν δαίμον(α) οὗτος κἂν πρέποντι χωρίῳ (D.-K. 88.B 25.27ff.).

satisfy an arbitrary, unspecified condition. In formal terms, the operand for Type VI is *N*, where *N* is the word which appears as subject of the existential εἰμί but the rest of the operand sentence is left quite undetermined.

In an earlier study I proposed alternative (3), the locative-existential source, as the most natural analysis for Type VI in Greek; and evidence has been cited by Lyons in support of a similar interpretation of existential sentences in many languages.[80] As against analysis (4), either (2) or (3) has the advantage of suggesting why it is precisely the verb εἰμί that appears as existential sentence operator in Type VI (and by extension, in Type IV as well). If we take a copula sentence as operand for the existential operator, we can regard this operator as lexically (though of course not syntactically) derived from the correlative elementary use of the verb as locative or nominal copula. Now, without abandoning the case for analysis (3) with its strong intuitive support in the connections between existence and location, I would like here to insist that the more general hypothesis (4) must also figure in any full account of the psychology or phenomenology of existence statements. For the freethinker who propounds a sentence like **120**, οὐδ' ἔστι Ζεύς "There *is* no Zeus", does not mean simply *There is no Zeus on Olympus, nor anywhere else* – though it may be correct to say that this is what he means *primarily* or that this is the most natural paraphrase of what he says. But the sentence itself means more. The speaker intends to deny that *anything* could be truly said about Zeus, that he is a possible subject for any reliable elementary statements: the stories of priests and poets are all a pack of lies. Despite its intuitive connections with location, ἔστι in Type VI functions as a pure semantic operator: it posits, and οὐκ ἔστι refuses to posit, an extra-linguistic subject of a specified kind (Zeus, god, centaur) *for any predication whatsoever*. The generality of this function of existence statements is best brought out by analysis (4), which leaves the form of the operand quite undetermined except for a specification of the subject noun.

Note that on this view, and indeed on any view considered here, the syntactical function of ἔστι in Type VI is essentially the same as in Type IV. In both types we have the existential sentence operator proper. But in Type IV the underlying structure is more transparent, since we are provided with a definite operand in the relative clause. In Type VI this operand clause has been generalized in a way that would be indicated in logic by the expression for a sentential variable or place-holder but which is indicated in natural language by *the omission of the clause as such*.[81]

---

[80] See "The Greek Verb *be*", pp. 257f.; Lyons, *Introduction*, 389f., *Foundations of Language 3* (1967), pp. 390ff.
[81] In Leśniewski's Ontology, singular and plural examples of Type VI are rendered differently, though both make use of his analogue to the (generalized) copula. Thus *Zeus*

§22. ON THE HISTORICAL ORIGINS OF TYPE VI

At the end of § 18 I suggested that Type VI, although independently attested in the Rigveda and in fifth-century Greek (and presumably elsewhere as well), appears to represent not an inherited sentence form from the common I.-E. tradition but rather a linguistic innovation produced by the rise of theological speculation. If, as proposed in the last section, we regard Type VI as a kind of generalization of the existential sentence operator that occurs in its clearest form in Type IV but also occurs less transparently in Types II and III, then the presence of Types II–IV in the common I.-E. tradition is sufficient to account for the parallel but independent creation of Type VI in two or more cognate languages. (We may compare the late and independent development of a verb *have* which replaces some or all of the old possessive uses of *es- in Greek, Latin, Hittite, Germanic, etc.) In this section I shall support my thesis of the late development of Type VI in Greek by considering some apparent counter-examples in Homer. In the next section we shall see that even in the mid-fifth-century prose of Herodotus there is no definite trace of Type VI.

When we analyze the use of εἰμί in a mixed or borderline case (such as a copula-existential or a locative-possessive) we find that several distinct constructions are realized in a single occurrence of the verb: the syntax is as it were overdetermined. (For a complex example of this, see **130** below in § 23.) The cases we are now concerned with represent the opposite phenomenon, where the verb seems to be *underconstrued*, so that we are tempted to regard it as an absolute existential use of Type VI. In § 13 we encountered a superficial example of this in **78** ἔστι μὲν ὕλη/παντοίη "There is timber of all sorts". Ignoring the optional adjectival adjunct, we might be tempted to take this as an instance of Type VI. But that would certainly be a mistake. The context of **78** in Athena's description of Ithaca makes it quite clear that the locative specification ἐν "here (in Ithaca)" is elliptically understood from the preceding lines; and ἐν occurs again in the next verse. There is no doubt that **78** is an ordinary case of the locative-existential.

In other cases the approximation to Type VI is less superficial. Consider ἦν δέ τις Εὐχήνωρ "There was a certain Euchenor" in **40** of § 7. In the three

---

exists becomes $(\exists x)$ Zeus ε x, i.e. something is true of Zeus, or "Zeus" is the subject for at least one true elementary sentence. This corresponds in its generality to my suggestion (4) above, although it has the superficial form of suggestion (2). The plural subtype, on the other hand, (*The gods exist*) is interpreted along the lines of suggestion (1) with *gods* in predicate position, as in classical quantification theory: $(\exists x)$ x ε god(s). Note that solution (4) cannot be extended to the plural form in Leśniewski's system because of his conditions on the epsilon: for x ε y to be true, x must be an unshared (i.e. singular) name. The existence of x is specified here not by the quantifier but again by this same condition, namely, that the expression to the left of "ε" must be unshared but *non-empty*.

parallel sentences quoted there – **38, 39, 41** – we have the locative or para-locative expression "among the Trojans." It is natural to regard **40** as an abridged version of the same formula, and hence to reconstruct a similar locative syntax: "There was a certain Euchenor (among the Achaeans)." This means construing **40** as a locative-existential. It is important to note that the words "There was a certain Euchenor" do not stand alone here: they serve to introduce the subject for the following predicates ("son of the prophet Polyidos, rich and noble", etc.) as well as for the demonstrative-relative clause which resumes the narrative ("him Paris struck"). Hence the structure of **40** is in any case closer to Type II than to the syntactically in-dependent, generalized statements of existence of Type VI.

Nevertheless, an initial clause like ἦν δέ τις Εὐχήνωρ, without any explicit locative or paralocative specification, shows how the sentence pattern of Type VI can arise in Greek (and presumably in other I.-E. languages) as a natural form of words which at least *suggests* the absolute use of the verb as existential predicate. And the same is true for other cases where a locative or paralocative specification remains implicit.[82] I cite two more examples, where we have at best a generalized locative specification understood from the larger context.

128 *Od.* 9.425

ἄρσενες ὄιες ἦσαν ἐϋτρεφέες, δασύμαλλοι,
καλοί τε μεγάλοι τε, ἰοδνεφὲς εἶρος ἔχοντες·
τοὺς ἀκέων συνέεργον

"Some rams there were of a good breed, thick in the fleece, handsome and large, which bore a dark gray wool. These I quietly bound."

(Palmer)

129 *Od.* 10.552

'Ελπήνωρ δέ τις ἔσκε νεώτατος, οὔτε τι λίην
ἄλκιμος ἐν πολέμῳ οὔτε φρεσὶν ᾗσιν ἀρηρώς,
ὅς μοι ἄνευθ᾽ ἑτάρων ἱεροῖς ἐν δώμασι Κίρκης
... κατελέξατο

"There was a certain Elpenor, the youngest of them all, a man not very staunch in fight nor sound of understanding, who, parted from his mates, lay down to sleep upon the magic house of Circe."

(Palmer)

In both cases we have the appearance of an absolute construction for the

---

[82] See ῥωχμὸς ἔην γαίης "There was a break in the ground (sc. in the racecourse)" in **110** and φύλλων ἔην χύσις, "There was a pile of leaves (sc. in the wood, under the inter-twined olive trees)" in **109**, both quoted in §16.

verb εἰμί, but in neither case do we have a general statement of existence. What is asserted is the *presence* of an extra-linguistic subject (or subjects) relative to a given situation, not their absolute presence somewhere in the world. The rams of **128** are present with Odysseus in the Cyclops' cave, among the other sheep mentioned a few verses earlier (ὄεσσι in 9.418). Elpenor in **129** is located in the house of Circe, among the companions of Odysseus mentioned in the preceding verse (ἑταίρους 10.551). In both cases these individuals serve as subject for immediately following descriptive predicates, and in both cases they are taken up into the narrative by relative-demonstrative clauses. As in the case of Type IIB, sentences like **128** and **129** seem to have the function of situating an individual in a given spatial and human (or animal) environment, so that the narrator may refer to this individual as an agent in the following action.[83] These sentences are best regarded as elliptical or degenerate cases of Type II. Their function is not to assert existence as such but to present or introduce their subjects by implicitly locating them within a previously mentioned place or group.

The fact remains that sentences like **128** and **129** represent a sentence pattern where the syntax of εἰμί is not quite clear and where one might well describe the construction as absolute. And this is also true for the use of ἔστι (ὅς τις...) as existential sentence operator in Type IV. Even in Type V the surface syntax of the verb is often absolute, for example, in ὅμαδος ἦν "There was an uproar." Although a deeper analysis shows that the use of the verb in Types IV and V is not "independent" of its construction with an operand sentence, the superficial analogy between the absolute use of εἰμί here and in sentences like **128** and **129** naturally gives rise to the impression that we have in Homer a use of the verb alone as existential predicate. It is this superficial impression of an absolute existential use in Homer which explains why philologists have failed to recognize the originality of a sentence type like εἰσὶ θεοί "The gods exist." And from the historical point of view this surface analogy to the existential predicate in Homer permits us to understand how the new Type VI could arise as a natural use of the verb in Greek, when general questions of existence are explicitly under discussion. And since Types IV and V probably belong to the uses of *es-* which Greek has inherited from earlier I.-E., it is easy to see how similar analogies could produce a parallel to Type VI in other I.-E. languages such as Sanskrit.[84]

---

[83] So again immediately after **128** for the ram which will carry Odysseus himself, 9.432 ἀρνειὸς γὰρ ἔην, μήλων ὄχ' ἄριστος ἁπάντων,/ τοῦ... λαβών "There was a ram, by far the best of all the flock, whose back I grasped" (Palmer).

[84] Another parallel to the absolute existential use of Type VI which occurs in early Greek, though perhaps not in other I.-E. languages, is the vital use of Type I. Thus θεοὶ αἰεὶ ἐόντες, which I take to mean "the gods who live forever", i.e. the ἀθάνατοι, could easily be reinterpreted as "the gods who exist forever." As I have pointed out (above, p. 299),

Still, it seems clear that Type VI as such does not occur in Homer. We recognize three characteristic features of Type VI: (a) the syntactical independence of the verb from surrounding sentences and sentential adjuncts (in contrast to the "bound" use of the existential verb in Types II and IV), (b) the syntactic simplicity of the subject term as a first-order nominal (in contrast to the nominalized subject of Type V), and (c) the semantic generality of the posing of the subject, that is to say, the assertion of existence independently of any limitation to a given time, place, or environment (in contrast to the vital use of Type I, which asserts that a person is or is not alive at a given time). It is this third feature which is uniquely distinctive of Type VI as a generalized statement of existence.

§23. APPENDIX ON MIXED EXISTENTIAL USES AND ON SOME APPARENT APPROXIMATIONS TO TYPE VI IN HERODOTUS

I offer Types I–V as an adequate basis for the analysis of all existential uses of the verb in Homer. Together with Type VI, they seem to suffice for an analysis of the existential uses in Greek generally, though a test of this claim would involve a study of much more material than can be considered here. And when we turn to the analysis of particular examples encountered at random, we must naturally take account of the phenomenon of mixed or overconstrued uses, where a single occurrence of the verb illustrates two or more distinct sentence types. Let us consider one Homeric passage that shows a complex interaction of sentence types for two consecutive occurrences of εἰμί.

130 *Od.* 19.344–348

οὐδὲ γυνὴ ποδὸς ἅψεται ἡμετέροιο	344
τάων αἵ τοι δῶμα κάτα δρήστειραι ἔασιν,	345
εἰ μή τις γρηῦς ἐστι παλαιή, κεδνὰ ἰδυῖα,	346
ἥ τις δὴ τέτληκε τόσα φρεσὶν ὅσσα τ' ἐγώ περ·	347
τῇ δ' οὐκ ἂν φθονέοιμι ποδῶν ἅψασθαι ἐμεῖο.	348

"Foot of mine shall not be touched by any of these maids who serve the palace – unless indeed there be some aged woman, sober-minded, one who has borne as many sorrows as myself. It would not trouble me that such a one should touch my feet."

(Palmer)

The construction of the first occurrence of the verb (ἔασιν in verse 345)

---

the distinction between a Type I and a Type VI use is hard to draw even in principle for the Homeric expression ἐσσομένοισι "for men to come."

is (i) possessive with τοι, (ii) locative with δῶμα κάτα, and (iii) copulative with δρήστειραι. There may also be an existential (i.e. locative-possessive-existential) nuance latent here and brought out by the second occurrence in the next verse. Note that Palmer's translation does not render ἔασιν either as copula or verb of possession but (in effect) construes its syntax (iii) as that of a verb operator with the agent noun δρήστειραι and thus renders the underlying verbal idea "(those maids) who serve", instead of the surface construction with copula: "who are servants." Although the locative phrase in (ii) is construed with ἔασιν in the surface syntax of **130**, the translation correctly reflects the deeper connections of this phrase with the verb underlying δρήστειρα. This is still clearer in Lattimore's version, "those (women) such as do your work for you in your palace," where we also have a rendering of the possessive dative in (i).

In the second occurrence of our verb, ἐστί in verse 346, we again have the convergence of at least three distinct constructions: (i) the possessive, with τοι understood from the preceding line (and emphatically reinforced by Penelope's answer at verse 353: ἔστι δέ μοι γρηῦς), (ii) an underlying copula construction with the following adjectives παλαιή, κέδνα ἰδυῖα, and (iii) an existential sentence operator of Type IV with the following clause "unless there is one who has borne sorrows", as brought out in the translation.[85] Furthermore, if we understand an implicit partitive or locative construction in verse 346, as the context encourages us to do, the use of the sentence operator ἔστι here approximates to Type II: "If (among the maidservants in your house) there is an old woman." Summing up, then, in the second occurrence in 346 we can count a mixed case of Types II and IV combined with a (locative-?) possessive-existential use of εἰμί; while in the first occurrence in 345 we have a locative-possessive (-existential?) use combined with a nominal copula.

This detailed analysis of a passage with two overconstrued occurrences of εἰμί makes clear that my theoretical description of sentence types involves an inevitable and desirable simplification, since it separates out constructions that are blended and defines boundaries that are blurred in the living usage of the language. Out of some 250 Homeric occurrences quoted in this study, and some 2000 occurrences which I have *not* quoted, perhaps half involve some overlap of the sort just illustrated.[86] And the same is of course true

---

[85] To be properly counted with Type IV the relative clause must be restrictive, not appositive or merely conjoined, as is the case in Penelope's response at 354: (ἔστι δέ μοι γρηῦς ...) ἥ κεῖνον... τρέφεν "There is one, she who nursed Odysseus."

[86] Since the copula construction is numerically predominant, the most frequent forms of overlap will be between (i) cop A and cop N, where a predicate noun is accompanied by an adjective, (ii) either or both of these together with a locative construction, (iii) one or more of the former plus a possessive (dative) construction.

for occurrences of the verb in post-Homeric literature. To give an intelligible description of the uses of εἰμί is precisely to make such a theoretical simplification. The test for adequacy of this description is not that we find more pure cases than mixed ones but rather that (i) the constructions recognized by the theory as "pure" sentence types must be defined with sufficient precision, in formal or syntactic terms, so that we can in general give a definite answer to the question: is a particular occurrence of εἰμί an instance of this theoretical use?, and (ii) in analyzing the syntax of other attested occurrences we do not require any new sentence types not recognized by our general description of the uses of the verb. I claim that my account satisfies the second requirement, and that it satisfies the first as well, except in the "mixed" cases of copula-existential and locative-existential. In these cases the copula or locative construction is defined precisely enough, but the existential component remains vaguely lexical, intuitive, or rhetorical. I do not think much further progress can be made here until we have a satisfactory over-all theory of quantifier words and quantifier morphemes (numbers, plural endings, indefinite pronouns like τις, words like "many", "other", etc.), which does not seem to be available even for English. Assuming that we had such a theory, it would probably turn out that the existential nuance in a copula sentence like εἷς κοίρανος ἔστω "Let there be one ruler" or "Let one (man) be ruler" is not a function of the verb εἰμί at all but of the quantifier word "one". I suggest, in short, that the verb *be* is no more (and no less) existential in the sentence just quoted than the verb *go* in the parallel sentence εἷς ἐρχέσθω "Let one (man) go" or (in a more archaic style) "Let there go one man." If we speak here of an existential nuance for *be* but not for *go*, it is because the same verb in other uses is existential in a clear sense, e.g. in my Type IV. It is for similar reasons that we regularly count the English phrase "there is..." but not "there goes..." as existential.

It is quite unfeasible to support my claim of adequacy by any extended sampling of the post-Homeric literature. The wider our corpus becomes, the greater will be the number not only of overlap or dubious cases but also of slight variants on the types here defined. For instance, there is no exact Homeric analogue to Alcman 1.36 (Page): ἔστι τις σιῶν (=θεῶν) τίσις "There is somehow retribution from the gods", nor to Sophocles *O.T.* 369: (Teresias) εἴπερ τί γ' ἐστὶ τῆς ἀληθείας σθένος. (Oedipus) ἀλλ' ἔστι, πλὴν σοί, "(I think to speak on in this way) if there is any strength in truth." "There is, but not for you." Both of these passages represent variants of Type V which are moving in the general direction of Type VI. (They are of course not standard examples of Type VI, since the subject in each case is a second-order nominal, a *nomen actionis*.) It would be easy to find new versions of our types, with or without direct roots in Homeric usage. (See the examples of post-Homeric forms of Types II, IV and V in §§10, 14 and 15.) Thus the Type V form οὐδὲν γὰρ ἄν μου ὄφελος εἴη "There would not be much good in me (if I could not do this)" (Plato, *Euthyphro* 4 E 9; cf. *Apol.* 28 B 7, *Crito* 46 A 2, 54 A 9, etc.) which is so common in Attic, is an exact parallel to our specimen 9 for Type V, though it does not occur in this form in Homer.[87]

I close this survey with a brief glance at Herodotus' use of existential εἰμί. The History of Herodotus may be taken as the earliest extant corpus of Greek prose, just as the Homeric poems are the earliest corpus of Greek generally. Although roughly contemporary with Protagoras, his language seems largely free of Sophistic influence of the sort which becomes predominant after 430 B.C. (e.g. in Euripides, Aristophanes, and Thucydides). As far as I can see, his nine books contain no authentic example of our Type VI. We may consider as a representative sample the 13 passages listed in Powell's *Lexicon to Herodotus* under the title "ἔστι III.1. emphatic *lives, exists.*" This may serve as a rough control on the adequacy of our sentence types as applied to post-Homeric prose. We may also see how a non-technical literary language approaches our Type VI without actually illustrating it. I list passages in the order in which they occur in Powell, and suggest an analysis after each example.

131 Hdt. I.120.2

ἔστι τε ὁ παῖς καὶ περίεστι

(In answer to the question εἰ ἐπέζωσε καὶ μὴ ἀπέθανε πρότερον, "if the boy lived on and did not die earlier," he answered:) "The boy lives and survives."

This is a clear case of Type I.

132 I. 210.2

Ὦ βασιλεῦ, μὴ εἴη ἀνὴρ Πέρσης γεγονὼς ὅστις τοι ἐπιβουλεύσειε, εἰ δ' ἔστι, ἀπόλοιτο ὡς τάχιστα

"King, may there be no Persian born who would conspire against you; but if there is, let him perish as soon as possible."

The general form is Type IV with operator and operand in the optative, as in **86** above in §14: "Let there be someone (no one) who...;" but this coincides with a periphrastic construction for the perfect optative of γίγνομαι.

---

[87] μοῦ ὄφελός ἐστι ← (ἐγὼ) ὀφέλλω, just like νεκύων κλαγγὴ ἦν ← νέκυες ἔκλαγξαν. In Homer we several times find a predicate use of ὄφελος with the suppletive γίγνομαι in much the same sense, e.g. *Il.* 13.236 αἴ κ' ὄφελός τι γενώμεθα. The Attic use quoted above could also be derived as a transform of this copula sentence rather than of the underlying verb ὀφέλλω. The Attic Type V construction of ὄφελός ἐστι is foreshadowed (but with a different sense) in *Il.* 22.513 οὐδὲν σοί γ' ὄφελος (εἶναι).

Furthermore, the contrast of birth and death may suggest a vital sense for εἰ δ' ἔστι: "if such a man lives."

133 II.28.1

 ταῦτα μέν νυν ἔστω ὡς ἔστι τε καὶ ὡς ἀρχὴν ἐγένετο

 (After various alternative explanations for the flood of the Nile:)
 "Let these things be as they are and as they were (occurred)
 from the beginning." (But no one claims to know the sources
 of the river.)

This is a variant on the veridical construction. See Chapter VII and **139** below.

134 III.155.2

 ὁ δὲ εἶπε· οὐκ ἔστι οὗτος ἀνὴρ ὅτι μὴ σύ, τῷ ἐστι δύναμις
 τοσαύτη ἐμὲ δὴ ὧδε διαθεῖναι

 "He said: There is no man, besides yourself, who has power
 enough to treat me in this way."

134 is one of the rare cases of Type IV where εἰμί occurs in the relative clause. Note, however, that its construction here is possessive, not copulative. (See above, p. 281, n. 47.)

135 IV.192.2

 ταῦτά τε δὴ αὐτόθι ἐστὶ θηρία καὶ τά περ τῇ ἄλλῃ, πλὴν ἐλάφου
 τε καὶ ὑὸς ἀγρίου· ἔλαφος δὲ καὶ ὗς ἄγριος ἐν Λιβύῃ πάμπαν
 οὐκ ἔστι

 "All these beasts are found here [sc. in Libya], and likewise
 those belonging to other countries, except the stag and the wild-
 boar; but neither stag nor wild boar are found in any part of
 Libya."

             (tr. Rawlinson)

Such reports on the fauna of a country naturally contain repeated examples of the locative-existential. The uses of εἰμί in **135** are typical of this and similar contexts in Herodotus. (See, e.g. the immediately preceding examples in IV.191.4ff.) The final example in **135** is an ordinary locative-existential, but (as we have noted above, pp. 273f.) a strong denial of presence for a species in a given region *seems* to differ only in degree from a general denial of existence as in Type VI.

136 VI.74.2

 ἐν δὲ ταύτῃ τῇ πόλι λέγεται εἶναι ὑπ' Ἀρκάδων τὸ Στυγὸς
 ὕδωρ, καὶ δὴ καὶ ἔστι τοιόνδε τι

 "In this city [sc. Nonacris], as the Arcadians say, are the waters
 of Styx. And in fact there is (or "it is"?) something of the
 following sort."

The first occurrence (εἶναι) is a normal example of the locative-existential; the construction of the second (ἔστι) is more ambiguous. It can be taken either as an emphatic reiteration of the same use with a veridical nuance ("there is in fact", in contrast to "there is said to be"), or simply as an emphatic copula with τοιόνδε τι as predicate.

137 VI.86. δ

> Γλαύκου νῦν οὔτε τι ἀπόγονον ἔστι οὐδὲν οὔτ᾽ ἱστίη οὐδεμία νομιζομένη εἶναι Γλαύκου, ἐκτέτριπταί τε πρόρριζος ἐκ Σπάρτης
>
> "There is at present no offspring of Glaucus, nor is there any family known as his – root and branch has he been removed from Sparta."

> (after Rawlinson)

This is perhaps as close as Herodotus ever comes to a Type VI existential. Still, the verb has neither the syntactic nor the semantic independence that is characteristic of statements like "The gods do not exist." The local specification ("in Sparta") is clearly implied, and the first use is also a variant on the possessive construction, with genitive for dative of possessor: "Glaucus at the present time has not a single descendant" (Rawlinson). The second occurrence can be construed as a variant on Type IV, with a participial clause in place of the restrictive relative: ⟨οὐκ ἔστι⟩ ἱστίη οὐδεμία νομιζομένη (=ἥτις νομίζεται).

The next two passages are cited together by Powell, although the syntax of the verb is really not parallel in the two cases:

138 III.17.2

> ἐπὶ δὲ τοὺς Αἰθίοπας κατόπτας πρῶτον (sc. ἀπέστελλε), ὀψομένους τε τὴν ἐν τούτοισι τοῖσι Αἰθίοψι λεγομένην εἶναι ἡλίου τράπεζαν εἰ ἔστι ἀληθέως.... ἡ δὲ τράπεζα τοῦ ἡλίου τοιήδε τις λέγεται εἶναι
>
> (Cambyses sent) spies first against the Aethiopians, to see if there is really the table of the Sun which is said to be among these Aethiopians.... The table of the Sun is said to be one of the following sort.

The first occurrence (εἶναι) is the locative-existential so common in Herodotus; the second (εἰ ἔστι) is an abbreviated repetition of the same construction, with a veridical nuance (and the suggestion of a veridical construction) added by ἀληθέως and by the contrast with λεγομένην εἶναι ("whether there was really what is called the table of the sun in Ethiopia," Rawlinson). The final εἶναι is of course the nominal copula with τοιήδε τις as predicate.

139 IV.195.2

> ταῦτα εἰ μὲν ἔστι ἀληθέως οὐκ οἶδα, τὰ δὲ λέγεται γράφω
>
> (After a report on a lake where girls dredge gold dust with birds' feathers:) "If this be true, I know not; I but write what is said."
>
> (Rawlinson)

139 is a variant of the veridical construction, with the nuance of truth underlined by ἀληθέως. Note that the antecedent of ταῦτα is not a concrete object, like the table of the Sun which is the most plausible subject of εἰ ἔστι ἀληθέως in **138**, but a sentential subject (namely, the content of the preceding sentences), just as in **133** above.

Powell's list contains three examples of the idiom οὐκ ἔστι μηχανή οὐδεμία as a variant on Type IV. (Other modifications of this Type appear in his Lexicon under ἔστι II: ἔστι τῇ, οὐκ ἔστι ὅτε οὐ, etc.)

140 I.209.5

> οὐκ ὦν ἔστι μηχανὴ ἀπὸ τῆς ὄψιος ταύτης οὐδεμία τὸ μὴ οὐ κεῖνον ἐπιβουλεύειν ἐμοί
>
> "On the basis of this dream there is no chance that he is not plotting against me."

141 II.181.3

> καὶ ἔστι τοι οὐδεμία μηχανὴ μὴ οὐκ ἀπολωλέναι κάκιστα γυναικῶν πασέων
>
> "And there is for you no chance not to die most miserably of all women."

In both **140** and **141** the operand sentence is presented as an infinitival rather than a relative clause; and, unlike the standard examples of Type IV, the subject of ἔστι here is not the subject of the operand clause. (For Homeric parallels on the latter point see above, §14, **95** and **96**.) In **141** the subject of the operand appears as "possessive" dative with the operator (ἔστι τοι).

142 VIII.57.2

> ἀλλ᾽ εἴ τις ἔστι μηχανή, ἴθι καὶ πειρῶ διαχέαι τά βεβουλευμένα
>
> "But if there is any way, go and try to annul the decision (sc. to withdraw the fleet from Salamis)."

In this variant on Type IV the operator occurs as an elliptical *if*-clause, and its operand ("to annul the decision") is taken up in a different construction with the verb operator "try".

As the last item in Powell's list we have an ordinary locative-existential with an emphatic repetition of the verb:

143 V.67.1

ἡρώιον γὰρ ἦν καὶ ἔστι ἐν αὐτῇ τῇ ἀγορῇ τῶν Σικυωνίων
Ἀδρήστου τοῦ Ταλαοῦ

"For there was and is in the very market-place of Sicyon a hero
shrine of Adrastus son of Talaus."

In sum, we find no radically new sentence types for the existential verb,
though some variants – for example, on Type IV in **140–142** – depart rather
far from their Homeric prototypes. Our Type I is represented in **131** and
perhaps as a secondary overlap elsewhere, for example in **132**. Variants on
Type IV are frequent, as in **132** and **133**. In **133** and **139** we have variants
on the veridical construction, whose characteristic syntactic form was not
recognized by Powell. Especially common is the locative-existential in **135**,
136, 138, 143 and probably in **137**. These locative-existential uses, which
occur constantly in Herodotus because of the very nature of his narrative,
correspond roughly to the Homeric Type IIA. Our Type III is naturally
absent from this sample since Powell's entry concerns the singular ἔστι
only, whereas Type III by definition takes a plural form. Type V happens
to be absent, but can be paralleled elsewhere in Herodotus.[88] Only in one
case (**137**) do we find a dubious approximation to Type VI. Elsewhere, for
example in **138**, the appearance of a Type VI sentence is altogether illusory,
since a definite locative completion is clearly implied by the context.

This sample from Herodotus thus confirms our conclusion from Homer.
The absolute use of εἰμί as existential predicate in Type VI – the syntactically
independent construction of the verb in a two-word sentence with a first-
order nominal as subject – has some analogues and approximations in
normal usage. But it becomes a fixed sentence form only in technical or
philosophical prose, just as sentences like *There are no unicorns* or *Electrons
exist* rarely occur outside of philosophic contexts in English. The first and
perhaps the only natural use for such sentences in non-technical discourse
is in the case of religious or mythical entities, from Zeus to Santa Claus,
whose reality is seriously maintained by some members of the community
and doubted or denied by others.

---

[88] See, e.g. I.11.5 ἐκ τοῦ αὐτοῦ μὲν χωρίου ἡ ὁρμὴ ἔσται. In general Herodotus seems
to prefer γίγνεσθαι in this construction with action nouns as subject: I.9.1 μή τί τοι ἐξ
αὐτῆς γένηται βλάβος; I.18.1 ἐν τοῖσι τρώματα μεγάλα διφάσια Μιλησίων ἐγένετο, etc.

CHAPTER VII

THE VERIDICAL USE

§1. VERIDICAL NUANCE AND VERIDICAL CONSTRUCTION. DIFFERENCE IN PRINCIPLE BETWEEN THE LATTER AND THE COPULA AND EXISTENTIAL USES OF THE VERB

In this chapter we survey a range of uses in which the Greek verb *be* has the sense (i.e. the translation value) "be true", "be so", or "be the case". This is what I call the veridical *nuance* or veridical *lexical value* of εἰμί. The term "veridical use" will apply to any sentence in which εἰμί has this lexical value. In accordance with the general method of this study, I shall try as far as possible to correlate this lexical value with one or more definite sentence forms. The most important of these is the sentence pattern I call the *veridical construction*, where a clause with εἰμί is joined to a clause with a verb of saying (less often, with a verb of thinking or perceiving) in a comparative structure that has the general form "Things are as you say". In Sections 2 and 3 I define this construction and show how it underlies many examples where the verb has a veridical value. In other cases we see that the veridical nuance is associated with an opposition between *being* and *seeming*; that is, we find a sentence pattern in which a construction with εἰμί is paralleled by and contrasted with a construction with δοκεῖν, φαίνεσθαι, or a verb of similar meaning. There are still other circumstances in which a veridical nuance is less strongly marked but where a translation of εἰμί as "is truly" can still be justified; for example, where εἰμί occurs in an indirect question or in an object clause governed by a verb meaning "to know," such as οἶδα. (See below, pp. 341f. and 351.) Only the first of these three patterns is covered by the term "veridical construction". In all three cases, I suggest, the veridical value of εἰμί rests upon the basic verbal function of truth claim discussed in Chapter V §§1–2.

It has long been recognized that our verb may in some passages be translated as "is true", "is so", or "is the case", in other words that it may by itself bear the meaning which is more fully paraphrased in Greek as ἐστὶν ἀληθές or, occasionally, ἔστιν ἀληθῶς.[1] The importance of this veridical

---

[1] For εἶναι ἀληθῆ, see the quotation from Melissus in Chapter VI p. 305, sentence **127**; for ἔστι ἀληθέως in Herodotus, see pp. 328f. sentences **138** and **139**. Related forms in Attic are cited below, §5 sentences **32–33**.

nuance is called to our attention by Aristotle, who lists it as one of the four philosophically relevant senses or uses of the verb *be*:

Met. Δ 7, 1017ᵃ31.

> ἔτι τὸ εἶναι σημαίνει καὶ τὸ ἔστιν ὅτι ἀληθές, τὸ δὲ μὴ εἶναι ὅτι οὐκ ἀληθὲς ἀλλὰ ψεῦδος
>
> "And also *being* and *is* signify that (something) is true, *not being* signifies that it is not true but false."

Examples of the verb with this sense, above all in the participle, are duly noted by Liddell and Scott (s.v. εἰμί A.III). Furthermore, comparative grammarians have pointed out that the neuter of the participle **sont-* from **es-* (i.e. the form corresponding to ἐόν or ὄν in Greek) serves quite generally in I.-E. languages to mean "the truth" or "what is the case". Derivative forms of this participle, cognate with ὄντως in Greek, *satya-* in Sanscrit, and *sooth* in English, still furnish the ordinary terms for "true" in several modern languages of India and Scandinavia.[2]

This veridical nuance for εἰμί and its participial derivatives, and more generally for **es-* in I.-E., is thus a matter of common knowledge; it is only the term "veridical" which is relatively new. But the veridical construction as a syntactic form, or a family of closely related forms, has apparently not been previously identified. It is, I suggest, this particular construction which exhibits the veridical value of εἰμί in its purest form and shows most clearly how the verb serves to convey the notion of truth. But although I want to put this veridical construction at the center of our analysis, we shall be concerned more generally with any occurrence of εἰμί with the lexical value "is true" or the like, regardless of the syntactic form of the sentence. So understood, a veridical use of εἰμί may sometimes coincide with an existential sentence and even with a copula construction. Thus Aristotle's example in *Met.*Δ.7, where he claims that ἔστι means "is true", is from the grammatical point of view an ordinary instance of the adjectival copula: ἔστι Σωκράτης μουσικός "Socrates *is* musical, he really is." The initial position of the copula has no syntactic significance. Insofar as we speak of Aristotle's example as a veridical use of εἰμί, we are referring only to the lexical nuance of the verb and not to a distinct sentence form.

Even in this wide lexical sense, however, the veridical use remains quite rare. It accounts for no more than 2 percent of all occurrences of the verb

---

[2] See H. Frisk, "'Wahrheit' und 'Lüge' in den indogermanischen Sprachen", *Götesborgs Hogskolas Arsskrift*, 41.3 (1935), 4ff. Notice the phrase *satyam ast* "really is (exists)" in the quotation from the *Rigveda*, Chapter VI, p. 304.

in the samples for which I have figures.[3] It may seem odd to devote a separate chapter to such an infrequent use of the verb, when the more common possessive and potential constructions were treated together with the existential verb in Chapter VI. But the theoretical interest of a given use cannot be measured by the statistics for its frequency of occurrence. If I single out the veridical in this way, that is because its distinct identity and significance have generally been overlooked.

I have elsewhere emphasized the importance of the veridical *nuance* for the development of the concept of Being in Greek philosophy beginning with Parmenides.[4] Considering the matter now from a more strictly linguistic point of view, I want to show that a careful definition of the veridical *construction* is equally fundamental for an adequate theory of the verb *be*. The linguistic importance of this use is suggested by the fact that the veridical lexical value, and probably also the veridical sentence form, is a prehistoric use of the verb *es-*, a heritage in Greek from common I.-E. And it is this sentence form, perhaps, that indicates better than any other evidence the inadequacy of the traditional dichotomy between copula and existential verb. For although the veridical use may overlap or coincide with existential and copula uses, the typical cases of the veridical *construction* are neither existential nor copulative.

In §20 of the last chapter I pointed out that the logical or semantic function of the verb in this construction is parallel to that of existential Types IV and V. In our concluding chapter we shall consider how the copula, existential, and veridical uses fit together in a system with a certain underlying conceptual unity. But first of all we must define the veridical construction in order to distinguish it clearly from the copula and existential sentence forms described in Chapters IV and VI. It cannot in general be identified with a copula use because the syntax of the veridical is typically "absolute", with no nominal or locative predicate expression. And it does not fall under any recognized existential type since the underlying subject of the verb is sentential rather than nominal in form; that is to say, the subject of εἰμί is represented by one or more distinct sentences in the context. Above all, in its fullest form the veridical construction is characterized by an explicit comparison between εἰμί and a verb of saying or thinking.

---

[3] I count 12 examples of the veridical use in 562 occurrences of εἰμί in *Iliad* 1–12. My short samples from Lysias and Xenophon show a ratio ranging from 0 to 2 examples of the veridical in 100 occurrences. Powell's *Lexicon to Herodotus* lists only a dozen instances of the veridical use in 923 occurrences of the participle ἐών, ἐοῦσα, ἐόν.

[4] "Greek Verb 'to be'", pp. 249–54, and "The Thesis of Parmenides", *Review of Metaphysics*, 22 (1969), pp. 700–24; cf. "More on Parmenides", *ibid.* 23 (1969), 333–40.

§2. ILLUSTRATION AND FORMAL DEFINITION OF
THE VERIDICAL CONSTRUCTION

In its most common appearance in classic Attic, the veridical use consists of a two-word sentence of either of the following forms: (a) ἔστι ταῦτα "That is true", or (b) ἔστι οὕτω "It is so." Both of these occur as standard forms of assent in the Platonic dialogues, for example. With these two forms are associated (c) a use of the neuter participle τὸ ὄν (Ionic ἐόν) or τὰ ὄντα for "the truth" or "the facts." The participial construction will be discussed in Section 4. The first object of our attention must be the more elementary forms with finite verb. We shall see that both (a) and (b) point to a fuller sentence form that permits us to give a syntactical definition of the veridical construction. I shall illustrate the Homeric usage in some detail, since the finite construction is used more freely in Homer than in later Greek, and there is some reason to suppose that these Homeric uses reflect the prehistoric circumstances which gave rise to the common I.-E. use of the participle *sont- for "truth" or "fact".

Earlier authors who took notice of the veridical use generally grouped it with existential uses of the verb. This assimilation of the veridical to the existential is in part justified, as we have seen, by a basic analogy or identity between the logical function of the verb in the two cases; both veridical and existential uses assert a semantic relation between language and the world (or, in some instances of the veridical, between cognition and the world). But if the distinct lexical value and syntactic structure of the veridical was often overlooked, that is due to the fact that no syntactic analysis of existential sentences had been undertaken, while the lexical account of the existential verb was given in the form of very general paraphrases such as "vorhanden sein, sich befinden, existieren" (Brugmann), or "to have or take place in the world of fact, to exist, occur, happen" (*Oxford English Dictionary*). For philologists operating with such a vague and generalized notion of an existential use of *es-, it was easy enough to count the veridical nuance ("is a fact") merely as a special case.[5] But as we see from the syntactic analysis of the preceding chapter, the verb εἰμί in the veridical construction takes

---

[5] Thus Brugmann remarks, after the paraphrase just quoted: "Diese Seite des Sinnes von *es*- bekundet sich auch in dem Gebrauch der partizipialen Formen ai. *sát* N. 'das Seiende, Wesen,' griech. ὄντως 'in Wirklichkeit', ai. *satyá-ḥ* 'wirklich, wahr,' got. *sunjis* aisl. *sannr* 'wahr.'" (*Syntax des einfachen Satzes*, p. 73). Similarly, the *O.E.D.* simply lists "to be the case or the fact" as one of the sub-entries under the general existential heading cited above. More recently Benveniste has characterized the existential value of *es*- in such a way that the veridical nuance is immediately included in it: "Le sens en est 'avoir existence, se trouver en réalité', et cette 'existence', cette 'réalité' se définissent comme ce qui est authentique, consistant, vrai" (*Problèmes de linguistique générale* p. 188).

a subject which is sentential in form, whereas in the existential constructions it takes as subject either a first-order nominal or a pronoun for a first-order nominal (in Types I–IV and VI) or an abstract action noun (in Type V). To these syntactical distinctions correspond certain lexical differences, namely that the verb in Types II–IV and VI expresses what I have called existence$_1$, the *being-there* of persons and things, while in Type V it expresses existence$_2$ or *occurrence* for actions and events. (And in the later use with quality nouns as subject, as in *Virtue exists, Beauty exists*, the verb may be said to express *instantiation*, a variant on existence$_2$.) In the veridical construction, on the other hand, the verb expresses the *truth* of statements and cognition or the *being-so* of facts and states-of-affairs. We will now see that these distinctions are grounded in the fuller, more specific structure of the veridical sentence form.

The two common forms ἔστι ταῦτα and ἔστι οὕτω may both be derived as alternative abbreviations for a single long form: (ταῦτα) ἔστι (οὕτω) "These things are so", where the underlying subject of ἔστι (that is to say, the antecedent of ταῦτα) is provided not by any single word but by a preceding sentence or sentences. (We note in passing that one or both of these alternative forms appear in a wide variety of I.-E. languages, from Homeric Greek and ancient Hittite to modern Greek, Russian, and English, e.g. in the form *It is so, So be it!*, French *c'est ainsi, c'est comme ça*, etc.)[6] In the most explicit cases, however, the syntax of the construction is more complex: the adverb οὕτω correlates the veridical clause with a verb of saying.

1 *Il.* 24.373

    οὕτω πη τάδε γ' ἐστί, φίλον τέκος, ὡς ἀγορεύεις

    "Yes, in truth, dear child, all this is much as you tell me"

                                              (Lattimore)

In **1** the pro-word τάδε refers back not to any preceding nominal form but to the whole dangerous situation in which Priam finds himself, the situation which has just been described by Hermes (in disguise) in a half-dozen sentences (verses 362–71). The underlying syntax of Priam's reply in **1** above can be analyzed as containing a double construction of εἰμί, with zeroing of the second occurrence of the verb: **1A** *Things are just as you say (that*

---

[6] Professor Benveniste has called my attention to the Hittite form *ešzi-at*, "cela est (vrai)" (≈ἔστι ταῦτα). See E. Benveniste, *Hittite et Indo-européén*, p. 42; A. Goetze, "Die Pestgebete des Muršiliš," *Kleinasiatische Forschungen* I (1930), p. 212 (§6.3 with commentary on p. 229). The formula for confession of sin is given as *ešzi-at iịanun-at* "it is (so), I did it." In Russian we have *taki yest* "So is it" (≈ἔστι οὕτω). Modern Greek has preserved both forms, with and without the adverb: δὲν εἶναι ἔτσι; "n'est-il pas vrai?" εἶναι ἢ δὲν εἶναι; "est-ce vrai ou non?" (quoted from H. Pernot, *Lexique Grec Moderne-Français*, s. vv. ἔτσι and εἶμαι).

they are). We can scarcely avoid noticing that this is precisely the colloquial equivalent of the classical formula for truth in Greek philosophy, the formula for which Tarski has provided a standard modern interpretation.[7] The philosophers had only to make explicit what was given in the idiomatic form of the veridical construction.

2 Plato (?) *Hippias Maior* 282 A 4

 ἔστι μὲν ταῦτα, ὦ Σώκρατες, οὕτως ὡς σὺ λέγεις

 "These things are just as you say, Socrates"

(The idiomatic status of this example is of course independent of the disputed question of Platonic authorship.)

3 Sophocles, *Trachiniae* 474

 πᾶν σοι φράσω τάληϑὲς οὐδὲ κρύψομαι.

 ἔστιν γὰρ οὕτως ὥσπερ οὗτος ἐννέπει

 "I shall tell you the whole truth and hide nothing: it is just as he says."

If we take the formula *Things are (in fact) as you say they are* as characteristic for a correspondence theory of truth, examples **1–3** show us that such a theory is prefigured in the veridical idioms of ancient Greek, and probably even earlier in the prehistoric I.-E. use of the verb **es-*.[8]

---

[7] See, above all, Arist. *Met*. Gamma 7, 1011ᵇ26 τὸ μὲν γὰρ λέγειν τὸ ὂν μὴ εἶναι ἢ τὸ μὴ ὂν εἶναι ψεῦδος, τὸ δὲ τὸ ὂν εἶναι καὶ τὸ μὴ ὂν μὴ εἶναι ἀληϑές "To say of what is (so) that it is not or of what is not (so) that it is, is falsehood; to say of what is (so) that it is and of what is not (so) that it is not, is truth." I have introduced the "(so)" to indicate the more strictly veridical or semantic use of the verb, which occurs in Aristotle's text as the participle ὄν. The infinitive εἶναι, on the other hand, in indirect discourse after λέγειν, represents the descriptive content of what is said, precisely that repeated occurrence of the verb which is normally zeroed even in the most explicit colloquial examples such as **1** above.

In an interesting article "On Concepts of Truth in Natural Languages" (*Review of Metaphysics* 23, 1969, p. 282), Fred Sommers proposes that we interpret "is" in Aristotle's formula as an elliptical copula: "saying of what-is-P *that* it is P...", for instance saying of snow (what-is-white) that it is white, is True." Since, as we see in §5, the copula and veridical construction may overlap, Sommers' interpretation is a possible reading of the Greek. Furthermore, it is a reading which Aristotle would himself accept, since in his view to say something is, in the elementary case, always to affirm or deny a predicate of an (existing) subject, τι κατά τινος. Nevertheless, the idiom which Aristotle uses in the formula quoted from Gamma 7, while it admits the copula interpretation for ὄν and εἶναι, does not require this. The use of *to be* here is general enough to permit any sentence as substituend, for example "to say (in reference to the fact that it is snowing) that it is snowing."

[8] In classic Attic the phrase οὕτως ἔχει is more common than ἔστι οὕτως, with essentially the same meaning. The former phrase does not concern us here except as an instance of the general tendency for ἔχει to serve as a functional equivalent of ἐστί, above all with adverbial forms. Compare εὖ ἔχει, καλῶς ἔχει "it is well", κακῶς ἔχει "it is ill," etc.; and see LSJ s.v. ἔχω (A) B.II.

We now have a formal, syntactic definition for the veridical construction of εἰμί. This is a use of the verb which satisfies the following three conditions: (1) the construction of the verb is absolute, that is, there is no nominal, locative or quasi-locative predicate, and no other complement to the verb except for the comparative adverb οὕτως, ὡς, or ὧδε; (2) the subject of the verb is sentential, e.g. ταῦτα or τάδε refers back not to a particular word or phrase but to what has just been said in one or more sentences; and (3) the adverb οὕτως and/or ὡς introduces a comparison between the clause with εἰμί and another clause with a verb of saying or, less often, of thinking. In typical cases such as sentences 1–3, the clause with εἰμί (which we may for brevity call the *essive* clause) serves to assert the truth of what is said or thought, the truth of the object of the associated verb of saying or thinking. But as we shall see, the use of this syntactical construction actually has a wider range than is covered by the notion of truth. If by "veridical construction" we mean an expression of the idea of truth, the above conditions are necessary but not sufficient for a definition. Before attempting to narrow the definition, let us consider the wider use.

In example 1 Priam agrees that the situation (τάδε) is in fact (ἐστί) just as Hermes has described it in his speech (οὕτω ... ὡς ἀγορεύεις). Introducing our semantic metaphors from Chapters VI §20, we may say that in such uses the veridical ἐστί *poses*, or affirms *as present in the world,* a descriptive content which has just been expressed in language. In other terms, Priam affirms that Hermes' linguistic picture of the situation fits the facts. But this specifically veridical use of ἐστί for the recognition of an alleged state of affairs as truly existing in the world is only one form of a more general semantic use to express the *realization of an intention*, that is to say, *of a projected situation*, where statement, wish, request, conjecture, and knowledge are counted as different modes of projecting or intending a situation. For the properly veridical use illustrated above, we may characterize the underlying subject of the verb as a *Sinn* in Wittgenstein's sense, an alleged or possible state of affairs as pictured in or specified by a sentence. But for the wider use now to be considered, we need a more general concept like Husserl's notion of a noematic content, a content which may be qualified by the various intentional modes of belief, desire, resolve, or the like. Let us extend our use of the term *descriptive content* to cover this wider intentional sense. In the properly veridical uses the descriptive content will be an alleged state of affairs formulated in a preceding statement, and the veridical ἐστί asserts that this situation is in fact realized (or, as philosophers sometimes say, that the state of affairs actually "exists" or "obtains"). In the variants which follow, the descriptive content may be formulated not only in a statement but also in a request or a proposal, and the corresponding use of εἰμί expresses a prediction, a promise, a wish, or an intention of any sort regarding this content.

4 *Il.* 24.669 (cf. 21.223)

ἔσται τοι καὶ ταῦτα, γέρον Πρίαμ᾽, ὡς σὺ κελεύεις
"Then all this, aged Priam, shall be done as you ask it."

(Lattimore)

In a use like **4** it is clear that the term "veridical" is no longer strictly appropriate, since the concept of truth or falsity is not directly involved. The clause ἔσται ταῦτα "this shall be (so)" is, in effect, the expression of a promise, and it is equivalent in meaning to ταῦτα τελέω "I shall carry out (what you request)."[9] This promissory use of ἔσται ταῦτα remains current in classic Attic. See, for example, Plato, *Philebus* 31 C 6 ἔσται ταῦτ᾽ εἰς δύναμιν "I will do my best (to give the explanation you ask for)."[10]

In example **4** the pro-word ταῦτα refers back to Priam's appeal to Achilles to delay battle twelve days for Hector's burial. In Achilles' answer this descriptive content – the content of Priam's request and the underlying subject of ἔσται (ταῦτα) – is further spelled out in the verse which follows our quotation: "I will hold back the war for as long as you have asked" (*Il.* 24.670). This function of referring back to the content of a preceding discourse, which is performed by ταῦτα in our last example, is performed by οὕτως in the next:

5 *Il.* 4.189

αἲ γὰρ δὴ οὕτως εἴη, φίλος ὦ Μενέλαε
"May it only be as you say, o Menelaos, dear brother!"

(Lattimore)

The Greek says simply "may it be so," but the translation naturally adds "as you say," since the reference is clearly to the content of Menelaus' preceding statement, namely, that his wound is a slight one. It is the realiza-

---

[9] For the sense compare *Il.* 23.96 πάντα μάλ᾽ ἐκτελέω καὶ πείσομαι ὡς σὺ κελεύεις. See also *Il.* 23.20 = 180 πάντα γὰρ ἤδη τοι τελέω τὰ πάροιθεν ὑπέστην. Note that τελέω may also be used like a strictly veridical εἰμί for the assertion of matters of fact: *Od.* 19.305 τάδε πάντα τελείεται ὡς ἀγορεύω "all this shall be accomplished exactly as I say" (Palmer), where the sentence structure is the same as in **1–3** above, except for the substitution of τελείεται for ἐστί.

[10] The Attic use of the formula ἔσται ταῦτα has been studied in detail by Eduard Fraenkel, *Beobachtungen zu Aristophanes* (Rome, 1962), pp. 77–89. Fraenkel does not discuss other forms of the veridical construction (e.g. he does not consider ἔστι ταῦτα), but he does mention our Homeric example **4**. He concludes that ἔσται ταῦτα originally served as the solemn confirmation of a wish or prophecy, but that in Attic tragedy (especially Euripides) and in the later works of Plato it becomes an habitual substitute for the more ordinary expression of promise or consent ποιήσω ταῦτα (or δράσω ταῦτα). The Homeric equivalent of the latter is πάντα (ἐκ-)τελέω, illustrated in the preceding note. See also ταῦτα μὲν οὕτω δὴ τελέω, γέρον, ὡς σὺ κελεύεις *Od.* 4.485, etc.

tion *in fact* of this descriptive content that is expressed by εἴη in **5**, where the optative form reflects the intentional modality of *wish* rather than confident assertion. Notice that here, where the verb is not provided with any subject expression, we may identify its underlying "real" (i.e. extra-linguistic) subject with *the actual state of affairs*, whatever that may be, as distinct from the alleged situation described by Menelaus. Some distinction between the situation as described and as it actually obtains *must* be made here in order for the wish to be intelligible: what Agamemnon wishes is precisely that the situation concerning the wound should be (in fact) as his brother claims it to be (in words). What the analysis of **5** brings to light is something like a correspondence theory of wishes. As in the earlier examples of correspondence for statements, the very concept of congruence between word and fact presupposes the logical distinctness and the possible divergence between fact and descriptive content.[11]

In sentence **5** we no longer have the full veridical construction with an explicit clause of comparison, containing a verb of saying or thinking. But it seems fair to say that οὕτως represents such a clause implicitly, just as in the familiar ἔστι οὕτω "it is so (just as you say)." In transformational terms the clause of saying has been zeroed here but can be reconstructed from the comparative adverb οὕτως. In the next example, however, the comparative construction is absent. We have no clause of saying, nor any clear hint of one. Instead, the content of what is said has itself become the subject of the verb εἰμί, as in the formula ἔστι ταῦτα "These things (which you say) are so." In answer to the sailor's offer to take her home to her parents, the Phoenician slave girl responds as follows:

6 *Od.* 15.435

εἴη κεν καὶ τοῦτ', εἴ μοι ἐθέλοιτέ γε, ναῦται,
ὅρκῳ πιστωθῆναι

"It may be, if you sailors pledge yourselves by oath (to take me home unharmed)."

(Palmer)

In this construction the potential optative (with κεν = ἄν) expresses not a

---

[11] I operate with the simplest possible distinction between facts, or states of affairs as they actually obtain in the world, and descriptive contents or alleged facts, as specified in sentences (whether true or false). This is the minimum distinction required in any concept of truth that can be used to analyze the veridical idioms described in this chapter. An adequate philosophic *theory* of truth may of course require more subtle distinctions, such as that between sentence and statement, on the one hand, or between facts and states of affairs on the other. (A distinction of the latter sort is proposed by Sommers in the article cited above, n. 7.) Apart from the question whether such distinctions are required elsewhere, I cannot find anything which corresponds to them in the Greek idioms under discussion.

simple wish but a conditional assent to a proposed line of action. In **6** τοῦτο refers back to the sailor's proposal; εἴη may be understood as expressing its realization in fact, subject to the condition stated in the second clause.

In an example like **6** we no longer have the veridical construction as I have defined it, but we have a close paraphrase equivalent and perhaps the same underlying structure. At any rate, "it may be as you say" is clearly what **6** *means*, just as ἔστι ταῦτα means "things are as you say". If we look only at the surface construction, however, we see that εἴη τοῦτο in **6**, like εἴη in **5** and ἔσται ταῦτα in **4**, can be assimilated to a Type V existential use of εἰμί as verb of occurrence: "let it take place", "this will happen". The difference is that in existential Type V the subject of the verb is an abstract (action) noun whereas in **4–6** it is a sentential structure. But since the action noun is itself a kind of sentence-nominalization, this distinction can vanish in some cases, when a pro-word like ταῦτα serves as generalized subject of a Type V existential. (See below, on sentence **16**.) Thus there is a genuine affinity between the use of εἰμί in the essive clause of a veridical construction and its use in a Type V existential like ὅμαδος ἦν "there was an uproar".

On the other hand, any resemblance between the veridical and a copula construction of εἰμί is superficial and misleading. The verb in *This is so* or *This is as you say* is not the copula as syntactically defined: there is no nominal, locative, or paralocative form to serve as predicate. The only real resemblance is to the problematic copula construction with predicate adverbs: κακῶς ἦν "It went badly", εὖ ἔσται "it will be well". (See Chapter IV §22). We shall return to this connection later, in §5. For the moment I observe only that the adverbial "predicate" in our construction does not stand alone but serves to introduce a coordinate clause of comparison: *as you say*. Furthermore, a fuller analysis of this coordinate clause will show that, within it, the (non-copulative) use of εἰμί makes a new appearance. *Things are (in fact) as you say (that they are)*. Except in the explicit philosophical formula for truth, we seem never to get the verb actually repeated in this way. But it (or some equivalent expression)is clearly embedded there in the underlying structure of indirect discourse after a verb of saying. It is simply that the usual idiomatic mechanisms of brevity and elegance lead to the zeroing of the second occurrence of εἰμί, and this tendency is overcome only by the philosophic desire for maximum clarity and explicitness.[12] But in this

---

[12] For the double occurrence of εἰμί in the formula for truth – one occurrence for the facts, one for the alleged facts or descriptive content that is supposed to correspond – see, in addition to the quotation from Aristotle in n. 7 above, Plato, *Crat.* 385 B 7 οὗτος (sc. ὁ λόγος) ὃς ἂν τὰ ὄντα λέγῃ ὡς ἔστιν, ἀληθής· ὃς δ' ἂν ὡς οὐκ ἔστιν, ψευδής "The statement which says of what is the case that it is (so), is true; the one which says that it is not (so) is false." The standard formula is also reflected in *Euthydemus* 284A–C, *Theaet.* 188D, *Soph.* 263B, but in these dialogues Plato gives the veridical construction a special twist

second occurrence, *(things are in fact) as you say that they are*, there is no semblance of a copula construction. Nor do we find any in the typical examples of the participial construction illustrated below, in §4.

I conclude this preliminary survey of the veridical construction and related forms with three examples to show how the verb may express a command, a prediction, or an indirect question concerning the future course of events.

7 *Il.* 8.523

ὦδ ἔστω, Τρῶες μεγαλήτορες, ὡς ἀγορεύω
(Let us camp in the plain, and keep a steady watch....)
"Let it be thus, high-hearted men of Troy, as I tell you."

(Lattimore)

8 *Il.* 18.266

ἀλλ' ἴομεν προτὶ ἄστυ, πίθεσθέ μοι· ὧδε γὰρ ἔσται
"Let us go into the town; believe me; thus it will happen"
(followed by a correct prediction by Polydamas of the disasters of the next day)

(Lattimore)

9 *Il.* 4.14

ἡμεῖς δὲ φραζώμεθ' ὅπως ἔσται τάδε ἔργα
"Let us consider then how these things shall be accomplished"
(namely, whether to renew the war or let the opponents be reconciled).

(Lattimore)

Only in **7** do we have a sentence form that satisfies our definition of the veridical construction, since only in this case do we find a clause of comparison with verb of saying. In **8** such a comparison is implicit in the use of ὧδε, and to this extent the construction is implicitly veridical. (In terms of formal syntax we may say that the underlying structure of **8** is "It will happen so, as I tell you," with zeroing of the second clause.) In **9**, however, we do not have a veridical construction, since ὅπως here introduces not a comparison but a clause of indirect question: "How will these things turn out? Let us think it over." (The following verses articulate two alternative courses of events between which the gods may choose.) The essive clause here is of the same form as in the veridical construction: the syntax of the verb is absolute and the underlying subject is sentential. But the third syntactic

---

in order to bring out the paradox of "saying or thinking what-is-not" (or in order to formulate his solution to this paradox, in the *Sophist*). We have the double occurrence earlier in Protagoras' formula for Man the Measure: πάντων χρημάτων μέτρον ... τῶν μὲν ὄντων ὡς ἔστιν, τῶν δὲ οὐκ ὄντων ὡς οὐκ ἔστιν. And compare Melissus' phrase in Chapter VI, sentence **127** εἰ γὰρ ἔστι ... ὅσα φασὶν οἱ ἄνθρωποι εἶναι ἀληθῆ.

condition of the veridical, the comparative construction of essive clause with clause of saying or thinking, is not present. We have in effect a generalized Type V existential use of εἰμί in **9**, closely related to but not actually an instance of the veridical construction.

§3. RESTRICTING THE DEFINITION OF
THE VERIDICAL CONSTRUCTION.
FORMAL VARIANTS, AND THE CONTRAST
WITH EXISTENTIAL TYPE V

The nine Homeric and classical examples cited so far exhibit a number of formal variations, and others will be noted in this section and the next. Some but not all of these variants have the effect of excluding the veridical nuance, so that the verb *be* no longer has the sense of "is true" or "is the case". Our problem is to restrict the definition in such a way that it picks out just those cases where the veridical construction (as defined above) and the veridical nuance coincide. Intuitively we see that these are the cases where the clause of saying or thinking refers to a statement or to its cognitive analogue, an act of knowing or thinking-so. But it is not clear how this restriction can be formulated in syntactic terms. If by "veridical proper" we mean the case where veridical construction and veridical nuance coincide, it may be that the veridical proper is an irreducibly semantic concept and that all we can do is locate it within the veridical construction as formally defined.

Of our nine examples so far, two may be ignored as dubiously veridical: neither **6** nor **9** exhibits the formal mark of a comparative construction. In **5** and **8** the comparison is implicit, but I assume that the implication is clear enough for this to make no essential difference. Thus we have seven examples illustrating a diversity of "propositional attitudes" on the part of the speaker, ranging from the admission that the facts are as stated in **1–3**, to a promise to fulfill a request in **4**, a wish that the facts may be as stated in **5**, a command that orders be carried out in **7**, and a prediction concerning things to come in **8**. Only in the first three examples, and to a lesser degree in **5** and **8**, is the term "veridical" strictly appropriate. However, for lack of a better term I shall continue to call "veridical construction" the sentence type already defined: namely, a comparative construction joining an essive clause (with εἰμί construed absolutely, with sentential subject) and a clause of saying or thinking, including predicting, requesting, commanding, knowing and believing. For simplicity we may describe the latter, which contains a verb of saying or thinking, as the *intentional* clause, where "intentional" points to the different ways in which a speaker may project or intend a situation or state of affairs. In every case the essive clause will express the realization of the situation so projected.[13]

In order to restrict our definition now to the veridical proper, we first note the cases which have been or should be excluded. Our formal definition already excludes examples like 9 above and 10 below, where the essive clause expresses the realization of the descriptive content of one or more sentences but without a comparative construction. Note that both the syntax and the logical function of the essive clause taken alone are the same here as in the veridical construction: the verb, construed absolutely, expresses the realization of a projected state of affairs. But the veridical construction requires something more: the comparison with an intentional clause. Such a comparison is present in 4 and 7 above, where the veridical *nuance* (i.e. the notion of truth) is nevertheless not present. Why not? Because in this case the intentional clause does not refer to an assertion, but to a request in 4 and a command in 7. It is not the mood of the essive clause that is decisive here. In 5 the verb appears in the optative (εἴη) and the idea is nonetheless veridical ("may it be as you say" or "may what you say be true"); in 4 the verb is in the indicative (ἔσται) and the idea is *not* veridical ("what you ask for will be carried out," not "what you say will be so"). What makes the difference here is the presence in 5 of a *statement* by the interlocutor and the absence of such a statement in 4.

We could give a formal definition of the veridical proper if we could specify in syntactic terms when the intentional clause represents a statement. Unfortunately this cannot be done by simply specifying which *verb* occurs in the intentional clause, since ἀγορεύω "I say" occurs both in 7 for a command and in 1 for an assertion. And in the implicit comparisons of 5 and 8 no verb of saying occurs. Still, the occurrence of certain verbs in the intentional clause may serve to rule out the veridical nuance: for example, verbs meaning "to order" or "to urge", like κελεύεις in 4. But the deep criterion for distinguishing the veridical proper from other sentences of the same general form is whether the verb of saying or thinking in the intentional clause takes as its object *a clause of the unmarked indicative*, i.e. of unqualified truth claim. (See Chapter V §§ 2–2a.) The possibility of a formal definition of the veridical proper thus depends upon the possibility of an adequate theory of moods for the deep structure of indirect discourse after verbs of saying or thinking. I cannot provide such a theory, and hence I cannot provide a formal definition of the veridical proper. What I have to offer is only the general principle that should guide such a theory. Insofar as the unmarked

---

[13] Ernst Tugendhat has pointed out to me that Wittgenstein envisaged just such a generalization of the notion of the realization of a projected state of affairs. See his *Philosophical Investigations* §§ 437–65 and *Philosophische Grammatik* §§ 85ff.

indicative is accepted as the fundamental case in a general theory of moods (as I proposed in Chapter V), the veridical proper represents the fundamental case of the general veridical construction as I have defined it. The notion of truth or the veridical nuance for εἰμί will coincide with the veridical construction in just those instances where the intentional clause implies a truth claim for the sentence or sentences that are imbedded as object for the verb of saying or thinking – a truth claim which is affirmed by the subject of the intentional verb, regardless whether he is the speaker of the whole sentence or the interlocutor or someone else, i.e. regardless whether the intentional verb is in first, second, or third person. This principle picks out those cases where the intentional clause means "I state that...," "I think that...," or "I know that...." In other words, within the veridical construction the veridical proper is found in those sentences where the clause with εἰμί is compared to a *clause of statement*, whether this statement occurs in uttered speech or in the silent discourse of the soul with itself (to borrow Plato's phrase).[14]

Beyond this we cannot give a general analysis but must stick to cases. We return to the formal variants on the veridical construction as defined.

The general structure is a compound sentence form joining an essive and an intentional clause. Formally, there are at least three possibilities for the connection between the clauses: (i) in the standard form, the essive clause is principal, with the intentional conjoined by comparative particles like οὕτω and ὡς; (ii) the intentional clause appears as principal with the essive clause as its object or parenthetical modifier, and (iii) the essive clause appears alone, and the intentional correlate must be understood from the context.

Type (i), with the *essive* as primary clause, is illustrated in **1–4** and **7** above. We have type (iii), with the essive alone expressed, in **5**, **6** and **8**. Type (ii), with the essive clause construed as object of or as parenthetical to the intentional verb, is perhaps the most common of all. In addition to **9** above we have sentences such as the following:

---

[14] The problem is complicated by the fact that in a clause of saying, like "I say to you that *p*," we have only the most basic, declarative operation on the underlying sentence *p*, whereas in a clause of thinking, like "I remember that *p*" or "I know that *p*," we have a more complex epistemic operator. The common feature, which is all that concerns us here, is that both the latter and the former operations affirm (or leave unaltered) the elementary truth claim of *p*, unlike "I wonder whether *p*," "I wish that *p*," or "Bring it about that *p*." It seems probable that this common semantic feature can be correlated with syntactic peculiarities in the treatment of the embedded sentence *p*, in Greek as in English. In English, these peculiarities will usually show up in verb ending or word order, but sometimes only in the intonation of *p*. I cannot undertake the analysis for Greek, except to point out that a clause of thinking will often be followed by an independent sentence (or sentences) in the unmarked indicative which spell out the thought, just as in the case of a clause of saying. See examples **11** and **13**.

10 *Il.* 2.252

οὐδέ τί πω σάφα ἴδμεν ὅπως ἔσται τάδε ἔργα,
ἦ εὖ ἦε κακῶς νοστήσομεν υἷες Ἀχαιῶν

"We do not even know clearly how these things will be accomplished,
whether we ... shall win home well or badly"

(Lattimore)

11 *Il.* 9.527

μέμνημαι τόδε ἔργον ἐγὼ πάλαι, οὔ τι νέον γε,
ὡς ἦν· ἐν δ᾽ ὑμῖν ἐρέω

"For I remember this action of old, it is not a new thing,
and how it went, ... I will tell it among you."

(Lattimore)

12 *Od.* 21.212

σφῶϊν δ᾽, ὡς ἔσεταί περ, ἀληθείην καταλέξω

"To you then I will truly tell what shall hereafter be"

(Palmer)

13 *Od.* 19.312

ἀλλά μοι ὧδ᾽ ἀνὰ θυμὸν ὀΐεται, ὡς ἔσεταί περ

"But yet the thought is in my heart how it will really be"

(Palmer)

Notice that the veridical word actually occurs in **12**, but the *truth* in
question happens to be a promise or resolve on Odysseus' part to reward his
faithful helpers. Thus it appears that the word "truth", like the veridical
construction itself, has promissory as well as declarative applications.

The last examples also show how the intentional clause may be constituted
by a verb of thinking – of memory in **11**, of imagination or conviction in **13** –
as well as by a verb of statement. The parallel is underscored in **11**, where
the verb of thinking is followed by one of saying (ἐρέω). **11-13** satisfy our
conditions for the veridical construction but **10** does not: instead of comparative syntax for the essive clause we have an indirect question, as in **9** above.

In **11–13** the speaker of the essive clause is also the subject of the intentional
verb of saying or thinking. This point deserves attention, since one might
suppose that the primary function of the veridical use of εἰμί was the endorsement in a dialogue situation of what the interlocutor had asserted, as when
ἔστι οὕτω functions like "Yes". (Compare *sic* as "Yes" in Latin.) So a
reader under the influence of the speech-acts theory of language might
conclude that the basic correspondence relation implied by the comparative
clauses with ἐστί was, after all, a correspondence between speaker and
speaker, or between an act of assertion and an act of endorsement or re-

assertion, and not at all a correspondence between saying-so and being-the-case. But this conclusion would be a mistake. As Alexander Mourelatos has observed, in a dialogue situation the communication of truth involves a relation between three terms: "*A*, the facts; *B*, the informer; *C*, the interested party."[15] We may formulate this more precisely as a triadic relation between *A* what is the case, *B* what the speaker asserts, and *C* what the hearer accepts. If *C* coincides with *B*, that is, if the hearer accepts the speaker's statement as true, that is because he believes that *B* coincides with *A*. So he can express his agreement by saying ἔστι οὕτω, "it is so (as you say it is)." But the speaker-hearer agreement between *C* and *B* is based upon the prior semantic agreement believed to obtain between *B* and *A*: the correspondence between word and deed, between statement and fact, remains decisive. This is clear in examples like **11–13**, where the speaker-hearer relation plays no direct part in the comparative construction. The speaker says how things were or will be, and he underscores his own statement by insisting "I tell it like it is".[16]

In a further variant we have the verb of saying taken up in nominalized form as subject of the essive clause:

14 *Il.* 24.56

    εἴη κεν καὶ τοῦτο τεὸν ἔπος
    "What you have said could be true"[17]

                                     (Lattimore)

In these variants we find an alternation between an adverb or adverbial conjunction ὡς (ὧδε, ὅπως) and the pro-word τά (τόδε, τοῦτο), with the latter occasionally filled out by the general dummy-noun ἔργα or ἔργον (as in later Greek by πρᾶγμα or χρῆμα).

It is not entirely a matter of convenience how many of these variants we classify under the veridical construction. In transformational terms, a construction which does not satisfy our definition of the veridical can be meaningfully described as a formal variant on this construction only if it can be derived from the veridical by a well-defined transformation. Thus **14** can count as a transform of the veridical construction because τεὸν ἔπος "your word" can be analyzed as a nominalization of the intentional clause

---

[15] *The Route of Parmenides* (New Haven, 1970), p. 63.

[16] In some circumstances, for example in the use of the veridical construction for the expression of a wish ("so be it!"), an interchange of speakers is normally required. But the triadic structure remains. What the hearer wishes (*C*) is for the facts (*A*) to be as the speaker has asserted or proposed (*B*). In other words, he expresses his acceptance of the content of the first speaker's utterance by wishing for its fulfillment in deed.

[17] So also in a promissory clause: *Od.* 11.348 τοῦτο μὲν οὕτω δὴ ἔσται ἔπος "The queen's word will be fulfilled (as I am king in Phaeacia.)". Again we have a parallel use of τελέω: *Od.* 19.309 αἲ γὰρ τοῦτο, ξεῖνε, ἔπος τετελεσμένον εἴη, which stands in immediate antithesis to the more properly veridical example in **13** above.

"(what) you have said," and the latter in turn derived from the comparative construction "as you have said." Although it does not have the surface structure of the veridical, the use of εἴη κεν in **14** is translated "could be true" just because the whole sentence can be understood as a paraphrase of "This could be as you say." (A similar analysis can be applied to **6** above.) On the other hand, examples **9** and **10** are not plausibly counted as veridical just because they cannot be derived from the comparative construction.[18] One might be tempted to suppose that every case where εἰμί bears the full veridical nuance is also a case where the sentence can be derived from an underlying veridical construction. And this may be correct for the veridical with verbs of saying, expressed or implied. (For exceptions with verbs of knowing and seeming, where the veridical nuance is independent of the veridical construction, see below, p. 351 and n. 23).

Without attempting to account for every case where εἰμί bears a veridical nuance, we can see that *some* formal variants illustrated here are plausibly derived from an underlying comparative construction. And this is often the case for the participial construction of ὄν and ὄντα as objects of verbs of saying and thinking, to be illustrated in the next section. What is essential for an analysis in terms of the veridical construction is not the explicit comparison but a clear articulation of the two terms in the semantic relation: on the one hand the intentional content, what is said, thought, or proposed; on the other hand, the semantic value of fulfillment, what is in fact the case or will actually be done. Where this coordination of intention and realization disappears from the construction, we move in the direction of an ordinary Type V use of εἰμί as verb of occurrence. I illustrate this shift from veridical to existential use by two Attic examples, only the first of which may properly be described as veridical.

15 Thucydides I.132.4

> ἐπυνθάνοντο δὲ καὶ ἐς τοὺς Εἵλωτας πράσσειν τι αὐτόν, καὶ ἦν δὲ οὕτως.
>
> "(The Spartan authorities) were informed that he (Pausanias) was even intriguing with the Helots; and such indeed was the fact (for he promised them freedom and citizenship)."
>
> (tr. Crawley)

Since, as the context shows, the phrase ἦν οὕτως functions here as a con-

---

[18] Note the interaction here between the syntactic and semantic analysis. Whether a given sentence has the surface syntax of the veridical construction can be decided on formal grounds alone. And the derivation of another given sentence from an underlying veridical can also be given in formal terms. But whether or not such a derivation is regarded as *plausible* depends upon whether or not it gives a satisfactory interpretation of the meaning of the alleged transform.

firmation of the charges against Pausanias, we have in **15** the essential
veridical correlation between what is alleged and what is the case. (On the
other hand, if ἦν οὕτως were to be understood simply as introducing the
detail of the charges without confirming their truth, we would *not* have an
implicit comparison and hence no veridical construction.) No such correlation or contrast is involved in the following case.

> **16** Xen. *Anabasis* III. 1.33
>
> ὅτε δὲ ταῦτα ἦν σχεδὸν μέσαι ἦσαν νύκτες
>
> "(The Greek officers were called to an emergency meeting.)
> When this took place, it was about midnight."

Here ταῦτα ἦν simply resumes the contents of the preceding sentences (ἐπεὶ
δὲ πάντες συνῆλθον,... ἐκαθέζοντο), without raising any further question
of truth or fulfillment. In this case ταῦτα ἦν is naturally regarded as a generalized transform of Type V, with ταῦτα as pro-word for the appropriate
action nouns (e.g. for *the meeting of the officers*). As a sentence on the model
of Type V with εἰμί as verb of occurrence, **16** has the semantic structure
described in Chapter VI §20: ταῦτα represents the descriptive content of
the preceding sentences, while ἦν assigns the positive semantic value together
with the tense of the underlying description (like the verb in κλαγγὴ ἦν in
our specimen for Type V). But this semantic structure of **16** is revealed only
by analysis, as in other cases of Type V. The correlation between word and
fact is not articulated by the sentence form itself, as it is in **1–8** and **11–14**
above. Thus we see that the line between a Type V existential and a veridical
construction cannot be drawn on the basis of the form of the subject
expression alone, since ταῦτα in **16** is formally indistinguishable from the
subject of a true veridical.

The distinction between a Type V and a veridical use of εἰμί is particularly
clear in the following example, where the two constructions would correspond to different lexical meanings.

> **17** *Il.* 19.242
>
> αὐτίκ᾿ ἔπειθ᾿ ἅμα μῦθος ἔην, τετέλεστο δὲ ἔργον
>
> "No sooner was the order given than the thing had been done."
>
> > (Lattimore)

In **17** the distinctively veridical or semantic idea is expressed by τετέλεστο,
not by ἔην which is here simply a verb of occurrence. In a different context,
however, we might be inclined to take μῦθος ἔην as "the word was true
(or fulfilled)", like εἴη ἔπος in **14** above. (And see τοῦτο οὕτω ἔσται ἔπος
in note 17 above.) This sense is excluded by the context in **17**, and perhaps

by the use of μῦθος in Homer generally. If acceptable, however, it would give us an underlying veridical construction for ἔην in **17**.[19]

Despite this sharp lexical contrast between the verb of occurrence in a Type V sentence like **17** and the superficially similar veridical use in **14**, certain deeper connections between the two constructions have emerged. In **16** ταῦτα ἦν "this took place" is not a veridical use as it stands, but all that is lacking for the veridical construction is some comparison to an utterance or thought which could be given in a coordinate clause.[20] The generalized Type V existential ταῦτα ἦν in **16** is indistinguishable from the essive clause of a veridical construction like ἔσται ταῦτα in **4** or τόδε ἔργον ... πάλαι (ὡς) ἦν in **11**, *if the essive clause is considered alone*, apart from the clause of saying or thinking. We might almost say that the essive clause of the veridical construction *is* a Type V existential use of εἰμί (with zeroing of the abstract subject noun or its replacement by τάδε or ταῦτα), and that the special feature of the veridical consists only in the inclusion of this clause within the comparative structure with a verb of saying or thinking. But although this seems a natural way to describe the veridical when εἰμί occurs in past or future tense, it does not fit so well for a present tense example like ἔστι οὕτω (ὡς σὺ λέγεις): "things are so (as you say)." To describe ἔστι here as a verb of occurrence is artificial, to say the least; and the same construction would scarcely occur with an action noun as subject of εἰμί. And this assimilation of veridical to existential will not work at all for examples like **14** and **17**, as we have seen. Hence we may admit a close affinity but not an identity between the use of the verb in the veridical construction and in a Type V existential.[21]

§4. THE VERIDICAL CONSTRUCTION IN PARTICIPIAL FORM

In the finite forms of the veridical use (as in existential Types II–VI and in certain sentence-operator uses of the copula) the verb occurs only in the third person singular. Its surface subject, if one is expressed at all, is normally in the neuter singular or neuter plural: τοῦτο, τάδε. The participial trans-

---

[19] For a post-Homeric passage where ὄντα μῦθον does mean "true tale", see the quotation from Euripides below, p. 354, under **27**.

[20] For an example of this, where the whole context suggests a veridical value for what might otherwise be taken as verb of occurrence, see Pindar *Nem.* 5.31 τὸ δ᾽ ἐναντίον ἔσκεν "It was the opposite that happened" (or "that was the case").

[21] This affinity is to be explained by the common semantic structure of veridical and existential uses, as pointed out in Chapter VI §20. Both in the veridical and in an existential Type V with generalized subject like ταῦτα, the function of the verb is to express semantic fulfillment, the realization in fact or in deed of a sentential content represented either by the underlying subject of the verb or (in a veridical with οὕτως) by the associated clause of saying or thinking.

formation of this construction will therefore give us the neuter form ἐόν or ἐόντα for the essive clause, in some syntactic connection with a verb of saying and thinking. In most cases the participle will be construed as direct object of a verb *tell*, *know*, *guess*, or the like; and it will have the translation-meaning "the truth", "the facts", or "what was actually the case."

This construction of the participle with a veridical nuance is familiar from Attic and particularly well attested in the Ionic prose of Herodotus. Since a similar use of the participle *sont- and its derivatives is found in many other I.-E. languages, it is natural to infer that the Attic-Ionic use of the participle represents an inherited form from prehistoric times.

The only objection to this inference is that the veridical participle is almost totally absent from Homer. But this objection will carry little weight, if one reflects upon the more abundant Homeric use of the finite verb in the veridical constructions illustrated in §§2–3. The participial variant on this finite construction is, after all, a natural syntactic possibility of the language, and it is likely to be only an accident (i.e. attributable to dialectical or stylistic influences, or to random variation) if Homer so rarely makes use of this possibility. That he *could* do so is confirmed by the single case in which he does:

18 *Il.* 1.70

> ὃς ᾔδη τά τ᾽ ἐόντα τά τ᾽ ἐσσόμενα πρό τ᾽ ἐόντα
> "(The prophet Calchas) who knew all things that were, the things to come and the things past."

> (Lattimore)

For those scholars who may be inclined to depreciate the value of a single occurrence, in deference to the powerful but rarely avowed philological axiom *Einmal ist "niemals", zweimal ist "immer"*, I might point out that **18** has a certain formulaic air about it and that two variants on the verse actually occur in Hesiod (*Theogony* 32,38).[22] However, this hexameter "formula" is not likely to be very old (indeed, no older than the complete *Iliad*, in my opinion), in view of the nearly classical use of τά as article. What is more important is the clear relation between this participial construction and the finite forms of the veridical discussed in §§2–3. In this example the essive clause has been nominalized as object of the intentional clause of knowing. The closest parallel is to **10**, where we have the same verb "know": οὐδὲ ... ἴδμεν ὅπως ἔσται τάδε ἔργα. But whereas we did not count **10** as strictly veridical because of its structure as indirect question ("How will these things be? We do not know"), in **18** we are free to understand the underlying

---

[22] My acquaintance with this axiom is due to my former teacher Ernst Kapp, who claimed to have heard of it from Wilamowitz.

structure as comparative. "He knew the things that will be" is a natural abbreviation for "These things will be, and he knows it", or in other words "He knows these things as they will be". On the other hand, if we derived **18** from the interrogative form, "He knows *which* things will be," the analysis would be exactly parallel to **10**. In general, the Greek construction of the participle as object of the verb *know* seems to be ambiguous in this regard. I prefer a standard veridical analysis for **18** because of the examples to follow from Herodotus, where verbs of knowing alternate with verbs of saying.[23]

In the participial construction of **18** we may, if we wish, identify the lexical value of εἰμί with the verb of occurrence of Type V: "what happens", "what is going on". But a greater formal affinity to the veridical construction is indicated by the conjunction of two features: the generalized sentential subject for εἰμί (instead of the action noun in Type V) and the syntax of the participle as the object of an intentional verb such as *know*. (The former condition alone is not sufficient, as we saw in sentence **16**; and the latter condition by itself gives us a quasi-veridical: see the preceding note.) But as we have seen, there is still an ambiguity as to whether the underlying structure is comparative (and hence veridical) or interrogative, as in **9** and **10**. A similar ambiguity characterizes the next example.

19 Lysias 1.42

νῦν δ' οὐδὲν εἰδὼς τῶν ἐσομένων ἐκείνῃ τῇ νυκτί

"But since I knew nothing of what was going to happen that night (I was unable to take precautions)."

In such uses we often find the suppletive verb of occurrence γίγνομαι with or without a specifically veridical suggestion.[24]

---

[23] For a Homeric example with verb of knowing where the sense is veridical but the construction clearly interrogative see *Od*. 24.159 οὐδέ τις ἡμείων δύνατο γνῶναι τὸν ἐόντα "None of us was able to recognize who he was" (namely, Odysseus when he returned in disguise), where we have a regular participial transform of the direct question τίς ἐστι; "Who is he?" (I owe this example to Friedrich Solmsen.) There is a clear affinity between this use and the veridical proper: the point of the remark was the difficulty of identifying Odysseus in disguise, i.e. of knowing *who he really was*. I would classify this with **9** and **10** among the near-veridicals. But whereas in **9** and **10** the subject of εἰμί is sentential in form, in *Od*. 24.159 it is a person. In fact the underlying syntax of ἐόντα here is the copula of personal identity described in Chapter IV §12. Hence this example satisfies none of our formal conditions for the veridical construction. Yet there is a clear contrast between "who he was" and "who he seemed to be," which accounts for the veridical nuance here. What is common to *Od*. 24.159 and to **18** above is the construction of the participle after a verb of knowing or perceiving. This construction, which is optional in Homer, becomes standard in later prose. And as a result we find a more generalized use of quasi-veridicals like γνῶναι ... ἐόντα: e.g. ἤκουσε Κῦρον ἐν Κιλικίᾳ ὄντα "He heard that Cyrus was in Cilicia" (Xen. *Anab*. I.4.5). Such quasi-veridicals represent a partial overlap between the veridical nuance and the copula construction; see further §5 below.

[24] See *Iliad* 12.69 ἐθέλοιμι καὶ αὐτίκα τοῦτο γενέσθαι ,where the reference of τοῦτο is spelled out by a following infinitival clause. This is a borderline case; the use of the

The dictionary examples of the veridical nuance, where the participle is translated as "truth", "fact" or the like, represent a special case of this participial construction where the participle is in present tense and hence will not usually be rendered as a verb of occurrence. In Attic the plural τὰ ὄντα (like τὰ ἐόντα in **18**) is well attested with the veridical sense, and we also find the singular form in adjectival agreement with λόγος. (See below on sentence **27**.) Herodotus uses only the singular in this sense, but he seems to use it more frequently than any other classical author. I shall illustrate the Herodotean use of the participle in detail, since it provides a relatively large and stylistically homogeneous sample that shows just how the participial syntax answers point for point to the construction of the finite verb which we have described in §§2–3, except that we rarely have a clear case of comparative structure with the participle.

Powell's *Lexicon* lists 10 examples of τὸ ἐόν as "the truth", and two occurrences of τὸν ἐόντα λόγον "the true story". Of the 10 instances of the veridical participle alone, three occur as direct object of a *verbum dicendi*, four more as direct object of a *verbum sentiendi* (including "hear" as well as "guess", "learn", etc.). In one case (**21**) we have the two constructions combined for a single occurrence of the participle.

20 Hdt. V. 50.2

> χρεὸν γάρ μιν μὴ λέγειν τὸ ἐόν, βουλόμενόν γε Σπαρτιήτας ἐξαγαγεῖν ἐς τὴν Ἀσίην
>
> "He should not have told the truth, if he wanted to lead the Spartans on an expedition into Asia."

21 VI.37.2

> μόγις κοτὲ μαθὼν τῶν τις πρεσβυτέρων εἶπε τὸ ἐόν
>
> "Finally one of the elders understood and said what it was (declared what the utterance meant: τὸ θέλει τὸ ἔπος εἶπαι)."

---

intentional verb "I would wish" suggests a veridical structure in the wider sense illustrated above by sentences **5** and **6**. But we might also regard this simply as a generalized Type V use of γενέσθαι as verb of occurrence, with sentential subject. (The standard Type V use, with an action noun as subject, appears in the immediately following context: *Il.* 12.71 παλίωξις δὲ γένηται.) In Attic γίγνομαι is frequently used as mutative-kinetic suppletive for εἰμί in a generalized Type V existential with sentential subject, analogous to ὅτε ταῦτα ἦν in **16** above: Lysias 1.10 οὕτως ἐγίγνετο, 13.15 οὐκ ἔφασαν ἐπιτρέψειν ταῦτα γενέσθαι. Only when the participle is construed with a verb of saying or thinking do we have a clear approximation to the veridical construction, as in **18** and **19**; so in Lysias 1.18 ὅτι ἐγὼ πάντα εἴην πεπυσμένος τὰ γιγνόμενα ἐν τῇ οἰκίᾳ "that I had learned everything that went on in the house." In this last case the context is explicitly veridical: κατειποῦσαν ἅπαντα τἀληθῆ, ... ψεύσῃ δὲ μηδέν etc.

22 VI.50.3

Κλεομένης... εἴρετο τὸν Κριὸν ὅ τι οἱ εἴη οὔνομα· ὁ δέ οἱ τὸ
ἐὸν ἔφρασε

"Cleomenes asked Crius his name, and the latter told him what
it was (told him the truth)."

Note that in **22**, and perhaps in **21**, the veridical ἐόν answers to an interrogative copula: τί οἱ εἴη οὔνομα; "What was his name?". We have here a quasi-veridical use and in **22** a case of the overlap between copula (or copula-possessive) construction and veridical nuance which is discussed in the next section.

23 VII.209.1

ἀκούων δὲ Ξέρξης οὐκ εἶχε συμβαλέσθαι τὸ ἐόν, ὅτι παρεσ-
κευάζοντο ὡς ἀπολεόμενοί τε καὶ ἀπολέοντες κατὰ δύναμιν

"When Xerxes heard this, he was unable to guess the truth (what
was going on), namely that the Spartans were preparing to die
and to kill to the best of their ability."

The other three Herodotean examples of the participle as object of *verba
sentiendi* are: εἰ ... σὺ τὸ ἐὸν ἀκήκοας "If what you have heard is true"
(V.106.4); τοῖσί τε λεγομένοισι πρότερον ... σταθμώμενος καὶ τῷ ἐόντι
"judging both by his former counsels and by the circumstances of the case"
(VII.237.2, after Rawlinson); ἐπειρόμενοι δὲ ἐξέμαθον πᾶν τὸ ἐόν "by
asking further they learned the whole story" (IX.11.3).

In an eighth occurrence, the participle is construed in close association
with a verb of speaking:

24 I.30.3

Σόλων δὲ οὐδὲν ὑποθωπεύσας, ἀλλὰ τῷ ἐόντι χρησάμενος λέγει

"Solon stooped to no flattery, but spoke in reliance on the truth."

In two remaining examples the veridical participle is construed adverbially;
in the first of these the underlying comparative construction is clear.

25 I.97.1

πλεῦνος δὲ αἰεὶ γινομένου τοῦ ἐπιφοιτέοντος, οἷα πυνθανομέ-
νων τὰς δίκας ἀποβαίνειν κατὰ τὸ ἐόν.

"The number of complaints brought before him (sc. Deioces)
continually increasing, as people learnt more and more the fair-
ness of his judgments."

(Rawlinson)

The construction is literally: *They learned that Deioces' judgments proceeded*

according to the facts (of the case), i.e. he judged the rights and obligations
of the contending parties to be *as they were in fact.*

26 IV.32

εἰ δὴ τῷ ἐόντι γε ῞Ομηρος ταῦτα τὰ ἔπεα ἐποίησε

"(Hesiod mentions the Hyperboreans, and Homer also does so
in the *Epigoni*,) if Homer is really the author of that poem."[25]

Sentence **26** illustrates the frozen, parenthetical use of the participle in dative
or adverbial form, like *in fact* or *actually* in English. So we find τῷ ὄντι and
ὄντως as standard adverbs in Attic. (See Thucyd. IV.28.2, VIII.92.11,
Ar. *Clouds* 86, etc. ἐόντως in this sense is an almost certain correction in
Hdt. VII.143.1.) The underlying veridical construction in **26** implies a
contrast between the questionable assignment of the *Epigoni* to Homer and
a positive semantic value (ἔστι οὕτως "it is so") which Herodotus is un-
villing to confirm.

Finally, we have two participial examples in Herodotus of a variant already
illustrated from Homer for the finite verb. In **14** we saw that the verb of
saying in nominalized form (in that case ἔπος) might be construed as subject
for a veridical εἰμί (meaning "is true", "is realized in fact"). In Herodotus
as in Attic authors this predicative construction with a finite form of εἰμί
is rare or unattested, but the corresponding attributive use of the participle
in ὁ ἐὼν λόγος is well known:

27 I.116.5

ὁ δὲ ἀγόμενος ἐς τὰς ἀνάγκας οὕτω δὴ ἔφαινε τὸν ἐόντα λόγον

"When he (sc. the cowherd) was brought to torture, he revealed
the true story."

So also τὸν ἐόντα λέγειν λόγον "to tell the true tale" in Hdt. I.95.1. For
Attic examples see οὐκ ὄντα λόγον ... ξυνέθηκα; in Ar. *Frogs* 1052, τὸν
ὄντα δ' εἴσῃ μῦθον Eur. *El.* 346 (cited LSJ s.v. εἰμί A.3).[26]

In this variant the verb εἰμί seems to predicate *truth* as a property of

---

[25] For the immediately preceding context of **26** see sentence **82** in Chapter IV §17.
[26] This variant or transform of the veridical construction is surely one ingredient among
others in the elaborately ambiguous syntax of the opening sentence of Heraclitus' own
λόγος: τοῦ δὲ λόγου τοῦδ' ἐόντος ἀεὶ ἀξύνετοι γίνονται ἄνθρωποι καὶ πρόσθεν ἢ
ἀκοῦσαι καὶ ἀκούσαντες τὸ πρῶτον (fr. 1), "Although this word is true (forever)...."
Note the typical connection of ἐών in this construction with λόγος on the one hand,
ξυνίημι and ἀκούω on the other. Compare Herodotus' phrase ἀκούων οὐκ εἶχε συμβαλέσθαι
τὸ ἐόν in **23** above.

statements: *The story which you tell is true*. But this is not logically distinct
from the more typical veridical construction with which we began in §2:
ἔστι ταῦτα οὕτω ὡς σὺ λέγεις "These things are (in fact) as you say."
A story is true if and only if it states the facts as they are. The use of veridical
εἰμί for expressing the truth of statements, as in **27**, may be lexically or
stylistically distinct from the use of the verb to express a fact, situation,
or event, as in **1–4** in §2 (or in a Type V construction as verb of occurrence).
But the underlying structure of the veridical use is the same in nearly every
case: *Things are (will be, were…) as you say (propose, believe…)*. And the
connections between the uses for truth and for occurrence, which were noted
in the last section, are fully confirmed from Herodotus. If we read through
the context that follows sentence **27**, we see that τὸν ἐόντα λόγον – the true
story of Cyrus' childhood – is rendered again by ἀληθείη in the next sentence
and two paragraphs later by τὸ γεγονός "what happened" and τὸ πρῆγμα
"the fact", "the deed" (Hdt. I.118.1). The λόγος is ἐών ("true") just because
it relates τὸ ἐόν "what is the case" or τὸ γεγονός "what has occurred".

§5. THE VERIDICAL USE AND THE COPULA CONSTRUCTION

At the end of Section 3 we noted that the essive clause of the veridical construction, considered alone, could often be interpreted as a generalized Type V
use of εἰμί as existential verb of occurrence: ταῦτα ἦν "these things took
place," ἔσται τάδε (ἔργα) "these things will take place." It is only the comparison with a clause of saying or thinking that distinguishes such a use as
properly veridical. The verb itself can be regarded simply as the sentence
operator ("it occurs that") defined in Chapter VI §15. But it would be a
mistake to assume that there is any necessary or general connection between
the veridical nuance and this particular existential use of the verb. The most
distinctive feature of the veridical construction is the correlation between
an intentional clause (of saying, thinking, etc.) and an essive clause with εἰμί.
The use of εἰμί in the essive clause may be a Type V existential, but it may
also be a locative-existential (as in sentence **138** in Chapter VI §23) or an
ordinary instance of the nominal copula. In the latter case what we have in
the essive clause is a use of the verb as copula, upon which a veridical nuance
has been superimposed by the expressed or implied comparison with a clause
of saying or thinking.

I shall illustrate this overlap between the veridical use and the copulative
construction both for first-order and for sentence-operator uses of the
nominal copula. First of all, however, let us consider a special case of what
I have called the adverbial copula, as an example of ambiguity between the
copula, existential, and veridical constructions.

28 *Il.* 11.838

πῶς τ᾿ ἄρ᾿ ἔοι τάδε ἔργα; τί ῥέζομεν, Εὐρύπυλ᾿ ἥρως;

"But how shall this be, my lord Eurypylos, what shall we do?"

(after Lattimore)

In Chapter IV §22 this verse was cited as specimen **111**, in the context of a discussion of the adverbial copula. We see now that it might better be regarded as a Type V existential with εἰμί as verb of occurrence: "How shall these things come about?" But we must also take note of the parallel to clauses of doubt and deliberation as in **10** above: ὅπως ἔσται τάδε ἔργα "(We do not know) how these things will be accomplished." In the present example τάδε ἔργα refers back to Eurypylus' request to Patroclus to heal his wound. In this context the first clause in **28** might be rendered "How can your proposal be carried out?" or "How can it be realized?" This rendering serves to bring out the similarity to the promissory or conditional use of the verb in response to a request, in **4** and **6** above. In **28** as in **6**, it is possible to describe the construction as veridical in a wide sense if we interpret τάδε ἔργα (and τοῦτο in the earlier example) as meaning "the action which you propose." In a passage of this kind we may speak at most of an *implicit* veridical construction, since the correlation between the essive clause and an understood clause of saying is not expressed in the surface structure of the text.

We have a direct case of overlap between veridical nuance and copula construction in sentence **22** cited in §4. There the apparently standard veridical use of the participle ὁ δέ οἱ τὸ ἐὸν ἔφρασε "He told him the truth" is indistinguishable from an indirect transformation of the preceding question εἴρετο ὅ τι (=τί) οἱ εἴη οὔνομα "He asked (Crius) what was his name." The answer might equally well be rendered "He told him what his name was." On this reading the underlying construction of the verb is copula-possessive: τὸ ὄνομα μοί ἐστι Κριός "My name is Crius". In the next example we have a pure case of the first-order nominal copula with a superimposed construction that again suggests the veridical value.

29 Aeschylus *Septem* 592

οὐ γὰρ δοκεῖν ἄριστος, ἀλλ᾿ εἶναι θέλει

"He wants not to appear but to *be* the noblest."

The underlying construction involves a contrast between *He is noblest* and the same kernel structure transformed by the verb operator *seems*: *He seems to be noblest.* (Both of these forms serve in turn as operands for a second verb operator *He wants (to be X)*, but we need not consider this second transformation here.) Now the operator *seems* is equivalent to a contrasted clause of thinking: *He seems (to them) to be X* is a paraphrase equivalent of

They believe that he is X. (This is even more obvious in Greek than in English because of the double use of δοκεῖν.) What makes **29** the most famous pre-Platonic expression of the contrast between Being and Seeming is the analogy to an underlying veridical structure: (What he wants is) *to be in fact X, just as men think he is.* But in this case Aeschylus has given the structure a special twist: Amphiaraus wants to be noble in fact, and he does not *care* what people think (hence he wears no blazon on his shield). Notice that this *seems-is* contrast can be imposed upon any copula use of *be*, and indeed upon any verb in the language. In such a contrast the veridical value of εἰμί is entirely independent of the veridical construction as defined in §2: it relies only on the fundamental truth claim of the sentential form (which need not be expressed by an indicative verb, as we see from the use of the infinitive εἶναι in **29**).

A more direct suggestion of the veridical construction in the use of a second-order copula (with a nominalized verb as subject) is illustrated by another passage in the same play:

30 *Ibid.* 224

> Et.   πειθαρχία γάρ ἐστι τῆς εὐπραξίας
> μήτηρ, γυνὴ Σωτῆρος· ὧδ᾽ ἔχει λόγος.
> Χο.   ἔστι· θεοῦ δ᾽ ἔτ᾽ ἰσχὺς καθυπερτέρα.
> "Eteocles: Obedience is the mother of success, the wife of safety.
>   So goes the tale.
> Chorus: It is (true). But the strength of god is higher still."

The isolated verb ἔστι here (like an emphatic εἶναι; or δὲν εἶναι; in Modern Greek) has in effect the syntax of the copula from the preceding construction: "Yes, obedience is indeed the mother of success." But probably it also receives the full lexical value of the veridical from the contrast with the verb of saying that is reflected in ὧδ᾽ ἔχει λόγος (=ὧδε λέγουσι "so they say"). The next example is the only non-philosophical passage listed in LSJ for the veridical value associated with a finite form of εἰμί:

31 Thucyd. I.10.2

> Ἀθηναίων δὲ τὸ αὐτὸ τοῦτο παθόντων διπλασίαν ἂν τὴν δύ-
> ναμιν εἰκάζεσθαι ἀπὸ τῆς φανερᾶς ὄψεως τῆς πόλεως ἢ ἔστιν
> "(If Sparta was left in ruins, one would find no visible evidence
> of her former power.) Whereas, if Athens were to suffer the same
> misfortune, I suppose that any inference from the appearance
> presented to the eye would make her power to have been twice
> as great as it is."
>
> (Crawley)

As the translation suggests, we have an underlying copulative use of ἐστί with δύναμις as subject and a predicate like μεγάλη "great" (understood from διπλασίαν, and from the general context): *The power of Athens is great, but it would be thought to be twice as great.* The concluding ἔστιν of the sentence as it stands represents this underlying copula syntax, but the lexical value of the verb is reinforced by the veridical correlation with the verb of thinking εἰκάζεσαι, just as εἶναι is contrasted with δοκεῖν in **29**.

I want to suggest that there is always some such contrast expressed or implied – between what a thing is and what it seems, between what it is and what it is said or thought to be – when the veridical value "is true" is associated with a copula construction. We can only speculate on the wider structure of Aristotle's example, οἷον ὅτι ἔστι Σωκράτης μουσικός, ὅτι ἀληθές "As when we say 'Socrates *is* musical', (meaning) that it is true" (*Met.*Δ.7,1017ᵃ33), since no context is provided. From this and the other two illustrations which he gives, we gather only that an initial ἔστι or οὐκ ἔστι (in a copula construction) is interpreted by Aristotle as affirmation or denial of the sentence as a whole, in other words as an assertion of its truth or falsity, in contrast with a non-initial negation that bears only on the predicate: ὅτι ἔστι Σωκράτης οὐ λευκός, ὅτι ἀληθές "When we say 'Socrates *is* not-pale', meaning that this is true." Initial negation, on the other hand, signifies sentence-negation or falsity: τὸ δ' οὐκ ἔστιν ἡ διάμετρος σύμμετρος, ὅτι ψεῦδος "or when we say 'The diagonal *is not* commensurable', meaning that it is false." The freedom of Greek word order here permits a diversity of stylistic nuance and emphasis which we must render by stress and intonation in English. But the initial position of ἔστι or οὐκ ἔστι will not by itself suffice to assign a distinct syntactic or logical value to such a sentence form. Although initial position for the copula always suggests a certain emphasis, it is easy to see by running through a few pages of Herodotus or Plato that this emphasis need not be strictly veridical, any more than it need be existential. The first example of an initial copula in Herodotus, at I.2.1, is εἴησαν δ' ἂν οὗτοι Κρῆτες "(certain Greeks, with whose names they are unacquainted,) but who would probably be Cretans" (transl. Rawlinson). The first Herodotean example of initial ἔστι as copula seems to be I.35.2, ἔστι δὲ παραπλησίη ἡ κάθαρσις τοῖσι Λυδοῖσι καὶ τοῖσι Ἕλλησι, which is simply a parenthetical statement of relevant information: "Now the Lydian method of purifying is very nearly the same as the Greek" (Rawlinson). As these examples show, in order to be able to recognize a veridical use of the copula, we need something more than its initial position in the sentence.[27]

At this point we may recall that every use of the copula in a declarative

---

[27] On initial ἔστι, see further Appendix A, pp. 424f.

sentence is closely associated with a truth claim that properly belongs to the sentence as a whole. (This holds more generally for *any* finite verb in a declarative sentence; see Chapter V §1.) Hence when the copula takes the conspicuous initial position, there is a natural tendency for this implicit truth claim to come to the fore. And it seems to be this fact which Aristotle is referring to in the remarks previously quoted. But we have the specifically veridical idea only if the sentence or its context suggests some correlation with an act of statement, belief or the like. If this correlation is lacking, we can speak only of a certain asseverative or assertive nuance that is associated with initial position for the copula.[28]

I list a few examples of the emphatic initial copula in Attic, some of which involve a direct expression of the notion of truth, some involve a veridical correlation in the context, while others may be regarded simply as an emphatic assertion:

32 Soph. *Ajax* 664

ἀλλ᾽ ἔστ᾽ ἀληθὴς ἡ βροτῶν παροιμία

"But the proverb of mankind is true" (namely, there is no profit in an enemy's gift).

33 Plato *Parmenides* 128 C 2

οὐ παντάπασιν οὕτω σεμνύνεται τὸ γράμμα, ὥστε ἅπερ σὺ λέγεις διανοηθὲν γραφῆναι... ἔστι δὲ τό γε ἀληθὲς βοήθειά τις ταῦτα τῷ Παρμενίδου λόγῳ.

"The work was not intended quite as solemnly as you say.... It is in fact (only) a defense of Parmenides' doctrine."

34 Xen. *Anab.* VI.1.6

ὁ δ᾽ ἔπεσε τεχνικῶς πως, καὶ... ἐξέφερον ὡς τεθνηκότα ·ἦν δὲ οὐδὲν πεπονθώς.

---

[28] A similarly emphatic assertive or affirmative role of the initial copula in Latin was recognized long ago as a stylistic device by Marouzeau, who called it "attribution affirmative". See *La phrase à verb "être" en latin* (1910), pp. 43–51; *L'ordre des mots en latin* (1953), pp. 35f. Marouzeau is careful to point out, however, that initial position for the copula may have several other stylistic motivations, including emphasis on the tense or delaying the repetition of a predicate expression from the end of a preceding sentence.

In connection with Latin we may also note the overlap of veridical and copula construction, or at least the strong asseverative use of the copula, that is suggested by the etymology of Latin *sons* (= I.-E. *sont-, the participle of *es-): "'coupable', terme juridique qui s'applique à 'l'étant', a celui 'qui est réellement' (l'auteur du délit)", Benveniste, *Problèmes de linguistique générale*, p. 188. So also Brugmann, *Syntax des einf. Satzes* p. 73: "*sons* 'schuldig, straflich' ('der es gewesen ist, der Täter')". For derivatives of the I.-E. participle *sont- which reflect a similar legal-religious use of "being" for "being the guilty one", see English *sin*, German *Sünde* (Ernout-Meillet, *Dict. étym.* s.v. *sons*). And compare the Hittite formula of confession cited above, n. 6.

"(The Thracian warrior in mock combat) fell in a tricky way....
And they carried him off as dead. But in fact he had suffered
no harm."

35 Soph. *Ajax* 466

οὐκ ἔστι τοὔργον τλητόν

"No, that cannot be borne."

36 Eur. *Iph. in Tauris* 721

ἀλλ' ἔστιν, ἔστιν, ἡ λίαν δυσπραξία

λίαν διδοῦσα μεταβολάς, ὅταν τύχῃ

"(The oracle of Apollo has not destroyed you yet, though you
stand near to death.) But in fact (or in possibility?) extreme
misfortune veers to the other extreme when the event arrives."

Only in **33** is the assertive force of initial ἔστι supported by an explicit
veridical contrast with a verb of saying (οὐ ... ἅπερ σὺ λέγεις). But in **34**
a similar contrast is clearly suggested: *They acted as if he were dead, and
the audience believed it for a moment, but in fact....* (For the use of the
periphrastic construction here precisely in order to exploit the veridical-
assertive value of εἰμί, see Chapter IV §17.) In **36** there is a vaguer contrast
between the despair of Orestes and the hopeful assertion of Pylades: *Your
death seems imminent, but the gods have (or may have?) surprises in store.*
(Again the periphrastic construction is motivated by the assertive – and
perhaps potential – value of ἔστι.) [29] In **32** the initial position for the copula
serves to underline the "veridical" recognition that what men proverbially
say has proved true in the present case of the sword which Ajax received
from Hector. In **35**, on the other hand, we have simply the violent rejection
of an envisaged course of action, where any intentional-essive correlation
is left entirely implicit.

§6. HOMERIC PARALLELS TO THE VERIDICAL USE OF THE COPULA

In the last section we saw how an explicitly veridical construction for the
copula shades off into cases which are scarcely more than emphatic assertions.
Since all of the examples cited are from classic prose and poetry, I here note
by way of appendix a few Homeric parallels. We have already mentioned the
quasi-veridical use of the participle after a verb of knowing or perceiving.

---

[29] In many cases a repeated initial ἔστι will have existential force, as in Soph. *Philoctetes*
1241 ἔστιν τις ἔστιν ὅς σε κωλύσει τὸ δρᾶν, Demosth. 18.308 ἔστι γάρ, ἔστιν ἡσυχία
δικαία καὶ συμφέρουσα τῇ πόλει ... ἀλλ' οὐ ταύτην οὗτος ἄγει τὴν ἡσυχίαν (cited by
Fraenkel, *Beobachtungen zu Aristophanes*, p. 79 n., who also quotes two examples of
repeated ἔσται τάδ' ἔσται in the promissory veridical from Euripides; for this use see
above, n. 10.

37 *Od.* 15.532

ἔγνων γάρ μιν ἐσάντα ἰδὼν οἰωνὸν ἐόντα
"I knew him at a glance to be a bird of omen"

(Palmer)

More interesting is the following example, where the idea of truth is expressed by the predicate adjective but underlined by an emphatic initial position for the copula. (The case is all the more striking since it is one of the very few instances in Homer of an initial ἔστι without existential force.)

38 *Od.* 23.62

ἀλλ᾽ οὐκ ἔσθ᾽ ὅδε μῦθος ἐτήτυμος, ὡς ἀγορεύεις
"But this is no true tale you tell"

(Palmer)

We have a famous echo of this in Stesichorus, fr. 15 (Page): οὐκ ἔστ᾽ ἔτυμος λόγος οὗτος "That tale is not true." Finally, there is a curious family of Homeric formulas some members of which illustrate a veridical nuance for the copula. The least problematic specimen is *Iliad* 23.643, where Nestor sums up an account of his youthful exploits with the clause ὥς ποτ᾽ ἔον "Such was I once". Here we have not the veridical but simply an adverbial copula with the anaphoric ὥς referring back to the content of the preceding narrative. However, in an earlier passage the same phrase in the mouth of the same speaker occurs with a curious conditional.

39 *Il.* 11.762

ὣς ἔον, εἴ ποτ᾽ ἔον γε, μετ᾽ ἀνδράσιν
"That was I among men, if it ever happened."

(Lattimore)

The literal sense of the conditional is "if I was really such" (*si revera talis fuit*, Ebeling). The idea expressed is less one of genuine doubt than of remoteness: it is probably not the accuracy of his memory which Nestor calls into question, but the reality of a past so far away. Thus Chantraine paraphrases our next example as "si ce passé a jamais été vrai" (*Gramm. hom.* I, 320). In this case we have an underlying construction of the verb as nominal copula:

40 *Il.* 3.180

δαὴρ αὖτ᾽ ἐμὸς ἔσκε κυνώπιδος, εἴ ποτ᾽ ἔην γε
"(Agamemnon) was my brother-in-law, slut that I am – if he ever was!"

(Lattimore, adapted)

In **39** and **40** the use of the verb is clearly copulative, with a superimposed veridical nuance: "can it have been so?" There is no question in either case of an existential or vital sense ("if he was ever alive"), since in **39** the speaker is referring to himself and in **40** Helen is referring to Agamemnon who is in plain sight. The situation is different in the next example, where Priam speaks of his dead son.

41 *Il.* 24.426

> ἐπεὶ οὔ ποτ᾽ ἐμὸς πάϊς, εἴ ποτ᾽ ἔην γε,
> λήθετ᾽ ἐνὶ μεγάροισι θεῶν
>
> "Because my own son, if ever I had one,
> never forgot in his halls the gods who live on Olympus."

(Lattimore)

Here we may hesitate between the copula construction suggested by the metrical parallel to **40** ("if Hector ever was my son") and the equally plausible reading of the verb as an existential Type I: "if he was ever alive". The three examples of related formulas in the *Odyssey* suggest that the poet was there influenced by this second, vital-existential reading of **41**.[30]

These examples may serve to confirm the possibility of an overlap between the copula construction and the veridical nuance in Homer, of the sort illustrated for post-Homeric literature in §5. The point is of some importance, since I will want to assume that the connection between copula and veridical uses of the verb is not a late development in Greek but forms part of the fundamental and permanent structure of the language, as do the connections between the veridical and the verb of occurrence.[31] Accordingly, I regard the rarity of the copula-veridical overlap in Homer as a literary accident, like the uniqueness of the veridical participle illustrated in **18**. Neither fact is particularly surprising, if we take into account the over-all rarity of the veridical use in Greek and the presence in Homer of an alternative expression for the veridical idea in the forms ἐτεόν, ἐτήτυμος, etc. The contrast between Homer and Herodotus is instructive in this connection. In Herodotus, where the veridical use of τὸ ἐόν is so common, the corresponding use of ἐτεόν and its cognates is altogether lacking.

---

[30] Thus in *Od.* 15.267 πατὴρ δέ μοί ἐστιν Ὀδυσσεύς,/εἴ ποτ᾽ ἔην· νῦν δ᾽ ἤδη ἀπέφθιτο λυγρῷ ὀλέθρῳ, the reference to death again suggests a vital sense for ἔην as in **41**: this looks like a secondary use of the formula which occurs as verse ending in **40** and **41** above. In *Od.* 19.315 both readings are possible: οἷος Ὀδυσσεὺς ἔσκε μετ᾽ ἀνδράσιν, εἴ ποτ᾽ ἔην γε, although there is an obvious parallel in thought to **39**. In the final example at *Odyssey* 24.289, ἐμὸν παῖδ᾽, εἴ ποτ᾽ ἔην γε, we have precisely the formula of **41** with the same ambiguity.

[31] For indirect evidence of the antiquity of the copula-veridical connections, see the parallels in Latin cited above, n. 28 §5.

§7. Some polemical reflections on the Greek notion of truth

The discussion of the concept of truth by the Greek philosophers falls outside the scope of this study. As we have seen, however, the classical formula given by Aristotle – to say of what is that it is and of what is not that it is not – merely articulates the pattern of the ordinary veridical idioms in Greek. Wherever their full structure is clear, these uses of εἰμί are characterized by an explicit comparison, formulated by οὕτως ... ὡς between an essive clause which expresses how things are, were, or will be, and an intentional clause with a verb of saying or thinking.[32] As in the most contemporary idiom so in Homer and Sophocles: the man who speaks the truth "tells it like it is", and the liar tells it otherwise.

This informal *façon de parler* leaves open many of the philosophic issues involved in a correspondence theory which conceives truth as some kind of relation between language and the world. The idioms specify only that there is some relation of this kind, such that it admits a comparison between its terms, that one term is to be found in *what is said or thought*, the other in *what is* or *what is actually the case*, and that the truth depends upon some point of similarity or agreement (οὕτως ... ὡς) between the two.

That this is the ordinary Greek notion of telling or knowing the truth, from Homer to Aristotle, the passages cited in this chapter should establish beyond reasonable doubt. (And the uses of **sont-* and its derivatives for "truth" in other I.-E. languages suggest that the view described here is a good deal older than Homer.) But the situation has been confused by much discussion of the meaning and etymology of the term ἀλήθεια, which we normally translate as "truth". First of all it should be noted that ἀλήθεια is not the only or the most typical word for "truth" in Homer. It occurs only twice in the *Iliad* (at 23.361 and 24.407); the corresponding neuter adjective ἀληθέα only once (6.382). (The form ἀληθής also occurs once, at 12.433 in a rather problematic application to a servant woman; in this case there is a respectable variant reading ἀλῆτις.) There are several other expressions for true or reliable statement that are at least as common in Homer, for example ἀτρεχέως and ἐτεόν (with its cognate ἐτήτυμος). Thus the problem of the

---

[32] I refer here to the veridical construction proper as the central case. As we have just seen, a comparable veridical value for the verb can be brought out by an opposition between what a thing is and what it seems or is thought to be, without the syntax of comparison. But this contrast either presupposes or reinforces the basic veridical comparison: to think correctly about a thing is to think about it as it is. Similarly, to know a thing is to know it as it is. Thus the veridical value tends also be to associated with εἰμί as object of verbs meaning "to know" (above, p. 351).

Homeric notion of truth is in no sense identical with the interpretation of
the word ἀλήθεια.

This fact has been obscured by Heidegger's very influential discussion of
the etymology of ἀλήθεια in connection with his own view of truth as
Unverborgenheit or "uncoveredness", a view which he attributes to the
Greeks. According to Heidegger, it is not λόγος – either as statement
(*Aussage*) or as judgment (*Urteil*) – that provides the primary locus for truth.[33]
The original phenomenon of verity lies rather in perception in the widest
sense, in νόησις, that is to say in the *Erschlossenheit* ("openness") which is
a fundamental constitution of *Dasein*: the openness of human existence in
virtue of which it can encounter beings in its world.[34] The derivative truth
of statements in language depends on, or consists in, the "pointing-out"
(*Aufzeigen*) or "uncovering" (*Entdecken*) of that which is encountered and
which "shows itself" (*sich zeigt*). Truth as *Unverborgenheit* means to take
things out of hiding, to let them be seen in their uncoveredness.[35]

I shall not discuss Heidegger's doctrine as a contribution to the theory
of truth. Nor shall I contest the etymological connection between ἀλήθεια
and the verbal root of λανθάνομαι "I escape notice," "(I do something)
without being perceived". The same root, with much the same meaning,
is found in Latin *lateo* "am hidden" "remain unnoticed." The question
is what light this etymology sheds on the conception of speaking the truth
(ἀληθέα μυθήσασθαι) in Homer, and how it can fit the veridical idioms
analyzed in this chapter.

J. B. Hofmann explains the connection as follows: the man is truthful
who is guilty of no forgetfulness, who hides nothing in silence.[36] Leaving
aside the question whether forgetfulness as such (λήθη, λαθέσθαι) plays a
role in the Homeric usage of ἀλήθεια, I find Hofmann's view entirely
compatible with the epic texts. But it implies that the *hiding* is an inter-
personal relationship between speaker and hearer, not an existential or
cognitive relation between an individual subject and the facts and beings
which it encounters in its world. Only the former view of ἀλήθεια as a
relation between one man and another, between what the speaker knows or
thinks and what he tells his interlocutor – only this view can do justice to
the Homeric evidence which regularly construes ἀλήθεια (and its opposite

[33] *Sein und Zeit*, p. 226.
[34] *Ibid*. 220f.
[35] *Ibid*. 219 "Das Wahrsein des λόγος als ἀπόφανσις ist das ἀληθεύειν in der Weise des
ἀποφαίνεσθαι: Seiendes – aus der Verborgenheit herausnehmend – in seiner Unverborgenheit (Entdecktheit) sehen lassen. Die ἀλήθεια ... bedeutet die "Sache selbst", das,
was sich zeigt, *das Seiende im Wie seiner Entdecktheit*."
[36] *Etymol. Wörterbuch des Griechischen* s.v. ἀληθής.

ψεῦδος) with verbs of saying, and implicitly contrasts it with expressions like κρύπτω "to hide".[37]

> ἐχθρὸς γάρ μοι κεῖνος ὁμῶς ᾽Αΐδαο πύλῃσιν
> ὅς χ᾽ ἕτερον μὲν κεύθῃ ἐνὶ φρεσίν, ἄλλο δὲ εἴπῃ
> "For as I detest the doorways of Death, I detest that man, who
> hides one thing in the depths of his heart, and speaks forth
> another."
> (*Il.* 9.312, tr. Lattimore)

In this passage the word ἀλήθεια does not occur; but the corresponding idea is perfectly expressed. What ἀλήθεια designates – etymologically, and in the archaic usage insofar as this reflects the etymology – is not the concept of truth as a relation between statements and the world, or between the subject and what he apprehends: it is rather the concept of *truthfulness* or *sincerity* in one man's speaking openly to another, *sans arrière-pensée*. To speak "truthfully" in Homer is to tell all (πᾶσαν ἀληθείην κατάλεξον *Il.* 24.407), to omit or suppress nothing so that it "escapes (the hearer's) notice" (λανθάνει), to hide nothing in one's heart. Why this word for subjective or personal truthfulness later became the general term for *truth*, I do not know. What the development shows is that the etymological associations of the word, if not entirely lost to sight, were no longer strong enough to determine its classical use. And even in the earliest use, in Homer, there is no trace of "the things themselves" emerging from their hiddenness or showing themselves.

The veridical idioms analyzed here indicate quite clearly that the Greeks regularly distinguish between the facts as they are and the facts as they are said or thought to be. This truism bears repeating, because some interpreters have suggested that a distinction of this kind is alien to the Greek view of the world.[38] A strange attribution to the people who invented the antithesis

---

[37] For the evidence, see W. Luther, *"Wahrheit" und "Lüge" im ältesten Griechentum.* Luther's interpretation, however, is confusing. On the one hand he accepts Heidegger's translation as "Unverborgenheit" and combats the views of Leo Meyers and Bultmann which resemble the account I have given (they suggest a basic meaning of "ohne verheimlichendes Täuschen"), p. 12. On the other hand, his own formula for the *Grundbedeutung* is compatible with the evidence and with my interpretation of it: ἀληθέα εἰπεῖν means "etwas berichten, mitteilen usw. so, dass nichts verborgen und verhüllt wird" (p. 26). This seems to imply that the hiding or uncovering takes place between speaker and hearer; and of course that is what *must* be meant by ἀληθέα εἰπεῖν.

On this point a more correct account is given by H. Boeder, who renders πᾶσα ἀληθείη as "rückhaltlose Offenheit"; see "Der frühgriechische Wortgebrauch von Logos und Aletheia" in *Archiv für Begriffsgeschichte* IV (1959), p. 97. For further discussion and literature see Alexander P. D. Mourelatos, *The Route of Parmenides* (New Haven, 1970), pp. 63–6.

[38] I have in mind Luther, *"Wahrheit" und "Lüge"*, p. 14: "Die ... Scheidung zwischen 'Aussage' und der in der 'Aussage' gemeinten 'Sache' hat aber für die griechische Welt-

of word (λόγος) and deed (ἔργον)! What is true is that the Greeks rarely – and
before Chrysippus, never systematically – distinguish the word or sentence as
a linguistic expression, as a mere utterance, from the meaning or content
which it expresses. But even in the case of true speech, where word and deed
must match, the idioms we have discussed make a clear distinction between
the statement of or belief in a fact and the fact itself.

§8. SOME USES OF VERIDICAL εἶναι IN GREEK PHILOSOPHY

I close this chapter with a few brief indications of the philosophical use of
εἶναι, ἔστι, or ὄν where the veridical nuance or construction is of importance.
One peculiar feature of the philosophic use is the attention given to the
negative form (τὸ) μὴ ὄν.

In the standard non-philosophical uses of the veridical, the essive clause
always refers to the facts as they really are (were, will be), regardless whether
we take the subject of εἰμί to be *the real situation* or *the situation as described*.
In either event the clause with εἰμί refers to what is, was, or may be the case.
The negative form of an essive clause is thus quite rare in ordinary usage.
Herodotus speaks 12 times of τὸ ἐόν and ἐὼν λόγος; never of τὸ μὴ ἐόν
or οὐκ ἐὼν λόγος. The Platonic dialogues do not have a formula of denial
that corresponds to ἔστι ταῦτα and ἔστι οὕτω as formulas of assent. In an
ordinary veridical it is just as unusual to negate the essive clause as it would
be for us to form a negative of *in fact* or *actually*. (Of course we may use
these parenthetical adverbs negatively, but normally the negation applies
not to them but to the sentence they modify: *not actually* will usually mean
actually, not.)

Still, it is clearly possible to use οὐκ ἔστι in a veridical construction or
with a veridical nuance. Aristotle cites a negative example of a veridical
copula in *Met.Δ*.7, and we have found parallel uses of the initial copula in
strong denials such as οὐκ ἔστι τλητόν or οὐκ ἔστι ἐτήτυμος (above,
pp. 360f.). What is hard to find – and I have found none – is an extra-
philosophic example of the absolute construction οὐκ ἔστι ταῦτα "that is
not so" or τὸ μὴ ὄν "What is not the case."[39] Yet even if it happens that the
non-technical literature contains no example of such forms, that would only

---

ansicht keine Gültigkeit; vielmehr gehört dort beides untrennbar zusammen." Again,
Luther's formulation is unclear: he *may* mean only that the Greeks do not distinguish
λόγος as a sentence or utterance from λόγος as a meaningful proposition or statement
of *alleged* fact. But in that case his use of this point against Heidegger is unjustified.

[39] The closest thing to this which I have noticed is the negative adjectival use of the
participle, as in Aristophanes, *Frogs* 1052 πότερον δ' οὐκ ὄντα λόγον τοῦτον περὶ τῆς
Φαίδρας ξυνέθηκα; "Was this a false story I made up about Phaedra?"; similarly in Soph.
Electra 584 ἀλλ' εἰσόρα μὴ σκῆψιν οὐκ οὖσαν τίθης "But take care not to offer a false

be another proof of the gap between our imperfect knowledge of the language, based exclusively upon written occurrences, and the native speaker's spontaneous mastery of the rules of grammatical acceptability. For the philosophic discussions make abundantly clear that the Greeks themselves found nothing incorrect or ungrammatical in an expression like τὸ μὴ ὄν, though they did find it full of logical traps.

It is above all the philosophers, then, who bring the veridical μὴ ὄν and οὐκ ἔστι (without predicate expression) into the clear light of attested usage, as known from the preserved literature. The first to do so was probably Parmenides, but I shall begin here with the less controversial formula of Protagoras (fr. 1): Man is the measure of all things, τῶν μὲν ὄντων ὡς ἔστιν, τῶν δὲ οὐκ ὄντων ὡς οὐκ ἔστιν. We have here the classical formula for truth, and ᾿Αλήθεια was in fact the title of Protagoras' book. (In view of Protagoras' doctrine, it is probably no accident that the corresponding formula for falsehood is omitted.) In this formulation the participles correspond to the essive clause of a veridical construction; the finite verbs represent indirect discourse after an understood verb of *judging* or *knowing* (understood from μέτρον): "Man measures what is so, (determining) that it is so." Thus we have here the recurrence of the veridical εἰμί embedded within the intentional clause of *dicendi vel sentiendi*, that recurrence which we illustrated earlier from Aristotle's formula for truth but which is suppressed in the idiomatic forms of the veridical. Thus both the expression of a second form of εἰμί and the symmetrical balance of affirmative and negative clauses distinguish the philosophical veridical from its idiomatic prototypes. What they have in common, however, is a generalized sentential subject for finite verb and participle: *what is* (or *what is the case*) can be any proposition or any fact whatever. In the philosophic formula the verb occurs twice: once for the fact as such (τὰ ὄντα), once for the fact as recognized and affirmed in human speech or cognition (ὡς ἔστι). In modern terminology we may say that here the participle τὸ ὄν represents an arbitrary fact; the finite verb ὡς ἔστι represents an arbitrary proposition (or the content of any "judgment"). In the formula quoted from Aristotle (above, p. 336 n. 7) we have the infinitive εἶναι instead of the finite verb, but the logic of the use is the same.

---

excuse." K. J. Dover points out a more complex example of μὴ οὖσαν προσποίησιν at Thuc. VI. 16.5. (See p. 458 for a Sophistic example of τὰ μὴ ἐόντα.)

Plato himself shows some caution in his introduction of the phrase τὸ μὴ ὄν. In the *Cratylus* he speaks first of τὰ ὄντα λέγειν, then of λέγειν τὰ ὄντα τε καὶ μή (385 B 7-10), later of τὸ μὴ τὰ ὄντα λέγειν (429 D 5-6). In the *Euthydemus* we have the transition from οὐ τὰ ὄντα λέγει to τὰ μὴ ὄντα (284 B 2-3). In the *Republic* the concept of τὸ μὴ ὄν puts in a serious philosophical appearance (478 B 6ff.; cf. *Symp.* 205 B 9). Then in the *Theaetetus* (188 Dff.) and the *Sophist* (236 Eff.), to say or think τὸ μὴ ὄν is posed as a problem.

This two-fold philosophic use of the verb, for an arbitrary fact and/or an arbitrary proposition, must be borne in mind when one encounters any form of εἰμί in Plato or in Aristotle – and particularly when one encounters the infinitive εἶναι without a predicate. It has occasionally been observed that the phrase τὸ εἶναί τι ἢ μὴ εἶναί τι in Aristotle "is not his way of referring to existence-propositions…. It is his way of including all statements or assertions or propositions whatever and excluding sentences which are not statements but prayers or commands or promises or the like."[40] As Robinson suggests, the infinitive εἶναι may not only refer to an arbitrary proposition but may indicate the propositional form as such, in semantic terms the truth claim (like ὡς ἔστι in the Protagorean and Aristotelian formulas for truth). It is this semantic value ("belongs to", "is true of") or its ontological correlate, and not predication considered merely as a syntactic connection, which is signified by εἶναι and μὴ εἶναι in the definition of the *terms* of a syllogistic premiss: ὅρον δὲ καλῶ εἰς ὃν διαλύεται ἡ πρότασις, οἷον τό τε κατηγορούμενον καὶ τὸ καθ᾽ οὗ κατηγορεῖται, προστιθεμένου [ἢ διαιρουμένου secl. Ross] τοῦ εἶναι ἢ μὴ εἶναι (*An. Pr.* I.1.24ᵇ16), "I call 'term' that into which a premiss is resolved, i.e. the predicate and that of which it is predicated, with *being* or *not being* added." By εἶναι here Aristotle means not (or not merely) the grammatical or formal link of terms in a sentence but the semantic claim that the predicate *belongs* or *applies* to the subject – the connection which he elsewhere expresses by ὑπάρχειν τινί. Aristotle's terminology does not explicitly distinguish the propositional claim (the attribution of P. to S.) from the fact that P. actually *belongs* to S. But if the definition quoted is general enough to apply to false premisses – as it should –, then it must be the former notion which is properly signified here by εἶναι and μὴ εἶναι.

The most important of all Aristotelian uses of εἶναι and μὴ εἶναι for an arbitrary fact or proposition is in the various statements of the laws of non-contradiction and excluded middle, e.g. *Phys.* 191ᵇ26 ἔτι δὲ καὶ τὸ εἶναι ἅπαν ἢ μὴ εἶναι οὐκ ἀναιροῦμεν "Furthermore (by this solution) we do not violate the principle that every thing either is or is not"; *Met.* 1005ᵇ24 ταὐτὸν ὑπολαμβάνειν εἶναι καὶ μὴ εἶναι ("It is impossible for anyone) to believe that the same thing is and is not", ᵇ35 ἐνδέχεσθαί φασι τὸ αὐτὸ εἶναι καὶ μὴ εἶναι "They say it is possible for the same thing to be and not to be," etc. Here the ambiguity between proposition and fact (as represented by εἶναι) may be systematic, insofar as Aristotle regards non-contradiction not only as a law of logic ("The propositions p and $\sim p$ cannot both be true")

---

[40] R. Robinson, *Plato's Earlier Dialectic*, 2nd. ed. 1953 p. 101, commenting on *Post. An.* I.2.72ᵃ20. See the parallel remarks of J. Hintikka, *Acta Philosophica Fennica* XIV (1962), pp. 13f., who cites several other examples in the *De Int.* and *Post. An.*

but also as a law of being ("An attribute P. cannot both belong and not belong to a subject S.")

The use of the veridical in Plato is a subject too vast to touch on here. I mention only one example, an important passage in the *Theaetetus*, where it seems certain that τὸ ἔστιν καὶ τὸ οὐκ ἔστι, οὐσία καὶ τὸ μὴ εἶναι stand for the general forms of affirmation and denial, that is for the forms and function of statement or judgment in general, in affirming and denying any fact or proposition whatsoever (186C). Plato's point is that this general propositional form – the form of a truth claim – is a necessary condition for truth and knowledge, and a condition which sense-perception as such cannot satisfy. Sensation cannot be knowledge because it cannot be true, and it cannot be true because it is non-propositional in form, that is, it does not assert anything, and hence it does not raise the question of truth. The commentators who understand οὐσία here as "existence" have made non-sense of the passage, and they have thus rendered unintelligible Plato's last and deepest argument against the identification of knowledge with sense-perception.

I note, finally, that it is typical of Aristotle (and probably of Plato as well) that he thought of truth-claim or assertion as two-valued, like true and false or affirmation and denial. This duality can be traced back to the Man-the-Measure formula quoted from Protagoras and, ultimately, to the "two ways" of Parmenides: ἔστι and οὐκ ἔστι. It seems to be the natural result of regarding affirmation and negation, Yes and No, as coordinate and equally elementary concepts.[41]

I should point out that these last examples from Aristotle and Plato (on pp. 368f.) are not strictly veridical insofar as they involve no correlation or contrast with a clause of saying, thinking, or seeming. Where εἶναι represents the propositional form as such or an arbitrary propositional content, what we have is the verb as sign of predication in the widest sense, that is to say, as sign of sentential truth claim. (See above, Chapter V § 12, p. 226 and below, Chapter VIII § 6 on predication₃.) It is this function of εἰμί, as verb par excellence, which underlies its veridical use generally and its use in the veridical construction in particular. We speak of the verb as veridical only when there is some hint of the metalinguistic concept of truth, and this hint is usually conveyed by some comparison or contrast with an act of saying, thinking, or seeming. But the implicit truth claim which is part of the sentential form is not meta-linguistic. On the contrary, it is the basis for

---

[41] For a consideration of the same point in Aquinas (who follows Aristotle), see A. Kenny, *Action, Emotion and Will* (London, 1963), pp. 226f.

any declarative object-language. The veridical use of εἰμί builds on this basis and thematizes the truth claim as such by means of a comparison between what is claimed and what is the case.[42]

---

[42] For an interesting idiom closely related in structure to the essive clause of the veridical but without any clear hint of the notion of truth, see the construction of ἔστι (τοῦτο) with ὥστε + *infinitive* as "clause of consequence": *Phaedo* 93 B 4 ἦ οὖν ἔστι τοῦτο περὶ ψυχήν, ὥστε... "Isn't this the case concerning soul, namely that (no soul is any more soul than another)?" Also *ibid.* 103 E 2 ἔστιν ἄρα, ἦ δ' ὅς, περὶ ἔνια τῶν τοιούτων, ὥστε... "Thus it is the case, he said, concerning some things of this sort, that (not only does the form itself always deserve its own name, but something else also deserves this name always)." Like the *that*-clause in the English idiom "it is the case that", the infinitival clause with ὥστε spells out the underlying sentential subject of ἔστι. This use of ἔστι is second-order but not meta-linguistic: the verb gives separate expression, in general form, to the notion of propositional or factual claim that is particularized in the specific sentential structure of the infinitival clause.

CHAPTER VIII

THE UNITY OF THE SYSTEM OF 'BE' IN GREEK

§1. THE PLAN OF THIS CHAPTER

Now that our description of the uses of εἰμί is complete, it is time to draw together the threads of the analysis and consider the system of the verb as a whole. How can a single verb perform so many different functions? Which meaning or use of the verb do we take as primary, and in what sense are the other uses to be "derived" from it? Should the joining together of such different functions in the use of the single lexeme *es- be regarded simply as a peculiarity of Indo-European, or as a fact of some general importance for the theory and philosophy of language? And what can be the philosophical interest of a concept of Being that is founded upon such an unusual and apparently arbitrary linguistic situation? We must, after all, meet the challenge of the linguistic relativists who point out that the systematic use of a single sign for both predication and existence is almost unknown outside of I.-E. And we must face the charges of Mill and others that this situation has been a source of endless confusion in Western philosophy.

In dealing with this wide range of questions I shall proceed by stages, shifting the point of view as we move along. The system of *to be* is too diversified to be grasped as a unified whole from any one standpoint or by any single method. My first line of approach will be a traditional one, an inquiry into the etymology and diachronic development of the system. If I begin with a quasi-historical search for a basic or original meaning for the verb, that is not because I have any serious hopes of finding one, or of penetrating to a prehistoric situation for I.-E. *es- which would be simpler or clearer than the situation for εἰμί in Homer. But the search for origins is a traditional method of lexical study, whose limitations must be made plain. Furthermore, the fiction of a development from primitive conditions, as in the creation myths or in the theory of a social contract, has the expository advantage of making quite clear just what is taken as *basic* and what as *derived*, since the distinction is drawn as one between temporally distinct phases in a gradual process. In §2 I shall suspend my disbelief and expound a theory of the development of the various uses from an original locative or locative-existential meaning (as exhibited in πάρ-ειμι "I am present", ἄπ-ειμι "I am absent"). In §3 I give my reasons for believing that such a view, if taken literally as a chronological development from a single source, is not only unsupported by the evidence but probably false in principle, since it is based upon a mistaken view of the original "simplicity" of meaning for words in the early state of a language. I shall also suggest (in §§3–4) how the facts which *seem* to support this diachronic theory can be reinterpreted in psychological terms as indicating a fundamental role played by bodily or spatial metaphors in concept formation, in expressive or poetic discourse, and perhaps in language-learning. In §5 I turn to a purely synchronic account of the system of εἰμί as unified by the static aspectual value that contrasts *be* with *become*. I shall here review and expand some of the points made in our discussion of the theory of the copula in Chapter V. Finally, in §§6–7 I turn to the more properly philosophical problem of the conceptual unity of a system that combines predicative, existential, and veridical functions in the uses of a single verb. In answering Mill's charge I shall of course not claim that the Greek philosophers drew every distinction that has become familiar to us, nor that their discussion of ontological issues is uniformly free of confusion and unclarity. But I shall contend that Parmenides, Plato and Aristotle were served rather than hindered by the fact that the language itself joins together the formal sign of predication with the notions of existence and truth.[1] Whatever errors the Greek philosophers may have committed in their doctrines of Being, it was not an error to suppose that predication, truth, and existence (or reality) belong together in a single family of concepts, the topic for a single body of theory. If we no longer use the term "Being" for this conceptual family, we do not hesitate to employ its correlate "ontology" for the corresponding field of philosophic study. To this extent we justify the tacit assumption of the Greek philosophers (and of many of their successors, from Islamic and medieval times to Hegel and Heidegger) that the key functions of the verb *to be* represent a unified conceptual system of great importance, just that system which is traditionally designated by the I.-E. verb or by its nominal derivatives: εἶναι, ὄν, οὐσία, *esse, Sein, Being.*

---

[1] Perhaps the *is* of identity should be included here. I omit it for two quite different reasons. In the first place, I do not believe this can be distinguished from an ordinary copula use on linguistic grounds. That is, neither in Greek nor in English does the natural language articulate the assertion of identity as a separate sentence form, with distinct syntactic features. (On this see below, p. 400, n. 33.) In the second place, it is hard to see how the failure to distinguish the *is* of identity was in any sense a philosophic advantage. But the case could be argued. Questions of identity in the strong sense – which go beyond knowing who is who – are essentially philosophic questions, and perhaps it is just as well that the language does not beg them for us.

§2. THE SEARCH FOR THE ORIGINAL MEANING OF
be (**es-*) IN INDO-EUROPEAN

We begin, then, with an exercise in diachronic speculation. In the search for an etymology or *Urbedeutung* of **es-*, an original meaning from which all attested uses can be derived, it has always been assumed that the existential uses of the verb are older and more fundamental than the use as copula. I gave reasons for rejecting this assumption in Chapter V, but we may ignore these reasons for the moment, in order to participate more sympathetically in the traditional hunt for a primary sense of the verb. In such an inquiry it is generally taken for granted that the original meaning must be concrete, sensible, or particularly "vivid" (*anschaulich*). In fact it has been the standard view of comparative linguistics that although *to exist* is the oldest attested meaning for **es-*, the notion of existence is itself too abstract and intellectual to count as the *original* sense of the verb.[2] The operative assumptions here are (1) that **es-* must once have been a verb like other verbs, and (2) that the primitive meaning of verbs and other basic lexemes must have been an idea with sensorial content, carrying a concrete spatial or bodily connotation. "Primitive languages, being almost entirely unfamiliar with abstraction, gave an exceedingly concrete form to the expression of thought." The communication of feelings and ideas, the expression of general categories was obliged to make use of "a form borrowed from sensation." The fundamental device by which primitive languages developed a wider and richer vocabulary was *metaphor* or, *transfer of meaning*, from a bodily to an emotional or moral sense, from sensible to intellectual, from concrete to abstract.[3]

---

[2] See the passages in Brugmann, Delbrück, Kühner-Gerth, and Schwyzer cited in Chapter V §4, n. 21. Also Benveniste (*Problèmes de ling. gén.* p. 160): "le verbe *esti* ... a dû avoir un sens lexical défini, avant de tomber – au terme d'un long développment historique – au rang de 'copule'. Il n'est plus possible d'atteindre directement ce sens, mais le fait que **bhū-*, 'pousser, croître', a fourni une partie des formes de **es-* permet de l'entrevoir."

[3] These views are taken from Ernest Renan, *De l'origine du language*, Ch. V, as typical of an attitude which was almost universal among scientific linguists in the nineteenth century and is still influential today. Renan's own position is more subtle than the citations suggest, since he insists that "ceux qui ont tiré le language exclusivement de la sensation se sont trompés, aussi bien que ceux qui ont assigné aux idées une origine purement matérielle." He sees the grammar of a language as the necessary element of rational form, whereas the vocabulary is a variable content that sensory experience has poured "dans les moules pré-existants de la raison". But as an item of vocabulary, the verb *to be* "dans presque toutes les langues, se tire d'une idée sensible." Renan recognizes the frequent connections of such verbs with *to stand* (and also, he supposes, with *to breathe*), but he is rather at a loss to identify the "sens primitivement concret" which he is sure **es-* must once have had. (See pp. 129f. in the 10th ed. *sans date*, Calmann-Lévy, Paris. The quotations in the text are from pp. 120–3.)

The bias in favor of such a view is at least as old as Locke, who wrote (in a section entitled "Words ultimately derived from such as signify sensible ideas") that "if we could trace them to their sources, we should find, in all languages, the names which stand for things that fall not under our senses to have had their first rise from sensible ideas"; from these they have been "transferred to more abstruse significations" (*Essay concerning Human Understanding*, Bk. III. ch. i.5).

It would be in the spirit of these assumptions to suppose that the root *weid- of οἶδα ("know") and ἰδεῖν ("see") in Greek originally meant simply "to see" (as in the Latin cognate *videre*), hence in the perfect form "to know from having seen," and finally "to know" (from any source). So we naturally take as basic for the root *gen- (γίγνομαι) the physical sense "to be born", for an infant emerging from its mother's body. By metaphorical extension the verb γίγνομαι is subsequently used for anything that *emerges* or *comes to light*, and finally (with a copulative construction) for anything which *comes to be* or *becomes* (such-and-such). Now since *be* and *become* are so closely parallel in usage, and since we know that εἰμί in Homer can sometimes mean "I am alive", it is tempting to assume that in this biological and as it were bodily sense of the verb we can recognize its primitive significance. This assumption has indeed left its trace in the etymological literature.[4] This view has the merit of explaining the fact that the vital use of εἰμί in our existential Type I appears as an archaism in Greek, while it finds some parallels in early Indo-Iranian.[5] And since "to live, be alive" (with the negative form meaning "to be dead") is surely the most definite and vivid of all senses attested for εἰμί, making it in this use a verb very much like other verbs (e.g. like ζώω or βιόω), why should we not accept this as the most primitive meaning of *es-?

The trouble is that this vital sense of the verb seems to be poorly attested for cognate verbs outside of Greek and, within Greek, there is no evidence to show that the vital use is older than the others. Only if we are fully

---

[4] Thus G. Curtius, *Griech. Etymologie*[5] (Leipzig, 1879), p. 375, citing Max Müller and Renan, posited three successive phases in the extension of meaning of *es-: "To breathe," "to live," and "to be". This etymology was accepted by Kühner-Gerth, (3rd ed., 1898), I. 3; but abandoned by Delbrück (1900). However, Delbrück's own presentation of the development of the copula implies an unknown, concrete *Urbedeutung* for the verb (*Vergl. Syntax* III. 12–4). Some sympathy for the etymology "be alive" can perhaps be felt in the remarks quoted from Benveniste above, n. 2.

[5] See H. Grassmann, *Wörterbuch zum Rig-Veda* s.v. *as*, with *ásu* ("Das Leben, besonders in seiner Regsamkeit und Frische") and *ásura* ("lebendig, regsam; aber nur vom Körperlosen, geistigen Leben gebraucht"). The sense of "Leben, Lebenskraft" is confirmed for the corresponding forms in Iranian; see Bartholomae, *Altiranisches Wörterbuch* (1904), pp. 106, 110, 283. (I owe this reference to the kindness of Professor Benveniste.) For the possibility of explaining some Old Persian and Avestan uses of the finite forms of *es-* as meaning "am alive", see Chapter VI, §18, n. 67.

committed in advance to a general semantic development from concrete to abstract, from bodily to intellectual, could we have any reason at all to believe that the nominal copula or the various uses of εἰμί which we find restricted to the third person (the second-order copula, existential Types II–V, the veridical) are all to be derived from an original use in which the verb applied only or primarily to persons. In the absence of definite evidence in its support, this view has been generally abandoned by comparatists in the twentieth century.

It might seem wise at this point to abandon not the hypothesis itself but only its diachronic form, and to admit that the vital value of εἰμί as "to be alive", if not a unique *Urbedeutung*, is at any rate very closely associated with the nuclear or core uses of the verb for personal subjects in Homer and elsewhere, as I tentatively suggested in Chapter V (§12). But at present we are looking for an etymology, and there is another possibility to be considered.

Let us postulate, then, a more general basic meaning, of which the vital use for persons might itself be a special case, and from which the copula construction in turn can be derived. The natural candidate is the strong or pregnant locative use, where the verb is construed as copula but has at the same time a kind of existential force: "is present", "is on hand", "is effectively (there)". This is the use illustrated in the compounds πάρ-ειμι, ἄπ-ειμι with their Latin cognates *prae-sens*, *ab-sens*. (The very early date of this particular construction is suggested not only by the parallels in Vedic and elsewhere, but also by the obsolete form of the Latin participle for *sum* which figures in the two compounds just quoted.) Enough has already been said on the intimate connections between the ideas of place, existence, and possession, in Greek and elsewhere. (See Chapter VI, §§8, 11–13.) Since our locative-existential use is itself copulative, being completed by an adverbial of place, and since the archaic vital use can in turn be interpreted as an elliptical locative (εἰμί "I am alive" meaning literally "I am on hand", "I am present among the living" or the like), it is natural to take this locative-existential use as the basis for an explanation of the entire system of uses for εἰμί. And this seems in fact to be the only view of an original or basic meaning for I.-E. *es- that still finds serious defenders.[6] This

---

[6] I quote again from the *O.E.D.*, s.v. "be", B., Vol. I, p. 717: "The primary sense appears to have been that of branch II below, 'to occupy a place' (i.e. *to sit, stand, lie*, etc.) in some specified place; thence the more abstract branch I ["to have or take place in the world of fact, to exist, occur, happen"] was derived by abstracting the notion of particular place, so as to emphasize that of actual existence, 'to be somewhere, no matter where, to be in the universe, or realm of fact, to have a place among existing things, to exist.'"

This was roughly my own view in "The Greek Verb 'to be' and the Concept of Being", *Foundations of Language* 1966, pp. 257f. A somewhat similar view has been proposed by J. Klowski, in "Zur Entstehung der Begriffe Sein und Nichts," *Archiv für Geschichte der Philosophie* 49 (1967), pp. 138ff. Klowski proposes as the oldest and most concrete meaning

locative view of εἰμί is an attractive one. Before renouncing the whole genetic approach to the meaning of the verb, let us see just what is implied in the proposal to take the locative-existential use as chronologically primary.

We postulate that there was once a time when the verb εἰμί (or its ancestor *es-) was used *exclusively* with a locative complement expressed or implied, and with the corresponding lexical value: "Here is X", "X is present here" (or "at such a place"), "X is found here", and the like. (For examples of the verb actually used in this way see Chapter VI §§11 and 13, sentences **51–58**, **73–79**.) We then assume that *at some subsequent time* speakers of the language felt the need to express existence without a local specification, in sentences such as *There is no one who can fight against Zeus* (Type IV), *There will be a time when...* (Type IV, variant), or *There will be retribution for the crime* (Type V). Under these new circumstances speakers of proto-Greek transferred (by instinct, not by covenant) the locative-existential verb to new, more abstract uses, in which the intuitive spatial connotations were preserved either metaphorically (as in our idioms *take place, be in a difficult situation*) or purely formally, without any noticeable imagery (as in *there is, be in love*). We have, in short, the double phenomenon of (a) the metaphorical extension of a verb of place to new, non-spatial applications, together with (b) a gradual and sometimes complete fading of the metaphor. The possessive construction ἔστι μοι shows precisely this gradation, for the most characteristic uses in Homer include a specification of place (ἔστι τοι ἐν κλισίῃ "You have in your hut"), whereas the more abstract uses drop this specification altogether (οὐδέ μοι ἔστι πατὴρ καὶ πότνια μήτηρ "I have no father, no honored mother"). (For these examples and others, see Chapter VI §12, sentences **59–63**.) And in the case of possession, this extension is intuitively obvious: to own something is to have it at hand, within one's house – and more generally, within one's control.

It is possible to imagine a similar extension of the locative verb to the

---

of εἶναι "vorhanden sein, sich befinden," where "vorhanden sein" signifies "dass sich etwas vor jemanden Händen befindet, und durch das Verb 'sich befinden' zum Ausdruck kommt, das in dem Gesichtskreis des jeweiligen Subjekts sich etwas findet, das von dem betreffenden Subjekt bewusst wahrgenommen wird." But this particular formulation brings in an element of perceptual relativism that seems quite foreign to the meaning of εἰμί. For example, in ἔστι πόλις Ἐφύρη "There is a city Ephyre (in a corner of Argos)", there is no question of Ephyre being within sight or hearing of the speaker. Insofar as we can spell out the intuitive force of the verb in locative and locative-existential uses, it means something like "to be effectively there, as a physical presence" – a presence which manifests itself in the capacity to act or be acted upon, or, in the case of topographical items, in the capacity to localize events and serve as the scene of action. Compare Plato's tentative definition of "being" in the *Sophist* 247 d 8: "the mark of τὰ ὄντα ὡς ἔστι is no other than δύναμις, the power to act or to be acted upon."

standard copula use with predicate nouns and adjectives. In this case we see that the local connotations have faded entirely and are preserved only in a lingering stative-durative aspect of the verb. In a sentence like Σωκράτης ἐστὶ σοφός "Socrates is wise", the original locative verb reaches the limit of its extended use, where every hint of spatial imagery has disappeared. But we may easily suppose that at one time the metaphorical force of the verb was felt, and that such a sentence meant "Socrates stands in the condition (of being) wise", "Socrates is in a state of wisdom". For we see that this development has actually taken place in the incorporation of forms of *stare* "to stand" within the conjugation of *be* in the Romance languages. Today *Está cansada* "She is tired" (in Spanish) or *Sono stato studente* "I have been a student" (in Italian) involves an almost colorless use of the cognates of *stare*. But there was surely a time in the development of these forms when the local imagery was still felt.[7] Furthermore, we know of cases from other languages where a verb of place is used as copula. Thus in Ewe the locative-existential verb *le* "is present" "is (somewhere)" serves in various predicative constructions. The metaphorical extension of the local verb to attributions of state can be illustrated by the following gradation:

> *mele ho me* "I am in the house"
>
> *mele dowofe* "I am at work" (lit., "in the work-place")
>
> *mele dzidzo kpom* "I am in a good mood" (lit., "in a state of seeing happiness")
>
> *alè mele* "I am in this state, I am so"
>
> *meli nyuie* "I am well"[8]

It would be easy to arrange the Greek uses of εἰμί according to a similar gradation, beginning with the locative copula and the local-existential uses, passing to the possessive and to the more abstract existential uses, and ending with the purely "formal" role of the verb in nominal predication. According to the diachronic hypothesis, this gradation would represent successive stages in an historical (or rather, prehistorical) development, in which the original local use of the verb was progressively extended to non-spatial concepts.

---

[7] Lest the reader find this analogy more compelling than it really is, I hasten to point out that this development for cognates of *stare* presupposes a language with an older copula verb, namely *esse*, for which *stare* became the (partial) suppletive. But what the analogy is supposed to explain is precisely the *original* development of such a copula for predicate nouns and adjectives, in a state of the language where there was *ex hypothesi* no generalized copula verb.

[8] For the data on Ewe see Chapter V §10 n. 46. The expression for possession in Ewe is also provided by *le*: "I have it" is *le asi-nye*, literally "it is in my hand".

To make this hypothesis plausible we must show how it can also account for the veridical and, above all, for the vital uses of εἰμί.

There is no definite trace of a locative idea in the expressions for the veridical construction described in Chapter VII. What we can see, nevertheless, is the psychological plausibility of such a development, by attending to our own metaphors that may serve to render the veridical ἔστι οὕτω "This is how things stand" or ἔστι ταῦτα "That is the situation".

For the vital use our etymological hypothesis can be regarded as more strongly confirmed, since it posits an underlying local value for the use of εἰμί in existential Type I that we would in some cases have to recognize anyway. That is to say, there are some passages in Homer and in later poetry which definitely support the view that follows necessarily from our hypothesis, namely that the most vivid of all uses of εἰμί, where it can be translated "am alive", must have originated from a metaphorical or pregnant use of the verb with the local sense "am present", "am at hand." On this view, ἔστι "is alive" will at first have meant "is present among men", is here among us in the light of day rather than below in the dark and gloomy house of Hades; "the one who is not" (in the sense of "the dead") would be an elliptical or euphemistic expression as in our phrases *the departed, the one who is gone (from among us)*. Now this connection between the vital use and the idea of location seems actually to be expressed in at least one passage in Homer:

> *Od.* 24.262 (=sentence **21** in Chapter VI §6)
>
> ὡς ἐρέεινον
> ἀμφὶ ξείνῳ ἐμῷ, ἤ που ζώει τε καὶ ἔστιν,
> ἤ ἤδη τέθνηκε καὶ εἰν ᾽Αΐδαο δόμοισιν
>
> "When I asked him
> about my friend from abroad, whether he still lives and is
> somewhere here,
> or is dead now and down in the house of Hades."
>
> (Lattimore)

Whereas Palmer (whom we quoted in the first citation of this passage, on p. 242 renders the two verbs ζώει τε καὶ ἔστιν by a single English phrase "if he were living", Lattimore translates ἔστιν separately, with the local sense: "is somewhere here." This translation can be justified by (i) the curious reduplication of ζώει τε καὶ ἔστιν, which makes the latter redundant if it means simply "is alive", and (ii) the parallelism of the two terms in the next verse where τέθνηκε "is dead" answers to ζώει, but εἰν ᾽Αΐδαο δόμοισιν (ἐστι) "(is) in the halls of Hades" answers to ἔστι alone.[9]

[9] See Klowski, *Archiv für Gesch. d. Phil.* 1967, p. 139, for a similar interpretation of ἔστι here. Unlike Klowski, I place absolutely no reliance on the occurrence of που in this

This passage shows that ἔστι in its vital use sometimes does clearly preserve a local-existential sense. And a moment's reflection will show that it is always possible to assume that this is the underlying force of the expression. For *being on earth, in the light of the sun* is a standard phrase in Homer for the life of man, as we can see from formulas that resemble the passage just quoted: εἴ που ἔτι ζώει καὶ ὁρᾷ φάος ἠελίοιο "if he yet lives and sees the light of the sun". (*Od.* 14.44 = 20.207, with three slight variants in the *Odyssey* and four parallels in the *Iliad*. Compare also *Il.* 1.88 ἐμεῦ ζῶντος καὶ ἐπὶ χθονὶ δερκομένοιο "as long as I live and see upon the earth.") That the traditional local definition of mortals as *earthlings*, ἐπιχθόνιοι, in contrast to the ("Olympian") immortals as *sky-dwellers*, οὐρανίωνες, goes back to I.-E. times is borne out by the etymology of Latin *humanus* from *humus*. (For parallels from Baltic, Germanic, and Celtic, see Ernout-Meillet, *Dict. ét. s.v. homo.*) This connection between human life and dwelling on the earth, in the light of day, is so well documented from earliest times that, when we encounter εἰμί for "am alive" without any local indication (as in our paradigm for Type I, ἔτ' εἰσί "they are still alive"), we may understand this as an elliptical expression for the pregnant locative that receives fuller statement in later poets:

Soph. *Philoct.* 415

    ὡς μηκέτ' ὄντα κεῖνον ἐν φάει νόει

    "Count him as one no longer in the light"

Ibid. 1312

    ἀλλ' ἐξ Ἀχιλλέως, ὃς μετὰ ζώντων θ' ὅτ' ἦν

    ἦκου' ἄριστα, νῦν τε τῶν τεθνηκότων

    "(You were not born from Sisyphus) but from Achilles, whose glory was greatest when he was among the living, as now among the dead."

Eur. *Hecuba* 1214

    ἀλλ' ἡνίχ' ἡμεῖς οὐκέτ' ἐσμὲν ἐν φάει

    "But since we are no longer in the light."

Here the sense of the old Homeric use of εἰμί for *being alive* seems to have been intuitively grasped and re-expressed in an unambiguous way. Even that most archaic of all uses of εἰμί for "the gods who are forever" (θεοὶ αἰὲν ἐόντες) may once have meant *the gods who remain forever in the light*, who do not go down into the darkness of death.

---

context, since the unaccented adverb is normally used in questions as an empty particle, without local connotations, i.e. as meaning "perhaps" rather than "somewhere". Notice, however, that this secondary value for που is itself a kind of evidence for the general concrete-to-abstract theory under consideration.

§3. SOME GENERAL REASONS AGAINST TAKING THE SUGGESTED
ETYMOLOGY OF *be* AT ITS FACE VALUE, AS A CHRONOLOGICAL
DEVELOPMENT OF "ABSTRACT" MEANINGS FROM
AN ORIGINAL WHICH WAS MORE "CONCRETE"

I have tried to present the hypothesis of an original local sense for εἰμί in the most favorable light possible, since I believe that it contains a valuable kernel of truth. The husk of error in which this is wrapped can be cleanly stripped away only if the theory is first stated in its most radical form, as a development of many different senses and uses from *one meaning alone*. For what is fundamentally false in this or any similar developmental account is the assumption that the basic words were originally univocal, that in the beginning their spatial or bodily meaning was their *only* meaning. In support of this assumption there is no evidence whatsoever, and in the nature of the case there can be none, since we have no way of getting back to "the beginning", either of I.-E. or of any other human language. And against it there are weighty considerations. Once we abandon this assumption of naive primitivism in the theory of meaning, we see that any quasi-historical account which explains the diversity of Homeric usage for εἰμί as the outcome of a chronological development must be regarded as a piece of fiction, an aitiological myth dressed up in historical clothes.

If we ask, in what sense are we to "believe" the theory of a gradual development of the different uses of εἰμί by the particularization or meta-phorical extension of a primitive local sense, my answer is that this theory must be treated in accordance with the device which it employs. It cannot be taken literally, as an account of the chronological development of the language in prehistoric times, only *figuratively*, as a suggestive formulation of certain facts in the psychology of language, including perhaps some facts about the way children develop their vocabulary and learn new meanings for words which they first understood in a "concrete" sense. It may be true, for example, that other uses of the verb *to be* come to be understood on the basis of a child's primary understanding of spatial relations.[10] And if

---

[10] It seems that Helen Keller first learned to use the copula *is* "in connection with" a lesson "on words indicative of place-relations", including *in* and *on*. *Helen is in wardrobe* and *Box is on table* are examples of her early use of the verb. (Report of Anne Sullivan in Helen Keller, *The Story of My Life*, ed. J. A. Macy, Doubleday and Co., 1954, p. 279.) Both before and for some time after, however, she seems to have made free use of nominal sentences like *Strawberries – very good* and *Helen wrong* (pp. 265, 269). The whole question can now be studied systematically in developmental psycho-linguistics.

I might add that in semi-systematic observation of my daughter Maria learning to speak, I found that the locative copula appeared several months before the nominal copula.

the child does regularly learn to use the copula and other "abstract" words in this way, the factors which make it so are no doubt still important for the intuitive basis of an adult's use of language. Indeed, what is true of the child is to some extent true of the race: much of our abstract philosophical terminology is historically derived from bodily or spatial metaphors. The root of *concept* means "grasping(-together)," *hypothesis* means "laying underneath (as a basis or foundation)," *subject* means "what lies underneath, as basis" (ὑποκείμενον), *object* is *what lies opposite, in front* (ἀντικείμενον). The terms *discern, discriminate,* and *certainty* are all derived from Latin versions of an I.-E. root **krei-* meaning "to divide, separate" physically, as in a sieve (Latin *cribrum,* French *crible*). Greek variants on the same root give us *crisis, criterion,* and a host of other words with wide use in science and philosophy.

Nevertheless, such striking parallels in ontogeny and phylogeny do not establish the thesis on which the genetic myth rests. Neither the psychological fact that if a word has several meanings a child will probably learn the more physical meaning first, nor the historical fact that expressions with bodily or spatial connotations gradually acquire technical uses from which these connotations disappear – neither fact is sufficient to establish, or even to make plausible, the assumption of original univocity. For example, nothing in comparative philology can prove that there was once a time when the root **krei-* meant *only "to separate spatially* (as with a sieve)", and did not *also* mean "to sift" in a wider sense, as when we sift evidence or select men we can trust. On the contrary, it is more reasonable to maintain that the more general notion was implicit "from the beginning" in the concrete application of the root **krei-* to operations with a sieve. For the sieve is designed to separate things according to some standard of purity or value, and the archetypal operation for the root **krei-* seems to be the winnowing or sifting of threshed grain.[11] For example, out of some fifteen occurrences of

---

(My notes begin when Maria, who is bilingual, was 23½ months old and mostly speaking French.) Sentences of the form *Où est maman?* and *Mama est là* occur before 24 months and are completely under control by 25 months. On the other hand the nominal copula is noted for the first time (*est chaud*) at 28½ months, at the same time as past tense (*a eu 'olypop* "I had a lolypop"), and 10 days later both *be* and *have* are in use as auxiliary verbs: *Papa a tourné café?* (I turn over the Italian coffee pot.) *N'est pas tombé café?* These observations suggest that command of the nominal copula is closely associated with a more general mastery of sentence form (including compound tenses with *be* and *have*), whereas the locative copula emerges earlier as an item of concrete vocabulary. For Maria at age two, *est là* ("Here it is") functioned as a basic concept answering to *parti!* ("Gone!" "Disappeared!"). For Maria at two-and-a-half, *est chaud, est tombé, est coming bientôt, est garçon* (for her brother) represent refinements on earlier forms without *be*.

11 For those who have never seen threshing under archaic circumstances let me report that the use of a sieve or strainer is one of the last steps in the operation, to sift the products

the cognate verb in the *Iliad* (or twice as many, if we count the compound forms in ἀπο- and δια-), only one refers to the actual operation of winnowing (5.501), one refers to the interpretation of dreams (5.150), and one refers to the rendering of crooked judgments in legal disputes (16.387), i.e. distinguishing right from wrong, the winner from the loser in the dispute. (This legal use, which is familiar from the post-Homeric words κρίτης "judge" and κρίσις "judgment", "trial", is likely to be prehistoric, since we find it also in Latin *crimen*.) The majority of uses for this verb apply to the separation of men from one another by tribes or the like, to the selection of brave men for a military assignment or a choice herd of cattle to pay a debt (2.362, 6.188, 9.521, 11.697, etc.). Even where the separation is understood literally in a local sense, it is based upon the recognition of some qualitative difference between the items separated. Thus the principle which is expressed in the more abstract senses of the root is implicit in the Homeric use of the verb. If the current meanings of *crisis* and *certainty* are clearly late and "secondary" in a chronological sense, that is not the case for *discern*, *discriminate*, or *criterion*, all of which (whether derived from Greek or from Latin variants of the root) express an idea that is present in the meaning of κρίνω in Homer. Even the sieve is a kind of criterion.

The example of **krei-* is worth pondering, for it shows how a true premiss, namely, that many philosophical or technical terms have lost an earlier connection with spatio-bodily meanings, has been used to draw a conclusion which is at least half false: (a) that the original meaning for any term was always spatio-bodily (or in some other way "concrete") and (b) that this was once the *only* meaning. The first conjunct of this conclusion (which may be slightly more plausible) does not really concern us here. It is (b), the thesis of original univocity, that I want to single out for conspicuous repudiation. For not only is there no good evidence in favor of (b); if one looks more closely at the facts which seem to support this thesis, they turn out to be incompatible with it. The thesis of original univocity is not only false in fact, as far as our evidence goes; it is false to the nature of language. It is false in general, because, as Aristotle put it, the vocabulary of a language is limited but it must be used to apply to an unlimited range of things and phenomena, so that a word will normally have several different uses. (*Soph. Elench.* 1, 165ᵃ10–13. Aristotle's point is a good one, though his pseudo-mathematical expression of it is misleading.) And it is false in detail because the most

---

of the cruder separation that relies upon the wind. The sieve which I observed in Crete in 1964 performs the same function as the winnowing-basket pictured by Cornford in *Plato's Cosmology*, p. 201; only it allows the grain to pass through and catches the straw.

concrete meaning of a term will often, if not always, contain within it an essential reference to some more abstract concept. The meanings of a language are not atomic, independent units; they belong together in a system, conceptually as well as formally. Thus the root *krei-, even when it applies to the action of sifting or winnowing, means *to select the valuable part* (the grain) *from an indiscriminate mass* (the grain with the chaff). This "abstract" meaning of *selecting, discriminating* is part of the concept of winnowing – though it is not part of the mechanical operation! There is a regrettable tendency to confuse the meaning of such a "concrete" term with the physical event it is true of. What winnowing means to the peasant is not understood by the wind, the pitchfork, and the laws of mechanics that do the job. Nor can the meaning of *to winnow* be captured by a description in terms of these factors alone, without reference to the qualitative or functional distinction between grain and chaff, in terms of edibility, nutritive value, what happens when one or the other is planted in the ground – and the importance of all this for a peasant's subsistence through the winter and for his harvest next year.

Thus the semantic structure of an archaic and "concrete" concept like *to sift* or *to winnow* (as expressed by the root *krei-) is not less complex and many-sided than that of an "abstract" concept like *criterion*, as used in analytical philosophy today. In fact the concrete sense of "to separate the grain from the straw" must – from the beginning – be understood as a case of the more general concept "to make a discrimination" (which will normally mean "to separate the better from the worse"). There is no reason to suppose that this more general concept is a *later* sense of the root *krei-; on the contrary, every reason to suppose that the two senses are coeval, equally primitive.[12]

In an example like *krei-, the logical relation between the two senses is one of asymmetric interdependence. Whereas the abstract sense "to discriminate" derives greater force and vividness from its archaic association with acts of spatial separation, it is not essentially tied to any *particular* spatial image and can survive the separation from all such imagery. This is presumably what we mean by calling it "abstract". The concrete spatial senses, however, whether applying to a harvest operation or to the arrangement of troops in battle order by kinship groups, cannot even be *understood* in isolation from the concept of distinguishing items according to some

---

[12] That is to say, *some* sense of physical separation will be as old as the root, though the particular application to winnowing or purifying grain cannot be older than farming. If I.-E. was spoken in a pre-agricultural society, the root *krei- may have meant "separate the good meat from the bad" or "the flesh from the entrails". But the more general or abstract connotations would be the same in any age.

definite criterion of value (e.g. edibility) or purposeful function (e.g. the bravest in front, each kinship group around the leader it will obey). To claim that this more general meaning of *krei- is chronologically later than the concrete sense to sift or separate is to maintain a position that is not only unsupported by evidence but is strictly absurd. For the more general sense is essentially part of the meaning of the word in its concrete application, though not conversely.

Applying this insight to questions more directly connected with the verb be, we may reconsider the case of the Greek word for become, γίγνομαι. How are the wider uses of this verb related to the literal sense "I am born"? The standard view is that the more general meanings "come into being" and "become (such-and-such)" are secondary extensions of this original bodily sense for the birth of a child. But again, this extension must have taken place in some remote prehistoric age, before the oldest preserved texts. In Homer, at any rate, we find the verb γίγνομαι in current use as suppletive copula and generalized verb of existence or occurrence, with the mutative aspectual value in contrast to εἰμί. I find only one use in the biological sense "am born" in six occurrences of γίγνομαι in the first book of the Iliad.[13] This sample is more or less representative of the Homeric use. Whereas the senses of "birth", "generation" and "kinship" dominate in the nominal forms from the same root (γένος, γενεή, etc.), for the verb the biological sense is only one use among others, and by no means the most common. The systematic use of γίγνομαι as suppletive copula for εἰμί is a special development in Greek (and still incomplete in Homer, where the verb shares this role with πέλω and others, as we have seen in Chapter V §11). But the wider use of the root *gen- for "becoming" or "emergence" is well attested elsewhere. For example, the Vedic use of the cognate verb jan- shows a similar profusion of abstract or figurative applications.[14] The sense of biological birth is no doubt one of the oldest and most basic meanings of the root *gen-. But a claim to the effect that this root once referred only to actual

---

[13] The first occurrence of the verb in the Iliad is a Type V existential: δεινὴ δὲ κλαγγὴ γένετο "a fearful clang arose (from the silver bow)", at 1.49; the second occurrence is copulative: ὁμηγερέες τ' ἐγένοντο "when they were assembled together" 1.57. I count one more generalized existential use, ἄχος γένετο at 1.188, before the first appearance of the verb in the sense of "birth" at 1.251: ἅμα τράφεν ἠδ' ἐγένοντο/ἐν Πύλῳ. There are two other "abstract" uses as verb of occurrence, with no literal sense of birth: 1.341 χρειὼ ἐμοῖο γένηται; 1.493 δυωδεκάτη γένετ' ἠώς.

[14] Among the senses for jan- listed in Grassmann's Wörterbuch zum Rig-veda (p. 465), in addition to "gebären", "zeugen", we find "erzeugen", "erstehen lassen", "schaffen", "hervorbringen". In Latin, on the other hand, Ernout-Meillet report that the verb geno/gigno meant (at first) "engenderer; puis par extension 'produire, causer' (sens physique et moral)". Since Homer and the Rigveda agree on the wider use, there is presumably no reason to project this alleged chronological development in Latin backwards into the I.-E. past.

birth would seem to rely on nothing more than the myth of univocity.

What the evidence from Homer and the Veda shows is not that the biological sense is older but that the archaic mind understood *birth* as a paradigmatic case of *coming to be*, the paradigm instance of the concept of becoming – just as persons are taken as paradigm subjects, so that abstract entities (as signified by any nominalized form) may also be "personified". And if we look again at our other alleged example of the concrete-to-abstract development, the root **weid-* of οἶδα "know", ἰδεῖν "see", and *videre* "see", we find here too that the more abstract sense of "knowledge" is archaic and pre-historic. The concordance of Greek, Vedic and other languages shows that the limitation of the root in Latin to what we call (by derivation) the *visual* sense is not the original I.-E. state of affairs but a special development.[15]

§4. THE REINTERPRETATION OF THE DEVELOPMENTAL HYPOTHESIS IN SYNCHRONIC TERMS: SPATIAL IMAGERY IS IN SOME SENSE FUNDAMENTAL IN OUR THINKING GENERALLY AND IN OUR CONCEPT OF EXISTENCE IN PARTICULAR

This long digression was needed to bring to light the underlying fallacy in the traditional assumption that the "abstract" uses of εἰμί must be later than, and chronologically derived from, some more "concrete" use for life or location. In order to separate this error from the truth with which it is generally associated, we were obliged to consider I.-E. roots like **krei-* and **gen-* where the etymological situation is particularly clear.

Of course nothing in the preceding section is intended as a denial of the fact that some words with bodily, spatial or sensory meaning come in the course of time to enjoy a figurative use, which in turn gradually fades into an abstract sense, as *conceptus* "grasping together", "gathering", "pregnancy", eventually becomes *conceptus animi* "grasping (conceiving) by the mind", and finally our term *concept*. What the considerations just presented do suggest is that such semantic development, where it occurs, is best understood on the basis of a synchronic cohabitation of special and general, concrete and abstract uses of a single lexeme side by side in the same state of the language. "Metaphor permeates all discourse, ordinary and special, and we should have a hard time finding a purely literal paragraph anywhere."[16]

---

[15] See Ernout-Meillet, *Dictionnaire étymologique* s.v. *video*: "la racine **weid-* où le sens de 'voir' est un cas particulier d'un emploi plus général: **weid-* indique la vision en tant qu'elle sert à la connaissance."

[16] Nelson Goodman, *Languages of Art. An Approach to a Theory of Symbols* (Indianapolis, 1968), p. 80.

I would add: even in the most *primitive* languages, at any rate, even in the most primitive known state of Indo-European. In fact, the *tendency* to metaphor is often part of what we grasp as literal meaning. Among diverse uses of a non-univocal word, the primacy of bodily and spatial imagery is real enough, but this primacy is not to be understood in chronological terms alone. We are confronted here with something quite fundamental in the psychology of language and concept-formation, a principle which must be taken into account in any theory of cognitive meaning as well as in any theory of poetic discourse. In some sense, visual imagery and spatial metaphors underlie much of our meaningful use of language as they underlie much of our conceptual thinking. As Aristotle put it, "the intellect grasps concepts in sensory images." In this sense, spatial or bodily meanings may be recognized as fundamental in language, just as the corresponding images seem to be psychologically fundamental in thinking. And this is scarcely surprising, since our experience as a whole and "from the beginning" is conditioned by the state or activity of our body, and in particular of our sense organs. Hence it is entirely natural that bodily associations or sensory images should often furnish an intuitive focus, a kind of psychosomatic basis for the system of meanings of a diversely used word. But it does not follow that the visual, spatial, or bodily meanings once existed naked and alone, outside of the conceptual framework of the language as a whole. There is no reason to take seriously the myth of original univocity.

From this point of view, we can accept all of the evidence that was alleged in support of the hypothesis of an original locative (or locative-existential) meaning for εἰμί and reinterpret it in purely synchronic terms. In this reinterpretation we take the Homeric system of uses as the primitive datum and abandon all hope of understanding this system on the basis of some earlier and supposedly simpler state of the language.[17] We recognize that within this system the local and local-existential uses of εἰμί are relatively rare, whereas the use of the verb as nominal copula is overwhelmingly more common. We may nonetheless regard the locative uses as primary or fundamental, in just the sense that spatial imagery is primary or fundamental in much of our conceptual thought, and perhaps also in our learning of language. Furthermore, these locative uses reinforce, and are reinforced by, the durative-stative aspectual value which characterizes the verb in *all* its uses. As a result of such connections and associations, a locative (or locative-existential) connotation colors the wider use of the verb in Homeric and

---

[17] I am referring to the system as a whole, of course. Some details of Homeric usage, for example the potential construction of ἔστι + *infinitive*, can be recognized as special developments in Greek. Special too is the use of γίγνομαι as suppletive; but common I.-E. must already have employed *some* mutative copula in contrast to *es-* (e.g. *bhū-*).

also in classical Greek, to an extent which we can hardly define. In a similar way, the connotations of birth color the use of γίγνομαι as mutative copula or verb of occurrence. We may speak of a locative *focus* for the meaning of εἰμί, just as we recognize the idea of birth as the intuitive focus for the various uses of γίγνομαι.[18] But to claim that the locative construction or the local-existential idea ("is present", *ist vorhanden*) constitutes the unique source from which all Homeric uses are to be derived, or the unique *Grundbedeutung* on which they all stand, is to go far beyond the evidence, and beyond all reason.

In concluding this discussion of the local sense of εἰμί, let me point out that the connections between the ideas of place and existence, which are so conspicuous in Greek, are by no means limited to that language. The need for spatial metaphors is a constant one in Western thought, and probably in human thought generally. A specialist in Indian logic could document the importance of the notion of *locus* (Sanskrit *adhikaraṇa* or *ādhāra*) in Indian theories of existence and predication. I have already mentioned an obvious psychosomatic explanation of this general connection between spatial and abstract ideas; though I do not pretend this is the *only* explanation. But whatever the full significance of such spatial imagery may be, its persistence in the case of the concept of existence is a remarkable fact in the history of Western philosophy. A few quotations will illustrate this point.

(Reasonable men) will say that what is capable of being present (παραγίγνεσθαι) and being absent (ἀπογίγνεσθαι) is by all means something (εἶναί τι).   Plato, *Sophist* 247 A 8.

We say that the essence is the structure (*ratio*) of a thing comprehended in its definition; its existence, on the other hand, is its presence in the nature of things.   Ficino, *Opera* p. 140 (= *Theol. Plat.* VI. 7)[19]

Existence and unity are two other ideas that are suggested to the understanding by every object without, and every idea within. When ideas are in our minds, we consider them as being actually there, as well as when we consider things to be actually without us: which is, that they exist, or have existence.   Locke, *Essay concerning Human Understanding*, Bk. II, ch. vii. 7.

No two ideas are in themselves contrary, except those of existence and non-existence, which are plainly resembling, as implying both of them an idea of the object; tho' the latter

---

18 There is a difference of course. The privileged position of the concept of birth among the meanings and uses of γίγνομαι is an obvious fact for anyone who knows Greek. Our assignment of a similar role to the locative use of εἰμί on the other hand, is the result of theoretical reflection. The decisive difference between the two cases lies in the presence for γίγνομαι of the cognate nominal forms, γένος, γένεσις, etc., whose use is more unambiguous. It seems that I.-E. verbs, by their very nature, are essentially more plurisignificant than the corresponding noun forms, where conditions of reference and denotation are more strictly defined.

19 "Essentiam quidem dicimus rationem rei quae definitione comprehenditur, esse vero ... quandum eius in rerum natura praesentiam." I am indebted to Paul O. Kristeller for this reference. See his *Il pensiero filosofico di Marsilio Ficino* (Florence, 1953), p. 32.

excludes the object from all times and places, in which it is supposed not to exist. Hume, *A Treatise of Human Nature*, Part I, Sect. v. 6 (ed. Selby-Bigge p. 15).

The so-called *existential quantifier* '(∃x)' corresponds to the words 'there is something such that'.... To say that [something of the form (∃x) Fx] is true is to say that there is at least one object in the universe such that when 'x' in ['Fx'] is thought of as naming it, ['Fx'] becomes true. Quine, *Methods of Logic*, 2nd ed. p. 83. (The expressions within brackets represent simplifications of the original.)

More recently, Jaakko Hintikka has offered an intuitive interpretation of the logical quantifiers in terms of "the language-game of seeking and finding" and has suggested that "all our knowledge of the existence of external objects is obtained by means of the activities of seeking and finding". In this view the universe of discourse is to be understood as "the relevant field of search".[20]

§5. THE UNITY OF εἰμί AS A LINGUISTIC SYSTEM

In intuitive or psychological terms we may thus recognize the locative and local-existential uses of εἰμί as the center of the whole system. In more strictly linguistic terms, however, it is the copula use as such – and not merely the locative copula – that imposes itself as the fundamental fact. Among the copula uses the construction with predicate nouns and adjectives is far more conspicuous than with adverbials of place. (Some statistics on this were cited in Chapter IV §1 and §7.) An account of the verb *be* is first and foremost an account of the nominal copula. It is this use which must provide the key to any attempt to see the uses of εἰμί as belonging together in a synchronic system.

In Chapter V we employed this key in defining the I.-E. verb **es-* as the central member of a family of verbs of station and posture (*stand, lie, sit*) that admit both locative and predicative constructions. As predicative verb of station, *be* functions in systematic aspectual opposition to a family of mutative or kinetic verbs whose central member is *become* (in Greek, γίγνομαι). The original definition of this stative-mutative system, which we borrowed from Lyons, consisted in the analogy between the three contrasting pairs of sentence forms for nominal predication, location, and possession:

---

[20] "Language-Games for Quantifiers", in *Studies in Logical Theory*, American Philosophi cal Quarterly Monograph No. 2 (Oxford, 1968), pp. 46–72. (Quotations are from pp. 51, 53 and 58). A similar intuition underlies Jack Kaminsky's suggestion that the existential quantifier be understood as "indicating that something is locatable" in some sense, though not necessarily locatable "in a space-time coordinate system". The predicate "exists" would be reserved for the latter use for presence in space and time, as in the quotation above from Hume. Thus it would be true to say "There is something called 'Hamlet'," since Hamlet is locatable as a character in Shakespeare's play. But "Hamlet exists" would be false. See J. Kaminsky, *Language and Ontology* (Carbondale, Ill. 1969), pp. 188–90, 207–8.

Stative	*Mutative*
X is wise (is president)	*X becomes wise (becomes president)*
X is in Chicago	*X goes (comes) to Chicago*
X has money	*X gets money*

We pointed out that in Greek the stative verb is provided by εἰμί in all three cases (since "I have" is expressed as ἔστι μοι); while the mutative counterpart may be provided by γίγνομαι throughout (ἐγένετο ἐν +*place*, "He came to", ἐγένετο αὐτῷ "He acquired"). We originally discussed this stative-mutative system in the context of a theory of the copula. We may now observe that the aspectual contrast stretches through the entire range of uses of εἰμί. The stative-mutative system has a vital branch in the opposition *am alive* (εἰμί), *am born* (γίγνομαι). It also has a generalized existential use in the opposition between *be there/endure* and *come to be/arise/take place*, for example in the Type V existential construction: κλαγγὴ ἦν "there was an outcry", as against κλαγγὴ ἐγένετο "an outcry arose" (This "existential" construction with action nouns is one of the most frequent of all uses of γίγνομαι.) There is even an opposition within the veridical use, as we see from the contrast of τὸ ἐόν "what is the case" with τὸ γεγονός "what has occurred", or τὰ γενόμενα "the facts". (See, e.g. Chapter VII, p. 355, and LSJ s.v. γίγνομαι I.3.). The very few uses of εἰμί that are not characterized by such an aspectual opposition, for example the potential construction ἔστι +*infinitive* or the periphrastic forms of the perfect (λελυκὼς ᾦ, εἴην) can be shown to be secondary or anomalous in some other respect as well.[21]

Thus it is the stative or static aspect that defines the unity of εἰμί as a linguistic system, if anything does. In Indo-European, the verb *to be* is the verb of state or station par excellence. Perhaps we may say that it is because it expresses being in a state generally that it can also express being in a place in particular. And if we ask the somewhat misleading question raised in Chapter V §3, "Why is it precisely the verb *es- that is introduced into a sentence without a verb – into a "nominal" sentence like *I – hungry* or *He – in bed*?" the only answer can be: because it is an essential feature of nominal and locative predication in its primary, neutral form to assign some attribute, property, or location that belongs to the subject in a static or (relatively) enduring way, in contrast to the secondary "mutative" form of predication for an attribute that is just being acquired or momentarily possessed (as expressed by *become hungry, get in bed*). As I argued in Chapter V §7, *be* is logically prior to *become*. In linguistic terms *be* is the unmarked, *become* the kinetically marked form of predication.

---

[21] Some examples of γίνεται + *infinitive* cited by LSJ suggest a marginal occurrence of aspectual opposition even in the potential construction.

But if it is this static aspect that provides the principle of unity in the system of εἰμί, it is the syntactic flexibility of the verb that explains the richness and diversity of the system. The verb *to be* is the jack-of-all-trades of the I.-E. languages. If we except its mutative twin *becomes*, perhaps the only I.-E. verb that displays a syntactic versatility comparable to *be* is the causative root **dhē-* (in Greek τίθημι), with its triple lexical value: (i) *to put (something somewhere)*, (ii) *to make (something such-and-such)*, and (iii) *to make absolutely, to produce, make to occur*. (This variety of lexical values for **dhē-* is largely the result of semantic developments in modern I.-E. languages. Unlike *be*, which still covers almost the whole range of **es-* as represented in Homer, modern cognates from **dhē-* – such as English *do*, German *tun*, French *faire* – have generally lost the locative construction with its corresponding sense "place, put", just as English *do* has in turn largely lost the sense of "make".) In Homeric Greek, we find that εἰμί, γίγνομαι and τίθημι form a vast system of interrelated uses, a tripartite system of *be*, *come to be*, and *make to be*, whose basis is provided by εἰμί. The underlying role of εἰμί as the central verb in the language will be clarified if we briefly consider the range of uses for τίθημι, which functions as a kind of causal operator on *be*.

Of the three principal divisions into which LSJ classifies the uses of τίθημι, let us look first at the branch that corresponds to the nominal copula: "B. *put in a certain state* or *condition*, much the same as ποιεῖν, ποιεῖσθαι, and so often to be rendered by our *make*." [22] In this construction the verb takes a double accusative, the second of which is an attributive noun or adjective, corresponding to the predicate form with εἰμί: "*make* one something, with the predicate [noun] in apposition, θεῖναί τινα αἰχμητήν, ἱέρειαν, μάντιν, etc. ... 2. with an Adjective for the attributive, θεῖναί τινα ἀθάνατον καὶ ἀγήρων *make him undying and undecaying*." In grammatical terms *I make him (to be) immortal* is the causal transform of *He is immortal*. Logically speaking, of course, the operation is oriented in the other direction: the second sentence describes the result of the action described by the causal "transform". The third constituent of our system, the mutative sentence *He becomes* (γίγνεται) *immortal*, describes this same causal action from the point of view of the subject of change, without reference to the cause. The tripartite system as a whole thus provides us with an expression for state (εἰμί), for change of state (γίγνομαι), and for cause of state (τίθημι).

These correlations can be followed throughout the system of τίθημι. The widest range of uses is that listed by LSJ under the first branch: "A. in local

---

[22] This use of τίθημι is essentially archaic: common in Homer and the poets, rare in classic prose where ποιέω normally takes over as verb "to make", both for the work of the craftsman and for this factitive use.

sense, *set, put, place.*" Here we find, in addition to ordinary expressions for putting something somewhere, such special uses as "II.1 θεῖναι τινί τι ἐν χερσίν ... *put* it in his hands"; IV with accusative and dative: *to assign, award*, e.g. honor to someone (τιμήν τινι) or to give a child a name (ὄνομα θέσθαι τινί); VII *dispose, order, ordain, bring to pass*, often with an adverbial modifier such as "thus" or "well", "successfully": οὕτω νῦν Ζεὺς θείη "May Zeus so dispose" (*Od.* 8.465: the content of the wish is spelled out by the following infinitives); οἶκον εὖ θέσθαι "to put one's household in good shape" (Hes. *Op.* 23); τὰ πρὶν εὖ θέμενοι "Having arranged things well so far" (Soph. *El.* 1434.) If we correlate these factitive phrases with their essive base, we see that II.1 corresponds to the pregnant locative use of εἰμί "be at one's disposal"; IV corresponds in part to the possessive construction with the dative, e.g. ὄνομα μοί ἐστι X "My name is X" (note, however, that for most possessive uses the corresponding causal is δίδωμι "give" rather than τίθημι); whereas VII corresponds to several different uses of εἰμί, including the essive clause of the veridical (ἔστι οὕτω) and the impersonal adverbial use εὖ ἔσται, καλῶς ἔσται (Chapter IV §22). What the Lexicon describes as the "local sense" of τίθημι thus shades off into figurative or abstract uses, culminating in the generalized sentence operator οὕτω θεῖναι "bring it about that...."

The third and final branch of uses for τίθημι is "C. without any attributive word following, *make, work, execute*, of an artist.... 2. *make, cause, bring to pass.*"[23]

These absolute uses of τίθημι as "to make" include what the Lexicon calls "periphrastic for a single Verb, μνηστήρων σκέδασιν θεῖναι *make* a scattering, *Od.* 1.116". In the construction σκέδασιν ἔθηκε + *genitive* we have an expressive transform of ἐσκέδασε + *accusative* "He scattered the suitors". Here the *make*-transformation corresponds closely to the *be*-transformation described in Chapter VI as a Type V existential. It so happens that we do not find *σκέδασις ἦν "a scattering occurred", but there are other cases of more exact parallelism, as between εἰ δὴ ὁμὴν Ἀχιλῆϊ καὶ Ἕκτορι θήσετε τιμήν "If you give like honor to Hector and Achilles", at *Il.* 24.57, and οὐ μὲν γὰρ τιμή γε μί' ἔσσεται "There shall not be the same honor (for both)," nine lines later.[24]

---

[23] The alternation between this absolute construction and the predicative use with two accusatives is of course shared by many causative verbs e.g. *Cut his hair, cut his hair short; paint the house, paint the house red.* There is a comparable option between "absolute" and determinate constructions of verbs for *to place*, e.g. *He set up an altar, He set up an alter in the precinct.*

[24] For these parallels see W. Porzig, *Namen für Satzinhalte* pp. 28–31. In the example cited the construction is not strictly absolute, but both the possessive dative and the pseudo-predicate "same" (ὁμή, μία) are superimposed upon a Type V use of εἰμί + *action noun*: τιμὴ ἔσσεται "Then will be honor" ← τιμήσομεν "We shall honor".

This wide range of uses for τίθημι is not peculiarly Greek. As Grassmann's *Wörterbuch zum Rig-Veda* points out for the cognate verb *dha-* in Vedic: "Der Begriff spaltet sich (schon vor der Sprachtrennung) in den örtlichen "an einen Ort hinschaffen", and den Causalen "thun, machen, schaffen" (p. 659). Grassmann adds that the causal-factitive concept is to be understood as a *later* development from the purely locative sense; but for this diachronic view there is no evidence. It merely reflects the sacred lexical myth of original univocity, which we have seen reason to doubt. Neither for **dhē-* nor for **es-* can we go back behind the primitive diversity of uses represented in Homer and the *Veda*. And the elaborate correlation between uses of *be*, *become*, and *put/make* in different languages suggests that the system as a whole is a common inheritance from I.-E. If, as we have seen, notions of place and location provide a kind of psychological focus for the system, its complex unity can be interpreted only in terms of the aspectual contrast: *state/change of state/cause of state*.[25] Over most of its range, τίθημι serves as stative-causal to εἰμί, just as the corresponding kinetic verb ἵημι "throw, send" serves as causal to εἶμι "go".

It would be possible to extend this discussion of the tripartite system *be-become-put/make*, in order to make clearer the fundamental role of **es-*. We could show, for example, that *be* shares one value with each of its counterparts which they do not share with one another. Thus **es-* shares with **dhē* its static value, in contrast to the mutative aspect of *become* (and it is this mutative aspect which characterizes the *send-go* system just mentioned). On the other hand, *be* shares with *become* its one- or two-term intransitive structure (without reference to a cause or agent), in contrast to the two- or three-term transitive construction of **dhē-*: *There is (occurs) X*, on the one hand, in contrast to *A makes X*, on the other; *X is (becomes) Y* in contrast to *A makes X (to be) Y*. (In terms of this contrast, *go* belongs as intransitive with *be* and *become*, while *send/throw* belongs as transitive with *put/make*.) But enough has been said to indicate the intricate complexity of the pattern of contrasts and analogies established around εἰμί as the fixed center or basis for the locative-predicative-existential system as a whole.

A fuller investigation of the place of *be* within the total system of the language would have to consider its relations with other sentence-operators that cover a range comparable to *put/make* and that function in systematic correlation or contrast to *be*. The most important of these is probably *seems*

---

[25] The underlying static value of **dhē-* is rightly characterized by Benveniste: "Là même où la traduction 'poser' est admissible, les conditions de l'emploi montrent que 'poser' signifie proprement 'poser quelque chose qui subsistera désormais, qui est destiné à durer': en grec, avec *themeilia* 'poser les fondements', avec *bômon*, 'fonder un autel'" (*Problèmes de ling. gén.* p. 291).

(to someone) that, which in Greek – and perhaps generally – belongs closely with *(someone) thinks that*. In Greek both concepts may be expressed by δοκέω, which has an etymological value (from **dek-*) "to take, accept (something as something)." Thus *X seems to me (to be Y)* and *I take (regard) X as Y* or *I believe X is Y* are related syntactically to the underlying sentence *X is Y* in precisely the same way that *I make X (to be) Y* is related to this same operand sentence with *is*. (I mean, the transformational relation is of the same type; the logical and semantic value of the two sentence-operators is of course quite different.) This allusion to *seems* and *believes* introduces a new dimension of the language, a vast superstructure of intentions or propositional attitudes erected on the base of sentences such as *N is Φ*. The epistemic and psychological richness of this superstructure (*I know that N is Φ, I hope that N is Φ, I wish that ..., I bet that ...*, etc.) scarcely requires comment.

What does deserve mention here is the fact that the wider systems indicated by *make (to be)* on the one hand, *take as/think (to be)* on the other, are in some respects much more general than the copula-locative-existential base provided by the verb *be*. From the point of view of these wider systems, *I make X (to be) Y* or *I believe X to be Y* is of the same form as *I make X do something* or *I believe X does something*, where the constituent *does something* may be replaced by any verb phrase in the language. Thus it might seem arbitrary to claim, as I have done, that these causal and cognitive-intentional superstructures are erected on the basis of stative sentence forms with *be*. Nevertheless, this way of describing the system is not entirely arbitrary. For one thing, this generalization of the verb εἰμί to include *doing* as a special case of *being* was carried out by the Greek philosophers themselves. This is the force of Aristotle's doctrine that there are as many uses of εἰμί as there are categories: one of the categories is *to do* (ποιεῖν). And this generalization of *to be* is largely prepared by the system of the language itself. In Homer, for example, there is no other verb *to do* with a range comparable to that of τίθημι; it is precisely this latter verb which means "to do" in the widest sense, and which functions systematically as the causative for εἰμί.[26] The fact that τίθημι as causative sentence operator actually has a wider range than its operand verb εἰμί serves, by a kind of reflex action, to widen the virtual range of the verb *be*. That is to say, the wider system of the causal sentence operator, because of its consistent pattern of connections with εἰμί, tends to suggest a generalization of εἰμί as underlying verb par excellence. The correlations *be-become-put/make* thus operate in the same

---

[26] The closest rival to τίθημι in Homer is perhaps τεύχω ("to produce", "to cause", "to make so and so"), which is similarly correlated with εἰμί and even provides a suppletive copula in the perfect: τέτυγμαι. Compare also τελέω as verb *to do* in Homer.

direction as the periphrastic uses of *be*, to generalize the conception of εἰμί as a universal (stative-intransitive) verb. Very much the same generalizing influence is exerted by the parallels of εἶναι and δοκεῖν *to be* and *to seem (to be)*. The philosophers did not have to construct the antithesis of Being and Becoming: it was given to them fully preformed, in the stative-mutative system already described. They had scarcely more to do with constructing the antithesis Being and Seeming (or Reality and Appearance): it was given to them *almost* preformed in the parallel tendency to regard εἶναι as universal operand for δοκεῖν, with the veridical value of εἶναι underscored by the uses discussed in Chapter VII. Grammatically speaking, the Appearance-Reality antithesis is given in the language as the contrast between *You take X to be so-and-so* and *X is (in fact) as you take it to be*.

It is perhaps only an accident that the Greek philosophers made no comparable use of the other contrast, between Being and Making (-to-be), which was just as fully prepared for them as Being-Becoming or Being-Seeming in the lexical and syntactic structure of the language.[27] We see once again that the structure of the language may condition but does not determine the development of philosophic ideas. It was only in Christian and Islamic times, under the influence of Biblical religion, that the distinction between eternal and created being, or between uncaused and caused existence, was worked out in terms that echo the archaic contrast between εἰμί and τίθημι (εἶναι), between Being and Making-to-be. It is not clear that there were any properly linguistic reasons either for the new importance of this antithesis in medieval philosophy or for the relative neglect of it in ancient thought.

§6. REVIEW OF THE SYSTEM OF USES OF εἰμί.
THE COPULA CONSTRUCTION TO BE TAKEN AS CENTRAL.
ELEMENTARY USES DISTINGUISHED FROM SECOND-ORDER USES,
AND THE LATTER ARE SUBDIVIDED INTO
"SYNTACTIC" AND "SEMANTIC" USES

We first attempted (in §2) to explain the various uses of εἰμί as developments from a hypothetical original sense; "is present", "is located (somewhere)". We then reinterpreted the alleged evidence for such a developmental account

---

[27] There are, of course, occasional developments of this conceptual connection, e.g. in Plato *Symp.* 205 B 8: "every causation of something passing from not being to being is Making". ἡ γάρ τοι ἐκ τοῦ μὴ ὄντος εἰς τὸ ὂν ἰόντι ὁτῳοῦν αἰτία πᾶσά ἐστι ποίησις. Parmenides had implicitly contrasted the unbegun Being of his true ἐόν with the erroneous "posits" of mortals (κατέθεντο, ἔθεντο, fr. 8.53 and 55). In the *Timaeus*, of course, the Being-Making antithesis is developed in a way that anticipates the medieval doctrine of created being: the realm of Becoming is reinterpreted as the work of a Craftsman who "establishes" the cosmos (συνέστησεν αὐτὸν [sc. τὸν κόσμον] ὁ συνιστάς 32 C 7).

as indicating rather the psychological or intuitive priority of spatial-bodily imagery in thinking generally (§§ 3–4). Having now reviewed and expanded our account of the aspectual system built around the *stative-mutative-factitive* correlations (in §5), we are ready to approach the final stage of our discussion, where we consider the question of systematic unity in the uses of εἰμί from the point of view of a philosophic concept of Being.

The traditional theory of the I.-E. verb *to be* was seriously handicapped by the assumption that the existential uses are primary and original, the copula uses secondary and derived. Once we carry out the modest Copernican Revolution which I propose, that is, once we reinstate the copula construction at the center of the system, the other uses of the verb will easily fall into place. As the locative use is *included* in the copula construction, the corresponding lexical value "is present, is located (there)" obviously occupies a central position within the system and exerts some influence over many uses of εἰμί which are not merely statements of place. (This influence is all the greater since there is no *rival* lexical meaning associated with the copula construction for predicate adjectives and nouns.) But the fact remains that the function of εἰμί in its copula uses is more syntactic than lexical in nature, even when the sentence as a whole is a statement of place. By this I mean that the "substance" of the sentence, its particular information content is specified by the predicate noun, adjective, or adverbial of place rather than by εἰμί, whereas the copula verb itself serves to indicate the "form" of the sentence, including the person and number of the subject, the tense, and the modalities of wish, command, conditional and the like. The functional associations of the verb – its "meaning" in a very broad sense – are thus connected with the general form of the subject-predicate sentence, rather than with any specific content. In some loose but intelligible sense of "means", the copula verb in its more elementary uses means *that some attribute* (property, location, etc.) *belongs to some subject*.[28] In its interrogative and modal uses, the copula indicates this same concept of belonging, only not as the object or content of a simple assertion but under special modifications (of possibility, doubt, wish, etc.). In meta-linguistic terms, the elementary copula signifies the truth-claim of a subject-predicate sentence, whereas the modified uses signify this claim under various epistemic or intentional

---

[28] This is presumably what Brugmann had in mind when he listed as one of the two earliest *Bedeutungen* of our verb (after "vorhandensein, existieren") "das Zutreffen eines dem Subjekt beigelegten Nominalbegriffs auf dieses Subjekt" (*Syntax des einf. Satzes*, p. 72). Brugmann describes this meaning as contributing to, but nonetheless distinct from, the later "rein formalen Geltung als Kopula". His formulation is distorted by the chronological hypothesis that I reject. But beneath it lies an intuitive grasp of the complexity of the copula function that I attempt to spell out here in the distinction between predication₁, predication₂, and predication₃.

modalities. Let us now limit ourselves to the most elementary case, in the unmarked indicative, and consider any declarative sentence of the form *N is Φ*. In this use the verb *be* serves to indicate (a) the person and number of the subject, (b) the tense of the sentence, and (c) the truth claim, as functionally associated with the indicative mood of the verb.[29] Speaking summarily, we may say that the copula as finite verb indicates the syntactic form of the sentence as a whole – its sentencehood – together with its truth claim. Let us designate this double function, syntactic and semantic, by describing the copula as *sign of predication*. Strictly speaking, of course, the copula verb serves as sign of predication only in copula sentences, i.e. in sentences of form *N is Φ*. Let us call predication restricted to this particular sentence form *predication₁*.

Insofar as εἰμί as copula comes to be thought of as the verb par excellence, its role in the sentence form *N is Φ* is easily generalized for any sentence of the form *NVΩ* or *noun phrase-verb phrase*. As a result, εἰμί can function as sign for the belonging of the predicate (i.e. attribute) to the subject quite in general, regardless whether the predicate phrase is provided by a copula construction or by any other verb in the language. This is the generalization taken for granted by Aristotle when he says "*Belonging* (ὑπάρχειν) signifies in just as many ways as *being* (εἶναι) and as *It is true to say this (is) that*" (*Pr. An.* I.36, 48ᵇ2). Let us call this generalized function of the copula, where *N is Φ* is regarded not as one sentence type among others but as a canonical rewriting of all subject-predicate propositions, *predication₂*.

Finally, εἰμί may be used to indicate sentencehood and truth claim quite generally, without specifying that the sentence in question need be of subject-predicate form. In this widest use, the content of an impersonal sentence like ὕει "it is raining", may also be represented by ἔστι, e.g. in the veridical construction: "it is the case". Here we can no longer properly speak of ἔστι as copula: it serves, as generalized verb, to suggest only the form of a state-

---

[29] For a fuller formulation of these points see Chapter V §§1–2, and above all §2a on the connection between the semantic interpretation of the verbal mood-ending and a general theory of intentional and epistemic modalities. Some of these modalities will modify the elementary truth claim (in a question, conditional statement, request, wish, etc.) in such a way that the notion of truth may no longer seem relevant – even when the syntax is that of the so-called veridical construction. (See Chapter VII pp. 338–43 for this generalization of the veridical construction beyond the case of assertion.) In the present discussion we are obliged to ignore these complications and focus our attention on the simplest case, where the indicative form serves for unconditional statement.

Notice that the concepts of person and tense, as well as the meaning of certain moods such as the optative of wish, are relative to the speaker and the time of speaking, i.e. to what I call the extra-linguistic situation of utterance. Hence certain features of this situation are involved as structural factors in the "form" of a sentence, insofar as that form is understood as what the copula indicates. I cannot pursue this point here; but see the discussion of Lakoff's theory of performative verbs in V §2a.

ment. But since this function is part of the traditional notion of a sign of predication, as a verb form indicating affirmation or assertion, let us call this *predication₃*.

We may note that predication₁, predication₂, and predication₃ all have the double aspect, syntactic and semantic: in every case εἰμί indicates both sentencehood and truth claim. The three forms of predication constitute progressive generalizations of this double function, so that each type of predication is contained in the one (or ones) that follow. Every use of εἰμί for predication₁ is also a use for types 2 and 3; every use for predication₂ is also a use for type 3; but not conversely.[30]

When I say that εἰμί as copula serves primarily to indicate the form of the sentence, I mean that (in addition to marking person, number, and tense) it serves as sign of predication in one or more of the senses just distinguished. We have been speaking of more or less elementary uses of the copula, such as *Socrates is wise, Socrates is in the agora*. We may now mention the wider use of the second-order copula, for example in the Greek periphrastic construction (*Socrates is condemned by the court*) or with non-elementary subjects (*Wisdom is a virtue*). Since in such sentences the role of εἰμί is that of verb or sentence operator, producing a transformation of a definite kind, its connection with the *form* of the sentence remains essential.

My claim is that if we begin with the use of εἰμί as copula and take into account its intuitive connections with the idea of *presence in a place* as well as its more abstract connections with the form of the sentence as such, as sign of predication and transformational operator, we will have no difficulty in understanding the use of the same verb for the expression of existence and truth. But if we begin with the existential use as primary and the copula construction as "derived", we are faced with a series of insoluble problems. Which existential use do we take as fundamental (since there are several, with very different structures)? And why are the "secondary" copula uses often syntactically elementary, whereas the existential uses are (always, or normally) the result of a grammatical transformation? And why are these "secondary" uses as copula so much more numerous than all the rest, even in the earliest period of the language? (See the statistics in Chapter IV §1 and Chapter V §4.) I shall not argue the case again. The theoretical rearrangement which I have proposed must be justified by its fruits. I hope these already seem attractive enough, and I will try to display them in an even more favorable light for the remainder of this chapter.

---

[30] These distinctions are essentially the same as those drawn more fully in Chapter V §12, for three concepts of *be* as sign of predication. For the generalized function of the verb as sign of predication₃ see the veridical use in Chapter VII and above all the examples from Plato and Aristotle in VII §8.

Before embarking on the final, most philosophical stage of our discussion of the unity of the system, let us review the uses of εἰμί once more according to the formal classification suggested by the syntactic analysis. In Chapter VI (pp. 297–300), we divided the functions of the verb into first-order and second-order syntax. A first-order use of εἰμί is either an elementary sentence form (including elementary copula sentences) or the result of a transformation that does not introduce the verb εἰμί. That is to say, the syntax of the verb is first-order wherever its occurrence can be derived from an elementary occurrence in an underlying kernel structure. In what follows, I shall employ the term "elementary use" more freely for what has just been defined as first-order syntax. Hence, as we saw in Chapter VI, an elementary use of εἰμί will always have a first-order ("concrete") noun as its subject, but not conversely. First-order nouns may also occur as subject of a derived (second-order) use of the verb, for example in the periphrastic construction of the copula or in the existential Type IV. But whenever the subject is a second-order term (that is, an abstract noun or a sentential subject), the syntax of the verb will also be second-order. This gives us the following classification, which I repeat from Chapter VI.

I. Elementary (first-order) uses of εἰμί

1. Elementary forms of the copula (with nominal, locative, or adverbial predicate)
2. Possessive construction with first-order noun as subject
3. Existential Type I (εἰμί = "I am alive")

II. Second-order (derived) uses of εἰμί

4. Various uses of the copula as verb-operator and sentence operator, including the periphrastic construction and the use of εἰμί as copula with abstract nouns or sentential subjects (See Chapter IV, §§ 19–20)
5. Type IV, with the verb as existential sentence operator: "There is (no)one who ...."
6. Type V, with εἰμί as surface predicate or operator of occurrence (κλαγγὴ ἦν)
7. Potential construction (ἔστι + *infinitive*)
8. Veridical use with sentential subject ("it is so")

As we saw, existential Types II–III and other forms of copula-existential sentences represent a mixed case, where the syntax of the verb can be regarded as elementary insofar as it is derived from an underlying copula sentence, but where it functions as a (second-order) existential operator insofar as it serves to introduce or posit a subject for this elementary copula. The underlying syntax of Type VI (εἰσὶ θεοί "There are gods") was recognized as problematic, but I proposed an analysis in which the verb functions *both* as elementary copula and also as existential operator. Hence we were able to conclude that every existential use of εἰμί is second-order *precisely to the extent that it is existential*. In this perspective the vital use of Type I, where εἰμί has the syntax of an ordinary verb like *live*, does not count as properly existential: not only is the syntax of the verb elementary, but the (previous) existence of the subject is presupposed even in a sentence which states that someone is no longer alive.

Thus we see that the two most vivid or concrete lexical values of εἰμί are associated with elementary uses of the verb: "am alive" with the vital use; "am present" with the locative copula. Furthermore, the concrete flavor of the possessive ἔστι μοι ("belongs to me" or "I have") is similarly connected with an elementary construction, and often reinforced by a local nuance. Hence we may count these three vivid values of εἰμί among the *primary* (or first-order) uses of the verb, in a sense which is now syntactically definite. But of course to say that these "concrete" uses are primary is not to say that they are older than the second-order uses. They are primary because their sentential structure is simpler and closer to the elementary building blocks of the language. But we have abandoned the myth of primitive beginnings, according to which the language once consisted only of the simplest blocks.

As part of our break with the myth of primitive origins, we also abandon the hypothesis of an I.-E. language without a copula sentence or without a copula verb. (This means that we abandon the theory of the nominal sentence as an originally independent predicative form from which the copula sentence could be historically derived.) In syntactical terms we include the more elementary forms of the nominal copula among the primary, underived uses of εἰμί, although the verb in this construction is generally felt as colorless and abstract. We can recognize this lexically "empty" value of the copula and nevertheless maintain that the verb here is not entirely meaningless. Even as nominal copula εἰμί preserves (1) the aspectual value *stative* (as opposed to *mutative-kinetic*), and (2) the sentential structure of predication, in the wider sense just specified as predication₂, with its double function: the indication of subject-predicate structure, and the corresponding truth claim.[31]

Among the second-order uses of εἰμί we pick out, as deserving special attention, those uses in which the function of the verb is to assign a semantical value to a sentential operand or descriptive content. These *semantic uses*

---

[31] Of course the copula verb may also indicate modal qualifications of this truth claim, for example in the optative. But throughout this discussion we ignore the problem of modalities. See above, n. 29.

include the veridical construction and existential Types IV, V and VI (on my analysis of VI). As was pointed out in Chapter VI §20, there are only two semantic values, positive and negative, as expressed by ἔστι (ἦν, ἔσται) and οὐκ ἔστι (ἦν, ἔσται) respectively.[32] The veridical and the various existential uses differ from one another according to the form of the descriptive operand to which the semantic values are assigned. And to these formal differences corresponds a variation in the lexical value associated with the semantic use of ἔστι: *true* and *false* (or *is the case, is not the case*); *exists* (or *there is*) and *does not exist* (*there is not*); *occurs* and *does not occur*.

The task which is waiting for us in the next section is to clarify the relation between these semantic uses of εἰμί and the more elementary function of the verb as copula.

§7. THE COPULA AND THE SEMANTIC USES OF *be*

Together with the copula construction, the veridical and existential uses (of which the most characteristic are Types IV, V, and VI) represent the three functions of the verb εἰμί that are of primary importance for any theory or concept of Being. From the philosophic point of view, the problem of the verb *be* is ultimately a question whether these three uses of the lexeme **es-* belong together in a conceptual system whose structure is of universal (or at least of very general) significance, or whether they represent a merely accidental grouping of distinct linguistic functions in I.-E., a fortuitous coming-together of heterogeneous elements that any rigorous philosophy of language must set asunder. (For the moment I treat the different existential uses together as a unit. We come to cases in a moment.) As a conclusion to this study of *be* in Greek, I shall present my case for the conceptual importance of the system.[33]

---

[32] It may be remarked that the semantic uses occur only in the third person singular form of the verb. But this limitation applies to most of the second-order uses of εἰμί, including the potential construction and the copula with abstract or sentential subject. Among second-order uses of εἰμί, only the periphrastic construction and other verb operator uses admit first and second person forms.

[33] In this context I consider only the copula (or "*is* of predication") and the semantic uses of εἰμί. As pointed out above, n. 1, I ignore the so-called "*is* of identity" since I have not succeeded in defining it as a grammatically distinct use of εἰμί. From the syntactical point of view, the *is* of identity is an ordinary use of the copula with predicate nouns (sometimes predicate adjectives, participles with the article, etc.). For example βασιλεύς ἐστι "He is king" is a statement of identity in ancient Persia, or in any society with only one king; but it is an ordinary use of the nominal copula in Homer, where many nobles bear the title βασιλεύς. So *She is his wife* illustrates the *is* of identity under conditions of monogamy, but not under polygamy. Surely the grammar of the sentence is the same in either case.

The three uses we are concerned with, then, are the predicative, existential, and veridical functions of εἰμί, as illustrated respectively by the three sentence schemes *X is Y*, *There is an X such that----*, and *----is so (or is the case)*, where the blanks illustrate a structure of sentential form, *X* ranges over nouns, and *Y* ranges over nouns, adjectives and adverbials of place. I submit that if we take the predicative function as primary, and if we limit our attention to elementary uses of the copula with first-order nominals as subject, the fundamental unity and quite general importance of this system will be clear. The convergence or interdependence of the concepts of predication, existence, and truth, as represented in these central functions of the I.-E. lexeme *es-*, is not an arbitrary fact of purely historical interest for the description of a particular language family. If we may rightly regard this fact as a kind of historical accident in I.-E., it is surely a happy accident, a lucky chance, which helped to make possible the rise of philosophy as we know it – in Greece, and perhaps also in India. The language facilitated the work of the Greek philosophers by bringing together "by chance" concepts which properly belong together in any general theory of language and the world.

Let me make clear just what it is I claim in arguing for the conceptual unity of the system of uses of *be*. We have recognized three primary uses of the verb defined by three or more distinct sentence types: the copula, the veridical, and the existential. To claim that these three uses belong together in a non-accidental way is not to claim that they are really one: that the *is* of predication is the same as the *is* of being-the-case or the *is* of existence. In arguing for a systematic unity here I do not conclude that the verb *be* is univocal or that all of its functions can be brought together under a single concept of Being. My thesis is rather like Aristotle's view that being is a πρὸς ἕν equivocal, which is to say that the verb has a number of distinct uses or meanings that are all systematically related to one fundamental use. But whereas for Aristotle's ontological theory the basic use of *be* is to designate "substance" (οὐσία), in my linguistic analysis the fundamental form of *be* is its use as copula or sign of predication.

My claim for the systematic unity of the verb *be* in Greek can be spelled

---

Thus the *is* of identity is a special case of the copula. And the conditions which make it *logically* special are not necessarily, or even usually, reflected in the grammar of the language. (We have seen a formal analogue to this in Leśniewski's system, where $A = B$ can be defined as a special case of $A \varepsilon B$, namely as the case where $A \varepsilon B$ and $B \varepsilon A$ are both true: above, Chapter I, p. 5.) Benson Mates calls my attention to a similar definition in Leibniz: *A* is the same as *B* if and only if *A* is *B* and *B* is *A*. See his "Leibniz on Possible Worlds" in *Logic, Methodology and Philosophy of Science* (Amsterdam, 1968), p. 518.

For special sentence forms where ἐστί has the value *is the one and only X*, see above, pp. 142–4 and compare the nuncupative use, pp. 35f. and p. 108.

out in three propositions: (1) if we take the copula construction as primary, the use of the same lexeme for truth and existence becomes intuitively clear and intelligible, that is, we can understand the linguistic fact of this triple function for εἰμί in terms of a natural connection of ideas which is not only psychologically plausible but to some extent conceptually justified; (2) this system of uses based on the copula is not only of historical interest, as a peculiarity of I.-E., but of permanent philosophical importance for the theory of language, just because (3) these three uses fundamentally belong together, in the sense that their interrelations define a set of problems that constitute the core of classical ontology and of contemporary ontology as well, insofar as the latter also deals with the theory of predication, existence, and truth. I will develop the second and third propositions first, before returning to my claim that the use of *be* for the existential and veridical functions becomes easy to understand once we accept the copula use as basic.

   In order to make clear what is at issue in my claim (2), that the triple function of εἰμί in Greek is of more than historical interest, let us consider two simpler cases where a single linguistic form does multiple duty. The first example, which I offer as a typical case of the historical accident, is the verb *voler* in French, which provides two dictionary entries: "*voler* to fly" and "*voler* to steal".[34] Since all of the forms for "*voler* fly" are identical with forms of "*voler* steal", we might wonder whether we have two distinct verbs or only one verb with two meanings (or two uses). If unity of etymology were decisive, we would recognize only one verb in this case. But etymology is not the whole story, and the absence of passive forms for "*voler* fly" points to the need for distinguishing two verbs. This is confirmed by the discrepancy between derivative forms: except for the action noun *vol* (which means both "flight" and "theft"), all of the derivatives belong to only one of the two verbs. Thus "*voler* fly" begets "*s'envoler*" ("take flight"), *survoler* ("fly over"), *volaille* ("fowl"), *volatile*, etc., whereas from "*voler* steal" there is only the agent noun *voleur* "thief". The historical study of French shows that the connection between these two verbs is provided by a special use in falconry, where the verb "to fly" for once takes a direct object: *Le faucon vole le perdix* means "The falcon catches the partridge in flight." Originally, then, "*voler* steal" was a special case, a technical idiomatic use, of "*voler* fly". In contemporary French, however, the two verbs have gone their separate ways, and the connecting use is now obsolete. This use of one set of forms for two distinct verbal ideas is a pure case of the historical accident, since the connection between the two uses is a matter of the past history of French in a period when falconry was common, and there is no reason to suppose

---

[34] My discussion of this example is based upon Benveniste, *Problèmes de linguistique générale*, pp. 290f.

that the notions of flying and stealing have deep conceptual connections that are likely to reappear in a wide variety of languages.

For a much less accidental case of multiple significance, consider the use of λόγος in Greek, which means (among other things) (1), "discourse", "speech"; (2), "rational account," "rational principle"; and also (3), "reason", "rationality" as a distinctively human capacity for thinking, calculating, making inferences, and the like. The connection of these three notions in the uses of a single lexeme is a peculiarity of Greek, which cannot be fully paralleled in other languages. Latin, for example, can use *ratio* for senses (2) and (3), but must resort to a different word, *oratio*, to render λόγος in sense (1). This disparity is of considerable historical importance, since the Greek definition of man as ζῶον λογικόν goes into Latin as *homo rationalis* and thus loses its original sense as "linguistic animal". (Bertrand Russell once remarked that he never met a man who answered to the definition. This objection will seem less plausible if we bear in mind the Greek formula rather than its Latin translation.) We do not have to suppose that the Greek word λόγος really has only one meaning in order to see that there is considerable philosophical advantage in a terminology that brings together the concepts of language and rationality as essentially related, as it were two sides of the same coin. The recognition of the deep connections between language and rationality, which was obscured in post-Cartesian philosophy of mind by an exclusive emphasis on introspection and immediate awareness and which comes almost as a rediscovery in more recent philosophy, was effortlessly provided for the Greeks by the multiple uses of their word λόγος. In general, ambiguity is not a conceptual advantage. But in this case an ambiguity peculiar to Greek is more than an historical accident: it contains the seed of an important philosophic insight.

It is in this sense that I claim the multiple uses of the I.-E. verb *be*, as present in ancient Greek, constitute a philosophical asset, a piece of good luck. The basic role of the copula construction in the system of *be*, and the use of the same verb in the expressions for truth and existence, meant that problems of reality or existence were for the Greeks inseparable from problems of truth and problems of predication. From a purely historical point of view these connections are of great interest, since they permit us to understand how the problem of falsehood as "saying what-is-not" (and the problem of error, as thinking what-is-not) could conjure up the fantastic paradoxes of not-being – quite different from, but for a time comparable in influence to those fantastic paradoxes of non-existence which haunted Russell, Moore, and other philosophers in this century, who wondered how "exists" could function as a predicate. Precisely because εἰμί was basically understood as copula, but also functioned like our verb *exist*, the major

Greek philosophers were never seriously tempted to conceive existence as a predicate.[35] From the historical point of view again, the system of εἰμί also permits us to see how the concepts of predication, truth, and existence are intertwined in Plato's theory of τὰ ὄντως ὄντα "the really Real" and in Aristotle's system of categories based upon the notion of οὐσία "substance" or "entity". But from a strictly philosophical point of view, the system of *be* had the advantage, first, of bringing the concepts of predication, truth, and existence (or reality) together in such a way as to facilitate the development of ontology as a coherent set of problems and topics – in Plato's *Sophist*, for example, and in the *Categories* and *Metaphysics* of Aristotle. And it had the further advantage of connecting the concepts of truth and reality with the fact or possibility of predication semantically understood – that is, with the possibility of making true and false statements *about* something non-linguistic. For those of us who find the development of modern metaphysics since Descartes radically bedevilled and distorted by the tyrannical influence of epistemology, with its prior concern with *how we know* and *how we can be sure*, it is always refreshing to turn to the calm objectivity of the Greek discussion of τὸ ὄν or "what there is". What might be described as the Cartesian curse on modern philosophy, the obsession with certainty and with the question of what we can know, leads almost inevitably to some form of idealism, even when it is conceived as radical empiricism. This is another temptation from which the Greeks are free, and free in part because of the guidance provided by their system of *be*. Problems of reality were articulated as problems concerning the conditions of rational discourse, of true and false statements. "What there is" was conceived as what made it possible and intelligible to say something about something. There was no temptation to suppose that *esse* meant *percipi*, that for something to be was for it to be known or knowable. If we may sum up the basic assumptions of Greek ontology from Parmenides to Aristotle in a single slogan, we might say: for the Greeks, *to be* meant *to be a subject* or *to be a predicate* for rational discourse and true statement.

Because of this intimate connection between Greek metaphysics and the theory of language, it is no accident that we have seen a rebirth of genuinely philosophical interest in Greek thought within the modern tradition characterized by the influence of Frege, of Wittgenstein's *Tractatus*, and some aspects of Russell's work. For here again the task of ontology – some would say, of metaphysics – is to analyze the logical structure of propositions in order to define the conditions for logic and science, conceived as a system

---

[35] This temptation was all the weaker in Greek because of the late and essentially marginal (almost exclusively philosophic) use of existential Type VI, where the verb has the apparent role of predicate: εἰσὶ θεοί "There are gods". See Chapter VI §§18 and 22.

of true propositions. And within this modern enterprise, the triadic structure of the Greek system of *be* reappears. It is this fact which justifies our claim that the Greek use of εἰμί brings together concepts that properly belong together in any account of how language manages to say something about the world.

Let me illustrate my point by an obvious analogy to a contemporary theory that shows no direct indebtedness to the Greek discussions of Being. In W. V. Quine's conception of ontological commitment, the notion of existence as formalized in predicate logic is applied to the general structure of a scientific theory. What exists, according to a given theory cast in Quine's canonical form – what the theory is *committed* to – is "the objects that some of the predicates have to be true of, in order for the theory to be true."[36] The theory may be true or false, the objects which it takes as values of its quantified variables may or may not exist. But *if* the theory is true, then the objects in question must exist. In such a view, predication is expressed in the formalized language of logic, and existential quantification figures as "a logically regimented rendering of the 'there is' idiom." (Quine, *op. cit.* p. 94.) But in this artificially disciplined form the essential link between predication, existence, and truth is clearly articulated. The three concepts are interdependent in the sense that any two of them may be used to give an explication of the third concept, and a thorough account of any one will involve all three.

I do not mean to suggest that in their strictly logical formulation these three concepts are equally primitive. The forms of predication and the notion of existence as expressed by the quantifiers are ordinarily taken as primitive and undefined, whereas the concept of truth and the related notion of *satisfaction* or *is true of* are defined in a metalanguage. The metalanguage itself presupposes the contents of an object language that will normally include the forms of predication and quantification. Formally speaking, then, existence and predication are logically prior to, and generally required for, the notion of truth. (This corresponds in my linguistic analysis to the fact that the essive clause of a veridical construction, considered by itself, can often be regarded as a Type V existential or a copula use of εἰμί.) But in an informal explication of the concepts of predication and existence, we can go the other way round. For example, in explicating existence we can start with the formal notion of a predicate and a variable – say *Fx* – and describe existing objects as the values of a variable which some predicate *is true of*.[37]

[36] "Existence and Quantification" in *Ontological Relativity and other Essays* (New York, 1969), p. 95.
[37] We can express this point of view by a formal definition of singular existence in Leśniewski's system, where *A exists* can be interpreted as $(\exists B) A\varepsilon B$, i.e. something is true of *A*. Note that in Leśniewski's use the quantifier does not express existence.

Alternatively, we can do as Russell once did and explain quantification in terms of predicate forms and truth for open sentences. Then $(x)Fx$ means "Fx is always true", and $(\exists x)Fx$ means "It is false that 'Fx is false' is always true".[38] Predication in turn can be described in terms of quantification, together with the notion of a sentence. "Predication and quantification... are intimately linked; for a predicate is simply any expression that yields ... an open sentence when adjoined to one or more quantifiable variables."[39] A fuller characterization of predication will involve the notion of truth, as in Quine's informal definition already quoted in Chapter V §1: "Predication joins a general term and a singular term to form a sentence that is true or false according as the general term is true or false of the object, if any, to which the singular term refers."[40]

The point to be made here is, or at any rate should be, philosophically banal. It is not that there is some one *right* way of relating the concepts of existence, predication, and truth. Different philosophers will formulate the relationship in different ways, depending upon their general outlook and their purpose at the moment. But in any account of how language succeeds in its enterprise of describing the world, these three concepts will belong together. There must be something there to talk about; there must be something said about it; and there must be some fitness or agreement – some truth or "satisfaction" – between what is said and what it is said of.

My allusion here to Quine and other moderns is intended both as polemical and as constructive. It is meant polemically as an objection to philosophers like Mill and Carnap, or to their allies among the linguists, who insist only

---

[38] Adapted from Russell, "On Denoting", in Feigl and Sellars, *Readings in Philosophical Analysis*, p. 104.

[39] Quine, *op. cit.* p. 95. For closed atomic sentences Quine adds: "When we schematize a sentence in the predicative way 'Fa', or 'a is an F', our recognition of an 'a' part and an 'F' part turns strictly on our use of variables of quantification; the 'a' represents a part of the sentence that stands where a quantifiable variable could stand, and the 'F' represents the rest."

[40] *Word and Object* p. 96. Notice how the three concepts of predication, truth, and existence (as "identified objects of reference") recur in the following rather different characterization of atomic sentences by Strawson: "The formally atomic proposition is something which is essentially determinable as true or false and which essentially involves ... predicating concepts of identified objects of reference" (*The Bounds of Sense*, pp. 81f.).

In the present context I make no distinction between the absolute "is true", as a predicate of sentences or propositions, and the relative "is true of", as a relation between phrases (or predicates) and things. The former use is more idiomatic, but I attach no philosophical importance to this fact. (The latter use is *also* idiomatic, as when we say "That is true of Joan but not of Jane", supposing that someone has just charged the two of them with being jealous.) What is important is that both "is true" and "is true of" express semantic properties, involving a relation between something in language and something in the world. The philosophical advantage of "is true of" is that it makes such a relation explicit.

upon the distinction between the various functions of *be* in I.-E. without seeing how profoundly these functions belong together. This allusion may also be taken constructively, in that it suggests how the logical notions of existence, predication and truth can provide a contemporary idiom in which some of the ancient ontological concerns may be reformulated and reinvigorated. But that is not my task here. I wish to show, in more strictly linguistic terms, how the existential and veridical uses of εἰμί may be understood not only as natural but as conceptually appropriate complements to the primary use of the verb as elementary copula. Hence I return to the first part of my thesis, concerning the intuitive coherence of the system of *be* in Greek.

We consider, then, elementary copula sentences with first-order (concrete) nouns as subject. We take the simplest case, where the subject expression is singular in form, and where it will most typically refer to a person as extra-linguistic subject. I assume that elementary sentences are in the indicative mood, with normal declarative intonation and with no suggestion in the context to modify their *prima facie* function as statements or assertions.

Let us begin with the connection between copula and veridical use, since in this case we have already seen how the two concepts are linked. If we take an elementary copula sentence like Σωκράτης ἐστὶ σοφός "Socrates is wise" or Σωκράτης ἐστὶν ἐν τῇ ἀγορᾷ "Socrates is in the agora", we have seen that one function of the copula verb is to carry the indicative mood marker which is the formal sign for the truth-claim of the sentence. (See Chapter V §1.) It is as finite verb, and not strictly as copula, that ἐστί performs this function. Nevertheless, the diverse uses of εἰμί, and in particular those uses by which it serves as basis for the entire stative-mutative-causative system sketched in §5, establish it without any doubt as the central verb in the language, the verb par excellence, both in elementary and in second-order uses. One of these non-elementary uses is of course the periphrastic construction with participles, where ἐστί can in principle replace any finite verb in the language. Since copula sentences are in any case among the most frequent types in actual discourse, it is easy for such a conspicuous and versatile verb to function as the symbol for the general form and truth claim of an arbitrary sentence.[41]

---

[41] I have no statistics for the frequency of εἰμί relative to other verbs in Ancient Greek, but one has the impression that it occurs far more often than any other. (This impression is confirmed by a glance at the space allotted to εἰμί in any complete lexicon or index to an ancient author.) For contemporary English we have the results of a recent computer check: *is* and *was* are the only verb forms listed among the ten most frequent words in the language. (The full list, in order of frequency, is *the, of, and, to, a, in, that, is, was* and *he.*) See H. Kučera, "Computers in Language Analysis and in Lexicography", in the new *American Heritage Dictionary of the English Language*, p. xxxix.

In an elementary copula sentence, as in any other elementary sentence, the truth claim is implicit in the declarative form. In the second-order veridical use of εἰμί, the truth claim becomes explicit and *thematized* (in Husserl's sense). This normally occurs in connection with a clause of statement or cognition ("as you say", "as you think"), which defines the informal analogue to a semantic metalanguage. In such a context, where the question of truth or of how things really stand is explicitly raised, the language needs a neutral verb to express the content of the truth claim in general or its validation in the corresponding "fact" – in abstraction from the *particular* content of the statement or fact in question. As we saw in Chapter VII, this is precisely the function of εἰμί in the essive clause of the veridical construction and in the participial transform of this clause as ὄν or ὄντα. And we noted there that the language makes no systematic distinction between the *truth* of what is said or thought and the *fact* or *reality* which is stated or perceived: ἐόν, like ἀληθές, may mean either.

I do not suggest that the veridical use as such, or any particular example of it, is derived from an underlying use of the copula. Such a derivation is the exception rather than the rule. (There are more frequent connections between the veridical and a Type V existential, and we shall consider the reason for this in a moment.) What I wish to show is that the verb whose primary and predominant use is that of the copula, but which has so many other uses as well, is uniquely suited to express the form of a (declarative) sentence in general, with its associated truth claim. In the terminology of §6, the sign of predication₁ is also the natural sign of predication₃; for this wider role is only a sort of generalization of its function as elementary copula, where it provides the verbal marker for sentencehood and for *prima facie* truth claim.

The link between the copula and veridical uses of εἰμί thus corresponds to a natural and conceptually justified transition from the primary (or "descriptive") function of the verb in elementary sentences to a second-order semantic use in the assignment of a truth value ("is so", "is the case") or in the expression for a fact as such. We can see this transition occurring, as it were, before our eyes when the copula takes the emphatic initial position, where it tends to underscore the truth claim of the sentence: ἔστι Σωκράτης σοφός "Socrates *is* wise." Formally speaking, this is not a veridical construction in the sense defined in Chapter VII §2. The use of the verb here is not properly semantic, since the syntax is still that of the elementary copula. But if we conceptualize what is expressed here as an emphatic nuance, we have just the notion of truth (or truth claim), as Aristotle observed. And so we see how this same verb *can* bear the sense of truth or fact in the essive clause of a veridical construction: ἔστι οὕτω "it is so". The veridical use simply makes general and explicit what is implicit and particularized in every use of the elementary copula.

The same explanation can be given for the existential uses, and first of all for Type IV. Again we consider the copula sentences Σωκράτης ἐστὶ σοφός "Socrates is wise" and Σωκράτης ἐστὶν ἐν τῇ ἀγορᾷ "Socrates is in the agora". And again we observe that bringing the copula to the head of the sentence will underscore the assertion as such, that is, the truth claim. But now we add that the very same shift in the position of ἐστί may also serve to focus attention on one *condition* for the truth of an elementary sentence: namely, the existence of an extra-linguistic subject. The sentences *Socrates is wise* and *Socrates is in the agora* are true only if "Socrates" refers to someone, that is to say, only if Socrates exists.[42] This is the intuitive content of the logical law $Fa \rightarrow (\exists x)Fx$ or, to fit our example more precisely, $Fa \rightarrow (\exists x)(x=a)$. It is logically necessary that *if* an elementary sentence is true then its subject must exist. In this sense it is not only natural, it is also logically appropriate that the same shift in word order which emphasizes the truth claim can also serve to assert the existence of the subject. As a rule, the emphasis produced by initial position tends to be associated with the assertion of the sentence as a whole. But there are linguistic as well as logical reasons why this emphasis *may* be focussed on the subject term. For the copula (like any verb) agrees with its subject in number and person. Since the copula as such has no lexical "content" but agrees formally with a subject term that *does* have content, emphasis on the copula may be felt (and intended) as emphasis on the subject as such. Hence the effect of an existential statement may be produced by initial position for the verb, without any other formal change in the copula construction. Examples of this kind belong to our mixed existential Types II and III.

(In the rest of this section I am concerned with an essentially philological question: How are we to understand the fact that the verb εἰμί is frequently used with existential force in Greek, given my assumption that the primary use of the verb is copulative? In principle the answer has already been stated: these semantic uses serve to express conditions and functions that are implicit in the copulative use of εἰμί. Our analysis of the copula function, which brings out these implications, thus provides a kind of *a priori* explanation of the linguistic fact that the same verb is also used for truth and existence. In the transition from copula to existential verb, as in the transition from copula to veridical, the move which is linguistically natural is also concep-

---

[42] Compare *Arist. Cat.* 13ᵇ18: οὔτε γὰρ τὸ νοσεῖν Σωκράτη οὔτε τὸ ὑγιαίνειν ἀληθὲς αὐτοῦ μὴ ὄντος ὅλως τοῦ Σωκράτους "Neither *Socrates is sick* nor *Socrates is well* is true if there is no Socrates at all." I leave open the question whether falsehood also requires the existence of the subject.

tually sound, at least in the elementary cases. It is precisely because of these genuine logical connections between predication on the one hand and truth and existence on the other that the triadic system of *be* is of permanent philosophic importance.

To spell out this general answer in more specific terms means to return to a rather detailed consideration of the various existential uses distinguished in Chapter VI. The philosophical reader may pass directly to §8 without loss of continuity.)

In what follows I give the citation number of sample sentences from Chapter VI for convenient cross-reference.

Od. 2.293 (=**54** in Chapter VI §11)

εἰσὶ δὲ νῆες
πολλαὶ ἐν ἀμφιάλῳ Ἰθάκῃ νέαι ἠδὲ παλαιαί
"There are many ships in the island of Ithaca, both new and old."

Although in this example **54** the existential force of the sentence is underlined by the presence of the quantifier-word πολλαί "many", the latter is certainly not required. There is no such factor in our specimen sentence for Type II:

Il. 6.152 (=**27** in Chapter VI §7)
ἔστι πόλις Ἐφύρη μυχῷ Ἄργεος ἱπποβότοιο
"There is a city Ephyre in a corner of horse-nourishing Argos"

In **27** the only formal difference from an ordinary copula use of ἐστί (as in *Ephyre is a city, Ephyre is in Argos*) is constituted by the initial position of the verb. More often there will be other formal changes as well, such as the introduction of an indefinite pronoun τις and a reshaping of the predicate words or phrases to suggest attributive rather than predicative syntax. This reshaping reflects the normal function of the clause with initial ἔστι, which is to introduce a subject term for *further* predication:

Plato *Ap.* 18 B 6 (=**46** in Chapter VI §10)
ἔστιν τις Σωκράτης σοφὸς ἀνήρ, τά τε μετέωρα φροντιστὴς καὶ...
"There is a certain Socrates, a wise man, a student of things aloft and...".

In these and other examples of Types II and III a copula use of ἐστί is remodelled as an existential assertion of the subject, although the verb does not *cease* to function as copula for predicate nouns and adverbials of place in the same sentence. Such sentences illustrate the natural transition from a copulative to an existential use of ἐστί, just as ἔστι Σωκράτης σοφός illustrates the transition from an ordinary copula to a quasi-veridical use.

In the more properly existential use of Type IV, however, the copula syntax has disappeared: an initial ἔστι serves *only* to assert the existence of an extra-linguistic subject for the following predication. And what follows is a relative clause, i.e. a (more or less) elementary sentence form from which the subject noun has been deleted, or replaced by the indefinite pronoun τις "(some)one":

Il. 21.103 (=**84** in Chapter VI §14)

 οὐκ ἔσθ' ὅς τις θάνατον φύγῃ

"There is no one who will escape death."

Examples of this purely existential use are relatively rare: my figures for *Iliad* 1–12 show only 5 instances of Type IV for 11 examples of the mixed uses of Types II–III. It would be unreasonable to suggest that either the mixed or the much more frequent "pure" copulative uses of the verb were histori-cally derived from such a rare construction. But neither do I assert that this properly existential use is itself derived from an *earlier* use of the verb as copula alone. I do not pretend to reconstruct a state of the language more primitive than what we find in Homer. Within this synchronic system we recognize the copula uses as primary, since they are syntactically more elementary and statistically much more frequent. What I claim to show is that the secondary use of the verb to assert the existence of its (extra-linguistic) subject is a natural extension of its use as elementary copula, as we see from the mixed cases, and that this extension is in principle justified, for the reasons given. Furthermore, it is *because* ἐστί as copula can assert the existence of its subject that the same verb may be used to assert existence independently of the copula construction, as in Type IV. It is in this sense that the use of ἐστί as copula *explains* its use as existential verb in Type IV, even though the latter construction cannot be derived from the copula by any syntactical transformation. (The relevant transformation would pre-suppose the existential operator, as latent in the use of ἔστι in Type II, but this operator is just what we are trying to derive.) Thus the existential presuppositions or implications of the elementary copula use fully explain the *logical* function of the existential use of ἔστι in Type IV, though nothing in the copula use can explain the syntactic role of the verb in Type IV. (In a similar way, the locative uses of ἐστί help to explain the rhetorical function of the verb in sentences of Types II and III, which serve to introduce their subject and "locate" it within the context of the narrative, as we have seen in Chapter VI.) For the purposes of a syntactic analysis the form of Type IV is primitive, and our explanation of it cannot go beyond the general descrip-tion of Chapter VI §14, together with the account of its semantic structure given there in §20.

Once we have understood this "absolute", non-copulative use of εἰμί as verb of existence in Type IV, the post-Homeric Type VI (εἰσὶ θεοί "The gods exist") poses no new problems of meaning or function. It does pose special difficulties for the syntactic analysis, but these we have attempted to resolve by interpreting Type VI as a generalized or elliptical version of Type IV: *There is no Zeus* may be seen as short for *There is no Zeus who* ---- with the blank to be filled in by any sentence one chooses. (If we choose to fill it with a copula sentence, we return in effect to the form of Type II where ἔστι functions twice, both as copula and as existential operator: ἔστι πόλις Ἐφύρη ἐν Ἄργει "There *is* a city (which *is*) in Argos.)

The only existential form yet to be considered is Type V, where the verb takes an abstract noun as subject: **97** ὅμαδος ἦν "There was an uproar"; **9** ἀμφὶ δέ μιν κλαγγὴ νεκύων ἦν "Around him was a clamor of the dead." (Again, I use the sentence numbers from Chapter VI §15.) This is the most frequent of all existential uses of εἰμί in Homer. I count 29 examples of Type V in *Iliad* 1–12, as against 25 examples of Type I–IV combined. In this construction we have no specific underlying connection with the elementary copula, although in a sentence like **9** there is a certain superficial resemblance to a copula sentence of locative form. If we took this surface similarity at face value, we could say that sentence **9** asserts the presence or existence of an event κλαγγή "clamoring", "outcry" in a certain location, just as the elementary copula in *Socrates is in the agora* asserts (or implies) the existence of Socrates. This analogy may indeed play some part in the intuitive understanding of a sentence like **9**. But it does not go to the heart of the matter. It cannot account for the function of the same verb in ὅμαδος ἦν "there was an uproar" **97**, unless we are prepared to add an implicit locative such as "in the agora". And in the case of some Type V existentials, like *Il.* 8.66 ὄφρα μὲν ἠὼς ἦν "while dawn lasted" or sentence **8** in Chapter VI ἔως ὁ πόλεμος ᾖ "as long as the war goes on" (Thucydides), it seems quite artificial to provide an adverbial of place. This artifice would become intolerable in the case of a generalized Type V use with sentential subject, like the example quoted from Xenophon (Chapter VII §3, sentence **16**): ὅτε ταῦτα ἦν "when these events took place", where there is no plausible connection with the copula construction in any form.

It is not to the elementary copula uses, then, that we must look for an explanation of the function of εἰμί in Type V, but rather to the generalized second-order uses of the verb (including the second-order copula), where it is construed with an abstract noun or sentential subject. The only feature which is common to the elementary copula and to the verb in a Type V existential is the aptitude of εἰμί to signify the general form of the sentence, including its truth claim. In Type V εἰμί functions as a kind of dummy predicate or "empty" operator to indicate that the action described in the operand sentence *takes place* or *occurs*, with a static-durative aspect (in contrast to the kinetic-inceptive, momentary or perfective aspect of the corresponding sentence with γίγνομαι as verb of occurrence, e.g. ὅτε ταῦτα ἐγένετο "When these events (had) occurred"). The content of a Type V sentence is fully expressible by the underlying operand sentence alone, without εἰμί; e.g. for sentence 9: ἀμφί μιν νέκυες ἔκλαγξαν "around him the dead clamored". The corresponding Type V use of εἰμί provides an emphatic or expressive stylistic variant on its operand, but adds no distinct idea. (That is why I call the verb here an "empty" operator or a dummy predicate.) The verb does not assert existence in the clear-cut sense in which it posits an extra-linguistic subject in Types IV and VI, and less unmistakably in Types II and III.

Still, it is customary to describe the verb in Type V as existential, and this can be justified by the natural rendering as "there is." Hence in Chapter VI §§ 19–20 I spoke of *existence₂* for sentences of this kind, and said that εἰμί here asserts the occurrence or realization of the underlying predicate concept: *clamoring*, *uproar*, or the like. (Similarly for the post-Homeric and largely philosophical variant on Type V with quality nominalizations as subject – e.g. ἔστιν ἀρετή "Virtue exists" – we may speak of the instantiation of the predicate concept *being virtuous*. However, most examples of this kind will perhaps best be assimilated to the philosophical Type VI εἰσὶ θεοί "The gods exist.") If we wanted to press our analysis of the existential use to the limit, we could say that just as Type IV asserts the existence₁ of an extra-linguistic subject for some predication, so Type V asserts the existence₂ (realization, occurrence, instantiation) of some predicate concept, in most cases applied to some definite extra-linguistic subject. Thus ἀμφὶ δέ μιν κλαγγὴ νεκύων ἦν would be analyzed as "The action of *clamoring* was realized (carried out) by the ghosts around Odysseus." Such an analysis could be developed in a coherent way, by analogy with the account of existential Type IV. We might argue that the truth of the underlying sentence *The ghosts clamored around Odysseus* implies or presupposes the existence₂ of clamoring just as it implies or presupposes the existence₁ of ghosts, and that the Type V existential in sentence 9 brings out the first implication just as a Type IV existential (*There are ghosts who clamor*) would bring out the second. (And we note that if $Fa \rightarrow (\exists F)\ Fa$ is not generally recognized as a logical law on the same footing as $Fa \rightarrow (\exists x)\ Fx$, that is because the interpretation of the second-order quantifier poses difficulties of all sorts. What the first formula *tries* to say seems valid enough, namely that for a predicate to be true of an object there must be at least one predicate as well as at least one object.)

But although this conception of existence₂ for predicates or predicate concepts is of some importance in philosophy, it takes us too far from the natural linguistic account of the function of εἰμί in sentences of Type V. For this account we need only consider the fundamental connection between a finite verb and the total truth claim of its sentence, a connection which is generalized in the case of εἰμί by its role as verb- and sentence-operator par excellence. As we have seen, this role as carrying the truth claim for a sentence of arbitrary form is scarcely distinguished (in Greek, at any rate) from the expression or designation of the facts as such, since to claim truth is just to state (what one takes to be) the facts. Thus the role of the verb as fact-expressing in the essive clause of the veridical ("This is how things stand") is in principle the same as that of the operator of occurrence in Type V: "It happened that...." And so we account for the close affinity between the veridical use of εἰμί and the "existential" use in a generalized example of Type V: ὅτε ταῦτα ἦν "When this took place". As operator of occurrence ἔστι expresses or affirms the truth claim of its operand sentence, just as the veridical use of the verb affirms its underlying sentential subject, or the corresponding fact. In both cases the role of the verb is to assign the semantic value "true" or "it is so" to an underlying sentence of more elementary form, in which the verb *to be* does not (or need not) appear. The existential use in Type IV (ἔστι ὅς τις ... "There is someone who...") has the same logical function of assigning a positive semantic value to an operand sentence, that is, it has the function of posing or asserting an extra-linguistic relation of fitness (realization, "satisfaction") between this sentence and the world to which it refers. The more properly existential use of ἔστι in Type IV differs from the wider semantic uses for occurrence and truth by virtue of the fact that in this use the verb assigns the positive semantic value not to a whole sentence but to an indefinite *subject* for the underlying sentence represented in the relative clause (or to some cases to the *object* of this clause). In formal terms, ἔστι in Type IV operates not on the operand sentence as such but on some noun in the sentence. In Type V εἰμί is construed with an abstract noun as subject in surface structure, but it operates on the corresponding *verb* or predicate phrase in the underlying sentence. In the veridical use (and in the generalized form of Type V) εἰμί operates on the underlying sentence as a whole. It is in this respect that the concept of existence (or existence$_1$) differs from that of occurrence (or existence$_2$) and truth. (See Chapter VI §20). But these differences should not blind us to the common logical character of the semantic uses of εἰμί, namely, that they express the fundamental concepts involved in the possibility of truth for elementary sentences, the necessary conditions for success in the attempt to use language to describe the world.

§8. CONCLUDING REMARKS ON THE STATIC CHARACTER OF *to be*,
AND ON THE ABSENCE OF A CONCEPT OF
EGO OR SELF IN GREEK ONTOLOGY

It remains only to say a word about the relevance of the stative aspect to the basic uses of εἰμί, and to close with a few remarks on the "objective" and impersonal character of Greek ontology.

As we noticed earlier, the appropriateness of the aspectual value *stative* or *static* to the central uses of the verb in copulative, existential, and veridical constructions seems to be reflected in a large number of modern idioms with static-locative connotations: "is in the state of", "is in the situation of" (for the copula), "there is" or "takes place" (for the existential uses), "this is how things stand" or "die Tatsache besteht" (for the veridical). I want now to suggest that these stative-locative metaphors are conceptually grounded in a fundamental static value that is indeed essential to the concepts of predication, truth claim, fact, and existence. It is no arbitrary whim or eccentricity to suppose that there must be some element of stability and constancy at the basis of any intelligible account of how things are or what things there are in the world, even if it turns out that the "things" themselves seem to undergo constant change.

There is an old argument, familiar from the *Cratylus*, to show that neither true description nor knowledge is possible at all if everything is in constant flux. The subject of a sentence, the object of a description must (it is claimed) have some relative stability, and the properties that figure in the description must themselves have some conceptual fixity, if the sentence or description is to have any lasting – or even any momentary – claim to truth. This argument can be formulated in such a way as not to beg the question against an ontology of process or a construal of objects in terms of space-time lines or "worms". We might insist that such ontological schemes differ from the usual (more or less Aristotelian) preference for solid entities only in the choice of units which they regard as fundamental, that is, as relatively fixed and stable: they do not disagree on the need for stable units. (On the other hand, the argument for stability could be developed as an attack on the coherence of any sense-datum ontology, on the grounds that such a view takes as its basic entity something intrinsically too momentary, too fleeting and evanescent to permit distinct identification or satisfactory description.) A view which recognizes predication, existence and truth as essentially static need not rest content with the common-sense acceptance of people, natural objects, and artefacts as the primary entities in the world. The original appeal of atoms was just that they seemed so much more stable. The present state of particle physics, with a large number of extremely short-lived "entities", suggests that modern science has given up the search for stability in the form of thing-like continuants. But in some form the principle of stability probably remains essential to the scientific enterprise. The various conservation laws seem to be a case in point. And certainly the laws of motion do not move. Or if they do change in the course of time, this change is only intelligible to us in terms of a formula that is itself constant.

So much for the need for stability in a scientific account of the world – what we may call the Eleatic tendency within science. As far as the notion of truth is concerned, the modern view is in some respects even more committed to permanence or fixity than were the Greek philosophers. The urge to banish egocentric particulars or indicator words (like *I*, *you*, *this*, *here*, and *now*) from logic and science springs from a basic refusal to accept a situation which Aristotle regarded with equanimity: namely, that the truth conditions of a proposition may depend upon its circumstances of utterance, so that its truth value will change as the circumstances are altered. Instead, the modern logician wants what Quine has called an *eternal* sentence: "a sentence whose truth value stays fixed through time and from speaker to speaker" (*Word and Object*, p. 193).

A modern reader who compares Greek ontology with the doctrine of Being presented in existentialist philosophy is struck by a disparity so great that the term "Being" itself seems to have become simply equivocal. How is the use of the terms ὄν, εἶναι, or οὐσία by Plato and Parmenides, for example, to be reconciled with a sense of *Sein* for which the primacy instance is *Dasein*: human existence as Heidegger portrays it, continually threatened by the slide into inauthenticity and finding itself only in the grim and anguished resolve to confront its own annihilation? The distance is so great between this view of existence and the Platonic and Parmenidean vision of Being as an eternal realm of changeless, untroubled Form that Heidegger's initial quotation from the Eleatic Stranger of the *Sophist* ("What do we mean when we say 'ὄν'?") has the effect of unconscious irony. And if we look back beyond Heidegger to Descartes, we see that the existential starting-point in *Cogito, ergo sum* is worlds away from anything in classic Greek thought. Since Descartes, the modern concern with Being has taken as its point of departure the thinking, existing subject characterized by the first-person form: *I* or *ego*. Greek ontology, by contrast, is always focussed on the third person – that is, the non-personal form, as in the veridical ἔστι ταῦτα "This is so". And this grammatical contrast between first and third person forms is simply the expression within language of a drastic difference of outlook and interest which distinguishes Greek ontology from the mainstream of modern metaphysics, from Descartes to the present day. (On the other hand, in the abstract ontology grounded in modern logic, beginning with Wittgenstein's *Tractatus*, we do find a systematic preference for "beings" – states of affairs, objects – that are to be described in third person language alone. In this impersonal and objective construal of ontology the early Wittgenstein and the Quine of "On what there is" stand closer to Greek interests than do the continental philosophers of Being.)

It is not our concern to explain why modern philosophy has been so largely dominated by the concept of the ego, the self, or the subject of experience. But it is relevant to our topic to point out that such concepts are strictly absent from the classical Greek theories of Being. Where the theory of the self does become central in later Greek thought, for example in Plotinus, this theory does not affect in any essential way the philosophical conception of Being as such (οὐσία), which remains fundamentally Platonic and impersonal. Nor does the great interest of the classical philosophers in the theory of human desire, action, and choice exert any noticeable influence upon their concept of Being.[43]

Of course Greek philosophy is not a monolithic block, and my generalizations would have to be qualified for each particular thinker. It is in Parmenides and Plato that the Greek notion of Being lies at the greatest possible distance from the concept of a personal subject or ego. In Aristotle's *Categories*, on the other hand, a human being is implicitly treated as the paradigm case of "entity" or substance (οὐσία). And in the *Metaphysics*, where only organisms are recognized as "entities" in the proper sense, the primary instance of Being is a self-regarding act of divine νόησις or intellection. Aristotle's God is, after all, a subject, though scarcely a person. (It can, for example, be referred to by a neuter or "non-personal" expression.) And nowhere in Aristotle any more than in Plato is the sentence form *I am* or *you are* granted an importance in ontology which is even remotely comparable to the form *it is*. (For the essential connection between first and second person as grammatical forms and extra-linguistic reference to persons, see Chapter IV §4.)

---

[43] There is of course a pre-modern background for the Cartesian *cogito* in Augustine and in the medieval Augustinian tradition. This subjective concern with self-consciousness and spiritual inwardness can be traced back through Neoplatonism to Seneca and later Stoics such as Marcus Aurelius. (It even has an archaic precursor in Heraclitus, who said ἐδιζησάμην ἐμεωυτόν "I sought my self.") The natural affinities of this tradition are with a religious concern for individual salvation and something like "peace of mind" whether epistemic or spiritual, whether secure or anguished. Thus the Western tradition of subjectivity, represented in different ways by Augustine, Descartes, and Heidegger, has its spiritual kinship elsewhere, for example in Indian religious philosophy. Behind the contrast which I am sketching between classical Greek and post-Cartesian modern philosophy there lies a deeper division between a metaphysics centered on science and a metaphysics centered in religious (or quasi-religious) personal experience.

I do not mean to suggest that this is an unmixed blessing in Greek thought. A doctrine of Being in which persons as such have no ontological status is a doctrine with grave weaknesses (as Aristotle's discussion of slavery shows). But for this neglect of persons in Greek ontology the verb *to be* is not responsible. εἰμί conjugates very well in the first and second person, and one use of the verb – what I have called the "vital" use, in sentences of existential Type I – is generally restricted to personal subjects. It was not for linguistic reasons that the Greek philosophers never propounded the thesis "I think, therefore I am." But our linguistic study does shed some light on the absence of personal forms in Greek ontology.

The uses of the verb εἰμί which determine its philosophical career are the semantic uses generally, and the veridical in particular, all of which are restricted to third person form, since they take sentential subjects (for the veridical), abstract subjects (for Type V existential), or in any case an entity which is neither the speaker nor the hearer (in existential Types II–IV and VI). Now I submit that the semantic uses of εἰμί were of such primary philosophical importance in Greece because philosophy, from its inception, was wedded to science, to mathematics, and to a general concern with *truth* in cognition and in statement. The Greek view of Being has the strength of its limitations. The absence of an ontology of persons is an omission which we can only regret. But this was perhaps the price to be paid for a theory of Being directly focussed on the most general conditions for rational discourse and for a true description of the world. The virtual non-existence of the concept of the self or subject in classical Greek metaphysics is as it were a negative consequence of the great positive achievement in this field: the serenely objective concern with the concepts of predication, existence, and truth in their most general form, as conditions for science, that is, for the cognitive or descriptive use of language in a theory of the world. It is this original union with science that defines the nature of philosophy in Greece, and in the West generally. And it is this original scientific interest which determines the impersonal form of the Eleatic-Platonic concept of Being, as the stable basis for true statement and cognition – just as a different but comparable scientific concern is reflected in the abstract ontology of our contemporaries.

It is another question how we are to reconcile the claims of scientific knowledge (including logic and mathematics) with the equally pressing, though entirely distinct need for an adequate ontology of persons. This is perhaps the central philosophical problem of the day, the basic challenge posed by the bewildering spectacle of two philosophic traditions – one "analytical" and one "continental" or "existentialist" – which seem unable and unwilling to communicate with one another.

But that is our problem. The Greeks have done their part. What they did was made possible or made easier for them by the language they spoke. In its second-order semantic uses of εἰμί the language had already brought to the fore, and articulated in easily recognizable form, the notions of "what there is" and "what is the case" that are present but latent in the more elementary, descriptive function of the verb in ordinary predication. What greater service could the Greek language render to philosophy than to bring together these three concepts – predication, existence, and truth – within the idiomatic system of uses of its most fundamental verb?

ON THE ACCENT OF ἐστί AND ITS POSITION
IN THE SENTENCE

According to the account given by comparative linguists since Wackernagel, following the information supplied by the best ancient grammarians, the accent of ἐστί depends exclusively upon its position in the sentence and upon the identity of the preceding word, if any. But insofar as the accent is a mechanical reflection of the word order, the accent as such can be of no importance for the syntax or meaning of ἐστί. It is only the phenomena of word order that might be of some interest in this connection.

Unfortunately this very simple conclusion has been obscured by a popular view, first formulated by Gottfried Hermann in 1801, according to which the difference between the weak or enclitic accent (namely, ἐστί) and the orthotone accent on the first syllable (ἔστι) depends upon a distinction between the use of the verb as copula and a stronger use where the verb is existential or has some other meaning of its own.[1] Since Hermann's theory continues to exert an influence by way of handbooks, school tradition, and even text editions, and since it has been taken for granted by many Hellenists including some of the best, a discussion of the matter is called for here. But it should be clear that our conclusion, as far as the accent is concerned, will be almost entirely negative: there is no reason to believe that any systematic distinction of sense or syntax was reflected in the accent as actually pronounced, or as described in the ancient grammarians. (For one or two possible exceptions see below, pp. 423f.) Such a distinction is sometimes taken for granted in the practice of a modern editor. Thus Burnet's text of Plato regularly accents the verb as orthotone in the standard formula for the Forms, for example, in αὐτὸ ὃ ἔστιν ⟨sc. τὸ ἴσον⟩ at *Phaedo* 74 B2, αὐτὸ τὸ ὃ ἔστιν at 74 D6, τοῦ ὃ ἔστιν ἴσον at 75 B1, αὐτοῦ τοῦ ἴσου ὅτι ἔστιν at 75 B6, and τὸ αὐτὸ ὃ ἔστι at 75 D2. In all five passages the MSS. have the enclitic accent, in agreement with Herodian's rule.[2] Burnet's accentuation

---

[1] See G. Hermann, *De emendanda ratione graecae grammaticae*, Leipzig 1801, pp. 84f.: "Verbum ἐστὶν enim duas habet significationes, unam, quae simpliciter copulae, quam logici vocant, munere fungitur, et praedicati alicuius accessionem requirat, ut τοῦτο ἐστὶν ἀληθές; alteram, quae ipsum in se conclusum habet praedicatum, ut ἔστι θεός. Harum significationum prior ubi obtinet, ultima syllaba acuitur, quo fit, ut minus audiatur verbum". (The eccentric accentuation here is Hermann's own.)

[2] I am relying on the facsimile edition of MS. "B", the Clarkianus (pp. 35r–35v), dated to 895 A.D. Burnet's apparatus for 74 B2 and 74 D6 shows that the verb is also enclitic here in "T" and "W". On the other hand, the Clarkianus (like Burnet) writes the copula as orthotone at 75 B8, where it occurs after punctuation, as first word in its clause: ἔστιν

of ἔστι in such passages reflects his own interpretation of the meaning of the verb in this formula ("what is *really* or *truly* so-and-so"); but this use of the accent presupposes Hermann's rule.

1. HERODIAN'S RULE AND THE MODERN THEORY OF THE ACCENT[3]

Among the personal forms of all Greek verbs, the present indicative of εἰμί and φημί stand alone in being normally enclitic. (This does not hold good for the second person singular forms, εἶ and φής: for the exception, see Vendryès, p. 117.) That is to say, the present forms of these two verbs will ordinarily bear no accent in non-final position (although they will be written with an acute accent on the last syllable when they occur at the end of the sentence and in various other circumstances specified by the rules for enclitics). This lack of accent is generally regarded as the survival of a prehistoric situation (attested in Sanscrit) where all finite verbs had an enclitic form in non-initial position in main clauses. The continuation of this enclitic treatment for εἰμί and φημί is apparently due to the purely mechanical fact that the present indicative forms of these two verbs alone never have a metrical length greater than three short syllables, or one long and one short. For verbs with longer forms, the old status as enclitic would be represented in Greek by an ordinary recessive accent according to the "rule of limitation"; and this is in fact what happens with all other finite verb forms. Short enclitics will have no accent or will take a secondary enclitic accent on the final syllable (like ποτέ). And this is the case for εἰμί and φημί.

In initial position, on the other hand, the present indicative forms of εἰμί and φημί would originally have been orthotones, with accent on the first syllable. There is some evidence for such an accent for forms like φῆμι (Vendryès, p. 110). The tradition prevailed, however, of writing these forms with enclitic accent even in initial position. It is only in the case of initial ἔστι that the verb is written as an orthotone, and explicitly recognized as such by the ancient grammarians. But there is a curious ambiguity as to

---

δὲ αὐτοῦ φαυλότερα. In both respects, then, the Clarkianus follows Herodian's rule: regardless of its veridical or existential value ἐστί is orthotone if initial (or quasi-initial), otherwise not.

The only exception I have noted in this section of the Clarkianus is the non-initial ἔστιν ὅτε ("sometimes") at 74 C1, which is orthotone in the MS. just as it is in Burnet's text. For this exception see below, p. 423.

[3] The account which follows is based on J. Vendryès, *Traité d'accentuation grecque* (Paris, 1904, reprinted 1945), who in turn follows J. Wackernagel, "Der griechische Verbalakzent", in *Kleine Schriften* II, 1058-1071, esp. pp. 1067f.

what is to count as initial position for ἐστί. The simplest rule is that ἔστι is orthotone only if the verb is first word in the sentence or in the verse, or if it is preceded by οὐ.[4] But other authors give a longer list. According to Herodian, we should write ἔστι not only after οὐ but also after καί, εἰ, ἀλλά, ὡς, and τοῦτο. (The rule in the *Etymologicum Magnum* adds μή to this list.) Why ἔστι should be orthotone in these quasi-initial positions is not entirely clear. Vendryès (p. 109) suggests that the accent of the verb in τοῦτ᾽ ἔστιν could be simply the acute accent of the elided syllable: τοῦτό ἐστιν. Wackernagel had pointed out that some of these words are not properly parts of the clause which they introduce (καί, ἀλλά) so that the ἔστι which follows these latter "ebenso gut am Satzanfang steht, als das in ἔστι πόλις Ἐφύρη" (*Kl. Schr.* II, 1068).

Whatever the historical explanation may be, the rule as formulated in Herodian and the scholia is a purely *formal* one: the accent of ἐστί depends only on its position in the sentence (or verse) and on the identity of the word which precedes it, if any.

2. HERMANN'S RULE

By Byzantine times and probably before, some scholars were dissatisfied with this mechanical account of the accent of ἔστι and were inclined to explain the orthotone accent by an appeal to the meaning of the sentence or to the intention of the speaker. Thus scholia T (cited by Laum, *op. cit.* p. 239) contain the following comment on *Il.* 23.549 (ἔστι τοι ἐν κλισίῃ χρυσὸς πολύς, ἔστι δὲ χαλκός): ἐπαγγελτικῶς τὸ ἔστι· διὸ ὀξέως. The word ἐπαγγελτικῶς is a rare one, but it presumably means something like "in the declarative manner," "assertively" or perhaps "imperiously", "dogmatically". The scholiast seems to be explaining the orthotone here by the confident or emphatic nature of the assertion. Two Byzantine texts go further, and propose a partial anticipation of Hermann's rule. Thus we find in the *Lexicon* of the ninth-century patriarch Photius (s.v. ἔστιν) a statement which recurs verbatim in the later commentary of Eustathius on the *Iliad* (p. 880, 22): the verb is accented ἔστι "when we state that something exists (or perhaps "is the case," ὡς ὑπάρχει), as in ἔστι πόλις Ἐφύρη"; it is enclitic "when we are answering a question." (See the passages cited by W. S. Barrett, *Euripides, Hippolytos*, Oxford 1964, p. 426 n. 2; also K. Lehrs, *Quaestiones epicae* p. 126. Since Eustathius assigns this doctrine to οἱ παλαιοί, it is presumably older than Photius.)

Strictly speaking, however, neither the ancients nor the Byzantines could

---

[4] See the Homeric scholia cited by B. Laum, *Das Alexandrinische Akzentuationssystem*, p. 239: Scholia A on *Il.* 6.152, H on *Od.* 14.99, BT on *Il.* 1.63.

formulate Hermann's rule, since they did not have available the concepts provided by Abelard's theory of the copula. As a pupil of the Enlightenment, Hermann set out to explain the facts of Greek grammar according to rational principles. In the case of the accent, what he probably wanted was a coherent linguistic account such as Wackernagel and Vendryès have provided. But comparative grammar did not exist in 1801, and for a rational explanation Hermann was obliged to fall back on the principles of medieval logic, as known to him from the writing of Christian Wolff.[5] Thus he distinguished two "significations" of ἐστί, one in which it simply performs the function of the copula and requires an additional predicate, and the other in which it contains the predicate within itself. He does not use the term "existence" in this connection, but his first example of the second sense is in fact an existential use: ἔστι θεός "God exists". In this second use, says Hermann, ἔστι means ἔστιν ὄν. (Later, p. 89, he says it may mean *exstat, revera est*, or *licet*.) And in this case the verb is orthotone, whereas in the copula use it has the less conspicuous accent on the second syllable.

Since Wackernagel, linguists who discuss this question have generally ignored or rejected Hermann's rule and accepted the evidence of Herodian and the Homeric scholia.[6] Every editor of a Greek text must decide how far he is to follow Herodian, Hermann, or the usage of the manuscripts. In the cases where the manuscript tradition deviates systematically from Herodian's rule, it should be possible to find a simple explanation which is not exposed (as Hermann's rule is) to obvious counter-examples from the same tradition. For example, if one can judge by modern editions ἔστι + *infinitive* in the potential construction is regularly orthotone in Homer, regardless of the position of the verb. This may well be a special development in pronunciation, overlooked by Herodian. If so, it can be explained by the fact that (1) the typical cases of the potential construction are negative, so that ἔστι follows οὐκ and is properly orthotone, and (2) the contrasting accent was generalized for this construction because of its distinct semantic value. Simi-

---

[5] For the influence of Wolff on Hermann, see Delbrück, *Vergl. Syntax* I (= Brugmann-Delbrück II), 25–7. Hermann makes clear in his preface (*De emendanda*, p. vi) that the *lumen philosophiae* should permit a modern grammarian to go much further than his ancient predecessors in articulating a rational theory. In stating his rule for the accent he explicitly appeals to the concept of "what logicians call the copula" (*ibid.* p. 84, cited above, p. 420, n. 1).

[6] For a strong rejection, see Vendryès, p. 110; Hermann's rule is simply ignored in Schwyzer, *Gr. Gramm.* I, 677. Delbrück seems to have been the last to resist Wackernagel's explanation (*Vergl. Syntax* III = Brugmann-Delbrück V, 78–80). Delbrück cites what he claims is a tendency in the MSS. of Homer to write ἔστι as orthotone in the vital, possessive, potential, and existential uses. Thus Delbrück, like Hermann and unlike Herodian, believed that the accent of ἔστι depended on the meaning. Of course some scribes may have been influenced by a rule like that quoted above from Photius and Eustathius. But I have found no general evidence of this in the Plato MS. described above, n. 2.

larly, we can explain the strong accent for ἔστιν ὅτε "sometimes" in non-initial position by remembering that ἔστιν ὅτε is after all a frozen sentence beginning, a variant of existential Type IV (ἔστιν ὅς τις ...) where the verb nearly always takes initial position. Again the orthotone pronunciation may have been generalized for this use of the verb as a convenient mark of its special meaning. (I have not examined the MSS. evidence in any detail, but Phillip DeLacy informs me that non-initial ἔστιν ὅτε is commonly orthotone in the best MSS. of Galen, and I have noted a similar example in the Clarkianus *Phaedo*.)

It is special evidence such as this which lends a certain plausibility to Hermann's rule. But it is simply false that there is any more general evidence for orthotone pronunciation of non-initial ἐστί, no matter how emphatic or existential its force may be. If an emphatic ἔστι is often orthotone, that is because emphasis on the verb is often connected with initial or quasi-initial position.[7]

3. The position of the verb

A glance at the examples of the existential use of εἰμί in Chapter VI will show that the verb often occurs in initial position, particularly in Types II and IV. But there are other cases where the verb is clearly existential though non-initial. (Aside from the vital use in Type I, where the verb is scarcely ever initial in Homer, consider sentences **34–37** of Type II, **51–52** of Type III, the very "existential" example **77** in §13, and almost any sample of Type V.) On the other hand, there are initial occurrences which are certainly not existential, though in some cases they may be emphatic. Thus we have εἴμ᾽ Ὀδυσεὺς Λαερτιάδης when Odysseus finally announces his identity in *Od.* 9.19. Similarly with the pronoun expressed: *Od.* 6.196 εἰμὶ δ᾽ ἐγὼ θυγάτηρ μεγαλήτορος Ἀλκινόοιο "I am the daughter of greathearted Alcinoös". (Also with identifications by place: *Il.* 21.154 εἴμ᾽ ἐκ Παιονίης; compare *Od.* 24.304.)[8] In classic prose as well an initial ἔστι may serve to introduce a dramatic disclosure of identity, as in Lysias I.16 ἔστι δ᾽ ἔφη

---

[7] A detailed consideration of Hermann's examples would show that his rule is really a recommendation to write as orthotone every emphatic use of the verb, regardless of the structure of the sentence. Thus he would write καὶ ἔστιν οὕτω ("ac revera est, nec non est, ita") but καὶ οὕτως ἐστίν ("atque ita, non aliter est"), *De emend.* p. 87. Note that the syntax can scarcely differ in the two cases, but that Hermann's judgment here conforms to Herodian's rule for the accent as based upon position. All Hermann really adds (in the application, as contrasted with the statement of his rule) is the connection between quasi-initial position and an emphatic or expressive force of the verb.

[8] It would be a mistake to suppose that initial εἰμί was standard or obligatory in self-identifications. Compare *Od.* 11.252 αὐτὰρ ἐγώ τοί εἰμι Ποσειδάων and 15.426 κούρη δ᾽ εἴμ᾽ Ἀρύβαντος ἐγώ.

Ἐρατοσθένης Ὀῆθεν ὁ ταῦτα πράττων "It is, she said, Eratosthenes of Oë who is doing these things (sc. committing adultery with your wife)." In other cases an initial ἔστι tends to convey a strong veridical or assertoric nuance, as in the example already quoted from Euripides: ἀλλ' ἔστιν, ἔστιν, ἡ λίαν δυσπραξία/λίαν διδοῦσα μεταβολάς. (See Chapter VII, sentence 36 and the parallels quoted there in §5.) But if we examine the cases of initial ἔστι in the first book of Herodotus, we see that the typical function of such a sentence is neither existential nor veridical. It normally serves to introduce a parenthetical bit of information concerning an item mentioned in the narrative, regardless of the syntax or meaning of the sentence, e.g. I.26.2 ἔστι δὲ μεταξὺ τῆς τε παλαιῆς πόλιος, ἣ τότε ἐπολιορκέετο, καὶ τοῦ νηοῦ ἑπτὰ στάδιοι "[The distance] between the old city [of Ephesus], which was then under siege, and the temple [of Artemis] is seven stades" (where we have the formulaic use of a singular ἔστι with plural "subject"); I.35.2 ἔστι δὲ παραπλησίη ἡ κάθαρσις τοῖσι Λυδοῖσι καὶ τοῖσι Ἕλλησι "The rite of purification is similar for the Lydians and for the Greeks" (interposed after Κροῖσος δέ μιν ἐκάθηρε in the story of Atys); I.84.3 ἔστι δὲ πρὸς τοῦ Τμώλου τετραμμένον τῆς πόλιος "[The section of the wall of Sardis where King Meles did not think fit to carry the lion child] is [the part] of the citadel turned towards the Tmolus river."

These examples should suffice to show that there can be no general rule, either syntactic or semantic, to explain every case of initial position for the verb. The prose of Plato and Aristotle is similarly full of initial occurrences of ἔστι which do not express any distinct existential or veridical force. For a stylistic or rhetorical analysis it would no doubt be possible to classify many cases of initial ἔστι according to typical features of context or content.[9] But that is not our task here. It is enough to have pointed out that there is no regular correlation between initial position and existential force.

It may be useful to add a few positive observations about the position of εἰμί within the sentence. I have already remarked (in Chapter VI pp. 255 and 264 n.) that word order, like omission of the verb, is primarily dependent upon stylistic or rhetorical factors (such as emphasis, contrast, variety, and brevity), and has no simple or direct connections with the syntax or meaning of the verb. If initial position represents the most conspicuous treatment, omission of the verb may be regarded as the *least* conspicuous. These are the two extreme cases, and they apply to the "mere" copula and to the existential or locative-existential uses alike. (For omission of the existential verb, see the examples

---

[9] See the interesting remarks of A. Bloch on the function of the verb *be* in introducing what he calls "der erläuternde Einschub" in Latin and Sanscrit as well as in Greek, *Museum Helveticum* I (1944), 243–51. The sentences just quoted from Herodotus are typical specimens of this rhetorical device.

from *Od.* 13.97, 102, and 103 cited above, p. 264 n.; and in detail see below, Appendix B, pp. 449-52.) For simplicity, however, I will limit the following remarks to the copula construction and to sentences in which the verb actually occurs.

The basic form of the copula sentence is N *is* Φ, where the predicate Φ will typically be an adjective, a noun, or a locative phrase, though it may also be a participle, a pronoun, or any prepositional phrase. If for the moment we ignore the complications arising from the omission of N and from the fact that either N or Φ may be represented by several words that are not immediately juxtaposed, we recognize that the N *is* Φ structure admits of six permutations of word order:

1	N *is* Φ
2	N Φ *is*
3	Φ N *is*
4	Φ *is* N
5	*is* Φ N
6	*is* N Φ

In English, as in most modern European languages, we know perfectly well what the standard order is. For declarative sentences it is **1**: N *is* Φ, *John is tall*; whereas the regular interrogative order is **6**: *is* N Φ, *Is John tall*? It is important to notice that patterns **2** *John tall is and **5** *is tall John are not mere deviations from the norm: they are grammatical mistakes. The speaker who produces such sentences in the course of ordinary conversation or written prose – whether as statements or as questions – must be ignorant of the language or he will recognize that he has misspoken.[10]

Thus word order in English is a matter of grammatical rule, that is to say, of acceptable and unacceptable sentence forms. There are no such rules in Greek, as far as the order of subject, predicate and copula is concerned. (Of course there are *some* rules governing word order, e.g. that postpositives such as μέν and δέ cannot occur as first word in the sentence.) Every one of the six permutations gives a sentence that is grammatically acceptable and may even be the most natural form under some circumstances. Hence if we speak of the "normal" word order of a Greek sentence we can refer only to general tendencies reflected in statistical frequencies: there is no question

---

[10] The other two patterns are possible under special circumstances. Thus **3** Φ N *is*, *Tall, John is* may serve as an expressive variant on **1**, with contrasting emphasis on the predicate; and it is the standard form for certain indirect questions (*I do not know how tall John is, I asked where he is*). Order **4** Φ *is* N, *Quiet is the night*, may occur as statement in poetry or archaic prose and also as *wh*-question: *Where is John*? **6** may serve not only for questions but, colloquially, for strong assertions: *Boy, is John tall!* But orders **2** and **5** are, as far as I can see, never acceptable as English sentences.

of a correct or incorrect order. A failure to grasp this distinction between the status of word order in ancient Greek and in modern languages such as English has led to much confusion and to futile requests for the "rule" of ancient usage.[11] There are no rules, and in this sense the order is "free". But there are certain preferences reflected in statistical frequencies. These frequencies seem to vary with the structure of the clause in some cases, and they may also vary between main clause and subordinate, between finite verb and participle or infinitival clause. In general, the order of the main clause seems to be freer, more variable; the subordinate clause tends to be arranged in a more mechanical and predictable way. (And this parallels the greater frequency with which εἰμί is omitted in principal clauses: see Appendix B, p. 441.) Furthermore, the tendencies are not quite the same in classic prose and in Homeric verse. Since the situation is so complicated, my remarks here are presented only as a tentative sketch: they will inevitably sound more dogmatic than they are meant to be.

There seems to be no doubt that the statistically favored order, both in Homer and in classic prose, is **2**: *N Φ is*.[12] This is the pattern illustrated by the first occurrence of εἰμί in the *Iliad* (1.63): καὶ γάρ τ᾽ ὄναρ ἐκ Διός ἐστιν "For a dream also is from Zeus"; and again by the first occurrence in the *Odyssey* (1.11): Ἔνθ᾽ ἄλλοι μὲν πάντες .../οἴκοι ἔσαν "Then all others... were at home." But although this is the most common pattern, both for main and subordinate clauses, and probably for participles and infinitival clauses as well, it does not follow that it must be recognized as the normal or standard order, in the sense usually supposed. I mean, it does not follow that, because (for whatever reasons) *N Φ is* is the statistically preferred order in Greek, every other order must be understood as the result of some special stylistic or rhetorical intention.[13] The statistical predominance of the

---

11 See the quotation from Thumb in Lasso de la Vega, *La oración nominal*, p. 139: "Greek has been taught and studied for centuries, and the most important descriptive grammar still cannot tell us what the usual position of the verb is: even for a schoolboy the correct rule (*die richtige Regel*) is useful." Thumb is criticizing Kühner-Gerth, probably unfairly. (See below, n. 22.) For literature in favor of different views of the "normal" order, see Schwyzer-Debrunner, p. 695.

12 This is, as we have noticed, not even a grammatical order in English or French. In German it is unacceptable in a main clause but, curiously enough, obligatory in the subordinate: *Wenn er zu Hause ist*....

13 This is the misleading assumption made, for example, by Lasso de la Vega, *loc. cit.*: "Once we have established a word order as statistically 'normal', the deviations from this order must be explained by the desire to give greater relief to the displaced elements." This implies that every Greek sentence is *first* conceived in a given order (e.g. *N Φ is*) and *then* rearranged. But the evidence for statistical frequency shows nothing whatsoever about the priority of a given form, whether this priority is interpreted psychologically or transformationally.

Lasso de la Vega's assumption about explaining all but one order as stylistically motivated deviations from a norm is to be found in a similar form in J. Marouzeau's

pattern *N Φ is* may itself be the result of several other factors. For example, it may be due in part to the fact that deictic elements tend to come first, combined with the fact that many clauses have deictic subjects (i.e. demonstrative or demonstrative-relative pronouns). Or it may also result from some more general tendency or statistical law that noun forms precede verbal and adjectival forms; and this in turn might be explained by a psychological tendency for nouns to represent ideas uppermost in the speaker's mind. On any such assumption, the predominance of this particular sentence pattern will not be a primary fact in linguistic experience but a secondary result of more fundamental factors, and hence the deviations from this pattern need not be felt as such by the speaker. His stylistic intention, insofar as we can divine it at all, will not be to deviate from some established norm but to produce diversity, vigor, surprise and the like by shifting back and forth between the different possibilities. He will be playing with *some* expectations on the hearers' part, but they need not be anything so fixed and simple as the assumption that *N Φ is* is the standard order.

Even the statistical predominance of this order is far from absolute. Lasso de la Vega claims that it accounts for more than two-thirds of all occurrences of the copula in Homer (*La oración nominal*, p. 156), but he does not give detailed statistics. My own figures suggest a fraction more like one-half. For *Iliad* 1, where there are about 30 examples of the copula construction in the indicative, I find that 10 cases leave the subject unexpressed. (For these 10, the order *Φ is* prevails over *is Φ* by a ratio of 9:1.) For the 20 cases where all three terms occur, I find 8 examples of *N Φ is* in main clause, 3 in subordinate, for a total of 11. Book 1 contains no cases of initial εἰμί, and hence no examples of patterns **5** or **6** (*is N Φ* and *is Φ N*) either for copula or for non-copula constructions. Thus the remaining 9 cases are divided about equally between patterns **1** *N is Φ* (2 examples in main clause, one in subordinate), **3** *Φ N is* (2 in main clause) and **4** *Φ is N* (2 in main clause, one in subordinate). The ninth case is ambiguous between patterns **4, 2,** and an existential construction (1.566 ὅσοι θεοί εἰσ' ἐν Ὀλύμπῳ), and it will therefore be ignored in my final count. It should be noted that all three examples of *Φ is N* in *Iliad* 1 are of the syntactical form *neuter adjective* + ἐστί + + *infinitive* (lines 169, 229, and 541).[14]

---

earlier studies for Latin. (See especially, *L'ordre des mots: Phrase à verbe être* (Paris, 1910), pp. 35 ff.). Marouzeau's findings suggest that some typical tendencies are the same for Latin and for Greek: in both cases the predicate precedes the copula much more often than not.

[14] The other examples from *Il.* 1 are: *N Φ is* in main clause, verses 63, 212, 259, 281, 325, 388, 563, 581; in subordinate 272, 280, 516; for *N is Φ*, 107, 239, 300 (though the last overlaps with possessive and might be discounted as copula); for *Φ N is* 573, 583.

In order to classify these examples for counting, I have been obliged to simplify the

For fuller data I have added examples from *Odyssey* 13, which happens to have only 11 clear cases of the copula construction in the indicative with subject expressed. (It also has 7 cases of the indicative copula without subject expression in the same clause; all of these are of the form *Φ is*.) The breakdown here is: *N Φ is*, 2 in main, 1 in subordinate = 3; *N is Φ*, 3 in main, 1 in subordinate = 4; *Φ is N*; 3 in main (2 of these with infinitival subject), 0 in subordinate; *Φ N is*, 1 in subordinate.[15] The predominance of *N Φ is* does not emerge in such a small sample; but it becomes apparent if we add the optative and imperative forms from *Odyssey* 13 (2 out of 3 for *N Φ is*), and the participles. (*N Φ is* accounts for all three participial examples where the noun "subject" occurs in the same case as the participle: verses 331 and 401 ≈ 433). An initial εἰμί occurs only once, in the locative-existential verse 246 ἔστι μὲν ὕλη, "There is timber (here)", where the locative predicate "in Ithaca" is in fact understood from the preceding lines (so that this example might be regarded as an elliptical version of *Φ is N*).

Thus my small samples confirm the chief conclusions of Lasso de la Vega: in Homer *N Φ is* is the most common word order; initial position for the copula is extremely rare.[16] Where no subject is expressed, the predicate nearly always precedes the copula (i.e. *Φ is* is vastly more common than *is Φ*). In the cases where the predicate precedes the copula and the subject *is* expressed,

---

data on word order in four cases (239, 259, 272, 583) out of 20. Thus in 239 ὁ δέ τοι μέγας ἔσσεται ὅρκος, if we count the *first* word of the predicate the order is *N Φ is*; I have counted it instead as *N is Φ* on the grounds that the noun ὅρκος is the principal predicate, on which μέγας depends. In 259 ἄμφω δὲ νεωτέρω ἐστὸν ἐμεῖο the same principle leads to the opposite result, i.e. to a classification as *N Φ is*, since ἐμεῖο depends upon the predicate adjective: the sentence type is adjectival copula. (For similar reasons I overlook the delayed position of ἡμῖν in 583 and count the sentence as *Φ N is*.) In 272 οἳ νῦν βροτοί εἰσιν ἐπιχθόνιοι I count βροτοί rather than ἐπιχθόνιοι as principal predicate on the grounds that it is more substantival. (Whenever there is serious doubt, as in this case, I try to count the *first* word in the predicate as principal.) Note that all four of these complex cases illustrate a secondary tendency for the copula *not* to occur as last word in the sentence, even where the general order is *N Φ is* or *Φ N is*. Or perhaps we should say: where the predicate expression is complex, it tends to split into two parts which occur on either side of the copula.

[15] The indicative examples classified in *Odyssey* 13 are: *N Φ is*, verses 129, 130, 295; *N is Φ*, 111, 297, 345, 351 (though the last two examples are debatable); *Φ is N*, 141, 210, 335, *Φ N is*, 223 (in subordinate clause with relative adjective: οἷοί τε ἀνάκτων παῖδες ἔασι). In the non-indicative moods we have examples of *N Φ is* at verses 46 and 412, *Φ is N* at 291. I omit verses 96, 105, 109, 144, 202, and 280 as existential, possessive, or otherwise too problematic to include in a classification of *copula* sentences with respect to word order.

[16] According to Lasso de la Vega, p. 156, the order *is Φ N* is a rarity whereas *is N Φ* is "practically nonexistent". He does cite one example of the latter (*Od.* 6.196 εἰμὶ δ' ἐγὼ θυγάτηρ). We could easily find more, except for the fact that when the verb precedes in this way there is a general tendency to classify it as existential. In fact *is N Φ* might be regarded as the standard pattern for a Type II existential: ἔστι πόλις Ἐφύρη μυχῷ Ἄργεος.

this subject is most likely to come first (*N Φ is*), least likely to be inserted between the other two terms (*Φ N is*); but it will often come last (*Φ is N*).

Looking at all six possibilities now, we recognize one as statistically preferred (*N Φ is*) and the two patterns with initial copula as most infrequent. This leaves us with three forms – *N is Φ*, *Φ is N*, and *Φ N is* – which are neither extremely common nor extremely rare. Of these three, pattern **4** *Φ is N* is the second most common order in Homer, according to Lasso de la Vega. (In my examples pattern **4** is no more common than **1**, *N is Φ*, but a larger sample might confirm Lasso's statement.) The same author suggests that **3**, *Φ N is*, is less common than the other two intermediate forms just because the subject term here interrupts the tight predicate-copula nexus. The fact that *N is Φ* occurs more frequently than *Φ N is* does show that, in Homer at any rate, the close tie between predicate and copula is more important than their relative order.

The complete picture for my sample of three-term sentences with the indicative copula in *Iliad* 1 and *Odyssey* 13 is as follows:

1	*N is Φ*	7
2	*N Φ is*	14
3	*Φ N is*	3
4	*Φ is N*	6
5	*is Φ N*	0
6	*is N Φ*	0

(but cf. *Od.* 13.246)

TOTAL   30

For copula clauses with no subject expressed, the order *Φ is* predominates over *is Φ* in the ratio of 16 to 1.

For a convenient though imperfect point of comparison in classic prose we may use the complete survey by H. L. Ebeling of 454 copula forms from Plato's *Protagoras*. His results are as follows:

1	*N is Φ*	32
2	*N Φ is*	104
3	*Φ N is*	20
4	*Φ is N*	62
5	*is Φ N*	5
6	*is N Φ*	13

TOTAL   236

For the copula uses without subject expressed, the order *Φ is* predominates over *is Φ* in the ratio of 195 to 23.[17]

[17] See H. L. Ebeling, "Some Statistics on the Order of Words in Greek", in *Studies in Honor of B. L. Gildersleeve* (Baltimore, 1902), 229–40. My figures are adapted from p. 233.

Unfortunately, Ebeling's statistics are not entirely appropriate for our purposes, since he counts not only εἰμί but all copula verbs, including γίγνομαι and φαίνομαι; and he considers only the nominal copula, not the locative or quasi-locative construction. Furthermore, he does not limit himself to indicative clauses, as I have done, but includes other moods and infinitival clauses as well. Still, it is unlikely that the relative frequencies would be seriously altered if Ebeling's statistics had been compiled only for indicative clauses with εἰμί: the other copula verbs are much less common than εἰμί, and I see no reason to believe that they behave very differently in regard to word order.[18] The non-indicative moods and infinitival clauses are likely to differ from indicative clauses above all in exhibiting less variety of order.

Admitting such qualifications, the similarity in these results from Homer and Plato is surely much more impressive than the differences. *N Φ is* remains the predominant pattern; *Φ is N* clearly emerges as the second most frequent order (just as Lasso says it is in Homer), and *Φ N is* is still the least common order for non-initial copula. The only interesting discrepancy from the Homeric data is the notable increase in the frequency of initial copula, and I think this will be confirmed by any extended sample of classical prose. (See the examples cited from Herodotus, above p. 425.)

Finally, I add my own figures for the first 30 occurrences of the indicative copula with subject expressed in Xenophon's *Anabasis*. Because of the special character of Xenophon's introductory narrative, which contains a large number of quasi-existential or possessive uses of the locative copula (such as I.2.7 ἐνταῦθα Κύρῳ βασίλεια ἦν "In that place was a palace belonging to Cyrus" or "There Cyrus had a palace"), I give my sample in two forms. The first covers only the first four chapters and includes copula sentences in the broadest sense, including those where the verb is used with existential or possessive nuance. The second version of this sample extends into the eighth chapter of the *Anabasis* but is restricted to rather clear-cut cases of the "mere" copula.

Xenophon, *Anabasis* I. 1–3: copula in broad sense

1	N is Φ	6 (in main clause)
2	N Φ is	7 (3 in main, 4 in subordinate clause)
3	Φ N is	1 (the possessive-existential example at 2.7, cited above)
4	Φ is N	7 (5 in main, 2 in subordinate; 5 of these are locative-existential, 3 of them introduced by ἐνταῦθα)

[18] In another connection K. J. Dover has observed that γίγνεσθαι and εἶναι "behave alike in respect of order" in construction with adjectival predicates. See his *Lysias and the Corpus Lysiacum* (Berkeley and Los Angeles, 1968), p. 127.

5	*is Φ N*	1 (2.10)
6	*is N Φ*	8 (6 in main, 2 in subordinate clause)
	TOTAL	30

This first sample is deviant in several respects. In addition to the large number of locative-existentials, we have an unusually high proportion of sentences with initial copula, mostly of the form *is N Φ*, which insert into the narrative a parenthetical statement of information; for example, 2.3 ἦν δὲ καὶ οὗτος καὶ ὁ Σωκράτης τῶν ἀμφὶ Μίλητον στρατευομένων. We can get a somewhat more representative sample if we exclude the existential-possessive examples and also omit a couple of ambiguous cases, and add instead 10 clearer cases of the copula from the following chapters.

Xenophon, *Anabasis* I.1–8.1: copula in the stricter sense

1	*N is Φ*	7 (main clause)
2	*N Φ is*	11 (5 in main, 6 in subordinate clause)
3	*Φ N is*	0
4	*Φ is N*	4 (main clause)
5	*is Φ N*	1 (main clause)
6	*is N Φ*	7 (5 in main, 2 in subordinate clause)
	TOTAL	30

Since this sample overlaps with the preceding one, the relatively high number of initial copulas (patterns **5** and **6**) still reflects the frequency of parenthetical insertions in the opening narrative. But if we ignore the sentences with initial copula and consider only the first four patterns, their relative frequency in the second Xenophon sample is about the same as in Plato and in my figures for Homer. In each author *N Φ is* is statistically preferred whereas *Φ N is* is the least favored form (for non-initial copula). The only point in which these authors tend to differ is whether or not *Φ is N* is more common than *N is Φ*, and on this point an author may well differ from himself, as in my two Xenophon samples. My own impression is that whether an author writes *Φ is N* or *N is Φ* depends to a large extent upon what other sentence types have just occurred; and therefore to speak of any general preference for one order over another is quite misleading, except in a special case like the sentence form *predicate* + ἐστί + *infinitival clause*. On the other hand, the overriding preference for the order *N Φ is* is so constant from author to author that it need not be qualified in this way.

My results suggest that the only respect in which the word order of copula sentences in classical prose differs significantly from the Homeric order is in the greater frequency of the initial copula. How far this difference is due to an actual change in practice from Homeric times, how far to the artistic stylization of the Homeric dialect, I cannot say. My evidence apparently offers no support for Dover's suggestion that Greek word order develops from a primary dependence on rhetorical factors (emphasis on what is new in contrast to what is expected) to a pattern determined by syntax (subject noun before predicate or verb). The order *Φ is N* seems to remain quite common; and the increased frequency of initial copula is certainly not due to syntactic considerations.[19]

We may view these results in a somewhat more general perspective by comparing them with Ebeling's figures for the relative order of subject, verb, and object in the three-term (*NVN*) sentence type in Plato's *Protagoras*, Xenophon's *Anabasis I*, and four speeches of Isocrates (numbers I, II, III, and IX). I symbolize the subject noun by *N*, as in the copula sentence, and the direct object by *O*.[20]

		Plato	Xenophon	Isocrates
1.	NVO	24	42	17
2.	NOV	62	45	73
3.	ONV	36	21	28
4.	OVN	9	11	3
5.	VON	10	12	1
6.	VNO	13	9	5
	TOTAL 154		140	127

In order to compare these results with those for copula sentences we must remember that εἰμί is after all a verb and that the two types *N is Φ* and *NVO* can be regarded as special cases of the general sentential formula *NVΩ*, where *Ω* represents both object and predicate. We thus get two generalizations that hold for both copula and transitive verb: (1) the statistically pre-

---

[19] See Dover's remarks in *Greek Word Order*, p. 31: "All patterns of order which are describable in syntactic terms are secondary phenomena"; also pp. 41ff. and 64f. I believe Dover has been misled by the attempt to find a primary *rule* to which there would be no (or very few) exceptions, where all we can hope for is a statistical generalization concerning relative frequencies.

Dover's thesis is not specifically formulated to apply to copula sentences. Still, if such a development had taken place for word order generally, we would expect to find some trace of it in copula sentences. The only chronological development which is clearly attested in the figures cited here is the post-Homeric use of initial copula to introduce parenthetical information. For this development see the study of A. Bloch cited above, p. 425, n. 9.) On the other hand, if Dover's claim about the increasing importance of syntactic factors was intended to contrast the situation in Hellenistic Greek with that of Classical Greek (as he points out to me in a letter, and see *Greek Word Order*, p. 10, n. 2), then my evidence is inconclusive, since I consider no author later than Xenophon.

[20] See Ebeling, "Some Statistics on the Order of Words in Greek," p. 235. Ebeling also gives statistics for Plato's *Gorgias*, but these correspond closely to those for the *Protagoras*, at least as far as the three preferred patterns are concerned: *NOV*, *ONV*, and *NVO*, in that order of preference.

ferred order is $N \, \Omega \, V$, with subject term first and verb last; and (2) the patterns with initial verb are among the least frequent. In other respects the preferences tend to diverge for the two sentence types. The transitive verb can be separated from its object much more easily than the copula from its predicate. Thus whereas the least preferred order for non-initial copula is $\Phi \, N \, is$, where the subject interrupts the copula-predicate nexus, for non-initial transitive verb the least preferred order is OVN, with subject in last place. The precedence of subject noun before transitive verb is much more clearly marked than in the case of the copula. In other words, even when the object comes first the subject tends to come before the verb, whereas when the predicate comes first the subject is generally last. Hence it is that the order $\Phi \, is \, N$, which is so common for the copula, has as its analogue here the much rarer form, OVN. In two respects, however, the practice for copula sentences can be subsumed under more general tendencies in Greek word order: a distinct preference for the order $N \, \Omega \, V$, and a statistical reluctance to put the verb in first place.[21]

Let me close by emphasizing the modesty of my statistical base, and the sketchy nature of my conclusions. A fuller study would be required for firm results, and a finer analysis would distinguish between the various cases, for example between first clause and second clause in a compound sentence, between main clause and subordinate, between relative clause and other kinds of subordinate construction. I have considered only three-term sentences with subject expressed, and have neglected infinitival clauses. Variations must be expected from author to author, and from context to context. Still, I would be very much surprised if a more careful and exhaustive study would lead us to reject either of the two generalizations formulated in the preceding paragraph.[22]

---

[21] Ebeling's study applies only to Attic prose. I have not found comparable figures for Homer. But see O. Behaghel, "Zur Stellung des Verbs im Germanischen und Indogerm." *Zeitschrift für vergl. Sprachforschung* 56 (1928), p. 280, who gives figures for 1200 verses in three books of the *Iliad* to show (1) that in Homer the verb tends to last place, but (2) that this preference is much more marked in subordinate clause (104 in last place to 9 in middle position) than in main clause (167 to 128).

[22] After completing this Appendix I find that my conclusions, which are based exclusively on the evidence cited above, can scarcely be regarded as novel. That the order $N\Omega V$ is "habitual" (i.e. most common) not only in Greek but in early I.-E. generally, was observed by Delbrück in his 1900 *Vergl. Syntax* III (= Brugmann-Delbrück V), p. 110. And Kühner-Gerth II.2, 595 asserts, correctly if dogmatically, that final position for the verb and initial position for the subject is customary ("gewöhnlich") in Greek. For more detailed confirmation, see P. Fischer, "Zur Stellung des Verbums in Griechischen," *Glotta* 13 (1924), 1–11 and 189–205. Fischer's work, like most studies in Greek word order, suffers from a failure to distinguish the statistical tendencies or relative frequencies, which is all that our data can provide, from the illusion of a grammatical rule or "law" that would require us to explain – or explain away – every apparent deviation.

ON THE THEORY OF THE NOMINAL SENTENCE

The omission of the verb *be* in Greek, in circumstances where the corresponding sentence in English and in most modern European languages would require the verb, is such a common phenomenon that no Hellenist can have missed it. The topic had already been discussed in the scholarly literature for two centuries before the appearance of Meillet's famous article in 1906.[1] Since Meillet, however, the nominal sentence has had a name and a certain theoretical importance in comparative linguistics. It is in fact almost exclusively in connection with the theory of the nominal sentence that we find any systematic discussion of the function of the verb *be* in the traditional literature.

The original problem, discussed by Meillet and earlier by Brugmann and Delbrück, was to determine whether and to what extent the nominal sentence could be traced back to common Indo-European, and how this phenomenon was related to the "development" of the verb *be* (**es-*) as copula. For comparative linguists whose task it was to reconstruct a "primitive" state of affairs, there was a natural tendency to suppose that the verbless form of nominal and locative predication is *older* than the use of **es-* as copula.[2] Recent discussions by Hjelmslev and Benveniste have attempted to formulate

---

[1] "La phrase nominale en indo-européen", *Mémoires de la Société de Linguistique de Paris* XIV (1906), 1–26. For a survey of the earlier literature see C. Guiraud, *La phrase nominale en grec*, pp. 21–5, and above all Jose S. Lasso de la Vega, *La oración nominal en Homero* (Madrid, 1955), pp. 13–5. Lasso de la Vega cites several studies from the eighteenth and early nineteenth centuries, the earliest of which is *Ellipses graecae* by Lamberto Bos, published in 1702. Throughout the nineteenth century this phenomenon was referred to as an "ellipse of the verb", although it is of course *not* a case of ellipse in the strict sense defined here. In our sense, an omission of εἰμί constitutes an ellipse only if there is a parallel occurrence of the verb in the immediate context. (See above, Chapter III § 4.) Ellipse in this sense can of course occur for εἰμί as for any Greek verb, as for example in *Il.* 2.204 εἷς κοίρανος ἔστω, / εἷς βασιλεύς "Let there be one ruler for us, one king."

The broader use of the term "ellipse" to describe what is now called the nominal sentence goes back to the Greek grammarians, for whom ἔλλειψις often means no more than "omission" (cf. ἐλλείποντος συνήθως τοῖς ἄρθροις τοῦ ποιητοῦ "Homer customarily omits the article," Apollonius, *Syntaxis* ed. Uhlig, p. 6, 6). So a sentence without a verb – including a "nominal" sentence without εἰμί – can be described as a case of ἔλλειψις. It is characteristic that Apollonius (*ibid.* p. 7, 1–3) cites *Il.* 9.247, where στῆθι is omitted after ἄνα "Up!", next to the nominal sentence *Od.* 16.45 (πάρα δ' ἀνήρ, ὃς καταθήσει "The man [is] at hand who will arrange it"). For Apollonius, both examples illustrate the same grammatical phenomenon: πάθη λόγου ἐλλείποντα ῥήματι "modifications of a sentence by omitting a verb".

[2] See the grammarians cited above p. 199 n. 21.

this problem within a more general perspective, independent of any historical development in Indo-European.[3] More recently still, two full-length studies have dealt with the nominal sentence in Homer and in other Greek authors of the archaic and early classical period.[4] An effort has been made not only to classify the types of sentences in which the verb is frequently omitted but also (above all by Benveniste and Guiraud) to define a difference in structure and meaning between comparable sentences with and without the verb.

From the transformational point of view adopted in the present study, the problem appears in a different light and its theoretical importance is considerably diminished. As I have argued above (Chapter III §2 pp. 65f. and Chapter V §8, pp. 210f.), the nominal sentence in Greek – and I dare say in other I.-E. languages – is best regarded as a phenomenon of surface structure only: the underlying sentence form or kernel will be reconstructed with a verb in every case. The problem of the nominal sentence becomes then simply the question under what circumstances the language permits or requires the omission of this verb. There are few if any sentence types in Greek where the zeroing of the copula is obligatory, that is, where the verb εἰμί never occurs. (For the special case of χρή see below, p. 442 n. 17.) The situation is different in Russian, for example, where the standard copula verb has no forms in the present indicative, so that zeroing is in this case obligatory.[5] This reinterpretation of the nominal sentence as a phenomenon of zeroing or deletion of the copula follows almost inevitably from the very nature of the transformational enterprise, understood as the attempt to derive all grammatical sentences from a small number of sentence forms, whose instances are themselves recognizable as sentences in the language under consideration.

It must be admitted that there is another solution which is compatible with our transformational point of view. It would be theoretically possible to take the verbless sentence καλὸς ὁ παῖς "The boy (is) beautiful" as the elementary form, and derive the corresponding copula sentence by an optional *insertion* of the verb: καλός ἐστι ὁ παῖς. But as a device for accounting for the Greek data, this solution is clearly uneconomical. Since the verbless sentence is frequent only in the third-person present indicative, this proposal would mean that we must normally insert the verb in first- and second-person sentences and that we must nearly always do so in past or future tenses, in oblique moods, and in indirect discourse. Instead of a rule for

---

[3] L. Hjelmslev, "Le verbe et la phrase nominale", *Mélanges Marouzeau* (1948), pp. 253–81; E. Benveniste, "La phrase nominale", *Bulletin de la Société de Linguistique de Paris* 46 (1950), 19–36, reprinted in *Problèmes de linguistique générale*, pp. 151–67.
[4] See the works of Lasso de la Vega (1955) and C. Guiraud (1962) cited above p. 435, n. 1.
[5] For a description of the Russian nominal sentence as containing a "zero verb-form", see the quotation from Lunt in Ch. III § 2, p. 65 n. 7.

optional omission of the verb in a relatively small number of cases (above all in third-person present indicative *singular*), we would have to specify a rule for its possible insertion in all cases and for its massive, well-nigh obligatory insertion in most cases. This way of describing the facts remains an open possibility for anyone who wishes to insist at all costs upon the primary status of the verbless form. But it is theoretically simpler to posit the verb in the underlying form and account for its absence by an appropriate rule for zeroing.[6]

This theoretical conclusion, that the nominal sentence represents an omission of the verb which is "understood" as such, seems to be in accord with the intuitive *Sprachgefühl* for ancient Greek so far as I can recapture it. It is also in accord with the description of the nominal sentence as a case of ἔλλειψις or "missing" verbs that we find in the ancient grammarians.[7] A parallel teaching of the classical Sanskrit grammarians suggests that this solution holds good for I.-E. generally. For although the nominal sentence is more widely employed in Sanskrit than in Greek, these grammarians accounted for it by "their notion of zero-occurrence of grammatical forms."[8]

If this view of the matter is accepted, the question remains: how are we to state the rule for zeroing? And this question can be divided into two parts. (1) Under what circumstances is the omission of the verb possible? (2) Given a sentence form in which the omission is possible, can we characterize in any general way the contexts in which the verb is actually omitted, so as to distinguish them from the sentences of similar form where the verb *could* be omitted but is in fact expressed?[9] Since we cannot appeal here to the in-

---

[6] Since the transformational theory used here requires that the elementary structures must be sentence forms of the language, I do not return to the question of a generative theory that would eliminate the verb *be* (as copula) from deep structure. This question was discussed above, Chapter V § 9. The proposal to eliminate *be* in this way is obviously more defensible in a generative account where the deep structures are abstract entities that need not have a direct correspondence with the form of actually occurring sentences. Thus Bach's proposal to eliminate *be* from deep structure is formulated for *English*, where the verbless sentence scarcely occurs!

[7] See the passage cited above, p. 435, n. 1, from Apollonius, *Syntaxis*, p. 7 ed. Uhlig.

[8] See B. K. Matilal, "Indian Theorists on the Nature of the Sentence," *Foundations of Language* 2 (1966), pp. 377–81. The grammarians in question (who belong to the third and second centuries B.C., apparently) gave as the definition or necessary condition of the sentence (*vākya*) "that [cluster of words] which possesses a finite verb [as an element]" (*ibid.* p. 377). On the other hand, Matilal also cites the view of later theorists who disputed this definition and defended the autonomy of the verbless sentence.

[9] Note that if we took the verbless form as elementary, precisely the same questions arise but from the opposite point of view. We would then ask (1A) under what circumstances can (or must) the verb be inserted? and (2A) for the optional cases, can we draw any general distinction between the passages in which the verb occurs and those in which it does not? Question (2A) is really identical with question (2) above. Hence to say that it is theoretically preferable to take the verbal sentence as elementary is just to say that question (1) is much easier to deal with than question (1A).

tuitions of any native speaker as to grammaticality or acceptability, our answer to either question can only be provided by a survey of the data in extant Greek literature. Any generalizations must be based on, and tested by, the statistical evidence from such a survey.

My own conclusion, based upon the results of earlier studies and upon a direct examination of the omissions in *Iliad* 1–12 and in selected passages of Attic prose, is that it is quite easy to formulate a general answer to question (1) but impossible to say anything about question (2) except in a piece-meal way – author by author, genre by genre, and ultimately sentence by sentence. Which is to say that the *possibility* of omission for the copula is a well-defined phenomenon of the language, of *la langue* in de Saussure's sense, whereas the *fact* of omission is a highly complex and variable phenomenon of *parole*, dependent upon a number of different factors that are in part syntactic but more often stylistic and in some cases even mechanical (for example, when metrical considerations affect the omission of forms in Homer). Hence we can usefully discuss the phenomenon of possible (optional) zeroing in general terms, but we cannot give any general account of when this option is exercised. We can, it is true, report statistical tendencies for given formulae (e.g. the frequent omission of the copula with ἀνάγκη or with τεκμήριον δέ), for given authors, and for given literary genres. Much of the work on the nominal sentence has been along these lines. But when it comes to explaining in any *particular* case why the verb was omitted here but not elsewhere in a comparable sentence of the same author, we cannot hope to find any general rules. Let me briefly develop these answers to our two questions, before citing examples to show how little difference of structure and meaning there may be between the verbal and the verbless forms.

I

To the question "When is the omission of the copula optional?" we can give the general answer: "Whenever the sentence structure is clear without an expression of the verb, in other words, whenever the hearer or reader can reconstruct (or 'supply') the appropriate form of εἰμί without difficulty." From this general principle we can deduce an explanation for the statistical fact that omission is very frequent only in the third-person present indicative forms (i.e. for ἐστί and εἰσί). On the same basis we can *also* explain how omission is possible in the more exceptional cases of first or second person, past or future tense, or subjunctive mood. For in these exceptional cases there is always some clue in the immediate context which permits us to reconstruct, say, the second-person singular form of the verb or the past tense.[10] This is necessarily so, since if there was no adequate clue in the context, we would not be able to say *which* form of εἰμί had been omitted. The most common case is an omission in third person present indicative. Hence, whenever we know (or assume) that a different form has been omitted, there must be some special clue in the context on which we are relying.

In general, the syntactic function of the verb is to furnish indications of person, tense, and mood. It becomes redundant whenever this information is provided by other clues, i.e., by other words in the sentence or in the immediate context. Thus the general rule for the zeroing of the copula is as follows: the copula can be omitted (or "understood") whenever it is uninformative. And this is true not only for the copula, but for the existential verb as well.[11]

As a matter of fact, the rule just stated — that a form may be left unexpressed whenever it has no additional information to contribute — applies quite generally to all cases of zeroing, including ellipse in the strict sense. The nominal sentence is, after all, only a special case of the omission of forms which are not indispensable to an understanding of the meaning (including the grammatical structure) of the sentence in question. The nominal sentence is a special case only because the third person present indicative forms of εἰμί are so frequently omitted. But they are so easily omitted just because they are so often redundant. And a moment's reflection will show why this is so.

In the absence of special clues, a verbless sentence of predicative form will be automatically "understood" in third person present indicative. This understanding may be based in part upon an expectation that naturally arises from the statistical frequency of omission for the verb in this form. But it is also based upon something else: namely, upon the fact that it is in the third person present indicative that the verb has least information to contribute to the sentence. The reasons for this are not hard to see. We can describe the present as the "zero" or unmarked tense in the sense that it provides the base point by reference to which the past and future tenses are defined; just as the indicative is the zero or unmarked mood in the same sense. The third person is the zero person in a somewhat different sense, as the neutral or unmarked form which lies outside the primary system of

---

[10] Thus if σύ occurs in a sentence with no verb expressed, we "understand" εἶ or ἐσσί; if an adverb of time occurs, like πάρος, πάλαι, or πρίν, we may easily understand an imperfect form (e.g. ἦν rather than ἐστί). For examples, see Guiraud, Ch. V; Lasso de la Vega, pp. 90–119.

[11] It is at least plausible to regard the omitted ἦν as existential in *Il.* 7.433 ἦμος δ᾽ οὔτ᾽ ἄρ πω ἠώς, ἔτι δ᾽ ἀμφιλύκη νύξ "But when the dawn was not yet, but still the pallor of night's edge" (Lattimore), cited by Guiraud, p. 319. For frequent omissions of the locative-existential verb in third person present, see below, pp. 449 ff.

contrast established by the dialogue structure of the speech situation: *I* and *you*.[12] If the third person present indicative is so easily omitted that is because (1) in the absence of other clues, the indicative mood is suggested by the predicative form of the sentence as such, with its implicit truth claim in the case of a declarative sentence and with a modified truth claim in the case of a question;[13] (2) the present form of the verb is functionally equivalent to the *absence* of any indication for past or future;[14] and (3) the third-person form is equivalent to the lack of any identification of the subject within the speaker-hearer framework. This latter point explains why the third person form is used not only for persons distinct from speaker and hearer but also for non-personal subjects such as inanimate objects, for nominalizations or sentential subjects, and also for impersonal or subject-less constructions. (See Chapter IV §§27–30.) Where the predicative structure of the sentence is clear, and where there are no indications either of past or future tense or of first or second person as subject, the only additional information that can be contributed by third person present indicative forms is the distinction between singular and plural subjects. (And this function is further reduced in Greek by the use of singular verbs for neuter plural subjects.) But since the number of the subject term is often indicated by the form of the predicate as well, for example if the latter is an adjective, and since the subject of the sentence is generally specified either by a word or phrase within the sentence or in the preceding context, there is no real need for a copula verb to distinguish singular and plural. Hence the plural verb is, in Homer at least, almost as frequently omitted as the singular ἐστί.[15]

[12] Compare Brøndal's definition of the third person as "neither the first nor the second" (cited by Guiraud, p. 14). Note that "zero form" as used in this context means not an underlying form which is left unexpressed (as when I speak of the zeroing of the copula), but simply a neutral form which either lies *outside* of a system of contrasts or serves within it as the standard or base from which the other elements are defined. In point of fact, the present tense is zero in both respects. It expresses the reference point for past and future (namely, the time of utterance); but it also provides the expression for untensed or "eternal" sentences (as in "Tyrants are suspicious" and "Homer is a poet"). For clarity, we might distinguish the latter use as the *unmarked* (tenseless) present from the former as the standard present, marked for tense.

[13] For this terminology see Chapter V §§ 1–2.

[14] The aspectual contrast of durative-aorist is not relevant here; or insofar as it is relevant, it explains why we translate a verbless sentence by "is" rather than by "becomes".

[15] This calls for qualification. According to Lasso de la Vega's figures, the overall ratio of omission to occurrence in the singular is about 5:3, whereas in the plural it is 4:5. If we consider only main clauses, the ratios are almost 2:1 for the singular, as against 1:1 for the plural. (I am combining statistics given in *La oración nominal en Homero*, pp. 71, 83 and 88.) Thus Homer omits the plural verb about as often as he expresses it, whereas in the singular he omits it much more often than not.

The relative proportions are quite different in Xenophon, according to the figures given by Erik Ekman, *Der reine Nominalsatz bei Xenophon*, Skrifter utgivna av K. Humanistika Vetenskaps-Samfundet i Uppsala 29.6, 1938.) For the singular form ἐστί the ratio of

These considerations show how the general rule, that the verb may be omitted wherever it is uninformative, will serve to explain the fact that it is so frequently omitted in the copula construction (where there is a predicate word or phrase to articulate the sentence structure), and why it is particularly common in the third person present indicative. Further considerations can account for other tendencies on the basis of the same principle. For example, the fact that the verb is less frequently omitted in subordinate clauses than in the principal construction is probably to be explained by the role which the verb plays in distinguishing such a clause from a noun phrase. The characteristic sentential structure of a subordinate clause would often be unrecognizable without a finite verb form, whereas the predicative structure of καλὸς ὁ παῖς "The boy (is) beautiful" is unmistakable without any further indication.

My statement and application of the general rule for optional omission of the verb may seem to provide little more than an *a priori* reformulation of the facts as to frequency of omission in Homer. The advantage of this reformulation is that it is designed to tie the facts of omission to the syntactic functions of the verb as described long ago by Meillet. For it is precisely when these functions are redundant that the verb is easily (i.e. frequently) omitted.

I believe that this is all there is to be said on the subject of the nominal sentence that is of any general interest for the theory of language. We can only explain, in principle and in general, why the verb can be omitted. But any more detailed consideration of the facts of actual omission – including the fact just noted, that the *plural* form is much less frequently omitted in Xenophon than in Homer (see preceding note) – belongs to a study of Greek literary style. I can scarcely do more than sketch the nature of the problems involved in this study. But in view of the extraordinary amount of attention devoted to the topic of the nominal sentence in the traditional literature, a few remarks may be appropriate here, in order to show that any detailed discussion of the topic belongs to the study of style rather than to linguistics as such.

II

Assuming that the verb *can* be omitted in a great variety of circumstances

---

omission to occurrence is almost 2:1 (896 to 535 cases noted), with a ratio closer to 3:1 for main clauses (719 omissions to 267 occurrences). In the plural, however, the nominal sentence is by comparison extremely rare: only 36 omissions for 258 occurrences, a ratio of about 1:7. (The plural form is almost never omitted in subordinate clauses: for main clauses the ratio of omission to occurrence is about 1:4).

Thus whereas Xenophon omits ἐστί even more frequently than Homer does, his omission of the plural from εἰσί is rare and restricted. For a comparison with some later authors, see below, p. 444 n. 21.

covered by the rule as formulated above, we may want to ask: under what circumstances is it *in fact* omitted? Here a distinction must be drawn between various types of answers to our question.

If we ask, in construction with what words is the verb most frequently omitted, we can compile a list of predicates – or more neutrally, nominal forms – that typically occur without the verb. The list will include nouns like ἀνάγκη, ὥρα, adjectives like αἰσχρόν and ἄμεινον, and verbals in -έος.[16] Now for every item on our list we can also find a sentence of this type where the verb occurs. (Some examples will be given below.) The single exception to this is χρή, when used in present tense. But χρή, precisely because it is unique in this respect, may reasonably be classified as a frozen verb form.[17] Since both types of sentence are found, and often in the same text, we are naturally inclined to ask "What distinguishes the sentences in which the verb appears from those in which it is absent?" But to this question there is in general no answer. Attempts to provide some systematic answer in semantic or rhetorical terms, as in the book of Guiraud, must encounter exceptions and difficulties at every step of the way, as Guiraud is obliged to recognize. For example, although we know that ἀνάγκη is frequently used without the verb, we do not know why ἀνάγκη ἐστί nevertheless occurs in a given passage (e.g. in Lysias XIII.44). We can only say that the author has a choice between two versions of the sentence, and it often makes very little difference which one he chooses. This is not to deny that in *some* contexts a clear stylistic motive for the omission or expression of the verb may be discerned. But in most cases the reasons or causes of the choice may be as complex or as trivial as for our choice to omit the word *that* in a sentence of the form *I know that he is here*. One may say that a speaker omits the word for the sake of brevity. But that is not saying much.

There is more to be said if, instead of taking passages one by one we compare the frequency of omission in different authors or in different styles and genres. It has been noted that Homer and the tragic poets omit the verb relatively often, whereas Herodotus almost never does so.[18] Lysias too

---

[16] See Guiraud, pp. 21f.; Meillet, "La phrase nominale", pp. 15–7. Compare Ekman, *Nominalsatz bei Xenophon*, pp. 11–7.

[17] In the case of χρή the regular omission of ἐστί is given a special significance by the occurrence in fifth-century Greek of declined forms such as χρῆσται, (ἐ)χρῆν, and χρείη. The non-occurrence of *χρῆστι or *χρή ἐστι in the same period shows that χρή by itself came to be regarded as syntactically equivalent to a present indicative verb form, whatever its remote origins may have been.

[18] See the statistics in Guiraud. Unfortunately, although Guiraud has studied the Homeric poems and seven other poets, Herodotus is the only *prose* author whom he treats. Hence we do not know whether the extreme scarcity of nominal sentences is a peculiarity of Herodotus' style or how it is to be correlated either with standard usage in Ionic prose or with the genre of historiography. But the frequency of the nominal sentence in Xenophon suggests that the explanation by literary genre cannot be right.

seems to be an author who is generally reluctant to use the nominal sentence, and the occurrence of the verbal form ἀνάγκη ἐστί which I have just cited from his thirteenth oration (Sect. 44) can be correlated with the very small number of verbless sentences to be found throughout my samples from Lysias. (In the first speech of Lysias I count only two omissions of the copula, both in the peroration [Sect. 48 and 49: I ignore χρή in Sect. 34], and only five or six omissions in XIII.1–95, which is about twice as long. Note that the form ἐστί *occurs* six times in Lysias I and thirteen times in Lysias XIII.) In my Xenophon samples, on the other hand, we repeatedly find ἀνάγκη followed by the infinitive, without a finite verb (*Anab.* I.3.5; II.1.17). And this fact can be correlated with a generally greater frequency of nominal sentences in Xenophon. (I count 10 or 12 examples in *Anab.* I.1–3.16, which covers twelve pages of the O.C.T. and is scarcely longer than Lysias' first speech; the latter, we have seen, contains only two verbless sentences.) Thus we can "explain" the occurrence of the verbal form ἀνάγκη ἐστί in one case, the verbless in the other by including both within a wider generalization: Lysias rarely omits the copula; Xenophon does so very frequently.[19]

In this form, however, the generalization probably conceals more than it reveals. In Xenophon the nominal sentences tend to cluster in the speeches or in special passages such as the formal eulogy of Cyrus (I.9.24, 29, 30). Omission of the copula thus seems to function as one among a number of devices which Xenophon utilizes to produce stylistic diversity between different parts of his work, notably between the narrative and the speeches.[20] Furthermore, if omission of the verb is relatively infrequent in the two courtroom speeches of Lysias that I have studied, the situation is entirely different in the *Epitaphios* (Lysias II). Here in twenty pages of Oxford text we do not find a *single* occurrence of ἐστί, whereas the nominal sentence confronts us in almost every paragraph. (I count four or five examples on the first page.) I conclude, not that the *Epitaphios* is written by a different author but that as an epideictic piece written for a solemn occasion it affects

---

[19] Ekman, p. 11, reports 58 examples of ἀνάγκη without ἐστί in Xenophon, for only 6 occurrences of the copula with ἀνάγκη in principal clause (and only one in the *Anabasis*: III.4.19).

[20] Ekman's conclusion (pp. 43 and 48) that the fewer nominal sentences one finds in Xenophon the closer one is to ordinary speech (*Umgangsprache*), seems to me far too simple. Indeed, until we have a careful study of the omission of ἐστί in Aristophanes, with quantitative comparisons for similar sentence types in Plato, Xenophon, and the orators, we cannot even make an intelligent guess about the actual practice in Attic conversation. And of course we will never have anything better than a guess.

What Ekman has apparently observed is an interesting deviation in the frequency of omission for different works of Xenophon (*Der reine Nominalsatz*, pp. 26, 32, 37). But the actual importance of this deviation could be made clear only from a study of selected samples of similar length, with figures for omission compared according to sentence type.

the "grand" style, and that one feature of this style is the frequent omission
of ἐστί as in the tragic poets.

On the other hand there is no reason to suppose that the omission of the
verb is *always* a mark of the high style. In Aristophanes and Plato, I suspect,
the verbless sentence will often reflect the economy of expression which is
natural to informal or animated conversation. My own suggestion would
be that a tendency to frequent omission of the verb may be correlated with
at least two distinct stylistic tendencies, the high style of tragedy and solemn
orations and the more relaxed usage of conversation, whereas ἐστί is more
often expressed in the formally correct prose of courtroom speeches and
historical narrative. But if this question is to be cleared up at all, we will
require more careful detailed studies of omission in passages of comparable
length from different works. And we will need comparisons not only between
different genres but also between different authors in the same genre and
even between different passages within the same work.[21]

III

I conclude by citing some examples of parallel sentences with and without
the verb. Most examples are taken from third person present indicative,
but a few other persons and tenses are cited to illustrate a similar parallelism.
Finally, I illustrate the omission of εἰμί for some non-copulative uses as well.

The aim of the following list is to show how insignificant the difference
will be between many cases of the nominal sentence and the corresponding
sentence form with the verb. It seems necessary to insist upon these parallels
since Benveniste, followed in part by Guiraud, has claimed that the nominal
sentence and the corresponding sentence with copula verb are essentially
different in structure and in function.[22] If Benveniste were right, it would

---

[21] The date of the text is likely to be a less significant factor than either author or genre,
as we can see from Lasso de la Vega's figures for Callimachus and Apollonius (*La oración
nominal*, p. 217). In the *Hymns* of Callimachus the third person present indicative of εἰμί
is *always* omitted, both in singular and in plural sentences. The usage of Apollonius is
entirely different. In the singular he follows (or rather exceeds) Homer in omitting the
verb more often than not, but is much less inclined to omit it in the plural. The evidence
cited for Apollonius suggests a ratio of omission to occurrence of 4:1 for the singular,
3:7 for the plural. (The corresponding ratios for Homer are 5:3 and 4:5.) This discrepancy
between singular and plural forms recalls that in Xenophon (above, p. 440, n. 15), although
for both forms the proportion of omissions is much higher in Apollonius. The point is that
Xenophon and Apollonius both deviate from Homer in the same direction: they omit the
singular more frequently than Homer does, the plural less frequently.

[22] See Benveniste, *Problèmes de linguistique générale*, pp. 158–69: "Au point de vue
indo-européen, ce sont deux énoncés de type distinct" (p. 159); "ils n'assertent pas de la
même manière" (p. 161). Of course I agree with Benveniste that we must accept the two
forms as coexisting in the earliest texts – in Greek as in Indo-Iranian – "sans chercher à les

be a mistake to interpret the verbless form as I have done, as a case of the zero copula (or, in transformational terms, as a case where the underlying copula has been zeroed). The Homeric evidence, where the verbless sentence is used with the greatest freedom, should provide the decisive test of Benveniste's thesis. I submit that, whatever interesting variation there may be in metre, in emphasis, or in other stylistic nuances, there can be no difference in syntax or semantic structure between the sentences with and without the verb in the following list of parallels.[23]

(1) μοῖρα followed by infinitival clause

A. with verb

Od. 5.41

ὣς γάρ οἱ μοῖρ᾽ ἐστὶ φίλους ἰδέειν καὶ ἱκέσθαι
οἶκον ἐς ὑψόροφον καὶ ἑὴν ἐς πατρίδα γαῖαν.

"Thus, then, it is his lot to see his friends and reach his high-roofed house and native land." (Palmer)

We have a variant on the same formula at *Od.* 5.114 and 9.532.

B. without verb

Od. 4.475

οὐ γάρ τοι πρὶν μοῖρα φίλους ἰδέειν καὶ ἱκέσθαι
οἶκον ἐΰκτίμενον καὶ σὴν ἐς πατρίδα γαῖαν, / πρίν...

"For now it is your lot neither to see your friends nor reach your high-roofed house and native land, until...."

(Palmer, adapted)

---

tirer l'un de l'autre par un processus génétique dont il n'y a aucune preuve." But admitting that the copula form is not to be derived diachronically from the nominal sentence as the supposedly earlier form, the question remains: given the synchronic coexistence of the two forms, is there any reason to reject the theoretical analysis of the verbless sentence as containing a zero occurrence of the copula? Benveniste's position seems to me not entirely consistent, since he claims that in the nominal sentence "le terme à fonction verbale [i.e. the predicate] se compose...de deux éléments: l'un, invariant, implicite, qui donne à l'énoncé force d'assertion; l'autre, variable et explicite," namely, the nominal form which constitutes the actual predicate expression (p. 158). In the case of the I.-E. nominal sentence I do not see how we can distinguish, either in fact or in theory, between Benveniste's implicit element of assertion and a zero copula, with zero person and tense – i.e., a third person present indicative verb form, which is unexpressed but "understood".

[23] Of course I do not mean to deny that there are certain kinds of sentences in which the verbless form tends to be preferred, e.g. in the expression of general truths or *sententiae*. But here too the copula form occurs with surprising frequency (in 27 percent of the cases in the *Iliad*, 45 percent in the *Odyssey*, according to Guiraud, p. 49). I have not noted exact parallels, but these two examples from the *Iliad* may serve to illustrate my claim that in every case where we find the nominal sentence, the copula form *could* appear without any difference of sense or syntax: *Il.*1.80 κρείσσων γὰρ βασιλεὺς ὅτε χώσεται ἀνδρὶ χέρηϊ, 2.196 θυμὸς δὲ μέγας ἐστὶ διοτρεφέων βασιλήων. Sentences introduced by γάρ are often verbless; but cf. *Il.* 4.323 τὸ γὰρ γέρας ἐστὶ γερόντων (with parallels cited by Lasso de la Vega, p. 62).

So regularly in the *Iliad* (7.52, 16.434, etc.)

  (2) θέμις followed by infinitival clause

    A. with verb

      Il. 23.44

        οὐ θέμις ἐστὶ λοετρὰ καρήατος ἆσσον ἱκέσθαι, / πρίν...

        "It is not right to let water come near my head, until...."

                                   (after Lattimore)

Similarly, *Il.* 14.384 and *Od.* 10.73. The affirmative form θέμις ἐστί occurs with preceding infinitive at *Od.* 16.91.

    B. without verb

      No examples. But we once have the verbless form ἡ γὰρ θέμις without infinitive expressed, at *Od.* 24.286. The corresponding verbal form (ἡ) θέμις ἐστί is very frequent in both poems (e.g. *Il.* 2.73, 11.778, *Od.* 3.45). I suspect that the metrical unit θέμις ἐστί was too convenient for the verb to be omitted.

  (3) αἴτιος (ἐπαίτιος) as predicate with personal subject

    A. with verb, in clausula

      Il. 1.153

        ἐπεὶ οὔ τί μοι αἴτιοί εἰσιν

        "Since to me they are in no way blameworthy."

      Il. 3.164

        οὔ τί μοι αἰτίη ἐσσί, θεοί νύ μοι αἴτιοί εἰσιν

        "To me you are in no way blameworthy; the gods are to blame."

      Od. 2.87

        σοὶ δ' οὔ τι μνηστῆρες Ἀχαιῶν αἴτιοί εἰσιν,

        ἀλλὰ φίλη μήτηρ,

        "To you the Achaean suitors are in no way to blame, but your own mother (is)."

      Il. 13.111

        ἀλλ' εἰ δὴ καὶ πάμπαν ἐτήτυμον αἴτιός ἐστιν

        "But even though he (Agamemnon) truly is utterly to blame"

    B. without verb.

      Il. 1.335

        οὔ τί μοι ὔμμες ἐπαίτιοι, ἀλλ' Ἀγαμέμνων,

        "To me you are in no way to blame, but Agamemnon (is)."

Il. 21.275

ἄλλος δ’ οὔ τίς μοι τόσον αἴτιος Οὐρανιώνων,
ἀλλὰ φίλη μήτηρ,

"To me no other of the Uranian gods is so much to blame, but my own mother."

Od. 1.347

οὔ νύ τ’ ἀοιδοὶ
αἴτιοι, ἀλλά ποϑι Ζεὺς αἴτιος, ὅς...

"The bards are not to blame, but rather Zeus is to blame, who..."

Note that the parallelism holds here in plural forms as well, and also in the second person.

(4) ἠώς as subject in expression of time

A. with verb

Il. 8.66

Ὄφρα μὲν ἠὼς ἦν καὶ ἀέξετο ἱερὸν ἦμαρ,
"As long as it was dawn, and the sacred daylight increasing"
(after Lattimore: I prefer the alternative rendering "As long as dawn lasted")

Il. 21.80

ἠὼς δέ μοί ἐστιν
ἥδε δυωδεκάτη, ὅτ’...
"This is the twelfth dawn since I...."

B. without verb

Il. 7.433

Ἦμος δ’ οὔτ’ ἄρ πω ἠώς, ἔτι δ’ ἀμφιλύκη νύξ,
"But when dawn was not yet, but still the pallor of night's edge"
(Lattimore)

Il. 24.413

δυωδεκάτη δέ οἱ ἠὼς / κειμένῳ,
"Now here is the twelfth dawn he has lain there"
(Lattimore)

(5) ἔμπεδος as predicate, μένος or φρένες as subject.

A. with verb

Il. 5.254 (≈ *Od.* 21.426)

ἔτι μοι μένος ἔμπεδόν ἐστιν
"My fighting strength is still steadfast"
(after Lattimore)

Od. 10.493

μάντιος ἀλαοῦ, τοῦ τε φρένες ἔμπεδοί εἰσι
"(the spirit of Teiresias), the prophet blind, whose wits are still steadfast"

(after Palmer)

B. without verb

Od. 22.226

οὐκέτι σοί γ᾿, Ὀδυσεῦ, μένος ἔμπεδον οὐδέ τις ἀλκή,
"Odysseus, your strength is no longer steadfast, nor is your valor."

Il. 6.352

τούτῳ δ᾿ οὔτ᾿ ἄρ νῦν φρένες ἔμπεδοι οὔτ᾿ ἄρ᾿ ὀπίσσω / ἔσσονται
"But this man's wits are not steadfast, nor will they be hereafter"

Od. 18.215

Τηλέμαχ᾿, οὐκέτι τοι φρένες ἔμπεδοι οὐδὲ νόημα.
"Telemachus, your wits are no longer steadfast, nor in your understanding."

Compare the verbal form five lines later in the same speech:
οὐκέτι τοι φρένες εἰσὶν ἐναίσιμοι οὐδὲ νόημα.

(6) γένος or γενέθλη as subject of subordinate clause introduced by "whence"

A. with verb

Il. 2.857

ὅθεν ἀργύρου ἐστὶ γενέθλη
"whence is the birthplace of silver"

Compare *Od.* 6.35 ὅθι τοι γένος ἐστὶ καὶ αὐτῇ
"(Phaeacia,) where is your birth (or race) as well"

Similarly *Od.* 17.523 ὅθι Μίνωος γένος ἐστίν

B. without verb

Il. 2.852

ὅθεν ἡμιόνων γένος ἀγροτεράων
"whence is the race of wild mules"

Compare *Od.* 15.175

ὅθι οἱ γενεή τε τόκος τε
"where is his birth and kin"

With patience, this list of parallels could be extended indefinitely. Although there are certainly other factors operating, it seems clear to me (as it has to others) that a chief determinant for the expression or omission of the verb in Homer is the question of metrical convenience. We can see this, for example, in parallel formulae with words meaning "better" and "best": ἀμείνων regularly occurs as verse ending, without the copula; φέρτερος and φέρτατος nearly always take ἐστί.[24] Let the theorist of the nominal sentence find whatever deeper meaning he can in such variation. The evidence cited shows that for many formulaic patterns in Homer, sentences which are otherwise of the same form may occur in contexts of very similar type *either with or without a form of* εἰμί *expressed*. But if this is true, there cannot be any *general* difference of structure or meaning between the nominal sentence and the sentence with the verb.

Most of the examples just cited are copulative in the general sense defined in Chapter IV, although there is room for doubt in some cases (such as μοῖρ᾽ ἐστί and θέμις ἐστί with infinitive). The examples under (6) might be considered locative-existential, and in several sentences (both in (5) and in (6)) we have a recognizable possessive construction of εἰμί with the dative. But only ὄφρα μὲν ἠὼς ἦν under (4)A seems to me clearly existential, of my Type V. (See above, Chapter VI, p. 287.) It is worth nothing that we have a parallel to this with the verb omitted: *Il.* 7.433, under (4) B. But other readers may prefer to construe ἠὼς ἦν as impersonal copula ("while it was dawn"). Hence I shall add a few verbless examples where it will, I hope, be generally agreed that the verb omitted represents an existential use of εἰμί.

The most common case is the omission of the verb in construction with locative preverbs like ἄγχι, ἀμφί, ἐν, ἔνθα etc. (The use of ἔνι for ἔνεστι is so regular as to count almost as an allomorph of the present indicative verb form.)

Od. 5.101

> οὐδέ τις ἄγχι βροτῶν πόλις, οἵ τε θεοῖσιν
> ἱερά τε ῥέζουσι
> "And there is no city of men nearby, who perform sacrifice to the gods"

> (after Lattimore)

This is a typical example of the locative-existential use illustrated in Chapter VI §13, where sentence **74** provides a good verbal parallel. But in this case

---

[24] Thus we have five examples of ἐπεὶ ἦ πολὺ φέρτερός ἐστι as clausula in the *Iliad*, plus many variants of person and tense. Only in one instance do we have the verbless form: *Il.* 4.307 ἐπεὶ ἦ πολὺ φέρτερον οὕτω. The copula is obviously omitted here to make room for οὕτω.

we also have an approximation to existential Type IV: "there is no one who...." In Homer I do not find a straightforward case of Type IV with verb unexpressed, although we have an even closer approximation to it in one of Meillet's classic examples of the nominal sentence:

Il. 1.174

πάρ᾽ ἔμοιγε καὶ ἄλλοι / οἵ κέ με τιμήσουσι
"There are others with me who will do me honor"

In Attic prose and poetry we do find a verbless form of Type IV in the frozen use of οὐδεὶς ὅστις οὐ for "everyone" (e.g. Eur. *Helen* 926 Ἑλένην γὰρ οὐδεὶς ὅστις οὐ στυγεῖ). The formula has become so mechanical that οὐδείς (ἐστι) can be attracted into the case of ὅστις: e.g. we find οὐδένα ὅντινα οὐ for "everyone" as object of a verb (see LSJ s.v. οὐδείς I.2).

In the next two cases of locative-existentials with verb unexpressed, the first example may count as an approximation to my Type III (πολλοὶ γὰρ ἀνὰ στρατόν εἰσι κέλευθοι: see Chapter VI §11.):

Il. 1.156

ἐπεὶ ἦ μάλα πολλὰ μεταξὺ
οὔρεά τε σκιόεντα θάλασσά τε ἠχήεσσα
"Since indeed there is much that lies between us, the shadowy mountains and the echoing sea"

(Lattimore)

Il. 5.740

ἐν δ᾽ Ἔρις, ἐν δ᾽ Ἀλκή, ἐν δὲ κρυόεσσα Ἰωκή,
ἐν δέ τε Γοργείη κεφαλὴ δεινοῖο πελώρου
(on the aegis of Athena:)
"And Hatred is there, and Battle Strength, and heart-freezing
Onslaught,
and thereon is set the head of the grim gigantic Gorgon"

(Lattimore)

(For similar uses of ἐν and ἔνι without the verb, see Chantraine, *Grammaire homérique*, II, p. 100.)

We see that the initial preverb (with, in the first case, πολλά as well) suffices to make the predicative structure clear, so that the verb may be omitted. But we also see that the verb, if expressed, would not serve merely to *locate* an object but to assert that such things are present ("are to be found") in the place or region indicated. This is true even when an adverb of place is used without its literal force of location, as in the poetic formula cited by Meillet from Plato's *Euthyphro* (21B1): ἵνα γὰρ δέος ἔνθα καὶ αἰδώς "Where (there is) fear, there also (is) reverence."

This example differs from most of the others in that the subject term is not a first-order nominal but an abstract nominalization. With subjects of this form we come to the neighborhood of existential Type V (ὅμαδος ἦν "There was an uproar."), where the verb form signifies that the action expressed by the noun *takes place*. A priori it would seem that the verb could not be omitted in sentences of this type. Guiraud has, however, listed a number of verbless sentences of existential force which may plausibly be classified under my Type V. (See *La phrase nominale en grec*, pp. 165–8.) Thus the verbless form οὐχ ἕδος "no sitting down!" in *Il.* 23.205 answers exactly to οὐχ ἕδος ἐστί in *Il.* 11.648, which we listed as sentence **114** under Type V (in Chapter VI, §17). Other examples follow.

Il. 4.13

ἀλλ᾽ ἤτοι νίκη μὲν ἀρηϊφίλου Μενελάου
"But now the victory is with warlike Menelaos"

(after Lattimore)

Il. 5.379

οὐ γὰρ ἔτι Τρώων καὶ ᾿Αχαιῶν φύλοπις αἰνή,
ἀλλ᾽ ἤδη Δαναοί γε καὶ ἀθανάτοισι μάχονται.
"For no longer it is the horrible war of Archaians and Trojans, but now the Danaans are fighting even with the immortals"

(after Lattimore)

Note that in both these cases we have the subjective genitive representing the subject of the underlying verb form – "Menelaos wins", "the Trojans and Achaeans fight" – precisely as in the standard example of Type V: κλαγγὴ ἦν νεκύων "There was a wailing of the dead". My last example is a famous locative-existential, in which three action nouns occur as subject of an unexpressed verb.

Od. 4.566

οὐ νιφετός, οὔτ᾽ ἄρ χειμὼν πολὺς οὔτε ποτ᾽ ὄμβρος[25]
"For there is no snow, nor much winter there, nor is there ever rain" (in the Elysian plain)

(Lattimore)

Although different analyses may be possible for some or most of these cases, I submit that in all of them the verb, if expressed, would be regarded as having some existential force and would naturally (in some cases, in-

---

[25] Since in the preceding verse we have a case of Type V with the suppletive verb πέλει (τῇ περ ῥηΐστη βιοτὴ πέλει ἀνθρώποισιν), one might suppose that the omission of the verb in *Od.* 4.566 is elliptical. The parallels just cited show that we are not obliged to construe it as an ellipse.

evitably) be translated by "there is". Furthermore, I claim that the non-expression of the verb in these existential sentences makes no more difference to the sense or syntax than it does for the copula examples considered earlier. There is of course a tendency to omit the verb less often in those constructions where it has a stronger value. And in some non-copulative uses the distinctive structure of the sentence would be obscured if the verb were left out. (Thus, in the vital, potential and veridical uses the verb is seldom if ever omitted.) But once these qualifications have been made, we must recognize the fact that the phenomenon of omission known as the nominal sentence extends to the existential as well as to the copulative uses of εἰμί. Omission does not characterize any particular sentence form nor any particular use or meaning of εἰμί.[26]

---

[26] Omission also applies to the possessive construction, but here the presence or absence of the verb may indeed make a difference. In some cases, at least, the possessive construction with εἰμί seems to correspond to indefinite syntax for the subject ("I have some *AN*") whereas the verbless form will give definite syntax ("My *N* is *A*"). Thus in *Od.* 8.320 οὕνεκά οἱ καλὴ θυγάτηρ, ἀτὰρ οὐκ ἐχέθυμος "Because his daughter (sc. Aphrodite) is fair but not temperate", the sense might be different with ἐστί: "Because he has a fair daughter." This is the only case I have noted where the meaning or structure of a sentence seems to be altered when ἐστί is expressed or omitted. But the difference may be greater in translation than in the original, since English makes a distinction between the definite and indefinite article that has no regular equivalent in Greek – above all not in Homeric Greek. A fuller study of the possessive construction would be required to show whether or not the omission of the verb here regularly makes a difference.

THE NOMINALIZED FORMS OF THE VERB:
τὸ ὄν AND οὐσία

It is in nominalized form, as articular participle and abstract noun, that the verb *be* serves not only to express but also to thematize the concept of Being as a distinct topic for philosophical reflection. Clearly, there can be no adequate study of this terminology apart from some detailed analysis of the ontological concepts and doctrines which it serves to articulate. And for such an analysis, this is not the place. What I propose to do is to sketch the linguistic background for this theoretical and conceptual development by summarizing the early use of these two nominal forms, both in ordinary literature and in the more technical language of philosophy.

1. τὸ ὄν

There would be no point in a full description of the uses of the participle ὄν (Ionic ἐών), since in general it behaves like any other participle in Greek. That is to say, it is the form taken by the verb in various subordinate or coordinate constructions, many of which can be translated into English as relative clauses of circumstance, cause, and the like. In these constructions the Greek participle has the surface syntax of an adjective but the underlying value of the finite verb: it agrees (in number, gender and case) with the noun that would figure as subject of the finite verb in the corresponding clause. For example, *Il.* 1.275 μήτε σὺ τόνδ᾽ ἀγαθός περ ἐὼν ἀποαίρεο κούρην "You, great man that you are, yet do not take the girl from him" (after Lattimore); *Il.* 2.27 ὅς σεῦ ἄνευθεν ἐὼν μέγα κήδεται "(Zeus) who cares for you greatly *from afar*"; Xen. *Anab.* I.1.11 Πρόξενον δὲ τὸν Βοιώτιον ξένον ὄντα ἐκέλευσε... παραγενέσθαι "He requested Proxenus the Boeotian, *who was his guest-friend*, to come to him." As the first two examples show, the participle of εἰμί often expresses a nuance (concessive, causal, adversative) that does not go smoothly into a relative clause in English; but the same could be said for the participle of any Greek verb. On the one hand, the participial forms of εἰμί can represent any construction of the copula, even in some cases where the finite verb scarcely occurs. (Thus we find in the Ionic of Democritus, fr. 174: ὅς ἄν... τὰ χρὴ ἐόντα μὴ ἔρδῃ "He that does not do the things that he should"; similarly Democritus fr. 256; whereas *χρή ἐστι does not occur. But note the article here.) But of course the participle is also used in constructions that do not count as copulative, for example in the vital (καὶ Ἕκτορος οὐκέτ' ἐόντος "even with Hector no longer alive" *Il.* 22.384), in the veridical (τὸν ἐόντα λέγειν λόγον "to tell the true story" Hdt.I.95.1), or in existential Type V: Thuc. IV. 103.5 ἅμα μὲν τῆς προδοσίας οὔσης, ἅμα δὲ καὶ χειμῶνος ὄντος "(Brasidas easily overcame the guard) since there was treachery (among them) and also a storm".

Somewhat more suggestive for the philosophical use are certain pregnant constructions of the participle in quasi-adjectival form, such as τὰ ὄντα χρήματα for "money on hand", cited in LSJ s.v. εἰμί A.1. We have an early example from the Attic inscription on finances, dated about 434 B.C. (Meiggs and Lewis, *A Selection of Greek Historical Inscriptions*, No. 58, p. 155 = *Inscr. Gr.* I, ed. minor 91.24), which reads in part: καὶ τὸ λοιπὸν ἀναγραφόντων οἱ αἰεὶ ταμίαι ἐς στήλην καὶ λόγον διδόντων τῶν τε ὄντων χρημάτων καὶ τῶν προσιόντων τοῖς θεοῖς.... ἐπειδὰν δὲ ἀποδεδομένα ἦ τοῖς θεοῖς τὰ χρήματα, ἐς τὸ νεώριον καὶ τὰ τείχη τοῖς περιοῦσι χρῆσθαι χρήμασ (ιν) "And in the future the treasurers in office each year shall inscribe on a stele and render account both of the money on hand (belonging) to the gods and also the money coming to them (i.e. current income).... And when the money has been paid to the gods, they shall use the remaining money for the dockyard and the city walls." Here τὰ ὄντα χρήματα is construed as parallel to τὰ προσιόντα τοῖς θεοῖς "incoming funds due to the gods" and also to τὰ περιόντα "money left over (when the debts have been paid)." The construction of ὄντα is thus both locative-existential ("money on hand") and possessive with θεοῖς ("money belonging to the gods"). The lexicon cites several more or less similar examples from later texts, of the form τὸ ἐσόμενον ἐκ+*genitive* "future revenue from", τοῦ ὄντος μηνός "in the current month", ἱερέων τῶν ὄντων "priests currently in office" or "those who are priests (at the time)", where the nuance points not to the locative but to the temporal present. It is apparently the locative, but perhaps the temporal as well, that we have in a passage from *Acts* 13.1 ἦσαν δὲ ἐν Ἀντιοχείᾳ κατὰ τὴν οὖσαν ἐκκλησίαν προφῆται καὶ διδάσκαλοι, which the King James Version renders as "Now there were in the church *that was at Antioch* certain prophets and teachers." These are all rather obvious transformations into adjectival form of standard uses of the finite verb, as documented above in Chapters IV and VI.

It is, however, not these adjectival uses of the participle but the more unusual substantival construction with the article that is of primary importance for the development of philosophical terminology. The earliest example has already been cited from Homer:

ὃς ἤδη τά τ' ἐόντα τά τ' ἐσσόμενα πρό τ' ἐόντα

"(Calchas) who knew the things that were, that had been, and those that were to be" (*Il.* 1.70)

In this context the participle denotes all actions and events which a soothsayer is supposed to divine, including the wishes and intentions of the gods. A similar generality is implied by the use of the participial form in Empedocles (fr. 129):

> ῥεῖ᾽ ὅ γε τῶν ὄντων πάντων λεύσσεσκεν ἕκαστον
> καί τε δέκ᾽ ἀνθρώπων καί τ᾽ εἴκοσιν αἰώνεσσιν
> "He gazed with ease on each of the things that are in ten and in twenty lifetimes of men."

As I suggested in Chapter VII §4, such constructions of the participle as an object of verbs of knowing may be regarded as parallel to its familiar veridical use as object of verbs of saying, for example in Thuc. VII.8.2 φοβούμενος δὲ μὴ οἱ πεμπόμενοι... οὐ τὰ ὄντα ἀπαγγέλλωσιν "fearing lest the messengers not report the facts" (or "the true situation"). The plural form seems to be standard in Attic but, as we have seen, Herodotus regularly uses the singular in the same way, with verbs of both types: λέγειν τὸ ἐόν "to tell the truth" or "say what is the case," ἐξέμαθον πᾶν τὸ ἐόν "they learned the whole story" (above, pp. 349–55).

This veridical construction for the nominalized participle is certainly the oldest and probably also the most common use of the articular form in non-philosophic literature; and I believe that it exerts a powerful influence on the meaning of the participle in philosophical contexts from Parmenides on. But the veridical is not the only pre-philosophic use. Thus the possessive construction (ἔστι μοι "I have") is reflected in the use of τὰ ὄντα for a man's property, e.g. ἀφαιρήσεται τὰ ὄντα (τινί) "He will take away (someone's) property," Plato *Gorgias* 511 A 7. (In this use χρήματα may originally have been understood as "subject" of ὄντα. See also below on οὐσία as property, p. 458.)

In principle, the articular participle can denote *what is* in any sense, including "the things that exist," whatever these may be. Such a generalized use of the participle for "the things that are (present in the world)" is not clearly attested before the late fifth century, and then only in semi-technical prose, for example in the Hippocratic Corpus: εἰ δέ ποτε κρατηθείη καὶ ὁκότερον [πρότερον], οὐδὲν ἂν εἴη τῶν νῦν ἐόντων ὥσπερ ἔχει νῦν "If either (fire or water) were to be dominated (by the other), none of *the things that are now* would be as it now is" (*De Victu* I.3, Loeb ed. of Hippocrates, Vol. IV, p. 232). In some cases the locative construction is explicit: πάντων τῶν ἐνεόντων ἐν τῷδε τῷ κόσμῳ "all the things which are contained in this world-order" (*De Natura Hominis* 7, *ibid.* p. 22). We find a similar use of πάντα τὰ ὄντα "all the things there are" in an occasional fragment of the Presocratics, such as Diogenes fr. 2. The context, both in Diogenes and in the Hippocratic treatises, suggests that τὰ ὄντα are *primarily* conceived as elemental powers and bodies, such as earth, water, air and fire, or hot and cold, dry and wet. But there is of course no reason to restrict the denotation of the participle to any specific set of entities. Whatever a given thinker recognizes as the contents and constituents of the world-order, these are for him τὰ ὄντα.

I have suggested elsewhere that this generalized, semi-technical use of the articular participle can be traced back to the earliest period of philosophical prose, and that there is no good reason to doubt the authenticity of the phrase τοῖς οὖσι in the earliest surviving monument of philosophical literature, the fragment of Anaximander.[1] But whenever the phrase was first used in this way, it marks a new departure. The attempt to give a unified explanation for the natural universe as a whole brings with it the need for a terminology to designate all the factors and contents of the world-order, whatever they may be. The neuter plural pronoun πάντα "everything," "all things," will often suffice. But when a fuller term is needed to suggest the physical presence and reality of these entities, what could be more appropriate than the phrase πάντα τὰ ἐόντα? Without assuming that the phrase actually

---

[1] See *Anaximander and the Origins of Greek Cosmology*, pp. 174f., where parallels are cited from Anaxagoras, Zeno, Melissus, and the Hippocratic treatise *De Carnibus*. In that context I did not distinguish the veridical use of ἐόντα, τὸ ἐόν and the like in Homer and Herodotus from this broader "existential" use in the philosophers and the medical treatises, where the sense is not "what is the case" but rather "what is present and effective in the world." For this I have been justly criticized by Jula Kerschensteiner, in *Kosmos*, Zetemata 30 (1962) pp. 63f. n. 4. I agree that there is in principle a clear distinction between the idiomatic use of the participle for "the facts" or "states of affairs" and this more technical use by the philosophers for the "entities" of the world or "what there is." (Clear as it is, the distinction is not always easy to apply. For example, in the *metron*-formula of Protagoras, which I quoted in the same context, τὰ ὄντα is ambiguous between the two uses, though it fits more naturally with the non-technical veridical use.) But I disagree with Dr. Kerschensteiner's implication that, since all attested technical uses of τὰ ὄντα – aside from the problematic occurrence in Anaximander's fragment – are later than Parmenides, they must reflect his influence. In the first place, we have practically no technical prose surviving from the period before Parmenides, and silence proves nothing either way. And furthermore, the concept of τὰ ἐόντα as the beings which compose the world-order forms no part of the doctrine of Parmenides: it belongs to the theories which he *attacks*. (In the difficult fragment 4 I take the plurals ἀπεόντα and παρεόντα to be rhetorically inspired: "what *you take* to be things absent and things present must be rigidly conceived together: and then you will recognize them as one.") The generalized use of ὅσα νῦν ἐστι and πάντα τὰ ὄντα, as we have it in Anaxagoras, Diogenes and the Hippocratic authors, can scarcely be derived from Parmenides' unitary conception of τὸ ἐόν. This use of the plurals is a perfectly natural expression for the Ionian (and originally Milesian) endeavor to construct a single explanatory scheme for the whole cosmos and for "everything there is."

arose in this way, we may regard it as a natural abbreviation for πάντα τὰ ἐνεόντα ἐν τῷδε τῷ κόσμῳ "all the things present in this world-order," quoted above from the Hippocratic *De Natura Hominis*.

With its locative-existential associations, this philosophical use of τὰ ὄντα is syntactically and semantically distinct from the more ordinary veridical use of the participle, which is apparently an Indo-European heritage in Greek. But the old poetic formula from Homer casts its shadow over the new terminology. This is clear from Anaxagoras' balance of "the things which were to be and the things that (previously) were but are not now, and all that are now and all that will be" (fr. 12: καὶ ὁποῖα ἔμελλεν ἔσεσθαι καὶ ὁποῖα ἦν, ἄσσα νῦν μὴ ἔστι, καὶ ὅσα νῦν ἐστι καὶ ὁποῖα ἔσται). The contents of the world-order are now conceived in the language which formerly served to express the seer's knowledge of things past, present, and to come. This hymnic diction (as it has been called) is only rarely heard in the Platonic and Aristotelian discussions of τὰ ὄντα. But if we recognize some interaction between the old use of the participle to refer to facts or events and the new use to designate whatever things there are in the world, this will help us to understand the persistent Greek refusal to make any sharp distinction between states of affairs or facts with a propositional structure, on the one hand, and individual objects or entities on the other. For the Greeks, both types count as "beings". Indeed the denotation of the participle is highly ambiguous, as Aristotle observed. In the first place τὰ ὄντα or "what is" means *what is the case*, facts or events that actually occur or will occur, as in the Homeric formula for prophecy. In the second place, τὰ ὄντα means *what is* in the locative-existential use of εἰμί, things which exist, things which are present, or which are to be found somewhere: for example, "things which are present in this world-order" τὰ ἐνεόντα ἐν τῷδε τῷ κόσμῳ. When the veridical nuance associated with the first use is combined with this thing-like existential use we get the typically Platonic conception of τὰ ὄντως ὄντα, the true entities which are "really real," but which need no longer be "in this world". Finally, since the participle can denote something *which is* in any sense, it can also refer to attributes like *being hot* or *being tall*, *being on hand* or *being priest*. Hence it is that Aristotle can say that τὸ ὄν is used in as many ways as there are categories of predication. In order to single out the kind of being that he regards as primary, being as a concrete entity or substantial thing, Aristotle relies upon another nominal derivative of the verb, to which we now turn.

2. οὐσία

An abstract nominalization or action noun for εἰμί seems to have come into current use at first in connection with compound forms of the verb. Thus ἀπουσία "absence" (from ἄπ-ειμι) and παρουσία "presence" (πάρ-ειμι) are both found in Aeschylus, whereas the simplex οὐσία is not attested before Herodotus. The nominal formation, based upon the participle οὖσα, is an unusual one. An alternative and equally irregular formation appears in Ionic (and perhaps in Doric): ἐστώ based upon the third-person indicative ἐστί. Here again the compound forms appear to be more common. ἀπεστώ "absence", συνεστώ "being-together," "banquet" (Hdt. VI.128.1, immediately after an occurrence of συνουσίη), εὐεστώ "well-being", are all found in Herodotus, and the latter occurs in Aeschylus also. In several of these compound forms a connection with the locative construction is obvious, but the existence of εὐεστώ shows that the nominalization (like the participle) may in principle represent *any* construction of the finite verb.

We are concerned here only with the simple form οὐσία, and its alternate ἐστώ.[2] οὐσία occurs in Herodotus and is common in Attic prose but only in the sense of "property", corresponding to the use of the participle τὰ ὄντα for a man's possessions. There is no direct connection between this idiomatic use of οὐσία (reflecting the possessive construction of εἰμί with the dative) and the more technical senses of οὐσία which we find in Plato and Aristotle. But there is at least one Sophistic treatise preserved in the Hippocratic Corpus which shows that the philosophic use of this form is older than Plato, and that it need not be connected with any particular theory of reality. Thus we find the author of the epideictic speech *On the Art (of Medicine)* making repeated use of οὐσία in his claim that medicine exists as a true τέχνη. This writer, who apparently belongs in the late fifth century, gives a popularized version of some Eleatic puzzles on what-is-not which are rather in the vein of Gorgias' treatise *On Not-being*, though presented with much less dialectical skill:

> καὶ γὰρ ἄλογον τῶν ἐόντων τι ἡγεῖσθαι μὴ ἐόν· ἐπεὶ τῶν γε μὴ ἐόντων τίνα ἄν τίς οὐσίην θεησάμενος ἀπαγγείλειεν ὡς ἔστιν;... ἀλλὰ τὰ μὲν ἐόντα αἰεὶ ὁρᾶταί τε καὶ γινώσκεται, τὰ δὲ μὴ ἐόντα οὔτε ὁρᾶται οὔτε γινώσκεται.

> "And it is unreasonable to believe that any of the things-that-are is not. For who can behold any *being* of the things-that-are-

---

[2] There is nothing to be said about the forms ἐσσία and ὠσία which Plato reports as dialectal variants on οὐσία in *Cratylus* 401C-D. There is no other trace of ἐσσία, and ὠσία is attested only in pseudo-Pythagorean writings of a later period. See the comment of Burnet on *Phaedo* 65 D 13, and P. Chantraine, *La formation des noms en grec ancien*, p. 117. For traces of the forms ἀπεστύς ("absence"), κακεστώ ("misery") and ἀειεστώ ("eternity", "eternal stability"), see P. Chantraine, *Dictionnaire étymologique de la langue grecque*, s.v. εἰμί.

not so as to declare that they are?.... But the things-that-are
are in every case seen and known, whereas the things-that-are-
not are neither seen nor known." (*De Arte* 2, Loeb ed. of Hippocrates, II, 192)

There would be no point in offering a philosophic analysis of such Sophistic
jargon. From the linguistic point of view we may simply note that the verb
and its nominal form οὐσίη tend here to have a sense which we may render
by "is real" or "exists." So in a later passage of the same treatise: ch. 5
(Loeb II, 196) καὶ τοῦτό γε τεκμήριον μέγα τῇ οὐσίῃ τῆς τέχνης, ὅτι
ἐοῦσά τέ ἐστι καὶ μεγάλη "And this is an important proof for the *being*
of the art, that it is real and great." (So also with the articular infinitive,
ibid. p. 198: μαρτύρια τῇ τέχνῃ ἐς τὸ εἶναι.) In Chapter 6 we read that
chance (τὸ αὐτόματον) has no existence or reality (οὐσίη) except as a name,
whereas medicine is shown in every case to have reality (φανεῖται αἰεὶ
οὐσίην ἔχουσα *ibid.* p. 200).

It is scarcely surprising that in rhetorical performances inspired by Parmenides, Zeno, and Melissus – and more directly by Gorgias – the abstract
nominalization of εἰμί should come to be used in a sense quite different
from its ordinary meaning of "property".[3] That a parallel development
may have taken place in more serious specimens of post-Eleatic philosophy
is suggested by the fragments of Philolaus, where ἐστώ (not otherwise
attested in this simple form for the classical period) occurs twice as an
expression for the "being" or "true reality" of the things which are organized
in the world-order:

> ἁ μὲν ἐστὼ τῶν πραγμάτων ἀίδιος ἔσσα καὶ αὐτὰ μὲν ἁ φύσις
> θείαν τε καὶ οὐκ ἀνθρωπίνην ἐνδέχεται γνῶσιν πλήν γα ἢ ὅτι
> οὐχ οἷόν τ' ἦν οὐδενὶ τῶν ἐόντων καὶ γιγνωσκομένων ὑφ' ἀμῶν
> γεγενῆσθαι μὴ ὑπαρχούσας τᾶς ἐστοῦς τῶν πραγμάτων, ἐξ ὧν
> συνέστα ὁ κόσμος, καὶ τῶν περαινόντων καὶ τῶν ἀπείρων.
> "The *being* of things, which is eternal, and their nature itself
> admit divine and not human knowledge, beyond the fact that
> none of the things which are and are known by us could have
> come to be if there did not exist as basis the *being* of those things
> from which the world-order is composed, both the limiting and
> the unlimited." (Philolaus fr. 6)[4]

---

[3] We may detect echoes of the Sophistic contrast of οὐσία and ὄνομα, "reality" and "name",
in other passages of late fifth-century literature. See Wilamowitz, *Herakles* (1959 ed.)
III, 78, à propos of Eur. *Heracles* 337f.
[4] I follow the text of Walter Burkert, *Weisheit und Wissenschaft* (Nürnberg, 1962), p. 233.

The authenticity of these fragments has been much contested. In my own judgment Walter Burkert has succeeded in showing that, for a group of citations including the one in question here, both the language and the concepts employed reflect the universe of discourse of the fifth century, before the revolutionary influence of Plato.[5] In any case, the use of ἐστώ here corresponds exactly to what we would expect in a serious philosophic conception of *being* after Parmenides. The existential force of the verb is combined with a distinct veridical nuance; for the ἐστώ of things is clearly conceived as an object of knowledge, even if this "true being" is fully knowable only for a divine power of cognition. That some Pythagoreans had in fact prepared the way for Plato to this extent is just what the testimony of Aristotle would lead us to believe. And that the nominalized form of εἰμί played some role in pre-Platonic discussion is in any case independently attested by the Hippocratic treatise *De Arte*.

Whatever the preliminaries may have been, the basically new conception of οὐσία in Plato is a function of its use as nominalization for the Socratic τί ἐστι; question, as in *Euthyphro* 11A7: καὶ κινδυνεύεις, ὦ Εὐθύφρων, ἐρωτώμενος τὸ ὅσιον ὅτι ποτ᾽ ἐστίν, τὴν μὲν οὐσίαν μοι αὐτοῦ οὐ βούλεσθαι δηλῶσαι, πάθος δέ τι περὶ αὐτοῦ λέγειν "It looks, Euthyphro, as though when you were asked *what the pious is*, you are unwilling to make clear to me its *being*, but you state some property of it." Here οὐσία represents neither the existence of the subject nor any predicate which happens to be true (even uniquely true) of it, but the very nature or essence of the thing, as revealed in definition. In the *Phaedo* the term applies in a special way to the being of the Forms, which are *what (a thing) really is*, αὐτὸ τὸ ὃ ἔστιν.[6] So the λόγος τῆς οὐσίας in Aristotle is the "statement of the essence," the formula which specifies *what a thing is*.

To follow the history of οὐσία further is no part of our present undertaking.[7] I close with one linguistic observation that may shed some light on the philosophic terminology. From Plato on, we can distinguish three as-

---

[5] See *Weisheit und Wissenschaft*, pp. 222–56; the book of Philolaus was "the first and perhaps the only written version of Pythagorean number doctrine before Plato" (p. 256).
[6] *Phaedo* 76 D 8 ἡ τοιαύτη οὐσία, 77 A 2 τὴν οὐσίαν ἣν σὺ νῦν λέγεις following αὐτὸ ὃ ἔστιν at 74 B 2, D 6, 75 B 1, D2. Similarly at 78 D 1–4, where τὸ ὄν is used synonymously with οὐσία and αὐτὸ ἕκαστον ὃ ἔστιν for "that being (οὐσία) of which we give an account of what it is (λόγον τοῦ εἶναι) in questions and answers." For Plato, of course, τὰ (ὄντως) ὄντα "the things that (truly) are" are just the Forms. And between the Forms and their essence or *what they are*, no distinction can be drawn. Hence in such Platonic contexts ἡ οὐσία (taken distributively for all the Forms) and τὰ ὄντα are strictly equivalent in meaning. In the *Sophist* Plato again uses οὐσία and τὸ ὄν as equivalent expressions for the kind Being.
[7] For a summary of the data, see R. Marten, ΟΥΣΙΑ *im Denken Platons* (1962). Marten refers to a monograph *OUSIA* by R. Hirzel (1913), which I have not been able to consult.

pects of the meaning of οὐσία which tend to interact, and which may on occasion produce some genuine ambiguity. (1) There is the new, specifically Platonic (or perhaps Socratic) use of οὐσία as nominalization for the verb in the "What is X?" question, so that οὐσία is in this sense properly used only for Platonic Forms or Aristotelian essences (τὸ τί ἐστι, τὸ τί ἦν εἶναι). (2) There is the less technical use of οὐσία for "being," "existence," or "true reality," however this may be conceived, as in the citation from the treatise *On the Art* and (with a stronger veridical nuance) in the use of ἐστώ in the fragment of Philolaus. (3) There is the possibility of a more concrete use of οὐσία as equivalent to τὰ ὄντα in the pre-Platonic sense: "the things there are (in this world)." Whereas the noun in (1) and usually in (2) as well serves as an "abstract" nominalization for the finite verb as predicate, i.e. for the being of what-is (and it is thus syntactically parallel to the articular infinitive τὸ εἶναι), οὐσία in (3) is used – like many other abstract nouns – for the subject so characterized. (This is what I call the concrete or agent nominalization, as typically illustrated by the articular participle τὸ ὄν or ὁ τρέχων "the runner", in contrast to the abstract action nominalization τὸ τρέχειν "running". This syntactic distinction corresponds in part to Heidegger's contrast between *das Seiende* and *das Sein der Seienden*.) The tendency to use οὐσία concretely, like the participle, to refer to *beings* or *what is*, was reinforced by the idiomatic sense of "property," "possessions". For in the latter use οὐσία and τὰ ὄντα are roughly synonymous. In the doctrine of οὐσία ("substance") in the *Categories*, Aristotle emphatically returns to such a concrete use of the noun to designate τὰ ὄντα as such. The οὐσία of the *Categories* is precisely a title for *the thing-that-is* in the strictest sense. (Compare *Met.* Z.1028ᵃ30 ὥστε τὸ πρώτως ὄν καὶ οὐ τὶ ὄν ἀλλ' ὄν ἁπλῶς ἡ οὐσία ἂν εἴη.) Since, however, Aristotle never abandons the more Platonic use of οὐσία for "essence" (where the noun designates not particular entities – other than Forms – but only the *being* which they have or in which they participate), the possibility of confusion is always present, and occasionally reflected in the translations. The troubled course of *Metaphysics* Z can be seen in part as an attempt, beginning with the concrete sense of οὐσία ("substance," as "the thing-which-is"), to reconcile this with the other notion of οὐσία as τὸ τί ἦν εἶναι ("what a thing is"). And there are passages in Aristotle where one is genuinely at a loss to know whether "substance" or "essence" is the appropriate rendering – or whether in this case the two concepts are in fact one. Consider, for example, *Met.* Λ.6 1071ᵇ20 δεῖ ἄρα εἶναι ἀρχὴν τοιαύτην ἧς ἡ οὐσία ἐνέργεια "Hence there must be a principle such that its being is activity." (In what precedes, 1071ᵇ5ff., we have the noun in the concrete sense of "substance": αἵ τε γὰρ οὐσίαι πρῶται τῶν ὄντων.) Similarly in the description of the Active Intellect at *DA* III.5 430ª18 τῇ οὐσίᾳ ὢν ἐνέργεια. It is probably no accident that this ambiguity between abstract and concrete readings of οὐσία is most acute – but also most harmless – in the case of immaterial entities such as the Active Intellect and the Prime Mover, where a genuine distinction between substance and essence can scarcely be drawn. For these, and for the πρῶται οὐσίαι of *Met.* Z.11, 1037ª5, ª28, ᵇ1–2, we have the case where the thing and its essence are strictly identical, just as a Platonic Form is in no sense distinct from the specific nature (φύσις) which it "has". In such a case there is no semantic distinction between the concrete (agent) and abstract (action) nominalization of εἰμί, that is, between τὸ ὄν and οὐσία, just because there is no conceptual distinction between the entity as such and its being-what-it-is.

BIBLIOGRAPHY

Abelard, Peter, *Logica 'Ingredientibus'*, ed. B. Geyer, in *Beiträge zur Geschichte der Philosophie des Mittelalters* XXI. 3 (1927).

Ackrill, John, *Aristotle's Categories and De Interpretatione*, Translated with Notes, Oxford, 1963.

Aerts, W. J., *Periphrastica*, Amsterdam, 1955.

Apollonius Dyscolus, *Syntaxis*, ed. Uhlig, Leipzig 1910 (Olms reprint, Hildesheim 1965).

Bach, Emmon, "*Have* and *be* in English Syntax," *Language* 43 (1967), 462–85.

Bach, E. and Harms, R. T., (eds.) *Universals in Linguistic Theory*, New York, 1968.

Bach, E., "Nouns and Noun Phrases," in Bach and Harms, *Universals in Linguistic Theory*.

Barbelenet, D., *De la phrase à verbe être dans l'ionien d'Hérodote*, Paris, 1913.

Barrett, W. S., *Euripides, Hippolytos*. Oxford, 1964.

Bartholomae, Christian, *Altiranisches Wörterbuch*, Strasbourg, 1904.

Behaghel, O., "Zur Stellung des Verbs im Germanischen und Indogermanischen," *Zeitschrift für vergleichende Sprachforschung auf dem Gebiete der indogermanischen Sprachen*. 56 (1928), 276–81.

Benveniste, Émile, "Catégories de pensée et catégories de langue," in *Problèmes de linguistique générale*.

Benveniste, É., "De la sujectivité dans le langage," in *Problèmes de linguistique générale*.

Benveniste, É., *Hittite et Indo-Européen*. Paris, 1962.

Benveniste, É., "La phrase nominale," in *Problèmes de linguistique générale*.

Benveniste, É., *Origines de la formation des noms*, Paris, 1935.

Benveniste, É., *Problèmes de linguistique générale*, Paris, 1966.

Benveniste, É., "Structure des relations de personne dans le verbe," in *Problèmes de linguistique générale*.

Bloch, A., "Über die Entwicklung der Ausdruckfähigkeit in den Sprachen des Altertums," *Museum Helveticum* I (1944), 234–57.

Boeder, H., "Der frühgriechische Wortgebrauch von Logos und Aletheia," in *Archiv für Begriffsgeschichte* 4 (1959).

Boyer, P. and Spéranski, N., *Manuel pour l'étude de la langue russe*, Paris, 1947.

Brugmann, K., *Kurze vergleichende Grammatik der indogermanischen Sprachen*, 3 Vols. Berlin, 1922.

Brugmann, Karl, *Die Syntax des einfachen Satzes im Indogermanischen* (Beiheft zum 43. Band der *Indogerm. Forschungen*), Berlin, 1925.

Burguière, P., *Histoire de l'infinitif en grec*, Paris, 1960.

Burkert, Walter, *Weisheit und Wissenschaft*, Nürnberg, 1962.

Chantraine, Pierre, *Dictionnaire étymologique de la langue grecque: Histoire des mots*, Tome II (E-K), Paris, 1970.

Chantraine, P., *Grammaire homérique*, Tome I: Phonétique et Morphologie, Paris, 1948; Tome II: Syntaxe, 1953.

Chantraine, P., *La formation des noms en grec ancien*, Paris, 1933.

Chomsky, Noam, *Aspects of the Theory of Syntax*, Cambridge, Mass., 1965.

Chomsky, Noam, "A Transformational Approach to Syntax," in Fodor and Katz, *The Structure of Language*.

Chomsky, Noam, "Current Issues in Linguistic Theory," in Fodor and Katz, *The Structure of Language*.

Chomsky, Noam, *Syntactic Structures*, The Hague, 1957.

Cunningham, Maurice P., "A Theory of the Latin Sentence," *Classical Philology* 60 (1965), 24–8.

Curtius, G., *Griechische Etymologie*, Leipzig, 1879.

Danto, Arthur, *Analytical Philosophy of Knowledge*, Cambridge, 1968.

Delbrück, Berthold, *Vergleichende Syntax der indogermanischen Sprachen* Vols. I–III (= Brugmann–Delbrück, *Grundriss* III–V), Strasbourg, 1893–1900.

Diels, H. and Kranz, W., *Die Fragmente der Vorsokratiker*. 7th ed. Berlin, 1954.

Dover, K. J., *Greek Word Order*, Cambridge, 1960.

Dover, K. J., *Lysias and the Corpus Lysiacum*, Berkeley and Los Angeles, 1968.

Dover, K. J., Review of Aerts, *Periphrastica*, in *Gnomon* 40 (1968). 87f.

Ebeling, H., *Lexicon Homericum*, Vol. I, Leipzig, 1880.

Ebeling, H. L., "Some Statistics on the Order of Words in Greek," in *Studies in Honor of B. L. Gildersleeve*, Baltimore, 1902.

Ekman, Erik, *Der reine Nominalsatz bei Xenophon*, Skrifter utgivna av K. Humanistika Vetenskaps-Samfundet i Uppsala 29.6, 1938.

Ernout, A. and Meillet, A., *Dictionnaire étymologique de la langue latine: Histoire des mots*, 3rd ed. Paris, 1951.

Ernout, A., "*Exstō* et les composés latins en *ex-*," *Bulletin de la Société de Linguistique de Paris* 50 (1950), 18–28.

Fillmore, Charles J., "A Case for Case," in Bach and Harms, *Universals in Linguistic Theory*.

Fischer, P., "Zur Stellung des Verbums in Griechischen," *Glotta* 13 (1924), 1–11 and 189–205.

Fodor, J. A. and Katz, J. J., (eds.) *The Structure of Language: Readings in the Philosophy of Language*, Englewood Cliffs, N. J., 1964.

Fraenkel, A. A., *Abstract Set Theory*, 2nd ed. Amsterdam, 1961.

Fraenkel, Eduard, *Beobachtungen zu Aristophanes*, Rome, 1962.

Frisk, H., *Griechisches etymologisches Wörterbuch*, Heidelberg, 1954.

Frisk, H., "'Wahrheit' und 'Lüge' in den indogermanischen Sprachen," in *Götesborgs Hogskolas Arsskrift* 41.3 (1935).

Geach, Peter T., "Assertion," *Philosophical Review* 74 (1965), 449–65.

Geach, Peter T., *Reference and Generality*, Ithaca, New York, 1962.

Gehring, A., *Index Homericus*, Leipzig, 1891–5.

Gilson, E., *L'être et l'essence*, Paris, 1948.

Goetze, A., "Die Pestgebete des Muršiliš," in *Kleinasiatische Forschungen* I (1930).

Goodman, Nelson, *Languages of Art: An Approach to a Theory of Symbols*, Indianapolis, 1968.

Goodwin, W. W., *Syntax of the Moods and Tenses of the Greek Verb*, Boston, 1897.

Graham, A. C., "'Being' in Classical Chinese," in *The Verb 'be' and its Synonyms* (ed. by John W. M. Verhaar), Part 1, Dordrecht, 1967.

Graham, A. C. "'Being' in Western Philosophy compared with *shih/fei* and *yu/wu* in Chinese Philosophy," *Asia Minor* (N. S.) 7 (1959), 79–112.

Grassmann, H., *Wörterbuch zum Rig-Veda*, 3rd ed. Wiesbaden, 1955.

Grensemann, Hermann, *Die hippokratische Schrift "Über die heilige Krankheit,"* text, translation, and notes, Berlin, 1968.

Guiraud, C., *La phrase nominale en grec d'Homère à Euripide*, Paris, 1962.

Hacking, Ian, "A Language Without Particulars," *Mind* 77 (1968), 168–85.

Harris, Zellig S., "Co-occurrence and Transformation in Linguistic Structure," in Fodor and Katz, *The Structure of Language*.

Harris, Zellig S., "The Elementary Transformations," in *Papers in Structural and Transformational Linguistics*.

Harris, Zelig S., "From Morpheme to Utterance," *Language* 22 (1946), 161–83, reprinted in Z. S. Harris. *Papers in Structural and Transformational Linguistics*.

Harris, Zellig S., *Mathematical Structures of Language*, New York, 1968.

Harris, Zellig S., "Transformational Theory," *Language*, 41 (1965), 363–401.
Harris, Zellig S., *Papers in Structural and Transformational Linguistics*, Dordrecht, 1970.
Hashimoto, A. Y., "The Verb 'to be' in Modern Chinese," in *The Verb 'be' and its Synonyms*, Part 4, Dordrecht, 1969.
Heidegger, Martin, *Kants These über das Sein*, Frankfurt A. M., 1962.
Heidegger, Martin, *Sein und Zeit*, 7th ed. Tübingen, 1953.
Hermann, Gottfried, *De emendanda ratione graecae grammaticae*, Leipzig, 1801.
Hermann, Ed, "Die subjektlosen Sätze bei Homer," *Nachrichten der Gesellschaft der Wissenschaften Göttingen*, Philol.-Hist. Klasse (1926), pp. 265–97.
Hintikka, Jaakko, "Language-Games for Quantifiers," in *Studies in Logical Theory*, American Philosophical Quarterly Monograph No. 2, Oxford, 1968.
Hippocrates, with an English translation by W. H. S. Jones, Loeb Classical Library, in 4 vols., London, 1923–31.
Hiż, Danuta and Joshi, A. K., "Transformational Decomposition: A Simple Description of an Algorithm for Transformational Analysis of English Sentences," in *Proceedings of the 2nd International Conference on Computational Linguistics, Grenoble, France, 1967.*
Hiż, Henry, "Referentials," *Semiotica* I (1969), 136–66.
Hiż, Henry, "The Role of Paraphrase in Grammar," *Monograph Series in Languages and Linguistics*, No. 17, ed. by C. I. J. M. Stuart (1964), 97–104.
Hjelmslev, L., "Le verbe et la phrase nominal," in *Mélanges J. Marouzeau*, Paris, 1948, 253–81.
Hofmann, J. B., *Etymologisches Wörterbuch des Griechischen*, Munich, 1950.
Humbach, H., *Die Gathas des Zarathustra*, Heidelberg, 1959.
Husserl, Edmund, *Ideen zu einer reinen Phänomenologie und phänomenologischen Philosophie*, Erstes Buch (ed. by W. Biemel), The Hague, 1950.
Italie, G., *Index Aeschyleus*, Leiden, 1955.
Jespersen, Otto, *Essentials of English Grammar*, London, 1960.
Jespersen, Otto, *A Modern English Grammar on Historical Principles*, Heidelberg 1909–1949.
Jespersen, Otto, *The Philosophy of Grammar*, London, 1929.
Kahn, Charles H., *Anaximander and the Origins of Greek Cosmology*, New York and London, 1960.
Kahn, C. H., "On the Terminology for *Copula* and *Existence*", in *Festschrift for Richard Walzer* (forthcoming).
Kahn, C. H., "The Greek Verb 'to be' and the Concept of Being," *Foundations of Language* 2 (1966), 245–65.
Kahn, C. H., "The Thesis of Parmenides," *Review of Metaphysics* 22 (1969), 700–24.
Kaminsky, J., *Language and Ontology*, Carbondale, Ill., 1969.
Keifer, Ferenc, "A Transformational Approach to the Verb *van* 'to be' in Hungarian," in *The Verb 'be' and its Synonyms* Part 3 (ed. by John W. M. Verhaar), Dordrecht, 1968.
Keller, Helen, *The Story of My Life*, ed. J. A. Macy, New York, 1954.
Kenny, Anthony, *Action, Emotion and Will*, London, 1963.
Kent, R., *Old Persian; Grammar, Texts, Lexicon*. New Haven, 1950.
Kerschensteiner, Jula, *Kosmos: Quellenkritische Untersuchungen zu den Vorsokratikern*, Zetemata 30, Munich, 1962.
Kinzel, Josef, "Die Kopula bei Homer und Hesiod," in *Jahresbericht des k.k.K. Franz Joseph Staatsgymnasium in Mährisch-Ostrau*, Schuljahr 1907–08.
Klowski, Joachim, "Zur Entstehung der Begriffe Sein und Nichts," *Archiv für Geschichte der Philosophie* 49 (1967), 121–48.
Kristeller, Paul O., *Il pensiero filosofico di Marsilio Ficino*, Florence, 1953.
Kučera, H., "Computers in Language Analysis and in Lexicography," in *American Heritage Dictionary of the English Language*, Boston, 1969, pp. xxxviii–xl.
Kühner-Gerth: *Ausführliche Grammatik der griechischen Sprache* by Raphael Kühner, Part Two (Syntax) ed. by Bernhard Gerth, in 2 vols., Hanover and Leipzig, 1898–1904.

Lakoff, George, "Linguistics and Natural Logic," *Synthese* 22 (1970), 165–75.

Lakoff, Robin T., *Abstract Syntax and Latin Complementation*, Cambridge, Mass., 1968.

Lambert, K. (ed.), *The Logical Way of Doing Things*, New Haven, 1969.

Langendoen, D. T., "The Copula in Mundari," in *The Verb 'be' and its Synonyms*, Part 1, Dordrecht, 1967.

Lasso de la Vega, José S., *La oración nominal en Homero*, Madrid, 1955.

Laum, B., *Das Alexandrinische Akzentuationssystem*, in Studien zur Geschichte und Kultur des Altertums, Paderborn, 1928.

Lehrs, K., *Quaestiones epicae*, Königsberg, 1837.

Lejewski, Czeslaw, "Logic and Existence," *British Journal for the Philosophy of Science* 5 (1954), 104–19.

Lejewski, C., "On Leśniewski's Ontology," *Ratio* 1 (1958), 150–76.

Lejewski, C., "Proper Names," *Proceedings of the Aristotelian Society*, 1958, 229–55.

Lewis, G. I., *Turkish Grammar*, Oxford, 1967.

LSJ: Liddell, H. G. and Scott, R., *A Greek-English Lexicon*, 9th ed. by H. S. Jones and R. McKenzie, Oxford, 1940.

Lunt, Horace G., *Fundamentals of Russian*, New York, 1958.

Luschei, E. C., *The Logical Systems of Lesniewski*, Amsterdam, 1962.

Luther, Wilhelm, *"Wahrheit" und "Lüge" im ältesten Griechentum*, Leipzig, 1935.

Lyons, John, "A Note on Possessive, Existential, and Locative Sentences," *Foundations of Language* 3 (1967), 390–6.

Lyons, John, "Existence, Location, Possession and Transitivity," in *Logic, Methodology and Philosophy of Science* III, ed. B. van Rootselaar and J. F. Staal (Amsterdam, 1968), 495–503.

Lyons, John, *Introduction to Theoretical Linguistics*, Cambridge, 1968.

Lyons, John, "Towards a 'notional' theory of the 'parts of speech'," *Journal of Linguistics* 2 (1966), 209–36.

Marouzeau, J., *L'ordre des mots en latin*, Paris, 1953.

Marouzeau, J., *L'ordre des mots: Phrase à verbe être*, Paris, 1910.

Marten, Rainer, ΟΥΣΙΑ *im Denken Platons*, Meisenheim am Glan, 1962.

Marty, A., "Über subjektlose Sätze, etc." *Vierteljahrschrift für wissenschaftliche Philosophie* 19 (1895), 19–87, 263–334.

Mates, Benson, "Leibniz on Possible Worlds," in *Logic, Methodology, and Philosophy of Science*, Amsterdam, 1968.

Meiggs, Russell, and Lewis, David, *A Selection of Greek Historical Inscriptions to the End of the Fifth Century B.C.*, Oxford, 1969.

Matilal, B. K., "Indian Theorists on the Nature of the Sentence," *Foundations of Language* 2 (1966), 377–81.

Meillet, Antoine, "La phrase nominale en indo-européen," *Mémoires de la Société de Linguistique de Paris* 14 (1906), 1–26.

Meillet, A. and Vendryès, J., *Traité de grammaire comparée des langues classiques*, 2nd ed. Paris, 1948.

Meyer-Lübke, W., *Grammaire des langues romanes*, French transl. by A. and G. Doutrepont, Paris, 1895.

Miklosich, F., *Subjektlose Sätze*, 2nd ed. Vienna, 1883.

Mossé, Fernand, *A Handbook of Middle English*, tr. by J. A. Walker, Baltimore, 1952.

Mourelatos, Alexander P. D., *The Route of Parmenides*, New Haven, 1970.

Munro, D. B., *A Grammar of the Homeric Dialect*, 2nd ed. Oxford, 1891. (Cited as *"Homeric Grammar".*)

Nemeth, J., *Turkish Grammar*, English adaptation by T. Halasi-Kun, The Hague, 1962.

Onians, R. B., *The Origins of European Thought*, 2nd ed. Cambridge, 1954.

Owen, G. E. L., "Logic and Metaphysics in Some Earlier Works of Aristotle," in *Aristotle and Plato in the Mid-Fourth Century*, ed. I. Düring and G. E. L. Owen, Göteborg, 1960.

Pernot, H., *Lexique Grec Moderne-Français*, Paris, 1933.

Port Royal *Grammar: Grammaire générale et raisonnée*, 3rd ed. Paris, 1769.

Port Royal *Logic: La logique ou l'art de penser*, 6th ed. Paris, 1709.

Porzig, W., *Die Namen für Satzinhalte im Griechischen und im Indogermanischen*, Berlin, 1942.

Powell, J. Enoch, *A Lexicon to Herodotus*, 2nd ed. Hildesheim, 1960.

Quine, Willard Van Orman, "Existence and Quantification," in *Ontological Relativity and other Essays*, New York, 1969.

Quine, W. V. O., *Mathematical Logic*, 2nd ed. Cambridge, Mass., 1951.

Quine, W. V. O., *Methods of Logic*, New York, 1959.

Quine, W. V. O., "On Carnap's Views on Ontology," in *The Ways of Paradox and other Essays*, New York, 1966.

Quine, W. V. O., *Word and Object*, Cambridge, Mass., 1960.

Redard, G., *Recherches sur XPH, XPHΣΘAI*, Paris, 1953.

Renan, Ernest, *De l'origine du langage*, 10th ed. *sans date*, Paris.

Robbins, Beverly L., *The Definite Article in English Transformations*, Papers in Formal Linguistics No. 4, The Hague, 1968.

Russell, Bertrand, *Introduction to Mathematical Philosophy*, London, 1919.

Russell, Bertrand, *Logic and Knowledge: Essays 1901–1950*, ed. R. C. Marsh, London, 1956.

Russell, Bertrand, "On Denoting," in H. Feigl and W. Sellars (eds.), *Readings in Philosophical Analysis*, New York, 1949.

Russell, Bertrand, *The Principles of Mathematics*, London, 1903; 2nd ed. 1937.

Sapir, Edward, *Language: An Introduction to the Study of Speech*, New York, 1921.

Saussure, Ferdinand de, *Cours de linguistique générale*, ed. by C. Bally and A. Sechehaye, 5th edition, Paris, 1960.

Schwyzer, Eduard, *Griechische Grammatik*, Vol. I (phonetics and morphology), Munich, 1938; Vol. II (syntax) completed by Albert Debrunner, Munich, 1950 (Vol. II is cited as "Schwyzer-Debrunner").

Searle, John, *Speech Acts*, Cambridge, 1969.

Smyth, H. E., *Greek Grammar*, rev. by G. M. Messing, Cambridge, Mass., 1956.

Sommers, Fred, "On Concepts of Truth in Natural Languages," *Review of Metaphysics* 23 (1969), 259–86.

Steinthal, H., *Geschichte der Sprachwissenschaft bei den Griechen und Römern*, 2 vols. 2nd ed. Berlin, 1890–1.

Strawson, P. F., *Individuals*, London, 1959.

Strawson, P. F., *The Bounds of Sense: An Essay on Kant's Critique of Pure Reason*, London, 1966.

Swadesh, M., "Nootka Internal Syntax," in *International Journal of American Linguistics* 9 (1939).

Toms, Eric, *Being, Negation and Logic*, Oxford, 1962.

Tugendhat, Ernst, "Die Sprachanalytische Kritik der Ontologie," in *Das Problem der Sprache*, Achter Deutscher Kongress für Philosophie, Heidelberg, 1966.

Vendler, Zeno, *Adjectives and Nominalizations*, Papers in Formal Linguistics No. 5, The Hague, 1968.

Vendler, Zeno, *Linguistics in Philosophy*, Ithaca, N. Y., 1967.

Westermann, D., *A Study of the Ewe Language*, transl. A. L. Bickford-Smith, Oxford, 1930.

Westermann, D., *Wörterbuch der Ewe-Sprache*, Berlin, 1905.

INDEX OF PASSAGES CITED

Passage cited	Page of citation (Numbers of sample sentences given in bold)	Passage cited	Page of citation (Numbers of sample sentences given in bold)
Aeschines		*Plutus*	
1.102	243n	1188	155 (**108**)
3.132	243n	Aristotle	
Aeschylus		*Categories*	
Agam.		ch. 2	47f.
940	169	10, 13b18	409 n. 42
958–61	140n	*De Int.*	
P.V.		ch. 1, 16a15	47 n. 15
88–92	91 n. 8	2–5	47 n. 14
291f.	279 (**91**)	3, 16b10	48
771	143 (**88**)	7	47 n. 15
846–8	259 (**47**)	12, 21b9	215n
Septem		*Prior An.*	
224–6	357 (**30**)	I.1, 24b16	368
592	356 (**29**)	I.27, 43a32–6	36n
Ammonius		I.36, 48b2	396
in De Int. p. 52,32–	47 n. 15	I.46, 51b13	215n
p. 53,7		*Post. An.*	
Anaxagoras		I.22, 83a1–21	36n
fr. 12 (D.-K.)	457	II.1, 89b32	303 (**126**)
Apollonius Dyscolus		*Physics*	
Syntaxis (ed. Uhlig)		185b29	215n
p. 7	68 n. 12	191b26	368
p. 6,6	435n	208a29	318 n. 78
Aristophanes		*De Anima*	
Acharnians		416b19	243
156f.	124 (**62**)	430a18	462
767	124 (**62**)	435b20	243
Clouds		*Met.*	
250f.	125 (**63**)	Γ.2, 1003a33–b10	6 n. 11
366f.	300 (**121**)	Γ.3, 1005b24, 35	368
1470f.	300f. n. 63	Γ.7, 1011b26	336n, 367
Frogs		Δ.7, 1017a27	215n
953	154n	Δ.7, 1017a31	332
1052	354, 366n	Z.1, 1028a30	461

Passage cited	Page of citation (Numbers of sample sentences given in bold)	Passage cited	Page of citation (Numbers of sample sentences given in bold)
Z.11, 1037a5, a28, b1–2	462	*Iph. in Tauris* 721f.	360 (**36**)
Λ.6, 1071b5ff., 20	461	*Medea* 89	155 (**107**)
Eud. Ethics 1215b26	243	*Troades* 1292	243
Politics			
1276b29	40 n. 2	Heraclitus	
1278b11	40 n. 2	fr. 1 (D.-K.)	354 n. 26
1283b42	40 n. 2	fr. 112	125n
Poetics		Herodotus	
1457a14–17	47 n. 15	I. 2.1	358
		6.1	260 n. 29
Critias		7.2–8.1	260 n. 29
fr. 25. 16–42 (D.-K.)	303 (**125**)	8.1	131 (**69**)
fr. 25. 27ff.	318n	8.2	154 (**106**)
		9.1	330n
Democritus		11.1	173
frr. 174, 256 (D.-K.)	453	11.5	330n
Demosthenes		12.1	173
IX.43	167	18.1	330n
XIV.19	168	26.2	425
XVIII.72	242 n. 18	30.3	353 (**24**)
XVIII.308	360n	32.4	92 n. 9
XXII.70	168	35.2	358, 425
LIX.30	155n	67.4	258n
Diogenes Laertius		84.3	425
VII.63	68 n. 12	93.2	168
VII.70	68 n. 13	95.1	354, 454
		97.1	353 (**25**)
Empedocles		107.2	168
fr. 128.1 (D.-K.)	258 n. 26	116.5	354 (**27**)
fr. 129	258 n. 26, 455	118.1	355
Euripides		120.2	242, 326 (**131**)
Bacchae		146.3	141n
395f.	39 n. 2	148.1	260 n. 28
Electra		152.1	141n
346	354	201	279 (**89**)
Hecuba		206.1	141n
284	242 (**23**)	209.5	329 (**140**)
532	151 (**97**)	210.2	326 (**132**)
1214	379	II. 15.4	141n
Helen		28.1	327 (**133**)
926	450	181.3	329 (**141**)
Hippolytus			
932	130 (**67**)		

Passage cited	Page of citation (Numbers of sample sentences given in bold)	Passage cited	Page of citation (Numbers of sample sentences given in bold)
Herodotus (*cont.*)		321	177
III. 17.2	328 (**138**)	415	146 (**90**)
108.4	120 (**54**)	732	180 (**150**)
113.1	273 (**76**)	Hippocrates	
152	156 n. 83	*De Arte*	
155.2	281n, 327 (**134**)	2–6	458f.
IV. 32	139 (**82**), 354 (**26**)	*De Natura Hominis*	
129.2	273 (**75**)	7	455f.
134.2	153 (**100**)	*The Sacred Disease*	
192.2	327 (**135**)	ch. 4	
195.2	329 (**139**)	(1.30 Grensemann)	302 (**124**)
V. 50.2	353 (**20**)	*De Victu*	
67.1	330 (**143**)	I.3	455
106.4	353	Homer	
VI. 5.39	281n	*Iliad 1*	
35.3	153	11–73	72f.
36.2	177	29	70
37	140 n. 66	49	237 (**10**), 384 n. 13
37.2	352 (**21**)	57	384 n. 13
50.3	353 (**22**)	63	160 (**123**), 427
65.2	131 (**71**)	70	143 n. 69,
74.2	327 (**136**)		350 (**18**), 454f.
86.δ	328 (**137**)	80	445 n. 23
VII. 34	177 (**143**)	91	90
52.7	321 (**142**)	107	96f. (**9**)
111.1	219n	114	89f. (**1**)
143.1	139 (**83**)	118	89f. (**2**)
209.1	353 (**23**)	131	90
237.2	353	144	166 (**136**)
VIII. 57.2	329 (**142**)	153	446
98.1	282n	156	166 (**135**), 450
IX. 11.3	353	174	160 (**120**), 450
115	133 (**75**)	176	94f. (**3**)
Hesiod		188	285, 384 n. 13
Erga		213	266 n. 35
11	236 (**6**)	251	384 n. 13
23	391	271	166 (**138**)
669	162	275	453
Scutum		287	162 (**127**)
230	147n	290 (≈ 494)	242 (**20**)
Theogony		300	165 (**132**),
32	350		266 n. 35
38	350	335	446
310	147n	338	105f. (**22**)

Passage cited	Page of citation (Numbers of sample sentences given in bold)	Passage cited	Page of citation (Numbers of sample sentences given in bold)
340f.	115 (48)	164	446
341	384 n. 13	180	361 (40)
356 (= 507)	128 (65)	229	105ff. (27)
388	131 (72)	384	153
416	114	429	105ff. (28)
493	384 n. 13	440	160 (119)
562	161 (125)	*Iliad 4*	
566	306f. n. 67, 428	13	451
573f.	111 (40)	14	341 (9)
583	90	20	101 (21)
Iliad 2		22	150
26 (= 63)	105f. (23)	51	276 (83)
27	158 (115), 453	84	221
73	112f. (41)	169	284
95	283 (97)	189	338 (5)
118	168	266	105f. (29)
119	242 n. 17	318	152 (99)
155	221	322f.	110 (38)
196	445 n. 23	323	445 n. 23
204	276 n. 43, 435 n. 1	478	206
226	266 n. 35	534	209 (4)
241	268 (66)	*Iliad 5*	
246	105ff. (24)	9f.	249 (38)
252	345 (10)	159f.	158 (116)
340	163	177	131 (68)
372	277	201	99 (15)
379f.	269 (67)	218	155 (110)
485	105ff. (25), 159 (118)	254	447
489	267 (64)	331	102n
618	276 (82)	349	153
641	241 (14)	360	158 (113)
687	278 (85)	379	451
760	105ff. (26)	402	221
811	246 (28)	740	450
852	448	873	132 (74)
857	448	877	166 (139), 306 n. 67
Iliad 3		*Iliad 6*	
3	221, 285	123	121 (55)
40f.	99 (16)	130	241 (15)
41f.	109 (34)	152	231, 246 (27), 410, 422
45	158n, 165 (131), 268 (65)	153	230, 243 (24)
114f.	165 (130)	206	122

Passage cited	Page of citation (Numbers of sample sentences given in bold)	Passage cited	Page of citation (Numbers of sample sentences given in bold)
Homer		277	160 (**121**)
Iliad 6 (cont.)		312f.	365
211	122 (**56**), 168	316	286 (**101**)
295	177	324	154 (**105**)
352	448	337	176n
410f.	99 (**17**)	364	266 (**60**)
413	267 (**62**)	395	261 (**52**)
434	206	415f.	287 (**104**)
462	285	474	173
488	132 (**73**)	527	345 (**11**)
Iliad 7		551	154 (**104**)
28f.	98ff. (**12**)	573	285
73	263 (**56**)	669	196 (**3**)
97f.	110 (**39**)	688	279 n. 44
102	163	*Iliad 10*	
282 (= 293)	220	66	261 (**51**)
424	154 (**103**)	113	158 (**112**)
433	439 n. 11, 447	172	115n
446	236 (**3**)	269	207
458 (≈ 451)	237 (**7**)	314–8	250 (**39**)
Iliad 8		357	159 (**117**)
1	292	378f.	266 (**61**)
16	158 (**114**)	383	95 (**7**)
66	174, 230, 287	*Iliad 11*	
	(**103**), 447	6	178 (**146**)
223	178 (**146**)	13	196 (**2**)
373	280 (**95**)	30–8	264n
456	158 (**113**)	73	221
473–7	98ff. (**13**)	84	287 (**103**)
521	166 (**137**)	339	178 (**145**)
523	341 (**7**)	443	269 (**68**)
Iliad 9		612	128 (**64**)
25	95 (**6**)	648	293 (**114**), 451
29	151 (**95**)	681	160 (**122**)
39	110 (**36**)	711–3	247 (**29**)
85	262	722f.	140 (**85**), 247
116	161 (**126**)		(**30**)
125	196 (**1**)	737	221
134	114 n. 33	762	152n, 361 (**39**)
135	160 (**121**)	793	96f. (**10**)
144	267 (**63**)	838	156 (**111**), 356
230	163		(**28**)
236	173	*Iliad 12*	
275f.	112f. (**43**)	12	94f. (**4**)

Passage cited	Page of citation (Numbers of sample sentences given in bold)	Passage cited	Page of citation (Numbers of sample sentences given in bold)
69	351 n. 24	224	221
71	352n	242	348 (**17**)
278	173	*Iliad 20*	
392	270	246	179 (**147**)
410	150	302	113 (**47**)
471	285	435	163
Iliad 13		*Iliad 21*	
32–4	247 (**31**)	80	447
111	446	103	278 (**84**), 411
114	294 (**116**)	109	168
236	326n	111	173, 280 (**96**)
312	279 n. 44	150	122 (**57**)
636	238n, 293 (**112**)	154	424
663f.	250 (**40**)	189	161 (**124**)
681	139 n. 63	193	294 (**115**)
789	236 (**5**)	275	447
814	178 (**144**)	281	116 (**50**), 292
817	280n	291	114
Iliad 14		322	115n
107	278 (**86**)	565	294
108	155n	*Iliad 22*	
113	168	153	264 (**58**)
122	153	199	75 n. 23
299	272 (**73**)	219	294 n. 56
313	295 (**118**)	318	218 (**8**)
Iliad 15		319	177
396	291	384	242 (**19**), 454
737	272 (**74**)	401	284 (**98**)
Iliad 16		513	326n
630	163	*Iliad 23*	
750	235 (**2**)	44	446
Iliad 17		103f.	274 (**77**)
147	286 (**101**)	205	451
446	275 (**80**)	420ff.	289 (**110**)
514	163	439	275 (**81**)
575f.	250 (**41**)	549f.	266 (**59**), 422
640	278 (**87**)	643	361
Iliad 18		*Iliad 24*	
266	341 (**8**)	56	346 (**14**)
549	206	57	391
Iliad 19		66	391
111	168	71	296 (**120**)
157	287 (**105**)	367	124
221	238n	373	81, 155, 335 (**1**)

Passage cited	Page of citation (Numbers of sample sentences given in bold)	Passage cited	Page of citation (Numbers of sample sentences given in bold)
Homer		*Odyssey 6*	
Iliad 24 (cont.)		35	448
387	122 (**58**)	82	231, 238 (**11**)
407	365	145f.	98ff. (**14**)
413	447	196	424, 429 n. 16
426	362 (**41**)	201	239 (**13**)
489	279 (**90**)	287	241 (**18**)
669	338 (**4**)	*Odyssey 8*	
763	267n	147	241 (**17**)
Odyssey 1		298	294 (**117**)
11f.	128 n. 50, 427	299	180 (**151**)
40	284 (**99**)	320	452
116	391	465	391
170	123 n. 42	511	114f.
261	294	549	99 (**18**)
267	163	550ff.	123 n. 41
347f.	447	*Odyssey 9*	
370	100 (**20**)	19ff.	123 (**59**), 424
Odyssey 2		52	114
82	151 (**96**)	118	220
87	446	136	115 (**49**)
203	181n	143	177
230–2	133 (**76**)	425	321 (**128**)
292f.	261 (**54**), 410	432	322 n. 83
Odyssey 3		508	243 (**25**), 250 (**42**)
180	174 (**140**)	*Odyssey 10*	
293ff.	247 (**32**)	44f.	124 (**60**)
Odyssey 4		73	112f. (**44**)
85	220	192f.	287 (**102**)
285	151 (**96**)	273	111, 114
354–60	248 (**34**)	469	174 n. 104
475f.	445	493	448
566	451	552	321 (**129**)
634	115n	*Odyssey 11*	
695	286 (**101**)	218	112f. (**42**)
771	270	252	424 n. 8
844–7	247 (**33**)	336	152 (**98**)
Odyssey 5		348	346 n. 17
8	133 (**76**)	444	284 (**100**)
41f.	113 (**46**), 445	456	180 (**152**)
101	449	605	237 (**9**), 283 (**9**)
189	115n	*Odyssey 12*	
474	98 (**14**)	80	165 (**129**)
483ff.	289 (**109**)	120	238 (**12**), 293 (**113**)

Passage cited	Page of citation (Numbers of sample sentences given in bold)	Passage cited	Page of citation (Numbers of sample sentences given in bold)
312	175 (141)	*Odyssey 19*	
320f.	288 (108)	172–80	248 (36)
Odyssey 13		309	346 n. 17
96–113	248 (35), 264n	312	345 (13)
105	264 (57)	315	362 n. 30
160	220	344–8	323f. (130)
234	218 (7)	353	324 (with n. 85)
243	206	409	108 n. 28
244–7	275 (78), 320 (78)	*Odyssey 20*	
		182	262 (55)
246	429f.	287	253
364	219n	*Odyssey 21*	
423	218 (5)	107	236 (4)
Odyssey 14		142	75
176	152n	212	345 (12)
231	222	251f.	261 (53)
255	218 (6)	426	447
334	222	*Odyssey 22*	
476	173	126	249 (37)
Odyssey 15		226	448
175	448	319	286 (101)
267	362 n. 30, 267n	*Odyssey 23*	
343	276 n. 42	62	361 (38)
403ff.	249n	371	174, 290 (111)
417	253f.	*Odyssey 24*	
426	424 n. 8	159	351 n. 23
433	230, 235 (1), 241 (1)	262–4	242 (21), 378
		289	362 n. 30,
435	339 (6)	298	123 n. 42
532	361 (37)	306	108 n. 28
533	275 (79)	351	244 (26)
Odyssey 16		289	362 n. 30
45	68 n. 12, 435 n. 1	Lysias	
91	113 (45), 446	I. 4	270 (69)
101	114	6	182
437	239n, 306 n. 67	10	176 (142), 352n
Odyssey 17		16	143 (86A), 424f.
523	448	18	352n
Odyssey 18		19	143 (86B)
79	241 (16)	22	260 (49)
215, 220	448	29	95f. (8)
275	114n	34	163
327	138 (81)	42	351 (19)

Passage cited	Page of citation (Numbers of sample sentences given in bold)	Passage cited	Page of citation (Numbers of sample sentences given in bold)
Lysias (cont.)		Euthydemus	
XII. 58	168	284A–C	340n
XIII. 1	105ff. (30)	284B 2–3	367n
7	153	Euthyphro	
15	352n	4E 9	326
16	285	9C 5, 10D 12	110n
23	96f. (11)	11A 7	460
28	280 (94)	21B 1	450
33	105f. (31)	Gorgias	
39	142n	511A 7	455
44	442f.	Hippias Maior	
55	260 n. 29	282A 4	336 (2)
58	181 (153)	Parmenides	
66	110 (37)	128C 2	359 (33)
71	286	Phaedo	
79	150	61C 4	182
80	286	70A 1–6, 70B 2, 70C 4,	
83	162 (128)	77A 10	274n
87	164	74B 2–75D 2	420
90	153	74B 2–78D 4	460n
92	149 (93)	74C 1	421n
		93B 4, 103E 2	370n
Melissus		108C 5	263
fr. 8.2 (D.-K.)	305 (127)	Philebus	
Menander		31C 6	338
Sententiae 258 (Jaekel)	101	Protagoras	
		311E 4	183
Parmenides		Republic	
fr. 4.1 (D.-K.)	456n	338C 1	110n
fr. 6.1	294 n. 57	478B 6ff.	367n
Philolaus		522A 3	236n
fr. 6 (D.-K.)	459	Sophist	
Plato		236E ff.	367n
Apology		247A 8	387
18B 6	259 (46), 410	247D–E	376n
20B	123	261D–263D	47 n. 14
Charmides		263B	340n
166D 8	143 (89)	Symposium	
Cratylus		205B 8–9	367n, 394n
385B 7	340n	Theaetetus	
385B 7–10, 429D	367n	144C	124
5–6		147B 10, 151E 2	110n
396A 6	282n	186C	369
401C–D	458n	188D ff.	340 n. 12, 337n

Passage cited	Page of citation (Numbers of sample sentences given in bold)	Passage cited	Page of citation (Numbers of sample sentences given in bold)
Timaeus		137.2	123
32C 7	394n	142.9	168
Protagoras		II. 14.2	153 **(102)**
fr. 1 (D.-K.)	341n, 367	41.1	109 **(35)**
fr. 4	302 **(123)**	44.3	243
		45.1	243
Sophocles		III. 70.5	167
Ajax		IV. 10.3	153 **(101)**
466	360 **(35)**	66.3	168
664	359 **(32)**	93.1	175
778, 783	242 **(22)**	103.5	454
1157f.	119 **(51)**	VI. 16.5	367n
Electra		VII. 8.2	455
584	366n		
1177	119 **(53)**	Xenophon	
1218f.	302 **(122)**	*Anabasis*	
1434	391	I. 1.4	164
O.C.		1.10	149
644	119 **(52)**	1.11	453
O.T.		2.3	167, 432
89f.	134 **(77)**	2.7	165 **(133)**
369f.	325	2.8	168
747	134 **(78)**	2.13	165 **(134)**
1146	137 **(80)**	2.21	131 **(70)**
Philoctetes		2.25	106ff. **(32)**
415	379	3.6	106ff. **(33)**
733, 751, 753	124 **(61)**	4.5	351 n. 23
1234	129 **(66)**	5.3	295 **(119)**
1241	279 **(88)**, 360n	5.7	279 **(92)**
1312	379	5.9	149 n.75
Trachiniae		6.6	280 **(93)**
474	336 **(3)**	6.8	149 n.75
		6.9	182 **(154)**
Thucydides		8.22	164
I. 8.4	163	8.25	285
10.2	357 **(31)**	9.14	270 **(70)**
24.1	260 **(48)**	9.15	270 **(71)**
38.4	136 **(79)**	9.27	95 **(5)**
58.2	237 **(8)**	10.6	149 **(94)**
78.2	155 **(109)**	10.14	125
78.4	164	II. 1.3	164
86.3	180 **(149)**	1.4	168
132.4	347 **(15)**	1.7	150
136.4	123	1.16	164

Passage cited	Page of citation (Numbers of sample sentences given in bold)	Passage cited	Page of citation (Numbers of sample sentences given in bold)
Xenophon		1.33	175, 348 **(16)**
Anabasis		2.29	243n
II (*cont.*)		2.37	182 **(155)**
1.21	285	3.11	288 **(107)**
1.22	125	IV. 1.5	175
2.10	270 **(72)**	V. 8.6	143 **(87)**
2.12	179 **(148)**	VI. 1.6	140 **(84)**, 359 **(34)**
2.13	142n	4.26	175
2.16	175	VII. 4.7	260 **(50)**
2.19	285	*Hellenica*	
2.21	285	VI. 5.39	281n
3.1	99 **(19)**	*Memorabilia*	
4.6	147 **(91)**	III. 6.3	147 **(92)**
III. 1.4	258 **(43)**	Xenophanes	
1.11	287 **(106)**	fr. 20 (D.-K.)	125n
1.26	259 **(45)**		

INDEX OF PROPER NAMES

Abelard, Peter, 36, 186n
Ackrill, John, 47n
Aerts, W. J., 127–43
Alexander of Aphrodisias, 170n
Ammonius, 47n
Aristotle, 6, 36, 43f., 46–8, 332, 336n, 358, 368f., 416–8

Bach, E., 211–3nn
Behagel, O., 434n
Benveniste, Émile, 1, 56f., 71n, 91n, 129n, 169 *and passim*
Bloch, A., 258n, 425n, 433n
Boeder, H., 365n
Brøndal, V., 440n
Brugmann, Karl, 115n, 156n, 178, 199n, 225n, 334, 395n
Burguière, P., 179n
Burkert, Walter, 459f.
Burnet, John, 421f.

Callimachus, 66n, 444n
Cardona, George, 257n, 304n, 306n
Carnap, Rudolph, 6
Chantraine, Pierre, 75n, 78n, 86n, 107n, 112n, 132 *and passim*
Chen, Chung-Hwan, 48n
Chomsky, Noam, 10–15, 38, 42n, 44f., 46n, 77n, 185n
Cunnigham, M. P., 62

Danto, Arthur, 310n
DeLacy, Phillip, 424
Delbrück, B., 199n, 304, 324n
Descartes, Renée, 416f.
Dover, K. J., 127nn, 291n, 367n, 431n, 433

Ebeling, H., 83f
Ebeling, H. L., 430–34.
Ekman, Erik, 440–43nn
Ernout, A., 232n, 385n

Ficino, Marsilio, 387
Fillmore, Charles A., 46n, 58, 62n, 93n, 171f., 211n
Fischer, P., 434n
Fraenkel, A. A., 314n
Fraenkel, Eduard, 338n
Frege, G., 44, 190n, 299, 404
Frisk, H., 151n, 332n

Gauthiot, R., 157n
Geach, P. T., 41n, 187n, 190n
Gehring, A., 206–8
Gilson, Étienne, 7–9, 232n
Goodman, Nelson, 385n
Goodwin, W. W., 236n
Graham, A. C., 2, 19n, 50n, 216n
Grassmann, H., 384n, 392
Guiraud, Charles, 116n, 119n, 188n, 266n, 435n, 439–42nn, 445n

Hacking, Ian, 54–6
Harris, Zellig S., 10–2, 18n, 20f. nn, 46nn, 51n, 60–2 *and passim*
Heidegger, Martin, 223n, 231, 314n, 364, 416
Hermann, Gottfried, 420–4
Hermann, Ed., 100n, 113n, 115–7nn, 169, 173f. nn
Hintikka, Jaakko, 368n, 388
Hiż, Danuta, 12n, 19n
Hiż, Henry, 7n, 21n, 31n, 72n, 229
Hjelmslev, Louis, 436n
Hockett, C. F., 45
Hofmann, J. B., 151n, 364
Hume, David, 388
Husserl, Edmund, 190, 215, 314n, 337

Italie, G., 83

Jesperson, Otto, 31n, 39, 40n, 136n, 195n, 201–5, 254
Joshi, A. K., 12n, 19n

Kaminsky, Jack, 388n
Keifer, F., 157n
Kenny, Anthony, 369n
Kerschensteiner, Jula, 456n
Kinzel, J., 62n
Klowski, J., 375n, 378n
Kneale, William, 108n
Kristeller, Paul O., 387n
Kühner-Gerth, 68n, 75n, 103n, 151n, 153n, 156f. *and passim*
Kuroda, Yuki, 31n

Lakoff, George, 190n, 193f.
Lakoff, Robin T., 10n
Lange, L., 62n
Langendoen, D. T., 28n, 216n
Lasso de la Vega, José S., 66n, 427–9, 435f.nn, 439–44nn
Lattimore, Richmond, 94n *and passim*
Leibniz, G., 401n
Lejewski, C., 5nn, 48n, 309n
Leśniewski, S., 4–7, 21n, 309n, 405n
Liddell-Scott-Jones, 82f., 156f., 390f.
Locke, John, 374, 387
Lunt, Horace G., 65n
Luschei, E. C., 5n
Luther, Wilhelm, 365nn
Lyons, John, 14n, 23n, 25, 31nn, 45n, 49–53 *and passim*

Marouzeau, J., 276n, 359n, 427f.n
Marten, R., 460n
Mates, Benson, 401n
Matilal, B. K., 437n
Meillet, Antoine, 62n, 85n, 156n, 174n, 179n, 188, 195, 199n, 223, 435
Meyer-Lübke, W., 223n
Miklosich, F., 170n, 172n, 174n
Mill, John Stuart, 4, 184–6
Mossé, Fernand, 32n
Mourelatos, Alexander P. D., 125n, 346, 365n
Munro, D. B., 62n, 100n, 103, 104n, 151, 152n, 181n, 221n

Newman, W. L., 40n

Onians, R. B., 163n, 292
Owen, G. E. L., 6

Palmer, G. H., 94n *and passim*
Parmenides, 333, 369, 416f.
Plato, 46f., 74n, 340n, 369, 416f.
Port Royal Grammar, 170, 184
Port Royal Logic, 8, 44, 213–5
Porzig, W., 78, 97, 391n
Powell, J. Enoch, 83, 326–30, 352
Protagoras, 302, 341n, 369

Quine, W. V. O., 8n, 69, 93, 184–6, 234, 308, 312, 388, 405f., 416f.

Rabassa, Gregory, 28n
Redard, G., 118n
Renan, Ernst, 373
Robbins, Beverly L., 15n, 93n, 201n
Robinson, Richard, 368
Russell, Bertrand, 4–7, 16, 21n, 36, 305, 403f., 406
Ryle, Gilbert, 77n

Sapir, Edward, 51f., 54–7
Saussure, Ferdinand de, 78n
Schwyzer-Debrunner, 75n, 78n, 85n, 104n, 149n, 167 *and passim*
Searle, John, 193n
Sellars, Wilfrid, 313n
Smyth, H. E., 145n, 149n
Solmsen, Friedrich, 351n
Sommers, Fred, 336n, 339n
Steinthal, H., 102n, 170n
Strawson, P. F., 2, 43 54–7, 308n
Swadesh, M., 54n, 56

Tarski, Alfred, 69, 336
Toms, Eric, 308n
Tugendhat, Ernst, 4n, 343n

Vendler, Zeno, 14n, 17n, 26n, 32n
Vendryès, J., 421–3
Vlastos, Gregory, 274n

Wackernagel, J., 420–3
Westermann, D., 216n
Whorff, B. L., 2
Wittgenstein, Ludwig, 186n, 190n, 215, 310f., 314n, 337, 343n, 404, 417

SUBJECT INDEX

Absolute Construction of εἰμί:
how defined, 240;
in existential Type I, 241; in Type IV, 281;
in Type VI, 297ff., 320–2;
in veridical use, 333–7
Abstract and concrete meaning, 380–7
Abstract noun, 16f., 94–7;
defined transformationally, 77ff.;
used metaphorically as predicate with
concrete subject, 109;
as subject or predicate of be, 109–18,
269f., 283–8;
used with concrete sense, 288–92, 461;
contrasted with infinitives, 295;
abstract nominalization of be (οὐσία),
457–62
Accent of ἐστί, 276n, 420–4
Adjectives:
as predicates of be, 89–102;
how distinguished from nouns, 102–4;
transformational status, 89f.;
most common form of predicate, 101f.;
agent adjectives, 145, 148;
quantifier-adjectives, 261–3, 276, 325
Adverbs as predicate with be, 150–6, 181,
228n, 356, 361
Agent nouns and adjectives, see Adjectives,
Nominalization
Ambiguity of meaning, 233f.;
can be a conceptual advantage, 403;
between concrete and abstract sense of
οὐσία, 461;
two senses of "exists"? 307–9;
see also Meaning, focal, Univocity
Apposition, transformationally derived
from copula construction, 201–3
Aspect, see Durative aspect, Static aspect
Assertion, see Truth claim

Become, verbs meaning, 196, 198 (with n.
20)–200, 204–7, 220–2;

in veridical use, 351f. n. 24, 355, 389;
original meaning of *gen-, 384f., 387;
see also Static aspect

Chinese, the copula in, 216
Comment, see Topic and comment
Concrete nouns, see under Noun: first-
order nominal; also Abstract nouns, used
with concrete sense
Copula, theory of, 4–9, and Chapter V
throughout;
according to Port Royal, 8, 213–5;
copula as represented in formal logic,
212f.;
formal definition of, 20, 38;
non-elementary, 21, 86, 89;
near-elementary, 25ff.;
different types in English, 22–30, 33;
first-order and second-order, 25ff., 398–
400;
copula uses in Greek: Chapter IV
throughout;
hypothetical development of, 199–204;
overlap with existential uses of be, 164–7
(and see under Existence);
associated with sentence form as such,
395–7, 412;
as expression of truth claim, 407f.,
412;
as basis for veridical and existential uses
of be, 407–14;
see also Predication

Declarative sentence, see Moods, Truth
Claim
Deep structure, xi;
elimination of be from, 195, 207, 211–4,
271, 437n;
see also Kernel sentence form, Transformational grammar
Deixis, identification of extra-linguistic sub-

ject by situation of utterance, 69–75 (with n. 16);
situational and contextual deixis, 120
Deletion, *see* Zeroing
Durative aspect of *be*, 196 (with n. 17), 219, 233–5, 237–9; *see also* Static (stative) aspect

Elementary sentences, *see* Kernel sentence forms.
Ellipse, 67–70, 158, 275, 435n; *see also* Zeroing
Enclitic ἐστί, *see* Accent
Essive clause, in veridical construction, 337
Ewe language, 215f., 377
Existence and the verb *be*, 4–9, Chapter VI *throughout*;
there is in English, 31–5, 229–32, 251f., 277;
copula vs. existential verb, an incoherent dichotomy, 80–4;
mixed uses (copula with existential sense), 164–7, 261–4, 272–7;
inappropriateness of term "existential", 231f.,
existential nuance in strict sense of quantifier, 233f., 238f., 277–82, 297–310;
existential sentence types, 239ff.;
rhetorical function of introducing subject, 246, 252–7;
problem of post-Homeric, "purely existential" sentence type ("There are gods"), 300ff.;
two concepts of existence, 307–10;
as presupposed by elementary copula uses, 309, 409;
expressed by spatial metaphors, 387f.;
English verb *exists*, 316n;
see also Locative construction, Spatial intuition

Factitive (causal) verb *dhē-* "put/make", 390–3
First-order and second-order uses of εἰμί, 297–300, 398–400
First-order nominals, *see under* Noun
Focal Meaning, *see under* Meaning

Genitive, as predicate with *be*, *see under* Predicate

Hittite, veridical use of *be* in, 335n
Homeric poems: use of *Iliad* and *Odyssey* as primary corpus, 9, 208, 240, 296f., 334;
see also Statistics on the uses of εἰμί

Identity, the *is* of, 4f., 39, 372n, 400f. n. 33;
as a function of special predicates, 120, 143f.;
in definitions, 121, 125f.;
questions of personal identity, 121–4
Impersonal construction: in general 57f., 61f., 169–81;
of copula in English, 35;
of εἰμί, 154f., 156n, 173–82, 296
Indicative, *see* Moods
Indo-European, the verb *be* in, 1–3, 9, 36, 214, 226f., 295, 297, 401;
hypothetical development of the copula in, 199ff., 435f.;
existential uses, 257n, 277, 320–2;
veridical value (especially with participle), 332–6, 350, 359n, 363;
etymology of *es-, 373ff.
Infinitive: not originally a dative form, 100 n. 17, 179n;
redundant infinitive, 181–3;
syntactic function and meaning, 295f.
see also Potential construction, Sentential subjects
Initial position for εἰμί,
in periphrasis, 139f.;
singular verb with plural "subject", 177, 279 n. 45, 425;
for existential verb, 245, 248, 251–6, 263, 274;
with veridical value, 332, 358–60
no regular correlation with existential sense, 260 n. 29, 424f.;
see also Accent
Intentional modalities, 191–4, 337–43, 393;
see also Moods, non-indicative.
Intonation, *see* Sentence intonation

Judgement, theory of: its connection with copula, 44, 169f.

Kernel sentence forms, 11–20, 61–7, 86, *and passim*;

in the analysis of periphrasis, 127ff.;
with verb and sentence operators, 144ff.;
existential verb in kernel, 244;
copula kernels for existential uses, 253–6,
    259;
existential uses without *be* in kernel, 281,
    283;
see also Sentence operators, Transforma-
    tional grammar
Kinetic aspect, *see* Static aspect

Lexical value,
for *be* as existential verb, 232–9, 307;
for *be* in veridical use, 331ff.;
see also Paraphrase
Locative construction of copula,
in English, 18, 27–9
in Greek, 156–67
paralocative and metaphorical uses, 159–
    64, 375–9
connected with existential sense, 164–7,
    233–7, 252–7, 262, 271–6, 288f., 314,
    376;
with vital sense, 378f.;
see also Possessive construction

Meaning, focal, 6f., 386f., 392;
meaning of *be* as copula, 194–8, 222–7,
    395–9;
of existential verb: how it is to be ana-
    lyzed, 229f., 307–14
see also Ambiguity, Lexical Value, Para-
    phrase, Semantics, Univocity
Metaphor, in use of locative construction,
    161–4;
in the development of meaning, 373–87
Moods: indicative-declarative, 187, as mark
    of truth claim 189–91, 343f.;
non-indicative ("oblique") moods, 189–
    94, 311n
Morphological derivation, how related to
    transformational derivation, 17, 78, 107,
    289f.
Mutative aspect, *see* Static aspect

Names, *see* Proper names
Nominalization as a transformation, 15–17,
    26;
abstract nouns as nominalizations, 16f.,

77–9, *and see* Abstract nouns;
agent (concrete) nominalization, 77, 106–
    8, 142, 144f., 148, 461;
sentential nominalization, 79f.;
nominalized forms of εἰμί: ὄν and οὐσία,
    453–62;
see also Abstract nouns, Sentential sub-
    jects
Nominal sentence, 63–7, 68 n.12, 188f.,
    195, Appendix B (435–52);
the term is confusing, 85f.;
not primitive, 200f.;
results from zeroing of *be*, 210f.;
the special case of χρή, 117f., 442
see also Omission of εἰμί
Non-copulative uses of *be*,
in English, 22f., 30–5;
in Greek, 80–4, 224, 228ff., Chapters VI
    and VII *throughout*;
see also Existence, Possessive construc-
    tion, Potential use, Veridical use
Nootka language, 54–8, 171
Noun: elementary nouns, 18f., 76f., 93;
in predicate position 107f.;
distinction of noun-verb correlated with
    subject-predicate structure, 47–59;
similarly for noun-adjective distinction,
    103f.;
personal nouns, 77, 91–4;
first-order nominals, 76f., 93f., 290–2,
    298;
so-called animate nouns, 77, 93;
see also Abstract nouns, Nominalization,
    Proper names, Sentential subjects
Nuncupative use of *be*, *see* Proper names

Omission of εἰμί, irrelevant for deep struc-
    ture, 65f., 264n, 274, Appendix B (435–
    52); applies to existential verb as well as
    copula, 249n, 449–52;
see also Nominal sentence
Ontology and the verb *be*, 1–8, 372, 402–6,
    416–9
Operand, *see* Sentence operator, Verb
    operator

Paralocative, *see* Locative construction
Paraphrase, as a method of defining lexical
    meaning, 229–33, 239, 307

Participle of *be*, philosophical use of, 367, 455–7

Performative use of language, 184; performative verbs and sentence operators, 193f.; *see also* Speech acts

Periphrastic construction of *be*, 126–48; definition of, 127–30;
philosophical interest of, as replacing any finite verb by *be*, 8 (with n. 13), 126, 214f. (with n. 45);
static aspect of, 137f.;
articular participle not periphrastic, 142f.

Person, grammatical, 70–5, 91f.;
in existential uses of *be*, 240, 400 n. 32, 418;
connections with persons as paradigm subjects, 92, 223, 416–8;
see also Noun, personal

Possessive construction of *be*, 62n, 80f., 228, 265–71;
combined with copula, 323f.;
parallel in Ewe, 215;
overlap with locative construction, 160, 265–8, (with n. 34), 323, with locative-existential, 165f., 273f., with copula-existential, 276f.;
reflected in sense of ὄντα and οὐσία ("property"), 455, 458, 461

Potential construction (ἐστί with infinitive), 80f., 178f., 228, 292–6

Predicate: broader and narrower definition of, 38f.;
ontological predicates in Aristotle, 43, 47f.;
predicate genitive, 161, 167–9, 228n;
predicate nouns and adjectives with verbs other than *be*, 202ff., 217–22;
see also Copula, Predication, Subject, *and* Chapter II *throughout*.

Predication and the verb *be*, 4–8, Chapter II *throughout*;
syntactic and semantic predication, 42, 69, 185, 227;
ontological, 43, 47f.;
judgmental (conceptual), 44f.;
verb as a sign of, 184–91, 226, 396ff.
is of predication, in formal logic and natural languages, 212–5;
connected with static aspect, 224, 415f.

sign of predication: three levels of generality, 226f., 396f.;
see also Copula

Prepositions, the use of εἰμί with, 161–4; *see also* Locative construction

Proper names,
as elementary nouns, 54n, 93 with n. 12;
as discriminating individuals, 73f. with n. 21;
as predicates of *be* (nuncupative use), 36, 108 with n. 29, 315;
nuncupative construction with *be*-replacer, 249n

Quantifier-adjectives, *see* Adjectives

Referential constancy and antecedent for pronouns, 71–4

Sanskrit: existential verb in initial position, 257n;
omission of *be* in, 437

Seem, its relation to *be*, 203f., 356f., 392–4

Semantical uses of *be*, 399–414;
as sentence-operators, restricted to third person, 400 n. 32, 418

Semantics, strong and weak, 7n, 229;
relation to syntactic analysis, 290, 307–13, 342–4, 347n;
semantic role of existential verb, 310–4;
see also Lexical value, Meaning, Paraphrase

Sentencehood and predication, 185–91

Sentence intonation, 187 with n. 5, 189, 191

Sentence operator: the verb *be* as, 23 (with n. 42), 116–8, 203;
in periphrasis, 146f.;
includes all cases of sentential subject for *be*, 150;
in impersonal construction, 178–81;
moods and modalities as sentence operators, 191–4;
existential verb as, 141, 258, 270, 277–82 (Type IV), 282–8 (Type V), 310–9;
veridical use of *be* as, 311–3;
quantifier words as, 263;
in potential construction, 293–6;
occurs only in third person, 400 n. 32, 418;
see also Kernel sentence forms

Sentential subjects (nominalized sentences), 79f., 94, 97–101, 110–8, 178; cf. 283ff.; in veridical use, 313, 335ff.

Situation of utterance (speech situation), distinguished from linguistic context, 70, 75
as factor in sentence form, 396n;
as affecting truth conditions, 416;
see also Deixis

Spatial intuition: underlying the concept of existence, 313f., 317f., 387f.;
underlying other abstract concepts, 373f., 380–6
see also Locative construction

Speech acts, theory of, 186f., 193 n. 11, 345f.

Statement, see Truth claim

Static (stative) aspect of be,
contrasted with kinetic (mutative) aspect, 195–207, 217–27, 238;
reinforced in perfect periphrasis, 132, 137f.;
characterizes the system as a whole, 388f.;
underlies the causal verb "put/make" (*dhē-), 390–3;
its philosophical significance, 415f.

Station, verbs of, as be-replacers, 217–9, 222–4

Statistics on the uses of εἰμί, 87 with n. 4, 92 n. 10, 102, 104, 142n, 158, 200, 324, 333 with n. 3, 412;
on word order, 427–34;
frequency of is and was in English, 407n

Stoic theory of lekta, 44, 48;
defective (elliptical) lekta, 68f;
theory of impersonal verbs, 170 with n. 26

Subject,
formal definition of (for English), 38;
grammatical and extra-linguistic, 42ff., 49ff., 312–4, 318f.;
logical subject and predicate, 44f.;
ontological subjects in Aristotle, 47f.;
understood subject, 61, 68–75, 90;
sentential subjects (nominalized sentences), 79;
distinction of subject and predicate lapses, 120, 144;
see also Predicate and Chapter II throughout

Topic and comment, 40n, 45f., 224;
in statements of identity, 120, 144

Transformational grammar, 10–35, 60–7, 88–90, etc.;
applied to periphrasis, 127ff., 144f.;
to impersonal verbs, 171ff.;
to the theory of moods, 191–4;
to apposition and quasi-predicatives, 201–3;
to existential sentence types, 251–8, 277–88, 298–301;
to possessive construction, 265–71;
see also Kernel sentence forms, Nominalization, Verb operator, Sentence operator, Zeroing

Truth (concept of) and the verb be, 5, 313, 331–70

Truth claim, 186f., 343f.,
associated with indicative verb and declarative sentence form, 189–91, 194, 226, 331, 357, 359;
expressed by εἰμί, 311, 359, 368–70;
contrasted with metalinguistic concept of truth, 369f.;
see also Veridical use

Turkish: moods and tenses in, 192;
copula in, 214

Univocity: the myth of primitive simplicity of meaning, 380ff.
see also Ambiguity, Metaphor

Verb:
as sign of predication, 47–53, 184–91;
the verb be as a theoretical entity, 207–10;
verbs of station, 217–24, 388;
see also Noun, Mood, Impersonal construction, Static aspect, Truth claim

Verb operator, 144–50, 163, 203

Verbals in -τός and -τέος, as used with εἰμί, 146f.

Verbless sentence, see Nominal sentence

Veridical use of be, 23, 155, 215, 228, 331–70;
connections with existential use, 309;
semantic analysis, 311–3;
veridical construction defined, 335–7, 342–4;
generalized for intentional modalities

other than statement, 337–42;
connections with copula, 356–62, 408;
see also Truth claim
Vital nuance ("am alive") for *be*, 22f., 224f.,
233–5, 240–5;
connection with locative use, 378f.

Word order: in formal definition of subject
and predicate for English, 38–40;
in Greek, of no syntactic significance, 113

139, 254f., 264n, 424–33;
see also Initial position

Zeroing:
of subject expression, 61, 63–8, 90, 98,
283f., 293f.;
of ἐστί, 63, 65f., 111, 210f., 335f., 436ff.;
other cases of zeroing, 158n, 209–11, 339;
zero forms of personal pronouns, 63–5;
see also Ellipse